Advanced PC Architecture

William Buchanan
and Austin Wilson

ADDISON-WESLEY

An imprint of Pearson Education

Harlow, England · London · New York · Reading, Massachusetts · San Francisco
Toronto · Don Mills, Ontario · Sydney · Tokyo · Singapore · Hong Kong · Seoul
Taipei · Cape Town · Madrid · Mexico City · Amsterdam · Munich · Paris · Milan

PEARSON EDUCATION LIMITED

Head Office: London Office:
Edinburgh Gate   128 Long Acre, London WC2E 9AN
Harlow CM20 2JE   Tel: +44 (0)20 7447 2000
Tel: +44 (0)1279 623623   Fax: +44 (0)20 7240 5771
Fax: +44 (0)1279 431059   Website: www.aw.com/cseng

First published in Great Britain in 2001

© William Buchanan and Austin Wilson 2001

The rights of William Buchanan and Austin Wilson to be identified as Authors of this
Work have been asserted by them in accordance with the Copyright, Designs and Patents
Act 1988.

ISBN 0 201 39858 3

British Library Cataloguing in Publication Data
A CIP catalogue record for this book can be obtained from the British Library

Library of Congress Cataloguing in Publication Data
Applied for.

The programs in this book have been included for their instructional value. The publisher does not
offer any warranties or representations in respect of their fitness for a particular purpose,
nor does the publisher accept any liability for any loss or damage arising from their use.

Many of the designations used by manufacturers and sellers to distinguish their
products are claimed as trademarks. Pearson Education Limited has made every
attempt to supply trademark information about manufacturers and their products mentioned
in this book.

10 9 8 7 6 5 4 3 2 1

Typeset by William Buchanan.
Printed and bound in the UK by Biddles Ltd of Guildford and King's Lynn.

The Publishers' policy is to use paper manufactured from sustainable forests.

Contents

Preface

The internal architecture of the PC is changing for many reasons, including:

- **Phasing-out of old legacy busses and devices**. PCs have, in the past, been difficult to configure and to add new equipment to, as they are still very much based on legacy systems. The worst offender of this is the ISA bus which requires the use of interrupt lines (IRQs) and special memory address (I/O ports). These have always been difficult to configure and normally require some degree of expertise before they can be correctly configured. New interfaces, such as the USB, allow for the automatic identification and configuration of a device and for addition and deletion of a device while the PC is still powered on.
- **Increase in the system data rate**. Over the years, the processor has increased its speed, but the system board has struggled to keep up with these increases. New architectures are now being developed which more closely match system memory and the graphics controller to the processor, while moving other devices and interfaces, such as the hard disk and communication ports, away from the processor. This allows high-speed devices to have direct access to the processor, allowing for increased data transfer to and from memory, and for enhanced 3D photorealisitic graphics.
- **New memory devices**. Traditional memory (DRAM) can be slow when compared with the processor speed. New memory devices, such as RDRAM, have now been developed which allows ultra-high data transfers between the processor and the memory.
- **New plug-and-play architectures**. USB provides a great deal of enhancements over traditional connections, and will be used extensively over the next few years to connect devices to the PC.
- **Increased usage of electronic bridges**. These segment the PCs into segments which are more closely matched to the speed of the device. A typical device is the PCI bridge.

This book provides a foundation on the understanding of previous, current and future PC systems. These principles will allow undergraduates and professionals to fully understand how the specification of each component of a PC affects overall system performance.

It outlines each of the main PC processors and contrasts their performance. It also examines each of the main interface devices and shows how they integrate into the complete system. In the motherboard material, previous, current and future motherboards are shown in some detail to allow undergraduates and professionals to understand how data is passed around the PC. The main objectives are to:

- Provide a complete understand of all PC systems, current or future. This helps in understanding the specifications of a computer so that users can purchase the required specification for their application.
- Provide an insight in how PC systems will involve in the future. This will allow hardware and software developers to properly understand how they design and develop their products to encapsulate new systems.
- Show how systems have evolved from the original PC to current and future systems. This shows how the PC has kept compatibility with previous systems, but increased its power.

One of the main aims of this book is to provide a foundation on the understanding of previous, current and future PC systems, and how the specification of each component of a PC affects the overall system performance. It shows where PCs have been in the past, where they are now, and how new architectures and interfaces devices will change the PC from a difficult-to-use, difficult-to-configure and difficult to add-to system into an easy-to-use supercomputer.

With new GHz processor speeds, and new memory and interfacing techniques, the PC is never going to be the same again. For the first time, the PC will discard the past and look towards the future. First in line in the discard pile will be the ISA bus, and gone forever will be IRQs and complex software set-ups. In will come true plug-and-play and hot addition/deletion.

The PC is dead. Long live, the PC. For 20 years the PC has struggled along with the same old system, and trying to be compatible with its famous father: the IBM PC. From now on, the PC will change, and things will never be the same again. In order to take it into the supercomputer range it must change. Thus everything is changing: its architecture, its memory, its graphics, its sound, in fact, almost everything. In will come a new shining system which will be one of the greatest achievements, ever!

So which chapters should you read if you really want to get a good understanding of the PC. Well we would recommend:

- **Motherboards (Chapter 27) and Hub-based architecture (Chapter 28)**. These chapters analyse typical motherboards and chipsets and show how each of the components interfaces together, and how the architecture affects the system performance.
- **Memory (Chapter 12)**. This chapter shows how cache memory and DRAM memory interfaces to the system, and the processor. It also outlines how SDRAM and RDRAM enhance the data transfer rate over traditional memory types, such as EDO RAM.
- **PCI bus (Chapter 18) and AGP bus (Chapter 24)**. This chapter discusses the fundamentals of the PCI bus and shows its importance in the architecture of modern PCs. This concept is then further enhanced in the AGP chapter, which has used the PCI bus as a foundation and then enhanced it to provide for high-speed graphics transfers.

As much as possible little interesting inserts have been added to the text. Maybe they should provide a light relief to the more academic material.

Contacts:

Dr William Buchanan
Address: School of Computing, Napier University, Edinburgh. UK.
Email address: w.buchanan@napier.ac.uk | w_j_buchanan@hotmail.com
WWW page: http://www.dcs.napier.ac.uk/~bill | http://ceres.dcs.napier.ac.uk/staff/bill
                 http//www.napier.ac.uk/Departments/Staff-detail.asp?StaffID=833
                 http://www.soc.napier.ac.uk/bill

Austin Wilson
Compaq Computers.

Introduction

1.1 Pre-PC Development

One of the first appearances of computer technology occurred in the USA in the 1880s, and was due to the American Constitution demanding that a survey be undertaken every 10 years. As the population in the USA increased, it took an increasing amount of time to produce the statistics. By the 1880s, it looked likely that the 1880 survey would not be complete until 1890. To overcome this, Herman Hollerith (who worked for the government) devised a machine that accepted punch cards with information on them. These cards allowed an electrical current to pass through a hole when there was a hole present.

1890 Hollerith's electromechanical machine was extremely successful and was used in the 1890 and 1900 censuses. He even founded the company that would later become International Business Machines (IBM): CTR (Computer Tabulating Recording). Unfortunately, Hollerith's business fell into financial difficulties and was saved by Tom Watson, a young salesman at CTR, who recognized the potential of selling punch card-based calculating machines to American businesses. He eventually took over the company, and, in the 1920s, he renamed it International Business Machines Corporation (IBM). After this, electromechanical machines were speeded up and improved, but electronic computers, using valves, would soon supercede these.

1943 The first electronic computers were developed, independently, in 1943; these were the 'Harvard Mk I' and Colossus. Colossus was developed in the UK and was used to crack the German coding system (Lorenz cipher), whereas 'Harvard Mk I' was developed at Harvard University and was a general-purpose electromechanical programmable computer. These led to the first generation of computers that used electronic valves and punched cards for their main, non-volatile storage.

1946 The world's first large electronic computer (1946), containing 19,000 valves, was built at the University of Pennsylvania by John Eckert during World War II. It was called ENIAC (Electronic Numerical Integrator and Computer) and it ceased operation in 1957. By today's standards, it was a lumbering dinosaur, and by the time it was dismantled it weighed over 30 tons and spread itself over 1,500 square feet. Amazingly, it also consumed over 25 kW of electrical power (equivalent to the power of over 400 60 W light bulbs), but could perform over 100,000 calculations per second (which is reasonable, even by today's standards). Unfortunately, it was unreliable, and would work only for a few hours, on average, before a valve needed to be replaced. Faultfinding, though, was easier in those days, as a valve that was not working would not glow, and would be cold to touch.

Valves were used in many applications, such as TV sets and radios, but they were unreliable and consumed great amounts of electrical power, mainly for the heating element on the cathode. By the 1940s, several scientists at the Bell Laboratories were investigating materials called semiconductors, such as silicon and germanium. These substances conducted electricity only moderately well, but when they where doped with impurities their resistance changed. From this work, they made a crystal called a diode, which worked like a valve but had many advantages, including the fact that it did not require a vacuum and was much smaller. It also worked well at room temperatures, required little electrical current and had no warm-up time. This was the start of microelectronics.

After ENIAC, progress was fast in the computer industry, and by 1948 small electronic computers were being produced in quantity within five years (2,000 were in use); in 1961, this figure had reached 10,000, by 1970 it was 100,000. At the time, IBM had a considerable share of the computer market, so much so that a complaint was filed against them alleging monopolistic practices in its computer business, in violation of the Sherman Act. By January 1954, the US District Court made a final judgment on the complaint against IBM. For this, a 'consent decree' was then signed by IBM, which placed limitations on how they conducted business with respect to 'electronic data processing machines'.

1948 One of the great computing revolutions occurred in December 1948, when William Shockley, Walter Brattain and John Bardeen at the Bell Laboratories produced a transistor that could act as a triode. It was made from a germanium crystal with a thin p-type section sandwiched between two n-type materials. Rather than release its details to the world, Bell Laboratories kept its invention secret for over seven months so that they could fully understand its operation. They soon applied for a patent for the transistor and, on 30 June 1948, they finally revealed the transistor to the world. Unfortunately, as with many other great inventions, it received little public attention and even less press coverage (the *New York Times* gave it 4½ inches on page 46). It must be said that few men have made such a profound change on the world, and Shockley, Brattain and Bardeen were deservedly awarded the Nobel Prize in 1956.

> "I think there is a world market for maybe five computers."
>
> Thomas Watson, chairman of IBM, 1943.

1952 Previously, in 1952, G.W. Dummer, a radar expert from Britain's Royal Radar Establishment, had presented a paper proposing that a solid block of materials could be used to connect electronic components, without connecting wires. This would lay the foundation of the integrated circuit.

Transistors were initially made from germanium, which is not a robust material and cannot withstand high temperatures. The first company to propose the use of silicon transistors was a geological research company named Texas Instruments (which had diversified into transistors). Then, in May 1954, Texas Instruments started commercial production of silicon transistors. Soon many companies were producing silicon transistors and, by 1955, the electronic valve market had peaked, while the market for transistors was rocketing. The larger electronic valve manufacturers, such as Western Electric, CBS, Raytheon and Westinghouse failed to adapt to the changing market and quickly lost their market share to the new transistor manufacturing companies, such as Texas Instruments, Motorola, Hughes and RCA.

1957 To commercialize on his success, Shockley, in 1955, founded Shockley Semiconductor. Then in 1957, eight engineers decided they could not work within Shockley Semiconductor and formed Fairchild Semiconductors, which would become one of the most inventive companies in Silicon Valley. Unfortunately, Fairchild Semiconductors seldom exploited its developments fully, and was more of an incubator for many of the innovators in the electronics industry. Around the same time, Kenneth Olsen founded the Digital Equipment Corporation (DEC), which would go on to become one of the key companies in the computer industry, along with IBM.

1958 In July 1958, at Texas Instruments, Jack St Clair Kilby proposed the creation of a monolithic device (an integrated circuit) on a single piece of silicon. Then, in September, he produced the first integrated circuit, containing five components on a piece of germanium that was half an inch long and was thinner than a toothpick.

1959 The following year, Fairchild Semiconductors filed for a patent for the planar process of manufacturing transistors. This process made commercial production of transistors possible and led to Fairchild's introduction, in two years, of the first commercial integrated circuit. Soon transistors were small enough to make hearing aids that fitted into the ear and within pacemakers. Companies such as Sony started to make transistors operate over higher frequencies and within larger temperature ranges. Eventually they became so small that many of them could be placed on a single piece of silicon. These were referred to as microchips and they started the microelectronics industry. The first two companies to develop the integrated circuit were Texas Instruments and Fairchild Semiconductors. At Fairchild Semiconductors, Robert Noyce constructed an integrated circuit with components connected by aluminium lines on a silicon oxide surface layer on a plane of silicon. He then went on to lead one of the most innovate companies in the world, the Intel Corporation.

1954 In 1954, the IBM 650 was built and was considered the workhorse of the industry at the time (which sold about 1000 machines, and used valves). In November 1956, IBM showed how innovative they were by developing the first hard disk, the RAMAC 305. It was towering by today's standards, with 50 two-foot diameter platters, giving a total capacity of 5 MB. Around the same time, the Massachusetts Institute of Technology produced the first transistorized computer: the TX-O (Transistorized Experimental computer). Seeing the potential of the transistor, IBM quickly switched from valves to transistors and, in 1959, they produced the first commercial transistorized computer. This was the IBM 7090/7094 series, and it dominated the computer market for years.

1957 Programs written on these mainframe computers were typically either machine code (using the actual binary language that the computer understood) or using one of the new compiled languages, such as COBOL and FORTRAN. FORTRAN was well suited to engineering and science as it was based around mathematical formulas. COBOL was more suited to business applications. FORTRAN was developed in 1957 (typically known as FORTRAN 57) and enhanced considerably the development of computer programs, as the program could be writing in a near-English form, rather than using a binary language. With FORTRAN, the compiler converts the FORTRAN statements into a form that the computer can understand. At the time, FORTRAN programs were stored on punch cards, and loaded into a punch card reader to be read into the computer. Each punch card had holes punched into it to represent ASCII characters. Any changes to a program would require a new set of punch cards.

> "I have traveled the length and breadth of this country and talked with the best people, and I can assure you that data processing is a fad that won't last out the year."
>
> Editor, Prentice Hall, 1957.

1959 In 1959, IBM built the first commercial transistorized computer, named the IBM 7090/7094 series, which dominated the computer market for many years. In 1960 in New York, IBM went on to develop the first automatic mass-production facility for transistors. In 1963 (DEC) sold their first minicomputer to Atomic Energy of Canada. DEC would become the main competitor to IBM, but eventually fail as they dismissed the growth in the personal computer market.

1961 The second generation of computers arrived in 1961, when the great innovator, Fairchild Semiconductors, released the first commercial integrated circuit. In the next two years, significant advances were made in the interfaces to computer systems. The first was by Teletype, who produced the Model 33 keyboard and punched-tape terminal. It was a classic design and was on many of the available systems. The other advance was by Douglas Engelbart, who received a patent for the mouse pointing device for computers.

1964 The production of transistors increased, and each year brought a significant decrease in their size. Gordon Moore, in 1964, plotted the growth in the number of transistors that could be fitted onto a single microchip, and found that the number of transistors that can be fitted onto an integrated circuit approximately doubled every 18 months. This is now known as Moore's law, and has been surprisingly accurate ever since. In 1964, Texas Instruments also received a patent for the integrated circuit.

> 'Sinclair ZX80: with an unusable keyboard and a quirky BASIC, this machine discouraged millions of people from ever buying another computer.'
>
> *PC World Magazine*, October 1985.

At the time, there were only three main ways of writing computer programs: machine code, FORTRAN or COBOL, which were often difficult for inexperienced users to use, so in 1964, John Kemeny and Thomas Kurtz at Dartmouth College developed the BASIC (beginners all-purpose symbolic instruction code) programming language. It was a great success, although it was not used much in 'serious' applications until Microsoft developed Visual BASIC, which used BASIC as a foundation language, but enhanced it with an excellent development system. Many of the first personal computers used BASIC as a standard programming language.

1965 The third generation of computers started in 1965 with the use of integrated circuits rather than discrete transistors. IBM again was innovative and created the System/360 mainframe, which in the course of history has been a true classic computer. Then in 1970, IBM introduced the System/370, which included semiconductor memories. Unfortunately, all of the computers were very expensive to purchase (approximately $1,000,000) and maintain, but were great computing workhorses at the time. Most companies had to lease their computer systems, as they could not afford to purchase them. As IBM clung happily to their mainframe market, several new companies were working away to erode their share. DEC were to be the first, with their minicomputer, but the PC companies of the future would finally overtake them. The beginning of their loss of market share can be traced to the development of the microprocessor, and to one company: Intel. In 1967, however, IBM again showed their leadership in the computer industry by developing the first floppy disk.

> **Magnetic tape**
>
> Around the middle of the 1970s, the growing electronics industry started to entice new companies to specialize in key areas, such as International Research who applied for a patent for a method of constructing double-sided magnetic tape utilizing a Mumetal foil inter layer.

1968 The beginning of the slide for IBM occurred in 1968, when Robert Noyce and Gordon Moore left Fairchild Semiconductors and met up with Andy Grove to found Intel Corporation. A venture capitalist named Arthur Rock provided the required start-up finance. This was mainly on the reputation of Robert Noyce as the person who first integrated more than one transistor on a piece of silicon.

At the same time, IBM scientist John Cocke and others completed a prototype scientific computer called the ACS, which used some RISC (reduced instruction set computer) concepts. Unfortunately, the project was cancelled because it was not compatible with IBM's System/360 computers. Along with this, several people were proposing the idea of a computer-on-a-chip, and International Research Corp. was the first to develop the required architecture, modeled on an enhanced DEC PDP-8/S concept. Wayne Pickette proposed to Fairchild Semiconductors that they should develop a computer-on-a-chip, but was turned down. So, he went to work with IBM and went on to design the controller for Project Winchester, which had an enclosed flying-head disk drive.

> **Winchester disks**
>
> Hard disks were at one time known as Winchester disks as they were initially available from IBM made from two spindles with 30 MB on each spindle. The 30-30 became known as Winchester disks after the 30-30 rifle.

In the same year, Douglas C. Engelbart, of the Stanford Research Institute, demonstrated the concept of computer systems using a keyboard, a keypad, a mouse and windows at the Joint Computer Conference in San Francisco's Civic Center. He also demonstrated the use of a word processor, a hypertext system and remote collaboration. His keyboard, mouse and windows concept has since become the standard user interface to computer systems.

> "DOS addresses only 1 megabyte of RAM because we cannot imagine any applications needing more."
> Microsoft, 1980, on the development of DOS.

1969 In 1969, Hewlett-Packard branched into the world of digital electronics with the world's first desktop scientific calculator: the HP 9100A. At the time, the electronics industry was producing cheap pocket calculators, which led to the development of affordable computers, when the Japanese company Busicom commissioned Intel to produce a set of between eight and 12 ICs for a calculator. Then, instead of designing a complete set of ICs, Ted Hoff at Intel designed an integrated circuit chip that could receive instructions and perform simple integrated functions on data. The design became the 4004 microprocessor. Intel produced a set of ICs, which could be programmed to perform different tasks. These were the first microprocessors and soon Intel (short for *Int*egrated *El*ectronics) produced a general-purpose 4-bit microprocessor: the 4004.

The 4004 caused a revolution in the electronics industry as previous electronic systems had a fixed functionality. With this processor the functionality could be programmed by software. Amazingly, by today's standards, it could handle only 4 bits of data at a time (a nibble), contained 2,000 transistors, had 46 instructions and allowed 4 kB of program code and 1 kB of data. From this humble start, the PC has since evolved using Intel microprocessors. Intel had previously been an innovative company, and had produced the first memory device (static RAM, which uses six transistors for each bit stored in memory), the first DRAM (dynamic memory, which uses only one transistor for each bit stored in memory) and the first EPROM (which allows data to be downloaded to a device, which is then stored permanently).

> In April 1970, Wayne Pickette proposed to Intel that they use the computer-on-a-chip for the Busicom project. Then, in December, Gilbert Hyatt filed a patent application entitled 'Single Chip Integrated Circuit Computer Architecture', the first basic patent on the microprocessor.

In the same year, Intel announced the 1 kB RAM chip, a significant memory increase over previously produced chips. Around the same time, one of Intel's major partners, and also, as history has shown, competitors, Advanced Micro Devices (AMD) Incorporated was founded. It was started when Jerry Sanders and seven others left Fairchild Semiconductors (the incubator for the electronics industry which produced many spin-off companies).

At the same time, the Xerox Corporation gathered a team at the Palo Alto Research Center (PARC) and gave them the objective of creating 'the architecture of information'. This would lead to many of the great developments of computing, including personal distributed computing, graphical user interfaces, the first commercial mouse, bit-mapped displays, Ethernet, client/server architecture, object-oriented programming, laser printing and many of the basic protocols of the Internet. Few research centers have ever been as creative and forward thinking as PARC was over those years.

> **Computer generations**
>
> | | |
> |---|---|
> | **1st** | Valves (ENIAC) |
> | **2nd** | Transistors (PDP-1) |
> | **3rd** | Integrated circuits/time-sharing (IBM System/360) |
> | **4th** | Large-scale integration (ZX81) |
> | **5th** | Systems-on-a-chip (Pentium). |

1971 In 1971, Gary Boone of Texas Instruments filed a patent application for a single-chip computer and the microprocessor was released in November. Also in the same year, Intel copied the 4004 microprocessor to Busicom. When released the basic specification of the 4004 was:

- Data bus: 4-bit
- Clock speed: 108 kHz
- Price: $200
- Speed: 60,000 operations per second
- Transistors: 2,300
- Silicon: 10μ technology, 3×4 mm^2
- Addressable memory: 640 bytes

> **Second-generation computer companies (Transistorized)**
> 1. IBM
> 2. Univac
> 3. Burroughs
> 4. NCR
> 5. Honeywell
> 6. Control Data Corporation
> 7. Siemens
> 8. Fuji
> 9. Bendix
> 10. Librascope

Intel then developed an EPROM, which integrated into the 4004 to enhance development cycles of microprocessor products.

Another significant event occurred when Bill Gates and Paul Allen, calling themselves the Lakeside Programming Group, signed an agreement with Computer Center Corporation to report bugs in PDP-10 software, in exchange for computer time. Other significant events at the time included:

- Ken Thompson at AT&T's Bell Laboratories wrote the first version of the UNIX operating system.
- Gary Starkweather at Xerox used a laser beam along with the standard photocopying processor to produce a laser printer.
- The National Radio Institute introduced the first computer kit, for $503.
- Texas Instruments developed the first microcomputer-on-a-chip, containing over 15,000 transistors.
- IBM introduced the memory disk, or floppy disk, which was an 8-inch floppy plastic disk coated with iron oxide.
- Wang Laboratories introduced the Wang 1200 word processor system.
- Niklaus Wirth invented the Pascal programming language. BASIC and FORTRAN had long been known for producing unstructured programs, with lots of GOTOs and RETURNs. Pascal was intended to teach good, modular programming practices, but was quickly accepted for its clean, pseudocode-like language. It still survives today, but it has struggled against C/C++ (mainly because of the popularity of UNIX) and Java (because of its integration with the Internet), but lives with Borland Delphi, an excellent Microsoft Windows development system.
- At XEROX PARC, Alan Kay proposed that XEROX should build a portable personal computer called the Dynabook, which would be the size of

> **All-time greats**
>
> One of the great revolutions of all time occurred on December 1948 when William Shockley, Walter Brattain and John Bardeen at the Bell Laboratories produced a transistor that could act as a triode. It was made from a germanium crystal with a thin p-type section sandwiched between two n-type materials. Rather than release its details to the world, Bell Laboratories kept its invention secret for over seven months so that they could fully understand its operation. Unfortunately, as with many other great inventions, it received little public attention and even less press coverage (the *New York Times* gave it 4½ inches on page 46).

an ordinary notebook; unfortunately, the PARC management did not support it. In future years, companies such as Toshiba and Compaq would exploit the idea. PARC eventually choose to develop the Alto personal computer.

- Texas Instruments introduced the TMS1000 one-chip microcomputer. It had 1 kB ROM, 32 bytes of RAM, and a simple 4-bit processor. In the following year (1973), Intel filed a patent application for a memory system for a multichip digital computer.

1973 In 1973, the model for future computer systems occurred at Xerox's PARC, when the Alto workstation was demonstrated with a bit-mapped screen (showing the Cookie Monster from Sesame Street). The following year at Xerox, Bob Metcalfe demonstrated the Ethernet networking technology, which was destined to become the standard local area networking technique. It was far from perfect, as computers contended with each other for access to the network, but it was cheap and simple, and it worked relatively well.

Also in 1973, before the widespread acceptance of PC-DOS, the future for personal computer operating systems looked to be CP/M (control program/monitor), which was written by Gary Kildall of Digital Research. One of his first applications of CP/M was on the Intel 8008, and then on the Intel 8080. At the time, computers based on the 8008 started to appear, such as the Scelbi-8H, which cost $565 and had 1 kB of memory.

IBM was also innovating at the time, creating a cheap floppy disk drive, and the IBM 3340 hard disk unit (a Winchester disk), which had a recording head that sat on a cushion of air 18 millionths of an inch above the platter. The disk was made with four platters, each 8-inches in diameter, giving a total capacity of 70 MB.

A year later (1974) at IBM, John Cocke produced a high-reliability, low-maintenance computer called the ServiceFree. It was one of the first computers in the world to use RISC technology and it operated at the unbelievable speed of 80 MIPS. Most computers at the time were measured in a small fraction of a MIP and were over 50 times faster than IBM's fastest mainframe. The project was eventually cancelled as a competing project named 'Future Systems' was consuming much of IBM's resources.

> "Since human beings themselves are not fully debugged yet, there will be bugs in the code no matter what you do."
>
> "We could conceivably put a company out of business with a bug in a spreadsheet, database, or word processor."
>
> Chris Mason, Microsoft.

1.2 8008/8080/8085

1974 In 1974, Intel was a truly innovative company, and was the first to develop an 8-bit microprocessor. These devices could handle eight bits (a byte) of data at a time and were:

- 8008 (0.2 MHz, 0.06 MIPS, 3,500 transistors, 10μ technology, 16 kB memory).
- 8080 (2 MHz, 0.64 MIPS, 6,000 transistors, 6μ technology, 64 kB memory).
- 8085 (5 MHz, 0.37 MIPS, 6,500 transistors, 3μ technology, 64 kB memory).

These were much more powerful than the previous 4-bit devices and were used in many early microcomputers and in applications such as electronic instruments and printers. The 8008 had a 14-bit address bus and could thus address up to 16 kB of memory, whereas the 8080 and 8085 had a 16-bit address buss, giving them a limit of 64 kB. Table 1.1 outlines the basic specification for the main 8-bit microprocessors. At the time, Intel's main product area was memory, and microprocessors seemed like a good way of increasing sales for other product lines, especially memory.

Excited by the new 8-bit microprocessors, two students from a private high school, Bill Gates and Paul Allen, rushed out to buy the new 8008 device. This, they believed, would be the beginning of the end of the large and expensive mainframes (such as the IBM range) and minicomputers (such as the DEC PDP range). They bought the processors for the high price of $360 (possibly a joke by Intel at the expense of the IBM System/360 mainframe), but even they could not make it support BASIC programming. Instead, they formed the Traf-O-Data company and used the 8008 to analyze tickertape read-outs of cars passing in a street. The company would close in the following year (1973) after it had made $20,000, but from this enterprising start, one of the leading computer companies in the world would grow: Micro-soft (although it would initially be called Micro-soft).

> "Computers in the future may weigh no more than 1.5 tons."
>
> *Popular Mechanics*, 1949.

Table 1.1   Popular 8-bit microprocessors

Processor	Release date (manufacturer)	Computer used in	Example computers
8008	April 1972 (Intel)	Mark-8	
8080	April 1974 (Intel)	Sol-20	
		MITS Altair 8800	
		IMSAI 8080	
8085	March 1976 (Intel)		
Z80	July 1976 (Zilog)	Radio Shack TRS-80	1. TRS-80 microcomputer, 4 kB RAM, 4 kB ROM, keyboard, black-and-white video display, tape cassette; $600, August 1977.
Z80A		Exidy Sorcerer	
		Sinclair ZX81	
		Osborne 1	2. ZX81 (1 kB), $200, March 1981. ZX81 (2 kB), $200, March 1981.
		Xerox 820	
		DEC Rainbow 100	3. Osborne 1, 5-inch display, 64 kB RAM, keyboard, keypad, modem, and two 5.25-inch 100 kB disk drives; $17, April 1981.
		Sord M5/ M23P	
		Sharp X1	
		Sony SMC-70	
6502/	June 1976 (MOS	Franklin Ace 1000	1. Atari 400/800, 8 kB, $550/1000, Oct 1979.
6502A	Technologies)	Atari 400/800	2. PET 2001,4 kB RAM, 14 kB ROM, key-board, display, tape drive; $600.
		Commodore PET	
		Apple II/III	3. Apple II, 4 kB RAM, 16 kB ROM, key-board, 8-slot motherboard, game paddles, graphics/text interface to color display (first ever), built-in BASIC; $1,300, April 1977.
			4. Apple II Plus, 48 kB, June 1979.
			5. Apple III, 5.25-inch floppy drive; $4,500–$8,000, May 1980.
			6. BBC Microcomputer System, 48 kB RAM, 73-key keyboard, 16-color graphics, September 1981.
6800/	1974 (Motorola)	MITS Altair 680	1. TRS-80 Color Computer, 4 kB RAM; $400.
6809			
780-1	NEC		1. ZX80, 1 kB RAM, 4 kB ROM; $200, February 1980.

In 1974, several personal computers began to appear, including the MITS-built (Micro Instrumentation and Telemetry Systems) computer based on Intel's new 8080 device, at the cheap price of $500, released as the Altair 8800 microcomputer. Unfortunately one of the first prototypes for the Altair computer was lost en route to New York where it was going to be reviewed and photographed for Popular Electronics. Eventually they did receive a new version and, at a selling price of $439, it received great reviews.

At PARC, the Bravo was developed for the Xerox Alto computer and demonstrated the first WYSIWYG (What You See Is What You Get) program for a personal computer. The Alto computer was then released onto the market. The following year Xerox demonstrated the Gypsy word processing system, which was fully WYSIWYG.

1975 Intel knew that providing a processor alone would have very little impact on the market. It needed a development system that would provide industrial developers with an easy method of developing hardware and software around the new processor. Thus, Intel introduced the Intellec 4 development system.

> "I'm glad to be out of that bag."
> "Hello, I am Macintosh. Never trust a computer you cannot lift."
>
> Quotes from the Macintosh computer when it introduced itself.

The main competitors to the 8080 were the Motorola 6800, the Zilog Z80 and the MOS Technology 6502. The Z80 had the advantage that it could run any programs written for the 8080 and, because it was also pin compatible, it could be easily swapped with the 8080 processor without a change of socket. It also had many other advantages over the 8080, such as direct memory access, serial I/O technology, and full use of the 'reserved' op-codes (Intel had used only 246 out of the 256 available op-codes). The Z80 was also much cheaper than the 8080 and had a 2.5 MHz clock speed. After the release of the Z80, Intel produced a quick response: the 8085, which used all the op-codes fully, but it was too late to stop the tide turning towards Zilog. Many personal computers started to appear that

> **Intel 4000-series**
> 4001 PROM (4096×8 bits)
> 4002 RAM (5120 bits)
> 4003 Registers
> 4004 Processor

were based on the Z80 processor, including the Radio Shack TRS-80, Osborne 1 and the Sinclair/Timex ZX81. The ZX81 caused a great revolution because of its cheapness but, unfortunately, most home users had to wait for many months to receive their kit or even longer for their prebuilt computer. However, as the computer was so original and cost-effective, users were willing to wait for their prized system. Another great challenger was the 6502, which, when released in June 1975, cost $25, which compared well with the 8080 (costing, at the time, $150). It was used in many of the great personal computer systems, such as the Apple II and Atari 400. At Motorola, Chuck Peddle and Charlie Melear developed the 6800 microprocessor, which was never really successful in the personal computer market, but was used in many industrial and automotive applications.

> "The PCjr is bound to be around for a while".
> Ken Williams, Serria On-Line founder.
>
> "We're just sitting here trying to put our PCjrs in a pile and burn them. And the damn things won't burn. That's the only thing IBM did right with it—they made it flame-proof."
> William Boman, Spinnaker Software chairman

For the first time, home users could actually build their own computers, and kits were available from Altair and Mistral. With the success of the Z80, many companies were demanding to produce a second-source supply for the Z80 processors. The Motorola processor was also more powerful than the 8080. It was also simpler in its design and required only a single 5V supply, whereas the 8080 required three different power supplies.

At the end of the 1970s, IBM's virtual monopoly on computer systems started to erode from both ends of their markers, from the high-powered end as DEC developed their range of minicomputers, and from the low-powered end due to companies developing computers based around the newly available 8-bit microprocessors, such as the 6502 and the Z80. IBM's main contenders other than DEC were Apple and Commodore, who introduced a new type of computer – the personal computer (PC). The leading systems at the time were the Apple I and the Commodore PET, which captured the interest of the home user and for the first time individuals had access to cheap computing power. These flagship computers spawned many others, such as the Sinclair ZX80/ZX81, the BBC microcomputer, the Sinclair Spectrum, the Commodore Vic-20 and the classic Apple II (all of which were based on the 6502 or Z80). Most of these computers were aimed at the lower end of the market and were used mainly for playing games, not for business applications. IBM finally decided, with the advice of Bill Gates, to use the 8088 for its version of the PC, and not, as they had first thought, the 8080 device. Microsoft also persuaded IBM to introduce the IBM PC with a minimum of 64 kB RAM, instead of the 16 kB that IBM had planned.

At the time, most people thought that personal computers would be used mainly for playing games. One of the major innovators in this was Atari, founded by Nolan Bushnell, which produced the first commercial game based on tennis, named Pong. By today's standards, Pong used simple graphics, and had just two paddle lines, which could be moved left and right, and a square ball that moved back and forward between the paddles. To many at the time it was the most amazing entertainment, ever. Atari and other companies would release many other classic games, such as Space Invaders, Asteroids and Frogger.

> "640K ought to be enough for anybody."
>
> Bill Gates, 1981.

While many of the processors at the time ran at 1 MHz or 5MHz at the most, RCA released the RISC-based 1802 processor, which ran at 6.4 MHz, and was used in a variety of systems, from video games to NASA space probes.

Until 1974, most programming languages had been produced either as a teaching language, such as Pascal or BASIC, or had been developed in the early days of computers, such as FORTRAN and COBOL. No software language had been developed that would properly interface with the operating system, and used both high-level commands, and supported low-level commands (such as AND, OR and NOT bitwise operations). To overcome these problems, Brian Kernighan and Dennis Ritchie developed the C programming language. Its main advantage was that it was supported in the UNIX operating system. C has since led a charmed existence by software developers for many proven (and unproven) reasons, and took off quickly in a way that Pascal had failed to do. Its advantages were stated as being both a high- and a low-level language, it produced small and efficient code, and that it was portable on different systems. The main advantage was probably that it was a standard software language that was supported on most operating systems, and for this the ANSI C standard helped its adoption, where a program written on one computer system would compile on another system, so long as both compilers conformed to a given standard (typically ANSI C). Eventually C moved from the UNIX operating system down to the PCs as they became more advanced. It normally requires a relatively large amount of storage space (for all of its standardized libraries), whereas BASIC requires very little storage space.

> **A great investment**
>
> **$10,000** invested in shares of Cisco Systems when they were initially floated on the stock market in 1990 was worth $6.5million at the end of the millennium.

Pascal always struggled because many compiler developments used non-standard additions to the basic language, and thus Pascal programs were difficult to port from one system to another. FORTRAN never really had this problem, as it only had a few standards, mainly FORTRAN 57 and FORTRAN 77.

BASIC also had few problems because of the lack of additional facilities, but many BASIC programs did not port well from one system to another, as they tended to use different methods to access the hardware (typically using the PEEK and POKE operation to read from and write to memory addresses, respectively). Also, BASIC accessed the hardware directly, whereas C has tended to use the operating system to access the hardware. The nondirect method had many advantages over direct access, such as allowing for multi-access to hardware, hardware independence, time-sharing, smoother running programs and better error control.

In 1975, Micro-soft (as it was known before the hyphen was dropped) realized the potential of BASIC for the newly developed 8-bit computers and used it to produce the first programming language for the PC. Their first product was BASIC for the Altair, which they licensed to MITS, their first customer. The MITS, Altair 8800 was a truly innovative system; it sold for $375 and had 1 kB of memory. Soon, Microsoft developed BASIC 2.0 for the Altair 8800, in 4 K and 8 K editions. The Altair was an instant success, and MITS begin work on a Motorola 6800-based system. Even its bus become a standard: the S-100 bus.

> In 1983, *Time* magazine selected the microcomputer as its Man of the Year.

At Xerox, work began on the Alto II, which would be easier to produce, more reliable, and more easily maintained, whereas IBM segmented their mainframe market and moved down-market, with their first briefcase-sized portable computer: the IBM 5100. It cost $9,000, used BASIC, had 16 kB RAM, tape storage, and a built-in 5-inch screen. Also at IBM, after the rejection of the ServiceFree computer, John Cocke began working on the 801 project, which would develop scaleable chip designs that could be used in small computers, as well as large ones.

1976 In 1976, the personal computer industry started to evolve around a few companies. For software development two companies stood out:

- **Microsoft**. The development of BASIC on the Altair allowed Microsoft to concentrate on software development (while many other companies concentrated on the cut-throat hardware market). Its core team of Paul Allen (ex-MITS) and Bill Gates (ex-Harvard) left their jobs and studies to devote their efforts, full-time, to Microsoft. In that year they employed their first employee, Marc McDonald, and registered the Microsoft trademark.
- **Digital Research**. Microsoft's biggest competitor for PC software was Digital Research who had copyrighted CP/M, which it hoped would become the industry-standard microcomputer operating system. Soon CP/M was licensed to GNAT Computers and IMSAI. But for a bad business decision at Digital Research, CP/M would have become the standard operating system for the PC, and the world may never have heard about MS-DOS.

For personal computer systems, five computers were leading the way:

1. **Apple**. Steve Wozniak and Steve Jobs completed work on the Apple I computer and, on April Fool's Day, 1976, the Apple Computer Company was formed. It was initially available in kit form and cost $666.66 (hopefully nothing to do with it being a beast to construct). With the success of the Apple I computer, Steve Wozniak began working on the Apple II, and he soon left Hewlett-Packard to devote more time to its development. Steve Wozniak and Steve Jobs proposed that Hewlett-Packard and Atari create a personal computer. Both proposals were turned down.

2. **Commodore**. Things were looking very good at Commodore, as Chuck Peddle designed the Commodore PET. To ensure a good supply of the 6502, Commodore International bought MOS Technology.

3. **Xerox**. The innovation continued at great pace at Xerox with the Display Word Processing Task Force recommending that Xerox produce an office information system, like the Alto (the Janus project). On the negative side, Xerox management had always been slightly suspicious about the change of business area, and rejected two proposals to market the Alto computer as part of an advanced word processing system.

4. **Cray Research**. Cray Research developed one of the first supercomputers with the Cray-1. It used vector-processing computers and was a direct attack on IBM's traditional computer market. This caused major rumbles in IBM, which was now seeing its market attacked from three sides: the personal computers (which started to show potential in lower-end applications), the minicomputer (which were cheaper and easier to use than the mainframes) and now the supercomputers (at the upper end). Processing power became the key factor for supercomputers, whereas connectivity was the main feature for mainframe computers. As DEC had done, Cray concentrated on the scientific and technical areas of high-performance computers.

5. **Wang Laboratories**. Wang emerged in the computing industry with its innovative word processing system, which used computer technology instead of traditional electronic typewriters. It initially cost $30,000.

6. **MITS**. After the success of the Altair 8800, MITS released the Altair 680, which was based on the Motorola 6800 microprocessor.

> "The 32-bit machine would be overkill for a personal computer."
>
> Sol Libes, ByteLines.

For microprocessors, there were five major competitors:

1. **Zilog**. Zilog released the 2.5 MHz Z80, an 8-bit microprocessor whose instruction set was a superset of the Intel 8080.

2. **AMD**. Intel realized that they must create alliances with key companies in order to increase the acceptance of the 8080 processor. Thus they signed a patent cross-license agreement with AMD, which gave AMD the right to copy Intel's processor microcode and instruction codes.

3. **MOS Technology**. MOS Technology released the 1 MHz 6502 microprocessor to a great reception, and started a wave of classic computers, such as the Apple II. The 6502A processor would increase the clock speed.

4. **National Semiconductor**. Released the SC/MP microprocessor, which used advanced multiprocessing.

5. **Texas Instruments**. After years of innovation at Intel in producing the first 4-bit (4004) and 8-bit processors (8008), it was TI who developed the first 16-bit microprocessor: the TMS9900. The processor was extremely advanced for the time but, unfortunately, TI failed to properly support it, mainly because there was no usable development system (something that Intel and Motorola always made sure was available for their systems). Its first implementation was within the TI 990 minicomputer.

1977   1977 belonged to Apple, Commodore and Radio Shack, who released the excellent Apple II, the Commodore PET and the TRS-80, respectively, to an eager market. In this year, the Apple Computer Company was incorporated, and the employees moved to California. They released the Apple II computer for $1,300; which used the 6502 CPU, had 4 kB RAM, 16 kB ROM, a QWERTY keyboard, 8-slot motherboard, game paddles, graphics/text interface to color display and came with the Applesoft system (built-in BASIC provided by Microsoft). Soon, Steve Wozniak was working on software for a floppy disk controller.

Over the years, it has been shown that a killer software application, or game, is required for the widespread adoption of a new computer system. This killer application for the Apple II was the VisiCalc spreadsheet program, which was initially developed by Dan Bricklin. The spreadsheet was a true inspirational product and unfortunately for Dan but fortunately for others such as Lotus and Microsoft, he never patented his technology. If he had done this, he would have become a multibillionaire. Dan got the idea of the electronic spreadsheet while he sat in a class at Harvard Business School. He designed the interface while his partner, Bob Frankston, wrote the code. Visi-Calc ran on the Apple II computer, and had a significant effect on the sales of the computer. It was released in 1979, and has since become the father of all other spreadsheet programs, such as Lotus 123 and Microsoft Excel (Lotus eventually bought the rights to VisiCalc for $800,000 in 1985).

Microsoft expanded their market by developing Microsoft FORTRAN for CP/M-based computers, and granted Apple Computer a license to Microsoft's BASIC.

> One of the main competitors to the Apple II was the Commodore PET 2001. It also based around the 6502 CPU, and had a simpler specification (4 kB RAM, 14 kB ROM, keyboard, display, and tape drive), but it cost only $600. Also in competition, and at the same price, was the Radio Shack TRS-80 microcomputer. It was based around the Z80 processor and had 4 kB RAM, 4 kB ROM, keyboard, black-and-white video display, and tape cassette, and sold well beyond expectations.

1.3 8086/8088

1978   The third generation of microprocessors arrived in June 1976 with the launch of the 16-bit processors, when Texas Instruments introduced the TMS9900. Unfortunately, it never took off as it lacked peripheral devices, and in May 1978, Intel released the 8086 microprocessor, which was mainly an extension to the original 8080 processor and thus retained a degree of software compatibility. Intel first introduced the 4.77 MHz 8086

> "Microcomputers are the tool of the 80's. BASIC is the language that all of them use. So the sooner you learn BASIC, the sooner you will understand the microcomputer revolution."
> 30 Hour BASIC Standard, 1981.

microprocessor, which had 16-bit registers, a 16-bit data bus, and 29,000 transistors, using three-micron technology. It also had a 20-bit address bus and could thus access 1MB of memory. As it could operate on 16 bits at a time, it had good performance (0.33 MIPS) and initially sold for $360 (perhaps a joke at the expense of the IBM System/360). Later speeds included 8 MHz (0.66 MIPS) and 10 MHz (0.75 MIPS).

It was important for Intel to keep compatibility with 8080. The difficulty was that the 8080 used a 16-bit address (64 kB or 65,536 locations), whereas the 8086 would use a 20-bit address bus, allowing up to 1MB of memory to be addressed. Thus, the 8086 was designed with a segmented memory, where the memory was segmented in 64 kB chunks. The 20-bit address was then made up of a segment address, and an offset address.

In February 1979, Intel released the 8086 processor as follows:

The Intel 8086, a new microcomputer, extends the midrange 8080 family into the 16-bit arena. The chip has attributes of both 8- and 16-bit processors. By executing the full set of

8080A/8085 8-bit instructions plus a powerful new set of 16-bit instructions, it enables a system designer familiar with existing 8080 devices to boost performance by a factor of as much as 10 while using essentially the same 8080 software package and development tools.

The goals of the 8086 architectural design were to extend existing 8080 features symmetrically, across the board, and to add processing capabilities not to be found in the 8080. The added features include 16-bit arithmetic, signed 8- and 16-bit arithmetic (including multiply and divide), efficient interruptible byte-string operations, and improved bit manipulation. Significantly, they also include mechanisms for such minicomputer-type operations as reentrant code, position-independent code, and dynamically relocatable programs. In addition, the processor may directly address up to 1 megabyte of memory and has been designed to support multiple-processor configurations.

The 8086 and 8088 were binary compatible with each other, but not pin compatible. Binary compatibility allowed either microprocessor to execute the same program. Pin incompatibility meant that you could not plug the 8086 into the 8088, or vice versa, and expect the chips to work. The new 'x86' devices implemented a CISC (complex instruction set computer design methodology). Many other companies, and academics, reckoned that RISC architecture was the best processor technology. Intel would eventually win the CISC battle with the release of the Pentium processor, many years later.

At the time, Intel Corporation struggled to supply enough chips to feed the hungry assembly lines of the expanding PC industry. Therefore, to ensure sufficient supply to the PC industry, they subcontracted fabrication rights of these chips to AMD, Harris, Hitachi, IBM, Siemens, and possibly others. Amongst Intel and their cohorts, the 8086 line of processors ran at speeds ranging from 4 MHz to 16 MHz.

The Z80 processor, which had beaten the 8080 processor in many ways, led the way for its new 16-bit processor: the Z8000. Zilog had intended that it was to be compatible with the previous processor. Unfortunately, the designer decided to redesign the processor so that it had an improved architecture but was not compatible with the Z80. From then on, Zilog lost their market share, and this gives an excellent example of compatibility winning over superior technology. The 8086 design was difficult to work with and was constrained by compatibility, but it allowed easy migration for system designers.

Top 20 computer people
1. Dan Bricklin (VisiCalc)
2. Bill Gates (Microsoft)
3. Steve Jobs (Apple)
4. Robert Noyce (Intel)
5. Dennis Ritchie (C Programming)
6. Marc Andreessen (Netscape Communications)
7. Bill Atkinson (Apple Mac GUI)
8. Tim Berners-Lee (CERN/WWW)
9. Doug Engelbart (Mouse/Windows/etc.)
10. Grace Murray Hopper (COBOL)
11. Philippe Kahn (Turbo Pascal)
12. Mitch Kapor (Lotus 123)
13. Donald Knuth (TEX)
14. Thomas Kurtz
15. Drew Major (NetWare)
16. Robert Metcalfe (Ethernet)
17. Bjarne Stroustrup (C++)
18. John Warnock (Adobe)
19. Niklaus Wirth (Pascal)
20. Steve Wozniak (Apple)
Byte, September 1995

IBM's designers, after discussions with Bill Gates, realized the power of the 8086 and used it in the original IBM PC and IBM XT (eXtended Technology). It had a 16-bit data bus and a 20-bit address bus, and thus had a maximum addressable capacity of 1 MB, and could handle either 8 or 16 bits of data at a time (although in a messy way). Its main competitors were the Motorola 68000 and the Zilog Z8000

Unlike many of their previous computer systems, IBM developed their version of the PC using standard components, such as Intel's 16-bit 8086 microprocessor. At the time, most PCs were sold as games machines or programming machines. IBM changed this by releasing their PC as a business computer, which could run word processors, spreadsheets and databases and was named the IBM PC. It has since become the parent of all the PCs since produced, and to increase the production of this software for the PC, IBM made information on the hardware freely available. This resulted in many software packages being developed and helped clone manufacturers to copy the original design. So the term 'IBM compatible' was born and it quickly became an industry standard by sheer market dominance.

On previous computers, IBM had written most of their programs for their systems. For the PC they had a strict time limit, so they first went to Digital Research who was responsible for developing CP/M, which was proposed as a new standardized operating system for microprocessors. Unfortunately, for Digital Research, they were unable to reach a final deal because they could not sign a strict confidentiality agreement. So IBM went to a small computer company called Microsoft. For this, Bill Gates bought a program called Q-DOS (often called the quick and dirty operating system) from Seattle Computer Products. Q-DOS was similar to CP/M, but totally incompatible. Microsoft paid less than $100,000 for the rights to the software. It was released on the PC as PC-DOS, and Microsoft released their own version called MS-DOS, which has since become the best selling software in history, and IBM increased the market for Intel processors a thousand times over.

To give users some choice in their operating system, the IBM PC was initially distributed with three operating systems: PC-DOS (provided by Microsoft), Digital Research's CP/M-86 and UCSD Pascal P-System. Microsoft understood that to make their operating system the standard, they must provide IBM with a good deal. Therefore, Microsoft offered IBM the royalty-free rights to use Microsoft's operating system forever for $80,000. This made PC-DOS much cheaper than the other two (such as $450 for P-System, $175 for CP/M and $60 for PC-DOS). Microsoft was smart in that they allowed IBM the use of PC-DOS for free, but they held the control of the licensing of the software. This was one of the greatest pieces of business ever conducted. Eventually CP/M and P-System died off, while PC-DOS became the standard operating system for the PC.

DOS was hardly earth shattering, but it has since gone on to make billions of dollars. It derived its name from its original purpose, that of controlling disk drives. Compared with some of the work that was going on at Apple and at Xerox, it was a very basic system, as it had no graphical user interface, and accepted commands from the keyboard and displayed them to the monitor. These commands were interpreted by the system to perform file management tasks, program execution and system configuration. Its function was to run programs, copy and remove files, create directories, move within a directory structure and to list files. To most people this was their first introduction to computing, but, for many, DOS made using the computer too difficult to use, and it would not be until proper graphical user interfaces, such as Windows 95, that PCs would truly be accepted and used by the majority.

> By the middle of the 1990s, Intel and Microsoft were so profitable that they accounted for nearly half of the entire profits in the world-wide PC industry (which was worth over $100 billion, each year).

It did not take long for the computer industry to start cloning the IBM PC. Many companies tried but most failed because their BIOS was not compatible with IBM PC BIOS. Columbia, Kayro and others went by the wayside because they were not totally PC compatible. Compaq eventually broke though the compatibility barrier with the introduction of the Compaq portable computer (they succeeded by totally rewriting their own version of the BIOS, which was functionally compatible but used a different coding structure). Compaq's success created the turning point that enabled today's modern computer industry. They become the fastest growing company in history, producing sales of $111 million in the first year of their operation.

Many companies recognized the potential for the 8086/8088, such as Microsoft who developed Microsoft COBOL and Microsoft BASIC for it. In Japan, NEC bought a license on the 8086/8088, after which they improved its design and produced two Intel clones: the V20 (8088-compatible) and the V30 (8086-compatible). The V-series ran approximately 20 per cent faster than the equivalent Intel chips and were therefore a cheap upgrade to owners of the IBM-PC and other cloned computers. Although these chips were pin compatible with the 8086 and 8088, they also had some extensions to the architecture, such as 'new' instructions on the 80186/80188, and were capable of running in Z80 mode (directly running programs written for the Z80 microprocessor). Much to Intel's embarrassment, NEC refused to pay royalties to Intel on the sale of their processors. Intel found that it was difficult to copyright the actual silicon design, and have since copyrighted the microcode, which runs on the processor. The microcode for the 8086/8088 consisted of 90 different mini-programs. However, in a courtroom, NEC showed that they had not copied these mini-programs but had designed their own.

At this time, Intel was losing a great deal of their memory product to Japanese companies. From then on, they decided to focus on the PC processor market (where large profits could be made). If they could always keep one step ahead of the cloners, then they would have a virtual monopoly. Eventually they would become so powerful as a market leader that they would overcome the basic rule that you always need a second source of processors for new processors to be accepted in the market. IBM had thus developed a system (the IBM PC) that would end up reducing their own market share, and create a quasi-monopoly at the end of the 1990s and the beginning of the millennium for Intel (with processors and support devices) and Microsoft (for operating systems, and eventually application software). IBM would eventually fail in its introduction of new industry standards, such as MCA bus technology, whereas Intel would gain acceptance of new standards, such as the PCI bus, and Microsoft would develop new standards in operating systems, such as Windows NT.

Apple was growing fast in 1978, and released a BASIC version of VisiCalc spreadsheet. They also produced their first Apple II disk drive and Disk II, which was a 5.25-inch floppy disk drive linked to the computer by a cable ($495). At the end of 1978, Apple Computer began work on an enhanced Apple II with custom chips, code-named Annie, a su-

---

The first of many

The world's first large electronic computer (1946), containing 19,000 values, was built at the University of Pennsylvania by John Eckert during World War II. It was called ENIAC (Electronic Numerical Integrator and Computer) and it ceased operation in 1957. By today's standards, it was a lumbering dinosaur and by the time it was dismantled it weighed over 30 tons and spread itself over 1,500 square feet. Amazingly, it also consumed over 25 kW of electrical power (equivalent to the power of over 400 60 W light bulbs), but could perform over 100,000 calculations per second (which is reasonable, even by today's standards). Unfortunately, it was unreliable, and would only work for a few hours, on average, before a valve needed to be replaced.

Compatibility v. Technology

While Intel was developing the 8086, they were also developing the 8800 processor, which was not compatible with the 8080, and would be a great technological breakthrough (as it would not have to be compatible with the older 8080 device). When the 8800 was finally released in 1981 as the iAPX432 (Intel Advanced Processor Architecture), it reached the market just as the IBM PC took off, and died a quick death, as everyone wanted the lower-powered 8086 device. The iAPX lives on as the x86 architecture.

supercomputer with a bit-sliced architecture, code-named Lisa, and also on Sara (the Apple III). Along with these developments, Atari released the Atari 400 and 800 personal computers, which used the 6502 processor. They were also responsible for creating a market for use of computer systems in social pursuits when they developed the Asteroids computer game, along with Taito, who developed the Space Invaders arcade game. They were classics of their time, but hardly powerful by today's bit-mapped three dimensional graphics.

> Around 1978, Epson, who had a successful market in typewriters, started to produce low-price, high-performance dot matrix printers (the MX-80). At the same time, Commodore released the CBM 2020 dot matrix printer (as well as a dual 5.25-inch floppy disk drive unit).

1979 At PARC, Xerox was the leader in developing a graphical user interface with their Alto computer. As a learning process, a group of engineers and executives from Apple were given a demonstration of the Alton, and its associated software, in exchange for Xerox spending $1 million buying 100,000 Apple Computer shares. The investment would pay off many times over for Apple as it helped in their development of the Apple Mac computer. Unfortunately, Xerox finally lost its foothold in the computer industry when the president decided to drop the development of the Alto, even although it had just been advertised on the TV. Microsoft, on the other hand, was going from strength to strength. Microsoft 8080 BASIC eventually broke the one million-dollar barrier, and was the first microprocessor product to do so. Soon, Microsoft had developed BASIC and FORTRAN for the 8086, along with their Assembler language system for 8080/Z80 microprocessors.

> In 1979, Apple Computer released DOS 3.2 and the Apple II Plus computer, which had a 48 kB memory and cost $1195. They also highlighted their growing strength by introducing their first printer, the Apple Silentype ($600).
>
> Radio Shack continued development of their TRS-80 computer, with the TRS-80 Model II, and Texas Instruments introduced the TI-99/4 personal computer ($1,500). Atari also started to distribute Atari 400 (8 kB memory, $550) and Atari 800 ($1,000) personal computers.

1979 also produced mixed fortunes for two of Intel's competitors: Zilog and Motorola. It was a bad year for Zilog when it distributed its new 16-bit processor, the Z8000. It main drawback was its incompatibility with its 8-bit predecessor, the classic Z80. For Motorola, it was a year of success as they released the excellent 68000, 16-bit microprocessor. It used 68,000 transistors (hence, its name).

In computer systems, 1979 saw Radio Shack (with their TRS-80 range), Commodore (with the PET range), Apple Computer (with their Apple II/III) and Microsoft come to the forefront of the personal computer market. These were joined by new companies, at different ends of the technological spectrum. At the bottom end, which covered the games and hobby market, Sinclair Research appeared, while at the top end (workstations), which was aimed at serious applications, came Apollo.

In the UK, Clive Sinclair created Sinclair Research, which was distended to develop classic computers, such as the ZX81 and the Sinclair Spectrum. He had already been a major innovator in the 1960s and the 1970s with watches, audio amplifiers and pocket calculators. In the main, these were extremely successful; however, he was also destined to develop an electric car (Sinclair C5), which had the

> **Supersonic**
>
> In their first year (1981), Compaq Computers generated $110 million, two years on it was $503.9 million, and two years after that it was $1 billion. The following year it was $2 billion. From zero to $2 billion, in six years (a world record at the time).

opposite effect on sales as he had had with his computer systems. Two other new companies were created in 1979, which would become important industry leaders in peripherals. These were Seagate Technologies (founded by Alan Shugart in Scotts Valley, California), and Hayes Microcomputer Products who produced the 110/300-baud Micromodem II for the Apple II ($380).

A key to the acceptance and the sales of a computer was its software. This was in terms of its operating systems and its applications. Initially it was games that were used with the PCs, but three important application packages were released which helped its acceptance in the business market:

- **Spreadsheet**. The VisiCalc software was released for the Apple II at a cost of $100. Apple Computer eventually tried to buy the company which developed VisiCalc for $1 million in Apple stock, but Apple's president refused to approve the deal. Its eventual rights would have been worth much more than this small figure.
- **Word processor**. MicroPro released the WordStar word processor (written by Rob Barnaby), which was available for Intel 8080A and Zilog Z80-based CP/M-80 systems. Apple Computer also released AppleWriter 1.0. The following year (1980) would see the release of the popular WordPerfect (from Satellite Software International).
- **Database**. The Vulcan database program, which become known at dBase II.

| 1980 | The major developments of the year were: |

- **Radio Shack**. Radio Shack followed up the success of the TRS-80 with the TRS-80 Model III, which was was based around the Zilog Z80 processor and was priced between $700 and $2,500. They also released the TRS-80 Color Computer, which was based on the Motorola 6809E processor and had 4 kB RAM. It was priced well below the Model III and cost $400. Radio Shack at the time were innovating in other areas, and produced the TRS-80 Pocket Computer, which had a 24-character display, and sold for $230.

> **An integrated circuit?**
>
> In 1952, G.W. Dummer, a radar expert from Britain's Royal Radar Establishment, had presented a paper proposing that a solid block of materials could be used to connect electronic components without connecting wires. This would lay the foundations of the integrated circuit.

- **Apple Computer**. Apple Computer accelerated their development work and released the Apple III computer, which was based on the 2 MHz 6502A microprocessor, and included a 5.25-inch floppy drive. It initially cost between $4,500 and $8,000. Work also began on the Diana project, which would eventually become the Apple IIe. The company was also floated on the stock market, where 4.6 million shares were sold at $22 a share. This made many Apple employees instant millionaires.
- **Sinclair Research**. Sinclair Research burst into the computer marketplace with the ZX80 computer. It was based on the 3.25 MHz NEC Technologies 780-1 processor and came with 1 kB RAM and 4 kB ROM. It was priced at a cut-down rate of $200, but was far from perfect. Its main drawback was its membrane type keyboard.
- **Intel**. Along with development of the 8086 processor, Intel released a number of support devices, including the 8087 math coprocessor.
- **Microsoft**. Microsoft released a UNIX operating system, Microsoft XENIX OS, for the Intel 8086, Zilog Z8000, Motorola M68000, and Digital Equipment PDP-11.
- **Hewlett-Packard**. HP had developed a good market in powerful calculators, and produced the HP-85, a hybrid of a computer and a calculator. It cost $3,250 and had a 32-character wide CRT display, a built-in printer, a cassette tape recorder, and a keyboard.

- **Commodore**. Commodore Business Machines enhanced their product range with the CBM 8032 computer, which had 32 kB RAM and an 80-column monochrome display. They also developed a dual 5.25-inch floppy disk drive unit (the CBM 8050). In Japan, Commodore released the VIC-1001, which would later become the VIC-20. It had 5 kB RAM, and a 22-column color video output capability.

- **Apollo**. Apollo burst onto the computer market with high-end workstations based on the Motorola 68000 processor. These were aimed at the serious user, and their main application area was in computer-aided design. One of the first to be introduced was the DN300, which was based around the excellent Motorola 68000 processor. It had a built-in mono monitor, an external 60 MB hard disk drive, an 8-inch floppy drive, built-in ATR (Apollo Token Ring) network card, and 1.5 MB RAM. It even had its own multiuser, networked operating system called Aegis. Unfortunately, for all its power and usability, Aegis never really took off, and when the market demanded standardized operating systems, Apollo switched to Domain/IX (which was a UNIX clone). It is likely that Apollo would have captured an even larger market if they had changed to UNIX at an earlier time, as Sun (the other large workstation manufacturer) had done. The Token Ring network was excellent in its performance, but suffered from several problems, such as the difficulty in tracing faults and the difficulty in adding and deleting nodes from the ring. Over time, Ethernet eventually became the standard networking technology, as it was relatively cheap and easy to maintain and install.

  Apollo attacked directly at the IBM/DEC mainframe/minicomputer market, and soon developed a large market share of the workstation market. The advantage of workstations over mainframes was that each workstation had its own local resources, including a graphical display and, typically, windows/graphics-based packages. Mainframes and minicomputers tended to be based on a central server with a number of text terminals. Apollo were successful in developing the workstation market and their only real competitor was Sun. Hewlett-Packard eventually took Apollo over. However, Apollo computers, as with the classic computers, such as the Apple II and the Apple Macintosh, were well loved by their owners and some would say that they were many years ahead of their time.

- **Seagate Technology**. Seagate become a market leader for hard disk drives when they developed a 5.25-inch Winchester disk, with four platters and a capacity of 5 MB.

- **Philips/Sony**. These companies developed the CD–Audio standard for optical disk storage of digital audio. At the same time, Sony Electronics introduced a 3.5-inch floppy double-sided double-intensity disk and drive, which had a capacity of 875 kB (less when formatted).

- **Texas Instruments**. TI were busy adding peripherals to their TI 99/4 computer, including a thermal printer (30 cps on a 5×7 character matrix), a command module ($45), a modem, RS-232 interface ($225), and a 5.25-inch mini-floppy disk drive that could store up to 90 kB on each disk. The floppy disk controller cost $300, and the disk drive cost $500.

- **Digital Research**. DR released CP/M-86 for Intel 8086- and 8088-based systems. Digital Research could have easily become the Microsoft of the future, but for a misunderstanding with IBM.

1.4 80186/80188

1982 Intel continued the evolution of the 8086 and 8088 by introducing the 80186 and 80188 in 1982. These processors featured new instructions and new fault tolerance protection, and were Intel's first of many failed attempts at the x86 chip integration game.

The new instructions and fault tolerance additions were logical evolutions of the 8086 and 8088, and the added instructions made programming much more convenient for low-level (assembly language) programmers. The original 8086 and 8088 would hang when they encountered an invalid computer instruction, whereas the 80186 and 80188 added the ability to trap this condition and attempt a recovery method.

Intel integrated this processor with many of the peripheral chips already employed in the IBM PC. The 80186/80188 integrated interrupt controllers, interval timers, DMA controllers, clock generators, and other core support logic. In many ways the 80186/80188 was a decade ahead of its time. Unfortunately, it did not catch on with many hardware manufacturers, and thus spelled the end of Intel's first attempt at CPU integration. However, it enjoyed a tremendous success in the world of embedded processors (often they can be found in a high performance disk driver or disk controller). Eventually, many embedded processor vendors began manufacturing these devices as a second source to Intel, or in clones of their own. Between the various vendors, the 80186/80188 was available in speeds ranging from 6 MHz to 40 MHz.

Intel had had considerable trouble providing enough 8086/80186 processors, and had created technology-sharing agreements with companies such as AMD. This also allowed companies to have a second source for processors, as many organizations (especially military-based organizations) did not trust a single-source supply for a product. In 1984, it was estimated that Intel could supply only between one-fifth and one-third of the current demand for the 80186 device. For the coming 80386 design, Intel decided to break the industry practice of second sourcing and go on their own.

1.5 80286

In 1982, Intel introduced the 80286. For the first time, Intel did not simultaneously introduce an 8-bit bus version of this processor (such as the 80288). The 80286 introduced some significant microprocessor extensions.

> "But what ... is it good for?" Engineer at the Advanced Computing Systems Division of IBM, 1968, commenting on the microchip.

Intel continued to extend the instruction set; more significantly, Intel added four more address lines and a new operating mode called 'protected mode'. The 8086, 8088, 80186 and 80188 all contained 20 address lines, giving these processors one megabyte of addressibility ($2^{20} = 1$ MB). The 80286, with its 24 address lines, gave 16 megabytes of addressibility ($2^{24} = 16$ MB).

For the most part, the new instructions of the 80286 were introduced to support the new protected mode. Real mode was still limited to the one megabyte program addressing of the 8086 et al. Essentially, a program could not take advantage of a 16 MB address space without using protected mode (16 MB was a typical memory address, at the time, but few programs could actually access the upper 15 MB of memory). Unfortunately, protected mode could not run real-mode (DOS) programs, and these limitations thwarted attempts to adopt the 80286 programming extensions for mainstream consumer use.

> "It is practically impossible to teach good programming style to students that have had prior exposure to BASIC; as potential programmers they are mentally mutilated beyond hope of regeneration." – Dijkstra

During the reign of the 80286, the first chipsets were introduced, which were basically a set of devices to replace dozens of other peripheral devices, while maintaining identical functionality. Chips and Technologies became one of the first popular chipset companies.

IBM was spurred by the huge success of the IBM PC and decided to use the 80286 in their next generation computer, the IBM PC-AT. However, the PC-AT was not introduced until 1985, three years after introduction of the 80286. IBM, it seems, were actually frightened by the thought of the 32-bit processors as it allowed PCs to challenge their thriving minicomputer market. A new threat to the PC emerged from Apple, who used the Motorola 68000 processor, with an excellent operating system to produce the Apple Mac computer. It had a full graphical user interface based around windows and icons, and had a mouse pointer to allow users to move easily around the computer system.

Like the IBM PC, the PC-AT was hugely successful for home and business use. Intel continued to second-source the device to ensure an adequate supply of chips to the computer industry. Intel, AMD, IBM and Harris were now producing 80286 chips as OEM products, whereas Siemens, Fujitsu and Kruger either cloned it, or were also second sources. Between these various manufacturers, the 80286 was offered in speeds ranging from 6 MHz to 25 MHz.

1.6 Post-PC Development

IBM dominated the computer industry in the 1950s and 1960s, and it was only in the 1970s that their quasi-monopoly started to erode. At the time, most of their competitors feared their power, and few companies had the sales turnover to match IBM in research and development. If a competitor released a new product, they would often sit back and wait for IBM to trump them with a better product that had the magical IBM badge. This was shown to great effect with the development of the System/360 range, which had one of the largest ever research and development budgets ($5 billion). After initial development setbacks, the System/360 range was a great success and paid off the initial investment many times over. IBM sold over 50,000 System/360 computers in a period of six years, and then replaced it with the System/370 series, which was one of the first computers with memory made from integrated circuits.

> "The use of COBOL cripples the mind; its teaching should, therefore, be regarded as a criminal offense."
>
> *Dijkstra.*

In 1981, IBM started the long slide from front-runner to also-ran and, within 10 years, their own child (the IBM PC) would eventually match the power of its own mainframes. For example, when the Pentium was released in 1989 it had a processing power of 250 MIPS, while the IBM System/370 mainframe had a processing power of 400 MIPS. IBM, in the development of the IBM AT computer, even tried to slug the power of the PC so that it would not impinge on their lucrative mainframe market. As will be seen, IBM, after the overwhelming success of the IBM PC, made two major mistakes:

- **The PCjr**. The PCjr sank quickly without trace, as it was incompatible with the IBM PC. The time and money spent on the PCjr was completely wasted and gave other manufacturers an opportunity to clone, and improve on the original IBM PC.
- **Missing the portable market**. IBM missed the IBM PC portable market, and when they did realize its potential, their attempt was inferior to the market leader, Compaq Computers. Later, though, they would produce an excellent portable, called the ThinkPad, but by that time they had lost a large market share to companies such as Toshiba, Compaq and Dell.

Along with making these mistakes, other factors continued to affect their loss of market share:

- Initially missing the market for systems based on 32-bit microprocessors (80386). IBM missed the 32-bit processor when they developed their AT and PS/2 ranges of computers, as initially they used the 16-bit 80286. This had been partly intentional, as IBM did not want to make their new computer too powerful, as they would start to compete with their lucrative mainframe market.
- Trying to move the market towards MCA. After IBM realized that they had lost the battle against the cloners, they developed their own architecture, MicroChannel Architecture (MCA), which would force manufacturers to license the technology from them. Unfortunately for IBM, Compaq took over the standard as they introduced a computer that used standard IBM PC architecture, but improved on it as they used the new Intel 80386 in their DeskPro range. IBM would, in time, come back into the fold and follow the rest in their architecture. From then on, IBM became a follower rather than a leader.

After losing a large market share, IBM soon realized, after the failure of MCA, that they had also lost the market leadership for hardware development. They then decided to try to turn the market for operating system software, with OS/2. It was becoming obvious that the operating system held the key to the hardware architectures and application software. In a perfect world, an operating system can hide the hardware from the application software, so the hardware becomes less important. Thus, if the software runs fast enough, the hardware can be of any type and of any architecture, allowing application programmers to write their software for the operating system and not for the specific hardware. Whichever company developed the standards for the operating system would hold the key to hardware architecture, and also the range of other packages, such as office tools, networking applications, and so on. OS/2 would eventually fail, and it would be

Top 20 computers of all time
1.   MITS Altair8800
2.   Apple II
3.   Commodore PET
4.   Radio Shack TRS-80
5.   Osborne I Portable
6.   Xerox Star
7.   IBM PC
8.   Compaq Portable
9.   Radio Shack TRS-80 Model 100
10. Apple Macintosh
11. IBM AT
12. Commodore Amiga 1000
13. Compaq Deskpro 386
14. Apple Macintosh II
15. Next Nextstation
16. NEC UltraLite
17. Sun SparcStation 1
18. IBM RS/6000
19. Apple Power Macintosh
20. IBM ThinkPad 701C
Byte, September 1995

left to one company to lead in this area: Microsoft. Not even the mighty Intel could hold the standards, as Microsoft held the key link between the software and the hardware. Their operating system would eventually decouple the software from the hardware. With the Microsoft Windows NT operating system, they produced an operating system that could run on different architectures.

Unfortunately for IBM, OS/2 was a compromised operating system that was developed for all their computers, whether they be mainframes or low-level PCs. Unlike the development of the PC, many of the organizational units within IBM, including the powerful mainframe divisions, had a say about what went into OS/2 and what was left out. For the IBM PC, the PC team at Boca Raton was given almost total independence from the rest of the organization, but the development of OS/2 was riddled with compromises, reviews and specification changes. At the time, mainframes differed from PCs in many different ways. One of the most noticeable ways was the way that they were booted, and the regularity of system crashes. Most users of PCs demanded fast boot times (less than a minute if possible), but had no great problems when it crashed a few times a day, which were typically due to incorrectly functioning and configured hardware, and incorrectly installed software. In the mainframe market, an operating system performs a great deal of system checks and tries to properly configure the hardware. This causes long boot-up times, which is not a problem with a mainframe that typically runs for many weeks, months or years without requiring a re-boot. However, for the PC, a boot time of anything more than a few minutes is a big problem. In the end, OS/2 had too long a boot time, and was too slow (possibly due to its complexity) to compete in the marketplace. In total, IBM spent over $2 billion on OS/2 with very little in return. It is perhaps ironic that new versions of the Microsoft operating system perform a great deal of system checks and try to configure the system each time it is booted. Now, though, this can be done in a relatively short time, as the hardware is a great deal faster than it was when graphical user interfaces first reached the market.

> **Another casualty**
>
> Another casualty of the rise of the IBM PC was DEC. As IBM had done with the System/360 range, DEC invested billions of dollars in their VAX range, which became an unbelievable success. As Compaq Computers would do in the 1980s, DEC achieved unbelievable growth, going from its foundation in 1957 to a sales turnover of $8 billion in 1986 (the peak year for DEC, before the PC destroyed the market for minicomputers).

The introduction of the PC would see the end of computer manufacturing for Osborne, Altair, Texas Instruments and Xerox. Going in the opposite direction were the new companies such as Compaq Computers, Sun Microsystems, Apollo (for a while), Cray and Microsoft. Compaq Computers generated $110 million in their first year (1981), a further two years on it was $503.9 million, two years after that it was $1 billion, and the following year it was $2 billion. From zero to $2 billion in six years–a world record, at the time.

Microsoft was another high-growth company going from $16 million in 1981 to $1.8 billion in 1991 (in most years, Microsoft doubled its size). Consistently, Microsoft was also highly profitable with at least 30 per cent of sales resulting in profit, and at least 10 per cent invested in research and development. The next 20 years would also see the creation of many computer-related multibillionaires, such as Bill Gates, who, within in 20 years, would be worth almost $100 billion.

Before the introduction of the IBM PC, the biggest threats to IBM came from DEC, at the top end and from Apple at the bottom. Both companies could do little wrong. DEC released their classic PDP-11 and then followed it up with the VAX range. Apple quickly developed their range of computers, and moved from a mainly game-playing computer to one that could be used for games and business applications. For Apple, the key to the move into the business environment was the introduction of VisiCalc. From the 1980s, software became the dominant driving force, and the best hardware in the world could not make up for a lack of application software.

1981 would become a pivotal year for the development of computers. Before this year, different computer standards thrived, and incompatibility reigned. After it, there would be only one main standard, which would be driven not by IBM, but by Intel and Microsoft.

At the time, the computer industry split itself into two main areas:

- **Serious/commercial computers**. Mainly IBM and DEC with their range of mainframe computers and minicomputers. Within 10 years, both IBM and DEC would change to be different companies. IBM would end up losing their quasi-monopoly on computers systems, and DEC would end up being taken over by Compaq, who would evolve from the new market created by IBM.

- **Hobby/home/game-playing computers**. These computers had grown from the basic 8-bit processors, such as the 6502 and the Z80. The main product leaders were Commodore, Sinclair, Apple, Osborne, Altair, Acorn, Radio Shack and Xerox.

Few of these computers, at the time, were compatible with each other, and it was a great advantage to a manufacturer that their computers were incompatible with others, as software written for one would not work on another. For example, the Apple II and the Commodore PET were based on the same processor, but had incompatible hardware, especially with the graphics system.

> **The Father of the PC**
>
> In 1981 IBM released, ahead of schedule, the IBM 5150 PC Personal Computer, which featured the 4.77 MHz Intel 8088 processor, 64 kB RAM, 40 kB ROM, one 5.25-inch floppy drive (160 kB capacity), and PC-DOS 1.0 (Microsoft's MS-DOS). It cost $3,000, and could be installed with Microsoft BASIC, VisiCalc, UCSD Pascal, CP/M-86, and Easywriter 1.0. Another version used a CGA graphics card, which gave 640×200 resolution with 16 colors.

At the time, many of the other computer companies were following up the success of their previous products, and few had any great worries of the business-oriented IBM PC. The main developments were:

> **The Real Apple**
>
> In 1981, Apple Computer got into a little bit of trouble over the Apple name, as The Beatles used it for their record company (Apple Corps Limited). Eventually, Apple Computer signed an agreement allowing them to use the Apple name for their business, but they were not allowed to market audio/video products with recording or playback capabilities.

- **Commodore**. After its release in Japan, Commodore eventually released the VIC-20 to an eager world market. It had a full-size 61-key keyboard, 5 kB RAM (expandable to 32 kB), 6502A CPU, a 22×23 line text display, and color graphics. It initially sold for $299, and at its peak, it was being produced at 9,000 units per day.
- **Sinclair**. Sinclair followed up the success of the ZX80 with the ZX81 (in the USA it was released as the TS1000), which cost just $150 and was based on the Z80A processor. Within 10 months, over 250,000 were sold.
- **Apple**. Apple was very much a market leader, and would eventually be the only real competitor to the IBM PC. In 1981, they reintroduced the Apple III, which was their first computer with a hard disk.
- **Osborne**. The Osborne Computer Corporation was going from strength to strength and, if it had not been for the release of the IBM PC, would have been a major computer manufacture. In 1981, they released the Osborne 1 PC, based on the Z80A processor, and included a 5-inch display, 64 kB RAM, keyboard, a keypad, modem, and two 5.25-inch 100 kB disk drives. It sold for $1,795, but included CP/M, BASIC, WordStar, and Super-Calc. Sales were much greater than expected; in fact they sold as many in a single month as they expected for their total annual sales (up to 10,000 per month).
- **Xerox**. Xerox continued to innovate, and released the Star 8010, which contained many of the features that were used with the Alto, such as a bit-mapped screen, WYSIWYG word processor, mouse, laser printer, Smalltalk language, Ethernet, and software for combining text and graphics in the same document. It sold for the unbelievably high price of $16,000. This price, especially up against the IBM PC, was too great for the market, and it quickly failed. At the same time, Xerox was planning the Xerox 820 (code named The Worm), which would be based on the 8-bit Z80 processor, whereas the new IBM PC was based on the 16-bit 8088. It, like the Star 8010, was doomed to fail. These were classic cases of releasing products at the wrong time for the wrong price.

- **Acorn**. In the UK, Acorn Computer released an excellent computer named the BBC Microcomputer System. It was quickly adopted for a UK TV program that the BBC was running to introduce microcomputers. Against the ZX81, it had an excellent specification, such as being based on the 6502A processor, addressing up to 48 kB RAM, and a 16-color graphics display. Its great advantage, though, was that it had a real keyboard (and not a horrible membrane keyboard, like the ZX81). The BBC TV program was a great success in the UK, as was the BBC Microcomputer.

Two other companies that became industry leaders developed products in 1981: Novell Data Systems and Aston-Tate. Novell created a simple networking operating system that allowed two computers to share a single hard disk drive. Soon Novell would develop their Novell NetWare operating system, which allowed computers to share resources over a network, especially disk and printer resources. Ashton-Tate released the dBase II package which, for many years, was the standard database package.

> **First microprocessor**
>
> In the late 1960s, the electronics industry was producing cheap pocket calculators, which led to the development of affordable computers when the Japanese company Busicom commissioned Intel to produce a set of between eight and 12 ICs for a calculator. Then, instead of designing a complete set of ICs, Ted Hoff at Intel designed an integrated circuit chip that could receive instructions and perform simple integrated functions on data. The design became the 4004 microprocessor. Intel produced a set of ICs that could be programmed to perform different tasks. These were the first ever microprocessors and soon Intel produced a general-purpose 4-bit microprocessor, named the 4004.

For Intel, the adoption of the 8088 in the IBM PC was a godsend, and they had great difficulty in keeping up with the supply of the processor. Unlike the 8080, though, they did not actively seek AMD as a second source for the processor, as they had learnt that some second-source rights caused problems when the second source company actually moved ahead of them in their technology. Typically, second-source companies were able to charge a lower rate, as they do not have to recoup the initial research and development investment. Intel would eventually seek other companies, and AMD sought out Zilog for second source rights for their up-and-coming Z8000 device. It seemed to AMD that Zilog would have greatest potential for their new device, as they had shown with their Z80 device.

Intel was starting to realize that the processor market was a winner as it had a great deal of intellectual effort added to it, and differed from the memory market where designs could be copied easily by competitors (one memory cell looks very much like any other one). With microprocessors, they could set new standards and protect their designs with copyrights. Also if they established a lead in the processor market, and kept one step ahead of the cloners, they could make a great deal of profit in releasing new products and producing support devices for their processors, especially for the 8086/8088. For this, Intel released the 8087 math coprocessor, which greatly speeded up mathematical calculations, especially floating point calculations. The use of floating-point long division would eventually come back to haunt Intel, when a college tutor discovered a bug in their Pentium processor.

Intel was an innovative company and had produced the first 4-bit and 8-bit processors, but in the 16-bit market they were beaten by Texas Instruments (TI). Unfortunately, the TMS 9900 was a rehash of an earlier product, and was generally underpowered. Intel, though, had the great strength in their 8088 processor of releasing a whole series of support devices, which made it easier for designers to integrate the new processor. No one could have guessed the impact that the IBM PC would have on the market. Intel was also beaten by National Semiconductor for the first 32-bit processor (the 32000).

1982 would see IBM throw open the market for computers through two great mistakes. Apart from IBM, five other companies would dominate the year: Commodore, Sinclair, Compaq, Apple and Sun. Commodore, Apple and Sinclair were from the old school, while Compaq and Sun Microsystems would learn to adapt to the new 'serious' market in computing that the IBM PC had created. In the same year, the US Justice Department threw out an anti-trust lawsuit filed against IBM 13 years earlier. Within 15 years, it would be Microsoft who was facing similar action.

> **Same old story**
>
> In the late 1940s, IBM had a considerable share of the computer market, so much so that a complaint was filed against them alleging monopolistic practices in its computer business, in violation of the Sherman Act. By January 1954, the US District Court made a final judgement on the complaint against IBM. For this, a consent decree was then signed by IBM, which placed limitations on how IBM conducts business with respect to 'electronic data processing machines'.

At IBM, the PC was taking off in ways that could never have been imagined. It had been a work of genius in which everything had been planned with perfection, and would sell over 200,000 computers within 12 months of its introduction, but the following year would see two major mistakes by IBM. The first was the introduction of the PCjr, which was intentionally incompatible with the IBM PC (because IBM did not want it to affect the IBM PC market), and the IBM AT. The PCjr failed because of its incompatibility; the AT failed because it used a 16-bit processor (the 80286) while other computers were released using the new Intel 32-bit processor (the 80386). IBM could have overcome these drawbacks easily but, as these developments involved a much wider team than the IBM PC, they were held back by the interests of other parties. For example, the mainframe division was keen for the AT to use 16-bit processors, rather than the more powerful 32-bit processors, as this could further erode their market. These two decisions would open the door to the new kid on the block – Compaq.

1983   Three former Texas Instruments managers founded Compaq Computer Corporation in 1982: Rod Canion, Jim Harris and Bill Murto. Their first product was Compaq Portable PC, which was released in 1983 and cost $3,000. The Compaq Portable was totally compatible with the IBM PC and used the Intel 8088 (4.77 MHz), had 128 kB RAM, a 9-inch monochrome monitor and had a 320 kB 5.25-inch disk drive (Sony Electronics in the same year demonstrated the 3.5-inch microfloppy disk system). A large part of the start-up finance was used to create a version of the ROM BIOS, which was IBM compatible but did not violate IBM's copyright – a stroke of genius that many failed to follow. Compaq would soon become the fastest growing company ever. Only in the computer industry could a company grow from zero to hundreds of millions of dollars within 12 months.

Compaq created a new market, which was based on IBM PC compatibility. They then waited for the great IBM to come along and sink their product, but when IBM did produce a portable, it was too late, too heavy, and failed to match the Compaq in its specification. Compaq were not in fact the first company to clone the IBM PC– that was achieved by Columbia Data Products with their MPC.

Two companies that would battle against the PC for market share were Sun and Apple. Sun Microsystems, which derived its name from an acronym from the Stanford University Network, would quickly become a major computer company. Their first product was the Sun 1 workstation computer. They, like Apple, fought the IBM PC in terms of architecture and operating system. Sun, almost single-handedly, made the UNIX operating system popular. Their computers succeeded in the market not because they were compatible with any other computer but because they were technically superior to anything that the IBM PC could offer. The software that ran on the system used the processing power of the processor fully, and the UNIX operating system provided an excellent robust and reliable operating system.

Compatibility can often lead to a great deal of problems, especially if the compatibility involves the 8088 processor.

At Apple, champagne corks were popping as they became the first PC company to generate $1 billion in annual sales, where the Apple II Plus and Apple II had sold over 750,000 units. After toying with the Lisa computer and new versions of the Apple II, Apple would have one more trump card up their sleeve: the Apple Macintosh.

Along with working with the IBM PC, Microsoft was also keen to work with Apple in case the relationship with IBM did not work out, and they signed an agreement to develop applications for the forthcoming Macintosh (of which Microsoft were given an initial prototype to work on). IBM had become slightly annoyed with the success of Microsoft, especially from the success of their own creation. For Microsoft, it was a no-lose situation. They were, in the main, sharing code across the two architectures, which would quickly become industry standards. One would become an open standard (the IBM PC), and the other a closed standard (the Apple Mac).

The year 1982 saw fantastic growth at Intel, and the only way that they could keep up with demand was to license their products to other silicon design companies. For this, they signed a 10-year technology exchange agreement with Advanced Micro Devices (AMD) that focused on the x86 microprocessor architecture. This agreement would be regretted later as AMD started to overtake them in the 80486 market. In the same year, Intel released an update to the 8086 processor, called the 80286, which was destined for the IBM AT computer. It ran initially at 6 MHz, which improved on the 4.77 MHz of the 8088 processor, and had a 16-bit data bus, like the 8086, but had an extended 24-bit address bus. This gave it an addressing range of 16 MB, rather than the 1 MB addressing range of the 8086/8088, or 1 GB of virtual memory. It outperformed the 8086 with a throughput of 0.9 MIPS, but this increased to 1.5 MIPS with a 10 MHz clock and 2.66 MIPS with a 12 MHz clock.

Commodore was never slow at developing their products, and after the success of the Vic-20 in 1981, they released the Commodore 64 in the following year. It sold for $600 and had an excellent specification based around the new 6510 processor, such as 64 kB RAM, 20 kB ROM, sound chip (the first PC to have integrated sound using an integrated synthesizer chip), eight sprites, 16-color graphics, and a 40-column screen. They then released a whole range of peripherals, such as the VIC Modem ($110). Commodore also moved into the business market, with the BX256 and BX128 computers for $3,000 and $1,700, respectively.

At Sinclair, the ZX81 had been an unbelievable success and, knowing that alone they could not succeed in the USA market, they signed an agreement with the Timex Corporation to license Sinclair computers in the USA. By the end of 1982, Sinclair Research had sold over 500,000 ZX81s in over 30 countries.

Hooray to Hollerith

One of the first occurrences of computer technology occurred in the USA in the 1880s. It was due to the American Constitution demanding that a survey be undertaken every 10 years. As the population in the USA increased, it took an increasing amount of time to produce the statistics. By the 1880s, it looked likely that the 1880 survey would not be complete until 1890. To overcome this, Herman Hollerith (who worked for the government) devised a machine that accepted punch cards with information on them. These cards allowed a current to pass through only when there was a hole present.

Hollerith's electromechanical machine was extremely successful and was used in the 1890 and 1900 Censuses. He even founded the company that would later become International Business Machines (IBM).

Atari also become a major computer company with the Atari 800, which had an advanced graphics display. Radio Shack also released the powerful TRS-80 Model 16, which used a

16-bit Motorola MC68000 microprocessor, a Z80 microprocessor, had 8-inch floppy drives, and an optional 8 MB hard drive. At the same time that Compaq were releasing their portable, Radio Shack produced the TRS-80 Pocket Computer; unfortunately, it was relatively slow as it used a 1.3 MHz 8-bit microprocessor, with a 26-character display.

DEC also decided finally to enter the personal computer market with the dual-processor Rainbow 100. It had an excellent specification with both a Z80 and an 8088 microprocessor, and could run CP/M, CP/M-86 or MS-DOS. Unfortunately, at $3,000 it was too expensive for the market, which was already hot for the IBM PC.

1983 was a mixed year for IBM, as they continued their success with the release of the IBM PC XT and released PC-DOS 2.1, but, on the downside, they released the IBM PCjr, which would soon become an expensive flop.

> **To the 4004 and beyond**
>
> The 4004 caused a revolution in the electronics industry as previous electronic systems had a fixed functionality. With this processor, the functionality could be programmed by software. Amazingly, by today's standards, it could handle only 4 bits of data at a time (a nibble); it contained 2,000 transistors, had 46 instructions and allowed 4 kB of program code and 1 kB of data. From this humble start, the PC has since evolved using Intel microprocessors. Intel had previously been an innovative company, and had produced the first memory device (static RAM, which uses six transistors for each bit stored in memory), the first DRAM (dynamic memory, which uses only one transistor for each bit stored in memory) and the first EPROM (which allows data to be downloaded to a device, which is then permanently stored).

The XT sold for $5,000 and had a 10 MB hard drive, three extra expansion slots, and a serial interface. In its basic form it had 128 kB RAM, and a 360 kB floppy drive.

The greatest winners in 1983 were the newly created Compaq Computers and Microsoft. In their first year, Compaq sold 47,000 computers, with a turnover of $111 million (and raised $67 million on their first public stock offering). They would eventually reach the $1 billion mark within five years of their creation.

Microsoft knew that they had to completely rewrite the MS-DOS operating system so that it coped better with current and future systems. For this, they introduced MS-DOS 2.0, which supported 10 MB hard drives, a tree-structured file system, and 360 kB floppy disks. They had realized quickly the potential of the IBM PC, and released XENIX 3.0 (a PC version of UNIX), Multi-Tool Word for DOS (which would eventually become Microsoft Word 1.0), as well as producing the Microsoft mouse (which sold for $200, with interface card and mouse). Microsoft also announced, in 1983, that it would be developing Microsoft Windows (initially known as Interface Manager), which would eventually be released in 1985.

At the same time as Microsoft announced Windows, IBM was developing a program called TopView, and Digital Research was developing GEM (Graphics Environment Manager). These programs would use DOS as the basic operating system, but would allow the user to run multiple programs. When released, the problem with TopView was that it was text-based and not a graphical user interface (GUI, or 'gooey'). Even allowing for this, most predicted, because of IBM's strength, that TopView would become the standard user interface. If IBM had won the battle for the user interface, they would have probably taken over the standard of both the user interface and the operating system, and then eventually the standard for the architecture. IBM, though, did agree to work with Microsoft on OS/2. Microsoft would eventually invest hundreds of millions of dollars on OS/2, with little in return. But organizations must learn from their mistakes, and Microsoft has always done this, and used the expertise gained in developing OS/2 in developing Microsoft Windows.

As Microsoft released their new version of MS-DOS, AT&T released the version of UNIX that would become a standard: UNIX System V. It was the first attempt at bringing together the different versions of UNIX, including XENIX, SunOS and UNIX 4.3 BSD. The two main families of UNIX were to become UNIX System V and BSD (Berkeley Software Distribution) Version 4.4. System V would eventually be sold to SCO (Santa Cruz Operation). Currently available UNIX systems include AIX (on IBM workstations and mainframes), HP-UX (on HP workstations), Linux (on PC-based systems), OSF/1 (on DEC workstations) and Solaris (on Sun workstations). Other attempts at standardizing UNIX occurred with X/Open, OSF, and COSE, but have mainly failed. The great strength of UNIX is its communications and networking protocols (such as TCP/IP, SMTP, SNMP, and so on), which provide the foundation for the Internet.

Many organizations have tried to create new operating systems, such as VMS (from DEC) and Aegis (Apollo), but only UNIX has become a serious competitor to Microsoft in operating systems. In the PC market, Microsoft would totally dominate the market, although Linux (a UNIX clone) created a small market share for the technical experts. UNIX-based systems used the standardized

Integration generations
1st 1 bit per module
2nd 1 register per module
3rd Register-on-a-chip
4th Processor-on-a-chip
5th System-on-a-chip

networking software that was built into UNIX, but the PC still lacked any proper form of networking. So, in 1983, Novell created one of the standards of the PC networking market: the Novell NetWare network operating system. The only other operating system that could have competed again Microsoft's DOS and Windows was the up-and-coming Mac OS from Apple, which was at least 10 years ahead of its competitors. However, Apple refused to license their system to other vendors or to other computer manufacturers.

Another significant event in software development occurred at AT&T, when Bjarn Stroustrup designed the new object-oriented language C++. Its great strength, but also one of its weaknesses, was that it was based on the popular C programming language. C++ is now widespread and many professional applications have been written using C++, whether they be for microcomputers, minicomputers or mainframe computers. The main drawback of C++ was that programmers could still use the C programming language, which, because of its looseness and simplicity, allowed the programmer to produce programs that would compile but could crash because of a run-time error due to badly designed software. Typical errors were running off the end of an array, bad parameter passing into modules, or using memory that was reserved for other purposes. Object-oriented programming languages are much tighter in their syntax and the things that are allowed to be done. Thus, the compiler typically catches more errors, whether they are run-time or syntax errors, before the program is run. Java has since overcome the problems of C++ as it is totally object-oriented and much tighter in the rules of software coding.

The great strength for the adoption of the PC was IBM's intention to allow software companies to quickly develop application software. They thus released information on the hardware of the computer so that software companies could write compatible applications. Like VisiCalc for the Apple II in 1983, the two killer applications to help boost the acceptance, and sales, of the IBM PC were:

1. **Lotus 1-2-3**. This was a spreadsheet designed and developed by Jonathan Sachs and Mitch Kapor at Lotus Development. Over $1 million was spent on its initial promotion but it paid back its original investment a thousand times over. It initially required an extremely large amount of memory (256 kB), but its sales hit Microsoft's Multiplan spreadsheet, which had sold over one million copies. Microsoft

"We could conceivably put a company out of business with a bug in a spreadsheet, database, or word processor."

Chris Mason, Microsoft.

learnt from this, and in the coming years would release Excel, which would become the standard spreadsheet.

2. **WordPerfect**. This was a word processing package developed by Satellite Software International (who would eventually change their name to the WordPerfect Corporation.). It initially cost $500, and was an instant success. Many believed that WordPerfect 5.1 was the classic touch-type program, as it used keystrokes instead of long-winded menu options. Many typists have since had real troubles moving from WordPerfect to WIMPs-based packages such as Microsoft Word, so much so that many current word processors support all of the WordPerfect keystrokes.

1983 was to be a bleak year for non-IBM PC compatible computers, and prices fell month upon month. It also spelt the end of the line, in different ways, for three great innovators in the personal computer industry: Zilog, Osborne and Texas Instruments. The beginning of the end for Zilog was when they released their 32-bit microprocessor, the Z8000, an advanced device that had a 256-byte on-chip cache, instruction pipelining, memory management, and 10–25 MHz clock speed. Unfortunately, it was incompatible with the great Z80 processor, and thus failed in the market against the strength of the Intel 8086 and the up-and-coming 80386 processor. Of the many computer manufacturers who rushed to the market and used the 8086/8088, only one, Commodore, introduced a Z8000-based system (Commodore Z8000). Apart from the failings at IBM and DEC, the release of the Z8000 processor must rank amongst the poorest decisions in computing history. No one could predict the effect that a Z80-compatiable 32-bit processor would have had on the market. Certainly a 32-bit processor that was functionally compatible with the 8086/8088 (as the Z80 had been with the 8080) would have blown the market wide open, and would have possibly stopped the slide to quasi-monopoly of the Intel processors. Another failure in the processor market was the extremely powerful 6 MHz, 32-bit NS32032 microprocessor from National Semiconductor.

As the PC sales increased in the business market, Commodore Business Machines was becoming dominant in the home computers market and highlighted their dominance with the release of the Commodore 64, for $400, which quickly fell to $200 and dropped the prices of the VIC-20 to below $100 (breaking this barrier for the first time). In 1983, the sales of the VIC-20 reached 1,000,000. Commodore was also keen to develop the business market, and released the Commodore Executive 64. It cost $1,000 and had 64 kB RAM, a detachable keyboard, a 5-inch color monitor, and a 170 kB floppy drive. In 1983, Commodore became the first personal computer company to sell over $1 billion worth of computers.

Many companies in the home computer market had made large profits, but one failure in a product range could spell disaster. The high profits for all would not last long as Commodore, Atari and Sinclair started slashing prices. Sinclair, through Timex, introduced the Timex/Sinclair 2000 in the USA (known as the Sinclair Spectrum in other countries). It cost $149 for a 16 kB model, while the ZX81 price was reduced to $49. The squeeze was on as prices, and profits, tumbled.

Atari released their 600XL for $199, and ceased production of the Atari 5200. The 600XL was based on the 1.79 MHz 6502C processor, had 16 kB RAM, 24 kB ROM, and an optional CP/M module. As the push was on from other manufacturers to reduce prices, they also did the same and reduced the Atari 800 to $400. Atari also released the 1200XL home computer, which had 64 kB RAM, and 256 color capability, and cost $900. Production eventually ended for the 1200XL, mainly because of compatibility problems.

At the time, Japanese companies had been making great advances in the electronics industry, and many, such as NEC and Fujitsu, were starting to overtake USA silicon companies, such as Texas Instruments, Intel and National Semiconductor, in their production of integrated circuits (although Intel had the x86 series of processors as their trump card).

They were also winning in producing peripherals and accessories for computer systems:

- Fujitsu produced the first 256 kbit memory chips.
- Sony developed a new standard for 3.5-inch floppy disks, with the Microfloppy Industry Committee, and thus created the first double-sided, double-density holding floppy disk system that could store up to 1 MB. Sony was also working with Philips in creating the CD-ROM, which was an extension of audio CD technology.

However, in computer manufacturing, Japanese companies struggled as the USA companies, such as IBM and Apple, were setting the standards. The IBM PC was relatively easy to clone, but the Apple computer required a license to manufacture, which, at the time, was almost impossible to gain. Compared with many USA-based companies, the Japanese companies were efficient and produced reliable electronics, but as long as they were one step behind the US-based computer companies, they could not gain a serious share of the home computer market. To overcome this, 14 Japanese companies and Microsoft joined an alliance to create the MSX standard. This used a standardized architecture based on the Zilog Z80, TI TMS9918A video processor, General Instruments AY-8910 sound processor, NEC cassette interface chip, Atari joystick interface, 64 kB RAM, and 32 kB ROM-based extended Microsoft BASIC. Unfortunately it was doomed to fail with the release of the IBM PC and because it was based on 8-bit technology. Several MSX computers did reach the market, but they quickly failed. It was a great idea, and one that should have worked. The key to its failure was that there was a better, more defined standard: the IBM PC.

Three casualties of 1983 were Osborne Computer, Radio Shack and Texas Instruments, all of which were caused by being non-IBM PC compatible. In a classic case of releasing the right product at the wrong time, Osborne Computer released their own portable computer, but, unlike the IBM PC or Compaq's portable, it was based on the Z80A processor. The computer quickly failed and Osborne eventually filed for bankruptcy. Around the same time, Radio Shack also produced a non-IBM compatible portable: the TRS-80 Model 100. They had following the tried and tested technique of improving their product line by releasing the TRS-80 Model 4. It would fail as it cost $2,000, and was non-IBM PC compatible (as it was based on the 4 MHz Zilog Z80A microprocessor). Against the IBM PC, and the lower-end computers such as the VIC-64 and the Sinclair Spectrum, it was vastly overpriced. Texas Instruments eventually withdrew from the personal computer market when their TI 99/1, which had sold well over the years (over one million), struggled against the new, cheaper computers.

1983 While the Apple II was still making vast profits, Apple took a big gamble with the LISA (local integrated software architecture) computer. It cost $50 million, and its software cost $100 million

> LISA was actually named after Steve Job's daughter.

Classic microprocessors

1. **Intel 4000/4040** (Nov 1971). First microprocessor. 46 instructions, with 2,300 transistors within a 16-pin device.
2. **TMS 1000** (1972). First microcontroller, and the first to include RAM.
3. **Intel 8080** (April 1974). 16-bit address bus and an 8-bit data bus, with seven 8-bit registers. Used in Altair 8800.
4. **Zilog Z-80** (July 1976). Vastly improved version of the 8080.
5. **MOS Technologies 650x** (1975). Vastly improved, and much cheaper, version of the 6800. The 6502 was used in the Apple II.
6. **Motorola 6809**. Enhanced version of the 6800. It had two 8-bit accumulators (A and B), which could combine into a single 16-bit register (D). It also had two index registers (X and Y) and two stack pointers (S and U).
7. **AMD Am2901**. Popular 4-bit-slice processor, which had sixteen 4-bit registers and a 4-bit ALU. They could be used for a modular design, where several processors could be combined to produce a larger system (for example, two Am2901s could produce an 8-bit system). It also contained the first integrated math coprocessor.

→ *Continued on Page 55.*

(showing that the costs of developing hardware were reducing, while software development costs were increasing).
LISA was released in 1984, unfortunately it was expensive
($10,000) and underpowered, but it was the first com-
mercial personal computer to have a proper graphical user
interface (GUI). Rather than going with the 8086 as most

> One of the first personal computers was the Altair which was named after a destination for the Star Ship Enterprise in an episode of Star Trek.

of the market was doing, it was based on the excellent 5 MHz 68000 microprocessor. LISA
would sell over 100,000 units, and had 1 MB RAM, 2 MB ROM, a 12-inch black/white
monitor, 720×364 graphics, dual 5.25-inch 860 kB floppy drives, and a 5 MB hard disk drive.
Apple was keen to develop the LISA computer, but it would be the new Mac that would become the focus for their operation.

Apple was investing a great deal of effort in the Mac, and gave its developers the best
environment possible. This caused considerable friction with the Apple II division, as all the
finances for the Mac facilities were generated from sales of the Apple II. Apple intentionally
kept the two divisions apart, which helped only to increase the friction. Within the year, the
Apple II highlighted its success by selling its one millionth unit, and they continued its development with the Apple IIe, which had 64 kB RAM, Applesoft BASIC, upper/lower case
keyboard, seven expansion slots, 40×24 and 80×24 text, 1 MHz 6502 processor, up to
560×192 graphics, and a 140 kB 5.25-inch floppy drive.

The software market, especially related to the IBM PC, was growing fast. Satellite Software International released WordPerfect 3.0 for $500, and Borland International, founded by
Philippe Kahn, created the first version of their excellent Turbo Pascal compiler, and single-
handedly saved Pascal from an early exit. Borland were, for years, the main company involved in producing software development tools for the PC, with Borland C++, Borland
Delphi and Borland JBuilder. Unfortunately, they would eventually struggle against the
might of Microsoft (who were able to invest a great deal of money into their development
tools, especially in Visual Basic and Visual C++). Microsoft had the privileged position of
being able to invest money in other areas of development, but redirecting them from profits
made from other areas. For example, they used profits from the DOS system to invest in
Windows, and profits from Windows to invest into office applications (Word, Excel and
PowerPoint), and profits from office applications to invest into software development tools
(Visual Basic, Visual C++ and Visual Java). Obviously, it is to Microsoft's advantage that
they keep their tools up-to-date, as this is the same development system that they use to generate their own applications.

1984   1984 obviously had futuristic connotations to it. However, it was more of a
nightmare for IBM when they released the IBM PCjr. It used the 8088 CPU,
included 64 kB RAM, a 'Freeboard' keyboard (IBM would eventually release a
free upgrade keyboard, to those who wanted it), and one 5.25-inch disk drive, and no monitor, for $1,300. A year later the PCjr was dropped.

As the market became more competitive, IBM started to show their teeth as the number
of cloners increased. IBM sued them over a copyright violation of the IBM PC's BIOS, and
easily won the case. The unfortunate companies who were the first to be taken to court were
Corona Data Systems and Eagle Computer. It was clear that, to avoid litigation, companies
had to rewrite the BIOS. This would not give any technical advantage, but would keep
IBM's lawyers away.

The next step for IBM was important in the development of the PC. IBM had learnt from
their mistakes with the PCjr, and made their new computer, the PC AT, which was compatible with the IBM PC. It used the new Intel 6MHz 80286 processor, and had a 5.25-inch
1.2 MB floppy drive, with 256 kB or 512 kB RAM, optional 20 MB hard drive, and a monochrome or color monitor, and initial cost was $4,000.

As the demand for IBM PCs increased, there was also an increase for demand for enhanced graphics. For this, IBM released the Enhanced Color Display (EGA) monitor with 640×350 resolution, and 16 colors, at a cost of $850. They also released TopView, which failed in the market because it was text-based rather than a GUI. If they had done, they may have captured the market that Microsoft Windows gained.

The battle for the processor market started to heat up when Intel released the 80188, which was an integrated version of the 8086. They also allowed IBM the legal rights to use microlithography masks to make x86 processor chips. Intel, having survived the new 32-bit processors from Zilog and National Semiconductor, faced their biggest threat from NEC and Motorola. NEC was the first to clone the 8088 (with the 8 MHz V20 microprocessor) and the 8086 processor (with the 8 MHz V30 microprocessor), and from Motorola who added the 68010 and 68020 32-bit processors to their range. Many non-PC-based developers adopted the Motorola processor in favor of the 8086, as it was typically easier to develop hardware for it, and much easier to write software (the 8086 had a segmented memory architecture). For most, it was the only way for a computer manufacturer to differentiate themselves from the clone market. Some, such as Radio Shack, followed the IBM PC market with the Tandy 1000/1200 HD, but there was little to differentiate their clone from any other clone.

New entries for the year included Silicon Graphics, who would go on to produce excellent workstations with state-of-the-art graphics power. In 1984, they produced the first three-dimensional graphics workstation. They were also involved, in the 1990s, in the development of the graphics for *Jurassic Park*.

1984 was to be the year of Compaq Computer and Apple Computers. Compaq introduced the Compaq Deskpro, a true classic, and Apple Computer unveiled their Macintosh computer. Apple knew that they had a very special creation which was not only technically superior, but it also looked beautiful. A great computer such as the Mac demanded an amazing advertising campaign and Apple created one of the most talked about adverts ever, when they ran a $1.5 million dollar advert during the NFL SuperBowl, and showed it only once.

The Macintosh was as brilliant a computer as anyone could have conceived, as it was designed by creative people, not just technocrats. It was a fully integrated unit that could be ported easily from place to place, and used the 8 MHz 32-bit Motorola 68000 processor, along with a 9-inch B/W screen, 512×342 graphics, 400 kB 3.5-inch floppy disk drive, mouse, and 128 kB RAM. It cost $2,500. Microsoft knew that they could not rely only on the IBM PC market, so they worked closely with Apple and released Microsoft BASIC (MacBASIC) and Microsoft Multiplan for the Macintosh. Just 74 days after their introduction, over 50,000 Macs had been sold; and after 100 days, they had sold 70,000 units. After six months, it was 100,000 units, and within the year, 250,000 units. This was a great disappointment to Apple as they had estimated that they would sell over two million units by the end of 1985. The main problem was that the computer lacked resources, especially memory. Apple Computer overcame this by releasing the Macintosh 512K for $3,200.

> **Xerox and PARC**
>
> In the early 1970s, the Xerox Corporation gathered a team at the Palo Alto Research Center (PARC) and gave them the objective of creating 'the architecture of information'. It would lead to many of the great developments of computing, including personal distributed computing, graphical user interfaces, the first commercial mouse, bit-mapped displays, Ethernet, client/server architecture, object-oriented programming, laser printing and many of the basic protocols of the Internet. Few research centers have ever been as creative and forward thinking as PARC was over those years. So why didn't Xerox fully exploit their research? Maybe it was because they had seen themselves as being a 'paper-based' organization, and distributing information by electronic methods went against this core business.

The Macintosh had everything going for it. It was a totally integrated system, compared to the IBM PC, which felt like a basic system that required lots of extra bits and pieces to make it work properly. A great confusion at the time was the number of application packages that were entering the market. Apple eased this problem with the release of AppleWorks, which integrated a word processor, database management program, and a spreadsheet.

Apple also continued developing the Lisa computer with Lisa 2, and the Apple II, with the Apple IIc computer (the Apple III computer had not sold well, and production of it soon stopped). The Apple IIc computer cost $1,300 and was based on the 6502A processor; it had 128 kB RAM and a 3.5-inch floppy disk drive. On the first day of its release, Apple received 52,000 orders. By the end of the year, over two million Apple II computers had been sold. The Lisa 2 computer came with 512 kB RAM and a 10 MB hard disk. Apple was also innovating in the printer market, with the color Apple Scribe printer and the LaserWriter. At the same time, Hewlett-Packard introduced the LaserJet laser printer with 300 dpi resolution for $3,600.

As Apple had done, in the following year Commodore would release a computer based on the 68000 processor (the Amiga, from the newly purchased Amiga Corporation). In 1984, they introduced the Com-

Open v. Closed systems

In 1985, Apple was having difficult times. The sales of the Macintosh were not as great as expected, and the Apple II was facing a great deal of competition from other manufacturers. Many people at the time, including Bill Gates, were advising Apple to open-up the market for Macintosh computers by allowing other manufacturers build their own systems, under strict license arrangements. Bill Gates had advised them that they should tie up with companies such as HP and AT&T. However, Apple held onto both their Mac operating system, and their hardware, which they believed were totally intertwined. A Mac could not exist without both its operating system and its hardware. Rather than open the market up, Apple decided to trample cloners, especially in software cloners. Apple's first target was Digital Research, who had developed GEM for the PC. Digital Research believed that they had borrowed the look-and-feel of the Mac operating system, but not the actual technology. Apple immediately shot GEM out of the water when Apple's lawyers, in 1985, visited Digital Research and threatened them with court action. At the time, IBM had been keen to license GEM for their own products, but they were frightened away over the fear of litigation, and that was the end of GEM.

Apple then turned to Microsoft to head off their attempt at producing a GUI. Bill Gates, though, had much greater strength than Digital Research against Apple. His main point was that the true originator of the GUI was Xerox. Thus, for its Microsoft Windows, it was Xerox's ideas that were being used, and not Apple's. Bill Gates, though, had another trump card: If Apple were going to stop Microsoft from producing Windows then Microsoft would stop producing application software for the Macintosh. Apple knew that they needed Microsoft more than Microsoft needed Apple. In the face of a lack of investment in their application software, Apple signed a contact with Microsoft which stated that Microsoft would:

'have a non-exclusive, worldwide, royalty-free, perpetual, nontransferable license to use derivate works in **present and future software programs**, and to license them to and through third parties for use in their software programs'

which basically gave Microsoft carte blanche for all future versions of their software, and were quite free to borrow which ever features they wanted. John Scully at Apple signed it, and gave away one of the most lucrative markets in history. Basically, Apple was buying peace with Microsoft, but it was peace with a long-term cost.

modore Plus/4 which used the 7501 microprocessor, and had 64 kB RAM and 320×200 pixel graphics with 128 colors. They also released the Commodore 16 with 16 kB of RAM, at a selling price of $100.

At Microsoft, development continued with both the Apple Mac and IBM PC systems. No one could have predicted, at the time, that the IBM PC market would eventually dwarf the Apple market. For many, the Macintosh looked to be the system of the future, so Microsoft stopped working on Excel, their new PC-based spreadsheet package, and switched their resources to developing software for the Macintosh. This included Excel for the Macintosh. From then on, Microsoft would concentrate on GUI applications for Microsoft Windows and for the Macintosh. There was still a great deal of profits to be gained from their DOS operating system, and they released MS-DOS 3.0/3.1, which supported larger hard disks, networks and high-capacity floppy disks.

Microsoft now held the largest part of the market for DOS, but Microsoft still felt that they would struggle if they did not have the support of a larger organization, so Microsoft held out an olive branch to IBM by demonstrating Microsoft Windows. IBM refused to become involved, mainly because it competed with its newly developed interface, TopView. The only other real competitor to Microsoft was Digital Research, who had missed out on the IBM PC market. In 1984, they released the Graphics Environment Manager (GEM) icon/desktop user interface for the IBM PC computer. Microsoft and Lotus Development also nearly agreed to merge their companies, but Jim Manzi at Lotus Development convinced Mitch Kapor to back out of it. Microsoft's Windows was superior to TopView as it used a graphical user interface

In the UNIX market, in 1984 the Massachusetts Institute of Technology (MIT) began to develop the X Window System. Their main objective was to create a good windows system for UNIX machines. Many versions evolved from this and, by 1985, it was decided that X would be available to anyone who wanted it for a nominal cost. X is a portable user interface and can be used to run programs remotely over a network. It has since become a de facto standard because of its manufacturer independence, portability, versatility and ability to operate transparently across most network technologies and operating systems. The main features of X-Windows are:

> "I don't think it's that significant"
>
> Tandy president, John Roach, on the IBM PC.

- It is network-transparent. The output from a program can be sent either to the local graphics screen or to a remote node on the network. Application programs can output simultaneously to displays on the network. The communication mechanism used is machine-independent and operating system-independent.
- Many different styles of user interface can be supported. The management of the user interface, such as the placing, sizing and stacking of windows is not embedded in the system, but is controlled by an application program that can be changed easily.
- As X is not embedded into an operating system, it can be transported easily to a wide range of computer systems.
- Calls are made from application programs to the X-windows libraries that control WIMPs. The application program thus does not have to create any of these functions.

1985 In 1985, Microsoft released their first version of Windows at a price of $100. It was hardly startling, and would take another two versions before it dominated the market completely. Windows 1.0 could only run one program at a time, and still used DOS (obviously this was a great advantage to Microsoft as it could result in double sales, of DOS and Windows. Also it would have been difficult for, at the time, a small company such as Microsoft to develop a new operating system). Another major failing was that it did not use the full capabilities of the new 32-bit processor (80386) or the enhanced 16-bit processor (80286), and could thus access only 1 MB of memory.

Just as IBM were releasing their AT computer with the 80286, Intel released their new 32-bit 16 MHz 80386DX microprocessor, and the 80287 math coprocessor. The 80386 used 32-bit registers and a 32-bit data bus, and incorporated 275,000 transistors (1.5 microns). The initial price was $299. It could access up to 4 GB of physical memory, or up to 64 TB of virtual memory. A worrying development for Intel came from the new start-up company, Chips & Technologies, which developed a set of five chips

> **New software for 1985**
>
> On the PC, new software versions were coming thick and fast. Lotus 1-2-3 had moved to 2.0, WordPerfect moved to Version 4.1, Novell NetWare was now at Version 2.0 and dBase was at Version 3. 1985 also saw the first CD-ROM drives for computer use.

that were equivalent to 63 smaller chips found on the IBM PC AT motherboard. This development meant that many of the support devices produced by Intel could be replaced by fewer devices, thus cutting production costs. At Motorola, the success of the 68000 led to the 68008 processor.

The year after Apple had released their 68000-based Macintosh, Commodore released their new flagship computer, the Amiga 1000. Unlike the IBM PC, it was fully multitasking and used a WIMPs (windows, icons, menus and pointers) system. In its basic form it cost $1300 and had 256 kB RAM, and an 880 kB 3.5-inch disk drive. The Commodore Amiga was a great introduction to computing as it had a proper graphical user interface, and could multitask programs. The Amiga felt more like a high-powered workstation, against the single-tasking, text command based IBM PC. Sales mushroomed, along with sales of Amiga-based games. In the same year, they also released the Commodore 128 computer, which was an upgrade of the Commodore 64, for which they tried to stop production (but public demand restarted production several times). As with other companies, Commodore were also trying to get into the PC market with the PC10 and PC20 computers (unfortunately there was little to differentiate these computers for the other IBM PC clones).

At Apple Computer, the success of the Macintosh continued. The battle was now on for the PC market, and they had the IBM PC in their sights. During the SuperBowl, Apple ran a TV advert for Macintosh Office, which showed blindfolded business executives walking off a cliff like lemmings. With the rapid growth of Apple, came turbulence as the company required to grow up and start to use formal business methods. John Sculley, the former Pepsi-Cola president who, in 1984, had been brought in to train Steve Jobs to become the CEO, actually ended-up forcing Steve (the co-founder of Apple Computer) out, who left, along with five senior managers, to form NeXT Incorporated. From then on, John Sculley was the man in charge of Apple.

In the face of the growth in IBM PC sales and with difficulties in keeping up with the demand for the Mac, the future for Apple looked difficult. The software for the Mac was being produced as quickly as the market was buying it. Microsoft released Microsoft Word 1.0 and the Microsoft Excel spreadsheet ($95). Apple were not impressed with the first version of Excel, and reckoned that Lotus Development's equivalent (Jazz) was better. Another key package for the Macintosh was Aldus PageMaker from Aldus, which created a new industry that integrated text and graphics with a design package: desktop publishing. For years, PageMaker was the de facto standard package for graphics design and desktop publishing. Microsoft obviously had a foot in both the IBM PC and the Macintosh market, as they released Microsoft Word 2.0 for DOS, and QuickBASIC 1.0.

> "... the 'irresistible tide' of AT&T's Unix now threatens to engulf the current microcomputer operating system standard, MS-DOS",
>
> – Datamation, 1984

The year produced many good deals for Microsoft, including:

- Microsoft signed a deal with IBM for a joint development agreement to work together on future operating systems and environments.
- Microsoft signed a deal with Apple to cover Apple's copyrights on the visual display of the Macintosh.
- Microsoft purchased all rights to DOS from Seattle Computer Products for $925,000.

Four companies that did not have a good 1985 were Atari, Radio Shack, Acorn and IBM. At IBM, there was despondency as they stopped production of their PCjr and released their first version of TopView for $150. Both flopped in the market. IBM also moved into networking with IBM Token Ring, but despite this being an excellent networking technology, the future would be Ethernet. Atari struggled on in face of the competition from Apple, Compaq, Commodore and the IBM PC, but with the might of Microsoft added to the equation, they had little chance in the profitable business market. They tried to continue their previous success in the home market with the 65XE, the 130XE and the 520ST, for $120, $400 and $600, respectively. Radio Shack also continued to swim against the tide with the release of the Tandy 6000 multiuser system (with up to nine users). It was extremely powerful and used both a Z80A and a 68000 processor. It had 512 kB RAM, 80×24 text, graphics, 1.2 MB 8-inch disk, an optional 15 MB hard drive, TRS-DOS, or XENIX 3.0. Another struggler with an excellent product was Acorn, who released The Advanced RISC Machine (ARM), which used a powerful 32-bit processor (many reckoned that its architecture was many years in advance of any PC on the market, at the time).

> ### Newcomers of the year (1985)
>
> Each year in the computer industry had seen the birth of a new significant company. In 1985, it was Nintendo, and Chip & Technologies. Nintendo would become one of the leading computer companies in the lucrative computer games market. They again highlighted the strength of the USA in generating new and innovative computer companies. Software companies were also being created, such as the Corel Corporation (by Michael Cowpland), and Quarterdeck Office Systems. One of the successes of the previous years was Sun Microsystems, who had started work on their SPARC processor.

One of the successes of the previous year, Compaq Computer, was jubilant as they reported second-year revenues of $329 million. They quickly followed up the success of the Compaq portable with the Compaq Deskpro 286 and Portable 286, which was similar in specification to the IBM AT.

1986   After a few frantic years, things started to settle down in 1986, as the IBM PC and the Apple Macintosh dominated the market, especially at the business end. One of the biggest winners was Compaq Computers who had seen their turnover for their third year rise to $503.9 million; by the middle of the year, they would sell their fifty thousandth computer. To further exploit the market that they had created, Compaq introduced the Compaq Portable II, which had such an excellent build quality and specification, that IBM would eventually withdraw from the portable computer for a while. It would take many years before IBM would regain some of the portable market with the excellent ThinkPad.

As IBM released the AT, which was based on the 8 MHz Intel 80286 processor, Compaq blasted the PC market wide open with the first 16 MHz Intel 80386-based PC: the Compaq Deskpro 386. This computer was already running at twice the clock speed of the AT and had the potential of running 32-bit software (as apposed to 16-bit software with the 80286). The 80386 also had significant improvements in the number of clock cycles that it took for an operation to be performed. Thus, the Deskpro 386 sprinted, while all the other PCs dawdled, and its full potential was yet to be realized.

IBM knew that the PC was a compromised system, and released the IBM RT Personal Computer, which was based on a 32-bit RISC-based processor, with 1 MB RAM, a 1.2 MB floppy, and 40 MB hard drive, and cost $11,700. Even with the RISC processor, it had a performance of only 2 MIPS, and thus its price/performance ratio was too great for the market to adopt it. Against these difficulties, IBM began work on a computer range that would become a classic: the IBM RS/6000 series.

Apple was starting to suffer against the growing power of the IBM PC developers. They still had a closed system, where it was up to them to develop the software and hardware for the Macintosh, whereas the IBM had hundreds, if not thousands, working and improving on it. The Apple Mac was now looking underpowered and lacking other facilities, especially in networking it onto IBM PC-based networks. Apple overcame the lack of processing power with the release of the Macintosh Plus, which was based around the 8 MHz 68000 processor with 1 MB RAM, SCSI-based hard disk connector (the first ever computer to have integrated SCSI interfaces) and an 800 kB 3.5-inch floppy drive. It cost $2,600 (a 512 kB version cost $2000). Unfortunately, it was still not possible to connect an Apple Mac onto an IBM PC-based network, unless connected by a telephone connection. This held it back from wider adoption in the commercial market. Apple, though, was starting to make great inroads into the publishing industry with the release of the innovative LaserWriter Plus printer. Networks become either totally IBM PC-based, totally UNIX-based or totally Mac-based. The protocol which would eventually break this mold, and allow differ computer types to intercommunicate, was TCP/IP (the truly global communications protocol). At that time, though, most of the protocols were vendor-supplied (such as AppleTalk for Mac networks, and IPX/SPX for PC networks).

Microsoft had, over the previous few years, initiated many new products for both the IBM PC and the Apple Macintosh. In 1985, they consolidated their market with new versions of their successful software, such as MS-DOS 3.2 and Microsoft Word 3.0. In MS-DOS 3.2, support was added for 3.5-inch 720 kB floppy disk drives (these disks were much more reliable than the older, 'floppy', 5.25-inch floppy disk, as they had a hard case to protect them). The initial investment of time and energy for those involved in Microsoft was rewarded when, for the first time, Microsoft sold its shares to the public. When floated, each share was worth $21, which raised $61 million for Microsoft and made Bill Gates the world's youngest billionaire.

Several computer manufacturers, such as Silicon Graphics, started to move towards the new range of RISC processors produced by MIP Technologies, such as the 8 MHz, 32-bit, R2000 processor. This used 110,000 transistors and gave a speed of 5 MIPS. At Motorola, they were working on the 68030 processor, which would have over 300,000 transistors. They also began work on the 88000 processor.

Newcomers of the year (1986)

The newcomer of the year was Gateway 2000, which shipped its first PC. In addition, after using the Small Computer System Interface (SCSI) on Apple's Macintosh (SCSI-1), it was standardized with the ANSI X3.131-1986 standard.

The Transputer

In 1985, the UK also showed that they could innovate in market niches with the release of the Inmos T800 Transputer, which was a powerful RISC processor that could be used in parallel processing applications. It had high-speed serial links between each of the processors.

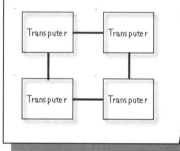

1.7 Top 15 Achievers and Under-achievers

Top brands (worth - $bn)		
1.	COCA-COLA	(72.2)
2.	MICROSOFT	(70.2)
3.	IBM	(53.2)
4.	INTEL	(39.0)
5.	NOKIA	(38.5)
6.	GENERAL ELECTRIC	(38.1)
7.	FORD	(36.4)
8.	DISNEY	(33.6)
9.	MCDONALD'S	(27.9)
10.	AT&T	(25.5)

Interbrand survey, 2000

Most of the chapters in this book are technically biased, but this chapter is slightly less so. It is intended to give a gentle introduction to computer systems, networks, the Internet and distributed systems. As a precursor to the more technical material in the following chapters, I've included my Top 15 achievers and under-achievers in the computer industry. Please excuse the usage of technical jargon, before it is introduced in later units. Most of the terms, such as TCP/IP and Ethernet, are well-known terms and are even used in the broadcasting industry.

The PC is an amazing device, and has allowed computers to move from technical specialists to, well, anyone. However, they are also one of the most annoying pieces of technology of all time, in terms of their software, their operating system, and their hardware. If we bought a car and it failed at least a few times every day, we would take it back and demand another one. When that failed, we would demand our money back. Or, imagine a toaster that failed half way through making a piece of toast, and we had to turn the power off, and restart it. We just wouldn't allow it.

So why does the PC lead such a privileged life. Well it's because it's so useful and multi-talented, although it doesn't really excel at much. Contrast a simple games computer against the PC and you'll find many lessons in how to make a computer easy-to-use, and easy to configure. One of the main reasons for many of its problems, though, is the compatibility with previous systems both in terms of hardware and software (and lots of dodgy software, of course).

The history of the PC is an unbelievable story, full of successes and failures. Many people who have used some of the computer systems before the IBM PC was developed, wipe a tear from their eyes, for various reasons, when they remember their first introduction to computers, typically with the Sinclair Spectrum or the Apple II. In those days, all your programs could be saved to a single floppy disk; 128 kB of memory was more than enough to run any program, and the nearest you got to a GUI was at the adhesives shelf at your local DIY store. It must be said, though, that computers were more interesting in those days. Open one up, and it was filled with processor chips, memory chips, sound chips, and so on. You could almost see the thing working (a bit like how it was in the days of valves). These days, computers lack any soul; one computer is much like the next. There's the processor, there's the memory, that's a bridge chip, and, oh, there's the busses, that's it.

As we move to computers on a chip, they will, in terms of hardware, become even more boring to look at. But, maybe I'm just biased. Oh, and before the IBM PC, it was people who made things happen in the computer industry; people like Steve Wozniak, Steve Jobs, Kenneth Olson, Sir Clive Sinclair, Bill Gates, and so on. These days it is large teams of software and hardware developers who move the industry. Well, enough of this negative stuff. The PC is an extremely exciting development, which has changed modern life. Without its flexibility, its compatibility, and, especially, its introduction into the home, we would not have seen the fast growth of the Internet.

> The Definition of an Upgrade: Take old bugs out, put new ones in.
>
> "We were called computer nerds. Anyone who spends their life on a computer is pretty unusual."
>
> – Bill Gates.

Here are my Top 15 successes (in rank order) in the computer industry:

- **IBM PC** (for most), which was a triumph of design and creativity. One of the few computer systems ever to be released on time, within budget, and within specification. Bill Gates must take some credit in getting IBM to adopt the 8088 processor, rather than the relatively slow 8080. After its success, every man and his dog at IBM had a say in what went into it. The rise of the bland IBM PC is an excellent example of an open-system triumphing over a closed-system. Companies which have quasi-monopolies are keen on keeping their systems closed, while companies which openly compete against other competitors prefer open systems. The market, and thus, the user, prefer open-systems.

- **TCP/IP**, which is the standard protocol used by computers communicating over the Internet. It has been designed to be computer-independent and operating system independent, thus any type of computer can talk to any other type (as long as both use TCP/IP communications). It has withstood the growth of the Internet with great success. Its only problem is that we are now running out of IP addresses to grant to all the computers that connect to the Internet. It is thus a victim of its own success. TCP/IP has proved the foundation for all the Internet applications, such as the World Wide Web, video conferencing, file transfer, remote login and electronic mail. It has also been followed by domain names (such as fred.com), which map symbolic names to IP addresses.

- **Electronic mail**, which has taken the paperless office one step nearer. Many mourned the death of letter writing, as TV and the telephone had suppressed its form. With e-mail it is back again, stronger than ever. It is not without its faults, though. Many people have sent e-mails in anger, or ignorance, and then regretted them

> Ethernet (n): something used to catch the etherbunny

later. It is just too quick, and does not allow for a cooling off period. My motto is: 'If you're annoyed about something, sleep on it, and send the e-mail in the morning'. Also, because e-mail is not a face-to-face communication, or a voice-to-voice communication, it is easy to take something out of context. So another motto is: 'Carefully read everything that you have written, and make sure there is nothing that is offensive or can be misinterpreted'. Only on the Internet could e-mail addressing (such as, fred@bloggs.com) be accepted, worldwide, in such a short time.

- **Microsoft**, which made sure that it could not lose in the growth of the PC, by teaming up with the main computer manufacturers, such as IBM (for DOS and OS/2), Apple (for Macintosh application software) and for its own operating system: Windows. Luckily, for Microsoft, it was its own operating system which became the industry standard. With the might of having the industry-standard operating system (DOS, and then Microsoft Windows), Microsoft captured a large market for industry-standard application programs, such as Word and Excel. For a company which never specialized in application software, it has done well to capture a larger market share than all of its competitors put together (many of whom specialize in application software).

- **Intel**, which was gifted an enormous market with the development of the IBM PC, but has since invested money in enhancing its processors, but still keeping compatibility with its earlier ones. This compatibility caused a great deal of hassle for software developers, but had great advantages for users. With processors, the larger the market you have, the more money you can invest in new ones, which leads to a larger market, and so on. Unfortunately, the problem with this is that other processor companies can simply copy your designs, and change them a little so that they are still compatible. This is something that Intel have fought against, and, in most cases, have succeed

> "The previous stars – Digital Research and Microsoft – may soon find themselves playing cameo roles as AT&T and IBM take center stage."
>
> ComputerWorld, 1984.

in regaining their market share, either with improved technology or with legal action. The Pentium processor was a great success, as it was technologically superior to many other processors on the market, even the enhanced RISC devices. It has since become faster and faster.

- **6502** and **Z80** (joint award), the classic 16-bit processors which became a standard part of most of the PCs available before the IBM PC. The 6502 competed against the mighty Motorola 6800, while the Z80 competed directly with the innovative Intel 8080.

- **Apple II**, which took computing out of the millionaires' club, and into the class room, the laboratory, and even the home.

- **Ethernet**, which has become the standard networking technology. It is not without its faults, but has survived because of its upgradeability, its ease-of-use, and its cheapness. Ethernet does not cope well with high capacity network traffic, because it is based on contention, where nodes must contend with each other to get access to a network segment. If two nodes try to get access at the same time, a collision results, and no data is transmitted. Thus the more traffic there is on a network, the more collisions there are. This reduces the overall network capacity. However, Ethernet had two more trump cards up its sleeve. When faced with network capacity problems, it increased its bit rate from the standard 10 Mbps (10BASE) to 100 Mbps (100BASE), which gave ten times the capacity and reduced contention problems. For network backbones it also suffered because it could not transmit data fast enough. So, it played its next card: 1000BASE, which increased the data rate to 1 Gbps (1000 MBps). Against this type of card player, no other networking technology had a chance.

- **WWW**, which is often confused with the Internet, and is becoming the largest database ever created (okay, 99% of it is rubbish, but even if 1% is good then it is all worthwhile). The WWW is one of the uses of the Internet; others include file transfer, remote login and electronic mail.

- **Apple Macintosh**, which was one of few PC systems which competed properly with the IBM PC. It succeeded mainly because of its excellent operating system (MAC OS), which was approximately 10 years ahead of its time. Possibly, if Apple had spent as much of its time in developing application software rather than its operating system it would have considerably helped the adoption of the Mac. Apple also refused, until it was too late, to license its technology to other manufacturers. For a long time it thus stayed a closed-system.

- **Compaq DeskPro 386**. Against all the odds, Compaq stole the IBM PC standard from the creators, who had tried to lead the rest of the industry up a dark alley with MCA.

- **Sun SPARC**, which succeeded against the growth of the IBM PC, because of its excellent technology, its reliable Unix operating system, and its graphical user interface (X-Windows). Sun Microsystems did not make the mistakes that Apple had made, and allowed other companies to license its technology. They also supported open systems in terms of both the hardware and software. Sun is probably the main reason that Unix is still alive, and thriving.

- **Commodore**, which bravely fought on against the IBM PC. It released many great computers, including the Vic range and the Commodore Amiga, and was responsible for forcing down the price of computers.

- **Sinclair Research**, which, more than any other company, made computing affordable to the masses. Okay, most of its computers had terrible membrane keyboards, memory adaptors that wobbled, took three fingers to get the required command (Shift-2nd Function-Alt-*etc*), required a cassette recorder to upload a program, would

> Computer message:
>
> 'C:\> Bad command or file name! Go stand in the corner.'

typically crash after you had entered one thousand lines of code, and so on. However, all of this aside, in the Sinclair Spectrum they found the right computer, for the right time, at the right price. Sometimes success can breed complacency, and so it turned out with the Sinclair QL and the Sinclair C-5 (the electric slipper).

- **Compaq**, for startling growth that is unlikely to ever be repeated. From zero to one billion dollars in five years, which it achieved, not by luck, but by shear superior technology, time-after-time, and by sharing its technology with others (which, at the time, was the only way to compete against the might of IBM).

> "Welcome IBM. Seriously.",
> Headline, produced by Apple, for the full page advert in the Wall Street Journal

Other contenders include:

- Unix, mainly for providing the communications protocol for the Internet: TCP/IP, and for being so reliable, and long lasting in a short-term industry. Also for being one of the strongest rivals to Microsoft Windows. For the technically minded, Unix allows the user to view the complete system, which is often hidden in Microsoft Windows.
- X-Windows, for lots of things, including its openness, and ability to share with others (*good old human attributes*).
- Hewlett-Packard, for its range of printers and their brand strength.
- CISCO, for its networking products and providing the backbone of the Internet (with CISCO routers).
- Java, for ignoring computer architecture, the type of network connection, and, well, everything.
- Power PC, for trying to head off the PC, at the pass, but not quite succeeding.
- Dell, for, like Compaq, achieving unbelievable growth, and creating a new market niche in selling computers directly from the factory.

Oh, and the Intel 80386, the Intel 8088, the Intel Pentium, Microsoft Visual Basic (for bringing programming to the masses), Microsoft Office, Microsoft Windows 95, Microsoft Windows NT, and so on. Okay, Windows 95, Windows NT, the 80386 and the Pentium would normally be in the Top 15, but, as Microsoft and Intel are already there, I've left them out. Here's to the Wintel Corporation. We are in their hands. One false move and they will bring their world down around themselves. Up to now, Wintel have made all the correct decisions.

When it comes to failures, there are no failures really, and it is easy to be wise after the event. Who really knows what would have happened if the industry had taken another route. So, instead of the Top 15 failures, I've listed the following as the Top 15 under-achievers (please forgive me for adding a few of my own, such as DOS and the Intel 8088):

- **DOS**, which became the best selling, standard operating systems for IBM PC

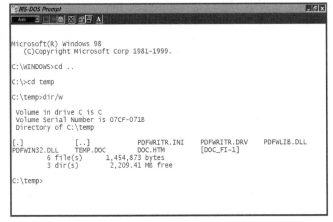

systems. Unfortunately, it held the computer industry back for at least ten years. It was text-based, command-oriented, had no graphical user interface. It could also only access up to 640 KB of memory, at 16 bits at a time. Many users with a short memory will say that the PC is easy-to-use, and intuitive, but they are maybe forgetting how it used to be, before Microsoft Windows. With Windows 95 (and to a lesser extent with Windows 3.x), Microsoft made computers much easier to use. From then on, users could actually switch on their computer without having to register for a higher degree in Computing (*sic*). DOS would have appeared fine, as it was compatible with all its previous parents, but the problem was MAC OS, which showed everyone how a user interface should operate. Against this competition, it was no contest. So, what was it that made the PC a success? It was application software. The PC had application software coming out of its ears.

- **Intel 8088**, which became the standard PC processor, and thus the standard machine code for all PC applications. So why, after being such a success, is it in the failures list? Well, like DOS, it's because it was so difficult to use, and was a compromised system. While Amiga and Apple programmers were writing proper programs which used the processor to its maximum extent, PC programmers were still using their processors in 'sleepy-mode' (8088-compatible mode), and could only access a maximum of 1 MB of memory (because of the 20-bit address bus limit for 8088 code). The big problem with the 8088 was that it kept compatibility with its father: the 8080. For this Intel decided to use a segmented memory access, which is fine for small programs, but a nightmare for large programs (basically anything over 64 kB).

- **Alpha** processor, which was DEC's attack on the processor market. It had a blistering performance, which blew every other processor out of the water (and still does in many cases). Unfortunately, it has never been properly exploited, as there was a lack of application software and development tools for it. The Intel Pentium proved that it was a great all-comer and did many things well, and was also willing to improve the areas that it was not so good at.

- **Z8000** processor, which was a classic case of being technically superior, but was not compatible with its father, the mighty Z80, and its kissing cousin, the 8080. Few companies have given away such an advantage with a single product. Where are Zilog now? Head buried in the sand, probably.

- **DEC**, which was one of the most innovate companies in the computer industry. It developed a completely new market niche with its minicomputers, but it refused, until it was too late, to believe that the microcomputer would have a major impact on the computer market. DEC went from a company that made a profit of $1.31 billion in 1988, to a company which, in one quarter of 1992, lost $2 billion. Its founder, Ken Olsen, eventually left the company in 1992, and his successor brought sweeping changes. Eventually, though, in 1998 it was one of the new PC companies, Compaq, which bought DEC. For Compaq, DEC seemed a good match, as DEC had never really created much of a market for PCs, and had concentrated on high-end products, such as Alpha-based workstations, batch processing and network servers.

- **Fairchild Semiconductor**. Few companies have ever generated so many ideas and incubated so many innovative companies, and got so little in return.

- **Xerox**. Many of the ideas in modern computing, such as GUIs and networking, were initiated at Xerox's research facility. Unfortunately, Xerox lacked commitment in their great developments. Maybe this was because it reduced Xerox's main market, which was, and still is, very much based on paper.

- **PCjr**, which was another case of incompatibility. IBM lost a whole year in releasing the PCjr, and lost a lot of credibility with its suppliers (many of whom were left with unsold systems) and their competitors (who were given a whole year to catch-up with IBM).

- **OS/2**, which was IBM's attempt to regain the operating system market from Microsoft. In conception it was a compromised operating system, and its development team lacked the freedom of the original IBM PC development. Too many people and too many committees were involved in its development. It thus lacked the freedom, flair and independence of Boca Raton development team who developed the IBM PC. At the time, IBM's mainframe divisions were a powerful force in IBM, and could easily stall, or veto a product if it had an effect on their profitable market.

- **CP/M**, which many believed would become the standard operating system for microcomputers. Digital Research had an excellent opportunity to make it the standard operating system for the PC, but Microsoft overcame it by making its DOS system so much cheaper.

- **MCA**, which was the architecture that IBM tried to move the market with. It failed because Compaq, and several major PC manufacturers, went against it, and kept developing using the existing x86 architecture to support the 80386 processor.

- **Seattle Computer Products**, which sold the rights of its QDOS program to Microsoft, and thus lost out of one of the most lucrative markets of all time.

- **Sinclair Research**, which after the success of the ZX81 and the Spectrum, threw it all away by releasing a whole range of under-achievers, such as the QL, and the C-5.

- **MSX**, which was meant to be the technology that would standardize computer software on PCs. Unfortunately, it hadn't heard of the new 16-bit processors, and most of all, the IBM PC.

- **Lotus Development**, which totally misjudged the market, by not initially developing its Lotus 1-2-3 spreadsheet for Microsoft Windows. It instead developed it for OS/2, and eventually lost the market leadership to Microsoft Excel. Lotus also missed an excellent opportunity to purchase a large part of Microsoft when it was still a small company. The profits on that purchase would have been gigantic.

1.8 History of Computer Systems

The highlights in the development of computer systems, the Internet and networks are:

1614   John Napier discovered logarithms, which allowed the simple calculation of complex multiplications, divisions, square roots and cube roots.

1642   Blaise Pascal built a mechanical adding machine.

1801   Joseph-Maire Jacuard developed an automatic loom controlled by punched cards.

1822   Charles Babbage designed his first mechanical computer, the first prototype for his difference engine. His model would be used in many future computer systems.

1880s   Hollerith produced a punch-card reader for the US Census.

1896   IBM founded (as the Tabulating Machine Company).

1906   Lee De Forest produces the first electronic value.

1946   ENIAC built at the University of Pennsylvania.

1948   Manchester University produces the first computer to use a stored program (the Mark I).

1948   William Shockley (and others) invents the transistor.

1954   Texas Instruments produces a transistor using silicon (rather than germanium). IBM produces the IBM 650 which was, at the time, the workhorse of the computer industry. MIT produces the first transistorized computer: the TX-O.

1957   IBM develops the FORTRAN (FORmula TRANslation) programming language.

1958   Jack St. Clair Kilby proposes the integrated circuit.

1959   Fairchild Semiconductor produces the first commercial transistor using the planar process. IBM produces the first transistorized computer: the IBM 7090.

1960   ALGOL introduced which was the first structured, procedural, language. LISP (LISt Process-

	ing) was introduced for the Artificial Intelligence applications.
1961	Fairchild Semiconductor produces the first commercial integrated circuit.
	COBOL (COmmon Business-Orientated Language) developed by Grace Murray Hopper.
1963	DEC produce its first minicomputer.
1965	BASIC (Beginners All-purpose Symbolic Instruction Code) was developed at Darthmouth College. IBM produced the System/360, which used integrated circuits.
1968	Robert Noyce and Gordon Moore start-up the Intel Corporation.
1969	Intel began work on a device for Busicom, which would eventually become the first micro-processor.
1970	Xerox creates the Palo Alto Research Center (PARC), which would become one of the lead-ing research centers of creative ideas in the computer industry. Intel release the first RAM chip (the 1103), which had a memory capacity of 1 Kb (1024 bits).
1971	Intel release the first microprocessor: the Intel 4004. Bill Gates and Paul Allen start work on a PDP-10 computer in their spare time. Ken Thompson, at Bell Laboratories, produces the first version of the UNIX operating system. Niklaus Wirth introduces the Pascal programming language.
1973	Xerox demonstrates a bit-mapped screen. IBM produces the first hard disk drive (an 8 inch diameter, and a storage of 70MB).
1974	Intel produces the first 8-bit microprocessor: the Intel 8008. Bill Gates and Paul Allen start-up a company named Traf-O-Data. Xerox demonstrates Ethernet. MITS produces a kit com-puter, based on the Intel 8008. Xerox demonstrates WYSIWYG (What You See Is What You Get). Motorola develops the 6800 microprocessor. Brian Kerighan and Dennis Ritchie pro-duced the C programming language.
1975	MOS Technologies produces the 6502 microprocessor. Microsoft develops BASIC for the MITS computer.
1976	Zilog releases the Z80 processor. Digital Research copyrighted the CP/M operating system. Steve Wozniak and Steve Jobs develop the Apple I computer, and create the Apple Corpora-tion. Texas Instruments produces the first 16-bit microprocessor: the TMS9900. Cray-1 supercomputer released, the first commercial supercomputer (150 million floating point op-erations per second).
1977	FORTRAN 77 introduced.
1978	Commodore released the Commodore PET.
1979	Intel releases the 8086/8088 microprocessors. Zilog introduced the Z8000 microprocessor and Motorola releases the 6800 microprocessor. Apple introduced the Apple II computer, and Radio Shack releases the TRS-80 computer. VisiCalc and WordStar introduced.
1981	IBM releases the IBM PC, which is available with MS-DOS supplied by Microsoft and PC-DOS (IBM's version).
1982	Compaq Corporation founded. Commodore releases the Vic-20 computer and Commodore 64. Sinclair releases the ZX81 computer and the Sinclair Spectrum. TCP/IP communications protocol created. Intel releases the 80286, which is an improved 8088 processor. WordPerfect 1.0 released.
1983	Compaq releases their first portable PC. Lotus 1-2-3 and WordPerfect released. Bjarn Stroustrup defines the C++ programming language. MS-DOS 2.0 and PC-DOS 2.0 released.
1984	Apple releases the Macintosh computer. MIT introduce the X-Windows user interface.
1985	Microsoft releases the first version of Microsoft Windows, and Intel releases the classic 80386 microprocessor. Adobe Systems define the PostScript standard which is used with the Apple LaserWriter. Philips and Sony introduce the CD-ROM.
1986	Microsoft releases MS-DOS 3.0. Compaq release the Deskpro 386.
1987	Microsoft releases the second version of Microsoft Windows. IBM releases PS/2 range. Model 30 uses 8088 processor, Model 50 and Model 60 use 80286, and Model 80 uses 80386 processor. VGA standard also introduced. IBM and Microsoft release the first version of OS/2.
1988	MS-DOS 4.0 released.
1989	WWW (World Wide Web) created by Tim Bernes-Lee at CERN, European Particle Physics Laboratory in Switzerland. Intel develops the 80486 processor. Creative Laboratories release Sound Blaster card.

1990   Microsoft releases Microsoft Windows 3.0.

1991   MS-DOS 5.0 released. Collaboration between IBM and Microsoft on DOS finishes.

1993   Intel introduces the Pentium processor (60 MHz). Microsoft release Windows NT, Office 4.0 (Word 6.0, Excel 5.0 and PowerPoint 4.0) and MS-DOS 6.0 (which includes DoubleSpace, a disk compression program).

1994   Netscape 1.0 released. Microsoft withdraws DoubleSpace in favor of DriveSpace (because of successful legal action by Stac which claimed that parts of it were copies of its program: Stacker). MS-DOS 6.22 would be the final version of DOS.

1995   Microsoft release Windows 95 and Office 95. Intel releases the Pentium Pro, which has speeds of 150, 166, 180 and 200MHz (400MIPs). JavaScript developed by Netscape.

1996   Netscape Navigator 2.0 released (the first to support Java Script). Microsoft releases Windows 95 OSR 2.0, which fixed the bugs in the first release and adds USB and FAT 32 support.

1997   Intel release Pentium MMX. Microsoft release Office 97, which creates a virtual monopoly in office application software for Microsoft. Office 97 is fully integrated and has enhanced version of Microsoft Word (upgraded from Word 6.0), Microsoft Excel (upgraded from Excel 5.0), Microsoft Access, Microsoft PowerPoint and Microsoft Outlook. IBM's Deep Blue beats Gary Kasparov (the World Chess Champion) in a chess match. Intel releases the Pentium II processor (233, 266 and 300 MHz versions). Apple admits serious financial trouble. Microsoft purchases 100,000 non-voting shares for $150 million. One of the conditions is that Apple drops their long running court case with Microsoft for copying the Mac interface on Microsoft Windows (although Apple copied its interface from Xerox). Bill Gate's fortune reaches $40 billion. He has thus, since 1975 (the year that Microsoft were founded), earned $500,000 per hour (assuming that he worked a 14 hour day), or $150 per second.

1998   Microsoft releases Microsoft Windows 98. Legal problems arise for Microsoft, especially as its new operating system includes several free programs as standard. The biggest problem is with Microsoft Internet Explorer, which is free compared to Netscape, which must be purchased.

1999   Linux Kernel 2.2.0 released, and heralded as the only real contender in the PC operating market to Microsoft. Intel releases Pentium III (basically a faster version of the Pentium II). Microsoft Office 2000 released. Bill Gates' wealth reaches $100 billion (in fact, $108 billion in September 1999).

2000   Millennium bug bites with false teeth.

and on   Microsoft release Windows NT Version 5/2000 in three versions: Workstation, Server and SMP Server (multiprocessor). It runs on DEC Alpha's, Intel *x*86, Intel IA32, Intel IA64 and AMD K7 (which is similar to an Alpha). Microsoft releases Office 2000, but lose court case.

1.9 Exercises

Using a WWW search engine (such as www.yahoo.com or www.altavista.com) or your own general knowledge, determine the answers to the following questions. Please select from a–d.

1.9.1   Which computer helped aid the British Government to crack codes in World War II:

    (a)   ENIAC   (b)   Harvard Mk I

    (c)   IBM System/360   (d)   Colossus

1.9.2   What is ENIAC an acronym for:

    (a)   Electronic Numerical Integrator and Computer

    (b)   Electronic Number Interface Analysis Computer

    (c)   Electronic Number Interface and Computer

    (d)   Electronic Numerical Interchange Computer

1.9.3   Which computer was the first to use integrated circuits:

    (a)   Apple   (b)   IBM System/360

    (c)   IBM PC   (d)   DEC PDP-11

1.9.4   Which one of the following formed Intel:
(a)   Bill Gates and Paul Allen
(b)   Robert Noyce, Gordon Moore and Andy Grove
(c)   Jerry Sanders   (d)   Steve Wozniak and Steve Jobs

1.9.5   Which one of the following formed Microsoft:
(a)   Bill Gates and Paul Allen
(b)   Robert Noyce, Gordon Moore and Andy Grove
(c)   Jerry Sanders   (d)   Steve Wozniak and Steve Jobs

1.9.6   Which one of the following formed Apple Computers:
(a)   Bill Gates and Paul Allen
(b)   Robert Noyce, Gordon Moore and Andy Grove
(c)   Jerry Sanders   (d)   Steve Wozniak and Steve Jobs

1.9.7   Which company did Kenneth Olsen help form:
(a)   Compaq   (b)   DEC
(c)   Microsoft   (d)   IBM

1.9.8   Which company developed the first microprocessor:
(a)   Texas Instruments   (b)   Motorola
(c)   Zilog   (d)   Intel

1.9.9   Which company was the first to demonstrate the usage of windows, mouse and keyboard:
(a)   IBM   (b)   Xerox
(c)   Microsoft   (d)   DEC

1.9.10   Which company was the first to demonstrate the WYSIWYG concept:
(a)   IBM   (b)   Xerox
(c)   Microsoft   (d)   DEC

1.9.11   What was the name of the Xerox famous research centre:
(a)   PARC   (b)   XRES
(c)   PERC   (d)   RESP

1.9.12   Which company did Bill Gates and Paul Allen initially create:
(a)   Micro-Traffic   (b)   Traf-O-Data
(c)   Traffic Software   (d)   Gates & Allen

1.9.13   Who developed the C programming language:
(a)   Bill Gates and Paul Allen   (b)   Brian Kernighan and Dennis Ritchie
(c)   Niklaus Wirth   (d)   Steve Wozniak and Steve Jobs

1.9.14   Who developed the Pascal programming language:
(a)   Bill Gates and Paul Allen   (b)   Brian Kernighan and Dennis Ritchie
(c)   Niklaus Wirth   (d)   Steve Wozniak and Steve Jobs

1.9.15   Which was the first ever commercial microprocessor:
(a)   4000   (b)   4004
(c)   8080   (d)   1000

1.9.16   Which processor did the Apple II use:
(a)   Zilog Z80   (b)   MOS Technology 6502
(c)   Intel 8080   (d)   NEC 780-1

1.9.17   Which processor did the Commodore PET use:
  (a)   Zilog Z80   (b)   MOS Technology 6502
  (c)   Intel 8080   (d)   NEC 780-1

1.9.18   Which processor did the TRS-80 use:
  (a)   Zilog Z80   (b)   MOS Technology 6502
  (c)   Intel 8080   (d)   NEC 780-1

1.9.19   Which processor did the ZX80 use:
  (a)   Zilog Z80   (b)   MOS Technology 6502
  (c)   Intel 8080   (d)   NEC 780-1

1.9.20   How did the Motorola 68000 gain its name:
  (a)   No reason   (b)   It was sold for $680.00
  (c)   It sounded like the 8008   (d)   It had 68,000 transistors

1.9.21   Which company produced the VAX range of computers:
  (a)   IBM   (b)   DEC
  (c)   Compaq   (d)   Apple

1.9.22   Which IBM product quickly failed because it was incompatible with its PC:
  (a)   PC AT   (b)   PC XT
  (c)   PCNext   (d)   PCjr

1.9.23   Which company released the first IBM PC-compatible portable:
  (a)   Compaq   (b)   IBM
  (c)   Radio Shack   (d)   Commodore

1.9.24   Which architecture did IBM try to develop an industry standard with:
  (a)   RS   (b)   MCA
  (c)   OS/2   (d)   PCI

1.9.25   Which IBM operating system failed to gain a large hold of the market:
  (a)   PC-DOS   (b)   OS/2
  (c)   Windows   (d)   Unix

1.9.26   Which company was the fastest growing of all time:
  (a)   IBM   (b)   Compaq
  (c)   DEC   (d)   Sun

1.9.27   Which processor did the first IBM PC use:
  (a)   8086   (b)   8088
  (c)   8085   (d)   8080

1.9.28   What was the clock speed of the first IBM PC:
  (a)   1 MHz   (b)   4.77 MHz
  (c)   8 MHz   (d)   16 MHz

1.9.29   Which company did Apple reach an agreement with about their name:
  (a)   Apple Corps Limited   (b)   Apple Beatles Limited
  (c)   Apple System Limited   (d)   Apple Records Limited

1.9.30   Which computer was used in the UK by the BBC to teach microcomputers:
  (a)   Acorn, BBC micro   (b)   Sinclair, ZX81
  (c)   Osborne, Osborne 1   (d)   Commodore, Vic-20

1.9.31   Which company is thought to be responsible for the first WYSIWYG application:
 (a) Apple   (b) IBM
 (c) Microsoft   (d) Xerox

1.9.32   Which was the first spreadsheet:
 (a) Excel   (b) VisiCalc
 (c) Lotus 1-2-3 (d) Top-Plan

1.9.33   What is Sun (as in Sun Microsystems) an acronym for:
 (a) Sale Unicode Network (b) Safe Universal Network
 (c) Stanford University Network (d) Salford University Network

1.9.34   Which company developed many of the standards for the 3.5-inch floppy disk:
 (a) IBM   (b) Sony
 (c) Microsoft   (d) Xerox

1.9.35   Which operating system did DEC initially use for its VAX range:
 (a) Mac OS   (b) AEGIS
 (c) VMS   (d) Unix

1.9.36   Which operating system did Apollo initially use for its workstations:
 (a) Mac OS   (b) AEGIS
 (c) VMS   (d) Unix

1.9.37   Which standard did several Japanese companies develop that was meant to be a standard for PC software:
 (a) DOS   (b) 1-2-3
 (c) MSX   (d) SCSI

1.9.38   Which university developed the X-Windows system:
 (a) Stanford   (b) MIT
 (c) UMIST   (d) New York

1.9.39   Which organization originally developed the Internet:
 (a) DARPA   (b) ISO
 (c) CERN   (d) IEEE

1.9.40   Which organization originally developed the initial specifications for the WWW:
 (a) DARPA   (b) ISO
 (c) CERN   (d) IEEE

1.9.41   Who invented the transistor:
 (a) Bill Gates   (b) Herman Hollerith
 (c) William Shockley (d) Lee De Forest

1.9.42   Which company did William Shockley form:
 (a) Shockley Semiconductor (b) Shockley Devices
 (c) Shockley Electronics (d) Shockley Electrics

1.9.43   Which company first proposed the integrated circuit:
 (a) IBM   (b) Texas Instruments
 (c) Motorola   (d) Fairchild Semiconductors

1.9.44   Which company developed the first 8-bit microprocessor:
        (a)   NEC (780-1)   (b)   Motorola (6800)
        (c)   Zilog (Z80)   (d)   Intel (8008)

1.9.45   Which company developed the first 16-bit microprocessor:
        (a)   Texas Instruments (9900)   (b)   Motorola (68000)
        (c)   Zilog (Z8000)   (d)   Intel (8086)

1.9.46   Which processor did Zilog produce:
        (a)   Z80   (b)   6502
        (c)   8080   (d)   6800

1.9.47   Which processor did MOS Technology produce:
        (a)   Z80   (b)   6502
        (c)   8080   (d)   6800

1.9.48   Which processor did Motorola produce:
        (a)   Z80   (b)   6502
        (c)   8080   (d)   6800

1.9.49   Which company is thought to be responsible for the first GUI:
        (a)   Apple   (b)   IBM
        (c)   Microsoft   (d)   Xerox

1.9.50   Which company developed the XENIX operating system:
        (a)   AT&T   (b)   IBM
        (c)   Microsoft   (d)   HP

1.9.51   Which company tried to standardize Unix with System V:
        (a)   AT&T   (b)   IBM
        (c)   Microsoft   (d)   HP

1.9.52   Who first produced an integrated circuit:
        (a)   John Cocke   (b)   Robert Noyce
        (c)   Gordon Moore   (d)   William Shockley

1.9.53   Create your own Top 15 computer industry achievers of all time, and your own personal under-achiever list, and complete Table 1.1. Possible ideas are computer games (such as Sonic the Hedgehog, Doom, and so on), or application packages (such as Microsoft Word, Lotus 1-2-3, and so on), Internet applications (such as Internet Explorer or Mirabillis ICQ), Computer Systems (such as Sony PlayStation or Sinclair Spectrum, and so on), and so on. Table 1.2 gives an example.

Table 1.2   Top 15 over-achievers/under-achievers

Position	Over-achiever	Under-achiever
1		
2		
3		
4		
5		
6		
7		

8		
9		
10		
11		
12		
13		
14		
15		

Table 1.3 Top 15 over-achievers/under-achievers (example)

Po.	Over-achiever	Under-achiever
1	IBM PC (for creating a global market, and changing modern life)	DOS (for being such as horrible, nasty operating system, that failed to use the full potential of the PC)
2	TCP/IP (for connecting computers to the Internet)	Intel 8088 (for having such a difficult internal architecture, and being so difficult to program for)
3	Electronic Mail (for being the best application, ever)	DEC Alpha (for failing to reach its potential)
4	Microsoft (for making all the right choices, and winning in virtually every market that it competed in)	Zilog Z8000 processor (for failing to be compatible with the Z80 processor)
5	Intel (for keeping the industry-standard for PC processors)	DEC (for missing the PC)
6	6502/Z80 processors (for providing excellent processors)	Fairchild Semiconductor (for failing to cash-in on its ideas)
7	Apple II (for being an excellent computer)	Xerox (as Fairchild Semiconductor)
8	Ethernet (for its ease of use, its robustness, its upgradeabliity, and so on)	PCjr (for completely failing to follow the success of the IBM PC)
9	WWW (for creating a global database)	OS/2 (for missing the point and trying to be an operating system which could be used on mainframes, minicomputers and PC)
10	Apple Macintosh (for a computer that was 10 years ahead of the PC)	CP/M (for missing the PC operating market)
11	Compaq DeskPro 386 (for its excellent specification, and stealing the market from IBM)	MCA (for failing to create a new standard, and losing IBM a great market share)
12	Sun SPARC (for its openness, its excellent specification, its Unix, and X-Windows)	Seattle Computer Products (for selling DOS to Microsoft)
13	Commodore Amiga (for being an excellent computer)	Sinclair Research (for the QL and C-5)
14	Sinclair Research (for the Sinclair Spectrum)	MSX (for failing to create a standard for PC software)
15	Compaq (for making all the right decisions, at the right time)	Lotus Development (for missing the market for Microsoft Windows)

1.9.54   Investigate the current value of Bill Gates' wealth. If possible, also determine some of the charitable organizations that Bill Gates has given money to.

1.10 DEC

The main rival to IBM before the advent of the PC was DEC (Digital Equipment Corporation), which was formed in 1957. DEC grew fast to become the second largest computer company in the world, but their unbelievable growth, and fall, is a lesson for any industry. It all began with brothers Kenneth Olson and Stanley Olson, and Harlan Anderson on a start-up capital of just $70,000 (which was 70% owned by American Research and Development Corporation). This should be compared with the start-up capital of Compaq, which was $10 million. At the time, IBM had a quasi-monopoly, and DEC did not have a chance to compete with them on a like-for-like product range, but they eventually thrived because they attacked a small market niche with technically superior products. When they started, DEC could not possibly compete with IBM in the larger commercial market, where IBM had made a considerable investment. So, DEC turned to the scientific and technical market, which required relatively small and configurable products. DEC could also not compete with the mighty IBM in terms of marketing and sales teams, as DEC was basically a company of engineers, and they were proud of it. Their main product was the minicomputer, which was much cheaper than mainframes, but had a great deal of power, and could be easily configured and managed by a small group.

DEC PDP range		
PDP-1	1960,	$120,000 18-bit, 50 sold.
PDP-2		24-bit. Prototype.
PDP-3		36-bit. Special build.
PDP-4	1962,	$60,000 18-bit, 45 sold.
PDP-5	1963,	$27,000, 12-bit, 1,000 sold.
PDP-6	1964,	$300,000, 36-bit, 23 sold.
PDP-7	1965,	$72,000, 18-bit, 120 sold.
PDP-8	1965,	$18,500, 12-bit, 50,000 sold.
PDP-9	1966,	$35,000, 18-bit, 445 sold.
PDP-10	1967,	$110,000, 36-bit, 700 sold.
PDP-11	1970,	$10,800, 16-bit, more than 600,000 sold.
PDP-12	1969,	$27,900, 12-bit, 725 sold.
PDP-15	1970,	$16,500, 18-bit, 790 sold.
PDP-16	1972,	8/16-bit, N/K sales.

The big winner for DEC was the PDP (Programmed Data Processor) series, which became the foundation of many scientific and engineering groups. No research group or industrial company was complete without a PDP computer. By today's standards, there was more power in a pocket calculator, as there was in the PDP-8. It was also relatively large, weighing 250 pounds, and came in a rack-mounted unit that was over 6 feet tall. However, the PDP range was much cheaper than IBM mainframes. For example, the PDP-1 sold for $120,000, while the comparable IBM computer cost millions. The PDP range also introduced computing to many young minds, such as two exceptional ones in Bill Gates and Paul Allen, who cut their teeth on a DEC PDP-8.

The next great winner for DEC was the VAX (Virtual Address eXtension) computer which cost billions to develop, but was a great technical and commercial success. The VAX range covered the complete spectrum of computer hardware from basic text terminals up to large mainframe computers. For the first time, DEC produced every part of the computer system: the operating system, the hardware and the software. One of the great successes of the VAX range was the VMS operating system (produced by David Culter), which allowed computer programmers to create programs which had more memory than the computer actually had (a virtual memory), and allowed several programs to run at the same time (multitasking). After the success of VMS, David Culter eventually went on to develop a RISC operating system, but DEC management cancelled the project. After this, he left DEC in disgust and went to Microsoft to lead the development of the Windows NT operating system (Microsoft and Intel have strong recruitment policies, and often hire the best brains in the computer industry).

In these days of networked computers, it is difficult to believe, but, at the time, the VAX range was a radical concept. The VAX range could even compete against IBM's mainframe market. The future looked destined to be DEC's, and not IBM's. In 1986, their sales reached $2 billion, but soon came the recession of the 1990s, which many companies had difficulty coping with. DEC could have coped with this if they had forecasted the changing market, and realized the power of the new 16-bit microprocessors. Their downfall was basically the IBM PC which beat both IBM's mainframes and DEC's minicomputers on performance, at a fraction of the price, from whichever company you wanted.

DEC actually, in 1979, had the opportunity to enter into the PC market when they allowed HeathKit to sell the PDP-11 minicomputer in kit form. At the time, DEC believed there was more profit to be made with corporate clients, thus didn't really believe there was a great market for PCs. Ken Olsen also believed that PCs were a passing fad that would never really evolve into proper computers. Many computers at the time were bought, played with, and then put in the cupboard, never to be used again. The great advantages with personal computers were that they were designed for individuals, whereas mini-computers were designed for businesses.

DEC struggled though the 1990s and could never regain their dominance. As with IBM's mainframe business, they relied on their existing customer base buying their new products. A well-known brand name, with its associated image is extremely important for corporate companies when they buy computers. Most companies believe that brand names such as DEC (as they were), IBM, Compaq and Dell are associated with reliable and well-built products. Companies buying the brand name kept DEC's brand alive in many cases. As many companies used DEC equipment, DEC in the 1990s was still a well-respected brand name. They showed that they could innovate and

Sinclair, RIP

The biggest failure of 1984 was Sinclair Research, after many years of success. They released the 16/32-bit QL microcomputer, which was their first attempt at the business market. It cost $500, and used the Motorola 68008 microprocessor, had 128 kB RAM, two built-in tape drives, and multi-tasking ROM-based operating system. It was their first attempt at the business marked, but unfortunately, the IBM PC now dominated that market.

In the following year, Sinclair Research, was struggling with disappointing sales of the QL, but still buoyed by the Sinclair Spectrum. The biggest disaster for Sinclair, though, was the C-5, which was to be a revolutionary electric vehicle. Unfortunately, it looked less like a motor vehicle, and more like a large plastic slipper. It was also powered by a washing machine motor, giving it a top speed of 15mph. Along with this it was heavy and short-ranged. Within a few short months, the production of the C-5 was stopped, and Sinclair faced large financial losses (£7 million). In the face of these losses, Sinclair sold his name and the rights to his computers to Amstrad. Clive Sinclair then went on to form a new company, Cambridge Computers. which created a laptop, which was not PC-compatible and based on the Z80-based machine and had an LCD screen. It was reasonability successful, but nowhere near as successful as the ZX-series of computers.

The C-5 was not Clive Sinclair's worse failure; it was the Zike (ultra-light electric bicycle), which only sold 2,000 units (as opposed to 17,000 C-5s). The Zeta (Zero-Emission Transport Accessory) has sold better with more than 15,000 units being sold. However, Clive Sinclair will always be remembered for classic computers, which were so popular you had to wait months to get one.

lead the market with one of the most respected RISC processors ever made: the Alpha. This had a blistering performance and is still used in many workstations. It would take several years before Intel could even match the power of the Alpha device. Unfortunately, DEC failed to support the processor with the required software. DEC, as IBM had, had always seen itself as a computer hardware company, and not a software one.

So from the 1980s to the 1990s, DEC had gone from being a fast-moving, innovative and enterprising company, to one which was entrenched in its existing product lines. As PCs grew in strength, DEC kept developing their minicomputers (as IBM was doing with their mainframes). DEC's other main problem was that, like IBM, they did everything, from writing software, design and making the processors, developing hard disk drives, and so on. This made them vulnerable from specialist companies who could beat DEC in each of the areas. A focused, specialist company will typically innovate faster than a large, generalized company. They also failed to become involved in alliances. This was because DEC felt that they could turn the market in whichever way they wanted, thus they did not need alliances.

> **PDP-8 Assembly Language Example**
>
> ```
> START,    CLA CLL
>           TAD X
>           AND I Y
>           DCA X
>           HLT
>
>           X, 1
>           Y, 7
> ```

DEC went from a company that made a profit of $1.31 billion in 1988, to a company that, in one quarter of 1992, lost $2 billion. Olsen eventually left the company in 1992, and his successor brought sweeping changes. Eventually, though, in 1998 it was one of the new PC companies, Compaq, who would buy DEC. For Compaq, DEC seemed a good match, as DEC had never really created much of a market for PCs, and had concentrated on high-end products, such as Alpha-based workstations and network servers.

Unlike IBM, DEC did not pull the walls down around themselves. They had found an excellent market share and were coping well. If not for the advent of the PC, DEC would probably be the market leader by now. Their VAX range would have probably evolved to include a closed-system personal computer in which DEC could have held control of (as IBM would have done). However, the open-system approach of the PC spelt disaster for both IBM and DEC.

> "This 'telephone' has too many shortcomings to be seriously considered as a means of communication. The device is inherently of no value to us."
>
> Western Union internal memo, 1876.

1.11 Note from the Authors

The history of the PC is an unbelievable story, full of successes and failures. Many people who used some of the computer systems before the IBM PC was developed, wipe a tear from their eyes, for various reasons, when they remember their first introduction to computers, typically with the Sinclair Spectrum or the Apple II. In those days, all your programs could be saved to a single floppy disk, 128 kB of memory was more than enough to run any program, and the nearest you got to a GUI was at the adhesives shelf at your local DIY store. It must be said that computers were more interesting in those days. Open one up, and it was filled with processor chips, memory chips, sound chips, and so on. You could almost see the thing working (a bit like it was in the days of valves). These days, computers lack any soul; one computer is much like the next. There's the processor, there's the memory, that's a bridge chip, and, oh, there's the busses, that's it.

> "Accessing memory using a segmented architecture holds many advantages over the earlier linear-addressing method."
>
> Intel quote.

As we move to computers on a chip, they will, in terms of hardware, become even more boring to look at. But, maybe I'm just biased. Oh, and before the IBM PC, it was people who made things happen in the computer industry, such as William Shockley, Steve Jobs, Kenneth Olson, Sir Clive Sinclair, Bill Gates, and so on. These days it is large teams of software and hardware engineers who move the industry. Well, enough of this negative stuff. The PC is an extremely exciting development, which has changed the form of modern life. Without its flexibility, its compatibility, and, especially, its introduction into the home, we would not have seen the fast growth of the Internet.

So was/is the IBM PC a success? Of course it was/is. But, for IBM it has been a double-edged sword. It opened up a new and exciting market, and made the company operate in ways that would have never been possible before. Before the IBM PC, their systems sold by themselves, because they were made by IBM. It also considerably reduced their market share.

Many questions remained unanswered: 'Would it have been accepted in the same way if it had been a closed system, which had to be licensed from IBM?' 'Would it have been accepted if it had used IBM components rather than other standard components, especially the Intel processors?', 'Would they have succeeded in the operating system market if they had written DOS by themselves?', and so on. Who knows? But, from now on we will refer to those computers based on the x86 architecture as PCs.

Winners in the Processor Race

4-bit (1971)
1st	Intel 4004
2nd	TI TMS1000

8-bit (1974)
1st	Intel 8008
2nd	Zilog Z80

16-bit (1976)
1st	TI TMS 9900
2nd	Intel 8086

32-bit (1981)
1st	NS 32000
2nd	Zilog Z8000

64-bit (1991)
1st	MIPS R4000
2nd	DEC Alpha

Classic microprocessors (cont.)

8. **Intel 8051**. Classic microcontroller, with data stored on-chip (128 bytes), and code stored off-chip. It was used in thousands of embedded products, and eventually reached sales of one billion.
9. **Microchip Technology PIC 16x/17x** (1975). Simple processor with RISC technology, and a large number of registers.
10. **TMS 9900** (1976). First 16-bit microprocessor, and featured a 15-bit address bus.
11. **Zilog Z-8000**. Innovative 16-bit microprocessor which failed due to initial bugs and lack of compatibility with the Z-80.
12. **Motorola 68000** (Sept. 1979). 32-bit internal architecture, with an external 16-bit data bus, and a 24-bit address bus. It contained 16 32-bit registers (8 for data, and 8 for address) and did not feature segmented addressing.
13. **National Semiconductor 32032**. Similar to 68000.
14. **Intel 8086** (1978). Based on 8080/8085, but expanded to cope with 16 bits. It was chosen over the 68000 for the IBM PC (possibly due to the availability of the CP/M operating system).
15. **SPARC** (1987). Scalable Processor ARChitecture designed by Sun Microsystems, for use on 68000-based workstations with the UNIX operating system.
16. **AMD 29000** (1987). RISC design, with a large number of registers.
17. **Siemens 80C166**. Low-cost embedded 8/16-bit load-store processor.
18. **MIPS R2000** (1986). MIPS (Microprocessor without Interlocked Pipeline Stages) R2000 was probably the first commercial RISC processor.
19. **HP PA-RISC** (1986). Large number of registers with RISC technology, for use in HP workstations.
20. **Motorola 88000** (1988). 32-bit processor, based on true Harvard architecture.
21. **Fairchild Clipper** (1998). Featured Harvard architecture.
22. **TMS 320C30** (1998). Popular DSP device.
23. **Motorola DSP96002**. Well-designed DSP device.
24. **Intel 860** (1988). 'Cray-on-a-chip'.
25. **IBM RS/6000** (1990). RISC processor for IBM workstations.
26. **DEC Alpha** (1992). 64-bit architecture, which created no limits to future performance improvements (such as the lack of any special registers).
27. **INMOS T-9000** (1994). Used to create parallel systems with point-to-point links between processors.

Other contenders: Acorn ARM (1986), Hitachi SuperH (1992), Motorola MCore (1998), Intel 960 (1988), Intel 432 (1980), Linn Rekursiv , MISC M17 (1988), AT&T CRISP (1987). Patriot Scientific ShBloom (1996), Sun picoJava (1997).

2 PC Basics

2.1 PC Systems

In selecting a PC many different components must be considered, especially in the way that they connect. Figure 2.1 outlines some of the component parts and the decisions that have to be made on each component. The most important components that affect the *general* performance of a PC (in ranked order) are:

1. **Processor**. The type of processor, its speed, its socket (which helps in upgrading in the future), its interface to level-2 cache, and so on. Additionally, MMX (which is an Intel trademark, but many read it as MultiMedia eXtension) can speed up multimedia applications.
2. **Local memory**. Most operating systems can run multiple programs, each of which requires its own memory space. When the system runs out of electronic memory (local memory), it uses the hard disk for an extra storage (to create a virtual memory). Hard disk accesses are much slower than electronic memory, thus the system is severely slowed down if there is a lack of local electronic memory. Most modern operating systems require a great deal of local electronic memory to operate.
3. **Graphics adaptor**. The graphics adaptor can be a major limiting factor on the performance of a system. New interfaces, such as AGP, speed up graphics performance considerably. Another limiting factor is the amount of local memory on the graphics adaptor. The greater the graphics memory, the higher the resolution that can be used, and the more colours that can be displayed. AGP is overcoming this limiting factor, as it allows the main electronic memory to be used to store graphics images.

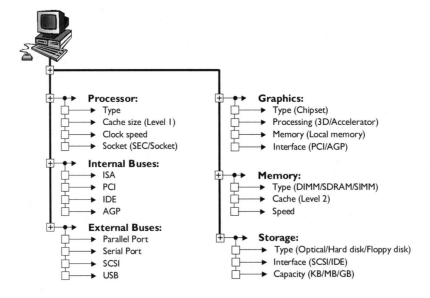

Processor:
→ Type
→ Cache size (Level 1)
→ Clock speed
→ Socket (SEC/Socket)

Internal Buses:
→ ISA
→ PCI
→ IDE
→ AGP

External Buses:
→ Parallel Port
→ Serial Port
→ SCSI
→ USB

Graphics:
→ Type (Chipset)
→ Processing (3D/Accelerator)
→ Memory (Local memory)
→ Interface (PCI/AGP)

Memory:
→ Type (DIMM/SDRAM/SIMM)
→ Cache (Level 2)
→ Speed

Storage:
→ Type (Optical/Hard disk/Floppy disk)
→ Interface (SCSI/IDE)
→ Capacity (KB/MB/GB)

Figure 2.1 PC components

4. **Cache capacity**. Cache memory has provided a great increase in the performance of a system. If a cache controller makes a correct guess, the processor merely has to examine the contents of the cache to get the required information. A level-1 cache is the fastest and is typically connected directly to the processor (normally inside the processor package) and runs at the speed of the processor; the level-2 cache runs at the speed of the motherboard.

5. **Hard disk capacity/interface**. The hard disk typically has an effect on the running of a program, as the program and its component parts must be loaded from the disk. The interface is thus extremely important as it defines the maximum data rate. SCSI has fast modes that give up to 40 MB/s, while IDE gives a maximum rate of 33 MB/s. The capacity of the disk can also lead to problems as the system can use unused disk capacity of a virtual memory capacity.

> **Factors which affect specific applications**
>
> More specific applications will be affected by other factors, such as:
>
> - **Internet access**. Affected mainly by the network connection (especially if a modem is used).
> - **CD-ROM access**. Affected by the interface to the CD-ROM.
> - **Modeling software**. Affected by mathematical processing.
> - **3D game playing**. Affected mainly by the graphics adaptor and graphics processing (and possibly the network connection, if playing over a network).

2.2 Practical PC System

At one time PCs were crammed full of microchips, wires and connectors. These days they tend to be based on just a few microchips, and contain very few interconnecting wires. The main reason for this is that much of the functionality of the PC has been integrated into several key devices. In the future, PCs may require only one or two devices to make them operate.

The architecture of the PC has changed over the past few years, and is now based mainly on the PCI bus (although hub-based systems are now becoming popular). Figure 2.2 shows the architecture of a modern PC. It can be seen that the system controller is the real heart of the PC, as it transfers data between the processor and the rest of the system. This data travels over bridges, which are used to connect one type of bus or interface to another. There are two main bridges: the system controller (the north bridge), and the bus bridge (the south bridge).

An example PC motherboard is illustrated in Figure 2.3. The main components are:

- **Processor**. The processor is typically a Pentium processor, which has a SEC (single-edge connector) or fits into a socket. The processor can run at a faster rate than the rest of the motherboard (called clock multiplication). Typically, the motherboard runs at 50 MHz, and the clock rate is multiplied by a given factor, such as 500 MHz (for a ×10 clock multiplier).
- **System controller**. Controls the interface between the processor, memory and the PCI bus.
- **PCI/ISA/IDE Xcelerated controller**. Controls the interface between the PCI bus and the ISA, USB and IDE buses.
- **I/O controller**. Controls the interface between the ISA and the other buses, such as the parallel bus, serial bus, floppy disk drive, keyboard, mouse and infrared transmission.
- **Flash memory**. Used to store the program that starts up the computer (the boot process).
- **Level-2 cache (SRAM)**. Used to store information from DRAM memory.

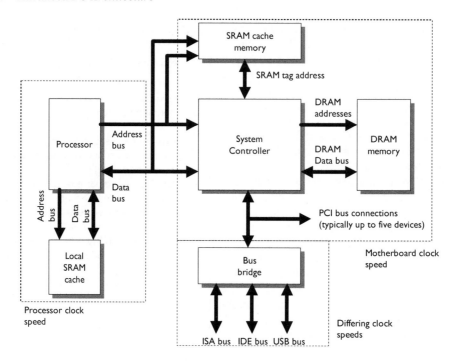

Figure 2.2   Local bus architecture

- **PCI connectors**. Used to connect to PCI-based interface adaptors, such as network cards, sound cards, and so on.
- **DIMM sockets**. This connects to the main memory of the computer. Typically it uses either EDO DRAM, SDRAM (Synchronous DRAM) or RDRAM. SDRAM transfers data faster than EDO DRAM as it uses the clock rate of the processor rather than that of the motherboard.
- **ISA connectors**. Used to connect to ISA-based interface adaptors, such as a sound cards.
- **IDE connectors**. Used to connect to hard disks or CD-ROM drives, where up to two drives can connect to each connector (IDE0 or IDE1) as a master or a slave. Thus the PC can support up to four disk drives on the IDE bus.
- **TV out socket**. Used to provide an output that will interface to a television, using either PAL (for the UK) or NSTC (for the US).
- **Video memory**. Used to store video information.
- **Graphics controller**. Used to control the graphics output.
- **Audio codec**. Used to process audio data.

2.3   Buses

The part that makes computers operate and allows devices to be plugged-in easily is the computer bus, which allows the orderly flow of data between one device and another. The PC, and other computer systems, has an amazing number of different types of interfaces and bus systems, including the PC bus, ISA bus, PCI bus, AGP bus, games port, parallel port and serial port.

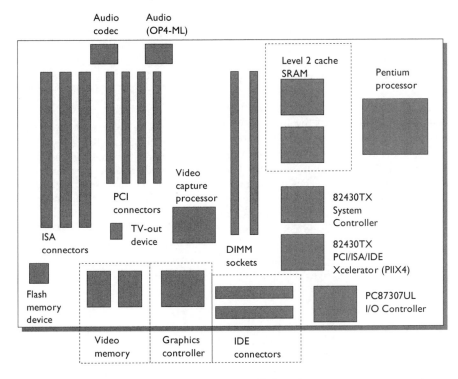

Figure 2.3   AN430TX board

The main elements of a basic computer system are a central processing unit (or microprocessor), memory, and I/O interfacing circuitry. Figure 2.4 shows a basic system. External devices such as a keyboard, display, and disk drives can connect directly onto the data, address and control buses, or through the I/O interface circuitry. These connect by means of three main buses: the address bus, the control bus and the data bus. A bus is a collection of common electrical connections grouped by a single name.

Electronic memory consists of RAM (random access memory) and ROM (read only memory). ROM stores permanent binary information, whereas RAM is a non-permanent memory and loses its contents on a loss of power. Applications of this type of memory include running programs and storing temporary information. RAM is normally made up of either DRAM (Dynamic RAM) or SRAM (Static RAM). DRAM uses a single capacitor and a transistor to store a single bit of data, whereas SRAM uses six transistors, arranged as a flip-flop device, to store a single bit of data. DRAM has the advantage that more memory can be crammed onto a microchip (as only one transistor is required for each bit stored). DRAM has two major disadvantages: it is relatively slow (because of the charging and discharging of the storage capacitors) and it requires that the complete contents of its memory be refreshed with power many times a second (because the tiny capacitors loose their charge over a short time). This power refresh is thus wasteful of electrical power and leads to heat dissipation.

The microprocessor is the main controller of the computer. It understands only binary information and

> **Processor classifications**
>
> The classification of a microprocessor relates to the maximum number of bits it can process at a time, that is their word length. The evolution has gone from 4-bit, to 8-bit, 16-bit, 32-bit and 64-bit architectures.

operates on a series of binary commands known as machine code. It fetches binary instructions from memory, decodes these instructions into a series of simple actions, and carries out the actions in a sequence of steps. A system clock synchronizes these steps.

To access a location in memory, the microprocessor puts the address of the location on the address bus. The contents at this address are then placed on the data bus and the microprocessor reads the data from the data bus. To store data in memory the microprocessor places the data on the data bus. The address of the location in memory is then put on the address bus and data is read from the data bus into the memory address location.

Monster or the Great Unifier?
With the growth in the Internet and global communications, we have created a global village, but have we also created an unregulated monster that is out of control. I think that Albert Einstein sums it best:

'Concern for man himself and his fate must always be the chief interest of all technical endeavors … in order that the creations of our minds shall be a blessing and not a curse to mankind. Never forget that in the midst of your diagrams and equations'

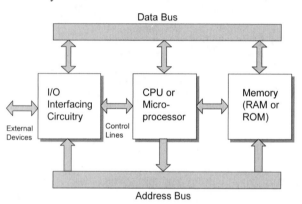

Figure 2.4   Block diagram of a simple computer system

2.3.1   *Bus specification*

The basic specification of a computer can be determined by analyzing the performance of the buses within the system. Each bus performs a specific function and is suited to the devices that connect to it. The basic specifications for buses include:

- **Data rate** (in bytes per second or bits per second). This defines the maximum amount of data that can be transferred at a time. For example, the ISA bus has a maximum data rate of 16 MB/s, Gigabit Ethernet has a maximum data rate of 125 MB/s, and the local bus that connects a PC processor to local memory can have a data rate of over 800 MB/s (64 bits at 100 MHz).

- **Maximum number of devices that connect to the bus**. The number of devices that connect to a bus can have a great effect on its performance as they all provide an electrical loading on the bus. The more that connect to the bus, the greater the overhead of bus arbitration will be. Standard SCSI allows a maximum of seven devices to be connected to the bus, whereas Ethernet can allow thousands of devices to connect to the bus.

- **Bus reliability**. This defines how well the bus copes with any errors that occur on the bus. Some buses, especially in industrial environments, can be susceptible to externally generated noise. A good bus should be able to detect if it has received data that has been corrupted by noise (or was sent incorrectly).

- **Data robustness**. This is the ability of the bus to react to faults within the bus or from the malfunctioning of connected devices. Buses such as the CAN bus can isolate incorrectly operating devices.

- **Electrical/physical robustness**. This is the ability of the bus to cope with electrical faults, especially due to short circuits and power surges. Problems can also be caused by open circuit electrical connections, although these tend not to cause long-term damage to the bus. The physical robustness of a bus is also important, especially in industrial or safety critical situations.

- **Electrical characteristics**. This involves the basic electrical parameters of the bus, such as the range of voltage levels used, electrical current ranges, short-circuit protection system, capacitance and impedance of cables, cross-talk (the amount of interference between local signal transmissions), and so on.

> Computer message:
> (A)bort, (R)etry, (T)ake down entire network?

- **Ease-of-connection**. This includes the availability of cables and connectors, and how easy it is to add and remove devices from the bus. Some buses allow devices to be added or removed while the bus is in operation (hot-pluggable). A good example of a hot-pluggable bus that is easy to connect to is the USB.

- **Communications overhead**. This is a measure of the amount of data that is added to the original data, so that it can be sent in a reliable way. Local, fast buses normally have a minimum of overhead, whereas remote, networked buses have a relatively large overhead on the transmitted data.

- **Bus controller topology**. This relates to the method that is used to control the flow of data around the bus. Some buses, such as SCSI, require a dedicated bus controller that is involved in all of the data transfers, whereas the PCI bus can operate with one or more bus controller devices taking control of the bus. Other buses, such as Ethernet, have a distributed topology where any device can take control of the bus.

- **Software interfacing**. This defines how easy it is to interface to the bus with software, especially when using standard interface protocols, such as TCP/IP or MODBUS.

- **Cable and connectors**. This defines the range of cables and connectors that can be used with the bus. There is a wide range of cables available, such as ribbon cables (which are light and are useful inside computer systems), twisted-pair cables (which are easy to connect to and are useful in minimizing cross-talk between transmitted signals) and fiber optic cables (which provide a high-capacity communications link and minimize cross talk between transmitted signals). For example, Ethernet can use BNC connectors with coaxial cables, RJ-45 connectors with twisted-pair cables and SNA connectors with fiber optic cables.

- **Standardization of the bus**. Most buses must comply with a given international standard, which allows hardware and software to interconnect in a standard form. There are normally standards for the electrical/mechanical interface, the logical operation of the bus, and its interface to software. For example, the IEEE has defined most of the Ethernet standard (especially IEEE 802.3), and the EIA have defined the RS-232 standard. International standard agencies, such as the IEEE, ISO, ANSI and EIA, provide a more secure standard than a vendor-led standard.

- **Power supply modes**. Some buses allow power-saving modes, where devices can power themselves down and be powered-up by an event on the bus. This is particularly useful with devices that have a limited power supply, such as being battery-supplied.

2.3.2   Bus components

Devices connect to each other within a computer using a bus. The bus can be either internal (such as the IDE bus, which connects to hard disks and CD-ROM drives within a PC) or external (such as the USB, which can connect to a number of external devices, typically to scanners, joypads and printers). Buses typically have a number of basic components: a data bus, an optional address bus, control lines and handshaking lines, as illustrated in Figure 2.5. Other lines, such as clock rates and power supply lines, are not normally displayed when discussing the logical operation of the bus. If there is no address bus or no control and handshaking lines, then the data bus can be used to provide addressing, control and handshaking. This is typical in serial communications, and helps to reduce the number of connections in the bus, although will generally slow down the communications.

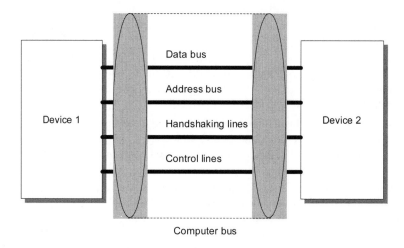

Figure 2.5   Model of a computer bus

Data bus

The data bus is responsible for passing data from one device and another. This data is either passed in a serial manner (one bit at a time) or in parallel (several bits at a time). In a parallel data bus, the bits are normally passed in multiples of eight. Typical parallel data buses are 8 bits, 16 bits, 32 bits, 64 bits or 128 bits wide.

The bus size defines the maximum size of the bus, but the bus can be used to transmit any number of bits that is less than the maximum size. For example, a 32-bit bus can be used to transmit 8 bits, 16 bits or 32 bits at a time. Most modern computer systems use a 64-bit address bus, although the software that runs on the computer uses a maximum of 32 bits (known as 32-bit software).

Parallel buses are normally faster than serial buses (as they can transmit more bits in a single operation), but require many more lines (thus requiring more wires in the cable). A parallel data bus normally requires extra data handshaking lines to synchronize the flow of data between devices. Serial data transmission normally uses a start and end bit sequence to define the start and end of

> All computers wait at the same speed.
>
> 2 + 2 = 5 for extremely large values of 2.

transmission. Figure 2.6 illustrates the differences between serial and parallel data buses. Parallel buses are typically used for local buses, or where there are no problems with cables with a relatively large number of wires. Typical parallel buses are SCSI and IDE, which are used to connect to hard disk drives, while typical serial buses are RS-232 and the USB.

Serial communications can operate at very high transmission rates; the main limiting factor is the transmission channel and the transmitter/receiver electronics. Gigabit Ethernet, for example, uses a transmission rate of 1 Gbps (125 MB/s) over high-quality twisted-pair copper cables, or over fiber optic cables (although this is a theoretical rate as more than one bit is sent at a time). For a 32-bit parallel bus, this would require a clocking rate of only 31.25 MHz (which requires much lower quality connectors and cables than the equivalent serial interface).

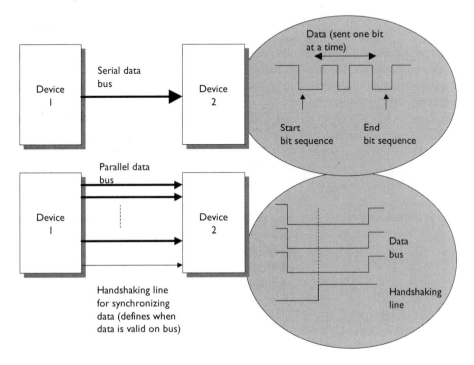

Figure 2.6 Serial/parallel data buses

Data transfer rates

The amount of data that a system can transfer at a time is normally defined either in bits per second (bps) or bytes per second (B/s). The more bytes (or bits) that can be transferred, the faster the transfer will be. Typically serial buses are defined in bps, whereas parallel buses use B/s.

The transfer of the data occurs at regular intervals defined by the period of the transfer clock. This period is defined either as a time interval (in seconds) or as a frequency (in Hz). For example, if a clock operates at a rate of 1,000,000 cycles per second, its frequency is 1 MHz, and its time interval will be one millionth of a second (1×10^{-6} s).

In general, if f is the clock frequency (in Hz), then the clock period (in seconds) will be

$$T = \frac{1}{f} s$$

> *Conversion from clock frequency to clock time interval*

For example, if the clock frequency is 8 MHz, then the clock period will be:

$$T = \frac{1}{8 \times 10^6} = 0.000000125\,\text{s}$$
$$= 0.125\,\mu\text{s}$$

> *Example of a calculation of clock time interval from clock frequency*

The data transfer rate (in bits/second) is defined as:

$$\text{Data transfer rate (bps)} = \frac{\text{Number of bits transmitted per operation (bits)}}{\text{Transfer time per operation (s)}}$$

If operated with a fixed clock frequency for each operation then the data transfer rate (in bits/second) will be:

$$\text{Data transfer rate (bps)} = \text{Number of bits transmitted per operation (bits)} \times \text{Clocking rate (Hz)}$$

For example, the ISA bus uses an 8 MHz (8×10^6 Hz) clocking frequency and has a 16-bit data bus. Thus the maximum data transfer rate (in bps) will be:

$$\text{Data transfer rate} = 16 \times 8 \times 10^6 = 128 \times 10^6\,\text{b/s} = 128\text{Mbps}$$

Often, it is required that the data rate be given in B/s rather than bps. To convert from bps to B/s, divide the bps value by eight. Thus to convert 128Mbps to B/s:

$$\text{Data transfer rate} = 128\text{Mbps}$$
$$= \frac{128}{8}\,\text{Mbps} = 16\text{MB/s}$$

> *Example conversion from bps to B/s*

For serial communication, if the time to transmit a single bit is $104.167\,\mu\text{s}$, then the maximum data rate will be:

> *Example conversion to bps for a serial transmission with a given transfer time interval*

$$\text{Data transfer rate} = \frac{1}{104.167 \times 10^{-6}} = 9600\,\text{bps}$$

2.3.3   Address bus

The address bus is responsible for identifying the location into which the data is to be passed. Each location in memory typically contains a single byte (8 bits), but could also be arranged as words (16 bits), or long words (32 bits). Byte-oriented memory is the most flexible as it also enables access to any multiple of 8 bits. The size of the address bus thus indicates the maximum addressable number of bytes. Table 2.3 shows the size of addressable memory for a given address bus size. The number of addressable bytes is given by:

$$\text{Addressable locations} = 2^n \;\text{B}$$

> *Addressable locations for a given address bus size*

where n is the number of bits in the address bus. For example (as defined in Table 2.1):

- A 1-bit address bus can address up to two locations (that is 0 and 1).
- A 2-bit address bus can address 2^2 or 4 locations (that is 00, 01, 10 and 11).
- A 20-bit address bus can address up to 2^{20} addresses (1 MB).

- A 32-bit address bus can address up to 2^{32} addresses (4 GB).

The units used for computers for defining memory are B (bytes), kB (kilobytes), MB (megabytes) and GB (gigabytes). These are defined as:

- Kilobyte: 2^{10} bytes, which is 1,024 B.
- Megabyte: 2^{20} bytes, which is 1,024 kB, or 1,048,576 B.
- Gigabyte: 2^{30} bytes, which is 1,024 MB, or 1,048,576 kB, or 1,073,741,824 B.

Table 2.1 Addressable memory (in bytes) related to address bus size

Address bus size	Addressable memory (bytes)	Address bus size	Addressable memory (bytes)
1	2	15	32 K
2	4	16	64 K
3	8	17	128 K
4	16	18	256 K
5	32	19	512 K
6	64	20	1 M†
7	128	21	2 M
8	256	22	4 M
9	512	23	8 M
10	1 K*	24	16 M
11	2 K	25	32 M
12	4 K	26	64 M
13	8 K	32	4 G‡
14	16 K	64	16 GG

* 1 K represents 1,024   † 1 M represents 1,048,576 (1024 K)
‡ 1 G represents 1,073,741,824 (1024 M)

Data handshaking

Handshaking lines are also required to allow the orderly flow of data. This is illustrated in Figure 2.7. Normally there are several different types of buses that connect to the system. These different buses are interfaced to with a bridge, which provides for the conversion between one type of bus and another. Sometimes devices connect directly onto the processor's bus; this is called a local bus, and is used to provide a fast interface with direct access without any conversions.

The most basic type of handshaking has two lines:

- Sending identification line – this identifies that a device is ready to send data.
- Receiving identification line – this identifies whether a device is ready to receive data.

Figure 2.8 shows a simple form of handshaking of data, from Device 1 to Device 2. The sending status is identified by READY? and the receiving status by STATUS. Normally an event is identified by a signal line moving from one state to another; this is described as edge-triggered (rather than level-triggered, where the actual level of the signal identifies its state). In the example in Figure 2.8, initially Device 1 puts data on the data bus, and identifies that it is ready to send data by changing the READY? line from a LOW to a HIGH level. Device 2 then identifies that it is reading the data by changing its STATUS line from a LOW to a HIGH. Next, it identifies that it has read the data by changing the STATUS line from a HIGH to a LOW. Device 1 can then put new data on the data bus and start the cycle again by changing the READY? line from a LOW to a HIGH.

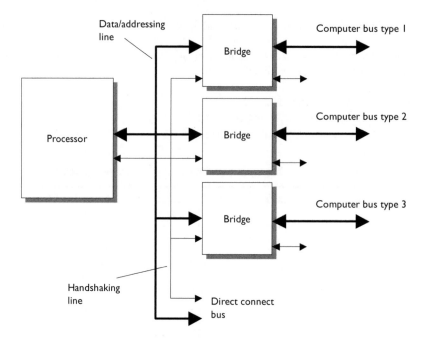

Figure 2.7   Computer bus connections

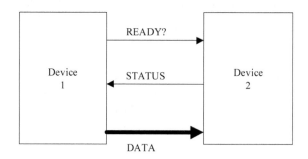

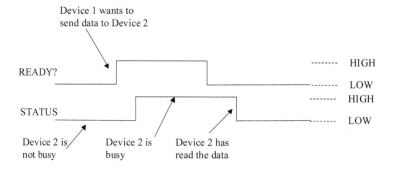

Figure 2.8   Simple handshaking of data

This type of communication allows communication in only one direction (from Device 1 to Device 2) and is know as simplex communication. The main types of communication are:

- **Simplex communication**. Only one device can communicate with the other, and thus requires handshaking lines for only one direction.
- **Half-duplex communication**. This allows communication from one device to the other, in any direction, and thus requires handshaking lines for either direction.
- **Full-duplex communications**. This allows communication from one device to another, in either direction, at the same time. A good example of this is in a telephone system, where a caller can send and receive at the same time. This requires separate transmit and receive data lines, and separate handshaking lines for either direction.

Control lines

Control lines define the operation of the data transaction, such as:

- Data flow direction – this identifies that data is either being read from a device or written to a device.
- Memory addressing type – this is typically by identifying that the address access is either direct memory accessing or indirect memory access. This identifies that the address on the bus is either a real memory location or an address tag.
- Device arbitration – this identifies which device has control of the bus, and is typically used when there are many devices connected to a common bus, and any of the devices are allowed to communicate with any other of the devices on the bus.

2.3.4 Cables

The cable type used to transmit the data over the bus depends on several parameters, including:

- The signal bandwidth.
- The reliability of the cable.
- The maximum length between nodes.
- The possibility of electrical hazards.
- Power loss in the cables.
- Tolerance to harsh conditions.
- Expense and general availability of the cable.
- Ease of connection and maintenance.
- Ease of running cables.

> Best file compression around:
>
> DEL *.* {DOS}
>
> or rm –r *.* {UNIX}
>
> gives 100% compression

The main types of cables used are standard copper cable, unshielded twisted-pair copper (UTP), shielded twisted-pair cable (STP), coaxial and fiber optic. Twisted-pair and coaxial cables transmit electric signals, whereas fiber optic cables transmit light pulses. Twisted-pair cables are not shielded and thus interfere with nearby cables. Public telephone lines generally use twisted-pair cables. In Local Area Networks (LANs) they are generally used up to bit rates of 10 Mbps and with maximum lengths of 100 m.

Coaxial cable has a grounded metal sheath around the signal conductor. This limits the amount of interference between cables and thus allows higher data rates. Typically, they are used at bit rates of 100 Mbps for maximum lengths of 1 km.

The highest specification of the three cables is fiber optic. This type of cable allows extremely high bit rates over long distances. Fiber optic cables do not interfere with nearby cables and give greater security, more protection from electrical damage by external

> "Welcome IBM. Seriously."
> Headline, produced by Apple, for a full page advert in the Wall Street Journal.

equipment and greater resistance to harsh environments; they are also safer in hazardous environments.

Cable characteristics

The main characteristics of cables are attenuation, cross-talk and characteristic impedance. Attenuation defines the reduction in the signal strength at a given frequency for a defined distance. It is normally defined in dB/100 m, which is the attenuation (in dB) for 100 m. An attenuation of 3 dB/100 m gives a signal voltage reduction of 0.5 for every 100 m. Table 2.2 lists some attenuation rates and equivalent voltage ratios; they are illustrated in Figure 2.9. Attenuation is given by:

$$\text{Attenuation} = 20 \log_{10}\left(\frac{V_{in}}{V_{out}}\right) \text{ dB}$$

> *Calculation of attenuation from input and output voltages*

For example, if the input voltage to a cable is 10 V and the voltage at the other end is only 7 V, then the attenuation is calculated as:

$$\text{Attenuation} = 20 \log_{10}\left(\frac{10}{7}\right) = 3.1 \text{ dB}$$

Coaxial cables have an inner core separated from an outer shield by a dielectric. They have an accurate characteristic impedance (which reduces reflections) and, because they are shielded, they have very low cross-talk levels. They tend also to have very low attenuation, (such as 1.2 dB at 4 MHz), with a relatively flat response. UTPs (unshielded twisted-pair cables) have either solid cores (for long cable runs) or are stranded patch cables (for short runs, such as connecting to workstations, patch panels, and so on). Solid cables should not be flexed, bent or twisted repeatedly, whereas stranded cables can be flexed without being damaged. Coaxial cables use BNC connectors while UTP cables use either the RJ-11 (small connector, which is used to connect the handset to the telephone) or the RJ-45 (larger connector, which is typically used in networked applications to connect a network adapter to a network hub).

The characteristic impedance of a cable and its connectors are important, as all parts of the transmission system need to be matched to the same impedance. This impedance is normally classified as the characteristic impedance of the cable. Any differences in the matching result in a reduction of signal power and produce signal reflections (or ghosting).

Cross-talk is important as it defines the amount of signal that crosses from one signal path to another. This causes some of the transmitted signal to be received back where it was transmitted. Capacitance (pF/100 m) defines the amount of distortion in the signal caused by each signal pair. The lower the capacitance value, the lower the distortion.

> Three kinds of people: those who can count and those who can't.

Table 2.2 Attenuation rates as a ratio

dB	Ratio	dB	Ratio	dB	Ratio
0	1.000	10	0.316	60	0.001
1	0.891	15	0.178	65	0.000 6
2	0.794	20	0.100	70	0.000 3
3	0.708	25	0.056	75	0.000 2
4	0.631	30	0.032	80	0.000 1
5	0.562	35	0.018	85	0.000 06
6	0.501	40	0.010	90	0.000 03
7	0.447	45	0.005 6	95	0.000 02
8	0.398	50	0.003 2	100	0.000 01
9	0.355	55	0.001 8		

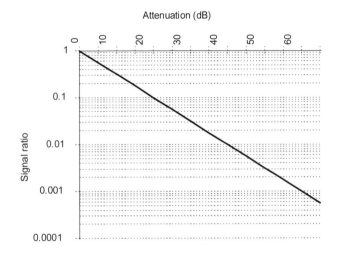

Figure 2.9 Signal ratio related to attenuation

Typical cables used are:

- Coaxial cable – cables with an inner core and a conducting shield having characteristic impedance of either $75\,\Omega$ for TV signal or $50\,\Omega$ for other types.
- Cat-3 UTP cable – level – 3 cables have non-twisted-pair cores with a characteristic impedance of $100\,\Omega$ ($\pm15\,\Omega$) and a capacitance of 59 pF/m. Conductor resistance is around $9.2\,\Omega/100$ m.
- Cat-5 UTP cable – level – 5 cables have twisted-pair cores with a characteristic impedance of $100\,\Omega$ ($\pm15\,\Omega$) and a capacitance of 45.9 pF/m. Conductor resistance is around $9\,\Omega/100$ m.

The Electrical Industries Association (EIA) has defined five main types of cables. Levels 1 and 2 are used for voice and low-speed communications (up to 4 Mbps). Level 3 is designed for LAN data transmission up to 16 Mbps, and level 4 is designed for speeds up to 20 Mbps. Level-5 cables have the highest specification of the UTP cables and allow data speeds of up to 100 Mbps. The main EIA specification on these types of cables is EIA/TIA568, and the ISO standard is ISO/IEC11801.

Table 2.3 gives typical attenuation rates for Cat-3, Cat-4 and Cat-5 cables. Notice that the attenuation rates for Cat-4 and Cat-5 are approximately the same. These two types of cable have lower attenuation rates than equivalent Cat-3 cables. Notice that the attenuation of the cable increases as the frequency increases. This is due to several factors, such as the skin effect, where the electrical current in the conductors becomes concentrated around the outside of the conductor, and the fact that the insulation (or dielectric) between the conductors actually starts to conduct as the frequency increases.

The Cat-3 cable produces considerable attenuation over a distance of 100 m. Table 2.3 shows that the signal ratio of the output to the input at 1 MHz will be 0.76 (2.39 dB), then at 4 MHz it is 0.55 (5.24 dB), until at 16 MHz it is 0.26. This differing attenuation at different frequencies produces not just a reduction in the signal strength but also distorts the signal (because each frequency is affected differently by the cable). Cat-4 and Cat-5 cables also produce distortion but their effects will be lessened because attenuation characteristics have flatter shapes.

Table 2.4 gives typical near-end cross-talk rates (dB/100 m) for Cat-3, Cat-4 and Cat-5 cables. The higher the figure, the smaller the cross-talk. Notice that Cat-3 cables have the most cross-talk and Cat-5 have the least for any given frequency. Notice also that the cross-talk increases as the frequency of the signal increases. Thus, high-frequency signals have more cross-talk than lower-frequency signals.

Table 2.3   Attenuation rates (dB/100 m) for Cat-3, Cat-4 and Cat-5 cables

Frequency (MHz)	*Attenuation rate (dB/100 m)*		
	Cat-3	*Cat-4*	*Cat-5*
1	2.39	1.96	2.63
4	5.24	3.93	4.26
10	8.85	6.56	6.56
16	11.8	8.2	8.2

Table 2.4   Near-end cross-talk (dB/100 m) for Cat-3, Cat-4 and Cat-5 cables

Frequency (MHz)	*Near end cross-talk (dB/100 m)*		
	Cat-3	*Cat-4*	*Cat-5*
1	13.45	18.36	21.65
4	10.49	15.41	18.04
10	8.52	13.45	15.41
16	7.54	12.46	14.17

2.4 Interrupts

An interrupt allows a program or an external device to interrupt the execution of a program. The generation of an interrupt can occur by hardware (hardware interrupt) or software (software interrupt). When an interrupt occurs an interrupt service routine (ISR) is called. For a hardware interrupt the ISR then communicates with the device and processes any data. When it has finished the program execution returns to the original program. A software interrupt causes the program to interrupt its execution and goes to an interrupt service routine. Typical software interrupts include reading a key from the keyboard, outputting text to the screen and reading the current date and time. The operating system must respond to interrupts from external devices, as illustrated in Figure 2.10.

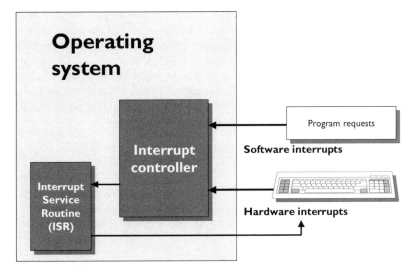

Figure 2.10 Interrupt service routine

2.4.1 *Software interrupts*

BIOS and the operating system

The Basic Input/Output System (BIOS) communicates directly with the hardware of the computer. It consists of a set of programs that interface with devices such as keyboards, displays, printers, serial ports and disk drives. These programs allow the user to write application programs that contain calls to these functions, without having to worry about controlling them or which type of equipment is being used. Without BIOS, the computer system would consist simply of a bundle of wires and electronic devices.

There are two main parts to BIOS. The first is the part stored permanently in a ROM (the ROM BIOS). It is this that starts up the computer (or bootstrap) and contains programs that communicate with resident devices. The second stage is loaded when the operating system is started. This part is non-permanent.

An operating system allows the user to access the hardware in an easy-to-use manner. It accepts commands from the keyboard and displays them to the monitor. The Disk Operating System, or DOS, gained its name from its original purpose of providing a controller for the computer to access its disk drives. The language of DOS consists of a set of commands that are entered directly by the user and are interpreted to perform file management tasks, program execution and system configuration. It makes calls to BIOS to execute these. The main functions of DOS are to run programs, copy and remove files, create directories, move within a directory structure and to list files. Microsoft Windows calls BIOS programs directly.

Interrupt vectors

Interrupt vectors are addresses that inform the interrupt handler as to where to find the ISR. All interrupts are assigned a number from 0 to 255. The interrupt vectors associated with each interrupt number are stored in the lower 1024 bytes of PC memory. For example, interrupt 0 is stored from `0000:0000` to `0000:0003`, interrupt 1 from `0000:0004` to `0000:0007`, and so on. The first two bytes store the offset and the next two store the segment address. Each interrupt number is assigned a predetermined task, as outlined in Table 2.5. An interrupt can be generated by external hardware, software, or the processor. Interrupts 0, 1, 3, 4, 6 and 7 are generated by the processor. Interrupts from 8 to 15 and interrupt 2 are generated by external hardware. These get the attention of the processor by activating a interrupt request (IRQ) line. The `IRQ0` line connects to the system timer, the keyboard to `IRQ1`, and so on. Most other interrupts are generated by software.

Processor interrupts

The processor-generated interrupts normally occur either when a program causes a certain type of error or if it is being used in a debug mode. In the debug mode the program can be made to break from its execution when a breakpoint occurs. This allows the user to test the status of the computer. It can also be forced to step through a program one operation at a time (single-step mode).

Table 2.5   Interrupt handling (codes followed by 'h' are in hexadecimal)

Interrupt	Name	Generated by
00 (00h)	Divide error	Processor
01 (00h)	Single step	Processor
02 (02h)	Non-maskable interrupt	External equipment
03 (03h)	Breakpoint	Processor
04 (04h)	Overflow	Processor
05 (05h)	Print screen	Shift-Print screen key stroke
06 (06h)	Reserved	Processor
07 (07h)	Reserved	Processor
08 (08h)	System timer	Hardware via IRQ0
09 (09h)	Keyboard	Hardware via IRQ1
10 (0Ah)	Reserved	Hardware via IRQ2
11 (0Bh)	Serial communications (COM2)	Hardware via IRQ3
12 (0Ch)	Serial communications (COM1)	Hardware via IRQ4
13 (0Dh)	Reserved	Hardware via IRQ5
14 (0Eh)	Floppy disk controller	Hardware via IRQ6
15 (0Fh)	Parallel printer	Hardware via IRQ7
16 (10h)	BIOS – Video access	Software
17 (11h)	BIOS – Equipment check	Software
18 (12h)	BIOS – Memory size	Software
19 (13h)	BIOS – Disk operations	Software
20 (14h)	BIOS – Serial communications	Software
22 (16h)	BIOS – Keyboard	Software
23 (17h)	BIOS – Printer	Software
25 (19h)	BIOS – Reboot	Software
26 (1Ah)	BIOS – Time of day	Software
28 (1Ch)	BIOS – Ticker timer	Software
33 (21h)	DOS – DOS services	Software
39 (27h)	DOS – Terminate and stay resident	Software

2.4.2 *Hardware interrupts*

Computer systems use either polling or interrupt-driven software to service external equipment. With polling the computer, continually monitors a status line and waits for it to become active, whereas an interrupt-driven device sends an interrupt request to the computer, which is then serviced by an interrupt service routine (ISR). Interrupt-driven devices are normally better in that the computer is thus free to do other things, whereas polling slows down the system as it must continually monitor the external device. Polling can also cause problems in that a device may be ready to send data and the computer is not watching the status line at that point. Figure 2.11 illustrates polling and interrupt-driven devices.

The generation of an interrupt can occur by hardware or software, as illustrated in Figure 2.12. If a device wishes to interrupt the processor, it informs the programmable interrupt controller (PIC). The PIC then decides whether it should interrupt the processor. If there is a processor interrupt then the processor reads the PIC to determine which device caused the interrupt. Then, depending on the device that caused the interrupt, a call to an ISR is made. The ISR then communicates with the device and processes any data. When it has finished, the program execution returns to the original program.

A software interrupt causes the program to interrupt its execution and goes to an interrupt service routine. Typical software interrupts include reading a key from the keyboard, outputting text to the screen and reading the current date and time.

Hardware interrupts allow external devices to gain the attention of the processor. Depending on the type of interrupt, the processor leaves the current program and goes to a special program called an interrupt service routine (ISR). This program communicates with the device and processes any data. After it has completed its task, program execution returns to the program that was running before the interrupt occurred. Examples of interrupts include the processing of keys from a keyboard and data from a soundcard.

As previously mentioned, a device informs the processor that it wants to interrupt it by setting an interrupt line on the PC. Then, depending on the device that caused the interrupt, a call to an ISR is made. Each PIC allows access to eight interrupt request lines. Most PCs use two PICs, which gives access to 16 interrupt lines.

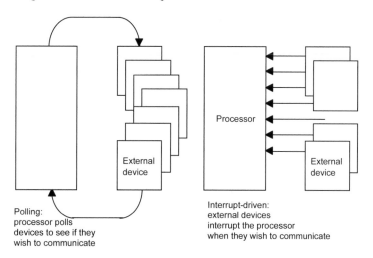

Figure 2.11 Polling and interrupt-driven communications

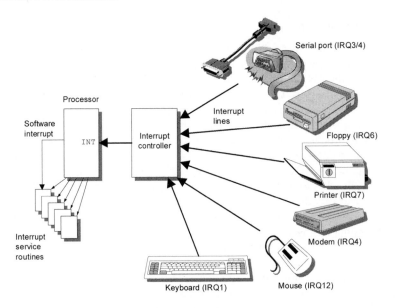

Figure 2.12   Interrupt handling

Interrupt vectors

Each device that requires to be interrupt-driven is assigned an IRQ (interrupt request) line. Each IRQ is active high. The first eight (IRQ0–IRQ7) map into interrupts 8 to 15 (08h–0Fh) and the next eight (IRQ8–IRQ15) into interrupts 112 to 119 (70h–77h). Table 2.6 outlines the use of these interrupts. When IRQ0 is made active, the ISR corresponds to interrupt vector 8. IRQ0 normally connects to the system timer, the keyboard to IRQ1, and so on. The standard set-up of these interrupts is illustrated in Figure 2.13. The system timer interrupts the processor 18.2 times per second and is used to update the system time. When the keyboard has data, it interrupts the processor with the IRQ1 line.

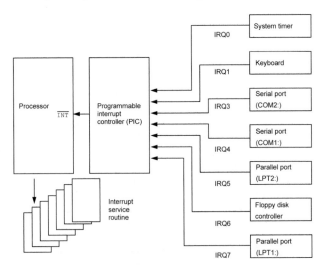

Figure 2.13   Standard usage of IRQ lines

Table 2.6 Interrupt handling

Interrupt	Name	Generated by
08 (08h)	System timer	IRQ0
09 (09h)	Keyboard	IRQ1
10 (0Ah)	Reserved	IRQ2
11 (0Bh)	Serial communications (COM2:)	IRQ3
12 (0Ch)	Serial communications (COM1:)	IRQ4
13 (0Dh)	Parallel port (LPT2:)	IRQ5
14 (0Eh)	Floppy disk controller	IRQ6
15 (0Fh)	Parallel printer (LPT1:)	IRQ7
112 (70h)	Real-time clock	IRQ8
113 (71h)	Redirection of IRQ2	IRQ9
114 (72h)	Reserved	IRQ10
115 (73h)	Reserved	IRQ11
116 (74h)	Reserved	IRQ12
117 (75h)	Math co-processor	IRQ13
118 (76h)	Hard disk controller	IRQ14
119 (77h)	Reserved	IRQ15

Data received from serial ports interrupts the processor with IRQ3 and IRQ4 and the parallel ports use IRQ5 and IRQ7. If one of the parallel or serial ports does not exist, then the IRQ line normally assigned to it can be used by another device. It is typical for interrupt-driven I/O cards, such as a soundcard, to have a programmable IRQ line mapped to an IRQ line that is not being used.

Note that several devices can use the same interrupt line. A typical example is COM1: and COM3: sharing IRQ4 and COM2: and COM4: sharing IRQ3. If they do share, then the ISR must be able to poll the shared devices to determine which of them caused the interrupt. If two different types of device (such as a soundcard and a serial port) use the same IRQ line, then there may be a contention problem as the ISR may not be able to communicate with different types of interfaces.

Figure 2.14 shows a sample window displaying interrupt usage. In this case it can be seen that the system timer uses IRQ0, the keyboard uses IRQ1, the PIC uses IRQ2, and so on. Notice that a sound blaster is using IRQ5. This interrupt is normally reserved for the secondary printer port. If there is no printer connected, then IRQ5 can be used by another device. Some devices can have their I/O address and interrupt line changed. An example is given in Figure 2.15. In this case, the IRQ line is set to IRQ7 and the base address is 378h.

Typical uses of interrupts are:

IRQ0: System timer

The system timer uses IRQ0 to interrupt the processor 18.2 times per second and is used to keep the time-of-day clock updated.

IRQ1: Keyboard data ready

The keyboard uses IRQ1 to signal to the processor that data is ready to be received from the keyboard. This data is normally a scan code.

IRQ2: Redirection of IRQ9

The BIOS redirects the interrupt for IRQ9 back here.

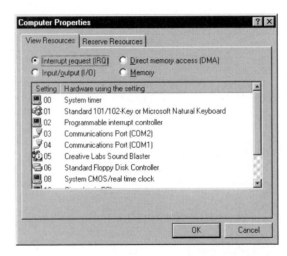

Figure 2.14   Standard usage of IRQ lines

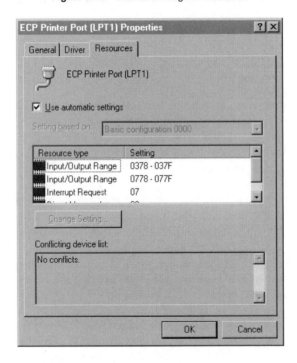

Figure 2.15   Standard set-up of IRQ lines

IRQ3: Secondary serial port (COM2:)   The secondary serial port (COM2:) uses IRQ3 to interrupt the processor. Typically, COM3: to COM8: also use it, although COM3: may use IRQ4.

IRQ4: Primary serial port (COM1:)   The primary serial port (COM1:) uses IRQ4 to interrupt the processor. Typically, COM3: also uses it.

IRQ5: Secondary parallel port (LPT2:)

On older PCs the `IRQ5` line was used by the fixed disk. On newer systems the secondary parallel port uses it. Typically, it is used by a soundcard on PCs that have no secondary parallel port connected.

IRQ6: Floppy disk controller

The floppy disk controller activates the `IRQ6` line on completion of a disk operation.

IRQ7: Primary parallel port (LPT1:)

Printers (or other parallel devices) activate the `IRQ7` line when they become active. As with `IRQ5,` it may be used by another device if there are no other devices connected to this line.

IRQ9

Redirected to `IRQ2` service routine.

Programmable interrupt controller

The PC uses the 8259 Programmable interrupt controller (PIC) to control hardware-generated interrupts. It is known as a programmable interrupt controller and has eight input interrupt request lines and an output line to secondary PIC, which are then assigned IRQ lines of `IRQ8` to `IRQ15`. This set-up is shown in Figure 2.16. When an interrupt occurs on any of these lines it is sensed by the processor. Originally, PCs had only one PIC and eight IRQ lines (`IRQ0-IRQ7`). Modern PCs can use up to 15 IRQ lines, which are set up by connecting a secondary PIC interrupt request output line to the `IRQ2` line of the primary PIC. The interrupt lines on the `IRQ2` line. The processor then interrogates the primary and secondary PICs for the interrupt line that caused the interrupt.

The primary and secondary PICs are programmed via port addresses 20h and 21h, as given in Table 2.7. The operation of the PIC is programmed using registers. The IRQ input lines are configured either as level-sensitive or edge-triggered interrupt. With edge-triggered interrupts, a change from a low to a high on the IRQ line causes the interrupt. A level-sensitive interrupt occurs when the IRQ line is high. Most devices generate edge-triggered interrupts.

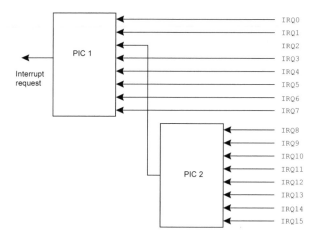

Figure 2.16 PC PIC connections

Table 2.7 Interrupt port addresses

Port address	Name	Description
20h	Interrupt control register (ICR)	Controls interrupts and signifies the end of an interrupt.
21h	Interrupt mask register (IMR)	Used to enable and disable interrupt lines.

In the IMR, an interrupt line is enabled by setting the assigned bit to a 0 (zero). This allows the interrupt line to interrupt the processor. Figure 2.17 shows the bit definitions of the IMR. For example, if bit 0 is set to a zero then the system timer on IRQ0 is enabled.

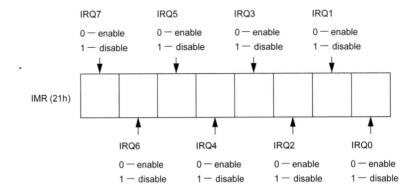

Figure 2.17   Interrupt mask register bit definitions

In the example code given below the lines IRQ0, IRQ1 and IRQ6 are allowed to interrupt the processor, whereas IRQ2, IRQ3, IRQ4 and IRQ7 are disabled:

```
_outp(0x21)=0xBC;  /* 1011 1100 enable disk
          (bit 6), keyboard (1) and timer (0) interrupts        */
```

When an interrupt occurs, all other interrupts are disabled and no other device can interrupt the processor. Interrupts are enabled again by setting the EOI bit on the interrupt control port, as shown in Figure 2.18.

The following code enables interrupts:

```
_outp(0x20,0x20); /* EOI command */
```

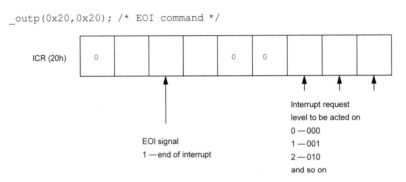

Figure 2.18   Interrupt control register bit definitions

2.5 Interfacing

There are two main methods of communicating with external equipment: either the equipment is mapped into the physical memory and given a real address on the address bus (memory mapped I/O), or it is mapped into a special area of input/output memory (isolated I/O). Figure 2.19 shows the two methods. Devices mapped into memory are accessed by reading or writing to the physical address. Isolated I/O provides ports that are gateways between the interface device and the processor. They are isolated from the system using a buffering system and are accessed by four machine code instructions. The IN instruction inputs a byte, or a word, and the OUT instruction outputs a byte, or a word. A high-level compiler interprets the equivalent high-level functions and produces machine code that uses these instructions.

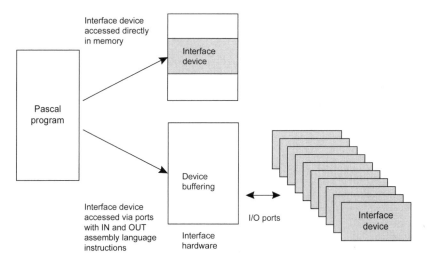

Figure 2.19 Memory mapping or isolated interfacing

2.5.1 Interfacing with memory

The 80×86 processor interfaces with memory through a bus controller, as shown in Figure 2.20. This device interprets the microprocessor signals and generates the required memory signals. Two main output lines differentiate between a read or a write operation ($R/\overline{W}$) and between direct and isolated memory access ($M/\overline{IO}$). The $R/\overline{W}$ line is low when data is being written to memory, and high when data is being read. When $M/\overline{IO}$ is high, direct memory access is selected, and when low, the isolated memory is selected.

2.5.2 Memory- mapped I/O

Interface devices can map directly onto the system address and data bus. In a PC-compatible system the address bus is 20 bits wide, from address 00000h to FFFFFh (1 MB). If the PC is being used in an enhanced mode (such as with Microsoft Windows) it can access the area of memory above 1 MB. If it uses 16-bit software (such as Microsoft Windows 3.1, then it can address up to 16 MB of physical memory, from 000000h to FFFFFFh. If it uses 32-bit software (such as Microsoft Windows 95/98/NT/2000), then the software can address up to 4 GB of physical memory, from 00000000h to FFFFFFFFh. Figure 2.21 gives a typical memory allocation.`

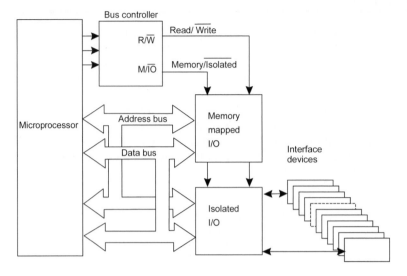

Figure 2.20 Access memory-mapped and isolated I/O

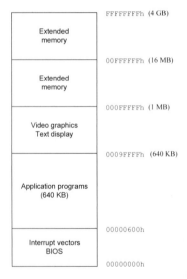

Figure 2.21 Typical PC memory map

2.5.3 *Isolated I/O*

Devices are not normally connected directly onto the address and data bus of the computer because they may use part of the memory that a program uses or they could cause a hardware fault. On modern PCs, only the graphics adaptor is mapped directly into memory, the rest communicate through a specially reserved area of memory known as isolated I/O memory.

Isolated I/O uses 16-bit addressing from 0000h to FFFFh, thus up to 64 kB of memory can be mapped. The left-hand side of Figure 2.22 shows an example for a computer in the range from 0000h to 0064h and the right-hand side shows from 0378h to 03FFh. It can be seen that the keyboard maps into addresses 0060h and 0064h, the speaker maps to address 0061h and the system timer between 0040h and 0043h. Table 2.8 shows the typical uses of the isolated memory area.

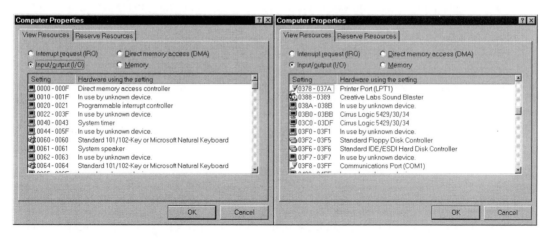

Figure 2.22 Example I/O memory map from `0000h` to `0064h` and `0378h` to `03FFh`

Table 2.8 Typical isolated I/O memory map

Address	Device
000h–01Fh	DMA controller
020h–021h	Programmable interrupt controller
040h–05Fh	Counter/timer
060h–07Fh	Digital I/O
080h–09Fh	DMA controller
0A0h–0BFh	NMI reset
0C0h–0DFh	DMA controller
0E0h–0FFh	Math coprocessor
170h–178h	Hard disk (secondary IDE drive or CD-ROM drive)
1F0h–1F8h	Hard disk (primary IDE drive)
200h–20Fh	Game I/O adapter
210h–217h	Expansion unit
278h–27Fh	Second parallel port (LPT2:)
2F8h–2FFh	Second serial port (COM2:)
300h–31Fh	Prototype card
378h–37Fh	Primary parallel port (LPT1:)
380h–38Ch	SDLC interface
3A0h–3AFh	Primary binary synchronous port
3B0h–3BFh	Graphics adapter
3C0h–3DFh	Graphics adapter
3F0h–3F7h	Floppy disk controller
3F8h–3FFh	Primary serial port (COM1:)

Inputting a byte from an I/O port

The assembly language command to input a byte is

```
IN AL,DX
```

where `DX` is the data register that contains the address of the input port. The 8-bit value loaded from this address is put into the register `AL`.

For Turbo/Borland C the equivalent function is `inportb()`. Its general syntax is as follows:

```
value=inportb(PORTADDRESS);
```

where `PORTADDRESS` is the address of the input port and `value` is loaded with the 8-bit value from this address. This function is prototyped in the header file `dos.h`.

For Turbo Pascal the equivalent is accessed via the `port[]` array. Its general syntax is as follows:

```
value:=port[PORTADDRESS];
```

where `PORTADDRESS` is the address of the input port and `value` the 8-bit value at this address. To gain access to this function the statement `uses  dos` must be placed near the top of the program. Microsoft C++ uses the equivalent `_inp()` function (which is prototyped in `conio.h`).

Inputting a word from a port

The assembly language command to input a word is

```
IN AX,DX
```

where `DX` is the data register that contains the address of the input port. The 16-bit value loaded from this address is put into the register `AX`.

For Turbo/Borland C the equivalent function is `inport()`. Its general syntax is as follows:

```
value=inport(PORTADDRESS);
```

where `PORTADDRESS` is the address of the input port and `value` is loaded with the 16-bit value at this address. This function is prototyped in the header file `dos.h`.

For Turbo Pascal the equivalent is accessed via the `portw[]` array. Its general syntax is as follows:

```
value:=portw[PORTADDRESS];
```

where `PORTADDRESS` is the address of the input port and `value` is the 16-bit value at this address. To gain access to this function the statement `uses  dos` must be placed near the top of the program. Microsoft C++ uses the equivalent `_inpw()` function (which is prototyped in `conio.h`).

Outputting a byte to an I/O port

The assembly language command to output a byte is

```
OUT DX,AL
```

where DX is the data register that contains the address of the output port. The 8-bit value sent to this address is stored in register AL.

For Turbo/Borland C the equivalent function is outportb(). Its general syntax is as follows:

```
outportb(PORTADDRESS,value);
```

where PORTADDRESS is the address of the output port and value is the 8-bit value to be sent to this address. This function is prototyped in the header file dos.h.

For Turbo Pascal the equivalent is accessed via the port[] array. Its general syntax is as follows:

```
port[PORTADDRESS]:=value;
```

where PORTADDRESS is the address of the output port and value is the 8-bit value to be sent to that address. To gain access to this function the statement uses dos requires to be placed near the top of the program.

Microsoft C++ uses the equivalent _outp() function (which is prototyped in conio.h).

Outputting a word

The assembly language command to input a byte is:

```
OUT DX,AX
```

where DX is the data register that contains the address of the output port. The 16-bit value sent to this address is stored in register AX.

For Turbo/Borland C the equivalent function is outport(). Its general syntax is as follows:

```
outport(PORTADDRESS,value);
```

where PORTADDRESS is the address of the output port and value is the 16-bit value to be sent to that address. This function is prototyped in the header file dos.h.

For Turbo Pascal the equivalent is accessed via the port[] array. Its general syntax is as follows:

```
portw[PORTADDRESS]:=value;
```

where PORTADDRESS is the address of the output port and value is the 16-bit value to be sent to that address. To gain access to this function the statement uses dos must be placed near the top of the program.

Microsoft C++ uses the equivalent _outp() function (which is prototyped in conio.h).

2.6 Exercises

The following questions are multiple choice. Please select from (a) to (d).

2.6.1   Which type of memory does not lose its contents when the power is withdrawn?
(a)	ROM	(b)	RAM
(c)	DRAM	(d)	SRAM

2.6.2   Which type of memory uses a single capacitor and a transistor to store a single bit of data?
(a)	EPROM	(b)	ERAM
(c)	DRAM	(d)	SRAM

2.6.3   Which type of memory requires its memory of be refreshed at regular intervals?
(a)	EPROM	(b)	ERAM
(c)	DRAM	(d)	SRAM

2.6.4   If a processor can operate on four bytes at a time, what is its classification?
(a)	8-bit	(b)	16-bit
(c)	32-bit	(d)	64-bit

2.6.5   Which of the following defines the amount of memory that can be accessed?
(a)	Address bus	(b)	Control lines
(c)	Handshaking lines	(d)	Data bus

2.6.6   Which of the following defines the number of bits that can be transmitted at a time?
(a)	Address bus	(b)	Control lines
(c)	Handshaking lines	(d)	Data bus

2.6.7   What is the maximum data throughput for a 32-bit parallel data bus with a clocked data rate of 10 MHz?
(a)	4 MB/s	(b)	40 MB/s
(c)	32 MB/s	(d)	320 MB/s

2.6.8   What is the maximum data throughput for a serial bus that has a bit transmission time of 69.44 µs?
(a)	6944 bps	(b)	9600 bps
(c)	1440 bps	(d)	14400 bps

2.6.9   How much memory can be accessed with a 20-bit address bus?
(a)	20 B	(b)	20 KB
(c)	1 MB	(d)	20 MB

2.6.10   How much memory can be accessed with a 32-bit address bus?
(a)	32 B	(b)	32 KB
(c)	1 GB	(d)	32 MB

2.6.11   Which interrupt does the primary serial port of a PC (COM1:) normally use?
(a)	IRQ0	(b)	IRQ3
(c)	IRQ4	(d)	IRQ7

2.6.12   Which interrupt does the secondary serial port of a PC (COM2:) normally use?
(a)	IRQ0	(b)	IRQ3
(c)	IRQ4	(d)	IRQ7

2.6.13   Which interrupt does the system timer on the PC use?
(a)   IRQ0   (b)   IRQ3
(c)   IRQ4   (d)   IRQ7

2.6.14   Which interrupt was used to increase the amount of interrupts from 8 to 16?
(a)   IRQ0   (b)   IRQ1
(c)   IRQ2   (d)   IRQ15

2.6.15   Which interrupt is used by the keyboard?
(a)   IRQ0   (b)   IRQ1
(c)   IRQ2   (d)   IRQ15

2.6.16   What does ISR stand for?
(a)   Interval status register   (b)   Interrupt status register
(c)   Interrupt service routine   (d)   Interrupt standard routine

2.6.17   How is isolated memory differentiated from memory added I/O?
(a)   Different address bus   (b)   Different data bus
(c)   Control line differentiates between them (memory/isolated)
(d)   There is no differentiation as they are physically the same

2.6.18   How many addresses can be accessed in the address range 0000h to FFFFh?
(a)   32,768 (32 kB)   (b)   6,536 (64 kB)
(c)   262,144 (256 kB)   (d)   1,048,576 (1 MB)

2.6.19   How much physical memory can a DOS-compatible program access?
(a)   32,768 (32 kB)   (b)   65,536 (64 kB)
(c)   262,144 (256 kB)   (d)   1,048,576 (1 MB)

2.6.20   What address is the interrupt control port register?
(a)   0002h   (b)   0020h
(c)   0200h   (d)   2000h

2.6.21   What is normally the base address for the primary parallel port?
(a)   0378h   (b)   0278h
(c)   03F8h   (d)   02F8h

2.6.22   Contrast the operation of polling and interrupt-driven software when interfacing to external equipment.

2.6.23   Access a PC and determine the following:

Interrupt	Device connected
IRQ1	
IRQ3	
IRQ5	
IRQ7	
IRQ9	
IRQ11	
IRQ13	
IRQ15	
I/O address	**Device connected**
0060h, 0064h	
0070h	
0090h	
00F0h	

0278h	
02F8h	
0378h	
03F8h	
DMA channel	**Device connected**
DMA0	
DMA1	
DMA2	
DMA3	

2.7 Note from the Author

This chapter has introduced some of the key concepts used in defining computer systems. So, what is it that differentiates one PC system from another? It is difficult to say, but basically it's all about how well systems are bolted together, how compatible the parts are with the loaded software, how they organize the peripherals, and so on. The big problem, though, is compatibility, which is all about peripherals looking the same, that is having the same IRQ, the same I/O address, and so on.

The PC is an amazing device that has allowed computers to move from technical specialists to, well, anyone. However, they are also one of the most annoying of pieces of technology of all time, in terms of their software, their operating systems, and their hardware. If we bought a car and it failed at least a few times every day, we would take it back and demand another one. When that failed, we would demand our money back. I could go on forever here, imagine a toaster that failed half way through making a piece of toast, and we had to turn the power off and restart it. We just wouldn't allow it.

So why does the PC lead such a privileged life? Well it's because it's so useful and multi-talented, although it doesn't really excel at much. Contrast a simple games computer against the PC and you find many lessons in how to make a computer easy to use, and configure. One of the main reasons for many of its problems is the compatibility with previous systems both in terms of hardware compatibility and software compatibility (and dodgy software, of course). The big change on the PC was the introduction of proper 32-bit software, Windows 95/NT.

In the future, systems will be configured by the operating system, not by the user. How many people understand what an IRQ is, or what I/O addresses are? Maybe if the PC faced some proper competition it would become easy to use and totally reliable. Then when they were switched on they would configure themselves automatically, and you could connect any device you wanted and it would understand how to configure (we're nearly there, but it's still not perfect). Then we would have a tool which could be used to improve creativity and you didn't need a degree in computer engineering to use one (in your dreams!). But, anyway, it's keeping a lot of technical people in a job, so, don't tell anyone our little secret. The Apple Macintosh was a classic example of a well-designed computer that was designed as a single unit. When initially released it started up with messages like 'I'm glad to be out of that bag' and 'Hello, I am Macintosh. Never trust a computer you cannot lift'.

> **Harvard architecture**
>
> Harvard architecture uses separate program and data spaces. It is also typically defined as architecture with uses separate program and data busses (and usually caches too). This architecture improves speed, though the address spaces are actually shared.
>
> The von Neumann architecture uses a stored program in the same writable memory that data is stored in.

3 Introduction to Intel Processors

3.1 Introduction

0th Generation
Intel marketed the first microprocessor, named the 4004, which caused a revolution in the electronics industry as previous electronic systems had fixed functionalities. With this processor, the functionality could be programmed by software. Amazingly, by today's standards, it could only handle 4 bits of data at a time (a nibble), contained 2000 transistors, had 46 instructions and allowed 4 k B of program code and 1 k B of data. From this humble start, the PC has since evolved using Intel microprocessors (Intel is a contraction of *Int*egrated *El*ectronics).

1st Generation
The next generation of Intel microprocessors arrived in 1974, which could handle 8 bits (a byte) of data at a time and were named the 8008, 8080 and the 8085. They were much more powerful than the previous 4-bit devices and were used in many early microcomputers and in applications such as electronic instruments and printers. The 8008 had a 14-bit address bus and can thus address up to 16 k B of memory (the 8080 has a 16-bit address bus giving it a 64 k B limit).

2nd Generation
The next generation of microprocessors began with the launch of the 16-bit processors. Intel released the 8086 microprocessor, which was mainly an extension to the original 8080 processor and thus retained a degree of software compatibility. It has a 16-bit data bus and a 20-bit address bus, and thus has a maximum addressable capacity of 1 MB. The 8086 could handle either 8 or 16 bits of data at a time (although in a messy way). IBM's designers realized the power of the 8086 and used it in the original IBM PC and IBM XT (eXtended Technology).

A stripped-down, 8-bit external data bus version called the 8088 was also available. This stripped-down processor allowed designers to produce less complex (and cheaper) computer systems. An improved architecture version, the 80286, was launched in 1982, and was used in the IBM AT (Advanced Technology).

3rd Generation
In 1985, Intel introduced its first 32-bit microprocessor, the 80386DX. This device was compatible with the previous 8088/8086/80286 (80×86) processors and gave excellent performance, handling 8, 16 or 32 bits at a time. It had a full 32-bit data and address buses and could thus address up to 4 GB of physical memory. A stripped-down 16-bit external data bus and 24-bit address bus version called the 80386SX was released in 1988, and could only access up to 16 MB of physical memory.

4th Generation
In 1989, Intel introduced the 80486DX, which was basically an improved 80386DX with a memory cache and math coprocessor integrated onto the chip. It had an improved internal structure making it around 50 per cent faster than a comparable 80386. The 80486SX was also introduced, which was merely an 80486DX with the link to the math coprocessor broken. As processor speeds increased, there was a limiting factor for the system clock speed, thus the system clock was doubled or trebled to produce the processor clock. Typically, systems with clock doubler processors are around 75 per cent faster than the comparable non-doubled processors. Example clock doubler processors were DX2-66 and DX2-50, which run from 33 MHz

and 25 MHz clocks, respectively. Intel have also produced a range of 80486 microprocessors, which ran at three or four times the system clock speed and are referred to as DX4 processors. These include the Intel DX4-100 (25 MHz clock) and Intel DX4-75 (25 MHz clock).

5th Generation   The Pentium (or P-5) is a 64-bit super-scalar processor. It can execute more than one instruction at a time and has a full 64-bit (8-byte) data bus and a 32-bit address bus. In terms of performance, it operates almost twice as fast as the equivalent 80486. It also has improved floating-point operations (roughly three times faster) and is fully compatible with previous 80x86 processors.

6th Generation   The Pentium II/III and Pentium Pro (or P-6) are enhancements of the P-5 and have a bus that supports up to four processors without extra supporting logic, with clock multiplying speeds of over 1 GHz. They also has major savings of electrical power and the minimization of electromagnetic interference (EMI). A great enhancement of the P-6 bus is that it detects and corrects all single-bit data bus errors and also detects multiple-bit errors on the data bus.

> **Strange but true**
>
> A customer phoned a customer support line, and stated that they were not able to send a fax. After several minutes, the support line operator finally traced the fault. The user had been holding the document to the screen and then pressing the send button.

3.2   Intel Range

In February 1979, Intel released the following press release:

> *The Intel 8086, a new microcomputer, extends the midrange 8080 family into the 16-bit arena. The chip has attributes of both 8- and 16-bit processors. By executing the full set of 8080A/8085 8-bit instructions plus a powerful new set of 16-bit instructions, it enables a system designer familiar with existing 8080 devices to boost performance by a factor of as much as 10 while using essentially the same 8080 software package and development tools.*
>
> *The goals of the 8086 architectural design were to extend existing 8080 features symmetrically, across the board, and to add processing capabilities not to be found in the 8080. The added features include 16-bit arithmetic, signed 8- and 16-bit arithmetic (including multiply and divide), efficient interruptible byte-string operations, and improved bit manipulation. Significantly, they also include mechanisms for such minicomputer-type operations as re entrant code, position-independent code, and dynamically relocatable programs. In addition, the processor may directly address up to 1 megabyte of memory and has been designed to support multiple-processor configurations.*

In 1979, Intel introduced the 8086 and 8088 microprocessor extensions to the 8080 product line. Since that time, the x86 product line has gone through six generations and become the most successful microprocessor in history. Much of this success was due to the success of the IBM-PC and its clones. Therefore Intel was at the right place at the right time when IBM made their historic decision to use the 8088. Today, the x86 market is a multibillion dollar industry, selling tens of millions of units per year.

The huge popularity of these x86 chips has lead to a prosperous x86 clone industry. AMD, Cyrix, IBM, TI, UMC, Siemens, NEC, Harris and others have all dabbled in the x86 chip industry. Today, AMD, Cyrix and Centaur are still actively competing.

3.2.1 The 8086/8088

The 8086 and 8088 used a CISC (complex instruction set computer) design methodology, and were binary compatible with each other, but not pin-compatible. Binary compatibility means that either microprocessor could execute the same programs, and pin-incompatibility means that you can't plug the 8086 into the 8088 or vice versa, and expect the chips to work.

The 8086 and 8088 both feature 20 address pins, and can thus give a total address space of one megabyte (2^{20} = one megabyte). The 8086 and 8088, though, had different data bus sizes, which determines how many bytes of data the microprocessor can read in each cycle. The 8086 featured a 16-bit data bus, while the 8088 featured an 8-bit data bus, at a transfer rate of between 4 MHz to 16 MHz. IBM chose to implement the 8088 in the IBM-PC, thus saving some cost and design complexity.

As IBM introduced the IBM-PC, a fledgling Intel Corporation struggled to supply enough chips to feed the hungry assembly lines of the expanding personal computer industry. To ensure sufficient supply, Intel subcontracted the fabrication rights of these chips to AMD, Harris, Hitachi, IBM, Siemens, and possibly others.

3.2.2 The 80186/80188

Intel continued the evolution of the 8086 and 8088 to the 80186 and 80188, which featured new instructions and new fault tolerance protection, and were Intel's first of many failed attempts at the x86 integration.

The new instructions and fault tolerance additions were logical evolutions of the 8086 and 8088. Intel added instructions that made programming much more convenient for low-level (assembly language) programmers. Intel also added some fault tolerance protection. The original 8086 and 8088 would hang when they encountered an invalid computer instruction. The 80186 and 80188 added the ability to trap this condition and attempt a recovery method.

3.2.3 The 80286

> **Intel Processors that shook the world**
>
> **4004:** November 1971, 108 kHz, 4-bit data bus, 2,300 transistors, 640 B of addressable memory.
>
> **8008:** April 1972, 200 kHz, 8-bit data bus, 3,500 transistors, 16 kB of addressable memory.
>
> **8080:** April 1974, 2 MHz, 8-bit data bus, 6,000 transistors, 64 kB of addressable memory.
>
> **8086:** June 1978, 5/8/10 MHz, 16-bit data bus, 29,000 transistors, 1 MB of addressable memory.
>
> **8088:** June 1979, 5/8 MHz, 8-bit data bus, 29,000 transistors, 1 MB of addressable memory.
>
> **80286:** 1982, 6-25 MHz; upgrade to 8086, with increased memory addressing (16 MB).
>
> **80386:** October 1985, 16/20/25/33 MHz, 32-bit data bus, 275,000 transistors, 4 GB of addressable memory.
>
> **80486:** April 1989, 25/33 /50 MHz, 32-bit data bus, 1.2 million transistors, 4 GB of addressable memory.
>
> **Pentium:** March 1993, 60/66 MHz, 64-bit data bus, 3.1 million transistors, 4 GB of addressable memory.
>
> **Pentium II/III:** March 1997, 200 MHz and on, 64-bit data bus, 7.5 million transistors, 64 GB of addressable memory.

In 1982, Intel introduced the 80286, and, for the first time, Intel did not simultaneously introduce an 8-bit bus version of this processor. The 80286 introduced some significant microprocessor extensions, such as a faster clock speed (6 MHz to 25 MHz), an extended instruction set, but more significantly, Intel added four more address lines and a new operating mode called protected mode. The 8086, 8088, 80186 and 80188 all contained 20 address lines, giving these processors one megabyte of addressibility (2^{20} = 1MB), while the 80286, with its 24 address lines, gives 16 megabytes of addressibility (2^{24} = 16 MB).

For the most part, the new instructions of the 80286 were introduced to support the new protected mode. Real mode was still limited to the one megabyte program addressing of the 8086 et al. For this SL compatibility, a program had to use protected mode in order to use up to 16-megabyte address space. Unfortunately, protected mode could not run real-mode (DOS) programs. These limitations thwarted attempts to adopt the 80286 programming extensions for mainstream consumer use. During the reign of the 80286, the first chipsets were introduced. The computer chipset was nothing more than a set of chips that replaced dozens of other peripheral chips, while maintaining identical functionality. Chips and Technologies became one of the first popular chipset companies.

IBM was spurred by the huge success of the IBM PC and decided to use the 80286 in their next generation computer, the IBM PC-AT. However, the PC-AT was not introduced until 1985 – three years after introduction of the 80286. Like the IBM PC, the PC-AT was hugely successful for home and business use, and Intel continued to second-source the chips to ensure an adequate supply of chips to the computer industry. Intel, AMD, IBM and Harris were known to produce 80286 chips as OEM products, while Siemens, Fujitsu and Kruger either cloned it, or were also second sources.

3.2.4   The 80386

In 1985, Intel introduced the 80386, which added significant programming and addressibility enhancements. Protected mode was enhanced to allow easy transitions between it and real mode (without resetting the microprocessor). Another new operating mode (v86 mode) was introduced to allow DOS programs to execute within a protected mode environment. Addressibility was further enhanced to 32 bits, giving the 80386 four gigabytes of memory addressibility (2^{32} = 4 GB).

Also like the 80286, the 80386 was not introduced in any computer systems for many years after its introduction. Compaq was the first mainstream company to introduce an 80386-based computer – beating IBM to market. Regardless, the 80386 enjoyed a very long life for home and business computer users. This long life was due largely to the programming extensions in the 80386 – namely the ability to create a protected mode operating system to take advantage of all 4 GB of potential memory while still being able to run legacy DOS applications.

Shortly after the 80386 was introduced, Intel introduced the 80386 SX, and to avoid confusion, Intel renamed the 80386 as 80386 DX. The SX was a cost-reduced 80386 with a 16-bit data bus, and 24-bit address bus. The 16-bit data bus meant the SX was destined to have lower memory throughput than its DX counterpart, while the 24-bit address bus mean that the SX could address only 16 MB of physical memory. Regardless of the address bus and data bus differences, the SX and DX were software compatible with each other. Intel also introduced the 80376 as part of the 80386 family. The 376 was an 80386 SX that ran exclusively in protected mode. Intel also made their second failed attempt at chip integration with the 80386 SL integrated core logic, chipset functionality, and power-saving features into the microprocessor.

During its long reign, the 80386-based computer began to evolve. Chipset vendors began dreaming of ways that would help improve the performance of the computer, thus giving their products competitive advantages. One of the innovations was the introduction of the memory cache. The memory cache within the chipset played a huge role in Intel's future product plans. First, Intel introduced a cache, and later they incorporated the cache into the microprocessor itself.

During this time, the popularity of the personal computer, and most notably their Intel microprocessors, didn't escape the notice of many entrepreneurs wishing to cash in on Intel's business. AMD began their own x86 microprocessor division. Other small start-ups, such as Cyrix and Nexgen, decided they too could design an Intel-compatible microprocessor. The aspirations of these companies didn't bode well within Intel. Shortly thereafter, Intel began taking measures to ensure their own dominance in the industry – to the exclusion of everybody else. Hence, Intel began what many believe are anti-competitive business practices. In spite of this, many 80386 clones began to appear. AMD marketed the Am386 microprocessors in speeds from 16 MHz to 40 MHz (although it was possible to overclock this chip up to 80 MHz). IBM introduced the 386 SLC, which featured a low-power 386 with an integrated 8-KB cache. IBM created other 386/486 hybrid chips – some that were pin-compatible with Intel, and others that were not.

3.2.5 *The 80486*

The 80486 offered little in the way of architectural enhancements over its 80386 predecessor, but had the integration of the 80387 math coprocessor into the 80486 core logic. Thus all software that required the math coprocessor could run on the 80486 without any expensive hardware upgrades. Like the 80386 SX, Intel decided to introduce the 80486 SX as a cost-reduced 80486 DX. Unfortunately, Intel chose to ensure that these processors were neither pin-compatible, nor 100 per cent software compatible with each other. Unlike the 80386 SX, the 80486 SX enjoyed the full data bus and address bus of its DX counterpart. Instead, Intel removed the math coprocessor, thereby rendering the 80486 SX somewhat software incompatible with its DX counterpart. To further complicate matters, Intel introduced the 80487 SX – the *math coprocessor* to the 80486 SX. Intel convinced vendors to include a new socket on the motherboard that could accommodate the 80486 SX and 80487 SX as an expensive hardware upgrade option. Unbeknownst to the consumer, the 80486 SX was an 80486 DX with a non-functional math unit (though later versions of the chip actually removed the math unit). The 80487 SX was a full 80486 DX with a couple of pins relocated on the package – to prevent consumers from using the cheaper 80486 DX as an upgrade option.

Also like the 80386, the Intel began to diversify their 80486 offerings, such as low-power versions and clock doulers/treblers (DX2 and DX4). The 80486 SL was introduced along with the 80386 SL as an integrated, low-power chip for notebook applications. Finally, after Intel introduced the Pentium chip, they produced a version of the Pentium that was pin-compatible with the 80486. They called this chip an *overdrive* processor.

Likewise, AMD and Cyrix continued to pursue their own 486-compatible chip solutions. AMD introduced many Am486 variants and Cyrix continued their nomenclature of calling an 80486-compatible chip the Cyrix 5x86. IBM began manufacturing for Cyrix, still pursuing their own microprocessor designs (the Blue Lightning series).

3.2.6 *The Pentium*

The Pentium processor was a big departure from all previous Intel x86 processors, and signaled the end to the 80x86 nomenclature (which was spurred by Intel losing a trademark dispute against AMD on the 386 processor). The Pentium processor contained more than one execution unit – making it superscalar. After release they rapidly diversified the Pentium product line with a range of different clock speeds from 60 and 66 MHz to 90, 100, 120 and 133 MHz. They also introduced low-power versions of the Pentium to be used in notebook computer applications. Finally, Intel introduced the MMX-enhanced processors for enhanced multimedia software development.

With the Pentium, Intel no longer needed (or wanted) any second-source fabrication manufacturing their microprocessors. Thus they kept many of the programming enhancements secret for the rest of the industry. However, AMD and Cyrix didn't sit by and watch

Intel expand and dominate the market. AMD introduced the K5 processor – their first in-house x86 design, but it was late to market and relatively slow. In response to their bleak outlook for the K5, AMD bought Nexgen, who had just created their own x86-compatible microprocessor, calling it the Nx586, and were near to completed their design of their next-generation processor core – the Nx686. AMD used the Nx686 core and created the successful K6 processor. AMD has continued to upgrade this processor to include MMX, and other enhancements. During this time, Cyrix introduced the 6x86, which was pin-compatible with the Pentium, though the 6x86 nomenclature might lead the consumer to believe that it is a sixth generation (Pentium Pro) compatible chip. The 6x86 has also been enhanced with MMX instructions as the 6x86 MX.

3.2.7 The Pentium Pro

The Pentium Pro was introduced in November 1995 as Intel's sixth generation x86 design – code-named the 'P6'. The Pentium Pro offered some minor programming enhancements, four more address lines (and could address up to 64 GB of main memory), and a large second-level cache. The addition of the second-level cache gave the Pentium Pro a good performance boost, but it was very expensive to manufacture.

Intel continued their attempts at closing the architecture to the exclusion and elimination of their competition, and they managed to gain patent protection for some pins on the Pentium Pro socket, thus making this chip very difficult to clone without substantial legal liability. However, Intel wasn't paranoid enough. Intel introduced the Pentium II under the impression that the Pentium Pro could never achieve their performance goals, as it was alleged that the Pentium Pro second-level cache could never run faster than 200 MHz, and therefore they must discontinue the development of this product line. The Pentium II also abandoned the socket approach to microprocessors, and introduced the slot concept, which was further enshrouded in patent protection, thereby further raising the bar to the cost of competition.

Regardless of Intel's continued monopolistic business practices, the P6 product line has diversified and flourished, and the Pentium II added MMX enhancements and a variety of second-level cache options. Intel has created the Celeron brand to compete in the sub-$1000 market. The Xeon was introduced to compete in the server market with a 100 MHz system bus. As time goes on, Intel will continue to diversify the P6 family product line, most likely with a 200 MHz system bus. Intel's competitors have stayed with a Pentium-compatible pin-out. AMD has continued to develop the K6 processor and added MMX enhancements. Cyrix has added MMX enhancements to the MII product line. Centaur products always contained MMX enhancements. These three companies combined their abilities to create a common set of MMX-3D instruction extensions, and created a 100 MHz system bus and an integrated second-level cache.

3.2.8 Pentium II/III

The Pentium II was a glorified Pentium Pro with MMX extensions, but used a different package to the Pentium Pro, known as Slot-1. Officially, Intel claimed technical reasons for needing Slot-1. The Pentium II can address up to 64 GB of main memory, but has cache limitations preventing memory use above 512 MB. Industry pundits claimed that it was devised to thwart competition with the Pentium Pro, and thus further the Intel monopoly. Strangely, the technical reasons for needing Slot-1 evaporated as soon as the Pentium Pro was dead. Slot-1 was also promised to be the upgrade path for consumers – leading many years into the future. As soon as Intel saturated the market with Slot-1 computers, they announced the future high-performance upgrade path would be Slot-2. The Pentium III further increased the clock speed to over 1GHz, and enhanced instructions that speeded Internet services. Other processors in the range include:

- **Celeron**. This is a stripped down Pentium II (sometimes affectionately known as the Castrated One, as was Intel's attempt at capturing the lower-end of the market). The Celeron had no second-level cache, making its performance lacklustre, and reportedly slower than a Pentium (with MMX) running at nearly one-half of its speed.
- **Xeon**. This is a fast Pentium II/III. The Pentium II contains a P6 (Pentium Pro) core with a half-speed second-level cache (L2 cache), whereas the Xeon has an L2 cache which runs at full processor speed. Pentium II connects to the motherboard in a slot named Slot-1, whereas the Xeon is not slot-compatible and uses Slot-2. Xeon is Intel's high-end microprocessor brand for the computer server market.
- **Merced**. Merced is Intel's future-generation microprocessor architecture. It is not the next-generation x86 microprocessor, but a completely new microprocessor design and instruction set. Merced will allow legacy x86 programs to run via a hardware translation mechanism, and is a further departure from its x86 predecessors. This translation mechanism enables Merced to run existing Windows and DOS applications. Intel claims that Merced will never run x86 programs as fast as the current state-of-the-art x86 microprocessors. Therefore, they are targeting Merced at the server and workstation market, and will offer x86 compatibility as a matter of convenience.

  Merced is not CISC (complex instruction set computer) or RISC (reduced instruction set computer), but closely resembles a VLIW (very long instruction word) design. Intel doesn't want to call this chip VLIW, ostensibly for political reasons (not invented here), and have instead defined it as EPIC (explicitly parallel instruction computing). For all intents and purposes, EPIC is VLIW. First versions of Merced will run between 600 MHz and 1 GHz.

3.3 Memory Addressing

Most modern operating systems allow processes to create a virtual memory made up of the physical electronic memory and, if required, hard disk storage. As far as the program is concerned, the program has the full memory resources of the system. The operating system then maps the addresses from the program onto an actual physical memory address (whether it be electronic memory or hard disk storage), as illustrated in Figure 3.1.

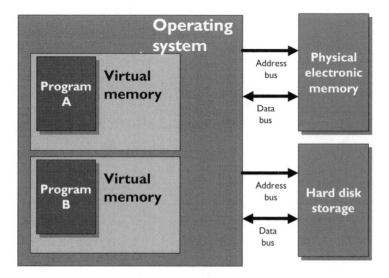

Figure 3.1   Virtual memory addressing

3.3.1   *Linear addressing*

Linear addressing simply maps linearly the memory address onto the physical memory address. For example, a 16-bit linear address ranges from 0000h to FFFFh (65,636 addresses), and a 32-bit linear address ranges from 00000000h to FFFFFFFFh (4,294,967,296 addresses). Figure 3.2 shows an example of 32-bit linear addressing. In this case, each of the memory addresses stores 8 bits (a byte) of data, and the output on the data bus depends on the number of memory locations accessed, after the base location.

3.3.2   *Segmented addressing*

Segmented addressing uses a segmentation address that points to a range of addresses. The actual address is then pointed to by an offset address. The address is then specified as:

$$Address = Segment : Offset$$

Figure 3.3 illustrates the concept of segmented addressing.

The Pentium processor run in one of two modes: virtual or real. In virtual mode, it acts as a pseudo-8086 16-bit processor (also known as the protected mode), and all DOS-based programs use the virtual mode. The 8086 has a 20-bit address bus so that when the PC is running 8086-compatible code it can address up to 1 MB of physical memory. It also has a segmented memory architecture and can directly address only 64 kB of data at any time. A chunk of memory is known as a segment, and hence the phrase 'segmented memory architecture'. In real-mode, the processor uses the full capabilities of its address and data buses. This mode normally depends on the addressing capabilities of the operating system, and uses a linear addressing structure.

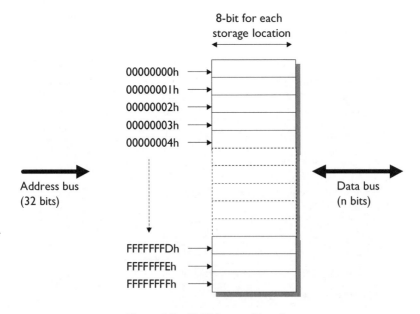

Figure 3.2   32-bit linear addressing

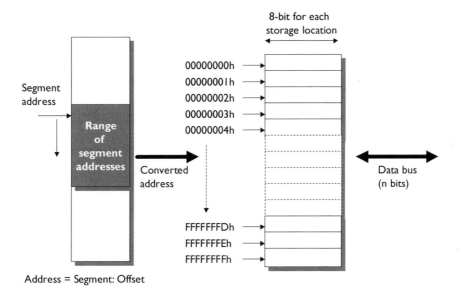

Figure 3.3 Segmented addressing

Memory addresses are normally defined by their hexadecimal addresses. For example, a 4-bit address bus can address 16 locations from `0000b` to `1111b`, which can be represented in hexadecimal as `0h` to `Fh`. An 8-bit bus can address up to 256 locations, from `00h` to `FFh`.

Two important addressing capabilities for the PC relate to a 16- and a 20-bit address bus. A 16-bit address bus addresses up to 64 kB of memory from `0000h` to `FFFFh` and a 20-bit address bus addresses up to 1 MB from `00000h` to `FFFFFh`. The Pentium processor has a 32-bit address bus and can address from `00000000h` to `FFFFFFFFh`.

A segmented memory address location is identified with a segment and an offset address. The standard notation is `segment:offset`. A `segment` address is a 4-digit hexadecimal address, which points to the start of a 64 kB chunk of data. The `offset` is also a 4-digit hexadecimal address, which defines the address offset from the segment base pointer.

The `segment:offset` address is defined as the logical address; the actual physical address is calculated by shifting the segment address 4 bits to the left and adding the offset. The example given next shows that the actual address of `2F84:0532` is `2FD72h`.

Segment (2F84):	0010	1111	1000	0100	0000
Offset (0532):		0000	0101	0011	0010
Actual address:	0010	1111	1101	0111	0010

3.4 8088 Microprocessor

Each of the PC-based Intel microprocessors is compatible with the original 8086 processor and is normally backwardly compatible. Thus, for example, a Pentium can run 8086, 80386 and 80486 code. The great revolution in processing power arrived with the 16-bit 8086 processor. This had a 20-bit address bus and a 16-bit address bus, while the 8088 had an 8-bit external data bus. Figure 3.4 shows the pin connections of the 8088 and also the main connections to the processor. Many of the 40 pins of the 8086 have dual functions. For example, the lines AD0–AD7 act either as the lower 8 bits of the address bus (A0–A7) or as the lower 8 bits of the data bus (D0–D7). The lines A16/S3–A19/S6 also have a dual function. S3–S6 are normally not used by the PC and thus they are used as the 4 upper bits of the address bus. The latching of the address is achieved when the ALE (address latch enable) which goes from a high to a low.

The bus controller (8288) generates the required control signals from the 8088 status lines $\overline{S0} - \overline{S1}$. For example, if $\overline{S0}$ is high, $\overline{S1}$ is low and $\overline{S2}$ is low, then the $\overline{MEMR}$ line goes low. The main control signals are:

- $\overline{IOR}$ (I/O read), which means that the processor is reading from the contents of the address that is on the I/O bus.
- $\overline{IOW}$ (I/O write), which means that the processor is writing the contents of the data bus to the address that is on the I/O bus.
- $\overline{MEMR}$ (memory read), which means that the processor is reading from the contents of the address that is on the address bus.
- $\overline{MEMW}$ (memory write), which means that the processor is writing the contents of the data bus to the address that is on the address bus.
- $\overline{INTA}$ (interrupt acknowledgement), which is used by the processor to acknowledge an interrupt ($\overline{S0}$, $\overline{S1}$ and $\overline{S2}$ all go low). When a peripheral wants the attention of the processor, it sends an interrupt request to the 8259, which, if it is allowed, sets INTR high.

The processor communicates either directly with memory (with $\overline{MEMW}$ and $\overline{MEMR}$) or with peripherals through isolated I/O ports (with $\overline{IOR}$ and $\overline{IOW}$).

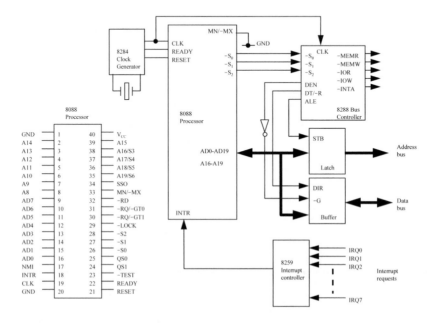

Figure 3.4 8088 connections

3.4.1 Registers

Microprocessors use registers to perform their operations. These registers are basically special memory locations within the processor that have special names. The 8086/88 has 14 registers, which are grouped into four categories, as illustrated in Figure 3.5.

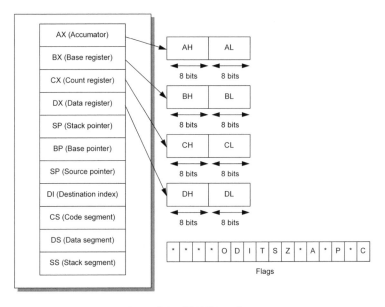

Figure 3.5 8086/88 registers

General-purpose registers

There are four general-purpose registers: AX, BX, CX and DX, each of which can be used to manipulate a whole 16-bit word or with two separate 8-bit bytes (which are called the lower- and upper-order bytes). Each of these registers can be used as two 8-bit registers, for example, AL represents an 8-bit register that is the lower half of AX and AH which is the upper half of AX.

The AX register is the most general of the four registers and is normally used for all types of operations. Each of the other registers has one or more implied extra functions. These are:

- AX is the accumulator, and is used for all input/output operations and some arithmetic operations. For example, multiply, divide and translate instructions assume the use of AX.
- BX is the base register, and can be used as an address register.
- CX is the count register, and is used by instructions that require to count. Typically, it is used for controlling the number of times a loop is repeated and in bit-shift operations.
- DX is the data register, and is used for some input/output and also when multiplying and dividing.

STRANGE, BUT TRUE

A customer phoned a customer support line, and complained that their computer would not work. All the wires were plugged in the right place, and it had been plugged-in. After many other questions the operator asked the user, "What happens when you press the power switch?", "What's a power switch?", came the reply.

Addressing registers

The addressing registers are used in memory addressing operations, such as holding the source address of the memory and the destination address. These address registers are named BP, SP, SI and DI:

- SI is the source index and is used with extended addressing commands.
- DI is the destination index and is used in some addressing modes.
- BP is the base pointer.
- SP is the stack pointer.

Status registers

Status registers are used to test for various conditions in an operations, such as 'is the result negative', 'is the result zero', and so on. The two status registers have 16 bits and are called the instruction pointer (IP) and the flag register (F):

- IP is the instruction pointer and contains the address of the next instruction of the program.
- Flag register holds a collection of 16 different conditions. Table 3.1 outlines the most used flags.

Table 3.1 Processor flags

Bit	Flag position	Name	Description
C	0	Set on carry	Contains the carry from the most significant bit (left-hand bit) following a shift, rotate or arithmetic operation.
A	4	Set on 1/2 carry	
S	7	Set on negative result	Contains the sign of an arithmetic operation (0 for positive, 1 for negative).
Z	6	Set on zero result	Contains results of last arithmetic or compare result (0 for nonzero, 1 for zero).
O	11	Set on overflow	Indicates that an overflow has occurred in the most significant bit from an arithmetic operation.
P	2	Set on even parity	
D	10	Direction	
I	9	Interrupt enable	Indicates whether the interrupt has been disabled.
T	8	Trap	

Segments registers

There are four areas of memory called segments, each of which are 16 bits and can thus address up to 64 kB (from 0000h to FFFFh). These segments are:

- Code segment (cs register). This defines the memory location where the program code (or instructions) is stored.
- Data segment (ds register). This defines where data from the program will be stored (ds stands for data segment register).

- Stack segment (ss register). This defines where the stack is stored.
- Extra segment (es).

All addresses are with reference to the segment registers.

The 8086 has a segmented memory, the segment registers are used to manipulate memory within these segments. Each segment provides 64 kB of memory, known as the current segment. Segmented memory was discussed in Section 3.2.2.

> **Strange but true**
>
> Some computer companies are considering changing the message "Press any key to continue" as some users phone up their support lines to ask where the "Any" key is.

Memory addressing

There are several methods of accessing memory locations:

- Implied addressing uses an instruction in which it is known which registers are used.
- Immediate (or literal) addressing, which uses a simple constant number to define the address location.
- Register addressing, which uses the address registers for the addressing (such as AX, BX, and so on).
- Memory addressing, which is used to read or write to a specified memory location.

3.4.2 *Accessing memory using C and Pascal*

In C the address `1234:9876h` is specified as `0x12349876`. Turbo Pascal accesses a memory location using the predefined array `mem[]` (to access a byte), `memw[]` (a word) or `memw[]` (a long integer). The general format is `mem[segment:offset]`.

3.4.3 *Near and far pointers*

A near pointer is a 16-bit pointer that can be used to address up to 64 kB of data, whereas a far pointer is a 20-bit pointer that can address up to 1 MB of data. A far pointer can be declared using the `far` data type modifier, as shown next.

```
char    far *ptr;      /* declare a far pointer          */
ptr=(char far *) 0x1234567;/*initialize far pointer      */
```

In the program shown in Figure 3.6 a near pointer `ptr1` and a far pointer `ptr2` have been declared. In the bottom part of the screen the actual addresses stored in these pointers is displayed. In this case `ptr1` is `DS:1234h` and `ptr2` is `0000:1234h`. Notice that the address notation of `ptr1` is limited to a four-digit hexadecimal address, whereas `ptr2` has a `segment:offset` address. The address of `ptr1` is in the form `DS:XXXX` where `DS` (the data segment) is a fixed address in memory and `XXXX` is the offset.

> Do witches run spell checkers?
>
> A computer's attention span is as long as its power cord.

There are several modes in which the compiler operates. In the small model the compiler declares all memory addresses as near pointers and in the large model they are declared as far pointers. Figure 3.7 shows how the large memory model is selected in Borland C (`Options` → `Compiler` → `Model` → `Large`). The large model allows a program to store up to 1 MB of data and code. Normally for a DOS-based program, the small model is the default and allows a maximum of 64 kB for data and 64 kB for code.

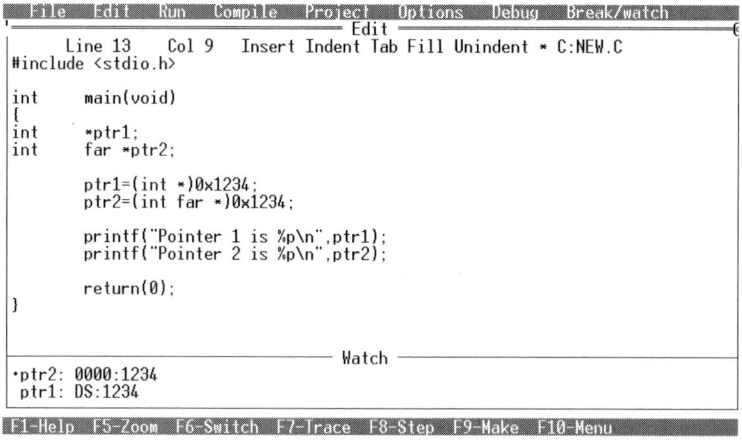

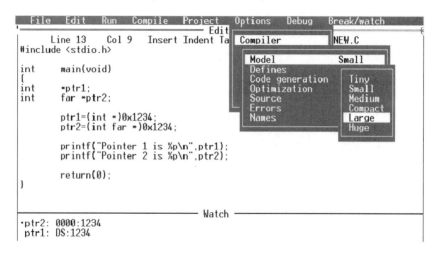

Figure 3.6   Near and far pointers

Figure 3.7   Compiling a program in the large model

3.5   View Inside the Processor

To be able to view the processor, the user must use a debugging program. Figure 3.8 shows an example of Turbo Debugger that is available with many of the Borland software development products and can be used to view the operation of a program. It can be seen that the machine code and equivalent assembly language macro appears in the top left-hand window. A sample code line is

```
cs:01FA→55              push    bp
```

which specifies that the memory location is 01FA in the code segment (cs:01FA). The machine code at this location is 55 (0101 0101) and the equivalent assembly language instruction is push bp. Note that the cs segment address in this case is 5757h, thus the actual physical address will be with reference to the address 57570h.

```
+-[_]-CPU 80486---------------Đ----1-[□][□]--+
¦                                            _   ax 0000   ¦c=0¦
¦  cs:01FA→55          push   bp             _   bx 062A   ¦z=1¦
¦  cs:01FB  8BEC       mov    bp,sp          _   cx 0009   ¦s=0¦
¦  cs:01FD  83EC08     sub    sp,0008        _   dx AB02   ¦o=0¦
¦  cs:0200  56         push   si             _   si 0145   ¦p=1¦
¦  cs:0201  57         push   di             _   di 060A   ¦a=0¦
¦                                            _   bp FFD2   ¦i=1¦
¦  cs:0202  B89401     mov    ax,0194        _   sp FFC8   ¦d=0¦
¦  cs:0205  50         push   ax             _   ds 58A0   ¦    ¦
¦  cs:0206  E8D40B     call   _puts          _   es 58A0   ¦    ¦
¦  cs:0209  59         pop    cx             _   ss 58A0   ¦    ¦
¦                                                cs 5757   ¦    ¦
¦  cs:020A  B8B501     mov    ax,01B5            ip 01FA   ¦    ¦
Ã□_____□¦               ¦    ¦
¦  ds:0000 00 00 00 00 54 75 72 62      Turb  ¦         ¦    ¦
¦  ds:0008 6F 2D 43 20 2D 20 43 6F  o-C - Co  +--------Â
¦  ds:0010 70 79 72 69 67 68 74 20  pyright   ¦  ss:FFCA 0001  ¦
¦  ds:0018 28 63 29 20 31 39 38 38  (c) 1988  ¦  ss:FFC8→011D  ¦
+----------------------¤--------+
```

Figure 3.8 Example screen from Turbo Debugger

The contents of the flag register is shown on the right-hand side. In this case the flags are

C=0, Z=1, S=0, O=0, P=1, A=0, I=1 and D=0.

The registers are shown to the left of the flag register. In this case the contents are

AX=0000h,   BX=062Ah,   CX=0009h,   DX=AB02h,   SI=0145h,
DI=060Ah,   BP=FFD2h,   SP=FFC8h,   DS=58A0h,   ES=58A0h, SS=58A0h,
CS=5757h,   IP=01FAh.

The data (in the data segment) is shown at the bottom left-hand corner of the screen. The first line

```
ds:0000 00 00 00 00 54 75 72 62     Turb
```

shows the first 8 bytes in memory (from DS:0000 to DS:0007). The first byte in memory is 00h (0000 0000) and the next is also 00h. After the 8 bytes are defined the eight equivalent ASCII characters are shown. In this case, these are:

```
Turb
```

The ASCII equivalent character for 5A (1001 1010) is 'T' and for 75 (0111 0101) it is 'u'. Note that in this case the data segment register has 58A0h. Thus the location of the data will be referenced to the address 58A00h.

The bottom right-hand window shows the contents of the stack.

3.6 Exercises

3.6.1   On its output pins, how many data bits does the 8086 have?
(a)   8   (b)   16
(c)   32   (d)   64

3.6.2   On its output pins, how many data bits does the 8088 have?

(a)   8   (b)   16
(c)   32   (d)   64

3.6.3   On its output pins, how many address bits does the 8088 have?

(a)   16   (b)   20
(c)   24   (d)   32

3.6.4   What is the maximum addressable physical memory with the 8088?

(a)   640 KB   (b)   1 MB
(c)   16 MB   (d)   64 MB

3.6.5   What is the actual address for 713F:0215?

(a)   713F0215h   (b)   71605h
(c)   7354h   (d)   928Fh

3.6.6   How much memory can a 16-bit address bus address?

3.6.7   Outline how the 8086 differs from the 8088. Also outline how the 80386DX differed from the 80386SX.

3.6.8   For the debug screen given in Figure 3.9, determine the following:

(i)   Contents of AX, BX, CX, DX, SI, DI.
(ii)   Contents of AH, AL, BH and BL.
(iii)   The first assembly language command.
(iv)   The physical memory address of the first line of code. (Hint: the cs:02C2 and the value in the cs register need to be used.)
(v)   The physical memory address of the data. (Hint: the ds:0000 and the value in the ds register need to be used.)

Note from the Authors

The **8086** and **8088** are the father of virtually every PC processor ever made, and they projected Intel from a small innovative company which specialized in memory devices into one of the most powerful companies in the world. The **8086/8088** had a fairly inconspicuous start to its life, until one day IBM decided that they would change many years of development, and use another organization's processor. So the first ever IBM PC used the **8086** processor.

It's amazing to think that the first IBM PC could have used the 8-bit 8080 processor, and it took a lot of persuasion by Bill Gates to make them change their minds, and adopt the 8086/8088 (which had a considerably enhanced specification).

```
+-[ ]-CPU 80486---------------Ð----1-[ ][ ]-+
¦                                      -  ax 0100   ¦c=0¦
¦   cs:02C2>55           push    bp        _  bx 02CE   ¦z=1¦
¦   cs:02C3 8BEC         mov     bp,sp     _  cx 0001   ¦s=0¦
¦                                          _  dx 02CE   ¦o=0¦
¦   cs:02C5 B8AA00       mov     ax,00AA   _  si 02C8   ¦p=1¦
¦   cs:02C8 50           push    ax        _  di 02CE   ¦a=0¦
¦   cs:02C9 E8F609       call    _puts     _  bp 0000   ¦i=1¦
¦   cs:02CC 59           pop     cx        _  sp FFF8   ¦d=0¦
¦                                          _  ds 5846   ¦   ¦
¦   cs:02CD 33C0         xor     ax,ax     _  es 5846   ¦   ¦
¦   cs:02CF EB00         jmp     #PROG1_1#10 (_ ss 5846 ¦   ¦
¦                                          _  cs 5751   ¦   ¦
¦   cs:02D1 5D           pop     bp        _  ip 02C2   ¦   ¦
Ã□-----------------------------------□¦               ¦   ¦
¦   ds:0000 00 00 00 00 42 6F 72 6C      Borl ¦       ¦   ¦
¦   ds:0008 61 6E 64 20 43 2B 2B 20 and C++  ¦  +--------Â
¦   ds:0010 2D 20 43 6F 70 79 72 69 - Copyri ¦  ¦ ss:FFFA 0000   ¦
¦   ds:0018 67 68 74 20 31 39 39 31 ght 1991 ¦  ¦ ss:FFF8□015B   ¦
+----------------------¤--------+
```

Figure 3.9   Example screen from Turbo Debugger

4 8086 Basics

4.1 Introduction

An important differentiation is between machine code and assembly language. The actual code that runs on the processor is machine code. This is made up of unique bit sequences that identify the command and other values which the commands operate on. For example, for the debugger screen from Figure 3.8, the assembly language line to move a value into the AX register is

```
mov     ax,0194
```

while the equivalent machine code is

```
B8 94 01
```

where the code B8h (1011 1000b) identifies the instruction to move a 16-bit value into the AX register and the value to be loaded is 0194h (0000 0001 1001 0100b). Note that the reason that the 94h value is stored before the 01h value is that on the PC the least significant byte is stored in the first memory location and the most significant byte in the highest memory location. Figure 4.1 gives an example of storage within the code segment. In this case the two instructions are mov and push. In machine code these are B8h and 50h, respectively.

In this case, the two instructions are mov and push. In machine code these are B8h and 50h, respectively. The MOV command is an important one, as it moves data between the processor and memory. A typical operation in a program is:

- Move data from a memory location into a processor register (for example, MOV BX,[*location*]).
- Process the data (for example, ADD BX, AX).
- Move results back into memory (for example, MOV [*location*], BX).

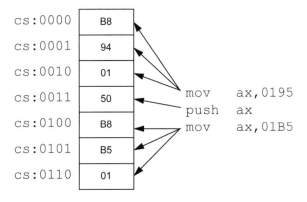

Figure 4.1 Example memory storage for code segment

The table in Section 4.9 outlines the assembly language mnemonics (in column 1) and the equivalent encoded bit values (in column 3). It also shows the number of cycles for a 8086 processor and a 80386 processor (columns 4 and 5). The explanation of the encoded bit values is given after the table.

4.2   Assembly Language Elements

Most modern C++ development systems use an inline assembler that allows assembly language code to be embedded with C++ code. This code can use any C variable or function name that is in scope. The __asm keyword invokes the inline assembler and can appear wherever a C statement is legal. The following code is a simple __asm block enclosed in brackets.

```
__asm
{
    /* Initialize serial port */
    mov dx,0x01;    /* COM2:                       */
    mov al,0xD2;    /* serial port parameters */
    mov ah,0x0;     /* initialize serial port */
    int 14h;
    line_status=ah;
    modem_status=al;
}
```

Note these statements can also be inserted after the __asm keyword, such as:

```
__asm mov dx,0x01;    /* COM2:                       */
__asm mov al,0xD2;    /* serial port parameters */
__asm mov ah,0x0;     /* initialize serial port */
__asm int 14h;
__asm line_status=ah;
__asm modem_status=al;
```

The following section outlines the usage of 8086 assembly language.

4.2.1   Characters and numbers

Integers can be represented as binary, octal, decimal or hexadecimal numbers; 8086 assembly language represents these with a preceding B, O, D or H, respectively. A decimal integer is assumed if there is no letter. Examples of numeric constants are:

```
01001100b   3eh   10b   ffffh   17o
```

Character constants are enclosed with single quotes when they have a fixed number of characters (such as 'b', 'fred', and so on); if they have a variable number of characters, they are enclosed with double quotes (such as "a", "fred", and so on).

For example:

```
'c'                'Press ENTER'
"Input Value> "    "x"
```

4.2.2   Comments

Assembly language programs probably need more comments than high-level language as some of the operations give little information on their purpose. The character used to signify a comment is the semi-colon (;) and all comments within a program are ignored by the assembler. For example, the following lines have comments:

```
                   ; This is a comment
      mov ax,1      ; move instruction will be discussed next
```

4.2.3 Move

The move instruction (mov) moves either a byte (8 bits) or a word (16 bits) from one place to another. There are three possible methods:

• Moving data from a register to a memory location.
• Moving data from a memory location to a register.
• Moving data from one register to another.

Real student answer

Handel was half German half Italian and half English. He was very large.

Note that in 8086/88 it is not possible to move data directly from one memory location to another using a single instruction. To move data from one memory location to another, first the data is moved from the memory location into a register, then it is moved from the register to the destination address.

Examples of moving a constant value into registers are:

```
      mov   cx,20         ; moves decimal 20 into cx
      mov   ax,10h        ; moves 10 hex into ax
      mov   ax,01110110b  ; moves binary 01110110 into ax
```

An address location is identified within square brackets ([]). To move data into a specified address the address location must be loaded into a register. For example, to load the value of 50h (0101 0000) into address location 200h the following lines are used:

```
      mov   bx,200h
      mov   [bx],50h     ; load 50 hex into memory location 200h
```

The general format of the mov instruction is:

```
      mov r/m , r/m/d        or
      mov sr , r16/m16       or
      mov r16/m16 , sr
```

where r/m stands for register (such as AH, AL, BH, BL, CH, CL, DH, DL, AX, BX, CX, DX, BP, SI, DI) or memory location, and r/m/d stands for a register, memory or a constant value. The register sr stands for any of the segment registers (CS, DS, ES, SS) and r16/m16 stands, for any 16-bit register (AX, BX, CX, SP, BP, SI, DI) and 16-bit memory address.

4.2.4 Addressing memory

An address location can be specified with the BX, BP, SI or DI register. Examples are:

```
      [BP]
      [SI]
      30 [BX]       ; which specifies the address BX+30
      [BP+DI]
      40 [BX+SI]    ; which specifies the address BX+SI+40
```

Program 4.1 on p. 106 gives an assembly language; it loads 1234h into address DS:0000h, 5678h into address DS:0002h and 22h into address DS:0005h.

Figure 4.2 shows a sample run of Program 4.2. It can be seen that the `mov [bx],1234` operation loads the value `34h` into address location `DS:0000h` and `12h` into address `DS:0001h`. This is because the processor loads the least significant byte into the lower address location.

Figure 4.2 shows that the associated machine code for the instructions is:

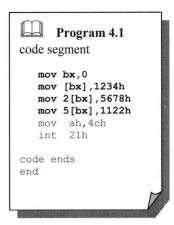

Program 4.1
code segment

```
    mov bx,0
    mov [bx],1234h
    mov 2[bx],5678h
    mov 5[bx],1122h
    mov  ah,4ch
    int   21h

code ends
end
```

BB	**0000**	mov	bx,0000
C707	**3412**	mov	word ptr [bx],1234
C747	**02 7856**	mov	word ptr [bx+02],5678
C747	**05 2211**	mov	word ptr [bx+05],1122
B4	**4C**	mov	ah,4C

Thus `BBh` is the machine code to load a value into the `BX` register, `C707h` loads a value into the address pointed to and `C747h` loads an offset value into an address location.

```
+-[_]-CPU 80486-------------------------------------Ð-------1-[ ] [ ]-+
¦  cs:0000 BB0000        mov    bx,0000            -  ax 0000  ¦c=0¦
¦  cs:0003 C7073412      mov    word ptr [bx],1234 _  bx 0000  ¦z=0¦
¦  cs:0007 C747027856    mov    word ptr [bx+02],5678_ cx 0000 ¦s=0¦
¦  cs:000C C747052211    mov    word ptr [bx+05],1122_ dx 0000 ¦o=0¦
¦  cs:0011>B44C          mov    ah,4C              _  si 0000  ¦p=0¦
¦  cs:0013 CD21          int    21                 _  di 0000  ¦a=0¦
¦  cs:0015 B253          mov    dl,53              _  bp 0000  ¦i=1¦
¦  cs:0017 018B7424      add    [bp+di+2474],cx    _  sp 0100  ¦d=0¦
¦  cs:001B 108B7C24      adc    [bp+di+247C],cl    _  ds 5707  ¦   ¦
¦  cs:001F 1483          adc    al,83              _  es 5707  ¦   ¦
¦  cs:0021 C404          les    ax,[si]            _  ss 5719  ¦   ¦
¦  cs:0023 56            push   si                 _  cs 5717  ¦   ¦
¦  cs:0024 E85337        call   377A               _  ip 0011  ¦   ¦
Ā                                                  ¦           ¦   ¦
¦  ds:0000 34 12 78 56 00 22 11 FE 4 xV " _        +--------------Â
¦  ds:0008 1D F0 E0 01 21 24 AA 01  -Ó !$¬         ¦ ss:0104 0000  ¦
¦  ds:0010 21 24 89 02 7C 1E EE 0F  !$ë |-¤        ¦ ss:0102 3D08  ¦
¦  ds:0018 01 01 01 00 02 FF FF FF                 ¦ ss:0100>C483  ¦
+-------------------------------------------------¤--------------+
```

Figure 4.2   Sample run of Program 4.1

4.2.5   *Addition and subtraction*

As they imply, the ADD and SUB perform addition and subtraction of two words or bytes. The ADD and SUB instructions operate on two operands and put the result into the first operand. The source or destination can be a register or address. Examples are:

```
mov ax,100
add ax,20    ;adds 20 onto the contents of ax
sub ax,12    ;subtracts 12 from ax and puts result into ax

mov bx,10    ;moves 10 into bx
add ax,bx    ;adds ax and bx and puts result into ax
```

The standard format of the add instruction is:

```
add r/m , r/m/d
```

where `r` is any register, `m` is memory location and `d` is any constant value.

4.2.6 Compare

The compare CMP instruction acts like the SUB instruction, but the result is discarded. It thus leaves both operands intact but sets the status flags, such as the O (overflow), C (carry), Z (zero) and S (sign flag). It is typically used to determine if two numbers are the same, or if one value is greater or less than another value. Examples are:

```
cmp 6,5        ;result is 1, this sets C=0 S=0; Z=0 O=0
cmp 10,10      ;result is 0, this sets Z=1 the rest as above
cmp 5,6        ;result is -1, this sets negative flag S=1
```

4.2.7 Unary operations

The unary operations (Inc, Dec and Neg) operate on a single operand. An INC instruction increments the operand by 1, the DEC instruction decrements the operand by 1, and the NEG instruction makes the operand negative. Examples are:

```
mov al,10
inc al         ; adds 1 onto AL, AL will thus store 11
inc al         ; AL now stores 12
dec al         ; takes 1 away from AL (thus it will be equal to 11)
neg al         ; make AL negative, thus AL stores -11
```

4.2.8 Boolean bitwise instructions

The Boolean bitwise instructions (And, Or, XOR and NCT) operate logically on individual bits. The XOR function yields a 1 when the bits in a given bit position differ. The AND function yields a 1 only when the given bit positions are both 1s. The OR operation gives a 1 when any one of the given bit positions are a 1. These operations are summarized in Table 4.1. For example:

```
        00110011            10101111            00011001
AND     11101110      OR    10111111     XOR    11011111
        00100010            10111111            11000110
```

Table 4.1 Bitwise operations

A	B	AND	OR	XOR
0	0	0	0	0
0	1	0	1	1
1	0	0	1	1
1	1	1	1	0

Examples of assembly language instructions which use bitwise operations are:

```
mov al,7dh     ;loads 01111101 into al
and al,03h     ; 01111101 AND 00000011 gives 00000001
               ;  al stores 00000001 or 1
mov ax,03f2h   ; loads 0000 0011 1111 0010 into AX
xor ax,ffffh   ; exclusive OR 1111 1111 1111 1111  with AX,
               ; AX now contain 1111 1100 0000 1101
```

4.2.9 Shift/rotate instructions

The shift/rotate instructions are:

SHL – shift bits left   SHR – shift bits right

SAL – shift arithmetic left   SAR – shift arithmetic right
RCL – rotate through carry left   RCR – rotate through carry right
ROL – rotate bits left   ROR – rotate bits right

The shift instructions move the bits, with or without the carry flag, and can be either an arithmetic shift or logical shift, whereas the rotate instructions are cyclic and may involve the carry flag. The SHL and SHR shift bits to the left and right, respectively. The bit shifted out is put into the carry flag and the bit shifted in is a 0. The rotate operations (ROL, ROR, RCL, RCR) are cyclic. Rotate with carry instructions (RCL and RCR) rotate the bits using the carry flag. Thus, the bit shifted out is put into the carry flag and the bit shift in is taken from the carry flag. The rotate bits (ROL and ROR) rotate the bits without the carry flag. The SAL instruction is identical to SHL, but the SAR instruction differs from SHR in that the most significant bit is shifted to the right for each shift operation. These operations are illustrated in Figure 4.3.

The number of shifts on the value is either specified as a unitary value (1) or stored in the counter register (CL). The standard format is:

```
SAR r/m, 1/CL    SAL r/m, 1/CL    SHR r/m, 1/CL    SHL r/m, 1/CL
ROR r/m, 1/CL    ROL r/m, 1/CL    RCR r/m, 1/CL    RCL r/m, 1/CL
```

where r/m is for register or memory and 1 stands for one shift. If more than one shift is required then the CL register is used. These operations take a destination and a counter value stored in CL. For example, with bit pattern:

Initial conditions: 01101011 and carry flag 1

Result after:

SHR	00110101	CF 1	→	SHL	11010110	CF 0		→
SAR	00110101	CF 1	→	SAL	11010110	CF 0		→
ROR	10110101	CF 0	→	RCR	10110101	CF 1		→
RCL	11010111	CF 0						

The following is an example of the SAR instruction:

```
mov cl,03          ; Contents of AX
mov ax,10110111b   ; (10110111b)
sar ax,1           ; shifted one place to the right (0101 1011b)
sar ax,cl          ; shifted three places to the right (0000 0101b)
```

After sar ax,1 stores 005Bh (0000 0000 0101 1011b) then the sar ax,cl instruction moves the contents of AX by three bit positions to the right. The contents of AX after this operation will be 0005h (0000 0000 0000 0101b).

The following shows an example of the SHR instruction:

```
mov cl,03          ; Contents of AX
mov ax,10110111b   ; (10110111b)

shr ax,1           ; Shift right one (01011011)
shr ax,cl          ; shift right three (00001011)
```

and an example of the ROR instruction:

```
mov cl,03                ; Contents of BX are :
```

```
mov bl,10110111b      ; 10110111
ror bl,1              ; rotate one place to the right(1101 1011b)
ror bl,cl             ; rotate three places to the right(0111 1011b)
```

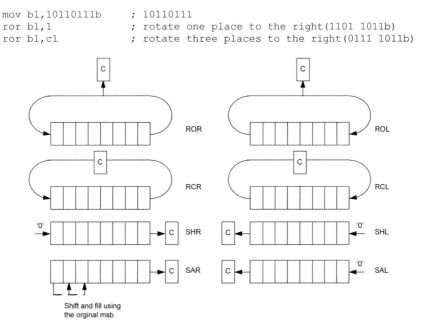

Figure 4.3 Rotate operations

4.2.10 Unconditional jump

The unconditional jump (JMP) instruction transfers program execution to another part of the program. It uses a label to identify the jump location; this is defined as a name followed by a colon. The JMP instruction is not conditional – the program will always jump. An example is

```
        mov al,10101010b
        jmp nextst
           : :
           : :
nextst: mov bx,10
```

4.2.11 Conditional jumps

With the JMP the program always goes to the label, but the unconditional jumps will branch only if a certain condition is met, such as if the result is negative, or the result is zero, and so on. Table 4.2 outlines the condition jump instructions.

A few examples are:

```
        mov     al,11
        cmp     al,10
        jle     fred  ; last operation was less than 10
                      ; then branch to label fred

fred2:  mov     ax,300
        sub     ax,1000 ; subtract 1000 from 300
        jg fred5        ; no jump since result was not greater

fred:   sub al,12       ;
        cmp al,0        ;
        jz fred2        ;no jump since not equal to zero
```

Table 4.2   Conditional jump instructions

Name	Description	Flag tests	Name	Description	Flag tests
JC	Jump if carry	C=1	JZ	Jump if zero	Z=1
JS	Jump if sign	S=1	JNC	Jump if not carry	C=0
JNS	Jump if not sign	S=0	JL	Jump if less than	
JNZ	Jump if not zero	Z=0	JLE	Jump if less than or equal to	
JGE	Jump if greater than or equal to	S=Ov	JG	Jump if greater than	Z=0 S=Ov
JA	Jump if above	C=0 and Z=0	JNB	Jump if not below	
JB	Jump if below				

4.2.12 Subroutine calls

Subroutines allow a section of code to be called and for the program to return back to where it was called. The instructions are CALL and RET. An example is given next:

```
        call   fred  ; Goto fred routine
        add    al,bl
         : :
         : :

fred:   mov    al,00h
        add    al,bl
        ret          ; return to place that called
```

> **Real student answer**
>
> Louis Pasteur discovered a cure for rabbis.

4.2.13 PUSH and POP

The PUSH and POP instructions are typically used with subroutines. A PUSH instruction puts the operand onto a temporary storage called a stack (this will be covered in more detail later). The stack is a LIFO (last in, first out), where the last element to be loaded is the first to be taken off, and so on. The POP instruction is used to extract the last value that was put on the stack.

Typically they are used to preserve the contents of various registers so that their contents are recovered after a subroutine is called. For example, if a subroutine modifies the AX, BX and CX registers, then the registers are put on the stack with:

```
    PUSH AX
    PUSH BX
    PUSH CX
```

Next, the subroutine can use these registers for its own use. Finally, within the subroutine, the original registers are restored with:

```
    POP CX
    POP BX
    POP AX
```

The order of the POP instructions must be the reverse of the PUSH instructions so that the contents are properly restored. For example:

```
    call sub1
    add   al,bl
     : :
```

> **Real student answer**
>
> The sun never set on the British Empire because the British Empire is in the East and the sun sets in the West.

```
sub1:    push ax
         push bx
         mov    ax,1111h
         mov    bx,1111h
         add    ax,bx
           : :
         pop bx
         pop ax
         ret              ; return to place that called
```

4.3 Timing

Each instruction takes a finite time to compete. The speed of operation is determined by the processor clock speed. To determine how long a certain instruction will take determine the number of clock cycles to execute it and multiply this by the clock period. For example, if the clock rate is 8 MHz then the clock period is 0.125 μs. Table 4.3 gives the number of clock cycles for various instructions. Note that different processors take differing number of clock cycles to execute each command. Notice also that the 80386 processor is around twice as fast as the 8086 for many of the commands. This is due to improved architecture.

> **Real student answer**
>
> Johann Bach wrote a great many musical compositions and had a large number of children. In between he practiced on an old spinster which he kept up in his attic.

For example, the `mov ax,1234` statement takes 0.5 μs assuming an 8 MHz clock. Note the great improvement in the 80286/386 over the 8086 in dealing with mathematics operations. In the 8086 it takes 144 clock cycles to perform a word divide while the 80386 takes only 22 clock cycles (nearly seven times faster). The following program outputs an incremented value every two seconds.

Table 4.3   Instruction timings for different processors

Command	Example	8086	80286	80386
mov	mov ax,1234	4	2	2
mov	mov dx,ax	2	2	2
out	out dx,al	8	3	11
inc	inc ax	3	2	2
dec	dec bx	3	2	2
and	and ax,0b6h	4	3	2
jne (nj)	jne fred	16(4)	7(3)	7(3)
div	div cx	80 (b)	14 (b)	14 (b)
		144 (w)	22 (w)	22 (w)
nop	nop	2	2	2

```
      (b) = byte divide, (w) = word divide, (nj) = no jump

loop:       mov    dx,1f3h    ; control register address
            mov    al,90h     ; set port A input, port B output
            out    dx,al

            mov    dx,1f0h
            in     al,dx      ;read byte from port A

            mov    dx,1f1h
            out    dx,al      ; send byte to port B
```

```
            call    delay
            jmp     loop

     ; two second delay loop for 8MHz clock
delay:  mov     ax,13
outer:  mov     bx,64777              ;;; ) outer
inner:  dec     bx          ;;;;; ) inner
            jnz inner       ;;;;; ) loop
            dec ax
            jnz outer                 ;;; ) loop
            ret
```

The second (inner) loop

```
        inner: dec bx
        jnz inner
```

will be executed 64,777 times. The number of cycles to do a `dec` and a `jnz` is 3+16 cycles. Thus it takes 19 cycles to complete this loop. The total time to complete this inner loop is thus

$$\text{number of cycles} \times \text{clock period} = 19 \times 0.125 \,\mu s = 2.375 \,\mu s$$

Total time to complete this loop is $64\,777 \times 2.375 \,\mu s = 0.1538 \,s$

This inner loop is executed 13 times, thus the total delay time is $13 \times 0.1538 = 2\,s$.

In general, for a general-purpose loop with A and B as the variables in AX and BX, then:

```
delay:  mov     ax,A        ; 4 clock cycles
outer:  mov     bx,B        ; 4
inner:  dec     bx          ; 3
            jnz inner       ; 16
            dec ax          ; 3
            jnz outer       ; 16
            ret
```

First the inner loop:

```
inner:          dec    bx       ; 3
                jnz inner       ; 16
```

then the number of cycles for inner loop will be $B \times 19$

```
inner:          dec    bx       ; 3
                jnz inner       ; 16
                dec ax          ; 3
                jnz outer       ; 16
```

Number of cycles is thus approximately $A \times ((B \times 19) + 16 + 3)$.

If $19 \times B$ is much greater than 19 then the following approximation can be made:

Number of cycles $= 19 \times A \times B$

Thus

$$\text{Time taken} = \frac{\text{Number . of clock cycles}}{\text{Clock Frequency}}$$

$$= \frac{19 \times A \times B}{\text{Clock Frequency}}$$

In the last example (assuming a 4 MHz clock), the values of A and B are 13 and 64 777, respectively thus:

$$\text{Time taken} = \frac{19 \times 13 \times 64\,777}{8 \times 10^6} = 2\,\text{s}$$

Typical processor clocks are:

8086	4.77 MHz, 8 MHz
80386	16 MHz, 25 MHz, 33 MHz
80486	33 MHz, 50 MHz, 66 MHz, 100 MHz
Pentium	60 MHz, 90 MHz, and above.

4.4 Moving Data Around in Memory

Program 4.2 loads the memory locations from DS:0000h to DS:00FFh with values starting at 00h and ending at FFh. After the AL and BX registers have been initialized to 00h then the code runs round a loop until all the memory locations have been loaded. The BX register contains the address the value will be loaded to. This increments each time round the loop. The AL register stores the value to be loaded into the currently specified memory location. Figure 4.4 shows a sample run.

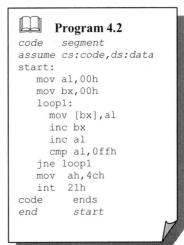

Program 4.2

```
code    segment
assume cs:code,ds:data
start:
    mov al,00h
    mov bx,00h
    loop1:
        mov [bx],al
        inc bx
        inc al
        cmp al,0ffh
    jne loop1
    mov ah,4ch
    int 21h
code    ends
end     start
```

```
+-[_]-CPU 80486--------------------------Ð-------1-[□] [□]-+
¦  cs:0000 B000          mov     al,00        -  ax 0020   ¦c=1¦
¦  cs:0002 BB0000        mov     bx,0000      _  bx 0020   ¦z=0¦
¦  cs:0005 8807          mov     [bx],al      _  cx 0000   ¦s=0¦
¦  cs:0007 43            inc     bx           _  dx 0000   ¦o=0¦
¦  cs:0008 FEC0          inc     al           _  si 0000   ¦p=0¦
¦  cs:000A>3CFF          cmp     al,FF        _  di 0000   ¦a=1¦
¦  cs:000C 75F7          jne     0005         _  bp 0000   ¦i=1¦
¦  cs:000E B44C          mov     ah,4C        _  sp 0100   ¦d=0¦
¦  cs:0010 CD21          int     21           _  ds 5705   ¦   ¦
¦  cs:0012 50            push    ax           _  es 5705   ¦   ¦
¦  cs:0013 6A01          push    0001         _  ss 5717   ¦   ¦
¦  cs:0015 9AB2467711    call    1177:46B2    _  cs 5715   ¦   ¦
¦  cs:001A FF76FE        push    word ptr [bp -  ip 000A   ¦   ¦
Ã□                                           □¦             ¦   ¦
¦  ds:0000 00 01 02 03 04 05 06 07  □□□□□□□□  ¦             ¦   ¦
¦  ds:0008 08 09 0A 0B 0C 0D 0E 0F  □       ¤ +---------------Â
¦  ds:0010 10 11 12 13 14 15 16 17  □□□□□¶§□□ ¦  ss:0102 C033  ¦
¦  ds:0018 18 19 1A 1B 1C 1D 1E 1F  □□□□□□□-  ¦  ss:0100□000C  ¦
+-------------------------------------------¤---------------+
```

Figure 4.4 Sample debug screen

4.5   Equates

To define a token to a certain value, the equates (EQU) statement can be used. For example:

```
one      EQU    1
outA     EQU    1f1h
PI       EQU    3.14159
prompt   EQU    'Type Enter'
```

The general format is:

```
name EQU expression
```

The assembler simply replaces every occurrence of the token with the value given.

Program 4.3

```
code segment
    mov bx,0
    mov [bx],1234h
    mov 2[bx],5678h
    mov 5[bx],1122h
    mov   ah,4ch
    int   21h
code ends
end
```

4.6   Exercises

In this tutorial the sample code should be inserted by replacing the highlighted code into Program 4.3.

4.6.1   Enter the following code and run the debugger to determine the values given next.

```
mov al,54h
mov bl,36h
add al,bl
```

AL

Sign flag

Carry flag

Overflow flag

Zero flag

4.6.2   Enter the following code and run the debugger to determine the values given next.

```
mov al,54h
mov bl,36h
sub al,bl
```

AL

Sign flag

Carry flag

Overflow flag

Zero flag

4.6.3   Enter the following code and run the debugger to determine the values given next.

```
mov al,47h
mov bl,62h
sub al,bl
```

AL

Sign flag

Carry flag

Overflow flag

Zero flag

4.6.4   Enter the following code and run the debugger to determine the values given next.

```
mov al,54h
mov bl,36h
```

```
and al,bl
```

AL
Sign flag
Carry flag

Overflow flag
Zero flag

4.6.5   Enter the following code and run the debugger to determine the values given next.

```
mov al,73h
mov bl,36h
xor al,bl
```

AL
Carry flag
Overflow flag
Sign flag
Zero flag

4.6.6   Enter the following code and run the debugger to determine the values given next.

```
mov al,54h
not al
```

AL
Carry flag
Overflow flag
Sign flag
Zero flag

4.6.7   Enter the following code and run the debugger to determine the values given next.

```
mov ax,1f54h
mov bx,5a36h
add al,bl
```

AL
Carry flag
Overflow flag
Sign flag
Zero flag

4.6.8   Enter the following code and run the debugger to determine the values given next.

```
mov ax,3a54h
mov bx,0236h
mov cl,3
shr ax,1
shl bx,cl
```

AX
BX
Carry flag

Overflow flag
Zero flag

4.6.9   Enter the following code and run the debugger to determine the values given next.

```
mov ax,3a54h
```

```
mov bx,0236h
mov cl,3
sar bx,cl
```

AX
BX
Carry flag

Overflow flag
Zero flag

4.6.10   Enter the following code and run the debugger to determine the values given next.

```
mov ax,3a54h
mov bx,0236h
mov cl,3
ror ax,cl
rcl bx,cl
```

AX
BX
Carry flag

Overflow flag
Zero flag

4.6.11   Enter the following code and run the debugger to determine the values given next.

```
mov al,54h
mov bl,66h
cmp al,bl
```

AL
BL
Carry flag

Overflow flag
Zero flag

4.6.12   Enter the following code and run the debugger to determine the values given next.

```
mov al,32
mov ah,53
mov bx,236
xor ax,bx
```

AX
BX
Carry flag

Overflow flag
Zero flag

4.6.13   Enter the following code and run the debugger to determine the values given next.

```
mov ax,3a54h
mov bx,100h
mov [bx],ax
```

AX
Contents of address 100h
Contents of address 101h

Overflow flag
Zero flag

4.6.14   Enter the following code and run the debugger to determine the values given next.

```
mov ax,3a54h
mov bx,120h
mov 20[bx],ax
```

Contents of address 100h		AX
Contents of address 120h		Zero flag
Contents of address 121h		

4.6.15   Enter the following code and run the debugger to determine the values given next.

```
mov al,'a'
mov ah,'b'
```

AL		Overflow flag
BL		Zero flag
Carry flag		

4.6.16   Write an assembly language program containing a function that adds the contents of the AX and BX registers and puts the result into the CX register.

4.6.17   Write a program that loads the values 00h, 01h, 02h,...FEh, FFh into the memory locations starting from address DS:0008h. A basic layout is shown below.

```
loop:
    mov al,00h
    mov bx,08h
      :    :
      :    :
    jne loop
```

📖   **Program 4.4**

```
data    segment
        val1 dw ?
        val2 dw ?
data    ends

code    segment
assume cs:code,ds:data

org 0100h

start:
    mov ax,1234h
    mov val1,ax
    mov val2,5678h

    mov ah,4Ch ; DOS exit
    int 21h
code    ends
end     start
```

4.6.18   Write a program that will load the values FFh, FEh, FDh,...01h, 00h into the memory locations starting from address DS:0000h.

4.6.19   Write a program that moves a block of memory from DS:0020h to 0100h to addresses that start at address 0200h.

4.6.20   Write a program that determines the largest byte in the memory locations 0000h to 0050h.

4.7   Data Definition

Variables are declared in the data segment. To define a variable, the DB (define byte) and DW (define word) macros are used. For example, to define (and initialize) a variable temp, which has the value 15 assigned to it, is declared as follows:

```
temp db 15
```

An uninitialized variable has a value that is a question mark, for example:

```
temp db ?
```

Other definition types are also used

• dd (define doubleword – 2 times 16 bits, which is 4 bytes).

- `dq` (define quadword, which is 8 bytes).
- `dt` (define 10 bytes).

The data definition is defined within the data segment. In Turbo Assembler (TASM) the data segment is defined after the `.DATA` directive (as shown in TASM Program 4.4). Microsoft Assembler (MASM) defines the data segment between the `data segment` and `data ends`, as shown in MASM Program 4.3.

Program 4.4 declares two variables named `val1` and `val2`. The value `val1` is loaded with the value `1234h` and `val2` is loaded with `5678h`. Figure 4.5 shows an example screen after the three `mov` instructions have been executed. It can be seen `val1` has been stored at `DS:0000` and `val2` at `DS:0002`.

> **Program 4.5**
> ```
> .MODEL SMALL
>
> .DATA
>
>     val1 dw ?
>     val2 dw ?
>
> .CODE
>     org 0100h
>     mov ax,1234h
>     mov val1,ax
>     mov val2,5678h
>
>     mov ah,4Ch ; DOS exit
>     int 21h
> end
> ```

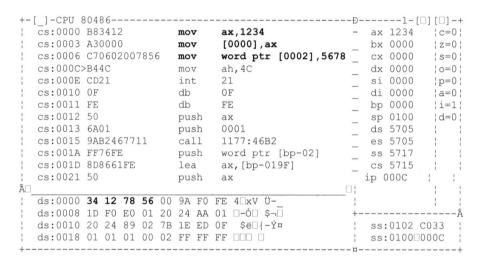

```
+-[_]-CPU 80486------------------------------------Đ-------1-[□] [□]-+
¦   cs:0000 B83412            mov     ax,1234            -  ax 1234  ¦c=0¦
¦   cs:0003 A30000            mov     [0000],ax          _  bx 0000  ¦z=0¦
¦   cs:0006 C70602007856      mov     word ptr [0002],5678 _ cx 0000 ¦s=0¦
¦   cs:000C>B44C              mov     ah,4C              _  dx 0000  ¦o=0¦
¦   cs:000E CD21              int     21                 _  si 0000  ¦p=0¦
¦   cs:0010 0F                db      0F                 _  di 0000  ¦a=0¦
¦   cs:0011 FE                db      FE                 _  bp 0000  ¦i=1¦
¦   cs:0012 50                push    ax                 _  sp 0100  ¦d=0¦
¦   cs:0013 6A01              push    0001               _  ds 5705  ¦   ¦
¦   cs:0015 9AB2467711        call    1177:46B2          _  es 5705  ¦   ¦
¦   cs:001A FF76FE            push    word ptr [bp-02]   _  ss 5717  ¦   ¦
¦   cs:001D 8D8661FE          lea     ax,[bp-019F]       _  cs 5715  ¦   ¦
¦   cs:0021 50                push    ax                    ip 000C  ¦   ¦
Ã□_____□¦               ¦   ¦
¦   ds:0000 34 12 78 56 00 9A F0 FE 4□xV Ü-_        ¦               ¦   ¦
¦   ds:0008 1D F0 E0 01 20 24 AA 01 □-Ó□ $¬□        +---------------Â
¦   ds:0010 20 24 89 02 7B 1E ED 0F  $ë□{-Ý¤        ¦  ss:0102 C033  ¦
¦   ds:0018 01 01 01 00 02 FF FF FF  □□□ □          ¦  ss:0100□000C  ¦
+------------------------------------------------¤---------------+
```

Figure 4.5   Sample debug screen

4.8   Assembler Directives

There are various structure directives that allow the user to structure the program. These are defined in Table 4.4.

Table 4.4   Assembler directives

Directive	Name	Description

SEGMENT and ENDS	Segment definition	The SEGMENT and ENDS directives mark the beginning and the end of a program segment. Its general format is:
		
		 `name segment`
		 `:    :`
		 `main program`
		 `:    :`
		 `name ends`
		 `end`

END	Source file end	The END directive marks the end of a module. The assembler will ignore any statements after the end directive.
GROUP	Segment group	
ASSUME	Segment registers	The ASSUME directive specifies the default segment register name. For example:

```
assume cs:code
```

The general format is

```
assume segmentregister:segmentregistername
```

| ORG | Segment origin | The ORG statement tells the assembler at which location the code should be located. |
| PROC and ENDP | Procedure definition and end | These statements define the start and end of a procedure. |

4.9 8086 Reference

Mnemonic	Description	Encoding	8086	386
AAA	Adjust after addition	00110111	8	4
AAD	Adjust before division	11010101 00001010	60	19
ADC *accum,immed*	Add immediate with carry to accumulator	0001010w *mod,reg,r/m*	4	2
ADC *r/m,immed*	Add immediate with carry to operand	100000sw *mod,reg,r/m*	4	2
ADC *r/m,reg*	Add register with carry to operand	000100dw *mod,reg,r/m*	3	2
ADC *reg,r/m*	Add operand with carry to register	000100dw *mod,reg,r/m*	3	2
ADD *accum,immed*	Add immediate to accumulator	0000010w	4	2
ADD *r/m,immed*	Add immediate to operand	100000sw *mod,000,r/m*	4	3
ADD *r/m,reg*	Add register to operand	0000010w *mod,reg,r/m*	4	2
ADD *reg,r/m*	Add operand to register	0000010w *mod,reg,r/m*	9	6
AND *accum,immed*	Bitwise AND immediate with operand	0010010w	4	2
AND *r/m,immed*	Bitwise AND register with operand	100000sw *mod,100,r/m*	4	2
AND *r/m,reg*	Bitwise AND operand with register	001000dw *mod,reg,r/m*	3	2
CALL *label*	Call instruction at label	11101000	19	7
CALL *r/m*	Call instruction indirect	11111111	16	7
CBW	Convert byte to word	10011000	2	3
CLC	Clear carry flag	11111000	2	2
CLD	Clear direction flag	11111100	2	2
CLI	Clear interrupt flag	11111010	2	3
CMC	Complement carry flag	11110101	2	2
CMP *accum, immed*	Compare immediate with accumulator	0011110w	4	2
CMP *r/m,immed*	Compare immediate with operand	100000sw	4	2
CMP *reg,r/m*	Compare register with operand	001110dw	3	2
CMPS arc,dest	Compare strings	1010011w	22	10
CMPSW	Compare strings word by word	1010011w	22	10

CMPSB	Compare string byte by byte	1010011w	22	10
CWD	Convert word to double word	10011001	5	2
DAA	Decimal adjust for addition	00100111	4	4
DAS	Decimal adjust for subtraction	00101111	4	4
DEC *r/m*	Decrement operand	1111111w	3	2
DEC *reg*	Decrement 16-bit register	01001 *reg*	3	2
DIV *r/m*	Divide accumulator by operand	1111011w	80	14
HLT	Halt	11110100	2	5
IDIV	Integer divide accumulator by operand	1111011w		
IMUL	Integer multiply accumulator by operand	1111011w		
IN *accum,immed*	Input from port	1110010w	10	12
IN *accum,DX*	Input form port given by DX	1110110w	8	13
INC *r/m*	Increment operand	1111111w *mod*,000,*r/m*	3	2
INC *reg*	Increment 16-bit register	01000 *reg*	3	2
INT *immed*	Software interrupt	11001101	51	37
INTO	Interrupt on overflow	11001110	53	35
IRET	Return from interrupt	11001111	32	22
JA *label*	Jump on above	01110111	4	3
JAE *label*	Jump on above or equal	01110011	4	3
JBE *label*	Jump on below	01110110	4	3
JC *label*	Jump on carry	01110010	4	3
JCXZ *label*	Jump on CX zero	11100011	4	3
JE *label*	Jump on equal	01110100	4	3
JG *label*	Jump on greater	01111111	4	3
JGE *label*	Jump on greater or equal	01111101	4	3
JL *label*	Jump on less than	01111100	4	3
JLE *label*	Jump on less than or equal	01111110	4	3
JMP *label*	Jump to label	11101011	15	7
JMP *r/m*	Jump to instruction directly	111111 *mod*,110,*r/m*	11	7
JNA *label*	Jump on not above	01110110	4	3
JNAE *label*	Jump on not above or equal	01110010	4	3
JNB *label*	Jump on not below	01110011	4	3
JNBE *label*	Jump on not below or equal	01110111	4	3
JNC *label*	Jump on not carry	01110011	4	3
JNE *label*	Jump on not equal	01110101	4	3
JNG *label*	Jump on not greater	01111110	4	3
JNGE *label*	Jump on not greater or equal	01111100	4	3
JNO *label*	Jump on not overflow	01110111	4	3
JNP *label*	Jump on not parity	01111011	4	3
JNS *label*	Jump on not sign	01111001	4	3
JNZ *label*	Jump on not zero	01110101	4	3
JO *label*	Jump on overflow	01110000	4	3
JP *label*	Jump on parity	01111010	4	3
JPE *label*	Jump on parity even	01111010	4	3
JPO *label*	Jump on parity odd	01111011	4	3
JS *label*	Jump on sign	01111000	4	3
JZ *label*	Jump on zero	01110100	4	3

LAHF	Load AH with flags	10011111	4	2
LOOP *label*	Loop	11100010	17	11
MOV *accum*,mem	Move memory to accumulator	101000dw	10	4
MOV mem, *accum*	Move accumulator to memory	101000dw	10	3
MOV *r/m*,immed	Move immediate to operand	1100011w *mod*,000,*r/m*	10	2
MOV *r/m*,reg	Move register to operand	100010dw *mod*,reg,*r/m*	2	2
MOV *r/m*,segreg	Move segment register to operand	100011d0 *mod*,sreg,*r/m*	2	2
MOV *reg*,immed	Move immediate to register	1011w *reg*	4	2
MOV seg*reg*,*r/m*	Move operand to segment register	100011d0 *mod*,sreg,*r/m*	2	2
MOVS dest,src	Move string	1010010w	18	7
MOVSB	Move string byte by byte	1010010w	18	7
MOVSW	Move string word by word	1010010w	18	7
MUL *r/m*	Multiply accumulator by operand	1111011w *mod*,100,*r/m*	70	9
NEG *r/m*	Negate operand	1111011w *mod*,011,*r/m*	3	2
NOP	No operation	10010000	3	3
NOT *r/m*	Invert bits	1111011w *mod*,010,*r/m*	3	2
OR *accum*,accum	Bitwise OR immediate with accumulator	000010dw *mod*,reg,*r/m*	3	2
OR *r/m*,immed	Bitwise OR immediate with operand	100000sw	4	2
OR *r/m*,reg	Bitwise OR register with operand	000010dw *mod*,reg,*r/m*	3	2
OR *reg*,r/m	Bitwise OR operand with register	000010dw *mod*,reg,*r/m*	3	2
OUT DX,*accum*	Output to port given by DX	1110111w	8	11
OUT *immed*,accum	Output to port	1110011w	10	10
POP *r/m*	Pop 16-bit operand	10001111 *mod*, 000,*r/m*	17	5
POP *reg*	Pop 16-bit register from stack	01011 *reg*	8	4
POPF	Pop flags	10011101	8	5
PUSH *r/m*	Push 16-bit operand	11111111 mem,110,*r/m*	16	5
PUSH *reg*	Push 16-bit register onto stack	010101 *reg*	11	2
PUSHF	Push flags	10011100	10	4
RCL *r/m*,1	Rotate left through carry by 1 bit	1101000w *mod*,010,*r/m*	2	3
RCL *r/m*,CL	Rotate left through carry by CL bits	1101001w *mod*,010,*r/m*	8+4n	3
RCR *r/m*,1	Rotate right through carry by 1 bit	1101000w *mod*,011,*r/m*	2	3
RCR *r/m*,CL	Rotate right through carry by CL bits	1101001w *mod*,011,*r/m*	8+4n	3
REP	Repeat	11110010	9	8
REPE	Repeat if equal	11110011		
REPNE	Repeat if not equal	11110011		
REPNZ	Repeat if not zero	11110011		
RET [*immed*]	Return after popping bytes from stack	11000010		
ROL *r/m*,1	Rotate left by 1 bit	1101000w *mod*,000,*r/m*	2	3
ROL *r/m*,CL	Rotate left by CL bits	1101001w *mod*,000,*r/m*	8+4n	3
ROR *r/m*,1	Rotate right by 1 bit	1101000w *mod*,001,*r/m*	2	3
ROR *r/m*,CL	Rotate right by CL bits	1101001w *mod*,001,*r/m*	8+4n	3
SAHF	Store AH into flags	10011110	4	3
SAL *r/m*,1	Shift arithmetic left by 1 bit	1101000w *mod*,100,*r/m*	2	3
SAL *r/m*,CL	Shift arithmetic left by CL bits	1100000w *mod*,100,*r/m*	8+4n	3
SAR *r/m*,1	Shift arithmetic right by 1 bit	1101000w *mod*,101,*r/m*	2	3
SAR *r/m*,CL	Shift arithmetic right by CL bits	1100000w *mod*,101,*r/m*	8+4n	3
SBB *accum*,immed	Subtract immediate and carry flag	0001110w	4	2

SBB *r/m,immed*	Subtract immediate and carry flag	100000sw *mod*,011,*r/m*	4	2
SBB *r/m,reg*	Subtract register and carry flag	000110dw *mod,reg,r/m*	3	2
SBB *reg,r/m*	Subtract operand and carry flag	000110dw *mod,reg,r/m*	3	2
SCAS dest	Scan string	1010111w	15	7
SCASB	Scan string for byte in AL	1010111w	15	7
SCASW	Scan string for word in AX	1010111w	15	7
SHL *r/m,*1	Shift left by 1 bit	1101000w *mod*,100,*r/m*	2	3
SHL *r/m,*CL	Shift left by CL bits	1100000w *mod*,100,*r/m*	8+4n	3
SHR *r/m,*1	Shift right by 1 bit	1101000w *mod*,101,*r/m*	2	3
SHR *r/m,*CL	Shift right by CL bits	1100000w *mod*,101,*r/m*	8+4n	3
STC	Set carry flag	11111001	2	2
STD	Set direction flag	11111101	2	2
STI	Set interrupt flag	11111011	2	3
STOS dest	Store string	1010101w	11	4
STOSB	Store byte in AL at string	1010101w	11	4
STOSW	Store word in AX at string	1010101w	11	4
SUB *accum,immed*	Subtract immediate from accumulator	0010110w	4	2
SUB *r/m,immed*	Subtract immediate from operand	100000sw *mod*,101,*r/m*	4	2
SUB *r/m,reg*	Subtract register from operand	001010dw *mod,reg,r/m*	3	2
SUB *reg,r/m*	Subtract operand from register	001010dw *mod,reg,r/m*	3	2
TEST *accum,immed*	Compare immediate bits with accumulator	1010100w	4	2
TEST *r/m,immed*	Compare immediate bits with operand	1111011w *mod*,000,*r/m*	5	2
TEST *reg,r/m*	Compare register bits with operand	1000011w *mod,reg,r/m*	3	2
WAIT	Wait	10011011	4	6
XCHG *accum,reg*	Exchange accumulator with register	100011w *mod,reg,r/m*	4	3
XCHG *r/m,reg*	Exchange operand with register	100011w *mod,reg,r/m*	17	5
XCHG *reg,accum*	Exchange register with accumulator	100011w *mod,reg,r/m*	4	3
XCHG *reg,r/m*	Exchange register with operand	100011w *mod,reg,r/m*	17	5
XOR *accum,immed*	Bitwise XOR immediate with accumulator	001110dw *mod,reg,r/m*	4	2
XOR *r/m,immed*	Bitwise XOR immediate with operand	001100dw *mod,reg,r/m*	4	2
XOR *r/m,reg*	Bitwise XOR register with operand	001100dw *mod,reg,r/m*	3	2
XOR *reg,r/m*	Bitwise XOR operand with register	001100dw *mod,reg,r/m*	3	2

Syntax:

reg	A general-purpose register of any size.
seg*reg*	A segment register, such as DS, ES, SS or CS.
accum	An accumulator of any size: AL or AX (or EAX on 386/486).
m	A direct or indirect memory operand of any size.
label	A labeled memory location in the code segment.
src,dest	A source of destination memory operand used in a string operand.
immed	A constant operand.

The bits are specified by:

d   **Direction bit**. If set (1), then the transfer is from memory to register or register to register, and the destination is a *reg* field. If not set, then the source is a register field and the transfer is from register to memory.

w   **Word/byte bit**. If set the 16-bit operands are used, else 8-bit operands are used.

s   **Sign-bit**. If set then the operand has a sign bit.

mod   **Mode**. Identifies the register/memory mode. These are:

    11   A two-register instruction is used; the reg field specifies the
              destination and the r/m field specifies the source.

reg   **Register**. Specifies one of the general-purpose registers. These are:

reg	16-bit, if w=1	8-bit, if w=0
000	AX	AL
001	CX	CL
010	DX	DL
011	BX	BL
100	SP	AH
101	BP	CH
110	SI	DH
111	DI	BH

r/m   **Register/memory**. Specifies a memory of register operand. If the mod file is
         11 then the register is specified with the *reg* field (as given above), else it
         has the following settings:

reg	Operand address
000	**DS:[BX+SI**+*disp*]
001	**DS:[BX+DI**+*disp*]
010	**SS:[BP+SI**+*disp*]
011	**SS:[BP+DI**+*disp*]
100	**DS:[SI**+*disp*]
101	**DS:[DI**+*disp*]
110	**DS:[BP**+*disp*]
111	**DS:[BX**+*disp*]

The instruction encoding has the form:

OPCODE	*mod,reg,r/m*	*disp*	*immed*
(1–2 bytes)	(0–1 byte)	(0–2 bytes)	(0–2 bytes)

where:

disp   **Displacement**. Specifies the offset for memory operands.

immed   **Register/memory**. Specifies the actual values for constant values.

5 80486

5.1 Introduction

The PC had grown from the 8086 processor, which could run 8-bit or 16-bit software. This processor was fine with text-based applications, but struggled with graphical programs, especially with GUIs. The original version of Microsoft Windows (Windows Version 1.0 and Version 2.0) ran on these limited processes. The great leap in computing power came with the development of the Intel 80386 processor and with Microsoft Windows 3.0. A key to the success of the 80386 was that it was fully compatible with the previous 8088/8086/80286 processors. This allowed it run all existing DOS-based program and new 32-bit applications. The DX version had full 32-bit data and address bus and could thus address up to 4 GB of physical memory. An SX version with a stripped-down 16-bit external data bus and 24-bit address bus version could access up to only 16 MB of physical memory (although at its time of release this was a large amount of memory). Most of the time, with Microsoft Windows 3.0, the processor was using only 16 bits, and thus not using the full power of the processor.

The 80486DX consisted of an improved 80386 with a memory cache and a math coprocessor integrated onto the chip. An SX version had the link to the math coprocessor broken. At the time, a limiting factor was the speed of the system clock (which was limited to around 25 MHz or 33 MHz). Thus, clock doubler, treblers or quadruplers allow the processor to multiply the system clock frequency to a high speed. Internal operations of the processor are then carried out at much higher speeds, but accesses outside the processor must slow down the system clock. As most of the operations within the computer involve operations within the processor then the overall speed of the computer is improved (roughly by about 75 per cent for a clock doubler).

5.2 80486 Pin Out

To allow for easy upgrades and to save space, the 80486 and Pentium processors are available in a pin-grid array (PGA) form. A 168-pin PGA 80486 processor is illustrated in Figure 5.1. It can be seen that the 486 processor has a 32-bit address bus (A0–A31) and a 32-bit data bus (D0–D31). Table 5.1 defines how the control signals are interpreted. For the STOP/special bus cycle, the byte enable signals ($\overline{BE0} - \overline{BE3}$) further define the cycle. These are:

- Write back cycle $\overline{BE0}$ =1, $\overline{BE1}$ =1, $\overline{BE2}$ =1, $\overline{BE3}$ =0.
- Halt cycle $\overline{BE0}$ =1, $\overline{BE1}$ =1, $\overline{BE2}$ =0, $\overline{BE3}$ =1.
- Flush cycle $\overline{BE0}$ =1, $\overline{BE1}$ =0, $\overline{BE2}$ =1, $\overline{BE3}$ =1.
- Shut down cycle $\overline{BE0}$ =0, $\overline{BE1}$ =1, $\overline{BE2}$ =1, $\overline{BE3}$ =1.

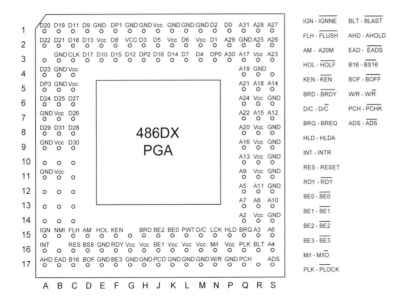

Figure 5.1 i486DX processor

The main 80486 pin connections are:

A2–A31 (I/O) — The 30 most significant bits of the address bus.

$\overline{\text{A20M}}$ (I) — When active low, the processor internally masks the address bit A20 before every memory access.

$\overline{\text{ADS}}$ (O) — Indicates that the processor has valid control signals and valid address signals.

AHOLD (I) — When active, a different bus controller can have access to the address bus. This is typically used in a multiprocessor system.

$\overline{\text{BE0}}$ – $\overline{\text{BE3}}$ (O) — The byte enable lines indicate which of the bytes of the 32-bit data bus are active.

$\overline{\text{BLAST}}$ (O) — Indicates that the current burst cycle will end after the next $\overline{\text{BRDY}}$ signal.

$\overline{\text{BOFF}}$ (I) — The backoff signal informs the processor to deactivate the bus on the next clock cycle.

$\overline{\text{BRDY}}$ (I) — The burst ready signal is used by an addressed system that has sent data on the data bus or read data from the bus.

BREQ (O) — Indicates that the processor has internally requested the bus.

$\overline{\text{BS16}}$, $\overline{\text{BS8}}$ (I)	The $\overline{\text{BS16}}$ signal indicates that a 16-bit data bus is used, the $\overline{\text{BS8}}$ signal indicates that an 8-bit data bus is used. If both are high then a 32-bit data bus is used.
DP0–DP3 (I/O)	The data parity bits gives a parity check for each byte of the 32-bit data bus. The parity bits are always even parity.
$\overline{\text{EADS}}$ (I)	Indicates that an external bus controller has put a valid address on the address bus.
$\overline{\text{FERR}}$ (O)	Indicates that the processor has detected an error in the internal floating-point unit.
$\overline{\text{FLUSH}}$ (I)	When active the processor writes the complete contents of the cache to memory.
HOLD, HLDA (I/O)	The bus hold (HOLD) and acknowledge (HLDA) are used for bus arbitration and allow other bus controllers to take control of the buses.
$\overline{\text{IGNNE}}$ (I)	When active the processor ignores any numeric errors.
INTR (I)	External devices to interrupt the processor use the interrupt request line.
$\overline{\text{KEN}}$ (I)	This signal stops caching of a specific address.
$\overline{\text{LOCK}}$ (O)	If active the processor will not pass control to an external bus controller when it receives a HOLD signal.
$\text{M}/\overline{\text{IO}}$, $\text{D}/\overline{\text{C}}$, $\text{W}/\overline{\text{R}}$ (O)	See Table 5.1.
NMI (I)	The non-maskable interrupt signal causes an interrupt 2.
$\overline{\text{PCHK}}$ (O)	If it is set active then a data parity error has occurred.
$\overline{\text{PLOCK}}$ (O)	The active pseudo lock signal identifies that the current data transfer requires more than one bus cycle.
PWT, PCD (O)	The page write-through (PWT) and page cache disable (PCD) are used with cache control.
$\overline{\text{RDY}}$ (I)	When active the addressed system has sent data on the data bus or read data from the bus.
RESET (I)	If the reset signal is high for more than 15 clock cycles then the processor will reset itself.

The 486 integrates a processor, cache and a math coprocessor onto a single IC. Figure 5.2 shows the main 80386/80486 processor connections. The Pentium processor connections are similar but it has a 64-bit data bus. There are three main interface connections: the memory/IO interface, interrupt interface and DMA interface.

The write/read ($\text{W}/\overline{\text{R}}$) line determines whether data is written to (W) or read from ($\overline{\text{R}}$) memory. PCs can interface directly with memory or can interface to isolated memory. The signal line $\text{M}/\overline{\text{IO}}$ differentiates between the two types. If it is high, then the processor accesses direct memory; if it is low, then it accesses isolated memory.

The 80386DX and 80486 have an external 32-bit data bus (D_0–D_{31}) and a 32-bit address bus ranging from A_2 to A_{31}. The two lower address lines, A_0 and A_1, are decoded to produce the byte enable signals $\overline{\text{BE0}}$, $\overline{\text{BE1}}$, $\overline{\text{BE2}}$ and $\overline{\text{BE3}}$. The $\overline{\text{BE0}}$ line activates when A_1A_0 is 00, $\overline{\text{BE1}}$ activates when A_1A_0 is 01, $\overline{\text{BE2}}$ activates when A_1A_0 and $\overline{\text{BE3}}$ actives when A_1A_0 is 11. Figure 5.3 illustrates this addressing.

The byte enable lines are also used to access either 8, 16, 24 or 32 bits of data at a time. When addressing a single byte, only the $\overline{\text{BE0}}$ line is active (D_0–D_7). If 16 bits of data are to be accessed then $\overline{\text{BE0}}$ and $\overline{\text{BE1}}$ are active (D_0–D_{15}). If 32 bits are to be accessed, then $\overline{\text{BE0}}$, $\overline{\text{BE1}}$, $\overline{\text{BE2}}$ and $\overline{\text{BE3}}$ are active (D_0–D_{31}).

Table 5.1 Control signals

M/$\overline{\text{IO}}$	D/$\overline{\text{C}}$	W/$\overline{\text{R}}$	*Description*
0	0	0	Interrupt acknowledge sequence
0	0	1	STOP/special bus cycle
0	1	0	Reading from an I/O port
0	1	1	Writing to an I/O port
1	0	0	Reading an instruction from memory
1	0	1	Reserved
1	1	0	Reading data from memory
1	1	1	Writing data to memory

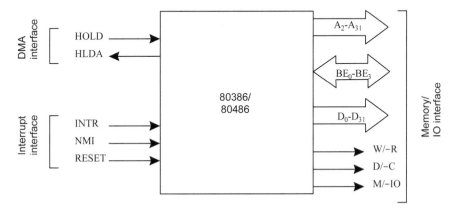

Figure 5.2 Some of the 80386/80486 signal connections

The D/$\overline{\text{C}}$ line differentiates between data and control signals. When it is high, then data is read from or written to memory; if it is low, then a control operation is indicated, such as a shutdown command.

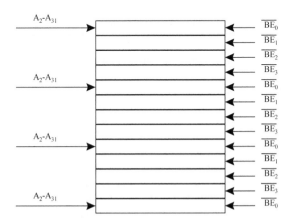

Figure 5.3 Memory addressing

The interrupt lines are interrupt request (INTR), non-maskable interrupt request (NMI) and system reset (RESET), all of which are active high signals. The INTR line is activated when an external device, such as a hard disk or a serial port, wishes to communicate with the processor. This interrupt is maskable and the processor can ignore the interrupt if it wants. NMI is a non-maskable interrupt and is always acted on. When it becomes active the processor calls the non-maskable interrupt service routine. The RESET signal causes a hardware reset and is normally made active when the processor is powered up.

5.3   80386/80486 Registers

The 80386 and 80486 are 32-bit processors and can thus operate on 32-bits at a time. They have expanded 32-bit registers, which can also be used as either 16-bit or 8-bit registers (mainly to keep compatibility with other processors and software). The general purpose registers, such as AX, BX, CX, DX, SI, DI and BP, are expanded from the 8086 processor and are named EAX, EBX, ECX, EDX, ESI, EDI and EBP, respectively, as illustrated in Figure 5.4. The CS, SS and DS registers are still 16 bits, but the flag register has been expanded to 32 bits and is named EFLAG.

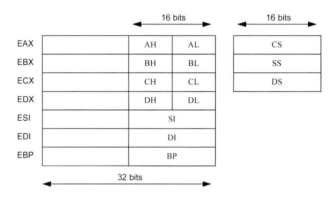

Figure 5.4   80386/80486 registers

5.4   Memory Cache

DRAM is based on the charging and discharge of tiny capacitors. It is thus a relatively slow type of memory compared with SRAM. For example, typical access time for DRAM is 70 ns and the motherboard clock speed can be over 100 MHz. This gives a clock period of 20 ns. Thus, the processor would require seven wait states before the data becomes available. A cache memory can be used to overcome this problem. This is a bank of fast memory (SRAM) that uses a cache controller to load

> **Importance of a cache**
>
> On a Pentium processor with a 500 MHz clock, the clock cycle will be 2 ns. If it uses 70 ns DRAM, it will take 35 processor clock cycles before the data from the DRAM will be valid.
>
> SRAM operating at 100 MHz will be seven times faster than 70 ns DRAM.

data from main memory (typically DRAM) into it. The cache controller guesses the data the processor requires and loads this into the cache memory. Figure 5.5 shows that if the controller guesses correctly, then it is a cache hit; if it is wrong then it is a cache miss. A miss causes the processor to access the memory in the normal way (that is, there may be wait states as the DRAM memory needs time to get the data). Typical cache memory sizes are 16 kB, 32 kB and 64 kB for 80486 processors, and 256 kB and 512 kB for Pentium processors. This should be compared with the size of the RAM on a typical PC, which is typically at least 32 MB.

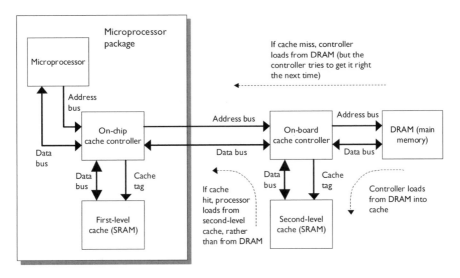

Figure 5.5 Cache operation

The 80486 and Pentium have built-in cache controllers and at least 64 kB (or over 256 kB for the Pentium) of local SRAM cache memory. This is a first-level cache and the total cache size can be increased with an off-chip (or near-chip) memory (second-level cache).

A cache subsystem consists of cache control logic, and cache SRAM located between the processor and system memory. The cache controller consists of two parts: a directory and cache management logic. The cache directory keeps track of what data is stored in cache SRAM and the cache management logic provides an interface between the cache controller and cache SRAM, as well as providing an interface between the processor and system memory.

5.4.1 Cache architecture

The main cache architectures are:

> **Methods of testing**
>
> - **Scenario-based testing**. Structured test scripts.
> - **Module/unit testing**. Testing small parts of the product.
> - **Stress tests**. Testing the product over the limits of its operation, such as over long time periods, or temperature limits.
> - **Beta testing**. Allowing users to test the product and document any problems found.
> - **Gorilla testing**. Testers do not follow a script, and do anything that they can to "break" the product.

- **Look-through cache**. In a look-through cache, the system memory is isolated from the processor address and control buses. In this case the processor sends a memory request directly to the cache controller, which then determines whether it should forward it to its own memory or the system memory. Figure 5.6 illustrates this type of cache. It can be seen that the cache controls whether the processor address contents are latched through to the DRAM memory and whether the contents of the DRAM's memory, is loaded onto the processor data bus (through the data transceiver). The operation is described as bus cycle forwarding.
- **Look-aside cache**. A look-aside cache is where the cache and system memory connect to a common bus. System memory and the cache controller see the beginning of the processor bus cycle at the same time. If the cache controller detects a cache hit, then it must inform the system memory before it tries to find the data. If a cache miss is found, then the memory access is allowed to continue.

- **Write-through cache**. With a write-through cache, all memory address accesses are seen by the system memory when the processor performs a bus cycle.
- **Write-back cache**. With a write-back cache, the cache controller controls all system writes. It thus does not write the system memory unless it has to.
- **Direct mapped cache**. When the contents of a new memory location have to be stored in the cache SRAM, there is only one possible place for it to be stored.
- **Set associative cache**. When the contents of a new memory location is to be stored, there is more than one place for it to be stored in the set associative cache environment. The number of places is referred to as ways. For example, in a two-way set associative cache there are two possible places; in a four-way set associative cache there are four possible places.

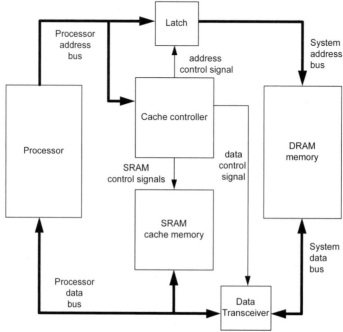

Figure 5.6   Look-through cache

Cache and memory read cycles

In a look-through cache design, when the processor executes a bus cycle the cache controller identifies the location being accessed and the bus cycle type by looking at the address and control buses. System memory has not seen the cycle yet.

If the cycle is a memory read, then the cache controller performs a directory search, that is, it looks in its directory to see if the requested data is stored in the cache SRAM. If the data is not in the cache SRAM, that is, a cache read miss, the cache controller generates:

- The address latch control signals – this provides the address and control signals to system memory.
- The data transceiver control signals – this routes the requested data back to the processor, once memory has provided it.

This is referred to as the cache controller forwarding the bus cycle. During a cache read miss:

- The processor is provided with the data read from system memory.
- At the same time, control signals are generated by the cache controller to write the data into the cache SRAM, and also update its directory.

If the data is in the cache SRAM, that is, a cache read hit:
- The cache controller generates SRAM control signals to provide the processor with the requested data.
- The bus cycle is not forwarded to the system memory.

5.4.2 Cache coherency and snooping

An important parameter in the cache is that the data in the cache must be the same as the data in the system memory, that is, cache coherency. For this reason, memory writes are forwarded on to system memory immediately in a write-through cache; for a cache write hit, both the cache SRAM and system memory are updated.

The cache controller must also be able to monitor writes to system memory by other busmasters. When the cache controller detects a write to system memory by another busmaster, it uses the address on the bus to perform a directory search. If a hit is detected, the directory entry is cleared. If the processor wants information from that same location later, a cache miss occurs, because the directory search results in a miss.

Snooping occurs when the cache controller monitors the address bus when another device is writing to system memory.

> **Sixers versus eighters**
>
> Before the advent of the 80486 which finally established the PC as the market leader, there was a gentle rivalry between the sixers (the Motorola and Mostec processors, which mainly began with a six), and the eighters (the Intel processors, which were part of the x86 series). Typical battles were (bold gives the possible winners):
>
> | 8-bit battle: | 8080 v. 6800 |
> | | [v. **Z80** .v. 6502] |
> | 16-bit battle: | **68000** v. 8086 |
> | 32-bit battle: | **68030** v. 80386 |
> | | 68040 v. **80486** |

5.4.3 Non-cacheable cycles

Some of the cycles that occur within the system are non-cacheable, as the required data will not be stored in the cache memory. These include interrupt acknowledgement cycles, and memory-mapped I/O reads and writes. The cache controller detects these by monitoring the address and control buses. These signals are then passed onto the system via the address latch and data transceiver.

5.4.4 Cache organization

A cache contains a table of data that are likely to be accessed by the processor. The cache controller makes guesses on these data and fills the cache memory. Along with these data, the cache must keep a record of the address that the data have been loaded from. The cache controller takes a 32-bit memory address and splits it into three parts:

> **Importance of a cache**
>
> It is generally considered that the processor spends 90 per cent of its time executing 10 per cent of a program, that is, recently used data and instructions that are likely to be used again in the near future.

- A 20-bit tag address (A12–A31).
- An 8-bit set address (A4–A11).
- A 4-bit byte address (A0–A3). A2–A3 identifies the 4-byte word and A0–A1 identifies the byte within the word.

Figure 5.7 illustrates a 4 kB memory cache. Each entry in the cache has a cache directory entry and a corresponding cache memory entry. The cache directory entry contains information on the actual address of the data in the memory cache. Each address of the entry is defined by the set address and, as this has 8 bits, there are 256 entries in the table. Each entry in the table contains the 20-bit tag address, a write protection bit (W) and a valid bit (V). The W and V bit are used as:

- The V bit identifies that cache memory entry is valid and can thus be used if there is a cache hit for the associated cache directory entry. Initially, at power on, the cache is flushed and all the valid bits are reset. Once data is loaded into the memory cache the valid bits for each entry are then set.
- The W bit identifies that the data in the associated memory entry should not be overwritten.

A cache hit is determined by comparing simultaneously all the tag addresses in the cache directory with the upper 20 bits of the address on the address bus. If a cache hit is found, then the address lines A2 and A3 are used to select the required 32 bits from the 128-bit cache memory entry (known as a cache line).

The cache in Figure 5.7 is a direct memory cache where data from a certain location is stored only at a single place within the cache. Unfortunately, an entry that has the same set address but a different tag address cannot be stored simultaneously. For example, the 32-bit addresses

> In 1984, Michael Dell started Dell Computer in his college dorm room. Within five years, Dell Computers had revenues of over one quarter of a billion dollars.

```
00000000000000000000 00101011 0000
10101010101010101010 00101011 1111
```

would both be stored at the set address 43 (00101011). As this address is the same, they could not be stored simultaneously in the cache.

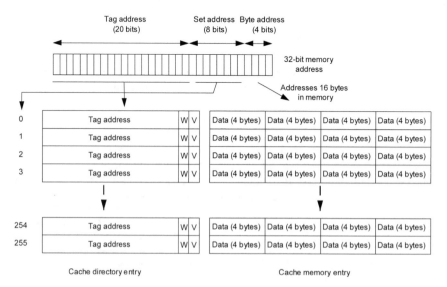

Figure 5.7 Cache directory and memory entries

To overcome this, a number of similar cache memories are built up into a number of ways. Typically this is two-, four- or eight-way. A four-way cache with 4 kB in each way gives a total cache size of 16 kB; this is illustrated in Figure 5.8. Multiway caches have an increased amount of logic, as they must check each of the ways to determine if there is a cache hit. The cache hit rate, though, increases with the number of ways, as it allows an increased number of addresses to be stored at the same time. A multiway cache is also known as a set associative cache (as opposed to a direct-mapped cache).

> In April 1989, *Inc.* selected Steve Jobs as the "entrepreneur of the decade" for his work on the Apple II, the Macintosh and the NeXT computer (his next venture after he left Apple).

The 486 processor has an integrated on-chip cache, which has a four-way, 16-byte cache line and 128 set addresses. This gives a capacity of 8192 bytes (8 kB). This type of cache is known as an L-1 cache and can significantly improve the performance of the processor, especially when loading code from memory and loading sequentially from memory (as is typical). A linefill sequence occurs when a cache read miss occurs and the 80486 internal cache reads 16 bytes from system memory.

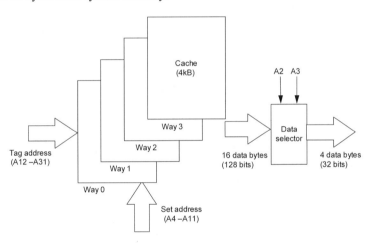

Figure 5.8 Cache with four ways

5.4.5 *80486 internal cache unit*

The 80486 internal cache unit is used to store frequently used data or instructions. It has an 8 kB four-way set associative look-through cache. The cache directory is made up of four tag directories and the LRU/valid, least recently used/valid directory. There are four banks of SRAM.

In Figure 5.9, each directory contains 128 locations (00h to 7Fh), and each way contains 128 locations, which stores one line of 16 bytes. Each directory location keeps track of one line and each directory keeps track of 2048 bytes. There are four directories, so the complete directory keeps track of 8192 bytes (8 kB).

> **First-level cache** (L-1 cache): runs at the speed of the processor.
> **Second-level cache** (L-2 cache): runs at the speed of the system.

If the processor requires data from memory, or performs a write to memory, the internal cache looks in its directories before the bus cycle is seen externally. The search is performed as follows:

Step 1:   Address bits [10:4] are used to identify a single location in each of the four directories and the LRU/valid directory. This is called a set. Note: each directory identifies the same location to look at.

Step 2:   The four tag directories compare the contents of the specified location with address bits [31:11]. This is called a tag. Note: if the contents of one of the tag directories matches what is on A[31:11], a tag hit occurs; this causes the cache controller to look at its LRU/valid directory. If no match is found, then the requested line is not in the cache SRAMs, and a tag miss occurs; the cache controller forwards the bus cycle on to main memory to retrieve the requested data.

Step 3:   A tag hit causes the cache controller to look at the bits in the LRU/valid directory. From these the cache controller decides whether the line associated with the tag hit is valid or not. Note: if the bits indicate that the line is valid, that is, a line hit, the cache controller provides the requested data to the processor. If the bits indicate that the line is invalid, or not an exact copy of what is in system memory, that is, a line miss, the cache controller forwards the cycle on to system memory.

The state will be one of the following:

- **Cache Read Hit**. When the processor requests information from system memory, a directory search of the cache occurs. If a hit occurs, there is no external bus cycle seen, and the internal cache provides the information.
- **Cache Write Hit**. When the processor writes to system memory, a directory search of the cache occurs. If a hit is detected, the internal cache SRAM location is updated, and the cycle is put out onto the buses as a memory write.
- **Cache Write Miss**. When the processor writes to system memory, a directory search of the cache occurs. If a miss is detected, the internal cache SRAM location is not updated, and the cycle is put out onto the buses as a memory write.

> **What's NeXT?**
>
> The NeXT computer developed by Steve Job's company was technically excellent, as was its software and operating system. Unfortunately, technical excellence does not necessarily win over the PC, and the market never adopted it. Its one claim to fame is that the World Wide Web was initially developed on it.

Snoop cycles

When another busmaster is writing to system memory, the processor uses A[10:4] to identify the directory entry to check. If the cache controller detects a hit, and the valid bit is high, then the processor has a copy of the system memory location being written to by another busmaster in its cache. The cache controller invalidates the entry by clearing the valid bit in the directory. If at a later time the processor then requests this information, it will be forced to go out to system memory, which contains the most up to date copy. Note: there are many complex algorithms, operations, and mechanisms used when the cache circuitry is operating. Depending on what happens, the cache controller applies the necessary permutations to ensure the cache information is correct; for example, scenarios where combinations of these permutations would be applied, include cache tag read miss, cache line read miss, and a cache read miss when the cache is full.

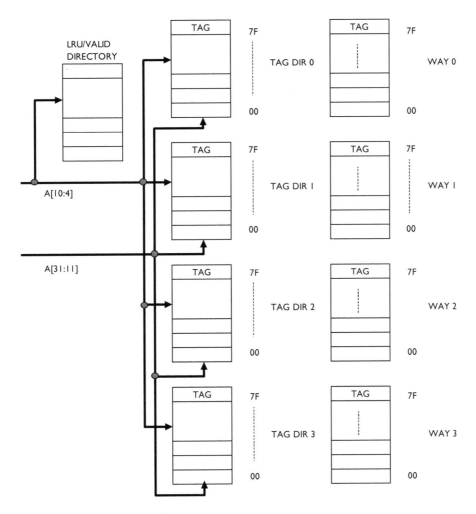

Figure 5.9   Tagging within the cache

Linefill operation address sequence

The processor puts out a dword (double word) address, with both A0 and A1 set to low. This address points to four sequential locations, that is, toggle A1, A0 from 00 to 11, which gives four combinations, 0, 1, 2, 3. When the processor performs a linefill, a sequence of dword addresses is formed by the processor using the following rules:

Bus cycle	Address formation
First	The dword address formed is dependent on the request.
Second	Toggle address bit 2.
Third	Toggle address bits 2 and 3.
Fourth	Toggle address bit 2 again.

For example, if the processor performs a linefill operation, and the first bus cycle dword address output is 34570h, the second cycle address will be 34574h, the third cycle address will be 34578h, and the fourth cycle address will be 3457Ch.

Cache example

1. The processor reads from memory location 46280h.

	4		6		2		8		0 h
A19		A15		A11		A7		A3	
0	1 0 0	0	1 1 0	0	0 1 0		1 0 0 0		0 0 0 0
0		8		C		2		8	

Set address = A[10:4] = 28h   Tag address = A[31:11] = 8Ch (leading 0s)

2. A linefill takes place starting at memory location 82480h. The cache controller stores the information in way 3. Tag directory 3 is updated.

   A[10:4] = set address = 48h
   A[31:11] = tag address = 104h

   Location 48h in tag directory 3 = 104h
   Location 48h in valid directory bit 3 = 1

3. The processor wants to read 32 bits, starting from 8248Ch.

   A[10:4] = set address = 48h
   A[31:11] = tag address = 104h

   Tag directory 3 = 104h at location 48h = tag hit.
   The cache controller looks at bit 3 of the valid directory = 1 = line hit. The cache provides the data to the CPU.

5.4.6   Second-level caches

An L1-cache (first-level cache) provides a relatively small on-chip cache, whereas an L2-cache (second-level cache) provides an external, on-board, cache, which provides a cache memory of 128–512 kB. The processor looks in its own L1-cache for a cache hit; if none is found then it searches in the on-board L2-cache. A cache hit in the L1-cache will obviously be faster than the off-chip cache.

An L2-cache for the Pentium has a maximum 512 kB-memory size, which has two ways. It is typically available as 128 kB, 256 kB or 512 kB. The cache controller internally takes a 32-bit memory address and splits it into three parts:

- A 13-bit tag address (A19–A31).
- A 13-bit set address (A6–A18).
- A 6-bit byte address (A0–A5).

Each cache line contains 64 bytes. A 13-bit set address gives a total of 8192 (2^{13}) addresses.

5.4.7   MESI states

A major problem occurs when there is more than one cache. This can happen when there is an L1-cache and an L2-cache, or when there is more than one processor, each of which has an on-chip cache. The MESI (modified, exclusive, shared, invalid) protocol implemented by the Pentium is used to synchronize cache operations. The four states defined in the protocol are:

- Modified (M) – in this state the data in the cache is more recent than the corresponding location in memory. The cache line is then marked that it is available only in a single cache of the complete system.

- Exclusive (E) – in this state the data in the cache is the same as the corresponding memory location. If new data is written to a cache location then the system memory is not updated automatically (write-back). On a multicache system, an exclusive cache line is stored on only one of the caches in a system. Thus it can be read and overwritten without the need for an external bus cycle.

- Shared (S) – in this state the data in the cache is the same as the corresponding location in memory. If new data is written to this cache location, system memory is updated at the same time (write-through). The shared cache line can be stored within other caches in the system; it is – as the name suggests – shared with a number of other caches. A shared cache line always contains the most up-to-date value; in this way, the cache always services read accesses. Write accesses to a shared cache line are always switched through to the external data bus independently of the cache strategy (write-through, write-back), so that the shared cache lines in the other caches are invalidated. The address given out during the bus cycle is used as an external inquiry cycle for invalidating the cache lines in the other caches. As the same time, the contents of the main memory are also updated. The write operation in the local cache itself only updates the contents of the cache; it is not invalidated.

> **Ctrl-Alt-Del defeats Trojan horses**
>
> Trojan horse viruses pretend to be valid programs and can either present a common user interface or pretend to be useful programs. One Trojan horse virus, which is available over the WWW, is said to contain over 100 active viruses. A computer running this program will quickly be infected with these viruses.
>
> The Happy99 virus typically attaches itself to emails and when the user runs the file it shows a lovely display of on-screen fireworks. Unfortunately, it also replaces the existing TCP/IP stack with its own version, and copies itself to the most used email addresses in a users address book (which is obviously embarrassing, as they tend to be friends or business colleagues).
>
> One method of determining a user's login ID and password is to create a program that displays the user login screen. When the user enters their password it can be sent to the hacker. Windows NT/2000 overcomes this by having a login screen that can be displayed only when the Ctrl-Alt-Del keystrokes are used. It is extremely difficult to override this, as many programs use these keystrokes to reboot the computer.

- Invalid (I) – in this state data in the cache location is not most recent data, or a flush has taken place. A cache line marked as invalid is logically not available in the cache, which could be because the cache line itself is empty or contains an invalid entry, that is, not updated. Invalid or empty tag entries also cause cache lines to be marked as invalid. Every access to an invalid cache line leads to a cache miss. In the case of a read access, the cache controller normally initiates a cache line fill (if the line can be cached and its transfer into the cache is not blocked). A write access, however, is switched through to the external bus as a write-through. The MESI protocol will not provide a write-allocate.

> The 80486 implemented write-through with shared (S) or invalid (I) states. This was enhanced by the Pentium to include write-back, with all the MESI states.

5.5   Exercises

5. 5.1   Outline the information that is stored in the processor internal cache.

5. 5.2   Define a set associative cache and a write-through cache.

5. 5.3   What signifies a cache read hit?

5. 5.4   Outline linefill technique.

5. 5.5   Define the sequence of addresses output by the processor if it requests data from memory location 4568h, and it is not in the internal cache.

5. 5.6   Outline how the processor changes the address during a linefill operation.

> **Common processor faults**
> Hang-ups
>
> **Possible cause:** internal processor timing problem.
>
> **Check:** if socketed, try a good processor. If an upgrade processor is supported, change the switch settings, and try a good processor in the upgrade socket.

5.6   80486 Microprocessor Signals

Refer to Figure 5.10 for the signal lines.

5.6.1   *Clock signal*

Pin symbol: CLK   **I/O: Input**
Function: Processor fundamental timing
Description: CLK is used to time all processor activity. A minimum of two CLK cycles are required for all external bus cycles, except burst cycles.

5.6.2   *Address bus signals*

Pin symbol: A[31:2]   **I/O: input/output**
Function: In conjunction with BE[3:0]#, identify the I/O or memory location or locations being accessed
Description: As outputs, A[31:2] identify a word address that points to four sequential locations. A word address is an address where A[31:2] are the same for four locations. The difference between the four locations is that A0 and A1 are different for each location; A0 and A1 are not output by the processor. For example, word address 8324h points to 8324h, 8325h, 8326h and 8327h. A[31:2], along with BE[3:0], form the address bus, and identify the exact location or locations in memory or I/O being accessed by the processor. As inputs, A[31:4] are used to provide an address to the processor when another bus master is writing to memory, recognized when EADS# is active. These signals are provided as inputs for cache invalidation purposes, that is, snooping.
Sampled or driven:
              As outputs, A[31:2] are driven in the same clock as ADS#. They remain active until the clock after the ready input is sampled active. As inputs, A[31:4] are sampled in the clock in which EADS# is sampled active.
Signal relationship:
              BE[3:0]# complete the definition of the location being accessed by the proces-

sor. The address bus is driven at the same time as ADS#. A20M# causes A20 to be low, regardless of the address formed in the processor. AHOLD causes A[31:2] to be tristated one clock after AHOLD is asserted. BOFF# causes A[31:2] to be tristated one clock after BOFF# is asserted. A[31:4] are sampled by the processor when EADS# is active, causing the processor to perform a snoop cycle. A[31:2] are tristated when HLDA is generated.

Pin symbol: BE[3:0]#   **I/O: output**

Function: Helps identify the location or locations being accessed by the processor. Also defines on what parts of the data bus the processor expects valid data to be on.

Description: The BE[3:0]#, in conjunction with A[31:2], form the address bus, and identify the exact location being accessed by the processor. Also identify what part of the data bus the processor expects data to be on.

Driven: BE[3:0]# are driven in the same clock as ADS#; same timing as A[31:2]. They remain active until the clock after the ready input is sampled active.

Signal relationship:

The address output by the processor is referred to as the word address. The processor does not output A0, and A1. The address output points to four sequential locations. The BE[3:0]# are derived internally from A[1:0], and identify which of the four sequential locations the processor is communicating with.

> **Common processor faults**
> Bad first fetch address, that is, not FFFFFFF0h
>
> **Possible cause:**
> - No processor RESET.
> - No processor clock.
> - The processor is outputting a bad address.
> - HOLD to the processor is active.
> - Bad switch or jumper settings.
>
> **Check:**
> - Switch/jumper settings.
> - RESET input.
> - CLK input.
> - Address outputs.

Example 1: Assume the processor wants to access 8 bits from location 2660h. The word address is 2660h. The dword address points to locations 2660h, 2661h, 2662h and 2663h. The processor wants only one byte. It only generates one BE# signal. The processor wants to access an address where A0 and A1 are both low, BE0# will be generated; the value represented by A1 and A0, (LSB), identify the BE# to be generated.

Example 2: Assume the processor wants to access 8 bits from location 6E26h. The dword address is 6E24h. The dword address points to the four locations, 6E24h, 6E25h, 6E26h and 6E27h. The processor wants only one byte. It only generates one BE# signal. The processor wants to access an address where A0 is low and A1 is high, BE2# will be generated; the value represented by A1 and A0, (LSB), identify the BE# to be generated.

Example 3: Assume the processor wants to access 16 bits starting from location 23CAh. The dword address is 23C8h. The dword address points to the four locations, 23C8h, 23C9h, 23CAh and 23CBh. The processor wants to access two sequential locations, 23CAh and 23CBh; it will generate two byte enables. The first location has A0 high, and A1 low, BE2# will be generated. The second location has both A0 and A1 high, BE3# will be generated. BE[3:0]# allows the processor to access four sequential locations in one bus cycle, as long as A[31:2] are the same for the four addresses.

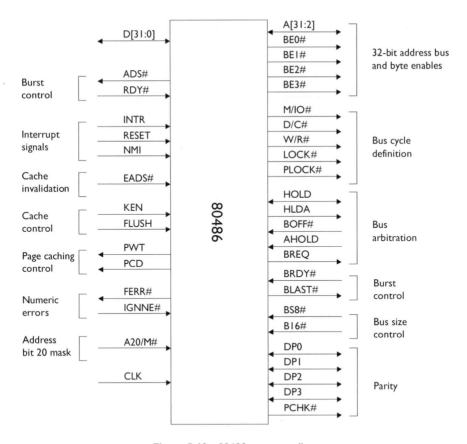

Figure 5.10   80486 processor lines

Pin symbol: A20M#   **I/O: input**

Function: Used to emulate the 1 MB address wraparound of the 8086.

Description: When A20M# is active, the processor forces address bit 20 low before per-
               forming a lookup to the internal cache or driving a memory cycle onto the bus.
               A20M# should be active only when the processor is operating in real mode.

Sampled: A20M# is sampled on every CLK, rising edge.

Signal relationship:

               When A20M# is active, the A20 output is forced low.

5.6.3   *Data bus signals*

Pin symbol: D[31:0]   **I/O: input/output**

Function: Forms a 32-bit data bus.

Description: The bidirectional lines, D[31:0] form the 32 bit data bus lines for the proces-
               sor. D[7:0], referred to as byte lane 0, define the least significant byte of the
               data bus and correspond to BE0#. D[31:24], referred to as byte lane 3, define
               the most significant byte of the data bus and correspond to BE3#. D[15:8], re-
               ferred to as byte lane 1, corresponds to BE1#. D[23:16], referred to as byte
               lane 2, correspond to BE2#.

Sampled or driven:

               D[31:0] are driven on processor write bus cycles during the second and subse-
               quent clocks of the write cycle. BE[3:0]# determine which bytes of the data

bus the processor will place the data on for a write bus cycle. D[31:0] are sampled during processor read cycles, when the ready input is sampled active. BE[3:0]# determine which bytes of the data bus to accept during a read bus cycle.

Relationship: BE[3:0] indicate which data byte or bytes are being driven or requested by the processor. D[31:0] are tristated when BOFF# is asserted. When either ready input is sampled active, this indicates that the data bus transfer is complete. DP[3:0], along with D[31:0], are driven for even parity on write bus cycles, and sampled for even parity on read cycles. The status of data bus parity is driven on PCHK# during read bus cycles.

> **Common processor faults**
> First fetch data is bad
>
> **Possible causes:**
> • Bad control signals output by the processor.
> • Bad data back to the processor.
>
> **Check:**
> • The data path between the ROM and the processor.
> • The bus cycle definition signals output by the processor.

Example 1: Assume the processor wants to read 8 bits from port 41h. The processor outputs the dword address 40h. The processor also generates BE1#; because A1 is low, and A0 is high, for the location being read. When one of the ready inputs is sampled active, the processor only accepts data on D[15:8], as it is associated with BE1#.

Example 2: Assume the processor wants to write 16 bits starting at address 234Eh. The processor wants to write 8 bits to 234Eh and 8 bits to 234Fh. The processor outputs the dword address 234Ch. The processor also generates BE2# and BE3#; directly related to A0 and A1 for the two locations. The low order 8 bits are placed on D[23:16], BE2#, the high order 8 bits are placed on D[31:24], BE3#.

5.6.4 Data parity signals

Pin symbol: DP[3:0]   **I/O: input/output**

Function: Bidirectional data parity pins for the data bus.

Description: There is one parity bit for each byte of the data bus. DP0 corresponds to D[7:0]. DP1 to D[15:8]. DP2 to D[23:16]. DP3 to D[31:24]. As outputs, DP[3:0] are driven during write bus cycles, so that the DP signal and its corresponding byte of the data bus contain an even number of highs. As inputs, DP[3:0] are checked during read cycles, so that each byte of the data bus and its corresponding DP signal contain an even number of highs. If an odd number of ones is detected on any byte of the data bus, including its corresponding DP bit, PCHK# is generated.

> **Common processor faults**
> Bad first jump address
>
> **Possible causes:**
> • Processor output address.
> • Bad data from ROM to form jump address.
>
> **Check:**
> • Processor address.
> • Data inputs to the processor forming the jump address

Sampled or driven:

DP[3:0] are driven during the same clock as the data on all write cycles. DP[3:0] are sampled, along with

D[31:0], during all read cycles when one of the ready inputs is sampled active.

Relationship: DP[3:0] are only checked or generated on data bytes enabled by BE[3:0]. DP[3:0] are tristated one clock after BOFF# is asserted. DP[3:0] are sampled when either ready input is sampled active. D[31:0] are used in conjunction with DP[3:0] to generate and check parity. DP[3:0] are tristated when HLDA is generated. The status of the data parity is driven on the PCHK# output.

Pin symbol: PCHK#   **I/O: output**
Function: Indicates the result of a parity check on a data read
Description: The data parity check signal indicates the result of a parity check on a data read. Parity is checked for all data bytes, indicated by the bus size and the byte enable signals. PCHK# low, indicates a parity error. PCHK# is valid in the clock immediately after read data is accepted by the processor.
Driven: PCHK# is driven in the clock after read data is returned to the processor.
Relationship: PCHK# is driven in the clock after one of the ready inputs was sampled active. DP[3:0] are used to create even parity with D[31:0] during write bus cycles. If even parity is not returned, PCHK# is generated.

5.6.5   *Bus cycle definition signals*

Pin symbol: M/IO#   **I/O: output**
Function: Distinguishes between a memory and an I/O bus cycle.
Description: The M/IO# signal when high, indicates that the current bus cycle is an access to memory, and when low, indicates that the current bus cycle is an access to I/O.
Driven: M/IO# is driven at the beginning of a bus cycle, at the same time as ADS#.
Relationship: M/IO# is driven at the same time as ADS#. M/IO# is tristated one clock after BOFF# is asserted. M/IO# is tristated when HLDA is generated.

Pin symbol: W/R#   **I/O: output**
Function: Distinguishes between a write and a read bus cycle.
Description: The W/R# signal when high, indicates that the current bus cycle is a write access, and when low, indicates that the current bus cycle is a read access.
Driven: W/R# is driven at the beginning of a bus cycle, at the same time as ADS#.
Relationship: W/R# is driven at the same time as ADS#. W/R# is tristated one clock after BOFF# is asserted. W/R# is tristated when HLDA is generated. KEN# determines cacheability only if W/R# indicates a read bus cycle.

Pin symbol: D/C#   **I/O: output**
Function: Distinguishes between a data access and a code access.
Description: The D/C# signal when high, indicates that the current bus cycle is a data access, and when low, indicates that the current bus cycle is a code access.
Driven: D/C# is driven at the beginning of a bus cycle, at the same time as ADS#.
Relationship: D/C# is driven at the same time as ADS#. D/C# is tristated one clock after BOFF# is asserted. D/C# is tristated when HLDA is generated.

The type of bus cycle being performed by the microprocessor is defined by M/IO#, W/R#, and D /C# as indicated next.

M/IO#	D/C#	W/R#	Bus cycle type
0	0	0	Interrupt acknowledge
0	0	1	Special (see next)
0	1	0	I/O read
0	1	1	I/O write
1	0	0	Instruction fetch
1	1	0	Memory data read
1	1	1	Memory write

Special cycles are defined further by the byte enable signals, as indicated below:

Type of special cycle	Active byte enable
Shut down	BE0#
Flush	BE1#
Halt	BE2#
Write back	BE3#

Interrupt acknowledge bus cycles occur as a result of the microprocessor INTR input going active. Flush, halt, write back, I/O read, I/O write, memory data read, and memory data write bus cycles occur as a result of a specific instruction seen by the microprocessor execution unit. Instruction fetches occur as a result of the prefetch mechanism having room for additional instructions, or being emptyas the result of a jump instruction. Shutdown bus cycles occur as a result of the microprocessor incurring multiple exceptions during the execution of an instruction.

5.6.6 *Bus lock*

Pin symbol: LOCK#   **I/O: output**
Function: Indicates to the system that the current sequence of bus cycle should not be interrupted.
Description: The bus lock output indicates to external logic that the current sequence of bus cycles being run by the processor should not be interrupted by another bus master. The microprocessor and external logic ignore hold requests by external busmasters when LOCK# is active. LOCK# is generated for interrupt acknowledge cycles, a cycle split due to a misaligned access, that is, a multiple byte access involving locations with different word addresses, or as a result of using the lock instruction. LOCK# is typically not used unless there is an external write-through cache in the system.
Driven: LOCK# goes active with ADS#, on the first locked bus cycle, and goes inactive after one of the ready inputs is sampled active during the last locked bus cycle.
Signal relationship:
              LOCK# is driven with ADS# on the first locked cycle. LOCK# is tristated one clock after BOFF#. LOCK# is deasserted after one of the ready signals is sampled active during the last cycle of a locked sequence. LOCK# is tristated when HLDA is generated. LOCK# is asserted for interrupt acknowledge bus cycles.

> **Common processor faults**
> Miscellaneous
>
> **Possible cause:** wrong type of processor or speed setting.
>
> **Check:** the processor type/ speed setting switches/ jumpers/resistors.

Pin symbol: PLOCK#   **I/O: output**

Function: Indicates to the system that the current bus transaction requires more than one bus cycle to complete, and should not be interrupted

Description: The pseudo-lock output indicates to external logic that the processor is running a sequence of cycles that should not be interrupted by another bus master. The microprocessor and external logic ignore hold requests by external busmasters when PLOCK# is active. PLOCK# is generated for operations like cache line-fills, (128 bits). PLOCK# is typically not used unless there is an external write-through cache in the system.

Driven: PLOCK# goes active during the second clock cycle of the first bus cycle and remains active until BLAST# is generated during the last cycle.

Signal relationship:

    PLOCK# is tristated when HLDA is generated. PLOCK# is deasserted when BLAST# is generated in the last cycle of a locked sequence.

5.6.7 *Bus control signals*

Pin symbol: ADS#   **I/O: output**

Function: Indicates that a new valid bus cycle is currently being driven by the microprocessor.

Description: The address strobe output indicates that a new valid bus cycle is being driven by the processor. A[31:2], BE [3:0]#, LOCK#, M/ IO#, D/C#, W/R#, PWT and PCD are driven to their valid levels, for the current cycle in the clock ADS# is generated. ADS# is used by external logic, as an indication that the processor has started a new bus cycle. ADS# tristates during a bus hold or backoff.

Driven: ADS# is driven active in the first clock of a bus cycle and driven inactive during the second and subsequent clocks of the cycle.

Signal relationship:

    A[31..2], BE [3..0]#, LOCK#, M/ IO#, D/C#, W/R#, PWT and PCD are driven to their valid levels, for the current cycle in the clock ADS# is generated. ADS# will not be generated if AHOLD is active. ADS# is tristated one clock after BOFF# is asserted. BREQ is generated at the same time as ADS# is generated. ADS# is tristated when HLDA is generated. An interrupt acknowledge bus cycle is driven as a result of INTR being sampled active; ADS# is generated.

Pin symbol: RDY#   **I/O: input**

Function: Indicates the transfer is complete.

Description: The ready input indicates that the current bus cycle is complete, as illustrated below. RDY# is ignored during the first CLK of a bus cycle, it is then sampled on the rising edge of subsequent CLK cycles until it is active. If RDY# is sampled inactive at the end of the second CLK cycle of the transfer, additional CLK cycles added are referred to as wait states. During read bus cycles, the microprocessor will accept data when RDY# is sampled active, and will then be able to begin the next bus cycle. When RDY# is sampled active during a write bus cycle, the microprocessor then knows the addressed device accepted the data, and will perform the next action. Note: RDY# is sometimes referred to as the non-burst ready input.

Sampled: On every bus cycle ready is sampled on the rising edge of CLK, at the end of the second bus cycle and subsequent CLK cycles until it is sampled active.

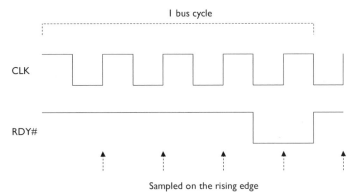

Sampled on the rising edge

Relationship: Once a bus cycle has been initiated, RDY# is sampled on the rising edge of the second and subsequent CLK until it is sampled active. During reads, DP[3:0] are sampled when RDY# is active. During reads, D[31:0] are accepted by the processor when ready is sampled active. If BOFF# and RDY# are active at the same time, BOFF# gets priority, meaning the current bus cycle will have to be started again later. LOCK# is deasserted after RDY# is sampled active during the last cycle of a locked sequence. PCHK# indicates the result of the parity check within the clock after RDY# is sampled active during read bus cycles.

5.6.8 *Interrupt signals*

Pin symbol: INTR   **I/O: input**
Function: Indicates that an external interrupt has been generated.
Description: The interrupt request indicates that an external device is requesting service. When INTR goes active, the processor finishes its current bus cycle, saves the contents of several registers to memory, performs two locked interrupt acknowledge bus cycles in order to get the type code which identifies the device requesting service. Uses the type code to form the start address of the devices interrupt service routine. Executes the service routine. Then returns to the previous program flow by retrieving the register values it saved to memory.
Sampled: INTR is sampled on every rising clock edge. The interrupt is handled when the current bus cycle is complete.
Relationship: In response to INTR, ADS# and the bus cycle definition signals are generated for an interrupt acknowledge bus cycle. LOCK# is generated for interrupt acknowledge bus cycles.

Pin symbol: NMI   **I/O: input**
Function: Indicates an external non-maskable interrupt has been generated.
Description: The non-maskable interrupt request indicates that an external non-maskable interrupt has been generated. NMI is not maskable within the processor. NMI is used to indicate a catastrophic error in the system. External logic allows NMI to be masked out. When NMI goes active, the processor finishes its current bus cycle, saves the contents of several registers to memory, uses a type code of 2 to form the start address of the devices interrupt service routine, executes the service routine, then returns to the previous program flow by retrieving the register values it saved to memory.
Sampled: NMI is sampled on every rising CLK edge.
Relationship: None.

Pin symbol: RESET   **I/O: input**
Function: Forces the processor to start executing from a known state
Description: When active, RESET causes the processor to stop all execution and bus activity, in order to be initialized as follows. The instruction pointer and code segment registers are loaded with set values, to ensure that the first address will be FFFFFFF0h. Other registers are cleared, to place them in a known state. The flags are cleared and the INTR input is masked out. A[31:20] are forced high. They remain high until one of the segment registers is loaded with a new value, occurs on the first jump instruction. The processor is placed in real mode. The internal cache is flushed. When RESET is deasserted, the processor fetches its first instruction from FFFFFFF0h.
Sampled: RESET is sampled on every rising edge of CLK. RESET must remain active for a minimum of 1 ms.
Relationship: RESET is sampled on every rising edge of CLK. If AHOLD is active on the falling edge of RESET, a built in self test, (BIST), is performed. HOLD is recognized by the processor, when RESET is active, that is, in the RESET state.

5.6.9 Bus arbitration signals

Pin symbol: HOLD   **I/O: input**
Function: The bus hold request input allows another bus master complete control of the system buses.
Description: The HOLD input provides other busmasters with a means of requesting ownership of the buses. When HOLD goes active, the processor finishes its current bus cycle, tristates most of its outputs, and asserts HLDA.
Sampled: HOLD is sampled on the rising edge of every clock.
Relationship: The following signals are tristated in response to an active HOLD: ADS#, A[31:2], BE[3:0]#, M/IO# ,W/R#, D/C#, D[31:0], DP[3:0], LOCK#, PCD, and PWT. HLDA is generated in response to HOLD, once the processor finishes its current bus cycle.

Pin symbol: HLDA   **I/O: output**
Function: Indicates externally that the processor has released the buses.
Description: The bus hold acknowledge output goes active in response to a bus hold request, HOLD. HLDA indicates to external logic that the processor has released the buses, that is, tristated itself from the buses. Note: although the processor has released itself from the buses, the processor can continue to execute instructions from cache as long as these instructions do not require use of the buses.
Driven: HLDA is driven in response to an active HOLD, once the current bus cycle is finished.
Relationship: The following signals are tristated in response to HLDA: ADS#, A[31:2], BE[3:0]#, M/IO#, W/R#, D/C#, D[31:0], DP[3:0], LOCK#, PCD and PWT. Asserting HOLD causes HLDA to be generated, once the processor finishes the current bus cycle. When HLDA is active, EADS# is recognized.

Pin symbol: BREQ   **I/O: output**
Function: Indicates to external logic that the processor has a bus cycle pending, and requires use of the buses.
Description: The bus request output is generated when the processor has a bus cycle pending that requires use of the buses; if the processor has control of the buses at that time it is still generated. BREQ is used by external logic to arbitrate be-

tween multiple busmasters. Note: BREQ is not often used in the ISA environment. It is used in the EISA environment.

Driven: BREQ is driven in the same CLK as ADS# when the processor owns the buses. If the processor is not driving the buses due to AHOLD, HOLD or BOFF# being active, BREQ is generated in the same CLK that ADS# would have been generated had the processor been driving the buses.

Relationship: BREQ is always asserted in the CLK that ADS# is, or should be asserted.

Pin symbol: BOFF#   **I/O: input**

Function: The backoff input is used to force the processor off the buses in the next clock

Description: In response to BOFF#, the processor will abort the bus cycle in progress, and tristate the buses in the next CLK. When BOFF# goes inactive the bus cycle will be restarted. If BOFF# and one of the ready inputs is active at the same time, BOFF# has priority. Note: BOFF# is not often used in the ISA environment. It is used in the EISA environment.

Sampled: BOFF# is sampled on every rising edge of CLK, including when RESET is active.

Relationship: The following signals are tristated when BOFF# is active: ADS#, A[31:2], BE[3:0]#, M/IO#, W/R#, D/C#, D[31:0], DP[3:0], LOCK#, PLOCK#, PCD and PWT. If one of the ready inputs is active at the same time as BOFF#, the ready input is ignored and the cycle will have to start later. When BOFF# is active, EADS# is recognized.

Pin symbol: AHOLD   **I/O: input**

Function: The address hold input is used to force the processor off the address bus in the next clock.

Description: In response to AHOLD being sampled active, the processor will tristate only its address bus in the next CLK. This is to stop the processor from driving the address bus when another bus master is writing to memory. EADS# is provided to force the processor to perform a snoop cycle. The processor completes the cycle it was performing when AHOLD goes active; the next cycle cannot begin until AHOLD is inactive. If AHOLD and RESET are active at the same time the processor will perform a built in self-test.

Sampled: AHOLD is sampled on every rising edge of CLK, including when RESET is active.

Relationship: A[31:2] are tristated when AHOLD is active. ADS# will not be driven if AHOLD is active. EADS# is recognized when AHOLD is active.

5.6.10 Cache invalidation signal

Pin symbol: EADS#   **I/O: input**

Function: Signals the processor to run a snoop cycle using A[31:4].

Description: The EADS# input indicates that an external busmaster is writing to memory and the processor should use A[31:4] to perform a snoop cycle on its internal cache, invalidating the entry if it is a hit.

Sampled: EADS# is sampled on the rising edge of clock when HLDA is active. It is also sampled on the rising edge of the clock two clocks after AHOLD or BOFF# is asserted.

Relationship: When HLDA is active, EADS# is recognized. When EADS# is active, A[31:4] are sampled. EADS# is recognized when BOFF# is active. EADS# is recognized when AHOLD is active.

5.6.11 Cache control signals

Pin symbol: KEN#   **I/O: input**
Function: Indicates to the processor that the current memory read is from a cacheable
               location.
Description: KEN# is used in conjunction with PCD to determine whether the current
               memory read cycle is cacheable or not. If KEN# is active and PCD is inactive
               during a memory read bus cycle, a linefill will occur.
Sampled: KEN# is sampled at the end of the first clock of a memory read bus cycle to
               determine if the cycle should be a linefill. KEN# is also sampled at the begin-
               ning of the last cycle of a linefill to determine if the information should be
               written into the internal cache.
Relationship: At the end of the first clock of a memory read bus cycle KEN# is sampled.
               M/IO# must be high, indicating a memory bus cycle is taking place. W/R#
               must be low, indicating a read cycle is taking place. PCD must be inactive and
               KEN# active for a linefill to occur.

Pin symbol: FLUSH#   **I/O: input**
Function: Indicates to the processor that it should invalidate every entry in the internal
               cache directory.
Description: When FLUSH# is active, the processor will invalidate every entry within its
               internal cache directory by clearing all valid bits. This forces the processor to
               go out to system memory to get data and instructions, and begin filling the in-
               ternal cache again.
Sampled: FLUSH# is sampled on the rising edge of every CLK. The flush occurs once
               the current bus cycle is finished.

Pin symbol: PCD   **I/O: output**
Function: Reflects the cacheability paging attribute within the processor for the current
               cycle.
Description: PCD is driven to reflect the cache disable paging attribute for the current cycle.
               PCD is an output to provide an external cacheability indication on a page by
               page basis. When active, the current page of memory is not cacheable; when
               inactive, the current page of memory is cacheable. PCD is used by the proces-
               sor in conjunction with KEN# to determine whether the current memory read
               bus cycle is cacheable or not. If PCD is inactive and KEN# is active during a
               memory read bus cycle, a cache linefill will occur. Note: PCD is often not
               connected in an ISA system unless there is an external or second-level cache.
Driven: PCD is driven out in the same CLK as ADS# and A[31:2], and remains active
               until one of the ready signals is sampled active.
Relationship: PCD is driven with ADS#. PCD is tristated one clock after BOFF#. PCD is
               tristated when HLDA is generated.

Pin symbol: PWT   **I/O: output**
Function: Reflects the write through paging attribute within the processor for the current
               cycle.
Description: PWT is driven to reflect the write through paging attribute for the current cy-
               cle. PWT is to provide an external page write through indication on a page by
               page basis. When active, the current page of memory is defined for cache pur-
               poses as write through. When inactive, the current page of memory is defined
               for cache purposes as write back. Note: PWT is often not connected in an ISA
               system unless there is an external or second-level write-back cache.

Driven: PWT is driven out in the same CLK as ADS# and A[31:2] and remains active until one of the ready signals is sampled active.

Relationship: PWT is driven with ADS#. PWT is tristated one clock after BOFF#. PWT is tristated when HLDA is generated.

5.6.12 Numeric coprocessor error reporting signals

Pin symbol: FERR#   **I/O: output**

Function: The floating-point error output is generated when an error occurs during the execution of a floating-point instruction by the internal numeric coprocessor

Description: When an error occurs during the execution of a floating-point instruction by the internal numeric coprocessor, the floating-point error output is driven active.

Driven: FERR# is driven in every CLK when necessary, and is not floated during HOLD or BOFF#.

Relationship: None.

Pin symbol : IGNNE#   **I/O: input**

Function: Determines whether floating-point errors should be ignored or not.

Description: When IGNNE# is active, the processor will ignore floating-point errors and continue executing floating-point instructions while IGNNE# is active. IGNNE# is generated by external logic when an I/O write to port F0h is detected.

Sampled: IGNNE# is sampled on every rising CLK edge.

Relationship: None.

5.6.13 Bus size signals

Pin symbol: BS8#   **I/O: input**

Function: This signal indicates to the processor that the addressed device is only 8 bits wide.

Description: The bus size signal indicates to the processor that it must run multiple signals when transferring more than 8 bits with the addressed device, and should use only D[7:0].

Sampled: BS8# is sampled on every CLK cycle.

Relationship: When BS8# is active, the processor should only transfer data over D[7:0].

Pin symbol: BS16#   **I/O: input**

Function: This signal indicates to the processor that the addressed device is only 16 bits wide.

Description: The bus size signal indicates to the processor that it must run multiple signals when transferring more than 16 bits with the addressed device, and should use only D[15:0].

Sampled: BS16# is sampled on every CLK cycle.

Relationship: When BS16# is active, the processor should only transfer data over D[15:0].

5.6.14 Burst control signals

Pin symbol: BRDY#   **I/O: input**

Function: Transfer complete indication.

Description: BRDY# performs a similar function to the non-burst ready input, RDY# (refer to the diagram below). The burst ready input indicates that the current bus cycle is complete. BRDY# is ignored during the first CLK of a bus cycle. It is sampled on the rising edge at the end of the second clock cycle and subsequent clock cycles of a burst cycle. Once sampled active data is transferred, BRDY# is sampled on the rising edge of subsequent clocks. Data is transferred each time BRDY# is sampled active. If sampled inactive during the second clock cycle of a transfer, additional clock cycles are referred to as wait states. The processor can only burst write up to four bytes, that is, the width of the data bus. When BRDY# is sampled active during a write bus cycle, the processor knows the addressed device accepted the data and is able to perform the next action. When BRDY# is sampled active during a read cycle, the processor knows to accept the data on D[31:0] as defined by BE[3:0]#. If KEN# has been sampled active, the processor knows it will be bursting four reads, and should sample BRDY# on the rising edge of every CLK.

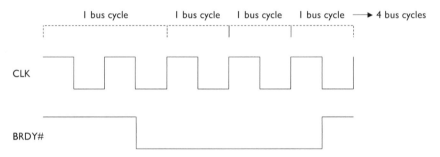

Sampled: BRDY# is sampled on the rising edge of CLK at the end of the second CLK cycle and subsequent CLKs until it is sampled active. When a burst cycle is being performed, BRDY# is sampled on the rising edge of each CLK at the end of the second, third and fourth bus cycles.

Relationship: During reads, DP[3:0] are sampled when BRDY# is active. During reads, D[31:0] are accepted by the processor when BRDY# is sampled active. If BRDY# and BOFF# are active at the same time, BOFF# has priority, meaning the current bus cycle has to be restarted later. LOCK# is deasserted after BRDY# is sampled active during the last cycle of a locked sequence. PCHK# indicates the result of a parity check within the clock after BRDY# is sampled active during read bus cycles.

Pin symbol: BLAST#   I/O: output

Function: Identifies the last cycle of a burst sequence.

Description: Burst last indicates that the next time BRDY# is sampled active, the burst bus cycles are complete. BLAST# is active for both burst and non-burst cycles. It is typically used to indicate to the memory bus control logic that this is the last access to memory. It may also be used by external cache circuitry to indicate when it should update its directory, during a linefill operation from system memory.

Driven: BLAST# is generated during cycle four of a linefill cycle. It is also generated during the second CLK cycle of a non-burst cycle to indicate the transfer is complete after a single cycle.

Relationship: PLOCK# is deasserted when BLAST# is generated in the last cycle of a locked sequence. During burst cycles, BLAST# is generated during the CLK representing the beginning of the fourth (last) cycle. During non-burst cycles, BLAST# is generated during the second CLK of the bus cycle.

6 Bus Cycles, Bus Controller and Direct Memory Access

6.1 Introduction

This chapter discusses the bus cycles for memory reads, memory writes and burst cycles. It does not discuss I/O bus cycles, as they occur in the same fashion, the only difference being the control signals generated by the processor. The chapter also discusses the system bus controller, which provides an interface between the processor and external devices, both memory and I/O. The system bus controller works with the processor to perform bus cycles.

6.2 Bus Cycles

This section analyzes some of the key bus cycles.

6.2.1 Zero wait state memory read cycle

Figure 6.1 shows a zero wait state memory data read cycle, which is assumed to be an access to a slave in the expansion bus. The shaded areas indicate that the state of these signals is irrelevant to the discussion of the current bus cycle. The stages are:

Stage 1: On the rising edge of CLK, the processor samples the RDY# input, it is active. The processor terminates the bus cycle marked 'previous cycle'. Note: this is shown only to indicate that before the processor can begin the next cycle, the current cycle must be finished.

Stage 2: The processor begins the memory read bus cycle by generating the following signals: M/IO# high, W/R# low and D/C# high; memory data read bus cycle. BE[3:0]# to correspond to the address or addresses of the device to be read from. The dword address of the memory device it wants to communicate with on the address bus.

Stage 3: The bus controller recognizes that ADS# is active, and generates SA0, SA1 and SBHE#. This provides the lower address bits to the expansion bus. BALE midway through address time; this ensures that the address is provided to the expansion bus.

Stage 4: At the end of address time the processor samples KEN#. If KEN# is active, the processor may turn this cycle into a linefill. The cache enable logic keeps KEN# active, except for processor memory accesses that are defined as non-cacheable. The programmer can use internal cache control registers to define areas of memory as non-cacheable. The cache enable logic monitors the address bus to determine how to control KEN#.

Stage 5: At the beginning of data time the bus controller generates the appropriate command signal, in this case MRDC#. This indicates to the slave being addressed that it should provide data.

Stage 6: Near the start of data time, the bus controller generates LOE# and the appropriate BCK[3:0] signals. This sets up the data latches to direct the data to the processor.

Stage 7:   The bus controller deasserts BALE; this latches SA[19:0].

Stage 8:   Midway through data time, the processor generates BLAST# to indicate to external logic that the next time the RDY# input is active, the current transaction is terminated.

Stage 9:   Midway through data time, the bus controller samples the NOWS# input. It is active, the bus controller will generate the RDY# signal. If the NOWS# signal was not active, then a wait state would have been inserted.

Stage 10:   The bus controller generates RDY# to indicate to the processor that the current bus cycle can be terminated.

Stage 11:   The processor samples RDY#. If it is active, it accepts the requested data.

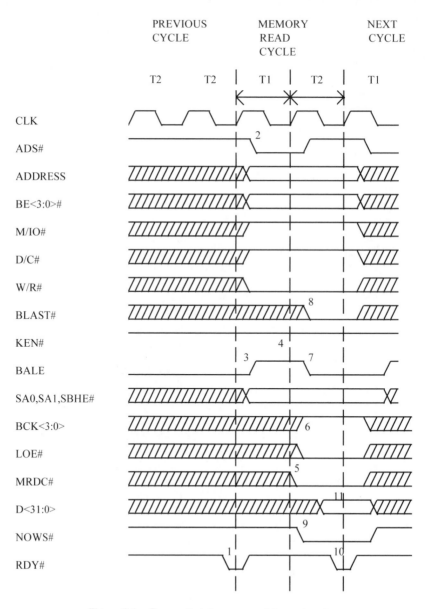

Figure 6.1   Zero wait state memory data read cycle

6.2.2 One wait state memory read cycle

Figure 6.2 shows a one wait state memory data read bus cycle. The cycle is assumed to be an access to a slave in the expansion bus. The shaded areas indicate that the state of these signals are irrelevant to the discussion of the current bus cycle.

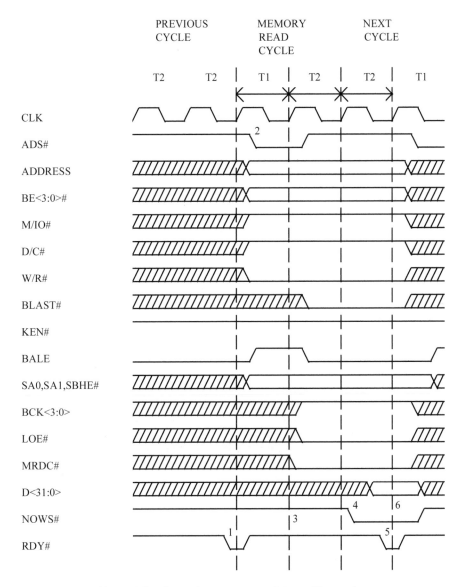

Figure 6.2   One wait state memory data read bus cycle

The stages are:

Stage 1:   On the rising edge of CLK, the processor samples the RDY# input; it is active.

The processor terminates the bus cycle marked 'previous cycle'. This is shown only to indicate that before the processor can begin the next cycle, the current cycle must be finished.

Stage 2:   The processor performs the memory read bus cycle in the same manner as described in steps 2 – 8 of the zero wait state memory read bus cycle.

Stage 3:   Midway through data time, the bus controller samples the NOWS# input; it is inactive. The bus controller does not generate the ready signal. Signals generated by the processor and bus controller prior to this time will remain active. A wait state is inserted into the bus cycle, that is, another data time.

Stage 4:   Midway through the wait state, the bus controller samples the NOWS# input; it is active. The bus controller generates the ready signal.

Stage 5:   The bus controller generates RDY# to tell the processor that the current bus cycle can be terminated.

Stage 6:   The processor samples RDY#; it is active. It accepts the requested data.

6.2.3 *Zero wait state memory write cycle*

Figure 6.3 shows a zero wait state memory data write cycle, which is assumed to be an access to a slave in the expansion bus. The shaded areas indicate that the state of these signals is irrelevant to the discussion of the current bus cycle. The stages are:

Stage 1:   On the rising edge of CLK, the processor samples the RDY# input; it is active. The processor terminates the bus cycle marked 'previous cycle'. This is shown only to indicate that before the processor can begin the next cycle, the current cycle must be finished.

Stage 2:   The processor begins the memory write bus cycle by generating the following signals: M/IO#, W/R# and D/C# high; memory data write bus cycle. BE[3:0]# to correspond to the address or addresses of the device to be written to. The dword address of the memory device it wants to communicate with on the address bus.

Stage 3:   The bus controller recognizes that ADS# is active and generates SA0, SA1 and SBHE#. This provides the lower address bits to the expansion bus. BALE midway through address time; this ensures that the address is provided to the expansion bus.

Stage 4:   At the beginning of data time, the bus controller generates the appropriate command signal, in this case MWTC#. This indicates to the addressed slave that it should accept data.

Stage 5:   Near the start of data time, the bus controller generates DIRW and the appropriate BEN[3:0]# signals. This sets up the data transceivers to move data towards the slave device.

Stage 6:   Approximately, midway through data time, the processor provides the data to be written.

Stage 7:   The bus controller deasserts BALE; this latches SA[19:0].

Stage 8:   Midway through data time, the processor generates BLAST# to indicate to external logic that the next time the ready input is active, the current transaction is terminated.

Stage 9:   Midway through data time, the bus controller samples the NOWS# input. It is active; the bus controller will generate the ready signal early.

Stage 10:   The bus controller generates RDY#, to indicate to the processor that the current bus cycle can be terminated. The slave accepts the data on the rising edge of the command signal, MWTC#.

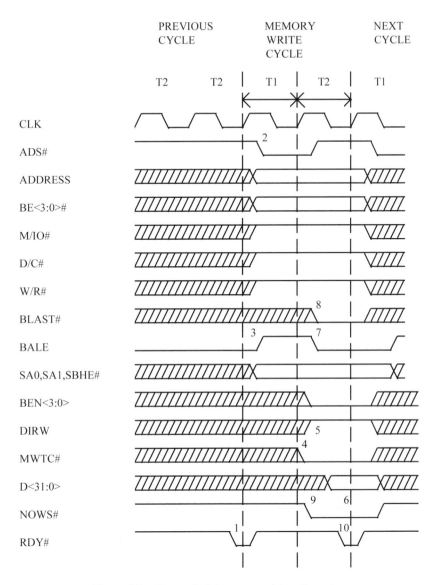

PREVIOUS   MEMORY   NEXT
CYCLE   WRITE   CYCLE
                  CYCLE

Figure 6.3   Zero wait state memory data write cycle

6.2.4   *Cacheable burst memory data read cycle*

Figure 6.4 shows a cacheable burst memory data read cycle. The cycle is assumed to be an access to local system memory. The shaded areas indicate that the state of these signals are irrelevant to the discussion of the current bus cycle. The stages are:

Stage 1:   On the rising edge of CLK, the processor samples the RDY# input; it is active. The processor terminates the bus cycle marked 'previous cycle'. This is shown only to indicate that before the processor can begin the next cycle, the current cycle must be finished.

Stage 2: The processor begins the memory read bus cycle by generating the following signals: M/IO# high, W/R# low and D/C# high; memory data read bus cycle. BE[3:0]# to correspond to the address or addresses of the device to be read from. The dword address of the memory device it wants to communicate with on the address bus.

Stage 3: At the end of address time the processor samples KEN# active. This tells the processor that the current access is to a cacheable memory location, and should be turned into a linefill cycle.

Stage 4: The bus controller generates BRDY# to indicate to the processor that the data for the first access is available.

Stage 5: The processor samples BRDY#; it is active. It accepts the data requested.

Stage 6: During the second access of the linefill the processor toggles A2. See Section 5.4.5.

Stage 7: The bus controller generates BRDY#; indicating to the processor that the data for the second access is available.

Stage 8: The processor samples BRDY#, it is active. It accepts the data requested.

Stage 9: During the third access of the linefill the processor toggles A2 and A3. See Chapter 5.

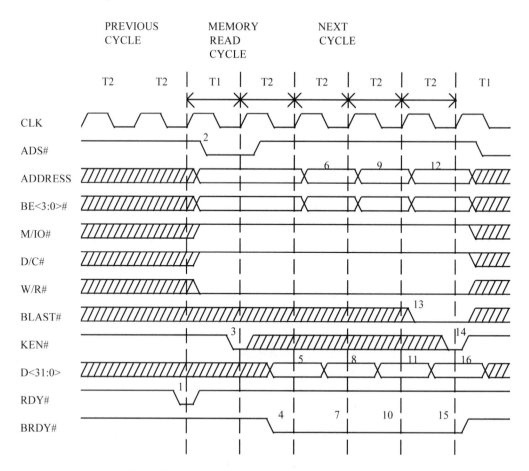

Figure 6.4   Cacheable burst memory data read cycle

Stage 10:   The bus controller generates BRDY#, indicating to the processor that the data for the third access is available.

Stage 11:   The processor samples BRDY# it is active. It accepts the third dword.

Stage 12:   During the fourth access of the linefill, the processor toggles A2. See chapter 5.

Stage 13:   Near the beginning of the fourth access, the processor generates BLAST# to indicate that the next time BRDY# is sampled active, the linefill operation is complete.

Stage 14:   The processor samples KEN# during the fourth cycle to ensure that the information retrieved during the linefill operation is to be placed in the internal cache.

Stage 15:   The bus controller generates BRDY#, indicating to the processor that the data for the fourth access is available.

Stage 16:   The processor samples BRDY#; it is active. It accepts the fourth dword.

6.2.5 Special cycles

Shutdown, halt, flush and write-back instructions are special cycles because no data is transferred between the processor and the slave device. The bus controller monitors the bus cycle definition and byte enable signals for these types of bus cycles; it handles them as follows:

- **When a shutdown cycle is detected,** the bus controller generates RESET to the processor. This forces the processor to start fetching data from the power on restart vector address, FFFFFFF0h. Note: BE0# is active for a shutdown bus cycle.

- **When a halt cycle is detected,** the bus controller generates a ready signal to the processor. After this, nothing will happen until the reset input or the INTR input to the processor goes active; interrupts have not been masked out. BE2# is active for a halt cycle.

- **When a flush cycle is detected,** the bus controller generates the ready signal to the processor, and a flush signal to any second level cache in the system. BE1# is active for a flush cycle.

- **When a write-back bus cycle is detected,** the bus controller generates a ready signal to the processor, and a write-back signal to any second-level cache in the system. BE3# is active for a write back cycle.

6.3   Bus Controller

The system bus controller provides an interface between the processor and external devices, both memory and I/O. The system bus controller works with the processor to perform bus cycles. Note that there is a separate bus controller for local DRAM, that is, the memory bus controller, as oppose to the system bus controller. These two devices are now generally integrated into the same ASIC on newer products.

The function of the bus controller is to:

- Generate the clocks for the processor and external devices.
- Provide the processor reset.
- Control the movement of addresses between the processor and slave devices.
- Control the movement of data between the current busmaster and the slave device, and to provide data steering when there is a difference in bus size between the busmaster and the slave.
- Generate the command signal translation between the processor and the slave.

- Generate the appropriate ready signal to the processor.
- Inform the processor when a memory address is cacheable.
- Inform the processor when a snoop cycle should occur.
- Arbitrate control of the buses when more than one busmaster requests them at the same time.

The embedded functions in the system bus controller are:

- **Clock generation**. The clock divider logic provides a clock to the processor, internal state machine, and a clock to the expansion bus; BCLK approximately 8 MHz.
- **Reset generation**. The reset logic generates RESET to the processor and RESDRV to the expansion bus. RESET is generated on power-up when PWRGOOD is low. RESDRV is a buffered version of RESET. RESET can also be generated under software control or when the processor executes a shutdown cycle.
- **State machine**. The state machine is the heart of the bus controller. It is a logic device that is stepped through a series of predefined states by a clock signal. Specific operations occur during each state, based upon input signals. There are three possible states the bus controller can be in at any given time, as illustrated in Figure 6.5. These are:

  - T_i is the idle state.
  - T_1 is the address state, that is, address time.
  - T_2 is the data state, that is, data time. It is during this time that data is transferred. If ready is not active at the end of data time, then an additional data time is added, that is, a wait state. Wait states are added until ready is sampled active. When ready is sampled active and there is no new cycle pending then the state machine returns to the idle state; if there is a cycle pending, then it enters the address time.

The CLK signal steps the bus controller through the states, and ADS# triggers the state machine. The timing diagrams in the bus cycle section give a description of what happens during each state.

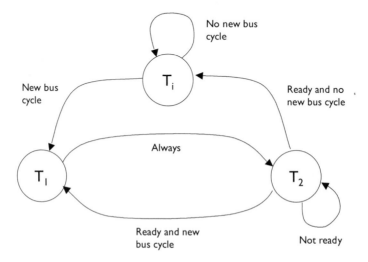

Figure 6.5   Bus controller states

6.3.1 Address movement

In the following discussion, the processor is always the busmaster, which is generally the case for debug. During T_1, the bus controller must move the address output by the processor to the expansion bus. The device used to do this is the address latch, as illustrated in Figure 6.6. Note that there are other components not shown on the diagram, which come into play more when the processor is not the busmaster. For debug purposes, the processor will generally be the busmaster.

The address latch is controlled by BALE. BALE is generated in the T1 state. This moves A[19:2] through to SA[19:2]. When BALE goes low, the address is latched; BALE is deasserted during the transition between T1 and T2.

When the processor is outputting a valid address, that is, ADS# is active, it drives the address lines, AD[31..2], and the byte enables, BE[3..0]#, out onto it's external bus lines. The bus controller then picks up this address and uses it to generate the system address lines, SA[19..0]. System address lines, SA[19..2], are just a direct copy of the processor address lines, AD[19..2]. They are either buffered through buffers, controlled by the bus controller, or buffered directly through the bus controller, dependent on board design. The bus controller decodes the byte enables and, from this, generates the system address bits, SA1 and SA0.

Note that depending on the amount of data requested by the processor, and the communicating devices data transfer size ability, the SA1 and SA0 lines may have to change during the processor access to provide it with all the data requested, for example, the processor requests 32 bits of data, but the communicating device has only an 8-bit data bus. The bus controller must fetch 4 bytes of data from the device, that is, do four cycles out on the system bus, before presenting all 32 bits of data back to the processor at the same time. This requires system address incrementing, and use of the data copy buffers.

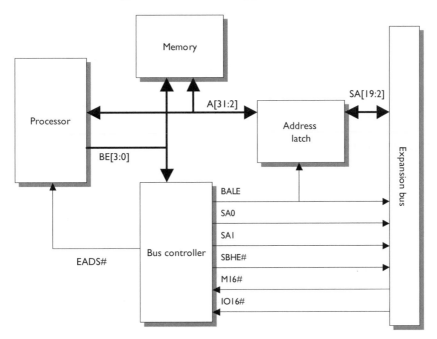

Figure 6.6　Bus controller

6.3.2   *Byte enable lines*

Specific addresses are associated with each byte enable, BE[3:0]#, and the processor expects data on specific data lines. The table below illustrates the end address, the byte enable associated with that end address, and the data bits associated with that byte enable.

From the table on the right it can be seen that:

C	D	E	F
8	9	A	B
4	5	6	7
0	I	2	3

BE0#	BE1#	BE2#	BE3#
D[7:0]	D[15:8]	D[23:16]	D[31:24]

Byte 0	Byte I	Byte 2	Byte 3

Word 0   Word I

Dword

- Even addresses ending in 0h, 4h, 8h, Ch correspond to BE0#. If the processor expects only one byte, SBHE# is high, SA0 and SA1 are both low, and the processor expects data on D[7:0].
- Odd addresses ending in 3h, 7h, Bh, Fh correspond to BE3#. If the processor expects only one byte, SBHE# is low, SA0 and SA1 are both high, and the processor expects data on D[31:24].

Using the same principle, addresses ending in 1h, 5h, 9h and Dh correspond to BE1#, and addresses ending in 3h, 7h, Bh and Fh correspond to BE2#. Note that SA0 and SBHE# may both be low if the processor is accessing sequential locations starting at an even address. In this case, more than one byte enable would be active. The relationship between the 16-bit ISA bus, SA0, and SBHE# is:

SA0	SBHE#	Data expected on
0	1	SD [7:0]
1	0	SD [15:8]
0	0	SD [15:0]

Note that this does not show where data would be placed when accessing an 8-bit device. The data steering examples shown later illustrate this. The following examples illustrate the address translation rules. By understanding the examples given, all address translation possibilities can be interpreted. Using the assumption given in each case, all of the following examples would be one cycle at the processor, and one cycle out on the system bus.

Byte transfer with an 8-bit slave at an even address

Writing a byte of data to address 38h, 0011 1000b (assume device data bus is 8 bits wide):

AD[31..2]	0000 0000 0000 0000 0000 0000 0011 10		
BE[3..0]#	1110		
Data transferred on D[7..0]		SA1, 0	00
SBHE#	1	IO16# and M16#	1

Byte transfer with an 8-bit slave at an odd address

If the address in the above example was changed to 39h, 0011 1001b, then the following changes would be observed:

AD[31..2]	As above		
BE[3..0]#	1101		
Data transferred on D[15..8]		SA1, 0	01
SBHE#	0	IO16# and M16#	1

Two-byte transfer with a 16-bit slave at an even address

Writing a word of data to I/O address 38h, 0011 1000b (assume device data bus is 16 bits wide):

AD[31..2]	0000 0000 0000 0000 0000 0000 0011 10		
BE[3..0]#	1100		
Data transferred on	D[15..0]	SA1, 0	00
SBHE#	0	IO16# = 0, M16#	1

Note that when transferring multiple bytes to/from an 8-bit device, there would still be only one cycle at the processor. The processor address would not change. Out on the system bus there could be more than one cycle. The system address would increment for each fetch from the device. This would be controlled by the bus controller.

For example, if the processor requests 32 bits of data from an 8-bit device, the processor puts out the address associated with a 32-bit transfer. This address does not change at the processor; there would be only one bus cycle on the processor bus. It would receive all 32 bits at the same time. Out on the system bus, four cycles will have been generated by the bus controller to get the full 32 bits to return to the processor, at the same time; the bus controller incorporates use of the copy buffers, in order to do this.

Read 32 bits from address FFFFFFF0, system ROM (note, the system ROM data bus is only 8 bits wide)

AD[31..2]	1111 1111 1111 1111 1111 1111 1111 00
BE[3..0]#	0000, all 4 byte enables are active

Out on the system bus side, four cycles will be performed by the bus controller, and SA1, SA0 will increment by 1, after each cycle, for example,

Cycle 0	SA1 0	SA0 0
1	SA1 0	SA0 1
2	SA1 1	SA0 0
3	SA1 1	SA0 1

Data is placed in each of the copy buffers as it is read from the ROM, and then passed to the processor as 32 bits.

6.3.3 *Data steering*

The 486 has a 32-bit data bus (the Pentium has a 64-bit data bus), and the expansion bus is 16 bits wide. Devices attached to the expansion bus can be either 8-or 16-bit. The bus controller is responsible for steering the data between the processor and the different sizes of slave device. The bus controller monitors BE[3:0]#, W/R#, M16#, and IO16# to determine the movement of data.

The data buffering logic is made up of a copy gate, a set of buffers, and a set of transceivers. The bus controller controls this logic using the following signals: CPYDIR, CPYEN#, BCK[3:0]#, LOE#, BEN[3:0] and DIRW.

If an 8-bit device is connected to SD[7:0], when the processor accesses the device the data will be placed on SD[7:0]. If the processor expects the data on a different byte lane, that is, data bits, then the data must be copied to another lane. Note that the data buffering logic will probably be embedded in an ASIC; it will not be seen as discrete latches and transceivers.

Note that transceivers are used for processor writes, and latches are used for processor reads, as illustrated in Figure 6.7. The following examples illustrate data steering control signal generation. By understanding the examples given, all data steering possibilities can be interpreted.

Byte transfer with an 8-bit device at an even address

SA0 and SA1 = 0, and SBHE# = 1, processor expects data on D[7:0], slave expects data on SD[7:0]. M16# and IO16# = 1. BE0# = 0, that is, only BE0# is active. The bus controller generates the following control signals:

For a read bus cycle:

BCK0 = 1   LOE# = 0

This allows data to move from SD[7:0] to D[7:0] through latch 0.

For a write bus cycle:

DIRW = 1   BEN0# = 0

This allows data to move from D[7:0] to SD[7:0] through transceiver 0.

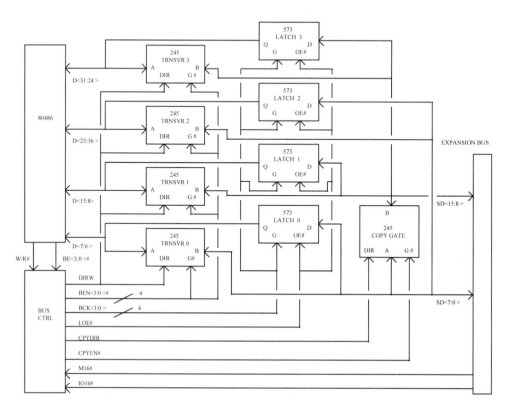

Figure 6.7   Transceivers

Byte transfer with an 8-bit device at an odd address

$SA0 = 1$, $SA1 = 0$, and $SBHE\# = 0$, processor expects data on $D[15:8]$, slave expects data on $SD[7:0]$. $M16\#$ and $IO16\# = 1$. $BE1\# = 0$, that is, only $BE1\#$ is active. The bus controller generates the following control signals:

    $CPYDIR = 1$ $CPYEN\# = 0$ $BCK1 = 1$ $LOE\# = 0$ **Read bus cycle**

This allows data to move from $SD[7:0]$ to $SD[15:8]$ through the copy gate, and then through latch 1 to $D[15:8]$.

    $DIRW = 1$ $BEN1\# = 0$ $CPYDIR = 0$ $CPYEN\# = 0$ **Write bus cycle**

This allows data to move from $D[15:8]$ to $SD[15:8]$ through transceiver 1, then move through the copy gate to $SD[7:0]$.

Two-byte transfer with a 16-bit device at an even I/O address

$SA0$ and $SA1 = 0$, and $SBHE\# = 0$, processor expects data on $D[15:0]$, slave expects data on $SD[15:0]$. $M16\# = 1$, $IO16\# = 0$. $BE0\#$ and $BE1\# = 0$. The bus controller generates the following control signals:

    $BCK0$ AND $BCK1 = 1$ $LOE\# = 0$ **Read bus cycle**

This allows data to move from $SD[15:0]$ through latches 0 and 1 to $D[15:0]$.

    $DIRW = 1$ $BEN0\#$ AND $BEN1\# = 0$ **Write bus cycle**

This allows data to move from $D[15:0]$ through transceivers 0 and 1 to $SD[15:0]$.

6.3.4 Byte lane boundary crossing

The following example illustrates the byte lane boundary rules, and how the bus controller handles the bus cycles when the boundary lanes are crossed.

Two-byte transfer with a 16-bit slave starting at an even address

When the processor wants to transfer 16 bits of data with a 16-bit device starting at an even address, $BE0\#$ and $BE1\#$, or $BE2\#$ and $BE3\#$, will be active, and either $I/O16\#$ or $M16\#$ will be active. This requires only one access to the slave device. The bus controller generates $SA0$, $SA1$, and $SBHE\#$ in the following manner:

$SA0$ is low, $SBHE\#$ is low. If $BE0\#$ is active, $SA1$ is low, or if $BE2\#$ is active, $SA1$ is high.

Two-byte transfer with a 16-bit slave starting at an odd address

When the processor wants to transfer 16 bits of data with a 16-bit device starting at an odd address, $BE1\#$ and $BE2\#$ will be active, and either $I/O16\#$ or $M16\#$ will be active. This type of transfer requires the bus controller to access the slave device twice. Even though there are two accesses to the slave device, it is just one bus cycle at the processor, with one ready signal, once both bytes have been transferred.

    The bus controller generates $SA0$, $SA1$, $SBHE\#$, and the data steering signals in the following manner:

In the first cycle, SA0 is high, SBHE# is low, and SA1 is low. RDY# is not generated in this cycle.

BCK1 is high and LOE# is low.

Read bus cycle

This allows data to be moved from SD[15:8] through latch 1 to D[15:8]; the data is latched in latch 1.

BEN1# is low, and DIRW is high.

Write bus cycle

This allows the data to be moved from D[15:8] through transceiver 1 to SD[15:8].

In the second cycle, SA0 is low, SBHE# is high, and SA1 is high. BCK2 is high and LOE# is low. RDY# is generated in this cycle.

BCK2 is high and LOE# is low.

Read bus cycle

This allows data to be moved from SD[7:0] through latch 2 to D[23:16].

BEN2# is low, and DIRW is high.

Write bus cycle

This allows the data to be moved from D[23:16] through transceiver 2 to SD[7:0].

Four-byte transfer with a 16-bit slave

When the processor wants to transfer 32 bits of data with a 16-bit device, it must always start at an even address. BE[3:0]# will be active, and either I/O16# or M16# will be active. This type of transfer requires the bus controller to generate two accesses to the slave. Although there are two accesses to the slave device, it is just one bus cycle to the processor with one ready signal once both words are transferred. The bus controller generates SA0, SA1, SBHE# and the data steering signals in the following manner:

In the first cycle, SA0, SBHE#, and SA1 are all low. RDY# is not generated in this cycle.

BCK0 and BCK1 are high, LOE# is low.

Read bus cycle

Data is moved from SD[15:0] through latches 1 and 2, to D[15:0].

BEN0# and BEN1# are low, DIRW is high.

Write bus cycle

Data is moved from D[15:0] through transceivers 0 and 1, to SD[15:0].

In the second cycle, SA0 is low, SBHE# is low, and SA1 is high. RDY# is generated in this cycle.

BCK2 and BCK3 are high, LOE# is low.

Read bus cycle

Data is moved from SD[15:0] through latches 2 and 3 to D[31:16].

BEN2# and BEN3# are low, DIRW is high.

Write bus cycle

Data is moved D[31:16] through transceivers 2 and 3 to SD [15:0].

6.3.5 Command signals

The command signals define the type of transfer taking place. They are used by the slave device to control the direction of data flow within the device; they are MRDC#, MWTC#, IORC# and IOWC#.

When the processor is in control, the command signals are generated during bus cycle data time; they are a decode of the M/IO#, D/C# and W/R# inputs.

The system bus controller generates RDY# to the processor to tell it that the current bus cycle is finished; during writes, the addressed slave has had enough time to accept the data, during reads the processor can accept the data.

Note that the bus controller generates ready at a certain time, that is, a default number of wait states based on the size of the slave device; bus cycles can be shortened by NOWS#, or lengthened by BUSRDY.

6.3.6 Arbitration and cache enable generation

The arbitration logic provides busmasters with a mechanism for requesting control of the buses. There are four possible busmasters in the ISA environment: processor, refresh, DMA or an ISA busmaster. The processor is the default busmaster.

The cache enable generation logic tells the processor whether the current memory bus cycle is cacheable or not, that is, if KEN#, cache enable, is active then the locations in memory are cacheable; the processor will turn the memory read cycle into a cache linefill cycle.

6.4   Direct Memory Access

Direct memory access (DMA) is a method in which an external device takes over the data and address buses for a short time. A DMA controller controls the transfers and makes the request to the processor to take over the transfer.

Two lines control the DMA interface: bus hold acknowledge (HLDA) and bus hold request (HOLD). When the DMA controller wants to take control of the local data and address bus lines, it sets the HOLD active, that is, a high level. When the processor has completed its current operation it sets the data and address buses into the high impedance state and then sets the HLDA line active high. The DMA controller can then transfer data directly to memory and when complete it sets the HOLD line inactive. When the processor senses this, it can then take over the control of the buses again.

6.4.1 Definition

DMA is the ability to transfer data between memory and I/O without processor intervention. Without DMA, the processor would have to read data from one device in one bus cycle, then write the data to the other device in another cycle. DMA was designed to free up the processor. During a DMA transfer, DMA logic takes control of the buses, and manages the transfer of data between memory and an I/O device in one bus cycle per transfer.

Once the DMA controller (DMAC) has control of the buses, it provides the memory address and control bus signals, IORC# and MWTC# or IOWC# and MRDC#. The DMAC manages the transfer of data between memory and an I/O device. The DMAC embedded in most of the DMA controller ASICs is similar to the Intel 8237.

6.4.2 Direct memory access signals

Figure 6.8 outlines the main DMA signals. The processor accesses the registers of the device using the following:

CS#   This input indicates to the DMAC that the processor is accessing one of its
                 internal registers.
A[3:0]   Three address inputs that identify which internal register is being accessed.
                 These are outputs when the DMAC is busmaster.
IORC#   This input indicates that an internal register is being read.
IOWC#   This input indicates that an internal register is being written to.
D[7:0]   Bidirectional data paths allowing transfer of data into and out of an internal
                 register.
RESET   This input resets the internal registers to a known good state.

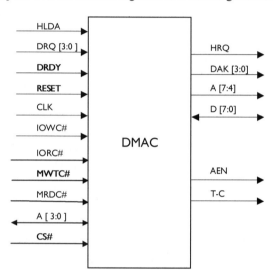

Figure 6.8   DMA signals

When the DMAC is a busmaster, the following are used:

CLK   This input times DMA transfers.
DRQ[3:0]   The DMA request inputs; each one corresponds to a different DMA channel.
                 An I/O device is attached to each signal. The I/O device indicates to the
                 DMAC that it is requesting a transfer through the DRQ signal, that is, it drives
                 the signal active.
HRQ   The hold request output is generated by the DMAC in response to an active
                 DRQ input. HRQ indicates to the arbitration logic that the DMAC wants con-
                 trol of the buses.
HLDA   This input tells the DMAC that it has been granted control of the buses in re-
                 sponse to its HRQ.
A[7:0]   Address outputs that provide the lower 8 bits of the address to memory. Note:
                 A[3:0] are inputs when the DMAC is a slave.
AEN   Address enable output is generated prior to outputting the address.
DAK[3:0]#   DMA acknowledge output is provided to the requesting I/O device as ac-
                 knowledgement to its DRQ.
IORC#   An output provided to the requesting I/O device, indicating that it should pro-
                 vide the data.
IOWC#   An output provided to the requesting I/O device, indicating that it should ac-
                 cept the data.

MRDC#   An output provided to memory, indicating that it should provide the data.

MWTC#   An output provided to memory, indicating that it should accept the data.

DRDY#   DMA ready input indicating to the DMAC that the current DMA bus cycle is complete.

T-C   An output generated by the DMAC after all bytes have been transferred, terminal count. It is provided to the I/O device to tell it that all bytes have been transferred.

6.4.3 Direct memory access Modes

Each DMA channel can be programmed to operate in one of three modes:

- **Single transfer mode**. In this transfer mode, the DMAC transfers one byte or word between memory and an I/O device, then releases control of the buses. The DMAC is programmed during post. DRDY indicates to the DMAC when the current transfer is finished. When DRDY is sampled active, the following happens within the DMAC:

    - The base address register increments; this register keeps track of the memory addresses.
    - The byte transfer count register decrements; this keeps track of how many bytes have still to be transferred. This register is sampled by the DMAC. If it equals FFFFh, the DMAC generates terminal count.
    - The DMAC releases the HRQ output regardless of the state of any DRQ inputs. This allows other busmasters to gain control of the buses.
    - Once HRQ has been released, the DMAC will generate HRQ again when one of its DRQ inputs is active.

- **Demand transfer mode**. In this mode, the DMAC transfers multiple bytes or words between memory and an I/O device, as long as the DRQ input is active.

- **Block transfer mode**. In this mode the DMAC transfers all bytes or words between memory and an I/O device until all transfers are complete.

6.4.4 Direct memory access cycles

ISA systems generally use a two-DMAC configuration, referred to as cascaded DMACs. One is the slave attached to DRQ [3:0] on the expansion bus. The other is the master attached to DRQ [7:5] on the expansion bus. DRQ4 is used to cascade the two controllers together; it is not available for an I/O device request channel.

The following discussion illustrates the use of the slave DMAC channel 2. The floppy disk controller is attached here. Other channel operations are similar; the addresses used to program the DMAC for the other channels are different.

To load the boot record from drive A into memory

Step 1:   Channel 2 of the DMAC is programmed as follows:

- The starting address is written to port 04h, base address register; the start address in memory for this operation is 7C00h
- The number of bytes to transfer is written to port 05h; the byte transfer count register 01FFh = 512 bytes.
- The mode and transfer type is written to port 0Bh; the mode register. The DMAC is programmed for single transfer write mode; the write is in reference to memory, that is, the data will be written into memory in this case.

Step 2:   The floppy disk controller (FDC) is programmed with the following information:

- The head to use.
- The track and sector to access.
- The transfer type in reference to the disk.
- A command for the FDC to go to the disk and get the data.

Step 3:   Once the FDC has the first byte, it generates DRQ2 to the DMA controller.

Step 4:   The DMA controller generates its HRQ to the bus controller.

Step 5:   The bus controller generates HOLD to the processor.

Step 6:   The processor tristates itself from the buses and generates HLDA to the bus controller.

Step 7:   The bus controller generates DMACK to the DMA.

Step 8:   The DMA generates AEN to make the address latches transparent.

Step 9:   The DMA provides the memory address 7C00h onto the SA bus.

Step 10: The DMA then generates the DAK2 output. This tells the FDC that its request is being serviced.

Step 11: The DMA then generates the two bus control signals, IORC# and MWTC#. IORC# and DAK2# cause the FDC to provide the data. MWTC# indicate to memory that it should accept data.

Step 12: The memory bus control logic has address, data and control signals; it handles the access to memory.

Step 13: The bus controller generates DRDY to terminate the transfer.

Step 14: When the DMAC samples DRDY active:

- The base address register increments to 7C01h.
- The byte transfer count register decrements to 1FEh.
- The byte transfer count register is sampled for terminal count; it has not been reached.

Step 15: The DMA releases the buses by deasserting HRQ to the bus controller. At this time refresh or the processor can gain control of the buses.

Step 16: When DRQ2 is active again, the DMA will request the buses; steps 4–15 occur again. The only difference is the register values at step 14 differ for each cycle.

Step 17: The process continues until terminal count is reached; T-C is generated at this time.

Step 18: In response to terminal count, the FDC generates IRQ6.

Common DMA faults

System board error or last write to milestone port is DMA controller test

Possible cause: Not accessing DMA controller correctly.

Check:

- CLK to the DMA controller.
- Using the single-step card or stimulus test equipment, trap on or loop on writes to, and reads from, DMA addresses; get the addresses from the I/O map.
- Check the chip select address is correct, IORC#, IOWC#, and the data is good; compare with a good board if required. Note that if the DMAC is embedded in an ASIC, there may not be a chip select signal; check the others indicated.

Step 19: The processor executes the FDC interrupt service routine; this is to determine whether the FDC transferred the data without any loss of data.

6.4.5 Direct memory access example

The following example demonstrates how to trap on the first DMA transfer cycle when loading the boot record, and how to display the data transferred from the last two locations of the boot record using the single-step card.

Common DMA faults
Common DMA faults
No boot
Possible cause:
• Bad DMA logic.
• Bad FDC logic.
Check:
• CLK to the DMA.
• Using the single-step card, trap on the first DMA transfer to 7C00h.
• Check the DMAC is providing the DAK# signals.
• Check that DRDY goes active before the trap using an oscilloscope.
• If the board does not trap at 7C00h, pull DRDY low and cycle the power.
• Check the DMAC is providing the correct address and control signals. If the board does not trap at 7C00h when DRDY is pulled low, using the single-step card trap on I/O writes to the DMA, and check the signals associated with programming the DMA registers.
• Check T-C is not open.

Step 1: Set the single-step card to trap on a memory write to address 7C00h. The boot record memory start address. Make sure the I/O read switch is also set up.

Step 2: Power-up the system.

Step 3: The card should trap on 7C00h when the DMAC becomes busmaster and is writing the first byte of the boot record into location 7C00h

Step 4: Set the single-step card to display last on a memory write to address 7DFEh; this is the second last boot record memory address. Make sure the I/O read switch is also set up.

Step 5: Power-up the system

Step 6: The card should display the last data written to 7DFEh when the DMAC is busmaster and has written the second last byte of the boot record data into location 7DFEh; the data value should be 55h.

Step 7: Set the single step card to display last on a memory write to address 7DFFh; this is the last boot record memory address. Note: make sure the I/O read switch is also set-up.

Step 5: Power-up the system

Step 6: The card should display the last data written to 7DFFh when the DMAC is busmaster and has written the last byte of the boot record data into location 7DFFh; the data value should be AAh.

Step 7: If the last two locations are not AA55h, the screen will show a diskette boot record error message.

6.4.6 Direct memory access summary

- Used to transfer data between peripheral devices, for example, floppy disk and local memory.
- DMA contains two embedded 8237 devices.

- DMA has to be programmed before it can perform a DMA transfer with: start address in memory; number of bytes/words to be transferred; type of transfer; read or write; and mode of operation.
- Byte DMA ctrl, slave, handles 8-bit device transfers; accesses through ports 00h– 0Fh.
- Word DMA ctrl, master, handles 16-bit device transfers; accessed through ports C0h– DFh.

6.5   Exercises

6.5.1   Identify the state of the following signals during a wait state when the processor is reading two bytes of data, starting at location 3456h in memory.

M/IO#	D/C#	W/R#	ADS#
BLAST#	DIRW	BE0#	BE2#
BEN2#	BEN3#	LOE#	

6.5.2   What affect does NOWS# being active have on a bus cycle?

6.5.3   If a processor bus cycle consists of the following states, what conclusion can be drawn?

T1, T2, T2, T2, T2

6.5.4   During a cache linefill, what is the condition of the following signals if the first memory location accessed is 345Ch?

Signal	1st	2nd	3rd	4th
A2				
A3				
M/IO#				
W/R#				
KEN#				
BLAST#				
BRDY#				

> **Microprocessor basics**
>
> **Accumulator.** A register with an implicit source and destination of an operation. This differs to RISC processors which use a load/store architecture, where to load a memory location into a register, it must first be loaded into an intermediate register.
>
> **Explicitly Parallel Instruction Computing.** HP/Intel term where fields are used in the instruction stream or in the actual instructions to group (specify instruction dependencies), rather than using a fixed length instruction word.
>
> **Microcode.** Microcode simplifies processor design as it allows hardware operations to operate as simple microinstructions to interpret more complex machine instructions. It is often slower than hardwired operations, and also increases the size of the processor, but leads to simpler designs.

6.5.5   Compare a zero wait state memory read with a zero wait state memory write. What processor signals are different? What bus controller signals are different?

6.5.6   What makes special cycles special?

6.5.7   How does the DMAC respond to DRDY?

6.5.8   What memory address does the DMAC transfer the first byte to during the boot process? Also, what signal tells the DMAC that the current transfer is complete, and what signal is generated by the DMAC that when all bytes have been transferred?

6.5.9   The DMAC IORC# and IOWC# signals are bidirectional; the MRDC# and MWTC# are not. Why?

6.5.10   What would be checked if the board would not boot, and the DMA logic is suspected?

CMOS, Memory and I/O

7

7.1 CMOS

The real-time clock, CMOS, chip provides the board with time-of-day clock, periodic interrupt, and system configuration information. It contains 64 (00h–3Fh) 8-bit locations of battery-backed up CMOS RAM. The split is:

- 00h–0Eh, used for real-time clock functions (time of day).
- 0Fh–35h, used for system configuration information, for example, hard drive type, memory size.
- 36h–3Fh, used for power-on password storage. Access to these locations is controlled through I/O port 92h (password protect bit).

Configuration faults that can be caused by CMOS are:

- Nonsystem disk.
- Hard drive mismatch.
- Memory mismatch.
- Serial port ID, parallel port ID, mismatch fails.

The CMOS can be cleared by removing the power jumper for a few seconds.

7.1.1 CMOS circuitry implementation

Figure 7.1 illustrates the CMOS signals and the internal structure of the CMOS array of locations; the locations are accessed through ports 70h and 71h, indexed pair of registers. The pins used are:

OSC	External frequency.
D[7:0]	Multiplexed pointer address/data bus.
RTCCS#	Active low chip select.
RTCWR#	Active low write signal; data writes.
RTCRD#	Active low read signal; data reads.

To access locations in the CMOS device, write to address 70h first, with a data value (in the range 0–3Fh) corresponding to the location to write to or read from. Then write to address 71h with the data value to be stored in the index pointer location, or read address 71h, to obtain the data stored in that index pointer location, for example, write address 70h, data 0Eh, read address 71h. The

---

Common CMOS faults

Fault: Last write to milestone checkpoint is CMOS test.

Possible cause: CMOS not getting correct control, address or data signals.

Check: Control inputs to CMOS. Address inputs to CMOS. Data bus to CMOS.

Fault: System does not boot.

Possible cause: CMOS may contain the wrong floppy drive configuration information.

Check: Clear the CMOS and retest the board.

Common CMOS faults

Fault: Hard drive failures

Possible cause: CMOS may contain the wrong hard drive configuration information.

Check: Clear the CMOS clear the board.

Fault: Memory error; memory not installed.

Possible cause: CMOS may contain the wrong memory configuration information.

Check: Clear the CMOS and retest the board.

data value obtained from this location is the diagnostic status byte whose bits indicate memory size error detected, CMOS checksum valid, time is valid.

7.1.2 *Writing to a CMOS location*

To write a value of 20h into the internal CMOS location 38h:

1. I/O write data 38h to port 70h (write the internal register location to the index register).
2. I/O write data 20h to port 71h (write the data value to be placed in location, 38h to the data register).

7.1.3 *Reading from a CMOS location*

To read the contents of internal CMOS location 0Eh:

1. I/O write data 0Eh to port 70h.
2. I/O read from port 71h (the contents of location 0Eh are read automatically by reading the data register, once the pointer has been set up using the index register).

> **Milestone checker**
>
> Most test systems use a milestone checker, where values are written to a special I/O memory port, By examining the contents of the port the tester can determine which device was the last to correctly start up. An example milestone checker port is Port B.

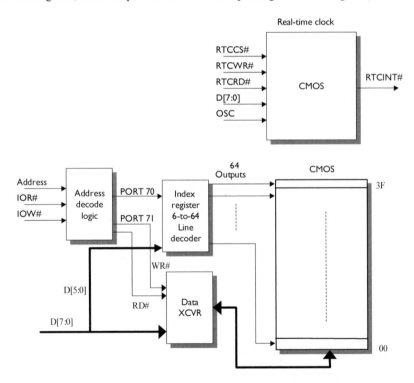

Figure 7.1   CMOS circuit

7.1.4 *High and extended CMOS*

Some of the newer systems have high CMOS locations, 40h–7Fh. A device with high CMOS registers will decode D[6:0] when writing to port 70h, to select a register. The function of the locations may vary from product to product; for a description of location and bit definition refer to the appropriate technical reference guide. Some of the newer systems also have extended CMOS locations. Extended CMOS can be found on some ISA systems, laptops, and EISA systems accessed using ports 800h–820h. The function of the locations may vary from product to product; for a description of location and bit definition, refer to the appropriate technical reference guide.

7.2 Memory

The memory devices used by microprocessor systems fall into two categories: ROM (read-only memory) and DRAM (dynamic random access memory). A memory map is made up of the memory addresses that are available to the processor. The processor outputs a memory cycle with a certain memory address on the address bus. The cycle type and address decode logic decode this and generate the relevant device control lines. Figure 7.2 shows the allocated memory space in an ISA system.

Notice that system ROM is mapped to two different locations. This is a function of the memory address decode logic. When an address in either of these two address ranges is presented to the memory decode logic, it decodes this address and generates the control lines required to access data from the system ROM. Also, notice that the processor reset vector address is FFFFFFF0 hex, that is, when the processor comes out of reset it will start fetching code from address location FFFFFFF0 hex. The address decode logic must be designed to map the system ROM address space at this address.

7.2.1 Read-only memory

Under normal system operations, the ROM device can only be read from. It is a nonvolatile device, that is, its contents are not lost when the power is removed. The type of information stored in ROM includes POST, BIOS and primary bootstrap routines. Many modern system use a flash ROM, for which the contents of this ROM device can be changed using a flash floppy disk

A ROM has two control inputs, address inputs and data inputs. Each ROM location is accessed using the address inputs. When chip select (CS#) is active, the ROM's internal decoder looks at the address inputs and identifies the location being accessed. When output enable (OE#) is active, the ROM's internal buffer is switched on, and data from the location being accessed is output. The data outputs provide the processor with the requested data.

To access ROM data:

1. The processor initiates a ROM read by generating a ROM address on the address bus (see figure 7.2) the correct bus cycle definition line conditions for a memory read or an instruction fetch, address strobe (ADS#) to validate the address, and bus cycle definition signals.

> **Classic software**
>
> **VisiCalc** (original authors: Dan Bricklin, Bob Frankston). VisiCalc is the classic case of a software package that helped sell a computer. It was released in 1979, and helped the Apple II to become adopted quickly. VisiCalc was the first spreadsheet, and preceded Lotus 1-2-3 by three years.

> **Classic software**
>
> **dBase II** (original author: Wayne Ratliff). Initially written for CP/M, dBase II was a massive success in its DOS version. It was bought by Aston-Tate, but has since lost its large market share, especially due to the bug-written dBase IV (1988) and their slowness to develop a Windows version (1994).

> **Classic software**
>
> **WordStar** (original author: Seymour Rubinstein). It was released in 1979, and quickly became the standard word processor. Often, other word processors imitated WordStar's keystrokes, such as Ctrl-Q-F to find a piece of text.

2. The address decoder monitors the upper address bits of the address bus and generates the ROM chip select (ROMCS#), indicating that the ROM is being accessed.
3. The bus controller generates SA0 and SA1 based on the byte enable BE[3:0]#, signals.
4. ROM decode logic identifies the location being accessed by its address inputs.
5. The bus controller generates the memory read and the appropriate data latch control signals based upon the BE[3:0]# signals.
6. ROM places the data on the system data (SD) bus.
7. The bus controller generates RDY# to the processor.
8. When the microprocessor samples RDY# active, it accepts what is on the data bus.

> **Classic software**
>
> **AutoCAD** (developer: Autodesk). Initially written for CP/M, and ported to DOS and Windows, it allowed designers to access powerful mechanical design software that was previously available only on mini and mainframe computers.

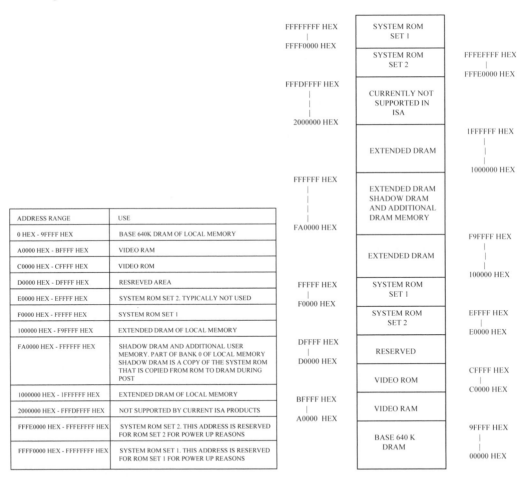

ADDRESS RANGE	USE
0 HEX - 9FFFF HEX	BASE 640K DRAM OF LOCAL MEMORY
A0000 HEX - BFFFF HEX	VIDEO RAM
C0000 HEX - CFFFF HEX	VIDEO ROM
D0000 HEX - DFFFF HEX	RESREVED AREA
E0000 HEX - EFFFF HEX	SYSTEM ROM SET 2. TYPICALLY NOT USED
F0000 HEX - FFFFF HEX	SYSTEM ROM SET 1
100000 HEX - F9FFFF HEX	EXTENDED DRAM OF LOCAL MEMORY
FA0000 HEX - FFFFFF HEX	SHADOW DRAM AND ADDITIONAL USER MEMORY. PART OF BANK 0 OF LOCAL MEMORY SHADOW DRAM IS A COPY OF THE SYSTEM ROM THAT IS COPIED FROM ROM TO DRAM DURING POST
1000000 HEX - 1FFFFFF HEX	EXTENDED DRAM OF LOCAL MEMORY
2000000 HEX - FFFDFFFF HEX	NOT SUPPORTED BY CURRENT ISA PRODUCTS
FFFE0000 HEX - FFFEFFFF HEX	SYSTEM ROM SET 2. THIS ADDRESS IS RESERVED FOR ROM SET 2 FOR POWER UP REASONS
FFFF0000 HEX - FFFFFFFF HEX	SYSTEM ROM SET 1. THIS ADDRESS IS RESERVED FOR ROM SET 1 FOR POWER UP REASONS

Figure 7.2   Memory map

7.2.2 *Dynamic random access memory*

DRAM can be either read from or written to. It is a volatile device, thus its contents are lost when the power is removed. It is typically used to store applications programs.

There are two simple ways of determining DRAM size:

- Read and interpret the part type printed on the device.
- Count the number of DRAM address lines connected to the chip, for example, if there were eight address lines connected to the DRAM, then the largest row or column address it could receive is FFh; as address 0 is valid, there are 256 row and 256 column addresses in the DRAM matrix. Therefore, the number of storage locations is 256×256 = 65,536 (64 kbit).

There are various sizes of DRAM device, indicating the number of addressable locations the device contains. The number of bits each location contains can also vary, for example, 1 bit or 4 bits per location. A DRAM circuit diagram marking may show $1\,\text{Mb} \times 4$; this means that the device contains 1M of storage locations each 4 bits wide, that is, it contains half a megabyte of data bits (500 kB or 4 Mbit).

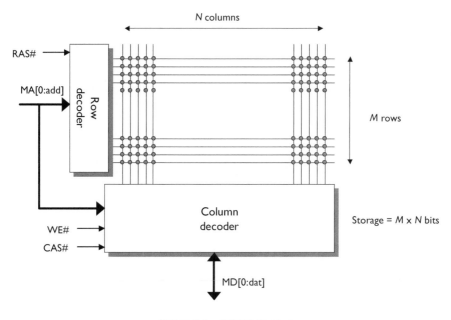

Figure 7.3 DRAM structure

Internally, a DRAM device is structured with a matrix of rows and columns (see Section 7.7). It has four control inputs, address inputs, and bidirectional data bus connections. These operate as follows:

- The memory address (MA) inputs provide the DRAM device with both the row and column address.
- When the row address strobe (RAS#) input goes low, the address on the MA inputs is latched into the DRAM device and identifies the row address being accessed.
- When the column address strobe (CAS#) input goes low, the address on the MA inputs is latched into the DRAM device and identifies the column address being accessed.

Classic software

Lotus 1-2-3 (developer: Lotus). Lotus 1-2-3 became the best selling application of all time. It considerably enhanced the VisiCalc program, and was written specifically for the IBM PC.

- When the write enable (WE#) input is active, it indicates to the DRAM that it should accept data on the rising edge of WE#, that is, a low to high transition. When the WE# is high, in conjunction with the OE# being low, it indicates that the DRAM should output data.
- When the output enable (OE#) input is active, it indicates to the DRAM that it should place the data onto the data bus lines. This line is usually tied permanently low through a pull-down resistor.

The memory data input/output lines provide a bidirectional data path for the transfer of data to and from the DRAM device.

Figure 7.4 illustrates the timing of DRAM access. The operation is as follows:

1. A row address is driven onto the MA inputs.
2. The DRAM latches the MA inputs when RAS# goes active.
3. The WE# state indicates the type of access:
   - WE# low indicates a write to the DRAM.
   - WE# high indicates a read from the DRAM.
4. A column address is driven onto the MA inputs.
5. The DRAM latches the MA inputs when CAS# goes active. Note: the intersection of the row and column addresses identifies the location being accessed.
6. Data is transferred:
   - If WE# is low, data is accepted on the rising edge.
   - If WE# is high once the row and column addresses have been decoded, the DRAM provides the data.

> **Classic software**
>
> **The Norton Utilities** (original author: Peter Norton). Early computers were difficult to use, and were often unreliable. DOS was always a very basic operating system and lacked a great deal of system tools. Norton Utilities allowed users to gain access to the hardware and firmware of the computer. A typical utility was one that recovered data from a corrupted hard disk (which often happened, as hard disks had to be parked before they were moved).

Note that if a sequential access is made to a DRAM device where the row address does not change, then the memory controller will keep RAS# active because the row address is the same, as it was for the previous access. The new column address is provided and latched in when CAS goes active. This is referred to as page mode DRAM accessing.

7.2.3   Bank concept

A single DRAM device on its own does not have the capability to provide the processor with as many data bits as the data bus is wide. For example, the Pentium has a 32-bit data bus. To optimize performance, DRAM should be 32 bits wide as well. To accomplish this, DRAM devices are grouped together to form banks, where the MA inputs to each DRAM in the bank are tied together; the MA0 input to each DRAM in the bank is attached to the same MA bit. The RAS# input to each DRAM in the bank are also tied together; the RAS# input to each DRAM in bank 0 is attached to RAS0#. Bank 1 RAS1#. The WE# input to each DRAM in the bank are tied together. Each DRAM is attached to different memory data bits, MD[31:0]; if the bank is made up of 1M×4 DRAM devices, each DRAM is connected to four different MD bits. The DRAMs are grouped together to form bytes within the data bus, using the CAS# signals; each byte has its own CAS# signal. The DRAMs that are attached to MD[7:0] are attached to CAS0#, MD[15:8] CAS1#, MD[23:16] CAS2# and MD[31:24] CAS3#. Note that the byte enables, BE[3:0]#, are decoded to drive the CAS[3:0]# signals directly.

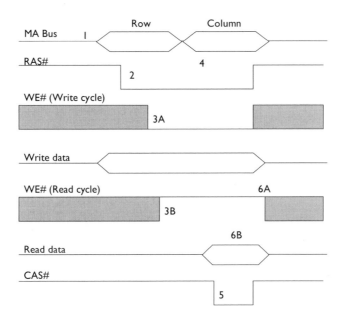

Figure 7.4 DRAM access cycle

7.2.4 *Refresh*

DRAM devices are manufactured using transistor/capacitor technology. As a result, to maintain data integrity, the data in the DRAM device must be periodically refreshed. A refresh cycle is basically a dummy read. The DRAM device reads the status of every location in the specified row, and recharges the cells that contained a charge.

There are different types of refresh cycles used that dependent on board design. Some examples are ras-only and cas-before-ras. For example, during a ras-only refresh cycle, the row address to be refreshed, an active RAS# signal and an inactive WE# signal must be provided to the DRAM device. Figure 7.5 illustrates a ras-only refresh cycle.

Note that when a refresh cycle is being performed, refresh has control of the buses. To get control of the buses refresh has to ask for them through the arbitration logic in the system bus controller. It does this by generating refresh CLK active; the bus controller recognizes this request, and asks the processor to release the buses.

The operation is as follows:

1. The timer generates an output called REFRESHCLK. This is generated at the refresh rate required by the DRAM design. A description of the set-up and operation of the timer can be found in Chapter 6.
2. The bus controller (arbitration logic inside) recognizes REFRESHCLK as a request by the refresh logic to gain control of the buses. In response to this, the bus controller generates HOLD to the processor.

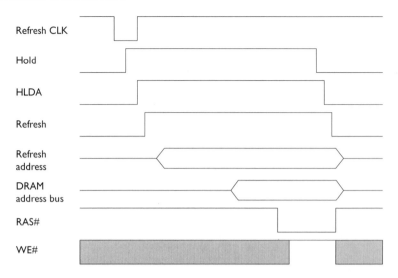

Figure 7.5   RAS-only refresh timing diagram

3. The CPU finishes it current instruction, tristates the buses, and generates hold acknowledge (HLDA).
4. In response to HLDA, the system bus controller gives control of the buses to the refresh logic by generating REFRESH#.
5. The refresh counter places the address to be refreshed onto the system bus.
6. The system bus controller generates the appropriate memory read signal.
7. The result of this is that all DRAM device locations with the selected row address are refreshed.
8. REFRESH# and HOLD are deasserted by the bus controller.

7.2.5 *Access time*

Manufactures define access time as the amount of time to transfer data between the processor and the slave device once the device has been chip selected. A DRAM device is selected when RAS# goes active. DRAM manufacturers define access time to be the time from the moment RAS# goes active until data can be transferred.

DRAM devices have the access time marked on them. It is the number to the right of the hyphen in nanoseconds (ns). It is important from a debug point of view that if DRAM devices are being changed, they are replaced with DRAM devices with the same access time or faster as the memory bus controller is designed around this timing constraint.

> **Classic software**
>
> **Flight Simulator (**developer: Microsoft). By today's standards, Microsoft's Flight Simulator was hardly startling, but in the 1980s its graphics were state-of-the-art. It led to a great market for supplying different terrains and cities to fly over. For many it was their first sight of New York from the sky.

> **Classic software**
>
> **Novell NetWare**(developer: Novell). NetWare became the first company to bring together PCs to make a local area network (LAN). For this, it used its own propriety protocol, IPX/SPX, and is the only networking operating system that can compete again the strength of UNIX (which uses the TCP/IP protocol) and Windows 95/98/NT/2000. It held an almost monopoly on networks in the commercial market, but has suffered recently due to the might of Microsoft Windows, as Windows can support many different networking protocols.

7.2.6 Pre-charge time and cycle time

Pre-charge time is the time it takes for the DRAM device to recover from a read operation. When read from, the DRAM device discharges the addressed cell to determine whether it contained a high or a low. To ensure that the data read is not lost, the DRAM must recharge the cell if it was discharged, normally close to the manufacturers access time. Cycle time is the access time plus the pre-charge time.

The memory bus controller is designed around cycle time. However, depending on the memory architecture the effect of cycle time can be reduced, that is, using an interleaved memory structure.

7.2.7 Parity

Some systems employ logic that checks that the data read from RAM is the same as the data that was written to RAM. This logic is the parity logic. When the processor writes to memory, it writes a combination of bytes; this could be one, two, three, and so on. For every byte of data written, a parity bit is generated and stored in DRAM along with the respective byte. When the data is read from memory, the byte and the parity bit are checked for data loss.

There are two types of parity, even and odd. For example, if even parity is being used, then the number of highs (logic 1) in the byte being written along with the parity bit itself must be an even number.

A 32-bit data bus will generate four parity bits. For example, one of the parity bits would be generated as follows:

1. The processor writes data 43h to memory location 3420h.
2. DRAM byte 0 is accessed; it is byte 0 because the address ends in 0.
3. The data value 43h is provided to both DRAM (on the MD bus) and the parity generator/checker logic. The parity logic counts the number of 1s in the data pattern, that is three and generates the MDP0 (memory data parity bit) high, giving a total number of four 1s, which satisfies the even parity rules.
4. The data value 43h is written into the DRAM. At the same time, a high, is written into the parity DRAM.

The parity bit checking would be:

1. The processor reads from memory location 3420h, expecting back the data that was previously written into that location.
2. The DRAM byte 0 is accessed, data 43h is placed onto the MD bus, and the parity DRAM provides the parity bit (high) associated with byte 0.
3. The parity generator/checker counts the number of 1s on its inputs, that is, a total of four, satisfying the even parity rules.
4. The PARITY# output remains inactive, indicating that no parity error has been detected.

For example, to write 34h to memory address 4680h:

D[7:0] =   0011 0100

Common memory faults

Fault: Bad first fetch data.

Possible cause: Unprogrammed or faulty ROM. Bad control signals at ROM. Bad address at ROM. Bad data path.

Check: ROMCS#. ROMOE#. Address bits. Data path between the ROM and the processor.

Fault: Bad jump address.

Possible cause: As above.

Check: Address bits. Data paths. Jump address output by the processor.

Parity output from parity DRAM =   1 during memory write

Data byte + parity o/p → parity generator

Parity generator activates its even output = 1; even output → parity input → parity DRAM = 1.
Location 4680h in parity DRAM = 1.
Location 4680h in DRAM = 34h.

When processor reads from memory location 4680h.

Data DRAM outputs 34h onto D[7:0].
Parity DRAM outputs 1 onto parity output.
Parity generators even output = 1; this disables IOCHK# = 1, so no NMI is generated.

With an error:

Read location 4680h, DRAM outputs 24h on D[7:0].
Parity DRAM outputs 1 onto parity output.

D[7:0] = 0010 0100

Parity generators even o/p = 0; enables IOCHK#
= 0, causes an NMI to be generated.

IOCHK# = 0, sets bit 6 of port 61h; during POST
(power on self test) processor checks for parity
errors by reading port 61h, IOCHK# indicates
parity errors on the expansion bus.

Local memory parity errors are detected when
PARIT# = 0, setting bit 7 of port 61h.

A parity error is considered to be catastrophic,
and through further decode logic an NMI would
be generated. The parity detection circuitry is not
100 per cent fool-proof. No errors are detected
with an even number of errors.
      The POST generally reports errors as follows:

        AAABBBB CC   memory error

This error code will normally be displayed on the
monitor if a memory error occurs.

> **Common memory faults**
>
> **Fault:** The post milestone hang is:
> 'check RAM refresh'.
>
> **Possible cause:** No REFCLK. I/O
> port 61hex is bad. The arbitration logic
> is bad.
>
> **Check:** REFCLK from the ASIC that
> contains the timers. HOLD to the
> processor. HLDA from the processor.
> The control signals to I/O port 61hex.
>
> **Fault:** The post milestone hang is:
> 'check on-board RAM'.
>
> **Possible cause:** Bad DRAM chip.
> DRAM chip not getting control signals.
> DRAM chip not getting correct ad-
> dress signals. Bad data path.
>
> **Check:** RAS#, CAS# and WE# inputs
> to the DRAM. The address inputs to
> the DRAM. Data paths from the
> DRAM chip back to the processor.

The AAABBBB is the memory address that failed, and identifies the failing bank and byte.
CC identifies the failing byte (when converted to binary); any highs represent the bit or bits
that failed within the byte, for example:

0, 4, 8, C = byte 0   1, 5, 9, D = byte 1
2, 6, A, E = byte 2   3, 7, B, F = byte 3

For example:

```
018643B    02    201 memory error
```
Byte 3   bit 1 → D25
and

```
009FF8C    30    201 memory error
```
Byte 0   bits 4 and 5 → D4 and D5

There are also memory faults that cause the board to hang up during the POST. Looking at the POST milestone checkpoint value indicates that the memory subsystem was being checked when the board hung; there are different approaches to tackling these faults. During POST, a walking 1 is written to and then read from memory to detect data faults. Parity errors can be detected by reading port 61h.

7.3   Input/Output Memory

I/O devices provide an interface with the user, for example, video, keyboard. I/O addresses are called ports. The M/IO# line is set to a 0 to select I/O memory. Section 7.6 gives an example of typical I/O address ports. The I/O address space range is from 0000h to FFFFh (64 KB), and are split into two main areas:

- 00h–FFh: embedded I/O addresses, such as DMA, interrupt control, programable timers, keyboard control, CMOS and coprocessor.
- 100h–FFFFh: expansion I/O addresses, such as video control, floppy control, hard drive control, parallel ports and serial ports.

Some I/O addresses are index or data register addresses. The data written to an index register indicates to the device which internal register is to be accessed. The data written to or read from a data register is the actual data value to be placed in the register or the data contained in the register, indicated by the preceding write to the index register. Chapter 7.1.1 gives some examples of how index and data registers are used.

The I/O address decode logic generates the appropriate chip select signal to the I/O device being accessed. For an I/O device to be accessed (read from or written to), it must have:

- An active chip select.
- An active IOW# or IOR#.
- Any address lines necessary to select the exact port within the device.

An I/O device will be selected when the processor is programming the device, writing or getting status information from the device reading. Once an I/O device has been programmed it will perform the appropriate function without being chip selected.

The I/O address decode logic decodes the address

Common I/O memory fault
Communication problems with any I/O device

Possible cause:
- No chip select.
- Bad control signals to the device.
- Bad address lines to the device.

Check:
- The address inputs to both the I/O device and the address decode logic.
- The data bus at the failing I/O device.
- The control signals to both the I/O device and the address decode logic.

put out by the processor, and generates the appropriate chip select signal to the I/O device being accessed. The I/O address decode logic is now generally embedded in the bus controller on ISA systems.

7.3.1 I/O address decode example

Using either the single-step card or test equipment that allows you to take control of the board and stimulate I/O cycles, perform the following procedure. This is useful when checking a failing I/O device, that is, the associated signals. The sequence is as follows:

1. Set the single-step card to trap on an I/O write to port 42h, that is, timer 1 counter 2, as indicated by the I/O map.
2. Power up the system.
3. Check the control signal logic levels.
4. Check the address bus logic levels, including the BE[3:0]#.

For the test equipment:

1. Connect the test equipment to the board, and power up the system.
2. Set the test equipment to loop on a write to port 42h.
3. Check the control signal logic levels.
4. Check the address bus logic levels, including the BE[3:0]#.

7.3.2 Example accesses

1. Keyboard controller has two registers at ports 60h and 64h

Address decode generates KEYCS# = 0. Keyboard ctrl decodes address bit 2 to determine which register is being accessed.

2. CMOS control has two registers at ports 70h and 71h

CMOS contains 64 registers from 0 to 3Fh. To access a CMOS register:

- Write the register value to port 70h (CMOS address register).
- Write data to or read data from port 71h (CMOS data register).

Processor reads from CMOS register 20h:

- Write 20h to port 70h.
- Read data from port 71h.

Processor writes to CMOS register 20h, with data E7h:

- Write 20h to port 70h.
- Write E7h to port 71h.

> **Classic software**
>
> **Unix System V** (distributor: AT&T). System V was the first real attempt at unifying UNIX into a single standardized operating system, and succeeded in merging Microsoft XENIX, SunOS, UNIX 4.3 BSD. Unfortunately, after this there was still a drift by hardware manufacturers to move away from the standard (and define their standards). Although it has been difficult to standardize UNIX, its true strength is its communications protocols, such as TCP/IP, which are now worldwide standards for communicating over the Internet. The biggest challenge to UNIX has been from Windows NT/2000, which has tried to create a hardware independent operating system. UNIX has, in the main, survived because of its simplicity and its reliability.

7.4 Port B

Port B allows for basic system testing. It is based at address 61h and consists of:

- A 4-bit register that can be written to.
- An 8-bit register that can be read from.

The table on the right-hand side gives the definitions for a general implementation of port B circuitry. For example, to drive a tone out to the speaker, and to enable parity and iochk logic, write data X3h to port 61h

During POST:

- Refresh test; bit 4 of port 61h is checked for toggling.
- Memory parity test; bits 6 and 7 are checked for parity errors.

Port B

Bit	I/O	Description
0	R/W	Speaker enable. Gate signal for interval timer 1, counter 2. 0 = disabled, 1 = enabled.
1	R/W	Speaker data. Allows the frequency from timer 1, counter 2 to drive the speaker. 0 = disabled, 1 = enabled
2	R/W	System board parity error NMI enable (parity). 0 = enabled, 1 = disabled and cleared; resetting an NMI.
3	R/W	Expansion board parity error NMI enable (IOCHK#). 0 = enabled, 1 = disabled and cleared; resetting an NMI.
4	R	Refresh detect bit; toggles to the opposite state each time a refresh cycle takes place.
5	R	State of timer 1, counter 2 output signal; frequency used to drive the speaker.
6	R	NMI status, expansion board parity error. 0 = no NMI from IOCHK#. 1 = IOCHK# active, NMI requested.
7	R	NMI status, local memory parity error. 0 = no NMI from system board parity error. 1 = NMI requested.

For example, display last read from port 61h on single-step card indicates data 40h, that is, bit 6 is set high.

Bit 6 = 1 → IOCHK# = 0, active, NMI interrupt requested, expansion bus memory error.

7.5 Exercises

7.5.1 The processor is fetching its first instruction from ROM. Data on the data bus is E6h, but it should be EAh. What possible faults could cause this?

7.5.2 What address is provided to the DRAM first?

7.5.3 Why is a refresh cycle necessary?

7.5.4 If the processor writes data AEh to memory address 6386h, what is the state of the parity bit?

7.5.5 If the POST hangs at the refresh checkpoint, what signals would you check?

7.5.6 What signal indicates to the DRAM that it should accept or provide data?

7.5.7   What is Intel's I/O address space range? How many ports are in that range?

7.5.8   What is the function of the address decode logic?

7.5.9   If the processor is writing to port address 42h, what will be the state of the following signals?

BE [3 : 0]# =   M/IO# =   W/R# =   D/C# =
A9 =   A8 =   A7 =   A6 =   A5 =   A4 =   A3 =   A2 =

7.5.10   When the processor is accessing port 64h, which CS line will be active?

7.5.11   If the processor is writing data to CMOS, what will be the condition of the following signals?

M/IO#   W/R#   D/C#   Address
bus

7.5.12   How many original CMOS locations are there?

7.5.13   Which locations are used for the real-time clock functions?

7.5.14   Which locations are used for system configuration information?

7.5.15   Which locations are used to store the power on password?

7.5.16   Show the bus cycles performed to read CMOS location 1Fh.

7.5.17   If the processor is writing data to port B, what is the condition of the following signals?

M/IO#   W/R#   D/C#   Address bus

7.5.18   State the values and the bits they must be written to ensure that the speaker tones will be heard.

7.5.19   If A3 is read from port B, what can be said about the system?

7.5.20   To disable an NMI, what values must be written to which bits of port B?

| **Common port B fault** |
| No speaker tone |

Possible cause:
- No speaker frequency from the timer.
- Port B is bad.

Check:
- Control signals to the timer.
- Control and data signals to, and from port B.

7.6   I/O Memory Map

Port	Device
000 ... 00F	DMA controller 1 (slave or byte)
020 ... 021	Interrupt controller 1 (master)
040	Timer 1/counter 0 (interval timer)
041	Timer 1/counter 1 (refresh request)
042	Timer 1/counter 2 (speaker output)
043	Timer 1 control word register
048	Timer 2/counter 0 (fail-safe timer)
049	Timer 2/counter 1 (not used)
04A	Timer 2/counter 2 (processor speed control)
04B	Timer 2 control word register
060	Keyboard data I/O register

061	Port B
064	Keyboard status/command register
065	Parallel port bidirectional enable (16 bit decode)
070	NMI enable register (bit [7] = 0)/CMOS index register(bits[6....0])
071	CMOS data register
07C	Reserved
080 ... 08F	DMA page registers
092	Password lock and alternate A20 switching
0A0 ... 0A1	Interrupt controller 2 (slave)
0C 0 ... 0CF	DMA controller 2 (master or word)
0F 0	Clear numeric coprocessor busy
0F 1	Not used
0F8 ... 0FF	Numeric coprocessor command ports
130	Peripheral configuration register
131	Option slot configuration register
132	Time register
133	Mapping register
134 ... 137	Telephone answering machine audio port
170 ... 177	Fixed disk drive controller 2
1F 0 ... 1FF	Fixed disk drive controller 1
201	Game port
204 (alt)	Peripheral configuration register
205 (alt)	Option slot configuration register
206 (alt)	Time register
207 (alt)	Mapping register
208 ... 20B (alt)	Telephone answering machine audio port
278 ... 27F	Parallel port 3
2F8 ... 2FF	Serial port 2
300 ... 30F	Ethernet controller
370 ... 377	Diskette drive controller 2
378 ... 37F	Parallel port 2
3A0 ...3AF	Not used
3B0 ... 3BB	Monochrome adapter
3BC ... 3BF	Parallel port 1
3C0 ... 3DF	Video graphics controller (VGA)
3F0 ... 3F7	Diskette drive controller 1
3F8 ... 3FF	Serial port 1
878 ... 87A	Memory diagnostic ports (later versions only)
A20 ... A3F	Token ring controller
C60 ... C62	DDF registers
C65 ... C66	Reserved
C67/C6FF	Miscellaneous configuration register
C6A	Processor control register
C6C	Reserved
C78 ... C7B	Reserved
C7C	ID Port
C7D ... C7F	Reserved
C80 ... C83	Peripheral ID Function
CA0 ... CA1	Reserved
1065	Reserved
3065	Reserved
C3C6	Reserved
C7C6	Reserved
CBC6	Reserved

7.7 Background on Memory

ROM is a permanent memory and is typically used to store programs and system data. A PC uses a ROM to store the BIOS (Basic I/O System) software. BIOS is a set of basic I/O procedures that allows the system to use the keyboard, monitor, hard disk, and so on. The BIOS also contains the software required to start the system (the bootstrap program).

There are four main types of ROM: mask-programmed ROM, erasable programmable ROM (EPROM), programmable ROM (PROM) and EEPROM (electrically erasable programmable ROM). A mask-programmed ROM has a fixed structure and cannot be erased or reprogrammed. It is normally cost-effective only when producing large quantities.

Classic software

Mac OS and System 7 (developer: Apple) .Microsoft have relied on gradual improvement to their software, especially in their operating systems, while Apple got it right first time with their Mac OS system. Many people believe that this was 10 years ahead of all other systems. With the PC there were many problems, such as keeping compatibility with the original DOS, difficulties with the Intel 8086/88 memory model, support for a great number of peripherals, and the slowness of its internal buses (including the graphics adaptor). These all made software development of the PC difficult. Apple did not have compatibility to deal when they designed the Macintosh as they had a blank piece of paper to work with. They spent as much money on the operating system as they did on developing the hardware for the Macintosh.

An EPROM is programmed by an EPROM programmer. It can be re-programmed by first erasing the data by exposing it to a high-intensity ultraviolet light (the EPROM device has a transparent quartz window). A PROM contains fusable links to store data. It is programmed by a PROM programmer but, unlike the EPROM, it cannot be erased. The best solution for flexibility is an EEPROM (or E^2PROM), which is programmed and erased electrically, typically without removing it from the installed system. Most modern PCs use E^2PROMs for their BIOS as they have the advantage of being updated by software. The main types of ROM are thus:

- **ROM.** Permanent memory that cannot be erased. Economical only in large quantities.
- **PROM.** Programmed by a PROM programmer, but cannot be reprogrammed.
- **EPROM.** Programmed using an EPROM programmer; can be unprogrammed using UV light.
- **EEPROM**. Programmed and erased electrically.

Some typical EPROMs are:

- 27256 (256kb or 262,144 bits);
- 27512 (512kb or 524,288 bits);
- 27101 (1024kb or 1,048,576 bits).

An n-bit addressable ROM has up to 2^n address locations, each of which stores a number of data bits. For example, a 9-bit addressable ROM has 512 different addressable locations, as illustrated in Figure 7.6. A decoder converts the 9-bit address code into one of 512 different address locations. In this case the ROM stores 8 bits for each address location. The presence or absence of a transistor defines a stored bit pattern. These transistors are either fixed (as in a ROM), are sensitive to UV light (as in an EPROM) or can be set up electrically (as in an E^2PROM). When a 0 is stored, then the line connecting the output to the address line is connected to ground via a transistor. If a 1 is stored there is no pull-down transistor present to ground the output line. Figure 7.7 shows a 9-bit addressable ROM with a 5-bit output. The pull-up transistors give a HIGH when there is no pull-down transistor present. In this case memory location 0 stores the bit pattern `11111`, location 1 stores `01110`, location 2 stores `10111`, and so on to location 511 which stores `10111`.

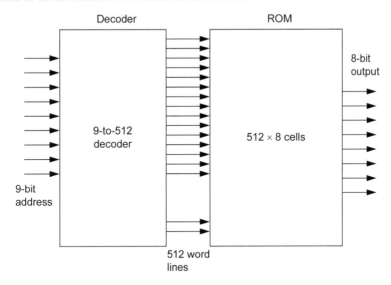

Figure 7.6   ROM addressing

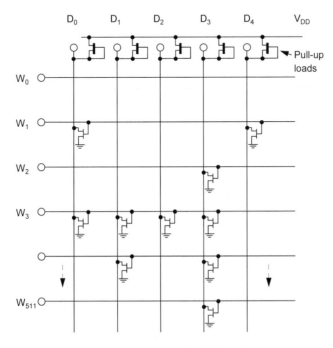

Figure 7.7   9-bit addressable NMOS ROM array

7.7.1   2D addressing

As the number of address lines increases, the address decoder becomes larger. This is unmanageable for large memories. For example, a 1 MB memory would require more than a million addressable memory locations (requiring a 20-to-1,048,576 decoder). An improved memory arrangement is to use a matrix of rows and columns. This technique is described as 2D addressing and is used to reduce the address decoder size.

Figure 7.8 shows an 11-bit addressable memory. Address lines A0–A6 accesses 128 rows of data. Each of these rows contains 128 bits of data. The address lines A7–A10 then select one of 16 lines to give the data lines D0–D7 (128 bits divided by 16 addressable lines gives 8 data bits). It contains 128×128 memory cells giving a total of 65,386 memory cells arranged into 16×128 locations in memory (2,048 locations). Each location holds 8 bits of data and the total storage is thus 2 kB.

7.7.2   Static random access memory

Static RAM (SRAM) retains its data for as long as the power is applied. This type of memory uses a number of transistors arranged as flip-flop storage cells. Each stored bit requires at least six transistors and it is thus difficult to get as much memory as a DRAM IC. Typically, the maximum available, memory on a single IC is 128 kB and is normally found in memories that are less than 512 kB

The left-hand side of Figure 7.9 shows a typical static RAM cell. Transistors Q_3 and Q_4 are pull-up transistors and are either NMOS depletion-mode or CMOS p-type transistors (depending on whether the technology is NMOS or CMOS). To store a bit the cell is selected with the Cell Select line (that is, it is set active HIGH). If bit is HIGH then Q_2 will be ON and Q_1 OFF as its gate is held LOW by Q_2. A LOW on the Bit line causes Q_1 to be OFF and Q_2 ON. When the Cell Select line is placed inactive the cell stores the state.

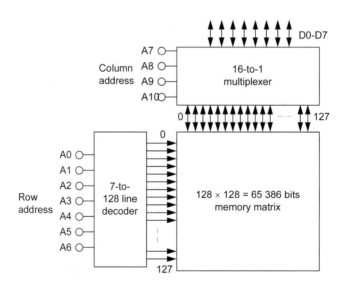

Figure 7.8   2D addressing of a 16kbit memory (2 KB or 2 048 × 8 bits)

7.7.3   Dynamic random access memory

A dynamic ram (DRAM) cell uses fewer transistors than an equivalent SRAM cell and it is thus possible to get a greater amount of DRAM memory on a single IC. This is because DRAM uses small capacitors to store electrical charge; a typical cell is shown on the right-hand side of Figure 7.9. Unfortunately, the capacitor loses its charge over a period of time and it must thus be refreshed every 2– 4 ms. Normally the DRAM array is configured such that a refresh automatically occurs internally for any read or write operation. Thus, because of the continual refreshing and the lost of charge, a DRAM IC consumes more power than a comparable SRAM. Another disadvantage is that the capacitors take a finite time to charge and discharge. This causes DRAMs to be considerably slower than SRAMs.

Memory arrays are made using DRAM cells arranged in rows and columns. A 256×256 (64 kbit) array is shown in Figure 7.10. This requires 256 rows and 256 columns. A DRAM cell is automatically refreshed every time it is read from or written to. It would be difficult to read the contents of every memory cell so DRAM cells are constructed in a way that a single read from memory refreshes a whole row of bits at the same time. The DRAM array in Figure 7.11 has 1,024 cells in each row. When a single row is selected, all 1,024 cells within it are automatically refreshed. Thus, in this case, only 256 refreshes are required to update the whole memory. These reads typically occur every 4 ms – one from each internal row.

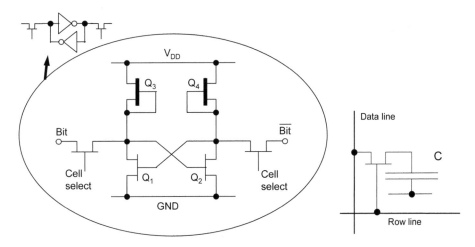

Figure 7.9   Static NMOS RAM cell and a DRAM cell

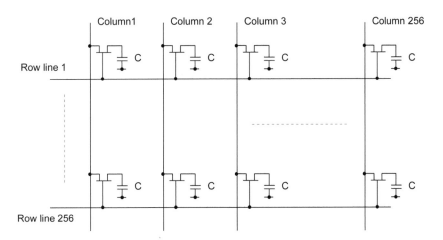

Figure 7.10   Basic DRAM memory array (256×256 bits = $65,536$ bits = 64 Kbit)

The array in Figure 7.11 is a $256\,\text{kb} \times 1$ DRAM memory. The address lines A0–A7 select one of 1,024 rows. These lines are fed into four 1-of-256 multiplexers. The address lines A8–A15 then select one bit from the each of the 1-to-256 multiplexers. One bit is then selected using the address bits A16 and A17. If the single bit is being written to the array then the R/W line is a HIGH and the input on Din is read. A LOW on the R/W line writes the bit to the output line Dout.

To reduce the number of pins on the device the address lines are reduced so that the row and column are latched in two separate operations. The RAS line allows the row address to be latched and CAS the column address. This is shown in Figure 7.11. A $256\,\text{kb} \times 1$ DRAM array thus only requires 16 pins (A0-A8, RAS, CAS, DIN, DOUT, R/W, VCC and GND).

DRAMs can be mounted on a single plug-in unit called a SIMM (single in-line memory module). A 30-pin SIMM is shown in Figure 7.12. It has a 10-bit address line input (A0–A9), an 8-bit data output/ input (D0–D7).

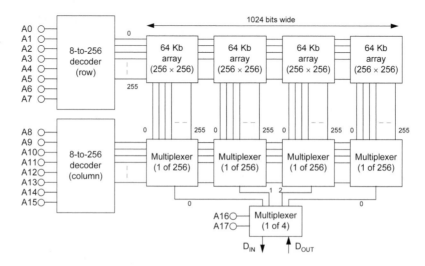

Figure 7.11   256 Kbit × 1 DRAM array

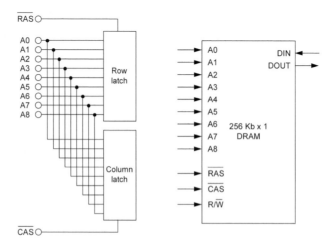

Figure 7.12   Row and column latching

8 UART and PIC

8.1 Introduction

The original PC was built around the 8086 processor, and Intel produced a whole host of devices that created the complete system, including:

- **8255**. Programmable peripheral interface (PPI), used to interface to digital equipment.
- **8259**. Programmable interrupt controller (PIC), used to generate hardware interrupts (such as IRQ3 and IRQ4) from connected devices. Modern PCs use two PICs to generate the interrupts from IRQ0 to IRQ15.
- **8250**. Universal asynchronous receiver transmitter (UART), used for serial communications. Typically, modern PCs contain two 8255-compatible devices, which gives up to two serial communications channels (COM1 and COM2).
- **8254**. Programmable timer counter (PTC), used to create timing intervals, such as the interrupt for DRAM refresh (once every 15 μs), and the interrupt for the time-of-day clock (15 times per second). Typically, modern PCs contain one 8254-compatible device, which gives three timer/counters.
- **8237**. Direct memory access controller (DMAC). Used to set up DMA transfers. Typically, modern PCs contain two 8237-compatible devices, which gives up to seven DMA channels.

These devices are normally mapped into the isolated I/O memory map, and now are integrated into multifunction devices (see chapter 27 for further details). The devices normally still function as they did on the original PC.

This chapter discusses two important devices: the UART and PIC. Their functionalities are now integrated into a multifunction device, but they still operate as if they were discrete devices. The UART transmits and receives characters using RS-232, and will be discussed in more detail in Chapter 25. The PIC is used to interrupt the processor.

8.2 Universal asynchronous receiver transmitter (8250)

The 8250 IC is a 40-pin IC that is used to transmit and receive asynchronous serial communications. Figure 8.1 shows the logic arrangement of the signals and their pin numbers. The connection to the system microprocessor is made through the data bus (D_0–D_7) and the handshaking and address lines ($\overline{DOSTR}$, $\overline{DISTR}$, A_2, A_1, A_0, RESET, and so on).

When the processor wishes to write data to the 8250, it sets the DOSTR and $\overline{DOSTR}$ (data output strobe) lines active, that is, high and low, respectively. When it wants to read data from the 8250, it sets the DISTR and $\overline{\text{DISTR}}$ (data input strobe) lines active, that is, high and low, respectively.

There are seven registers with the device: TD/RD buffer, interrupt enable, interrupt identify, and so on (refer to Figure 8.1). They are selected using the three addressed lines: A_2, A_1 and A_0. If the address $A_2A_1A_0$ is a 000, then the TD/RD register is address, an address of 001 selects the interrupt identify register, and so on. The timings of the transfers are controlled by the write (DOSTR) and read (DISTR) control signals.

The main input RS-232 handshaking lines are

$\overline{\text{RI}}$ (ring indicate), $\overline{\text{DSR}}$ (data set ready) and $\overline{\text{CTS}}$ (clear to send), and the main output handshaking lines are $\overline{\text{RTS}}$ (ready to send) and $\overline{\text{DTR}}$ (data terminal ready). Serial data is output from SOUT and inputted from SIN. Refer to Chapter 25 for more information on RS-232 handshaking.

The clock input lines XTAL1 and XTAL2 connect to a crystal to control the internal clock oscillator. Normally on a PC this clock frequency is set at 1.8432 MHz . The BAUDOT line is the clock frequency divided by 16, and is equal to the Baud rate. As the 1.843 MHz clock is divided by 16, then the maximum Baud rate will thus be 1,843,000 divided by 16, which gives 115,200 Baud.

The 8255 generates hardware interrupts on the INT line. A low input on the RESET input initializes the device and causes the internal registers of the 8250 to be reset. It is normally connected so that at power-up the RESET line is low for a short time. The 16550 is the 16-bit equivalent of the 8250.

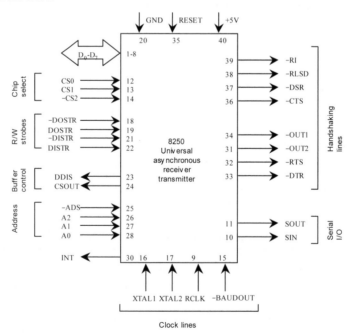

Figure 8.1   8250 pin connections

8.2.1 Frame format

RS-232 uses asynchronous communications, which has a start–stop data format, as shown in Figure 8.2. Each character is transmitted one at a time with a delay between them. This delay is called the inactive time and is set at a logic level high (–12 V), as shown in Figure 8.2. The transmitter sends a start bit to inform the receiver that a character is to be sent in the following bit transmission. This start bit is always a '0'. Next, 5, 6 or 7 data bits are sent as a 7-bit ASCII character, followed by a parity bit and finally either 1, 1.5 or 2 stop bits. Figure 8.2 also shows a frame format and an example transmission of the character 'A', using odd parity. The timing of a single bit sets the rate of transmission. Both the transmitter and receiver need to be set to the same bit-time interval. An internal clock on both sets this interval. These have to be only roughly synchronized and approximately at the same rate as data is transmitted in relatively short bursts.

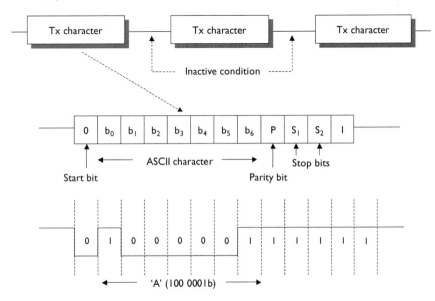

Figure 8.2 Asynchronous communications and RS-232 frame format

Example

An RS-232 serial data link uses 1 start bit, 7 data bits, 1 parity bit, 2 stop bits, ASCII coding and even parity. Determine the message sent from the following bit stream.

First bit sent
⇓
11111010000010110000011111111111111000001111111100011001111010100111111111111

The format of the data string sent is given next:

{idle} 11111 {start bit} 0 {'A'} 1000001 {parity bit} 0 {stop bits } 11 {start bit} 0 {'p'} 0000111 {parity bit} 1 {stop bits} 11 {idle} 11111111 {start bit} 0 {'p'} 0000111 {parity bit} 1 {stop bits} 11 {idle} 11 {start bit} 0 {'L'} 0011001 {parity bit} 1 {stop bits} 11

The message sent was thus 'AppL'.

Error control is data added to transmitted data in order to detect or correct an error in transmission. RS-232 uses a simple technique known as parity to provide a degree of error detection.

A parity bit is added to transmitted data to make the number of 1s sent either even (even parity) or odd (odd parity). It is a simple method of error coding and requires only exclusive OR (XOR) gates to generate the parity bit. The parity bit is added to the transmitted data by inserting it into the shift register at the correct bit position.

A single parity bit can detect only an odd number of errors, that is, 1, 3, 5, and so on. If there is an even number of bits in error then the parity bit will be correct and no error will be detected. This type of error coding is not normally used on its own where there is the possibility of several bits being in error.

Table 8.1	Bits per second related to characters sent per second

Speed (bps)	Characters/second
300	30
1200	120
2400	240

Baud rate

One of the main parameters that specifies RS-232 communications is the rate of transmission at which data is transmitted and received. It is important that the transmitter and receiver operate at roughly the same speed.

For asynchronous transmission, the start and stop bits are added in addition to the 7 ASCII character bits and the parity. Thus a total of 10 bits are required to transmit a single character. With 2 stop bits, a total of 11 bits are required. If 10 characters are sent every second, and if 11 bits are used for each character, then the transmission rate is 110 bits per second (bps).

Table 8.1 lists how the bit rate relates to the characters sent per second (assuming 10 transmitted bits per character). The bit rate is measured in bits per second (bps).

In addition to the bit rate, another term used to describe the transmission speed is the Baud rate. The bit rate refers to the actual rate at which bits are transmitted, whereas the Baud rate relates to the rate

Bits transmitted for each character

	Bits
ASCII character	7
Start bit	1
Stop bit	2
Total	10

at which signaling elements, used to represent bits, are transmitted. Since one signaling element encodes one bit, the two rates are then identical. Only in modems does the bit rate differ from the Baud rate.

Bit stream timings

Asynchronous communications is a stop–start mode of communication and both the transmitter and receiver must be set up with the same bit timings. A start bit identifies the start of transmission and is always a low logic level. Next, the least significant bit is sent followed by the rest of the 7-bit ASCII character bits. After this, the parity bit is sent followed by the stop bit(s). The actual timing of each bit relates to the Baud rate and can be determined using the following formula:

$$\text{Time period of each bit} = \frac{1}{\text{Baud rate}} \text{ s}$$

For example, if the Baud rate is 9,600 Baud (or bps), then the time period for each bit sent is 1/9,600 s, or 104 µs. Table 8.2 shows some bit timings as related to the Baud rate. An example of the voltage levels and timings for the ASCII character 'A' is given in Figure 8.3.

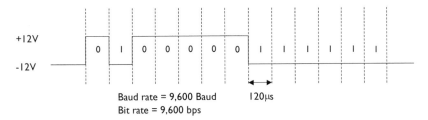

Baud rate = 9,600 Baud
Bit rate = 9,600 bps

Figure 8.3 ASCII 'A' at RS-232 voltage levels.

8.2.2 Programming RS-232

Normally, serial transmission is achieved via the RS-232 standard. Although 25 lines are defined usually only a few are used. Data is sent along the TD line and received by the RD line with a common ground return. The other lines, used for handshaking, are RTS (ready to send) which is an output signal to indicate that data is ready to be transmitted, and CTS (clear to send), which is an input indicating that the remote equipment is ready to receive data.

Table 8.2 Bit timings related to Baud rate

Baud rate	Time for each bit (µs)
1200	833
2400	417
9600	104
19200	52

The 8250 IC is commonly used in serial communications. It can either be mounted onto the motherboard of the PC or fitted to an I/O card. This section discusses how it is programmed. The main registers used in RS-232 communications are the line control register (LCR), the line status register (LSR) and the transmit and receive buffers (see Figure 8.4). The transmit and receive buffers share the same addresses.

The base address of the primary port (COM1:) is normally set at 3F8h and the secondary port (COM2:) at 2F8h. A standard PC can support up to four COM ports. These addresses are set in the BIOS memory and the address of each of the ports is stored at address locations 0040:0000 (COM1:), 0040:0002 (COM2:), 0040:0004 (COM3:) and 0040:0008 (COM4:). Program 8.1 can be used to identify these addresses. The statement

```
                    Program 8.1
#include <stdio.h>
#include <conio.h>
int    main(void)
{
int    far *ptr; /* 20-bit pointer */
       ptr=(int far *)0x0400000; /* 0040:0000 */
       clrscr();
       printf("COM1: %04x\n",*ptr);
       printf("COM2: %04x\n",*(ptr+1));
       printf("COM3: %04x\n",*(ptr+2));
       printf("COM4: %04x\n",*(ptr+3));
       return(0);
}
```

```
ptr=(int far *)0x0400000;
```

initializes a far pointer to the start of the BIOS communications port addresses. Each address is 16 bits, thus the pointer points to an integer value. A far pointer is used, as this can access the full 1 MB of memory; a non-far pointer can only access a maximum of 64 kB.

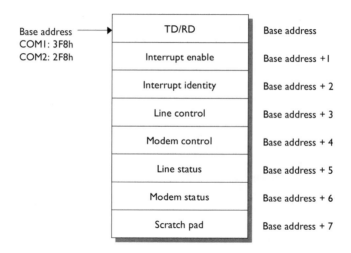

Figure 8.4   Serial communication registers

Sample run 8.1, there are four COM ports installed on the PC. If any of the addresses is zero then that COM port is not installed on the system.

Line status register

The LSR determines the status of the transmitter and receiver buffers. It can only be read from, and all the bits are set automatically by hardware. The bit definitions are given in Figure 8.6. When an error occurs in the transmission of a character one (or several) of the error bits is (are) set to a '1'.

🖥 **Sample run 8.1**

```
COM1: 03f8
COM2: 02f8
COM3: 03e8
COM4: 02e8
```

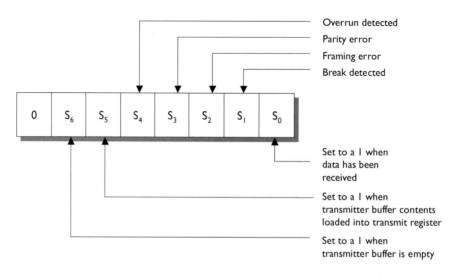

Figure 8.5   LSR

One danger when transmitting data is that a new character can be written to the transmitter buffer before the previous character has been sent. This overwrites the contents of the character being transmitted. To avoid this, the status bit S_6 is tested to determine if there is still a character still in the buffer. If there is, then it is set to a '1', else the transmitter buffer is empty.

To send a character:

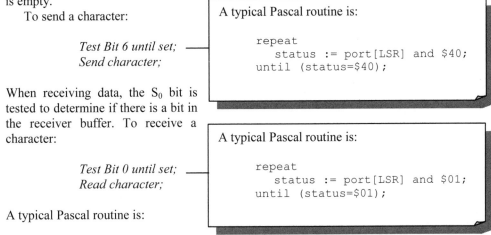

A typical Pascal routine is:

```
repeat
    status := port[LSR] and $40;
until (status=$40);
```

Test Bit 6 until set;
Send character;

When receiving data, the S_0 bit is tested to determine if there is a bit in the receiver buffer. To receive a character:

A typical Pascal routine is:

```
repeat
    status := port[LSR] and $01;
until (status=$01);
```

Test Bit 0 until set;
Read character;

A typical Pascal routine is:

Figure 8.6 shows how the LSR is tested for the transmission and reception of characters.

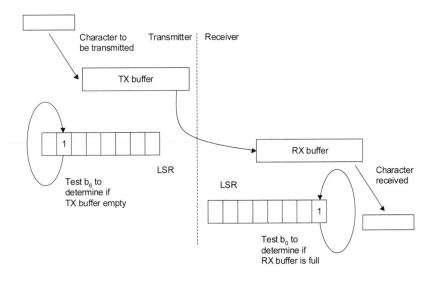

Figure 8.6   Testing of the LSR for the transmission and reception of characters.

Line control register

The LCR sets up the communications parameters. These include the number of bits per character, the parity and the number of stop bits. It can be written to or read from and has a similar function to that of the control registers used in the PPI and PTC. The bit definitions are given in Figure 8.7.

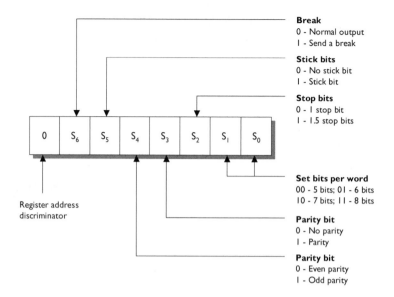

Figure 8.7   LCR

The msb, C_7, must to be set to a '0' in order to access the transmit and receive buffers (TX/RX buffer); if it is set to a '1', the Baud rate divider is accessed. The Baud rate is set by loading an appropriate 16-bit divisor, with the lower 8 bits of the divisor put into the TX/RX buffer address and the upper 8 bits put into the next address after the TX/RX buffer. The value loaded depends on the crystal frequency connected to the IC. Table 8.3 shows the divisor for a crystal frequency is

Table 8.3   Baud rate divisors

Baud rate	Divisor (value loaded into Tx/Rx buffer)
110	0417h
300	0180h
600	00C0h
1200	0060h
1800	0040h
2400	0030h
4800	0018h
9600	000Ch
19200	0006h

1.8432 MHz. In general the divisor, N, is related to the Baud rate by:

$$Baud\ rate = \frac{Clock\ frequency}{16 \times N}$$

For example, for 1.8432 MHz and 9,600 Baud, $N = 1.8432 \times 10^6 / (9600 \times 16) = 12$ (000Ch).

Register addresses

The addresses of the main registers are given in Table 8.4. To load the Baud rate divisor, first the LCR bit 7 is set to a '1', then the LSB is loaded into divisor LSB and the MSB into the divisor MSB register. Finally, bit 7 is set back to a '0'. For example, for 9600 Baud, `COM1` and 1.8432 MHz clock then `0Ch` is loaded in `3F8h` and `00h` into `3F9h`.

When bit 7 is set at a '0' then a read from base address reads from the RD buffer and a write operation writes to the TD buffer. An example of this is shown in Figure 8.8.

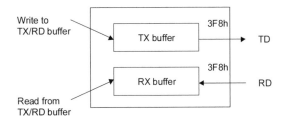

Figure 8.8 Read and write from TD/RD buffer

8.3 Programmable Interrupt Controller (8259)

The 8259 IC is a 28-pin IC used to generate processor interrupts. Figure 8.9 shows the logic arrangement of the signals and their pin numbers. The connection to the microprocessor is made through the data bus (D_0–D_7) and the handshaking and address lines ($\overline{\text{RD}}$, $\overline{\text{WR}}$, A_0, INT and $\overline{\text{INTA}}$).

Table 8.4 Serial communications addresses

Primary	Secondary	Register	Bit 7 of LCR
3F8h	2F8h	TD buffer	'0'
3F8h	2F8h	RD buffer	'0'
3F8h	2F8h	Divisor LSB	'1'
3F9h	2F9h	Divisor MSB	'1'
3FBh	2FBh	LCR	
3FDh	2FDh	LSR	

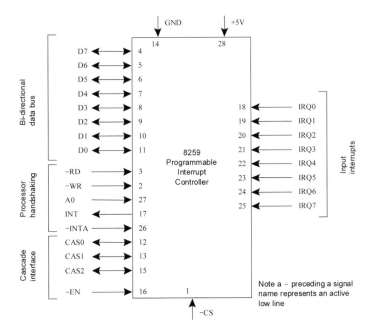

Figure 8.9 8259 pin connections

It has two registers: interrupt control port (ICP) and the interrupt mask register (IMR). The IMR enables and disables interrupt from interrupting the processor. As there are only two registers, there is only one address line, A_0. If A_0 is a 0, then the ICP is addressed; if A_0 is 1, then the IMR is selected. The timing of the transfers is controlled by the read ($\overline{RD}$) and write ($\overline{WR}$) control signals.

When one of the interrupt lines becomes active, and if that interrupt has been enabled, then the 8259 line generates an interrupt on the processor by setting the interrupt line (INT) high. If the processor accepts the interrupt, then it returns an acknowledgement with the $\overline{INTA}$ line. When the PIC receives this acknowledgement, it outputs the type number of the highest priority active interrupt on the data bus lines D0–D7. The processor then reads this.

The chip select signal ($\overline{CS}$) must be a low for the device to be activated.

8.3.1   PCs and interrupts

Interrupts are used when a specific program is to be run. For example, the interrupt service routine designed to determine which key was pressed on the keyboard. When the processor receives an interrupt it:

- Stops executing the current program.
- Saves its current place by pushing register values and flag settings onto its stack pointer (a stack is an area in memory used with push and pop instructions.).
- Runs the interrupt service routine associated with the interrupt that occurred.
- Returns to the place in the program that it was executing before the interrupt occurred; by popping the register and flag values to the back of the stack.

The main elements of interrupts are:

- **Interrupt vector table**. When the processor receives an interrupt it has to find out what the interrupt service routine start address is. The interrupt vector table is an area in memory that contains the starting address of each interrupt service routine.
- **Hardware interrupts**. A hardware interrupt is an interrupt that comes from the system hardware. The two types of hardware interrupt are maskable and non-maskable interrupts.
- **Maskable interrupts**. Maskable interrupts can be masked out by the processor. Many I/O devices have their own interrupt request lines to signal to the system that their own interrupt service routine needs to be run.
- **Interrupt controller**. The interrupt controller keeps track of the interrupt request inputs, and sends the processor an interrupt when one or more devices has an interrupt pending.

> **Classic software**
>
> **Excel for the Macintosh** (developer: Microsoft). Microsoft stole the thunder from VisiCalc and Lotus 1-2-3 when they produced a graphical version of a spreadsheet. Microsoft saw the potential of a graphical spreadsheet and quickly ported it to the PC. In the end, Lotus was too slow to convert Lotus 1-2-3 to Windows (going initially for an OS/2 version), and lost a considerable market share that would never be recovered.

The PC uses two Intel 8259 interrupt controller devices, which are cascaded together and embedded in the interrupt controller (Figure 2.16). Each 8259 has two sets of registers, which are used to program it: initialization command words and operation command words. The patterns written to these registers define the way the device functions. Some of these functions are edge/level triggering for IRQ inputs, single/multiple 8259s in the system, base ID, identify which master IRQ input a slave is attached to, and the interrupt mask settings. The PIC controllers can be set up in many different modes using ICW (initialization command words). Refer to an Intel data book for more information on these modes. The following code initializes the PICs with edge-triggered interrupts and interrupt lines IRQ8–IRQ15 enabled.

```
#define     ICR    0x20   /* Interrupt control port              */
#define     IMR    0x21   /* Interrupt mask register port        */

outportb(ICR,0x13);   /* edge triggered, one 8259, ICW4 required    */
outportb(IMR,8);      /* use interrupt vectors 08h-0Fh for IRQ0-IRQ7 */
outportb(IMR,9);      /* ICW4: buffered mode, normal EOI, 8088       */
```

Note that this initialization is normally carried out when the system is rebooted and there is thus no need to reinitialize it in a user program (unless any of the initialization parameters need to be changed). After initialization, these ports are used to either enable or disable interrupt lines using the IMR or to control the interrupts with the ICR.

In the IMR, an interrupt line is enabled by setting the assigned bit to a 0 (zero). This allows the interrupt line to interrupt the processor. Figure 2.17 shows the bit definitions of the IMR. For example, if bit 0 is set to a 0 then the system timer on IRQ0 is enabled.

Once initialized, the master MR can be accessed at port 21h. Setting an IMR bit = 1 masks out the associated IRQ. Trap on a read from port 21h = BAh (10111010b), IRQ 7, 5, 4, 3, and 1 are masked out.

The 8259 has four internal registers used during operations (as illustrated in Figure 8.10):

> **Common interrupt faults**
> I/O system board failure
>
> **Possible causes:**
> - No chip select.
> - Bad control signals at the interrupt controller.
> - Bad address lines at the interrupt controller.
>
> **Check:**
> - Address inputs to the interrupt controller.
> - Data bus to the interrupt controller.
> - Control signals to the interrupt controller.

- **IMR**. This register allows each of the eight INTR inputs to be disabled individually (see Table 2.7).
- **IRR.** This register keeps track of the interrupt requests that have to be serviced.
- **Priority logic register**. This determines which interrupt should be serviced first, i.e has the highest priority. Generally ISA systems currently use fixed priority. IRQ0 has the highest priority, IRQ1 next, and so on.
- **In-service register (ISR)**. This indicates the level of the interrupt to service, determined by the priority logic.

8.3.2 *Cascaded interrupt controllers*

If the system needs to handle more than eight interrupt requests, multiple interrupt controllers must be used. The interrupt controllers will be cascaded; one will be the master, the others will be slaves. Each slave will use one of the master's IRQ lines. The master is programmed to tell it which IRQ lines are attached to slaves. The slave is programmed to tell it which of the masters IRQ lines it is attached to. Important parameters are:

> **Common interrupt faults**
> Stack overflow
>
> **Possible cause**: Bad interrupt line
>
> **Check**: Interrupt line to the processor, stuck high.

- **Base address**. This is a number assigned to an 8259. The base address of the respective interrupt controller is added to the IRQ number to produce the type code.
- **Type code**. This is the value placed on the data bus by the interrupt controller. The processor multiplies the type code by four. This new value is a memory address used to point to a location in the interrupt vector table and is four bytes wide. These four bytes are the start address of the interrupt service routine to be run.

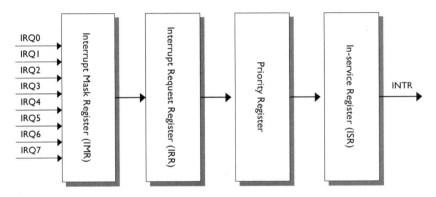

Figure 8.10   8259 registers

8.3.3   Interrupt example

The following example shows the sequence of events when an interrupt request is generated. IRQ 1 is used in the example. Assume the master base address is 08h. The sequence will be:

1. The user presses a key on the keyboard, and a scan code is sent to the keyboard interface.
2. The keyboard controller generates IRQ1.
3. The interrupt controller generates INTR active to the processor.
4. The processor finishes its current instruction, and saves register values and flags onto the stack.
5. The processor and the bus controller as a pair generate an interrupt acknowledge bus cycle (two back-to-back cycles).
6. The interrupt controller sees the first cycle, and starts to form the type code, i.e. base address + IRQ number, 08h + 01h = 09h.

Hardware maskable interrupt assignment/priority

The priority and typical usage of the hardware interrupts is:

Priority	Number	Interrupt source
Highest	IRQ0	Timer 1, counter 0 output, (time of day)
	IRQ1	Keyboard
N/a	IRQ2	Interrupt request from controller 2 (slave)
	IRQ8	Real-time clock
	IRQ9	Expansion bus
	IRQ10	Expansion bus
	IRQ11	Expansion bus
	IRQ12	Mouse
	IRQ13	Coprocessor error
	IRQ14	Hard drive controller
	IRQ15	Expansion bus
	IRQ3	Serial port (COM1)
	IRQ4	Serial port (COM2)
	IRQ5	Parallel port 2
	IRQ6	Floppy controller
Lowest	IRQ7	Parallel port 1

7. On the trailing edge of the second cycle, the interrupt controller places the type code onto the data bus.
8. The processor multiplies the type code by four: 09h × 4 = 24h.

9. The processor reads four bytes from the interrupt vector table at the address formed from the previous multiplication: 24h, 25h, 26h, and 27h.

10. This provides the processor with the start address of the interrupt service routine for keyboard operations; the ISR is run by the processor.

11. At the end of the ISR, the processor retrieves the flag and register values from the stack pointer, and continues to execute the original program from the previous point before the interrupt.

8.3.4 *Non-maskable interrupts*

A non-maskable interrupt cannot be masked within the processor, but can be masked by external hardware on the system board. A non-maskable interrupt (NMI) is caused by:

- Parity errors on expansion memory boards (IOCHK#).
- Parity errors from local memory or DIMMs/SIMMs (PARITY#).
- Fail-safe timer timeout on some systems.

NMIs are enabled through I/O port 70h, with data bit 7 set to a zero (if it is a 1 it disables NMIs). If NMIs are enabled, port B indicates the source of the hardware NMI interrupt.

8.4 Exercises

8.4.1 Which device can be used to create serial communications?

(a) 8255 (b) 8259
(c) 8254 (d) 8250

8.4.2 Which device can be used to create timing and counting operations?

(a) 8255 (b) 8259
(c) 8254 (d) 8250

8.4.3 How many data bits can the 8250 transfer at a time?

(a) 4 (b) 8
(c) 16 (d) 32

8.4.4 What is the clock frequency used with the 8250?

(a) 1.8432MHz (b) 10MHz
(c) 18.432MHz (d) 100MHz

8.4.5 With a Baud rate of 9,600 Baud (or 9,600bps), what is the maximum number of characters that can be transmitted?

(a) 96 (b) 960
(c) 9600 (d) 96000

8.4.6 With a Baud rate of 4,800 Baud (or 4,800bps),

(a) 2.083µs (b) 20.83µs
(c) 208.3µs (d) 2.083ms

8.4.7 How many data bits can the 16550 transfer at any one time?

(a) 4 (b) 8
(c) 16 (d) 32

8.4.8 How many interrupts does the 8259 support?

(a) 4 (b) 8
(c) 16 (d) 32

8.4.9   In the 8250, which register is used to determine whether a character has been received?
    (a)   Transmit register   (b)   Receiver register
    (c)   Line status register   (d)   Line control register

8.4.10   In the 8250, which register is used to determine whether there has been an error in receiving a character?
    (a)   Transmit register   (b)   Receiver register
    (c)   Line status register   (d)   Line control register

8.4.11   In the 8250, which register is used to set up the parity type?
    (a)   Transmit register   (b)   Receiver register
    (c)   Line status register   (d)   Line control register

8.4.12   Which of the following has the highest priority on a PC?
    (a)   IRQ0   (b)   IRQ15
    (c)   IRQ7   (d)   IRQ1

8.4.13   Which interrupt does the system time use?
    (a)   IRQ0   (b)   IRQ15
    (c)   IRQ7   (d)   IRQ1

8.4.14   Which interrupt does the primary parallel port normally use?
    (a)   IRQ5   (b)   IRQ3
    (c)   IRQ7   (d)   IRQ4

8.4.15   Which interrupt does the primary serial port normally use?
    (a)   IRQ5   (b)   IRQ3
    (c)   IRQ7   (d)   IRQ4

8.4.16   Which interrupt does the keyboard use?
    (a)   IRQ0   (b)   IRQ1
    (c)   IRQ12   (d)   IRQ7

8.4.17   Which signal line is used to select the 8259 device?
    (a)   INT   (b)   CS#
    (c)   RD#   (d)   IRQ

8.4.18   Which of the following would generate a non-maskable interrupt (NMI)?
    (a)   Parity error from memory   (b)   Keyboard interrupt
    (c)   Serial port interrupt   (d)   Hard disk interrupt

8.4.19   What is the first thing the processor does in response to an interrupt request?
    (a)   Save the current status of the current program
    (b)   Runs the interrupt service routine
    (c)   Stops the execution of the current program
    (d)   Pushes register values of the current program onto the stack

8.4.20   Which signal line is used to select the 8259 device?
    (a)   INT   (b)   CS#
    (c)   RD#   (d)   IRQ

8.4.21   Which addresses are used by the interrupt mask register and the interrupt request register?
    (a)   20h/21h   (b)   200h/201h
    (c)   20h/30h   (d)   2F8h/3F8h

8.4.22 If the interrupt mask register contains the value of 0110 0010h, which interrupts are masked?

  (a)   IRQ1, IRQ5 and IRQ6
  (b)   IRQ0, IRQ3, IRQ4, IRQ5 and IRQ7
  (c)   IRQ1, IRQ2 and IRQ6
  (d)   IRQ0, IRQ2, IRQ3, IRQ4 and IRQ7

8.4.23 Show that a value of 18h in the Baud rate divisor will give a Baud rate of 4,800 Baud (assume a 1.8432MHz clock).

8.4.24 Explain the purpose of the interrupt controller. If the processor's INT line was stuck active, what would happen?

8.4.25 Name the four registers in the 8259, and briefly describe their functions.

Microprocessor basics

Out-Of-Order Execution. A superscalar processor can issue instructions in an order that is different than the normal sequence. This can only happen if state conflicts can be resolved (with can be achieved with register renaming). For example:

  1. add regA,regB $\rightarrow$ regH
  2. sub regH,regC $\rightarrow$ regC
  3. add regD,regE $\rightarrow$ regH
  4. sub regH,regF $\rightarrow$ regF

can become:

  A. add regA,regB $\rightarrow$ regH (renamed) ⎤ Executed in
  A. add regD,regE $\rightarrow$ regH   ⎦ parallel
  B. sub regH,regC $\rightarrow$ regC   ⎤ Executed in
  B. sub regH (renamed),regF $\rightarrow$ regF   ⎦ parallel

Thus instruction 1 and 3 can be executed in parallel if regH is renamed (thus instruction 3 is executed before instruction 2.

Speculative Execution. In a pipelined processor, branch instructions in the execute stage affect the instruction fetch stage. On a decision there are two possible paths of execution, and the correct one cannot be known until the conditional branch executes. If the processor waits until the conditional branch executes, the stages between fetch and execute are unused, which leads to a delay before execution can resume after the branch (the time taken for new instructions to fill the pipeline again). Speculative execution improves this by choosing an execution path. If this is a correct path there is no branch delay, else any results from the speculative execution have to either be discarded or undone.

PPI and PTC

9.1 Introduction

The PPI and PTC are important devices that are either built into the functionality of the PC, or are available as plug-in cards, and their programming has been standardized around a standard set of I/O registers. The Intel 8254 provides for timer/counter functionality, with three counter/timers. Within the PC, the 8254 is used extensively to generate timing signals, such as the time-of-day interrupt, and the DRAM refresh rate signal. The Intel 8255 provides digital interfacing to peripheral devices, and contains 24 bits of input and/or output in three input/output ports.

9.2 Programmable Peripheral Interface (8255)

The 8255 IC is a 40-pin IC used to input and/or output digital signals. Figure 9.1 shows the logic arrangement of the signals and their pin numbers. The connection to the system microprocessor is through the data bus (D0–D7), and the handshaking and address lines ($\overline{RD}$, $\overline{WR}$, A1, A0 and RESET).

There are four registers in the device: port A, port B, port C and the control register. Port A, port B and port C link to the input/output lines PA0–PA7, PB0–PB7 and PC0–PC7, respectively. The register is selected using the two address lines, A0 and A1, by setting A1A0 to:

- 00 for port A.
- 01 for port B.
- 10 for port C.
- 11 for control register.

The other signal lines are:

- $\overline{RD}$, $\overline{WR}$. These control transfers for read ($\overline{RD}$) and write ($\overline{WR}$) operations.
- RESET. A low input on the RESET input initializes the device and causes a reset of the internal registers of the 8255. This is normally connected so that at power-up the RESET line is low for a short time.
- $\overline{CS}$. This is the chip select signal and must be a low to activate the device.

9.2.1 Programming the PPI

Each 8255 has 24 input/output lines. These are grouped into three groups of 8 bits and are named port A, port B and port C. A single 8-bit register, known as the control register, programs the functionality of these

Table 9.1 PPI addresses

Port address	Function
BASE_ADDRESS	Port A
BASE_ADDRESS+1	Port B
BASE_ADDRESS+2	Port C
BASE_ADDRESS+3	Control register

ports. Port C can be split into two halves to give port C (upper) and port C (lower). The ports and the control register map into the input/output memory with an assigned base address. The arrangement of the port addresses with respect to the base address is given in Table 9.1.

Figure 9.2 shows the functional layout of the 8255. The control register programs each of the ports to be an input or an output and also programs their mode of operation. There are four main parts that are programmed: port A, port B, port C (upper) and port C (lower).

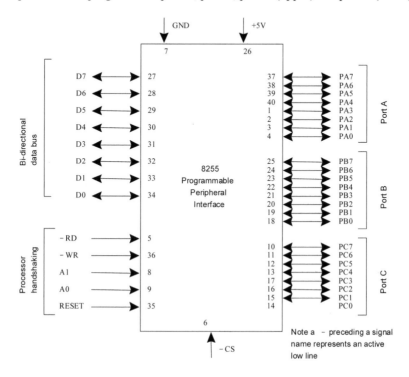

Figure 9.1 8255 pin connections

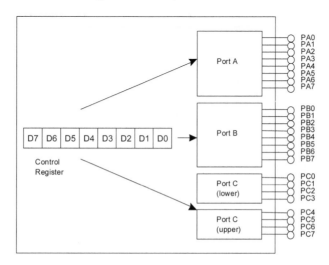

Figure 9.2 Layout of PPI

Figure 9.3 shows the definition of the control register bits. The msb (most significant bit) D7 makes the device either active or inactive. If it is set to a 0 it is inactive, else it will be active. The input/output status of port A is set by D4. If it is a 0, then port A is an output, else it is an input. The status of port B is set by D1, port C (lower) by D0 and port C (upper) by D3.

Port A can operated in one of three modes – 0, 1 and 2. These are set by bits D5 and D6. If they are set to 00 then mode 0 is selected, 01 to mode 1 and 10 to mode 2. Port B can be used in two modes (modes 0 and 1), which are set by bit D2. Examples of bit definitions and their modes of operation are given in Table 9.2.

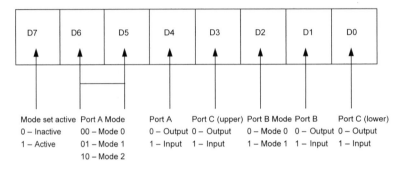

Figure 9.3   PPI control register bit definitions

Mode 0

Mode 0 is the simplest mode and has no handshaking. In this mode the bits on port C can be programmed as inputs or outputs.

Mode 1

Mode 1 allows handshaking for data synchronization. Handshaking is normally required when one device is faster than another. In a typical handshaking operation the originator of the data asks the recipient if it is ready to receive data. If it is not, then the recipient sends back a 'not ready for data' signal. When it is ready, it sends a 'ready for data' signal. The originator then sends the data and the recipient sets the 'not ready for data' signal until it has read the data.

If ports A and B are inputs then the bits on port C have the definitions given in Table 9.3.

When inputting data, the $\overline{\text{STB}}$ going low (active) writes data into the port. After this data is written into the

Table 9.2   Example bit patterns for control register

Bit pattern	Mode of operation
01101000	Device is inactive as D7 set to 0
10011000	Mode 0 Port A input, Port C (upper) input, Mode 0 Port B output, Port C (lower) output
10101000	Mode 1 Port A output, Port C (upper) input, Mode 0 Port B output, Port C (lower) output

Table 9.3   Mode 1 handshaking lines for inputting data

Signal	Port A	Port B
Strobe ($\overline{\text{STB}}$)	PC4	PC2
Input buffer full ($\overline{\text{IBF}}$)	PC5	PC1

port, the IBF line automatically goes high. This remains high until the data is read from the port.

If any of the ports are outputs, then the bit definitions of port C are as given in Table 9.4. In this mode, writing data to the port causes the $\overline{OBF}$ line to go low. This indicates that data is ready to be read from the port. The $\overline{OBF}$ line stays low until $\overline{ACK}$ is pulled low (the recipient has read the data).

Table 9.4 Mode 1 handshaking lines for outputting data

Signal	Port C	Port B
Output Buffer Full ($\overline{OBF}$)	PC7	PC1
Acknowledge ($\overline{ACK}$)	PC6	PC2

Mode 2

This mode allows bidirectional I/O. The signal lines are given in Table 9.5.

Table 9.5 Mode 2 operation for bidirectional I/O

Signal	Port A
$\overline{OBF}$	PC7
$\overline{ACK}$	PC6
$\overline{STB}$	PC4
IBF	PC5

9.2.2 Digital I/O programs

Program 9.1 outputs the binary code from 0 to 255 to port B with a one-second delay between changes. The program exits when the output reaches 255. A delay routine has been added which uses the system timer. Figure 9.4 shows a typical set-up to test the program where port B has been connected to eight light-emitting diodes (LEDs).

In 8086 Assembly Language a macro is defined using the equ statement. Program 9.1 uses these to define the port addresses. This helps to make the program more readable and makes it easier to make global changes. For example, a different base address is relatively easy to set up, as a single change to BASE_ADDRESS automatically updates all port defines in the program. In this case, the base address is 3B0h. This address should be changed to the required base address of the DIO card.

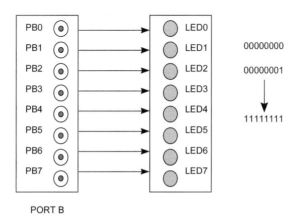

Figure 9.4 Possible system set-up

The statements

```
        mov dx,CNTRLREG      ; set up PPI with
        mov al,90h           ; Port B as Output
        out dx,al
```

Output the value 90h (1001 0000b) to the control register (CNTRLREG). The statements

```
        mov ax,00h
loop1:
        mov dx,PORTB
        out dx,al             ; output to Port B
        call delay
        inc ax
        cmp ax,100h
        jnz loop1             ; repeat until all 1s
```

initially set the AL register to 00h. The next two statements (mov dx, PORTB and out dx,al) output the value of AL to port B. Next, the delay routine is called (with call delay). This routine delays for a period of 1 second. Next, the AL register is incremented (inc al). After this, the AL register value is compared with 100h (0001 0000 0000b). The result of the compare statement is not equal to zero, then the program loops back to the loop1: label.

📖 Program 9.1

```
code            SEGMENT
                ASSUME cs:code
BASEADDRESS EQU     03B0h ; change this as required
PORTA       EQU     BASEADDRESS
PORTB       EQU     BASEADDRESS+1
CNTRLREG    EQU     BASEADDRESS+3
;    program to output to Port B counts in binary until from 00000000
;    to 11111111 with approximately 1 second delay between changes
start:
        mov dx,CNTRLREG      ; set up PPI with
        mov al,90h           ; Port B as Output
        out dx,al
        mov ax,00h
loop1:
        mov dx,PORTB
        out dx,al             ; output to Port B

        call delay
        inc ax
        cmp ax,100h
        jnz loop1             ; repeat until all 1s

        mov ah,4cH            ; program exit
        int 21h               ;

        ; ROUTINE TO GIVE 1 SECOND DELAY USING THE PC TIMER
DELAY:  push ax
        push bx
        mov ax,18             ; 18.2 clock ticks per second;
        ; Address of system timer on the PC is 0000:046C (low word)
        ; and 0000:046E (high word)
        mov bx,0
        mov es,bx
        ; Add the number of required ticks of the clock (ie 18)
        add ax,es:[46CH]
        mov bx,es:[46EH]
```

```
loop2:    ; Compare current timer count with AX and BX
          ;  if they are equal 1 second has passed
          cmp bx,es:[46EH]
          ja loop2
          jb over
          cmp ax,es:[46CH]
          jg loop2

over:     pop bx
          pop ax
          ret

code      ENDS
          END     start
```

> **Common timer faults**
>
> Board hangs at initialize time of day milestone checkpoint.
>
> **Possible cause:** No IRQ0 from the timer to the interrupt controller. Note that this is generally now embedded in an ASIC.
> No INTR to the processor.
>
> **Check:** Control signals to the timer. The INTR input to the processor.

Program 9.2 reads the binary input from port A and sends it to port B. It will stop only when all the input bits on port A are 1s. It shows how a byte can be read from a port and then outputted to another port. Port A is used in this example as the input and port B as the output. Figure 9.5 shows how port A could be connected to input switches and port B to the LEDs. Loading the bit pattern 90h into the control register initializes the correct set-up for ports A and B.

Programs 9.3 and 9.4 show an example of how a C/C++ program interfaces with the isolated I/O. They use the functions `_outp()` to output a byte to a port and `_inp()` to input a byte from a port.

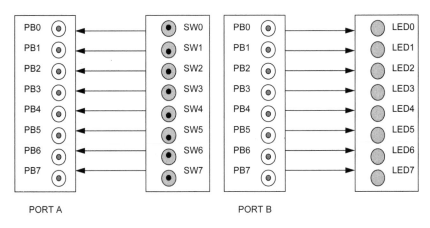

PORT A   PORT B

Figure 9.5 Typical system set-up

📖 Program 9.2

```
code        SEGMENT
            ASSUME cs:code
; program to read from Port A and send to
; Port B. Program stops with all 1's
start:
            mov dx,3B3h
            mov al,90h
            out dx,al
loop:       mov dx,3B0h
            in al,dx        ; read from Port A
```

```
            mov dx,3B1h
            out dx,al        ; output to Port B

            cmp al,ffh
            jnz loop:        ; repeat until all 1s
            mov ah,4cH       ; program exit
            int 21h          ;
code        ENDS
            END     start
```

📖 Program 9.3

```
/*    ppi_1.c                                                     */
/*    Program that will count from 0 to 255                       */
/*    and display it to PORT B. One second between counts         */

#define    BASE_ADDRESS    0x3B0 /* change this as required       */
#define    PORTA           BASE_ADDRESS
#define    PORTB           (BASE_ADDRESS+1)
#define    PORTC           (BASE_ADDRESS+2)
#define    CNTRL_REG       (BASE_ADDRESS+3)

// #include    <dos.h>      /* required for outportb() */
#include    <conio.h>   /* required for _outp() */
#include    <time.h>    /* required for time() */
#include    <stdio.h>   /* required for printf() */

void my_delay(int secs);

int    main(void)
{
/*    NOTE: It may be better to define i is an integer (int)      */
/*    as it is easier to display the value in the debugger        */
unsigned char   i=0;

      _outp(CNTRL_REG,0x90);

      // for Turbo C use outportb(CNTRL_REG,0x90); /*set A input, B output*/
      for (i=0;i<=255;i++)
      {
         _outp(PORTB,i);
         // for Turbo C use outportb(PORTB,i);
         my_delay(1);                   /* wait 1 second */
         printf("%d ",i);
      }
      return(0);
}

void my_delay(int secs)
{
time_t oldtime,newtime;

      time(&oldtime);
      do
      {
         time(&newtime);
      } while ((newtime-oldtime)<secs);
}
```

Common timer faults

No speaker tone

Possible cause: No speaker frequency from the timer. Port B bad.

Check: Control signals to the timer. Port B signals; see port B section.

📖 Program 9.4

```
/*    ppi_2.c                                                     */
#define    BASE_ADDRESS    0x3B0 /* change this as required       */
#define    PORTA           BASE_ADDRESS
```

```
#define      PORTB           (BASE_ADDRESS+1)
#define      PORTC           (BASE_ADDRESS+2)
#define      CNTRL_REG       (BASE_ADDRESS+3)

// #include   <dos.h>       /* required for outportb() */
#include    <conio.h>       /* required for _outp() */
#include    <time.h>        /* required for time() */
#include    <stdio.h>       /* required for printf() */

void  my_delay(int secs);

int    main(void)
{
unsigned char  i=0;

     _outp(CNTRL_REG,0x90);
     /*     for Turbo C use outportb(CNTRL_REG,0x90); */
     /*     set A input, B output                     */
     do
     {
       i=_inp(PORTA);     /* read from Port A    */
       _outp(PORTB,i);    /* output to Port B    */
       /* for Turbo C use i=inportb(PORTA) and   */
       /* outportb(PORTB,i);                     */
       my_delay(1);                   /* wait 1 second */
       printf("Input value is %d\n",i);
     }  while (i!=0xff)
     return(0);
}

void my_delay(int secs)
{
time_t oldtime,newtime;
     time(&oldtime);
     do
     {
       time(&newtime);
     } while ((newtime-oldtime)<secs);
}
```

9.3   Programmable Timer Controller (8254)

The 8254 IC is a 24-pin IC used to count pulses and in timing applications. Figure 9.6 shows the logic arrangement of the signals and their pin numbers. The connection to the system microprocessor is made through the data bus (D0–D7) and the handshaking and address lines ($\overline{RD}$, $\overline{WR}$, A1 and A0).

There are four registers in the device: counter 0, counter 1, counter 2 and the control register. The register is selected using the two address lines, A0 and A1, which are selected by setting A1A0 to:

- 00 for counter 0.
- 01 for counter 1.
- 10 for counter 2.
- 11 for control register.

The other signal lines are:

Common timer faults

Board hangs at the timer test milestone checkpoint.

Possible cause: Timer not getting correct address, data, or control signals.

Check:
- Address inputs to timer.
- Data bus to timer.
- Control signals to timer.

- $\overline{RD}$, $\overline{WR}$. These control transfers for read ($\overline{RD}$) and write ($\overline{WR}$) operations.
- RESET. A low input on the RESET input initializes the device and causes a reset of the internal registers of the 8254. This is normally connected so that at power-up the RESET line is low for a short time.
- $\overline{CS}$. This is the chip select signal and must be a low to activate the device.

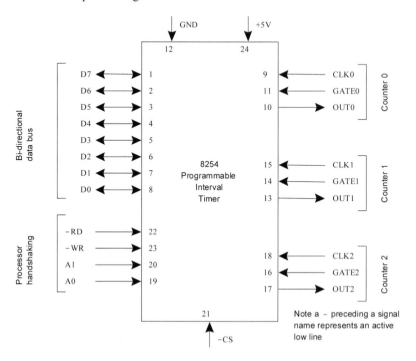

Figure 9.6   8254 pin connections

PC systems can be fitted with an 8254 PTC (programmable timer/counter) integrated circuit (IC) to give timing and counting capabilities. Each IC has 24 pins and contains three timer/counters, each of which can be programmed with differing functions. Typically, they are fitted onto a multifunction DIO interface card, or are fitted to a counter/timer I/O board. In-line switches or wire jumpers normally set the base address at which these ICs map into the isolated memory. The connections to each timer/counter are:

- **CLOCK INPUT**. Line input.
- **GATE**. Disables/enables timer/counter. A high level on the GATE enables the timer, else it is disabled. If the GATE is not connected then the input level floats. This is sensed as a high input and the counter will be active.
- **OUTPUT**. Line output.

Each counter has a 16-bit counter register which gives a count range of 0000000000000000b   (0   or   0000h)   to

> **Classic software**
>
> **Adobe Type** (developer: Adobe). An important change in desktop publishing was the use of enhanced fonts, such as the Type 1 PostScript fonts available from Adobe. Adobe has also produced one of the standard methods to transfer files around computer systems, without losing any layout information. This form is named PDF (portable document format), and is now well integrated with the World Wide Web.

111111111111
1111b (65 535
or FFFFh),
and it always
counts down.
A diagram of
a counter is
given in Fig-
ure 9.7. The
control regis-

Table 9.4 PTC addresses		
Function	*Address*	*Used as*
Counter 0 Read/Write Buffer	BASE_ADDRESS	16-bit register
Counter 1 Read/Write Buffer	BASE_ADDRESS+1	16-bit register
Counter 2 Read/Write Buffer	BASE_ADDRESS+2	16-bit register
Counter Control Register	BASE_ADDRESS+3	To program the counters

ter programs each of the three timer/counters on each IC. Its address is set with respect to the base address, as given in Table 9.6.

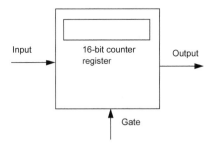

Figure 9.7 Diagram of counter/timer circuit

9.3.1 *Control register*

The control register programs the functionality of each of the three counters/timers. Figure 9.9 shows the format of this register. The counter to be programmed is set up by setting bits SC1 and SC0. If a PC card is used, then only 8 bits can be loaded to or read from the PTC at any time. Thus, to access the 16-bit counter register there must be two read or write operations. Bits RL1 and RL0 control the method of access. If these are set to 11 then the first byte written/read to/from the counter register is the LSB (least significant byte). The next write/read accesses the MSB (the most significant byte). Mode bits M2, M1 and M0 control the mode of the counter; these are discussed in the next section.

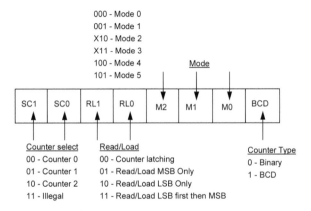

Figure 9.8 Timer control register bit definition

9.3.2 Modes

The bits M2, M1 and M0 in the counter control register program the PTC mode. These are:

- **Mode 0** (interrupt on terminal count). In this mode the output is initially low and stays low until the number of clock cycles has been counted. If the gate is low then the output is disabled. Figure 9.9 shows an example of mode 0 with a counter value of 4.
- **Mode 1** (programmable one-shot). The programmable one-shot mode is similar to mode 0, but the output starts initially high. The output goes low at the start of the count and remains low until the count finishes. It then goes high. A low-to high-transition on the GATE input initiates the count. A low or high level on the GATE after this has no effect on the count. Figure 9.10 shows an example of mode 1 with a counter value of 4.
- **Mode 2** (rate generator). In this mode the inputted CLOCK pulses are divided by the value in the counter register. The output goes low for one cycle and high for the rest of the cycle. Figure 9.11 shows an example of mode 2 with a counter value of 4. In this case the output is high for three cycles and low for one. As with mode 1, the count is initiated by a low-to-high transition on the GATE.
- **Mode 3** (square wave generator). The square wave generator is similar to mode 2 but the output is a square wave when the value in the counter is even, or is high for an extra cycle when the value of the count is odd. Figure 9.12 shows an example of mode 3 with a counter value of 4. In this case the output is low for two cycles and high for two cycles. If the counter is loaded with 5 the output is high for three cycles and low for two cycles. As with mode 1, the count is initiated by a low-to-high transition on the GATE.
- **Mode 4** (software triggered strobe). This is similar to mode 2, except that the GATE does not initiate the count. The output goes high for the count and goes low for one clock cycle. The output then goes back to high.
- **Mode 5** (hardware triggered strobe). This mode is similar to mode 2, except that the GATE input has no effect on the count. It starts counting after the rising edge of the input and then goes low for one clock period when the count is reached. Table 9.7 summarizes the control that the gate has on the mode.

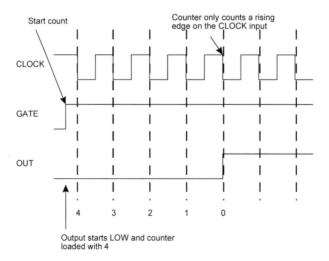

Figure 9.9   Mode 0 operation

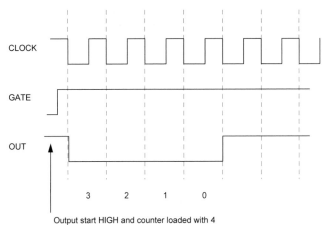

Output start HIGH and counter loaded with 4

Figure 9.10   Mode 1 operation

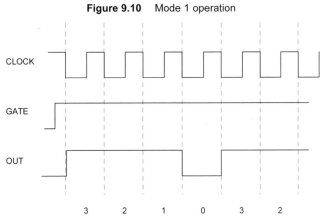

Count HIGH for 3 counts and LOW for 1

Figure 9.11   Mode 2 operation

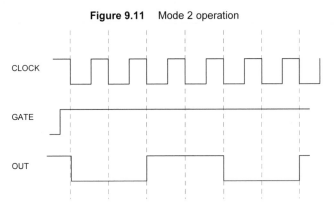

Count HIGH for 2 counts and LOW for 2

Figure 9.12   Mode 3 operation

Table 9.5   Gate control

Mode	GATE low	GATE low–high transition	GATE high	Output signal
0	Disable	None	Enable	See Figure 9.9
1	None	Initiate counting	None	See Figure 9.10
2	Disable; set output high	Initiate counting	Enable	See Figure 9.11
3	Disable; set output high	Initiate counting	Enable	See Figure 9.12
4	Disable	None	Enable	As mode 2
5	None	Start count	None	As mode 2

9.3.3   *Producing timer programs*

Program 9.5 uses mode 3 to produce a square wave of a frequency that is the input clock divided by an entered value. This clock input can be taken from an electronic clock output (for example, 25 kHz) or could be taken from a switched input. An oscilloscope (or LED if the input is relatively slow) can be used to display the input and output. Note that the GATE must be high in order for the counter to be active; a low disables the count and sets the output to a high.

The mode of counter 0 is set up using the statement

```
_outp(CNTRL_REG, 0x36);
```

which loads the bit pattern 0011 0110b into the control register. Taking each of the bits in turn, starting from the most significant bit, then 00 sets up counter 0, 11 specifies that the LSB will be loaded into the counter register then the MSB, 011 selects mode 3 and 0 specifies a binary count.

The statement

```
_outp(COUNTER0, d & 0x00FF);
```

masks the LSB of the variable d and puts it into the LSB of the counter register. The MSB byte of d is then loaded into the MSB of the counter by the following statement:

```
_outp(COUNTER0, d >> 8);
```

This uses the shift right operator (>>) to move the MSB bits eight positions to the right (that is, into the LSB positions).

Program 9.5

```
/*    This program divides the input clock on counter 0     */
/*    by an entered value. The GATE is set to a high and    */
/*    the output is OUT0.                                    */
#include <stdio.h>

#define  BASE_ADDRESS    0x3B8 /* change for system used on */
#define  COUNTER0        BASE_ADDRESS
#define  COUNTER1        (BASE_ADDRESS+1)
#define  COUNTER2        (BASE_ADDRESS+2)
#define  CNTRL_REG       (BASE_ADDRESS+3)

void  set_up_PTC(int);  /* ANSI C prototype definitions */
int   main(void)
{
```

```
int    Divide;

       puts("Enter the value the clock to be divided by>");
       scanf("%d",&Divide);
       set_up_PTC(Divide);
       puts("The Programmable counter is programmed");
       return(0);
}

void set_up_PTC(int d)
{
       outportb(CNTRL_REG, 0x36);
       /*0011 0110 - Binary Select (0)                                    */
       /*Mode Select 3 (011) Square wave generator                        */
       /*Read/Load Low Byte then High Byte (11)                           */
       /*Counter 0 selected (0)                                           */
       _outp(COUNTER0, d & 0x00FF);/*Load low byte into counter           */
       _outp(COUNTER0, d >> 8);   /*Load high byte into counter           */
}
```

Program 9.6 uses mode 2 to produce a rate generator.

Program 9.6

```
/* ·  This program divides the input clock on counter 0               */
/*    by an entered value to produce a rate generator.                */
/*    The GATE is set to a high and the output is OUT0.               */
/*    The output goes low for one cycle then high for the rest        */
#define  BASE_ADDRESS    0x3B8 /* change for system used on            */
#define  COUNTER0     BASE_ADDRESS
#define  COUNTER1    (BASE_ADDRESS+1)
#define  COUNTER2    (BASE_ADDRESS+2)
#define  CNTRL_REG       (BASE_ADDRESS+3)

#include <stdio.h>
#include <dos.h>

void  set_up_PTC(int);  /* ANSI C prototype definition   */
int   main(void)
{
int    Divide;
       puts("Enter value clock to be divided by>>");
       scanf("%d",&Divide);
       set_up_PTC(Divide);
       puts("The Programmable counter is programmed");
       return(0);
}

void  set_up_PTC(int d)
{
       outportb(CNTRL_REG, 0x34);
       /*0011 0100 - Binary Select (0)                                    */
       /*Mode Select 2 (010) Rate generator                               */
       /*Read/Load Low Byte then High Byte (11)                           */
       /*Counter 0 selected (0)                                           */

       _outp(COUNTER0, d & 0x00FF);/*Load low byte into counter           */
       _outp(COUNTER0, d >> 8);   /*Load high byte into counter           */
}
```

Program 9.7 is an assembly language program; divide by 10 counter.

📖   Program 9.7

```
code            SEGMENT
                ASSUME cs:code
BASEADDRESS     EQU     03B8H     ; change this as required
COUNTER0        EQU     BASEADDRESS
COUNTER1        EQU     BASEADDRESS+1
CNTRLREG        EQU     BASEADDRESS+3
; 8088 program to set up divide by 10 counter.
start:
        mov dx,CNTRLREG         ; Control Reg.
        mov al,36h              ;
        out dx,al              ; Square wave, etc.
        mov dx,COUNTER0
        mov dx,10              ; Low byte
        out al,dx
        mov al,00              ; High byte
        out al,dx
        mov ah,4cH             ; program exit
        int 21h               ;
code    ENDS
        END     start
```

9.3.4   Pulse counting programs

In Program 9.8, the PTC counts a number of clock pulses on counter 0. These pulses could be generated by many means, such as from switches, clock pulses, and so on. The counter always counts down and is initialized with 1111 1111 1111 1111b with the lines

```
_outp(CNTRL_REG,0x30);
_outp(COUNTER0,0xff);     /* load LSB   */
_outp(COUNTER0,0xff);     /* load MSB   */
```

This is latched into the counter register using the statement

```
_outp(CNTRL_REG, 0x00);
```

The getcount() function contains the statements given next. It reads the LSB and MSB of the counter register, then scales them so that the MSB is placed above the LSB. This is achieved by shifting the bits in the MSB by eight positions to the left. The scaled value is then subtracted from the initialized value to produce the final count.

```
lsb=inportb(portid);
msb=inportb(portid);
return(0xffff-(lsb+(msb<<8)));
```

📖   Program 9.8

```
/* Program which will determine the number of            */
/* clock pulses on Counter 0                             */
#include <stdio.h>
#include <conio.h>   /* required for clrscr() and kbhit() */

#define  BASE_ADDRESS   0x3B8 /* change for system used on   */
#define  COUNTER0       BASE_ADDRESS
#define  COUNTER1       (BASE_ADDRESS+1)
#define  COUNTER2       (BASE_ADDRESS+2)
#define  CNTRL_REG      (BASE_ADDRESS+3)

int      getcount(int portid);
void     set_up_PTC(void);
```

```
int     main(void)
{
int     count;
        set_up_PTC();
        do
        {
            clrscr();
            count=getcount(COUNTER0);
            printf("count is %d\n",
                            count);
            delay(1000);
        } while (!kbhit());
        return(0);
}

void set_up_PTC(void)
{
        _outp(CNTRL_REG, 0x30);
        _outp(COUNTER0,0xff);
                /* reset counter  */
        _outp(COUNTER0,0xff);      /* reset counter */
        _outp(CNTRL_REG, 0x00);    /* latch counter */
}
int     getcount(int portid)
{
int     lsb,msb;
        /* Count starts from 0xffff and then counts down    */
        lsb=inportb(portid);
        msb=inportb(portid);
        return(0xffff-(lsb+(msb<<8)));
}
```

Common timer faults

Board hangs at refresh milestone checkpoint.

Possible cause:

- Arbitration logic.
- Bad port B.
- No refresh signal.

Check:

- HOLD to and HLDA from the processor.
- Refresh output.
- Control signals to port B; see port B section

9.4   Timers and the PC

9.4.1   Timer 1

The first timer has a base address of 40h. The functions and addresses are:

- **40h (counter 0).** This is used as an interval timer. It is programmed as a square wave generator with an output frequency of approximately 18 Hz (one clock period every 55 ms). It is attached to IRQ0, and is used for DOS time of day.
- **41h (counter 1).** This is used as the refresh request timer. It is programmed as a rate generator with an output frequency of approximately 66kHz (one clock period every 15µs). It is used to initiate a refresh cycle for memory, and provides an input to REFCLK.
- **42h (counter 2).** This is used as the frequency for the speaker. It is programmed as a square wave generator; the programmer varies the output frequency to change the tone. Note that to drive the speaker, port B bits 0 and 1 must be high.
- **43h (control).**

CLASSIC SOFTWARE

Windows 3.x (developer: Microsoft). The first two versions of Microsoft Windows were pretty poor. They had poor interfaces, and still had all of the constraints of DOS (which are, of course, great). Microsoft Windows 3.0 changed all that with an enhanced usage of icons and windows, greater integration, increased memory usage. It was still 16-bit, but started to make full use of the processor, and gave a hint of the forthcoming multitasking (two processes at a time using time sharing). Other enhancement were OLE, True Type fonts, and drag-and-drop commands. Windows for Workgroups was Microsoft's first attempt at trying to network PCs together, but it was too complicated to set up, and not very powerful.

For example, to test counter 1:

- I/O write 54h to port address 43h.
- I/O write 12h to port address 41h.

The results should be:

- On the refresh pin, a 66-kHz square wave should be seen.
- Continually read from port 61h (port B). Bit 4 should toggle (the refresh detect bit). This is discussed in more detail in section 7.5.

For the interval timer, the following produces an 18-Hz square wave signal:

> **Classic software**
>
> **Lotus Notes 3.0.** Lotus had been losing a large market share for both their word processors (to Word) for their spreadsheets (to Excel). They thus had to come up with something that was innovative, easy to use, but powerful, in a business environment. Their answer was truly inspirational: Lotus Notes. It successfully integrates electronic mail and other standard applications in an easy-to-use manner.

- Write to port 43h, data 36h (00110110b – gives 00b –counter 0, 11b –load LSB followed by MSB, 011 –mode 3 for square wave, 0b – binary count). Refer to Figure 9.9.
- Write to port 40h, data 00h. LSB
- Write to port 40h, data 00h. MSB.

The input frequency is 1.2 MHz, thus the counter will count from 0000h to FFFFh for a single count. The frequency of the output will thus be:

$$\text{Frequency} = \frac{1.2}{65636}\text{MHz} = 18.3\text{Hz}$$

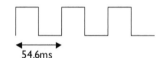

54.6ms

For the refresh request timer, the following produces a 15 µs pulse period:

- Write to port 43h, data 54h. (01110100b – gives 01b – counter 1, 01b – load LSB followed by MSB, 010 – mode 2, low for one clock cycle, and high for the rest of the pulse period, 0b – binary count). Refer to Figure 9.9.
- Write to port 41h, data 12h.
- Write to port 41h, data 00h.

The input frequency is 1.2 MHz, thus the counter will count from 12h (18 in decimal) to 00h for a single count. The period of the output will thus be:

$$\text{Time period} = \frac{18}{1.2}\mu s = 15\mu s$$

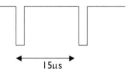

15µs

9.4.2   *Timer 2*

The first timer has a base address of 40h. The functions and addresses are:

- **48h (counter 0).** This is used in some systems as a fail-safe timer (watchdog timer).
- **49h (counter 1).** This is reserved.
- **4Ah (counter 2).** Counter 2 is used to control the speed at which the processor processes instructions.
- **4Bh (control).**

9.5 Exercises

Using C, Pascal, BASIC or Assembly Language, complete the following.

9.5.1 Write a program to input a byte from port A.

9.5.2 Write a program that will send to port B all 1s.

9.5.3 Write a program that will read a byte from port A. This byte is then sent to port B.

9.5.4 Write a program that sends a 'walking-ones' code to port B. The delay between changes should be one second. A 'walking-ones' code is as follows:

```
00000001
00000010
00000100
00001000
   : :
10000000
00000001
00000010,  and so on.
```

9.5.5 Write separate programs that output the patterns in (a) and (b). The sequences are as follows:

```
(a)    00000001    (b)    10000001
       00000010           01000010
       00000100           00100100
       00001000           00011000
       00010000           00100100
       00100000           01000010
       01000000           10000001
       10000000           01000010
       01000000           00100100
          ::
       00000001
       00000010
```

9.5.6 Write separate programs that output the following sequences:

```
(a)    1010 1010    (b)    1111 1111
       0101 0101           0000 0000
       1010 1010           1111 1111
       0101 0101           0000 0000
```

```
(c)    0000 0001    (d)    0000 0001
       0000 0011           0000 0011
       0000 1111           0000 0111
       0001 1111           0000 1111
       0011 1111           0001 1111
       0111 1111           0011 1111
       1111 1111           0111 1111
       0000 0001           1111 1111
       0000 0011           0111 1111
       0000 0111           0011 1111
       0000 1111           0001 1111
       0001 1111           0000 1111
```

(e)   The inverse of (d) above.

9.5.7   Write a program that reads a byte from port A and sends the 1s complement representation to port B. Note that 1s complement is all bits inverted.

9.5.8   Change the program in exercise 9.7 so that it gives the 2s complement value on port B. *Hint*: either complement all the bits of the value and add 1, or send the negated value.

9.5.9   Write a program that will count from 00h to ffh will 1s delay between each count. The output should go to port B.

9.5.10   Write a program that will sample port A every 1s then send it to port B.

9.5.11   Write a program that will simulate the following logic functions.

> NOT   PB0 = not (PA0)
> AND   PB0 = PA0 and PA1
> OR   PB0 = PA0 or PA1

where PA0 is bit 0 of port A, PA1 is bit 1 of port A and PB0 is bit 0 of port B.

9.5.12   Write a program that will simulate a traffic light sequence. The delay between changes should be approximately 1.

> PB0 is RED   PB1 is AMBER   PB2 is GREEN

and the sequence is:

> RED   →   AMBER   → GREEN   →   AMBER →
> RED   →   AMBER   → GREEN

9.5.13   Modify the program in 9.12 so that the sequence is:

> RED   →   RED and AMBER→   GREEN   →
> AMBER →   RED   →   RED and AMBER →
> GREEN

9.5.14   Write a program that will input a value from port A. This value is sent to port B and the bits are rotated with a delay of 1 second.

9.5.15   Write a program that will sample port A when bit 0 of port C is changed from a 0 to a 1. Values are then entered via port A by switching PC0 from a 0 to a 1. These values are put into memory starting from address 100h. The end of the input session is given by PC1 being set (that is, PC1 is equal to a 1). When this is set all the input values are sent to port B with a 2 - s interval.

9.5.16   If the processor is writing data to the control word of timer 1, what is the condition of the following signals?

> M/IO#   W/R#   D/C#   Address on the bus

Classic software

Microsoft Windows 95/98/NT/2000 The debate about whether Microsoft Windows 95 was just a copy of the Mac operating system will continue for years, but as Windows 3.x was a quantum leap from the previous versions, so Windows 95 was to Windows 3.x. The main problems with Windows 3.x was that it still used DOS as a basic operating system, and it also used 16-bit code (and most PCs used 32-bit processors, such as the 80386 and 80486 processors). Windows 95 was totally rewritten using mostly 32-bit software, and thus used the full power of the processor, and the full memory addressing capabilities. It could now address up to 4GB of virtual memory, and supported a great deal more devices, such as CD-ROMs and back-up resources. It also had networking capabilities built into it properly. The trump card for Microsoft, though, was that its networking supported many different network protocols, such as TCP/IP (for Internet traffic), IPX/SPX (for Novell NetWare traffic), and AppleTalk. It could thus live with any type of network (and, Microsoft hoped, would eventually replace the existing network with one based on Microsoft networking, and not the existing network (this is called gradual network migration). Windows 95/98 Workstation allowed for a peer-to-peer network where computers could share resources, whereas Windows NT/2000 allowed for the creation of a network server, which gave network-wide log-in, administration, global file systems, and so on. Windows NT 4.0 integrated the networking from Windows NT 3.0 and the user interface found in Windows 95. Its other enhancements were support for pre-emptive multitasking and multithreading of Windows-based and MS-DOS-based applications, enhanced robustness and clean-up when an application ended or crashed, and enhanced dynamic environment configuration. Windows 2000 builds on the success of NT.

9.5.17 If the processor is writing to the initial count register counter 2, timer 2, what is the condition of the following signals?

IORC#   IOWC#
A1   A0

9.5.18 What is timer 1 counter 0 used for? And what is the output frequency? Also, What is timer 1 counter 1 used for? And what is the output frequency?

Microprocessor basics

Register Renaming. These are additional registers which can be assigned to contain data that would normally be written to the destination register. One of the main uses is with speculative execution of branches (see Page 205), the branch uses renamed registers, which can be renamed back to the original registers if the branch prediction is successful, otherwise the data is discarded. Another application is with out of order execution (see p. 205) where renamed registers can be used to modify the execution of a program by renaming registers to avoid write conflicts.

Segment. This is an area of memory that is accessed through an identifier tag.

Stack Frame. A stack segment which contains parameters, local variables, previous stack frame pointer and return address, created when calling a subprogram (such as a procedure, a function (which is a procedure which returns a value), or a method (function or procedure which can access private data in an object).

Superscalar. A processor that can execute more than one instruction, at a time.

Very Long Instruction Word (VLIW). Instructions which include more than one operation, which are to be executed concurrently. This can be achieved with a fixed number of operations per instruction, or with a variable number of operations (Variable Length Instruction Grouping or Explicitly Parallel Instruction Computing (EPIC)).

Introduction to the Pentium

10.1 Introduction

Intel have gradually developed their range of processors from the original 16-bit 8086 processor to the 32-bit processors such as the Pentium II. Table 10.1 contrasts the Intel processor range. It can also be seen from this table that the Pentium II processor is almost a thousand times more powerful than an 8086 processor. The original 8086 had just 29,000 transistors and operated at a clock speed of 8 MHz. It had an external 20-bit bus and could thus access up to only 1 MB of physical memory. Compare this with the Pentium II, which can operate at over 300 MHz, contains over 6,000,000 transistors and can access up to 64 GB of physical memory.

Table 10.1 Processor comparison

Processor	Clock (when released)	Register size	External data bus	Maximum external memory	Cache	Power (MIPs)
8086	8 MHz	16	16	1 MB		0.8
286	12.5 MHz	16	16	16 MB		2.7
386DX	20 MHz	32	32	4 GB		6.0
486DX	25 MHz	32	32	4 GB	8 kB L-1	20
Pentium	60 MHz	32	64	4 GB	16 kB L-1	100
Pentium Pro	200 MHz	32	64	64 GB	16 kB L-1 256 kB L-2	440
Pentium II	200 MHz	32	64	64 GB	16 kB L-1 512 kB L-2	700

10.2 Intel Processor Development

The 80386 processor was a great leap forward in processing power after the 8086 and 80286, but it required an on-board math coprocessor to enhance its mathematical operations and it could execute only one instruction at a time. The 80486 brought many enhancements, including:

- The addition of parallel execution with the expansion of the Instruction decode and execution units into five pipelined stages. Each of these stages operates in parallel with the others on up to five instructions in different stages of execution. This allows up to five instructions to be completed at a time.
- The addition of an 8 kB on-chip cache to greatly reduce the data and code access times.
- The addition of an integrated floating-point unit.
- Support for more complex and powerful systems, such as off-board L-2 cache support and multiprocessor operation.

With the increase in notebook and palm-top computers, the 80486 was also enhanced to support many energy and system management capabilities. These processors were named the

80486SL processors. The new enhancements included:

- **System Management Mode.** This is triggered by the processor's own interrupt pin and allows complex system management features to be added to a system transparently to the operating system and application programs.
- **Stop Clock and Auto Halt Powerdown.** These allow the processor to either shut itself down (and preserve its current state) or run at a reduced clock rate.

> **Intel Inside**
>
> Few companies have ever managed to get their logo on other manufacturers' products. The Intel Inside logo was one of these successes. Others include:
>
> - Dolby noise reduction.
> - Teflon nonstick material.
> - Nutrasweet.

The Intel Pentium processor added many enhancements to the previous processors, including:

- The addition of a second execution pipeline. These two pipelines, named u and v, can execute two instructions per clock cycle. This is known as superscalar operation.
- Increased on-chip L-1 cache, 8 kB for code and another 8 kB for data. It uses the MESI protocol to support write-back mode, as well as the write-through mode (which is used by the 80486 processor).
- Branch prediction with an on-chip branch table that improves looping characteristics.
- Enhancement to the virtual-8086 mode to allow for 4 MB as well as 4 kB pages.
- 128-bit and 256-bit data paths are possible (although the main registers are still 32 bits).
- Burstable 64-bit external data bus.
- Addition of advanced programmable interrupt controller (APIC) to support multiple Pentium processors.
- New dual processing mode to support dual processor systems.

The Pentium processor has been extremely successful and has helped support enhanced multitasking operating systems such as Windows NT and Windows 95/98. The Intel Pentium Pro enhanced the Pentium processor with the following:

- Addition of a three-way superscalar architecture, as opposed to a two-way for the Pentium. This allows three instructions to be executed for every clock cycle.
- Enhanced prediction of parallel code (called dynamic execution micro-

Process league table	
Processor	Speed (MIPS)
Pentium III, 1 GHz	1500
Pentium III, 500 MHz	850
Pentium II, 333 MHz	770
Pentium II, 233 MHz	560
Cyrix 6x86MX, PR233	510
AMD K6, 233 MHz	480
Pentium Pro, 200 MHz	440
Pentium, 233 MHz MMX	435
AMD K5-PR166	260
Pentium, 133 MHz	240
Am5x86	150
Pentium, 66 MHz	100
486DX4/100, 100 MHz	60
486DX 2-50, 50 MHz	35
486DX, 25 MHz	20
68030 40 MHz	10
386DX, 33 MHz	10
68030, 25 MHz	6.3
386SX, 20 MHz	6
68030, 16 MHz	3.9
80286, 12 MHz	2.7
68020, 16 MHz	2.6
68000, 16 MHz	1.3
8086, 8 MHz	0.8
68000, 8 MHz	0.7
8080, 2 MHz	0.5
4004, 108 KHz	0.06

architecture) for the superscalar operation. This includes methods such as micro-data flow analysis, out-of-order execution, enhanced branch prediction and speculative execution. The three instruction decode units work in parallel to decode object code into smaller operations called micro-ops. These micro-ops then go into an instruction pool, and when there are no interdependencies they can be executed out of order by the five parallel execution units (two integer units, two for floating-point operations and one for memory). A retirement unit retires completed micro-ops in their original program order and takes account of any branches. This recovers the original program flow.

- Addition of register renaming. Multiple instructions not dependent on each other, using the same registers, allow the source and destination registers to be temporarily renamed. The original register names are used when instructions are retired and program flow is maintained.

- Addition of a closely coupled, on-package 256 kB L-2 cache that has a dedicated 64-bit full clock speed bus. The L-2 cache also supports up to four concurrent accesses through a 64-bit external data bus. Each of these accesses is transaction-oriented where each access is handled as a separate request and response. This allows for numerous requests while awaiting a response.

- Expanded 36-bit address bus to give a physical address size of 64 GB.

> **First bug**
>
> The first computer bug really was a bug. Grace Murray Hopper, who also invented COBOL, coined the term 'bug' when she traced an error in the Mark II to a moth trapped in a relay. She carefully removed the bug and taped it to her logbook.

The Pentium II processor is a further enhancement to the processor range. Apart from increasing the clock speed, it has several enhancements over the Pentium Pro, including:

- Integration of MMX technology. MMX instructions support high-speed multimedia operations and include the addition of eight new registers (MM0 to MM7), four MMX data types and an MMX instruction set.
- Single-edge contact (SEC) cartridge packaging. This gives improved handling performance and socketability. It uses surface mount component and has a thermal plate (which accepts a standard heat sink), a cover and a substrate with an edge-finger connection.
- Integrated on-chip L-1 cache, 16 kB for code and another 16 kB for data.
- Increased size, on-package, 512 kB L-2 cache.
- Enhanced low-power states, such as AutoHALT, Stop-Grant, Sleep and Deep Sleep.

10.3 Terminology

Before introducing the Pentium Pro (P-6) various terms have to be defined:

Transaction	Used to define a bus cycle. It consists of a set of phases that relate to a single bus request.
Bus agent	Devices that reside on the processor bus, i.e. the processor, PCI bridge and memory controller.
Priority agent	The device handling reset, configuration, initialization, error detection and handling; generally the processor-to-PCI bridge.
Requesting agent	The device driving the transaction, i.e. the busmaster.

Addressed agent	The slave device addressed by the transaction i.e. the, target agent.
Responding agent	The device that provides the transaction response on $\overline{RS2} - \overline{RS0}$ signals.
Snooping agent	A caching device that snoops on the transactions to maintain cache coherency.
Implicit write-back	When a hit to a modified line is detected during the snoop phase, an implicit write-back occurs. This is the mechanism used to write-back the cache line.

10.4 Pentium II and Pentium Pro

A major objective of electronic systems design is the saving of electrical power and the minimization of electromagnetic interference (EMI). Thus gunning transceiver logic (GTL) has been used to reduce both power consumption and EMI as it has a low voltage swing. GTL requires a - V reference signal, and signals that use GTL logic are terminated to 1.5 V. If a signal is 0.2 V above the reference voltage, that is, 1.2 V, then it is considered high. If a signal is 0.2 V below the reference voltage, that is, 0.8 V, then it is considered low.

The Pentium Pro and II support up to four processors on the same bus without extra supporting logic. Integrated into the bus structure are cache coherency signals, advanced programmable interrupt control signals and bus arbitration.

A great enhancement of the Pentium Pro bus is data error detection and correction. The Pentium Pro bus detects and corrects all single-bit data bus errors and also detects multiple-bit errors on the data bus. Address and control bus signals also have basic parity protection.

The Pentium Pro bus has a modified line write-back performed without backing off the current bus owner, where the processor must perform a write-back to memory when it detects a hit to a modified line. The following mechanism eliminates the need to back off the current busmaster. If a memory write is being performed by the current bus owner, then two writes will be seen on the bus, that is, the original one followed by the write-back. The memory controller latches and merges the data from the two cycles, and performs one write to DRAM. If the current bus owner is performing a memory read, then it accepts the data when it is being written to memory.

Other enhanced features are:

Top 10 IC manufacturers

Ranking (prev.)	Company	Sales in billions (growth, %)	Market share (%)
1 (1)	Intel	25.810 (13.3)	16.1
2 (2)	NEC	9.216 (12.0)	5.8
3 (3)	Toshiba	7.594 (28.4)	4.7
4 (6)	Samsung	7.095 (49.5)	4.4
4 (5)	Texas Instruments	7.095 (22.0)	4.4
6 (3)	Motorola	6.425 (–9.4)	4.0
7 (7)	Hitachi	5.521 (18.3)	3.4
8 (9)	STMicroelectronics	5.080 (21.0)	3.2
9 (8)	Philips	5.065 (13.9)	3.2
10 (10)	Infineon	5.010 (28.2)	3.1

Dataquest, 1999.

- Deferred reply transactions stop the processor from having to wait for slow devices; transactions that require a long time can be completed later (deferred.)
- Deeply pipelined bus transactions where the bus supports up to eight outstanding pipelined transactions.

10.5 System Overview

Figures 10.1 and 10.2 outline the main components of a Pentium system and Table 10.2 gives its main pin connections. A major upgrade is the support for up to four processors. The memory control and data path control logic provides the memory control signals, that is, memory address, $\overline{RAS}$ and $\overline{CAS}$ signals. The data path logic moves the data between the processor bus and the memory data bus. The memory interface component interfaces the memory data bus with the DRAM memory. Both interleaved and non-interleaved methods are generally supported. The memory consists of dual-in-line memory modules (DIMMs). A DIMM module supports 64 data bits and 8 parity or ECC bits. The PCI bridge provides the interface between the processor bus and the PCI bus. The standard bridge provides an interface between the PCI bus and the EISA/ISA bus. EISA/ISA support component provides the EISA/ISA bus support functions, for example, timers, interrupt control, flash ROM, keyboard interface, LA/SA translation and XD bus control.

> ### Changes from 80486 to Pentium
>
> 1 Additional internal pipeline.
> 2 External data bus increased from 32 bits to 64 bits.
>
> ### Change from Pentium to Pentium Pro
>
> New bus protocol where the old address and data time bus cycle is replaced with a six-phase transaction.
>
> ### Change from Pentium Pro to PII/PIII
>
> PII/PIII is basically a Pentium Pro (P6) core module with MMX.

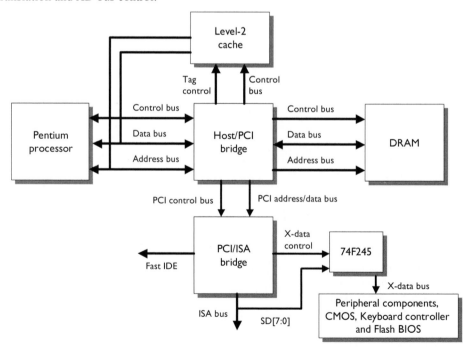

Figure 10.1   Pentium architecture (a more detailed version is given in Figure 10.7)

Table 10.2 Pentium signal lines

Signals	I/O	Description
$\overline{\text{BSEL}}$	I/O	Bus select is for future use.
DP0–DP63	I/O	64-bit data bus.
$\overline{\text{ADS}}$	O	Indicates that the processor has valid control signals and valid address signals.
AHOLD	I	When active a different bus controller can have access to the address bus. This is typically used in a multiprocessor system.
$\overline{\text{BE0}} - \overline{\text{BE3}}$	O	The byte enable lines indicate which of the bytes of the 32-bit data bus are active.
$\overline{\text{BLAST}}$	O	Indicates that the current burst cycle will end after the next $\overline{\text{BRDY}}$ signal.
$\overline{\text{BOFF}}$	I	The back-off signal informs the processor to deactivate the bus on the next clock cycle.
$\overline{\text{BRDY}}$	I	The burst ready signal is used by an addressed system that has sent data on the data bus or read data from the bus.
BREQ	O	Indicates that the processor has internally requested the bus.
$\overline{\text{BS16}}$, $\overline{\text{BS8}}$	I	The $\overline{\text{BS16}}$ signal indicates that a 16-bit data bus is used; the $\overline{\text{BS8}}$ signal indicates that an 8-bit data bus is used. If both are high, then a 32-bit data bus is used.
DP0–DP3	I/O	The data parity bits gives a parity check for each byte of the 32-bit data bus. The parity bits are always even parity.
$\overline{\text{EADS}}$	I	Indicates that an external bus controller has put a valid address on the address bus.
$\overline{\text{FERR}}$	O	Indicates that the processor has detected an error in the internal floating-point unit.
$\overline{\text{FLUSH}}$	I	When active, the processor writes the complete contents of the cache to memory.
HOLD, HLDA	I/O	The bus hold (HOLD) and acknowledge (HLDA) are used for bus arbitration and allow other bus controllers to take control of the buses.
$\overline{\text{IGNNE}}$	I	When active the processor ignores any numeric errors.
INTR	I	External devices to interrupt the processor use the interrupt request line.
$\overline{\text{KEN}}$	I	This signal stops caching of a specific address.
$\overline{\text{LOCK}}$	O	If active, the processor will not pass control to an external bus controller when it receives a HOLD signal.
$\text{M/}\overline{\text{IO}}$, $\text{D/}\overline{\text{C}}$, $\text{W/}\overline{\text{R}}$	O	See Table 5.1.
NMI	I	The non-maskable interrupt signal causes an interrupt 2.
$\overline{\text{PCHK}}$	O	If it is set active then a data parity error has occurred.
$\overline{\text{PLOCK}}$	O	The active pseudo-lock signal identifies that the current data transfer requires more than one bus cycle.

PWT, PCD	O	The page write-through (PWT) and page cache disable (PCD) are used with cache control.
$\overline{\text{RDY}}$	I	When active, the addressed system has sent data on the data bus or read data from the bus.
RESET	I	If the reset signal is high for more than 15 clock cycles, then the processor resets itself.

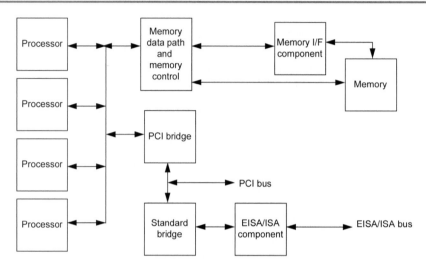

Figure 10.2   Pentium Pro architecture with multiple processors

A Pentium bus cycle is a transaction that takes place, read or write, between the processor and another device on the board. It can be split into two parts:

1. **Address time**. During the first part of the cycle, the processor will output the address and cycle type. This defines the type of transfer taking place. The system logic decodes this information and generates the data steering enables and a chip select for the slave device being communicated with.

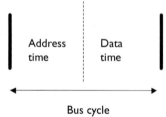

2. **Data time**. During the second part of the cycle, the data is transferred. For a write cycle, the data is latched into the target device. For a read cycle, the slave device outputs the requested data, and it is accepted by the processor.

10.5.1 Bus transactions

A Pentium Pro bus transaction contains up to six phases; each of these uses a particular set of signals to communicate particular information. The six phases are:

- **Arbitration**. A transaction begins with the arbitration phase when the requesting agent does not already own any of the buses. The bus agent generates the appropriate bus request signals to get ownership of the buses. This phase is skipped if the bus agent already owns the buses.
- **Request**. The bus agent enters the request phase once it owns the buses. This phase con-

sists of two clocks. During the first CLK, the bus agent drives $\overline{\text{ADS}}$ and an address on the bus; this allows other agents to snoop. During the second CLK, other transaction information is driven, for example, byte enables. All bus agents latch the information provided during the request phase, and store it in their in-order queues.

- **Error**. If a bus agent detects an address or control bus parity error, it must generate the appropriate error signals during the error phase time frame. If an error is indicated during the error phase, then the rest of the transaction phases are cancelled.

- **Snoop**. If a transaction is not cancelled during the error phase, then it will have a snoop phase. During this phase all snooping agents indicate if a hit was detected to a line in the shared or modified state.

- **Response**. If the transaction is not cancelled during the error phase, then it will have a response phase. The response phase indicates the status of the transaction. A hard failure response is provided if a transaction is retired due to an error, and then fails again on a retry. A no-data response will be provided if the transaction is complete, for example, a write transaction. A normal data response will be provided if the transaction has to contain a data phase, for example, a read transaction. A deferred response is provided if the transaction is to be completed later, for example, an I/O read from a slow device. An implicit write-back response will be provided if modified data has to be written back, for example, a snooping agent detects a hit to a modified line during a read from or a write to memory. A retry response is provided if a bus agent decides that a transaction must be retired.

- **Data**. If a transaction is not cancelled during the error phase, and did not get a hard failure, deferred or retry response during the response phase, then it will contain a data phase. Data is transferred during the data phase, for example, read data, write data, or implicit write-back data.

10.5.2 Transaction types

The P-6 can perform the following types of transaction:

- **I/O write**.
- **I/O read**.
- **Memory write**.
- **Memory read**.

Top 20 influential computer companies

1   Microsoft Corp.
2   Intel Corp.
3   IBM Corp.
4   Compaq Computer
5   Hewlett-Packard
6   Cisco Systems
7   Sun Microsystems
8   America Online
9   Dell Computer
10 Netscape
11 Oracle Corp.
12 3Com Corp.
13 Yahoo! Inc.
14 Gateway Inc.
15 Adobe Systems
16 Apple Computer
17 Novell Inc.
18 Toshiba Corp.
19 Macromedia Inc.
20 Intuit Inc.

PC Magazine, 1998.

More influential computer companies

21 Packard Bell NEC
22 Softbank Corp.
23 Canon Inc.
24 RealNetworks Inc.
25 Sony Corp.
26 Bay Networks Inc.
27 Corel Corp.
28 Symantec Corp.
29 Silicon Graphics
30 Seiko Epson Corp.
31 Lucent Technologies
32 Seagate Technology
33 Amazon.com Inc.
34 Network Associates
35 Micron
36 Autodesk Inc.
37 Creative Technology
38 GT Interactive
39 Ascend
40 CAI

PC Magazine, 1998.

- **Interrupt acknowledge**.
- **Special**. The type of special transaction being requested is determined by the byte enables, $\overline{BE8} - \overline{BE15}$. Special transaction types are:

  - Shutdown.
  - Flush.
  - Halt.
  - SMI acknowledge.
  - Flush acknowledge.
  - Sync.
  - Stop CLK acknowledge.

> **Most admired computer companies?**
>
> Microsoft (2)
> Dell Computer (3)
> Cisco Systems (4)
> Intel (8)
> Lucent Technologies (10)
>
> (Number indicates the position in Fortune 500 most admired companies list, 2000).

- **Deferred**. This allows the processor to move onto the next transaction instead of waiting for a response from a slow device. The processor is notified by a bus agent during the response phase of the current transaction that the transaction will be deferred and will be completed at a later time. The deferring bus agent then performs a deferred reply transaction and when the original transaction can be completed the deferred reply transaction returns data to complete the earlier I/O transaction. During the request phase of a deferred reply transaction, the bus agent identifies who the original requesting agent was, and which transaction the reply is for.

  If the original transaction was a read, then a normal data response would be provided during the deferred reply transaction, that is, a data phase would follow the response phase. If the original transaction was a write, then a no data response would be provided during the deferred reply transaction, that is, the deferred reply transaction will not contain a data phase because the write took place during the data phase of the original transaction.

10.6 Pentium Details

The 80486 was an excellent processor that allowed GUIs to properly run on a PC, but it was the Pentium that really lifted the PC into the serious computer market. Table 10.3 gives a comparison between the 80486 and Pentium, and Figure 10.3 outlines the functional blocks within the Pentium processor.

> **Pentium bug**
>
> The Pentium bug was found in October 1994 by Thomas Nicely, a mathematician from Lynchburgh College, Virginia. He found that one divided by 824,633,702,441 gave the wrong answer. This bug eventually cost Intel over half a billion dollars, as they offered to replace bug-ridden Pentiums with correctly operating ones.

Table 10.3   Pentium signal lines

Pentium	80486
64 bit data bus; allows access to eight sequential locations.	32- bit data bus; allows access to four sequential locations.
Eight sequential locations can be identified by a quadword output address.	Four sequential locations can be identified by a doubleword output address.

Address pipelining.	No address pipelining.
Two 8-kB internal cache: one for instructions, and one for data.	One 8-kB internal cache; stores both instructions and data.
Controls burst cycles with CACHE# output.	Controls burst cycles with BLAST# output.
Does not change the lower address bits during burst cycles.	Changes the lower order address bits during burst cycles.
Can reset the processor without clearing its internal cache.	Resetting the processor clears the internal cache.
BIST (built-in, self-test) caused by RESET and INIT.	BIST caused by RESET and AHOLD.
Both address and data parity supported.	Only data parity supported.
Two instruction pipelines; allows two instructions to be executed simultaneously, (as long as the result of one is not dependent on the result of the other).	One instruction pipeline; only one instruction can be executed at a time.
Snoops during busmaster writes and reads.	Snoops during busmaster writes to memory.
Supports system management mode.	No system management mode.

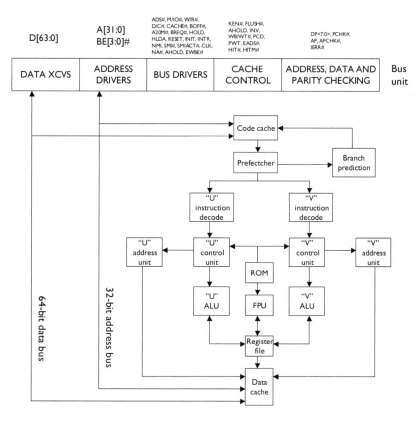

Figure 10.3 Pentium functional blocks

The functional units are:

- **Bus unit**. The bus unit handles all the processor transactions that involve accessing I/O devices and external memory. The bus unit interface contains the following blocks:

  Data transceivers provide a bidirectional data path between the processor and external devices.

  Address drivers provide a bidirectional address path between the processor and external devices. When the processor is in control, A[31:3] and BE[7:0]# are outputs. During snoop cycles, only A[31:5] are inputs.

  Bus control controls the bus cycles executed by the processor; it also provides an arbitration and interrupt interface.

  Cache control controls the cache interface, snooping, flushing and memory cycle cacheability.

  Address and data parity generation and checking generates and checks for even data parity on all memory writes and reads. It also generates even address parity on all write cycles, and checks for even address parity on all snoop cycles.

- **Code cache**. The code cache is a two-way set associative look-through design, with a line size of 32 bytes. It is used for storing frequently used instructions.

- **Prefetcher**. The prefetcher works in conjunction with the bus unit and branch prediction block to retrieve instructions from memory before they are requested. The prefetcher has two 32-B prefetch queues. Prefetches are fetched sequentially by the prefetch queue until a branch instruction is fetched, i.e. the next fetch location may not be a sequential one.

  > **Gunning Transceiver Logic**
  >
  > The Pentium Pro and later processors use a low-voltage swing in order to reduce both power consumption and electromagnetic interference. It also makes high frequency communications easier and cheaper to design.
  >
  >   Signals that use the Gunning Transceiver Logic (GTL) are terminated to 1.5 V. GTL relies on a reference voltage of 1 V. A signal is considered high if the signal is 0.2V higher than the reference voltage (1.2 V). A signal is considered low if the signal is 0.2V lower than the reference voltage (0.8V).

- **Branch prediction**. Based on the previous instructions executed, this logic predicts whether or not a branch instruction will be executed; if the branch is predicted to be taken, then the prefetch queue that is not being used begins to be filled with prefetches.

- **Instruction decoders**. The instruction decoders get instructions out of the prefetch queue and decodes them. Before the instruction is decoded completely, the U instruction decoder determines whether the next two instructions can be executed simultaneously; if they can be paired the first one is sent to the U pipeline and the second one is sent to the V pipeline. This is possible as long as the result of the second instruction is not dependent on the result of the first instruction. If the instructions cannot be paired, then the U pipeline is used. Once the instructions have been decoded they are passed onto the control unit.

- **Control units and ROM**. The ROM provides the processor with the microcode necessary to execute instructions and the control unit guides it through the operations.

- **Arithmetic logic units**. The arithmetic logic unit carries out the instruction provided to it by the rom and control unit. There are two ALUs, one for each pipeline.

- **Floating-point unit**. The FPU performs numeric calculations on numbers that contain decimal points.

- **Register file**. The register file provides the processor with temporary locations to store and manipulate data.
- **Data cache**. The data cache is an 8 kB cache used to store frequently used data. It is a two-way set associative look-through cache with a line size of 32 B, which supports the MESI protocol discussed in the next section.
- **Address unit**. The address unit computes the address that will be sent to memory by the bus unit.

The Pentium processor has a 64-bit data bus (D[63:0]) and eight byte enables (BE[7:0]#). A quadword address on A[31:3] points to eight sequential locations, and the number of byte enables active depends on the size of the transfer. The byte enable line will active an address location depending on the least significant four bits, as given next:

Quadword address ending in "8"	8	9	A	B	C	D	E	F
Quadword address ending in "0"	0	1	2	3	4	5	6	7

BE0#   BE2#   BE4#   BE6#
    BE1#   BE3#   BE5#   BE7#

For example:

The processor writes 32 bits to memory location 10804h

Quadword address = 10800h on A[31:3];   Active BE# signals = [7:4]

The processor writes 16 bits to memory location 1007h (a 16-bit write crosses the byte lanes)

First bus cycle:
Quadword address = 1000h;   BE7# = 0

Second bus cycle:
Quadword address = 1008h;   BE0# = 0

Processor writes 32 bits to memory location 8024Ah

Quadword address = 80248h;   BE[5:2]# = 0

10.6.1 Address pipelining/cache operation

Address pipelining is implemented and uses NA# (next address input). The Pentium has two 8-kB caches, one for code (a write-through cache) and one for data (typically, write-back cache). The data cache can be configured as write-back or write-through using the PWT signal, where:

PWT = 1, data cache is write-through
PWT = 0, data cache is write-back

The KEN# is activated only once during burst cycles and the CACHE# signal is used to control burst cycles. In a burst sequence, the low-order address bits do not change. For example:

Burst sequence = 4×64-bit data transfers, 32 bytes.

Processor reads 64 bits from memory location 10000h

First cycle qword	=	10000h	memory address	=	1000h
Second cycle qword	=	10000h	memory address	=	10008h, A3 toggles
Third cycle qword	=	10000h	memory address	=	10010h, A3, and A4 toggle
Fourth cycle qword	=	10000h	memory address	=	10018h, A3 toggles

10018h	8	9	A	B	C	D	E	F
10010h	0	1	2	3	4	5	6	7
10008h	8	9	A	B	C	D	E	F
10000h	0	1	2	3	4	5	6	7

If the information is not in cache, this results in a cache read miss. The processor then executes a 'linefill' from system memory (32 bytes) or second level cache. Pentium can be reset without clearing or flushing its internal caches; the INIT input is used to control this.

10.6.2 BIST

The BIST (built-in self-test) is initiated by RESET and INIT signals.

10.6.3 Data parity

The Pentium supports address and data parity and uses even parity mechanism for both. It generates DP[7:0] during memory writes, and checks for even parity during memory reads. If odd parity is detected, PCHK# = 0. For example:

Processor writes AAh to memory location 83214h

D[39:32] = 1010 1010 ; DP4 = 0

BE4# = 0

10.6.4 Address parity

The Pentium generates even parity when it is busmaster; this generates the AP signal. For example:

Processor accesses memory location 10000h
A[31:3] = 00010000h, AP = 1

Pentium looks at A[31:5] to generate and check for even address parity. It also checks for address parity when another device is busmaster. When EADS# = 0, an external busmaster is outputting an address. The system or memory controller will generate the AP signal to the Pentium. If odd parity is detected, APCHK# = 0.

10.6.5 Internal parity

Pentium generates and checks for even data parity when accessing its internal data cache. If an internal parity error is detected, the IERR# signal is set to a 0.

10.6.6 Pipelining

Pentium can execute two instructions simultaneously if the first instruction does not affect the second one. There are two instruction pipelines: 'U' and 'V'. For example:

```
Mov  AL, AA            ;   load AL register with AAh
Out  64, AL            ;   write to port 64h with the value AAh
```

These instructions could not be executed at the same time. The Pentium has branch prediction logic, which decides whether or not a conditional instruction will be executed. If it is, then this logic tells the processor to begin prefetching instructions from the jump location. The Pentium has two 32-B prefetch queues.

10.6.7 Boundary scan

Pentium has boundary scan support using TMS, TDI, TDO, TCK and TRST# signals. A boundary scan test technique feeds in a serial test pattern (Scan-in), which is clocked-in using an external clock (Clock), as illustrated in Figure 10.4. This test pattern can be clocked through the Pentium and onto other ASICs, and then eventually clocked out of the system (using Scan-out).

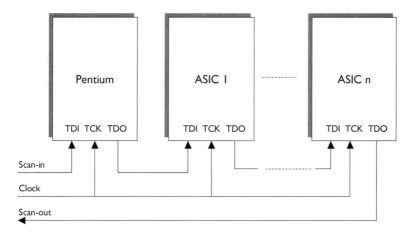

Figure 10.4   Boundary scan technique

10.6.8 Bus control

The bus control manages all external bus cycles and generates ADS#; M/IO#; D/C#; W/R# at the start of each new processor bus cycle. It also looks at interrupt type inputs:

INTR; NMI; RESET; SMI#

The processor outputs the address of the next cycle when NA# = 0.

If AHOLD = 1, the processor must tristate its address outputs within one clock cycle.
If BOFF# = 0, the processor must give up control of all its buses within one clock cycle.

10.6.9 Cache control

To determine whether or not an access is to a cacheable location:

> PCD = 0 from processor
> KEN# = 0 from external system

To determine the type of cache:

> PWT from processor
> WB/WT# from 2nd/3rd level cache

This indicates whether the requested information has been found in cache:

> HIT# and HITM#, hit modified.

Pentium bug

To determine *x* divided by *y*, the following are implemented:

1. Pick the first four binary digits of *y* and the first seven binary digits of *x*.
2. Produce a guess by looking up a multiplication table.
3. Multiply the answer by *y* to see how near the answer is.
4. If the answer is zero, the guess is correct, otherwise divide the remainder by *y* and continue.
5. Eventually the answer becomes more accurate, and the result of Step 3 becomes zero, giving the result.

The answer is normally accurate to 15 decimal places. Unfortunately, the Pentium chip had five incorrect entries out of 2,048 entries in the multiplication table. Under certain conditions the division gave incorrect answers. Intel calculated that the Pentium device would give only one wrong answer in 9 billion calculations, and that the mean time between incorrect answers was 27,000 years (much longer than the lifetime of any computer). In fact the Pentium chip had a MTBF (mean time before failure) of 200 years.

When cache is flushed, FLUSH# = 0, all cache directory entries are marked invalid.

10.6.10   Code cache

The 8-kb, two-way, set associative cache supports, s (shared) and i (invalid), are features of the MESI protocol. It is treated as a write-through cache.

10.6.11   Data cache

The 8-kb two-way set associative cache supports all features of MESI protocol when configured as a write-back cache. It can also be configured as write-through. The MESI states are:

- **M** (modified). Data in cache is more recent than the corresponding location in memory.
- **E** (exclusive). Data in cache is the same as the corresponding location in memory. If new data is written to this cache location, system memory is not updated automatically (write-back).
- **S** (shared). Data in cache is the same as the corresponding location in memory. If new data is written to this cache location, system memory is updated at the same time (write-through).
- **I** (invalid). Data in cache location is not most recent data or a flush has taken place.

Write-through

Processor reads from memory location 1000h, and the data is not in cache. Linefill operation reads from memory and updates cache; cache location is shared. For example:

- Processor writes 55h to memory location 1000h; processor updates cache and system memory; data is classed as shared (See Figure 10.5).
- DMA during floppy transfers writes FFh to memory location 1000h.
- Processor snoops on A[31:5] when EADS# = 0; processor marks cache data corresponding to memory location 1000h as invalid.
- Processor reads from memory location 1000h. Data in cache is invalid so processor performs a linefill from system memory.
- This updates the cache with the latest data. Cache entry will be marked as shared.

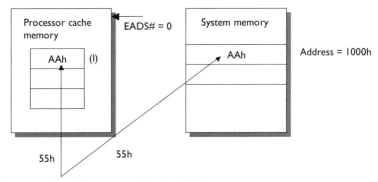

Figure 10.5 Write-through example

Write-back

Processor reads from memory location 1000h, and data is not in cache. Linefill operation reads from memory and updates cache. Cache location is marked as exclusive. Processor writes 55h to memory location 1000h. Processor updates cache location only, and marks it as modified (See Figure 10.6). DMA during a floppy transfer reads from memory location 1000h. When EADS# = 0, processor snoops A[31:5]. When processor detects it has modified data in its cache, it performs a write-back cycle. This involves holding off the busmaster access until the processor has updated system memory. BCLK is held low while the processor updates memory. Cache location is marked as exclusive again.

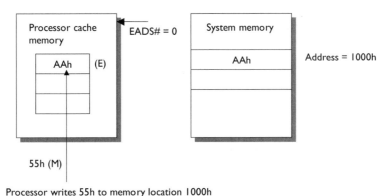

Figure 10.6 Write-back example

10.6.12   Prefetcher

Pentium has two prefetch queues. One prefetch queue is used in conjunction with the branch prediction logic to store instructions from the jump area of memory. There are two instruction decoders: control address and arithmetic logic units, 'U' and 'V'. The 'U' instruction decoder decides whether two instructions can be executed simultaneously. If they can, then the 'U' pipeline executes one instruction while the 'V' pipeline executes the other.

10.7 Exercises

10.7.1   Which bridge provides an interface between the host bus and the PCI bus?
  (a)   North bridge
  (b)   West bridge
  (c)   South bridge
  (d)   East bridge

> **MMX Technology**
>
> MMX technology has been added to the Pentium processor to enhance multimedia and communications software. It uses new data types and 57 new instructions to accelerate calculations that are common in audio, 2D and 3D graphics, video, speech synthesis and recognition, and data communications algorithms. The new instructions uses a technique known as SIMD (single instruction multiple data), which allows a single instruction to operate on multiple pieces of data, in parallel. For example, a single MMX instruction can add up to eight integer pairs, in parallel, using 64-bit registers.

10.7.2   Which bridge provides an interface between the PCI bus and the ISA bus?
  (a)   North bridge   (b)   West bridge
  (c)   South bridge   (d)   East bridge

10.7.3   The Pentium Pro has a 36-bit address bus; how much physical memory can it address:
  (a)   4 GB   (b)   16 GB
  (c)   64 GB   (d)   128 GB

10.7.4   What is the main difference between a level-1 cache and a level-2 cache?
  (a)   The level-1 cache runs at the processor speed while the level-2 cache runs at the system clock speed.
  (b)   The level-2 cache runs at the processor speed while the level-1 cache runs at the system clock speed.
  (c)   The level-1 cache contains SRAM while the level-2 cache contains DRAM.
  (c)   The level-1 cache contains DRAM while the level-2 cache contains SRAM.

10.7.5   What signals create the X-bus (used to interface to the keyboard, CMOS, and so on)?
  (a)   Cache control signals   (b)   Processor address and data bus
  (c)   SD[7:0] and X-bus control   (d)   All the ISA signals

10.7.6   Which phase do devices use to obtain access to a bus?
  (a)   Request   (b)   Arbitration
  (c)   Snoop   (d)   Response

10.7.7   What does the deferred transaction allow the processor to do?
  (a)   Move onto the next transaction without awaiting a response from a device.
  (b)   Perform a shutdown operation.
  (c)   Perform an I/O read or an I/O write.
  (d)   Acknowledge all known.

10.7.8   How is error checking implemented on the processor?
  (a)   Complex error checking and correction algorithm.
  (b)   A single parity bit on each byte on the data bus.

(c)   Error handshaking.
(d)   Sampling of the address and data.

10.7.9   Which signal line becomes active when a different bus controller can have access to the bus?
(a)   AHOLD   (b)   ADS#
(c)   EADS#   (d)   RDY#

10.7.10   Which signal line is used by an external device to indicate that there is a valid address on the address bus?
(a)   AHOLD   (b)   ADS#
(c)   EADS#   (d)   RDY#

10.7.11   Which of the following was a major difference between the 80486 and the Pentium?
(a)   Improvement in interrupt handling.
(b)   Increase in the size of the external address bus from 32 bits to 64 bits.
(c)   Support for a maths coprocessor.
(d)   Increase in the size of the external data bus from 32 bits to 64 bits.

10.7.12   Which of the following is **not** a difference between the Pentium and the Pentium Pro (P6)?
(a)   Register renaming.
(b)   Increase in the size of the external address bus from 32 bits to 36 bits.
(c)   Support for up to four processors.
(d)   Superscalar architecture.

10.7.13   Which of the following best describes superscalar architecture?
(a)   Processors run at a multiple of the system clock.
(b)   Instructions are not dependent on the clock.
(c)   There can be more than one processor on the motherboard.
(d)   Processor can execute more than one instruction at a time.

10.7.14   What is/are the main objective(s) of GTL?
(a)   It saves power and reduces electromagnetic interference (EMI).
(b)   It allows more devices to be interfaced to the processor
(c)   It allows more address and data lines.
(d)   It allows for faster interrupts.

10.7.15   What are the voltage swings for GTL?
(a)   From –0.2V (LOW) to +0.2V (HIGH), with a 0V reference.
(b)   From 0V (LOW) to +5V (HIGH), with a 2.5V reference.
(c)   From +0.8V (LOW) to 1.2V (HIGH), with a 1V reference.
(d)   From –5V (LOW) to +5V (HIGH), with a 0V reference.

10.7.16   What is the termination voltage for a GTL signal?
(a)   0V   (b)   +1.5V
(c)   +1.5V   (d)   Open-circuit

10.7.17   Which signal is used to inform the processor that it should deactivate the bus on the next clock cycle?
(a)   RESET#   (b)   BOFF#
(c)   INT#   (d)   BYE#

10.7.18   Which byte enable line will be used to identify the byte at address 4324h?
(a)   BE2#   (b)   BE3#
(c)   BE4#   (d)   BE5#

10.7.19   Which byte enable line will be used to identify the byte at address 432Dh?
     (a)   BE2#   (b)   BE3#
     (c)   BE4#   (d)   BE5#

10.7.20   What is the function of the branch prediction unit?
     (a)   It gets instructions out of the prefetch queue and decodes them.
     (b)   It is used as a temporary storage location.
     (c)   It predicts whether or not a branch instruction will be executed.
     (d)   It provides the processors with microcode required to execute the operation.

10.7.21   What is the function of the instruction decoder?
     (a)   It gets instructions out of the prefetch queue and decodes them.
     (b)   It is used as a temporary storage location.
     (c)   It predicts whether or not a branch instruction will be executed.
     (d)   It provides the processors with microcode required to execute the operation.

10.7.22   If the Pentium processor is reading 16 bits starting at memory location $4C36A_h$,
     (i)   What is the quadword address?
     (ii)   Which two BE* signals will be active?
     (iii)   What data bits does the processor expect data to be on?

10.7.23   If the Pentium processor is writing one byte to Port 84_h, what will be the state of the following signals (1 or 0)?

     (i)   AP   _____
     (ii)   BE0*   _____
     (iii)   BE4*   _____
     (iv)   What data bits does the processor expect data to be on?____

10.7.24   If the Pentium processor is writing a value of 45_h to memory location $2C328_h$, what will be the state of the following signals (1 or 0)?

     (i)   DP0   _____
     (ii)   AP   _____
     (iii)   BE4*   _____
     (iv)   BE0*   _____

10.7.25   Match the MESI state with its cause by placing the appropriate letter (a, b, c, or d) next to the state.

     _____Exclusive
     _____Modified
     _____Shared
     _____Invalid

     (a)   A read miss to a line that is cacheable and has been defined as write-through.
     (b)   Reset, flush or snoop write hit.
     (c)   A read miss to a line that is cacheable and has been defined as write-back.
     (d)   A write to a line that is in cache and has been previously defined as Exclusive.

10.7.26   Match the description that best describes each MESI state by placing the appropriate letter (a, b, c) next to the state.

_____Exclusive
_____Modified
_____Shared
_____Invalid

(a) The data stored in cache is a duplicate of the data stored in system memory
(b) The data stored in cache is newer than the data stored in system memory.
(c) The data stored in cache is older than the data stored in system memory.

10.7.27 List four new features that the Pentium processor provides that the 80486 processor does not provide.

10.7.28 When the Pentium processor writes to a memory location in the Shared state, what processor input determines whether the state should be changed?

(a) PCD
(b) HIT
(c) EADS*
(d) WB/WT*

10.7.29 List four things one should check if the first fetch after power up is to an address other than FFFFFFF0$_h$.

10.7.30 What two input signals are provided to the processor when another busmaster is accessing memory?

(a) AHOLD and EADS#
(b) INIT and EADS#
(c) PEN# and BUSCHK#
(d) HIT# and HITM#

10.7.31 How wide (in bits) is the data bus of an interleaved memory system in a Pentium processor system?

10.7.32 In a non-interleaved memory system, what memory data bits are associated with an address of 487D$_h$?

10.7.33 In an interleaved memory system, what memory data bits are associated with an address of 2616$_h$?

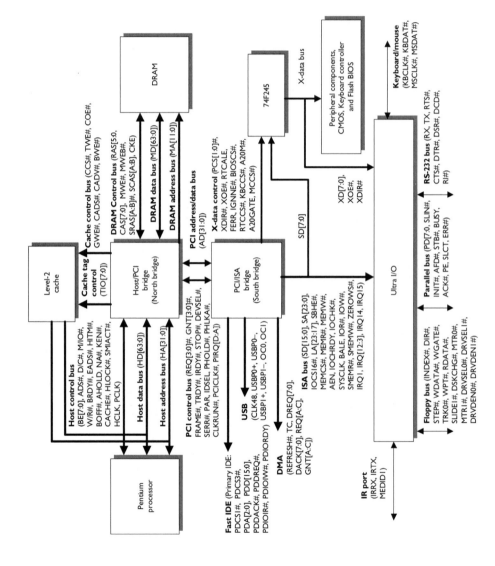

Figure 10.7 Pentium architecture

Transaction Phase Signals

11.1 Introduction

A key feature of modern computer systems is for any device to gain control of the bus. In order to do this there must be control signals that allow orderly control of the bus. This requires some form of arbitration, when a PCI master, EISA master, or DRAM wants control of the buses and the processor is the current bus owner.

Figure 11.1 shows how a DMA, PCI and EISA device would request control of the bus (the broken arrow gives the request/acknowledge path for a PCI device). For example:

Debug hints
Bad first fetch address

- No ADS#: check ADS# and BNR#.
- Wrong address or bad address path between the processor and the bridge: check A[35:3]#.
- Processor is not in control of the buses: check BPRI#.

- If an I/O device requires a DMA transfer, it will generate the appropriate DRQ signal.
- If a PCI device want control of the buses, it will generate the appropriate PREQ# signal.
- If an EISA busmaster wants control of the buses, it will generate the appropriate MREQ# signal.

As a result of a device requesting control of the buses, the south bridge (PCI/ISA bridge) generates REQ#, this then causes the north bridge (Host/PCI bridge) to generate the BPRI. The processor then finishes its current transaction and releases the BREQ#. The north bridge then generates a GNT#. The south bridge can then give the bridge to the requesting master.

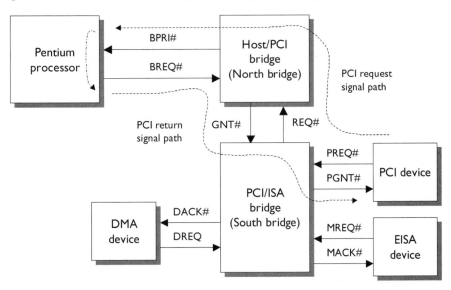

Figure 11.1   Transaction phase signals (see Figure 11.12 for a Pentium system)

The Pentium Pro supports up to four processors, where any processor can gain access to the system. At reset, each agent samples BR[3:1]# to determine its ID (rotating ID set to 3; 0 - 1 - 2 - 3, priority order). On the bus:

- A processor asserts its BR# signal.
- All the processors sample the BR#s on the rising edge of clock.
- The processor with the highest priority gets control.
- The rotating ID is changed to the ID of the processor in control.

Figure 11.2 shows the Pentium Pro transaction phase signals.

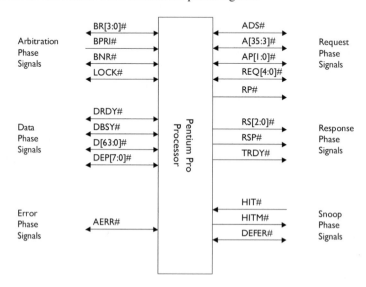

Figure 11.2   Transaction phase signals

The classifications are:

- **Arbitration phase**. The arbitration phase signals are used to get control of the bus.
- **Data phase**. A transaction that is going to transfer data will contain a data phase. During the data phase, data and parity or ECC information are provided.
- **Request phase**. The current busmaster starts a transaction in the request phase, which is two clocks long. During these two clocks, signals are driven that provide address, agent ID, control, parity and cacheability information about the transfer.
- **Error phase**. Once a transaction has been started by a bus agent, the other bus agents check parity on the supported signals. If an error is detected, the AERR# signal must be generated during the error phase.
- **Response phase**. During the response phase, the responding agent provides information about the current transaction back to the requesting agent. The information indicates whether the current transaction should be deferred or retired, a hard failure has been detected, an implicit write-back will occur, and if there will be a data phase.

> **Debug hints**
> Bad first fetch data
>
> - Data path between the processor and the bridge: check D[63:0]#.
> - Bad cycle type output by the processor: check REQ[4:0]#.

- **Snoop phase**. All snooping agents must provide the result of their snoop during the snoop phase.

11.1.1 Arbitration phase

The arbitration phase signals are defined in this section.

BR[3:0]# – bus request signals
BR[3:0]# are the physical bus request pins that drive the BREQ[3:0]# signals in the system. The BREQ[3:0]# signals are interconnected in a rotating manner to individual processors. Table 11.1 shows the rotating interconnect between the bus signals and the processor.

Table 11.1 Interconnection between bus signals and the processor

Bus signal	Agent ID0	Agent ID1	Agent ID2 pins	Agent ID3 pins
BREQ0#	BR0#	BR3#	BR2#	BR1#
BREQ1#	BR1#	BR0#	BR3#	BR2#
BREQ2#	BR2#	BR1#	BR0#	BR3#
BREQ3#	BR3#	BR2#	BR1#	BR4#

Symmetric agents have equal arbitration with more than one other device. The central agent has a higher arbitration priority than any other device. During reset the central agent asserts BREQ0#, that is, BREQ0# is driven low. The processors, symmetric agents, sample their BR[3:0]# pins on a low-to-high transition of RESET#; the value on the BR[3:0]# pins at this time identifies the agent's ID number, as shown below:

Active on RESET#	Agent ID
BR0#	0
BR3#	1
BR2#	2
BR1#	3

> **Debug hints**
> Bad first jump address
>
> - Wrong address output by the processor, bad address or data path between the processor, and the bridge chip: check A[35:3]#, D[63:0]#.

At reset, a rotating ID value of 3 is set in all the processors; the rotating ID identifies the processor with the lowest priority, that is, after reset processor 0 has the highest priority. A round-robin rotating priority scheme is used. The BR[3:0]# signals are used by the processors to keep track of the rotating ID number, and determine which processor should get the buses next. The processor requests bus ownership by generating its BR0# signal. All processors in the system sample the BR[3:0]# signals on the rising edge of the next clock; the new bus owner is determined by the rotating priority. The rotating ID changes as long as BPRI# remains inactive. The requesting processor owns the buses when its agent number equals the rotating ID.

For example, if the rotating ID is 3, this means that agent 0 has the highest priority, followed by agent 1, 2 and 3. If agent 1 wants control of the buses it drives its BR0# pin active, that is, Board signal BREQ1#. All processors sample their BR# pins and decide that the next bus owner will be agent 1. All processors change the rotating ID to 1; agent 1 can begin its transaction. The priority order is now agent 2, 3, 0 and 1, starting from the agent with the highest priority. If agents 2 and 3 want control of the buses they will generate their BR0# signals. The processors sample their BR# signals and decide that the next bus owner is agent 3, because the rotating ID is

> **Debug hints**
> First milestone checkpoint is not written to
>
> - Correct cycle type not being output: check REQ[4:0]#.

currently 1. On the next clock, the rotating ID is set to 3,and the priority order becomes, starting with the highest, 0, 1, 2, 3, and agent 3 begins its transaction.

Each processor in the system is identified by its agent ID number. The processor provides its agent ID during the transaction phase of a transaction; this allows all bus agents to track each transaction.

If one processor owns the buses when another one requests them by generating its BR0# signal, the current bus owner must deassert its BR0# signal when the current transaction is finished.

Note that if functional redundancy checking is being used on the system, then the processors are combined in pairs: agents 0 and 1 form an FRC master and slave respectively, and agents 2 and 3 form an FRC master and slave respectively. Also, in the single-processor environment, the agent is configured to have an agent ID number of 0. When the processor wants control of the buses it monitors the BPRI# signal and, if it is inactive, takes control automatically of the buses.

If AERR#, BINIT# or RESET# go active, BR[3:0]# must be deasserted in the next clock, and the BPRI# signal has priority over the BR[3:0]# signals.

BPRI# – Bus request priority
The BPRI# signal going active indicates that a device with higher priority than those connected to the BR[3:0]# signals, that is, processor(s), wants control of the buses. The device could be a PCI master, DMA, EISA master etc. If the processor is performing an un-locked transaction, and the BPRI# signal is sampled active, then it must release the buses when the transaction is complete. The central agent is always the next bus owner.

Note that the processor-to-PCI bus bridge chip is generally the central agent, that is, it drives BPRI# to get control of the buses from the processor.

Also, if a processor is busmaster and a PCI master, EISA master ISA master or DMA wants control of the buses then REQ#, MREQ# or DRQ generated respectively. For EISA, ISA or DMA masters, the standard bridge (PCI-to-EISA bridge) generates a request for the buses to the processor-to-PCI bridge chip. It will back the processor off and respond with a grant signal (GNT#), allowing the requesting master to get control of the buses.

If AERR#, BINIT# or RESET# go active, BPRI# must be deasserted in the next clock and the BPRI# signal has priority over the BR[3:0]# signals.

BNR# – block next request
The BNR# signal is driven by a bus agent to assert a bus stall. The current bus owner cannot start a new transaction because the agent that is driving the BNR# signal is indicating that it is unable to accept new transactions to avoid an internal queue overflow.

After RESET#, bus agents who wish to stall the buses to perform hardware initialization must assert BNR# in the clock after reset is sampled inactive. After BINIT#, bus agents who wish to stall the buses to perform hardware initialization must assert BNR# four clocks after BINIT# is sampled inactive.

LOCK# – lock
LOCK# indicates that new bus requests should not be generated because the current bus owner is performing a locked transaction. It takes priority over an active BPRI# or BR[3:0]# signal(s).

11.1.2 Request phase signals

The current busmaster starts a transaction in the request phase, which is two clocks long. During these two clocks, signals are driven that provide address, agent ID, control, parity, and cacheability information about the transfer.

ADS# – address strobe

The current bus owner generates ADS# for one clock, which identifies the beginning of a new transaction. The transaction address and control signals, A[35:3]#, RP#, AP[1:0]# and REQ[4:0]#, are generated at the same time and validated by the active ADS#. Other transaction phases, (error, snoop, response) and data are defined with respect to the active ADS#. The signals A[35:3]#, RP#, AP[1:0]# and REQ[4:0]# are all sampled with respect to ADS#.

> **Debug hints**
> Stuck at the first fetch
>
> • The end of the transaction is not seen by the processor: check HIT#, HITM#, RS[2:0]# and DRDY#.

A[35:3]# – address bus

A[35:3]# form the quadword address that identifies the location being accessed. This allows the processor to address 64 GB of address space. The current bus owner drives the quadword address of the location being accessed on A[35:3]# during the first clock of the request phase.

A[35:3]# contain byte enables, transaction length information, cache attributes connected with the location being accessed, deferred ID information, and other information related to the transaction during the second clock of the request phase.

During the second clock of the request phase, A[35:3] are defined as follows:

• A[31:24]# are outputs that contain cache attribute information, ATTR[7:0]#. The lower 3 bits are defined below, the rest are reserved for future expansion.

    ATTR[2:0]#
000	Write-back
001	Write-protected
010	Write-through
011	Write-combining, (reads are non-cacheable, writes can be delayed and combined)
111	Non-cacheable

• A[23:16]# contain deferred ID information, DID[7:0]#; they are valid only if DEN# is active. If the transaction is deferred, DID[7:0]# keep track of the transaction. DID[7:0]# are provided in the first clock of the request phase during a deferred reply transaction. The deferred ID provides

    DID[7:0]#
7#	Requesting agent type, low for symmetric, high for priority
[6:4]#	Requesting agent ID, defined at reset
[3:0]#	Transaction ID, used to track the transaction

• A[15:8]# contain byte enable information, BE[7:0]#. They identify the location in the quadword address being accessed. During special cycles they identify the type of special cycle being run:

    Active BE#s
None	No operation
0	Shutdown
1	Flush
1,0	Halt
2	Sync
2,0	Flush acknowledge

2,1   Stop clock acknowledge
2,1,0   SMI acknowledge

- A[7:3]# contain current transaction information, EXF[4:0]#.

Extended Function pin		Signal	Function
EXF4#	SMMEM#	smram	Space is being accessed in system management mode
EXF3#	SPLCK#		Indicates that a locked transaction is split
EXF2#			Reserved
EXF1#	DEN#		Defer enable indicates that the transaction can be deferred by the responding agent
EXF0#			Reserved

During the snoop phase, HIT# is generated if a hit is detected by snooping A[35:3]#. Also during the snoop phase, HITM# is generated if a hit to a modified line is detected by snooping A[35:3]#. A[23:16]# carry the deferred ID for deferred reply transactions, defined by REQ[4:0]# = 0h. A[11:5]# contain processor configuration information during RESET#.

AP[1:0]# – address parity bits
AP[1:0]# provide address bit, A[35:3]#, parity protection during both clocks of the transaction request phase. AP0# is the parity bit for A[23:3]#, and AP1# is the parity bit for A[35:24]. The parity bit is high if the number of zeros in the covered range is even. The parity bit is low if the number of zeros in the covered range is odd.

For example:

Address 13C1C6928h
A[35:24]# contains seven lows, AP1# is low, and A[23:3]# contains 12 lows, AP0# is high.

AERR# is generated in the error phase of a transaction if a bus agent detects an address parity error. AP[1:0]# are driven in the same clock as address strobe.

> **Debug hints**
> Lock-up
>
> - Processor timing or transaction is stuck in the snoop phase: replace the processor if socketed, and retest; check HIT# and HITM#.

REQ[4:0]# – request command signals
The REQ[4:0]# signals are generated during the request phase by the current bus owner. During the first clock, REQa[4:0]# identify the type of transaction taking place, and during the second clock, REQb[4:0]# identify the data transfer length (Table 11.2).

Table 11.2   Request command signals

Type of transaction	REQa[4:0]# 4 3 2 1 0	REQb[4:0]# 4 3 2 1 0
Deferred reply	1 1 1 1 1	x x x x x
Interrupt acknowledge	1 0 1 1 1	x x x 1 1
Special transaction	1 0 1 1 1	1 1 x 1 0
Branch trace message	1 0 1 1 0	1 1 x 1 1
I/O read	0 1 1 1 1	1 1 x LEN#
I/O write	0 1 1 1 0	1 1 x LEN#
Memory read and invalidate	ASZ# 1 0 1	1 1 x LEN#
Memory read	ASZ# 0 D/C# 1	1 1 x LEN#
Memory write	ASZ# 0 W/WB# 0	1 1 x LEN#

ASZ# indicates the memory address space being accessed, that is, 11 [4GB, 10] 4GB. LEN# identifies the length of the transaction, that is, 11 0-8 bytes, 01 32 bytes. D/C# indicates data or code read. W/WB# indicates write or write-back.

REQa[4:0]# are generated in the same clock as ADS#. RP# provides parity protection for REQ[4:0]#, and ADS#. AERR# is generated by any bus agent who detects a parity error during either of the two request phase clocks.

> **Debug hints**
> Divide overflow or illegal opcode
>
> * Bad processor: retest with another processor if socketed.

RP# – request parity
Parity protection on ADS# and REQ[4:0]# is provided by RP# during both clocks of the request phase. RP# is high if the number of zeroes in the covered signals is even, and low if the number of zeroes in the covered signals is odd.

For example:

* During the first clock of the request phase, ADS# is active. Assume REQ[4:0]# is 2h. The number of zeroes is odd; RP# will be low.
* During the second clock of the request phase, ADS# goes inactive; the number of zeroes is even; RP# will be high.

AERR# is generated in the error phase of a transaction if a bus agent detects a parity error in either of the two request phase clocks.

11.1.3 Error phase signals

Once a transaction has been started by a bus agent, the other bus agents check parity on the supported signals.

AERR# – address parity error
If an address parity error or request parity error occurs, AERR# is generated during the error phase. All bus agents abort the transaction and remove it from their in-order queue when AERR# is sampled active. The current bus owner will retry the transaction once. If AERR# is sampled active on the retry, the processor treats it as a hard error, goes into shutdown, and generates BERR#.

AERR# is generated if an address parity error is detected; A[35:3]# and AP[1:0]#, and also if a request parity error is detected; ADS#, REQ[4:0]# and RP#.

11.1.4 Snoop phase

All snooping agents must provide the result of their snoop during the snoop phase.

HIT# and HITM# – hit and hit modified
A snooping agent performs a cache directory search when it observes the beginning of a memory transaction, that is, the generation of ADS#, REQ[4:0]# and A[35:3]#. The snoop result is provided using HIT# and HITM#, during the snoop phase.

HIT# will be active when the directory search results in a hit to a line in the exclusive or shared state. It will also be active when the directory search results in a hit to a line in the modified state. The implicit write-back data is provided by the agent that detected the hit. If a write transaction is in progress, the bus owner provides the write data, the snooping agent provides the implicit write-back data, and the memory agent merges the data before writing it to memory. If a read transaction is in progress, the bus owner accepts the data, and the memory agent writes the modified data to memory.

DEFER# – defer

DEFER# can be used to suspend the current transaction with the corresponding transaction reply being completed later. It indicates to the processor that the current transaction will not be completed in order on the processor's bus.

DEN# and DID[7:0]# are sent out during the second clock of the request phase (refer to the A[35:3]# signals in the request phase section) and are latched by the responding agent. The deferred ID, DID[7:0]#, identifies the transaction ID, and the agent ID. The agent ID identifies the requester, and the transaction ID is different for each transaction, allowing the transaction to be tracked if it is deferred. DEN# indicates whether the processor will allow the transaction to be deferred.

Once the addressed agent is able to complete the transaction, the PCI bridge will become the bus owner and perform a deferred reply transaction. The bus agent that originated the original transaction will use the information in the current transaction to locate the original one, and the transaction is retired.

The transaction will not be deferred if HITM# and DEFER# are both active during the snoop phase; HITM# has priority, ensuring that the implicit write-back will occur.

RS[2:0]# – response status signals

RS[2:0]# are driven by the agent responsible for the completion of the transaction, that is, the response agent, at the top of the in-order queue. Table 11.3 shows possible response codes and their meanings.

RSP# – response phase

RSP# provides parity protection for RS[2:0]#. For example RS[2:0]# value is 3h, RSP# will be low. If an odd number of covered signals are low, then RSP# is low; if an even number of covered signals are low, then RSP# is high.

If a parity error is detected by a bus agent then BINIT# will be generated if the function has been enabled during configuration.

TRDY# – target ready

The target agent generates TRDY# during the response phase when it is ready to accept write or write-back data; the requesting or snooping agent can begin the data transfer.

During a write or write-back transaction, TRDY# active enables the requesting agent to provide D[63:0]# and DRDY#.

Table 11.3 Response codes

RS[3:0]#	Description	HITM#	DEFER#
7h	Idle state, the current transaction is not in the response phase.	NA	NA
6h	Retry response. RS[2:0]# indicate the end of the transaction; it has been cancelled, and must be reissued by the initiator.	1	0
5h	Defer response. RS[2:0]# indicate the end of the transaction; it has been suspended, and the defer agent will complete it with a defer reply.	1	0
4h	Reserved.		
3h	Hard failure. RS[2:0]# indicate the end of the transaction; a hard error was received, and exception handling is required by the initiator.	1	0
2h	No data. RS[2:0]# indicate the end of the transaction; it is completed at this time.	1	1
1h	Implicit write-back response; snooping agent will transfer the modified cache data.	0	X
0h	Normal with data; transaction completed.	1	1

11.1.5 Data phase

A transaction that is going to transfer data will contain a data phase. During the data phase, data and parity or ECC information are provided.

> **Debug hints**
> Processor bus signals are not static when single stepping. The processor bus cannot be compared with the single-step card. The first fetch address seen is FFFFFFE0h; the processor is fetching 32 bytes from FFFFFFE0h to FFFFFFFFh.

DRDY# – data ready

DRDY# indicates that valid data has been placed on the bus by the agent driving the data. When TRDY# is sampled active during a write transaction, the processor generates DRDY#. During a processor read transaction, DRDY# is driven by the memory controller or the processor to PCI bridge when valid data has been placed on the processor's data bus.

During multiple data transfers, DBSY# is generated before the first DRDY# and between DRDY# assertions.

DBSY# – data bus busy

DBSY# is asserted by the agent responsible for driving the processor's data bus when the data phase requires more than one clock, for example, cache linefill. It is driven at the start of the data phase.

DBSY# is generated during a processor write transaction when TRDY# is sampled active if the transaction requires multiple data transfers. During a processor read transaction, DBSY# is driven by the memory controller or the processor to PCI bridge if the transaction requires multiple data transfers.

A hold is placed on the data bus, D[63:0]#, that is, no other agent will try to use it when DBSY# is active.

D[63:0]# – data bus

D[63:0]# provide a bidirectional data path for the transfer of information between the processor and other devices on the processor bus.

During the second clock of the request phase, A[15:8]# represent the byte enables. The byte enables indicate which data bits are transferring valid information.

A15#, BE7# – byte lane 7, D[63:56]#   A14#, BE6# – byte lane 6, D[55:48]#
A13#, BE5# – byte lane 5, D[47:40]#   A12#, BE4# – byte lane 4, D[39:32]#
A11#, BE3# – byte lane 3, D[31:24]#   A10#, BE2# – byte lane 2, D[23:15]#
A9#, BE1# – byte lane 1, D[15:8]#   A8#, BE0# – byte lane 0, D[7:0]#

DEP[7:0]# provide parity or ECC protection, determined by configuration, for the data bus. DBSY# indicates that the data bus is in use. DRDY# indicates that information on the data bus should be latched.

DEP[7:0]# – data bus error correction/parity bits

DEP[7:0]# signals provide data bus parity or ECC protection. The POST software sets up the type of protection required.

If parity protection is required, then each DEP# signal is associated with one byte of the data bus. If an odd number of covered signals are low, then the DEP# bit should be low. If an even number of covered signals are low, then the DEP# bit should be high.

If ECC protection is required, then an algorithm is used to generate, check and correct errors. The DEP# signals are not associated with specific data bus bytes. If a single bit ECC error is detected by the processor, it can correct the error; a record of the error is kept in an error log.

If a double-bit ECC error is detected by the processor, a record of the error is kept in an error log. The processor cannot correct double-bit errors, and BERR# is generated. The processor, processor-to-PCI bridge, and the memory controller can all generate and check ECC data errors; they can correct single-bit errors. The DEP[7:0]# signals provide parity or ECC protection for the data bus, D[63:0]#. BERR# is generated if multiple-bit ECC data errors are detected.

11.2 Transaction Examples

The section illustrates different processor transactions.

11.2.1 Processor read transaction

Figure 11.3 outlines the processor read transaction, and Figure 11.4 gives an example timing diagram.

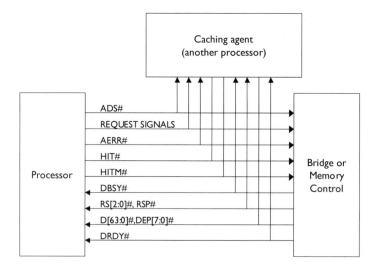

Figure 11.3   Processor read transaction block diagram

The states are:

T_1 The processor generates ADS# and the request phase signals beginning the transaction (A[35:3]# – address; AP[1:0]# – address parity; REQ[4:0]# – transaction type and; RP# – request parity signal). All bus agents latch the information and place it in their in-order queues. Caching agents can begin snooping their internal caches.

T_2 The processor generates the rest of the request phase signals, for example, byte enables, attribute information, deferred ID information on the address lines, and the length of transfer on REQ[4:0]#. All bus agents latch the information and place it in their in-order queues.

T_3 If the transaction is at the top of the in-order queue, the bus agent responsible for it will begin the cycle on its buses. For a transaction to a device other than memory the bridge chip would be the controlling agent. For a memory transaction, the memory controller would be the bus agent in control.

T_4 This is the transaction error phase. AERR# would be generated by the device detecting an address parity error, or a request parity error. In the timing diagram, no error was detected; if an error was detected, the transaction would have been re-moved from the in-order queue, and the remaining phases would be cancelled.

T_5 This is the transaction snoop phase; if a hit is detected by a caching agent, for ex-ample, another, processor, then HIT#, (or HITM# if appropriate) would be gener-ated. In the timing diagram example, a hit was not detected.

T_6 All bus agents sample HIT# and HITM#; if HITM# was active then a write-back cycle would be performed. In the timing diagram shown, no write-back cycle is performed.

T_7 This is the transaction response and data phase. The response parity signal, RSP#, is provided, along with a normal data response on RS[2:0]#. DRDY# active indi-cates that valid data is on the bus; if multiple data transfers were required then DBSY# would be active. The response and data phases begin in the same clock for a read transaction.

T_8 DRDY# is sampled active by the processor, and the requested data is accepted. This is the end of the transaction.

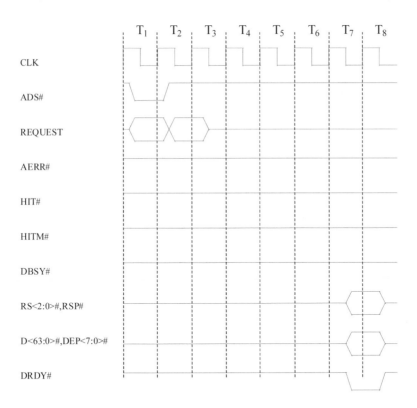

Figure 11.4   Processor read transaction timing diagram

11.2.2 Processor write transaction timing diagram

Figure 11.5 outlines the processor write transaction, and Figure 11.6 gives an example timing diagram. The states are:

T_1 The processor generates ADS# and the request phase signals beginning the trans-action (A[35:3]# – address; AP[1:0]# – address parity; REQ[4:0]# – transaction type; and RP# – request parity signal). All bus agents latch the information and place it in their in-order queues. Caching agents can begin snooping their internal caches.

T_2 The processor generates the rest of the request phase signals, for example, byte enables, attribute information, deferred ID information, on the address lines, and the length of transfer on REQ[4:0]#. All bus agents latch the information and place it in their in-order queues.

T_3 If the transaction is at the top of the in-order queue, the bus agent responsible for it will begin the cycle on its buses. For a transaction to a device other than memory, the bridge chip would be the controlling agent. For a memory transaction, the memory controller would be the bus agent in control.

T_4 This is the transaction error phase. AERR# would be generated by the device detecting an address parity error or a request parity error. In the timing diagram no error was detected; if an error was detected, the transaction would have been removed from the in-order queue, and the remaining phases would be cancelled.

T_5 This is the transaction snoop phase: if a hit is detected by a caching agent, for example, another processor, then HIT# (or HITM# if appropriate) would be generated. In the timing diagram example, a hit was not detected.

T_6 All bus agents sample HIT# and HITM#; if HITM# was active then a write-back cycle would be performed. In the timing diagram shown, no write-back cycle is performed. The processor places the write data on the data bus, D[63:0]#, and generates DRDY#, indicating that valid data is on the bus.

T_7 This is the transaction response phase. The response parity signal, RSP#, is provided, along with a no-data response on RS[2:0]#. The data phase begins before the response phase for a write transaction.

T_8 RS[2:0]# are sampled by the processor, and the result is a no data response. This is the end of the transaction.

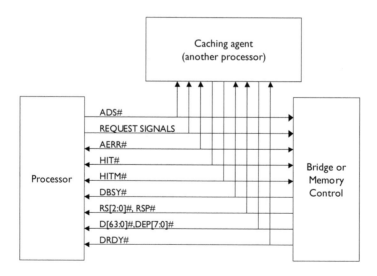

Figure 11.5   Processor write transaction block diagram

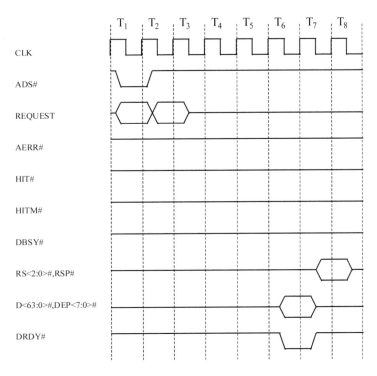

Figure 11.6   Processor write transaction timing diagram

11.2.3 Deferred transaction

Figure 11.7 outlines the deferred transaction, and Figure 11.8 gives an example timing diagram. The states are:

T_1 The processor generates ADS# and the request phase signals beginning the transaction (A[35:3]# – address; AP[1:0]# – address parity; REQ[4:0]# – transaction type; and RP# – request parity signal). All bus agents latch the information and place it in their in-order queues. Caching agents can begin snooping their internal caches.

T_2 The processor generates the rest of the request phase signals, for example, byte enables, attribute information, deferred ID information on the address lines, and the length of transfer on REQ[4:0]#. DEN# deferred enable, A4#, will be active. All bus agents latch the information and place it in their in-order queues.

T_3 If the transaction is at the top of the in-order queue, the bus agent will begin the cycle on its buses. The bridge chip begins the cycle on the PCI bus.

T_4 This is the transaction error phase. AERR# would be generated by the device detecting an address parity error or a request parity error. In the timing diagram, no error was detected; if an error was detected, the transaction would have been removed from the in-order queue, and the remaining phases would be cancelled.

T_5 This is the transaction snoop phase. If a hit is detected by a caching agent, for example, another processor, then HIT# (or HITM# if appropriate) would be generated. In the timing diagram example, a hit was not detected. DEN# was active in T_2, DEFER# is generated to tell the processor that the transaction may be deferred. The transaction does not have to be completed in order because DEFER# was generated.

T$_6$ DEFER# is sampled active, and HITM# is sampled inactive, indicating that the transaction will be completed later, that is not in order. Note that the transaction would not be deferred if HITM# was active. It would have to be completed in order to ensure that the write-back takes place.

T$_7$ This is the transaction response phase. The response parity signal, RSP#, is provided, along with a deferred response on RS[2:0]#. The transaction is removed from the processor's in-order queue but retains a copy of the transaction information in the outstanding transaction queue. There is no data phase because the transaction is being deferred.

T$_8$ The transaction is still in progress outside the processor bus. The shaded bar indicates that there could be one or more clocks before the data is available. The bus agent begins a deferred reply transaction when the data is available.

T$_9$ The deferred reply transaction is started by the bus agent when it generates ADS# and the request phase signals. The address bus bits, A[23:16]#, contain the deferred ID latched from the original transaction.

T$_{10}$/T$_{11}$ The processor knows that it will receive the response from the original request because it matches the deferred ID stored in the outstanding transaction queue with the DID[7:0]# signals.

T$_{12}$ This is the transaction error phase. AERR# would be generated by the device detecting an address parity error or a request parity error. In the timing diagram, no error was detected; if an error was detected, the transaction would have been removed from the in-order queue, and the remaining phases would be cancelled.

T$_{13}$ HIT# is generated by the bus agent to indicate what state the cache line should be saved in: HIT# active – saved in the shared state; HIT# inactive – saved in the exclusive state.

T$_{14}$ HIT# is sampled by the processor to determine the final state of the cache line.

T$_{15}$ This is the transaction response and data phase. The response parity signal, RSP#, is provided, along with a normal data response on RS[2:0]#. DRDY# active indicates that valid data is on the data bus, D[63:0]#.

T$_{16}$ The processor sampled DRDY# active and accepts the requested data.

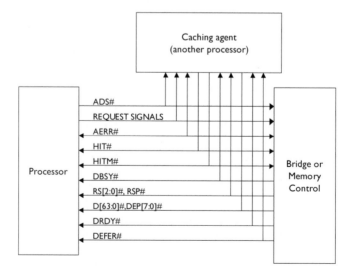

Figure 11.7   Deferred transaction block diagram

Note that for a write transaction, data would have been provided during T_6, and the deferred response would have been normal without data during T_{15}, telling the processor that the write took place.

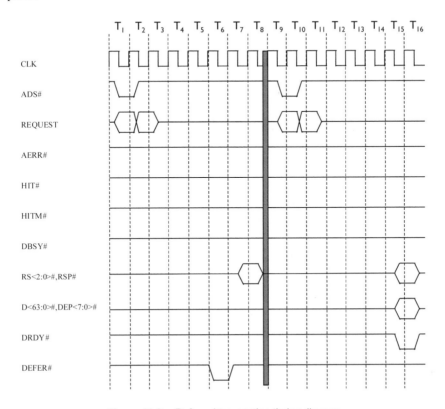

Figure 11.8 Deferred transaction timing diagram

11.2.4 Write-back transaction

Figure 11.9 outlines write-back transaction, and Figure 11.10 gives an example timing diagram. The states are:

T_1 The processor generates ADS# and the request phase signals beginning the transaction (A[35:3]# – address; AP[1:0]# – address parity; REQ[4:0]# – transaction type; and RP# – request parity signal). The memory controller and other processors latch the information and place it in their in-order queues. Caching agents can begin snooping their internal caches.

T_2 The processor generates the rest of the request phase signals, for example, byte enables, attribute information, deferred ID information on the address lines, and the length of transfer on REQ[4:0]#. The memory controller and other processors latch the information and place it in their in-order queues.

T_3 If the transaction is at the top of the in-order queue, the memory controller will begin the cycle on the memory bus.

T_4 This is the transaction error phase. AERR# would be generated by the device detecting an address parity error or a request parity error. In the timing diagram, no error was detected; if an error was detected, the transaction would have been removed from the in-order queue and the remaining phases would be cancelled.

T$_5$ The processor knows that the responding agent is ready to accept the write data because TRDY# is active. This is the transaction snoop phase. A caching agent detected a hit to a modified line and generates HITM#.

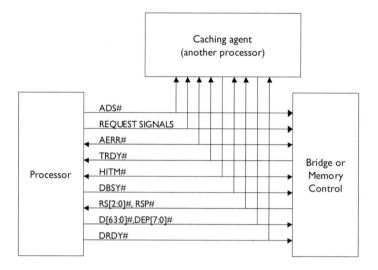

Figure 11.9   Write-back transaction block diagram

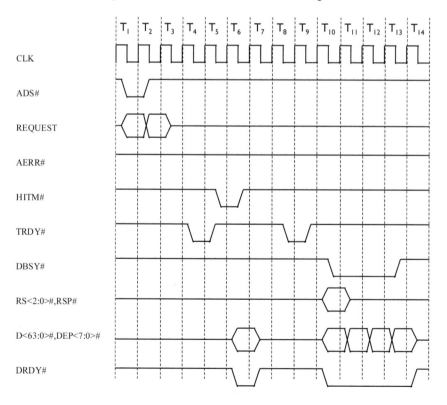

Figure 11.10   Write-back transaction timing diagram

T$_6$ HITM# is sampled active by the processor and the memory controller. The processor places the write data on the data bus, and generates DRDY#. The memory controller knows that it has to accept both the write and the write-back data.

T$_7$ This is the transaction data phase. The memory controller accepts the write data from the processor. The memory controller does not write the data to memory yet, but stores it in an internal buffer.

T$_8$ The memory controller indicates that it is ready to accept the write-back data by generating TRDY#.

T$_9$ The caching agent samples TRDY# active, and knows that the memory controller is ready to accept the write-back data.

T$_{10}$–T$_{14}$ The caching agent that detected the hit generates DRDY# and DBSY# and provides the modified cache line on the data bus a quadword at a time. The memory controller merges the original data with the modified data, and writes the modified line to memory.

11.3 Additional Pentium Pro Signals

This section discusses additional Pentium Pro signals that were not covered in sections 11.1 and 11.2. The additional signals cannot be associated directly with a particular transaction phase. Figure 11.11 shows that they can be split into four groups.

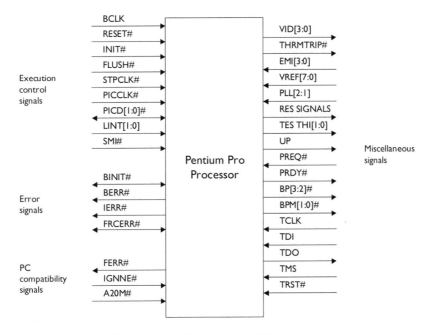

Figure 11.11   Pentium Pro additional signals

11.3.1 Execution control group

The execution control signals control how the processor handles the flow of transactions.

BCLK – bus clk (input)
Bus clk determines the Pentium Pro bus frequency, and determines indirectly the processor's

internal clk frequency, that is, the processor's core frequency is a multiple of BCLK. The Pentium Pro samples
LINT1/NMI, LINT0/INTR, IGNNE# and A20M# on a
high-to-low transition of RESET# to determine the ratio

> **Debug hints**
> Lock-up
>
> Internal error detected: check
> IERR#.

of the bus frequency to the processor core frequency; these values are latched on a low-to-
high RESET# transition, so that the signals can then be used for their normal function. Table
11.4 shows the bus core frequency ratio determined by the power-on configuration conditions.

Reset# – reset (input)
The registers are set to their default values, the internal caches are invalidated, and certain
signals are sampled for configuration purposes when RESET# is active.

INIT# – initialize (input)
The processor registers are set to their default values when INIT# goes active; the internal
caches are not invalidated.

FLUSH# –flush (input)
The processor writes back all cache lines in the modified state to memory, and then invalidates all lines in both caches, when FLUSH# is sampled active. A flush acknowledge transaction is performed to indicate to external logic that the cache flush operation is complete.

The processor enters tristate test mode if FLUSH# is active on a low-to-high reset transition. In a multiprocessor system, FLUSH# is generated in an attempt to allow another processor to take over as the boot processor if the boot processor fails to boot.

STPCLK# – stop clock (input)
The processor is placed in a low-power state by STPCLK#; most of the processor's internal
clks are stopped by this operation. The processor still snoops on bus transactions in the stop
clock state. The processor restarts its internal clock to all units and continues executing when
STPCLK# is deasserted.

LINT[1:0] – local interrupt signals (inputs)
The processor contains a local advanced programmable interrupt controller (APIC) with two
interrupt inputs, LINT[1:0]. The LINT[1:0] are local interrupt inputs that default to INTR,
LINT0, and NMI, LINT1, when the APIC is disabled. LINT[1:0] are programmed as local
interrupt inputs when the APIC is enabled; the system requires an I/O APIC, which handles
EISA and PCI interrupts to make full use of the local APIC, (EISA and PCI interrupts are
then handled via PICD[1:0]#).

Table 11.4 Power-on configuration conditions

Bus/core frequency ratio	LINT1/NMI	LINT0/INTR	IGNNE#	A20M#
2/4	0	0	0	0
2/5	0	1	0	0
2/6	0	0	1	0
2/7	0	0	1	0
2/8	0	0	0	1
2/9	0	1	0	1
2/10	0	0	1	1
2/11	0	1	1	1

PICCLK – programmable interrupt controller clock (input)

PICD[1:0]# – programmable interrupt controller data bus (bidirectional)

The processor APIC bus operations are synchronized by the PICCLK input. The PICCLK is used as a reference for sampling the APIC data signals, PICD[1:0]#. The PICD[1:0]# signals provide a bidirectional serial data path for the processor to read messages from, and send messages to another APIC. APIC logic allows any interrupt to be serviced by any processor in a multiprocessor environment. The APIC logic consists of a local APIC and an I/O APIC.

The I/O APIC resides in the I/O subsystem and has interrupt input pins that allow I/O devices to request servicing. The local APIC resides in the processor and decides who should service the interrupt when a message is received from the I/O APIC. The processor handles the interrupt in the normal manner.

The advantages of using an APIC are that the processor does not have to perform an interrupt acknowledge cycle to get the interrupt vector ID because it is part of the message sent and that interrupt servicing is shared by all the processors.

SMI# – system management interrupt (input)

SMI# is generated by an I/O agent that wants to be placed in power conservation mode, or wants to come out of power conservation mode.

The processor saves its registers and enters system management mode when SMI# is active. An SMI acknowledge transaction is issued by the processor. It then executes the SMM handler.

11.3.2 Error group

The error signals group indicate that a catastrophic error has occurred.

> **Debug hints**
> Video post lock-up
>
> Interrupts not functioning correctly: check LINT[:0].

BINIT# – bus initialization (bidirectional)

BINIT# resets the bus state machines when an error occurs that prevents reliable operation. As an output, BINIT# is out put by a bus agent, if enabled, when an error is detected, for which BINIT# is a valid response, for example:

- ADS# active when the in-order queue is full.
- HIT# or HITM# active outwith the snoop phase.
- Response parity error is detected.

As an input, BINIT# is an input to all bus agents. If a bus agent sees BINIT# active, it must:

- Deassert all signals on the bus.
- Reset the transaction queues.
- Reset the arbitration IDs to the power-on reset value, and begin a new arbitration sequence to request the buses.

Note that if the processor samples BINIT# active, it fetches it first instruction from the power-on restart vector address.

BERR# – bus error (output)

BERR# is generated by the processor when a bus protocol violation occurs. The processor will shut down, and the priority agent will generally generate an NMI. Examples of when BERR# would be generated are:

- Multiple-bit ECC errors on the data bus.
- On a transaction retry when AERR# is active.
- A hard error response during a transaction.
- An internal parity error.
- An FRCERR error.

IERR# – internal error (output)

IERR# is generated by the processor when it detects an internal error. IERR# would be generated in the same situations as BERR#.

FRCERR – functional redundancy check error (bidirectional)

If there are two processors in a system, they can be configured as an FRC pair. The master processor executes all the instructions, while the second processor (checker) mirrors the operations but does not drive the buses. The checker compares the master's outputs with its own internally sampled ones when a transaction is being performed. If the checker detects an error, it generates FRCERR to the master FRCERR input. The master enters into a machine check.

11.3.3 PC compatibility group

These signals keep compatibility with 8086-compatable systems.

FERR# – floating-point error (output)

FERR# is generated by the processor when an unmasked floating-point error is detected.

IGNNE # – ignore numeric error (input)

The processor ignores numeric errors and continues to execute floating-point instructions when IGNNE# is active.

A20M# – address 20 mask (input)

A20M# goes active only in real mode. It ensures that the processor masks out A20#, that is, it is low, before it performs a transaction. A20M# is used to emulate the 8086 address wrap-around at 1 MB.

11.3.4 Miscellaneous group

The miscellaneous group of signals provides a boundary scan interface and other miscellaneous functions.

> **Debug hints**
> Bad first fetch address
>
> - No processor RESET#: check RESET#.
> - No processor CLK: check BCLK.
> - Processor is in stop clock mode, tristate mode, or shutdown mode: check STPCLK#, FLUSH# and BERR#/IERR# for each fault respectively.
> - Overheating: check THRMTRIP#.

VID[3:0] – voltage Id signals (outputs)

The processor generates the VID[3:0] signals to an adjustable DC to DC converter, to set its voltage reference requirements. The following VID[3:0] patterns identify the voltage settings:

0000h : 3.5V incrementing in steps of one to 1110h : 2.1V. As the hex patterns increment, the voltage settings decrement in steps of 0.1V, for example, 0100 : 3.1V.

For example:

Operating frequency : 133MHz : 2.9V   Operating frequency : 150MHz : 3.3V

THRMTRIP# – thermal trip (output)

If the processor's internal temperature reaches about. 130°C, it shuts down to prevent any damage.

EMI[3:0] – emissions signals (inputs)

These pins are tied to the package heat spreader, and should be connected to ground.

VREF[7:0] – voltage reference signals (input)

These are voltage reference signals used by the internal gunning transceiver logic.

PLL[2:1] – phase lock loop signals (input)

These pins provide decoupling for an internal phase lock loop; they should be attached to a $0.1\mu F$ capacitor.

TESTHI[2:1] – test high

These should be pulled high.

UP – upgrade present

UP (if fitted) is linked to the voltage regulators to prevent harmful voltages from damaging the overdrive processor.

PREQ# – probe request (input)

This signal places the processor in probe mode for emulation purposes.

PRDY# – probe ready (output)

This signal indicates that the processor is in probe mode, and its test access port is ready to accept a boundary scan command.

BP[3:2]# – break point bits (output)

These bits indicate when a condition identified by the debug registers has occurred.

BPM[1:0]# – break point performance bits (output)

When programmed as breakpoint bits, these indicate when a condition identified by the debug registers has occurred. These bits can also be configured as performance monitoring bits.

TCK – test clock (input)

This clock is used to clock data into and out of the processor during boundary scan mode operation.

TDI – test data in (input)

This is the boundary scan serial data input. On the rising edge of TCK, data is shifted into the processor.

Debug hints
Processor speed fails

Switch settings: check the processor frequency switches.

Debug 1: crowbar test on motherboards

Check the electrolytic capacitors fitted across the power supplies for visual damage, e.g. charring, or using a multi meter set to the ohms range check for short circuits, i.e. buzz out each power rail to ground.

Debug 2: visual checks on motherboard

Inspect the board for:
1. Damaged/cracked components.
2. Damaged/unsoldered component pins.
3. Damaged connectors.
4. Damaged/unsoldered connector pins.
5. Damaged SIMM/DIMM sockets. If SIMMs/DIMMs are fitted, check that they are fitted correctly and making good contact.
6. Damaged tracks.
7. Insufficient solder/dry joints.
8. Short circuits.
9. Check that components fitted into sockets are inserted properly and making good contact, e.g. processor and ROM.

Check: Switch setting and Jumpers (if fitted) are not damaged, and are all in the correct positions, making good contact.

TDO – test data out (output)

This is the boundary scan serial data output. On the rising edge of TCK, data is shifted out of the processor.

TMS – test mode select (input)

Check that no components on the board are overheating (or) cracked when the power is applied. This is a boundary scan test logic control input.

TRST# – tap reset (input)

This is a boundary scan test logic asynchronous reset or initialization pin.

> **DEBUG 3: Thermal checks on motherboard**
>
> Check there are no components on the board overheating/cracked when the power is applied.

11.4 Exercises

11.4.1 In which phase can a device get control of the bus?

(a)	Arbitration	(b)	Data
(c)	Snoop	(d)	Request

11.4.2 Which signal is used by the processor to identify that it grants the bus to another device?

(a)	BNR#	(b)	BPRI#
(c)	LOCK#	(d)	ADS#

11.4.3 Which signal is used to inform the processor that another device wishes to take control of the bus?

(a)	BNR#	(b)	BPRI#
(c)	LOCK#	(d)	ADS#

11.4.4 Identify which of the P6, OPB and OMC would correspond for each of the following terms.

(i)   Bus agent
(ii)   Central agent
(iii) Requesting agent
(iv)   Addressed agent
(v)   Responding agent
(vi)   Snooping agent

11.4.5 Place the following phases in the order in which they occur: request phase, snoop phase, error phase, arbitration phase.

11.4.6 What address lines carry BE[7:0]*?

11.4.7 If the rotating ID is 2, what is the priority order?

> **Debug 4: POST and milestones**
>
> Systems boards go through a sequence of milestone check points as they boot up, that is, the board runs through the POST (power on self test) program checking out different areas of the system hardware. As it passes through the checkpoints, it writes a value out to an unused DMA page register, often port 80h (this address is dependent on the motherboard manufacturer). When testing, observe this sequence of events, and see whether the board goes through a checkpoint that a good one does not go to and continues, or hangs up at a particular checkpoint. Familiarity with the tests being carried out at the checkpoints gives a pointer to the area of the circuit then needs further testing.

11.4.8 How do the following improve P6 performance?

(i)	Superscalar model?	(ii)	Superpipelined model?
(iii)	Speculative execution?	(iv)	Integrated L2 cache?
(v)	Register renaming?	(vi)	Out-of-order execution?

11.4.9 During a write transaction, what input to the P6 indicates that the P6 can drive the data on the bus?

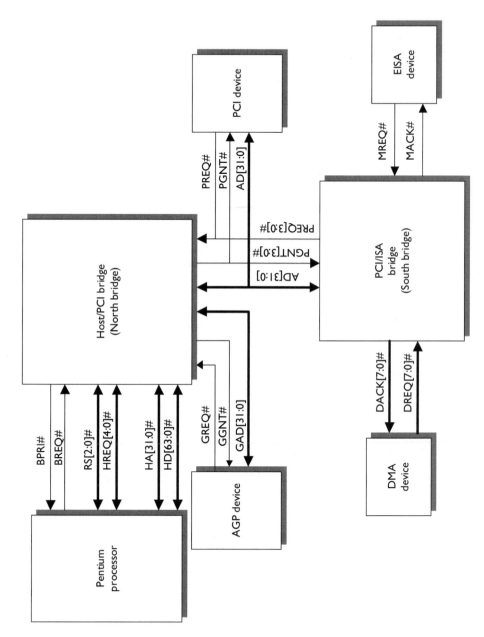

Figure 11.12 Main Pentium bus request signals (including AGP)

12   Memory

12.1 Introduction

Memory is a component that typically must be easily upgraded and installed, as many systems support a very large memory capacity. DRAM memory is typically used for the main memory of the computer as it is cheaper than SRAM for a given memory requirement. The first attempt at producing an easy-to-install memory component was as single in-line memory modules (SIMMs). These SIMMs were either 30-pin or 72-pin modules. Dual in-line memory modules (DIMMs) are typically 168-pin (EDO or SDRAM). The basic types are:

- 30-pin SIMMs have 10 addressing lines (A0-A9) and eight data lines (D0-D7). The ac-tual address is selected using the row address select (RAS) and the column address se-lect (CAS).
- 72-pin SIMMs have 12 addressing lines (A0-A11) and 32 data lines (D0-D31). The ac-tual address is selected using four row address strobe lines (RAS0-RAS3) and four col-umn address strobe lines (CAS0-CAS3). Tables A.1 and A.2 in the appendix define their pin connections.
- 168-pin are the most popular type of memory module for desktop systems, and have independent signal lines on each side of the module. They are available with 72 (36 tabs on each side), 88 (44 tabs on each side), 144 (72 tabs on each side), 168 (84 tabs on each side) or 200 tabs (100 tabs on each side). DIMMs give greater reliability and density than SIMMs: which provide only a 16-bit (30-pin) or 32-bit (72-pin) data interface. DIMMs provide a 64-bit data interface. Figures 12.16 and 12.17 (Section 12.6) show two common interfaces to DIMM modules (EDO, SDRAM and RDRAM).

12.2 Memory Basics

Most systems use DRAM as their main electronic memory storage. This type of memory uses a switching transistor to charge or discharge a tiny capacitor. Each capacitor represents a single bit of storage. Figure 12.1 outline the internal structure of DRAM memory. The memory is ac-cessed using:

- **RAS# (row address select).** These are used with the memory address lines (MA) to either initiate a memory cycle or address a row of memory. The amount of time that the RAS must be low for a memory refresh is known as the precharge time. There can be a number of RAS# as the memory is organized as a number of modules. In the example in Figure 12.1, there are four modules of memory, thus there are four RAS# lines (RAS0#, … RAS3#). Each of these access rows a bank of memory.

- **CAS# (column address select)**. These are used with the memory address lines (MA) to access a column within the memory. In the example shown in Figure 12.1, there are four modules of memory, thus there are four CAS# lines (CAS0#, … CAS3#). Each of these access columns with each module of memory.

- **MA[add:0]**. These are the address lines that locate the memory location on the device, and are used to access either the row or the column (multiplexing). If the RAS# line is active, a row address is latched, and if the CAS# line is active, a column address is latched (the minimum time that these must be active for is known as the hold time).

- **WE# (write enable).** Used to define a write or a read operation. An active low identifies a write operation, while a high level indicates a read operation.

- **OE# (output enable).** The output from the memory becomes available only when this line is active.

- **MD[dat:0] (memory data).** The lines that are used to define the data to be read or written to or from memory (sometimes referred to as DQ lines).

DIMMs are normally available in banks, typically with a bank of two or three banks. In Figure 12.2, the data bus of each bank is 64 bits wide. The first module provides the least significant 32 bits, and the second module provides the upper 32 bits. Each module also provides four parity bits (MP0–MP3 and MP4–MP7). Together, the modules provide the full 64 bits. The address lines MRAS0# and MRAS1# select module 0 and module 1, while MRAS2# and MRAS3# select module 2 and module 3. The columns are selected with the memory column address lines (in this case, MCAS0# … MCAS7#).

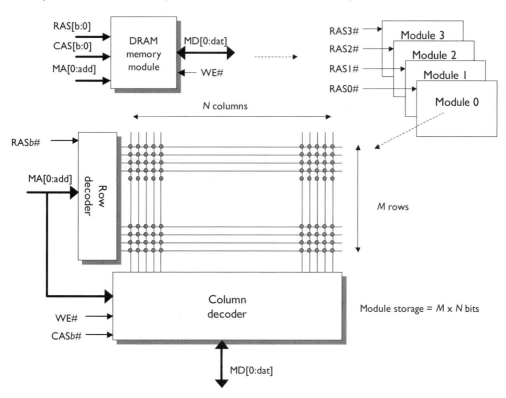

Figure 12.1 DRAM memory showing modules

The tiny capacitors within DRAM quickly lose their electrical charge, thus the memory is organized into rows (wordlines) and columns (bitlines) so that each DRAM cell in a row can be refreshed automatically with its state every time the row is accessed. The refresh is done through refresh cycles, which are hidden to the system. This is achieved using a sense amplifier which refreshes a whole row of data. Figure 12.3

Chipsets: a designer's best friend

Gordon Campbell started Chips & Technologies, who produced the first chipset in 1984 when they took 200 chips that made up an 80286-based PC, and reduced them to five or six devices (ASICs). These chipsets considerably reduced the design complexity.

shows a basic sense amplifier. Each column has a single sense amplifier. First the bit lines (Bit and $\overline{\text{Bit}}$) are charged to a high level by making the **Precharge** active HIGH. Next **Precharge** is made inactive. After this the memory cell is selected and the sense line is made active. If the bit stored was a HIGH then it will be charged up via **Q3** to refresh its level, else if it is a LOW then it will be discharged via **Q1**. The sense amplifier aids the charging and discharging of the cells.

Figure 12.4 shows the arrangement of the sense amplifier within the memory. Each column has an associated sense amplifier so that when a row is selected the whole row will be refreshed. The **Column select** line only allows a single to reach the **IO Bus**.

Each memory cell has a unique location or address defined by the intersection of a row and a column. These are addressed using the row address select (RAS#) and column address select (CAS#) signals.

Unfortunately, DRAM is relatively slow compared to modern clock speeds. A typical access time is around 60–70 ns. SRAM cache has improved the access time, as the SRAM loads data from DRAM into a fast SRAM memory. The processor will then (most of the time) access the cache rather than the DRAM memory. Unfortunately this is still not fast enough for fast transfers, thus several memory types have been designed to overcome the weaknesses. These are explained below.

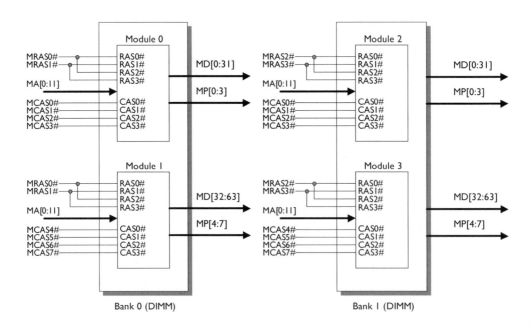

Figure 12.2   DIMM banks

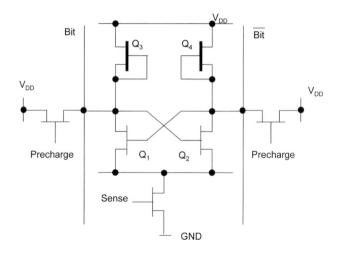

Figure 12.3 Basic sense amplifier circuit

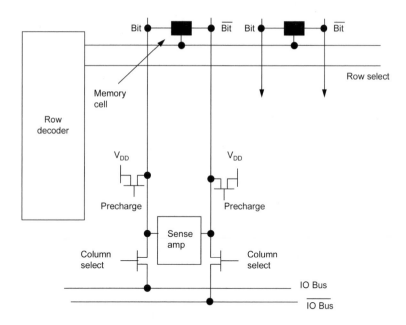

Figure 12.4 Memory arrangement with sense amplifier

DRAM uses an array of rows and columns. In standard DRAM (for fast paged memory DRAM) the access time is around 60–70ns. When accessing the memory, the memory management unit:

- Reads data by first activating the appropriate row of the array.
- Activates the appropriate column, then validates the data and transfers the data to the system.
- The column is then deactivated, which introduces an unwanted wait state during which the processor has to wait for the memory to finish the transfer.

- The output data buffer is then turned off, ready for the next memory access.

If the system clock that access the memory is running at 66 MHz, the clock period will be 15 ns. Thus, if the DRAM has a delay of 70 ns, there must be five clock delays (waits) before the data will be ready for the system to read. These delays are known as wait states. The best that FPM can achieve in a burst rate timing is 5-3-3-3, which means it takes five clocks cycles to read the first element of data (with four wait-states), with the next three elements each taking three clock cycles. The controller is thus forced to wait for four wait-states before it reads the data from the output from the memory.

12.2.1 Extended data out DRAM

Extended data out (EDO) memory allows for faster accesses, as it does not require the column to be deactivated and the output buffer to be turned off before the next data transfer starts. It can thus give a burst timing of 5-2-2-2 (at a bus speed of 66MHz). As this takes 11 cycles for four elements of data, rather that 14 clock cycles, there is a speed improvement of 27 per cent over FPM DRAM.

12.2.2 Burst extended data out DRAM

Burst extended data out (BEDO) DRAM improves the EDO DRAM principle by including a pipeline stage and a 2-bit burst counter. BEDO eliminates the wait states by accessing further data and can achieve system timings of 5-1-1-1. Unfortunately, BEDO DRAM has never really been supported by many DRAM controller vendors, and has been overtaken largely by synchronous DRAM (SDRAM). BEDO can use a transfer rate of up to 100MHz.

12.2.3 Synchronous DRAM

SDRAM allows for pin compatibility with EDO DRAM, but works in a different way. Most memory accesses in the PC are sequential, thus SDRAM is designed to fetch all the bits in a burst as fast as possible. For this, an on-chip burst counter allows the column part of the address to be incremented very rapidly, which helps speed up retrieval of information in sequential reads. The memory control thus provides the initial location of the block and its size, and the SDRAM provides the data as fast as the CPU can read them. This output process is synchronized by the system clock (typically at 100MHz). This is an important feature, as previous memory systems (such as FPM DRAM and EDO DRAM) have used asynchronous transfers (stop–start). After the data transfer has been set up, the SDRAM data burst can transfer at a rate of up to 100MHz, and thus uses a 10-ns clock transfer period. This gives a burst rate of 5-1-1-1, giving an improvement of around 18 per cent on EDO methods (for some types of memory transfer).

PC100 SDRAM devices (100MHz transfer rates) have since been developed onto PC133 SDRAM, which are capable of transferring data at up to 1.6GB/s (which is almost double previous transfer rates). As with PC100 SDRAM, there is no requirement for upgrades to the motherboard, as they are totally pin-compatible with previous DIMM banks. These types of devices are now popular in servers.

The greatest weakness of SDRAM is that it has been forced to be compatible with older memory systems. Thus, because of its legacy architecture, it cannot transfer it rates well above 133 MHz. The main weakness is separate address, control and data (now named DQM lines) lines, all controlled by the same clock.

Figure 12.5 outlines the main connections to SDRAM. SDRAM uses the same 168-pin connector as EDO and FPM DRAM, but the pin names and their functions have been changed. Table 12.1 outlines the main changes. It should be noticed that each of the physical banks has its own independent clock. This clock will typically be 66 MHz (15 ns), 100 MHz (10 ns) or 133 MHz (7.5 ns). The connection to the motherboard and to the DRAM controller will be outlined in Chapter 27.

Table 12.1 Changed pin connections for SDRAM

EDO DRAM	*SDRAM connection*	*SDRAM description*
CAS0#–CAS7#	DQMB0–DQMB7	Enables byte blocks. When reading from memory, DQMB controls the output buffers like an output enable. In Write mode, DQMB operates as a byte mask by allowing input data to be written when low, but blocks the write operation when high.
RAS0#–RAS3#	S0#-S3#	SDRAM selects. When low, enables the associated SDRAM command decoder, and disables it when high. S0# and S2# select module 0 (physical bank 0) and S1# and S3# select module 1 (physical bank 1).
Not used	CK0–CK3	DIMM clocks.
A0–A11	A0–A9, A11, A12, A10/AP	During the bank activate command cycle, A0–A11 define the row address (RA0–RA11) when sampled at the rising clock edge.
		During a read or write command cycle, A0–A9 define the column address (CA0–CA9) when sampled at the rising clock edge. A10 is the also /AP (auto-precharge) and is used in the auto-precharge operation at the end of the burst read or write cycle. When A10 is high, BS0 and BS1 define the bank to be precharged.
	CKE0	Activates the SDRAM CK signal when high and deactivates the CK signal when low. By deactivating the clocks, CKE low initiates the power down mode, suspend mode, or self-refresh mode.
Not used	/RAS, /CAS /WE	When sampled at the positive rising edge of the clock, /CAS, /RAS and /WE define the operation to be executed by the SDRAM.
A11, A12	BA1, BA0	Defines which SDRAM, out of four, is selected.

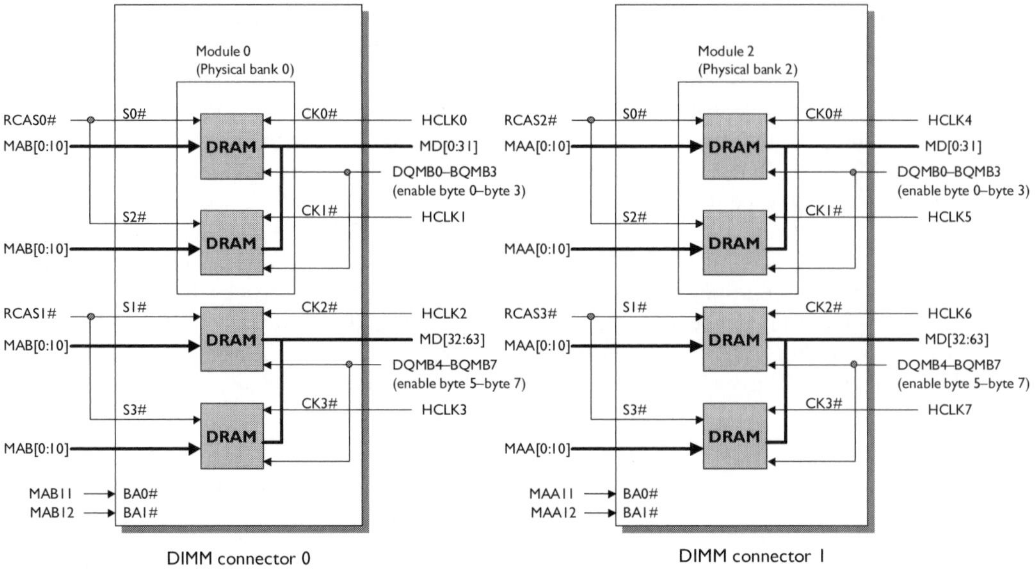

Figure 12.5   Connections to DIMM connector 0 and connector 1

Serial presence detect

Serial presence detect (SPD) allows for 256 bytes of serial data from an EEPROM that is mounted on the DIMM. It provides information on speed, density, architecture and functional information. Table A.4 in the appendix outlines some of the byte definitions. The first 128 bytes are locked by the manufacturer, and the other 128 byte can be used by the system.

The information is provided using the serial presence pins (three address, one data and one clock) and is used by the system BIOS to configure the system correctly. SPD is used with 168-pin unbuffered SDRAM and DRAM DIMMs and registered 168-pin SDRAM, whereas buffered DRAM uses parallel presence detect. An example of an SPD for a 168-pin unbuffered SDRAM DIMMs using 8M×8 SDRAM devices includes (with examples in brackets):

What's the difference between buffered and unbuffered?

Buffered devices have buffering on most of the pin connections (apart from data lines and RAS). They support only FPM/EDO. Unbuffered devices are a second generation development. The buffering is removed in order to speed the flow of data. Unbuffered devicessupport FPM, EDO and SDRAMs.

Buffered provides presence information in a parallel form (see Section 12.2.4); unbuffered is available in a serial form.

What if I plug an unbuffered DIMM in to a buffered slot?

It's not possible as they have different guide keys.

- Number of SPD bytes written during production (80h – 128 bytes).
- Total number of bytes in SPD device (08h – 256 bytes)
- Fundamental memory type (04 – SDRAM).
- Number of row addresses on assembly (0C – 12 rows).
- Number of column addresses on assembly (09 – 9 columns).
- Number of DIMM banks (01 – 1 bank).
- Data width of assembly (4800 – 8M×72×72).

- Voltage interface level of assembly (01 – LVTTL).
- Minimum row precharge time (1E – 30ns).

Figure 12.6 shows the pin connections of a system with two DIMM connectors. The address of the device is set by the SA0, SA1 and SA2 pins, while the SDA and SCL pins are used to read the data from the DIMM.

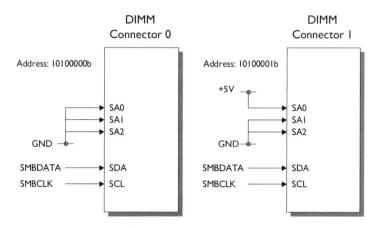

Figure 12.6 SPD pin connections

12.2.4 Double data rate DRAM

Double data rate(DDR) DRAM is an alternative to direct RDRAM, and provides high-speed memory transfers. DDR uses both the rising and falling edge for the synchronizing logic, whereas traditional memory transfers use either the rising or the falling edge of the signal. The output operations can thus be transferred at twice the normal rate as they use both edges.

12.2.5 Direct RDRAM

The next stage in increasing the data rate is direct Rambus DRAM (DRDRAM), which will allow higher rates. The transition to full DRDRAM can

> **Background to RDRAM**
>
> Direct RDRAM was the result of a collaboration between Intel and Rambus. Their brief was to develop a new type of RAM architecture that would run at many hundreds of megahertz. The new architecture uses bus mastering (with the Rambus Channel Master) and a new pathway (with the Rambus Channel) between memory devices (the Rambus Channel Slaves). Newer versions of the specification run at 700MHz in the second iteration (known as Concurrent RDRAM). RDRAM is the future!

be achieved through the S-RIMM specification, which allows for pin compatibility with existing DIMM sockets.

Processor speeds have evolved to over 1 GHz, and there is a need for faster accesses to DRAM than 66 MHz (528 MB/s), 100 MHz (800 MB/s), or even 133 MHz. A major objective is to achieve DRAM speeds that approach the speed of the processor. This would allow fast transfers between the processor and DRAM (without the need for a SRAM caches).

A direct Rambus channel includes:

- **One or more direct DRAMs**. These connect to a common bus, and can include microprocessors, memory, DSP devices, graphics processors and other fast transfer devices. Data is handshaked using Rambus signaling logic (RSL), where each RSL signal wire has equal loading, and fan-out is routed parallel to each other on the top surface of a

PCB, with a ground plane directly underneath it.

- **A controller**. The controller is located at one end with a parallel termination at the other end. In between the RDRAMS are distributed along the bus. The channel is 16 bits wide and uses a small number of very-high-speed signals to carry all address, data and control information at up to 800 MHz, which should increase to over 1 GHz with improvement in PCB design.

> ### To ECC or not ECC?
>
> ECC (error correction code) modules allow for basic error checking and correction for an odd number of bits in error that occur in memory (that is, single- and treble-bit errors). The output from 168 pins is either 64 bits of data or 72 bits (64 bits of data, and 8 parity bits for each of the bytes).

Figure 12.7 shows that the 16-bit channel gives a transfer rate of 1.6 GB/s. Higher data rates, such as 3.2 GB/s and 6.4 GB/s, are possible with parallel multiple channels. This new architecture allows the system bus to operate at speeds up to 133 MHz.

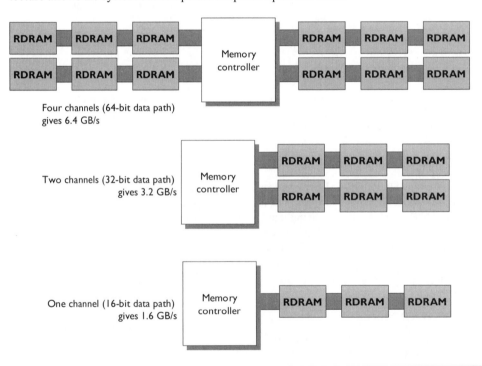

Figure 12.7   RDRAM configurations

Direct RDRAM memory controller

The direct Rambus memory controller acts as the bus master for the memory subsystem, and is the interface between the logic chip and the direct Rambus channel. It is typically integrated either into the microprocessor or its chipset (or video controller), and is responsible for generating requests, controlling the flow of data and keeping track of the direct RDRAM states and refresh.

> ### Objectives of DRDRAM
>
> - High bandwidth (1.6GB/s).
> - Maximum data bus utilization.
> - Minimum system cost.
> - Minimum system latency (delay).
> - Pluggable upgrades.
> - Same form factor as SDRAM solutions.
> - Scalable with device density and power supply.

. The specification supports up to four direct Rambus controllers on the single device, and each controller consists of two separate units:

- Rambus ASIC cell (RAC). This is the physical and electrical interface to the channel and is clocked at the channel frequency, which can be as high as 400MHz. It consists mainly of I/O buffers, multiplexers and clocking circuitry for the channel. The RAC also tracks RDRAM states and optimizes channel performance. If integrated in a chipset it requires 76 pin connections.
- Rambus memory controller (RMC). This is the control logic for the channel and acts as the interface between the logic chip and the RAC. It provides the logic between the controller and the memory, and takes memory access requests from the logic chip and translates them into the direct Rambus protocol.

> **PCs become microwaves?**
>
> As the clock speeds within PCs reach into the gigahertz region, the design of PCBs and the interconnecting wires must be designed properly, normally using transmission line technology. All fast-transfer signal lines must be matched with their transmission system. High data rates are achieved with RDRAM as:
>
> - High-quality terminated transmission lines.
> - Small difference in voltages between high and low logic states.
> - Well-defined channel topology.
> - Precise differential clocking.
> - Current mode drivers.
> - Dense device packing with short stub lengths.

Direct Rambus channel

The direct Rambus channel is the electronic connection between the controller and direct RDRAM. It uses 30 high-speed signals, which use both edges of the 400MHz clock, giving rates of over 800MB/s for each pin. The channels use RSL and have three independent buses: a 16/18-bit bidirectional data bus, a 3-bit unidirectional row control bus, and a 5-bit unidirectional column control bus for column and row commands to the RDRAMs from the controller. Separate and independent bus signals for column and row commands (along with the pipeling of the RDRAMs) allow for data bus of up to 95 per cent.

To achieve high clock speeds, all the signal lines must be properly terminated at the other end of the controller. This consists of a pull-up resistor connected to a 1.8V supply rail. These resistor values should match the impedance of the channel so that no reflections occur.

The channel uses differential clocks (which consist of two lines that are not ground). Differential signals improve noise immunity and reduce jittery. The clocks used are clock-to-master (CTM and CTMN) and clock-from-master (CFM and CFMN), as illustrated in Figure 12.8. This clock is 400 MHz. It can be seen that the signals for the RIMMs (RDRAM DIMM modules) run along and through each of the modules. Most of the signals run from the controller to the terminator.

At A, the differential 400 MHz is generated by a separate clock chip. This clock is then connected sequentially to each of the RIMMs (B). When it reaches the controller, it loops back out (D) and is changed from CTM to CFM, which is then routed back to all the

> **CBR**
>
> CBR is short for CAS before RAS. It is a fast refresh technique where the DRAM keeps track of the next row it needs to refresh, thus simplifying what a system would have to do to refresh the part.
>
> **Interleave**
>
> This is the process of taking data bits (singly or in bursts) alternately from two or more memory pages (on an SDRAM) or devices (on a memory card or subsystem).

RIMMs, until it is terminated (E). The CTM differential clock operates as the direct RDRAM transmit clock (TCLK) and the controller receive clock. All read data is aligned to the CTM clock. The CFM clock operates as the direct RDRAM receive clock (RCLK) and the controller send clock. All write data, as well as column and row packet data, are aligned to the CFM clock.

> **Page**
>
> A page within DRAM is the number of bits that can be accessed from one row address. Page size is determined by the number of column addresses. For example, a device with 10 column address pins has a page depth of 1,024 bits.

As illustrated in the lower part of Figure 12.8, data and the corresponding clock are aligned and always flow in the same direction through the Rambus channel. This allows the controller and direct RDRAMs to be able to operate at high speed, at 800 MB/s (two bytes at 400 MHz) in each direction (giving 1.6 GB/s).

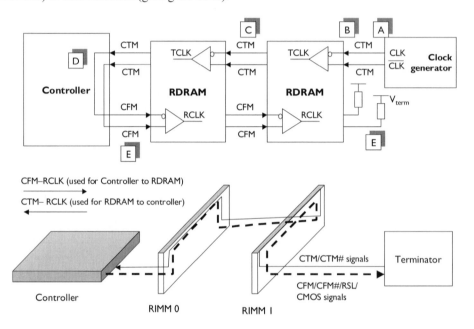

Figure 12.8   RDRAM connections

Interface signals

The direct RDRAM channel consists of 33 signals including clocks:

DQA[8:0] (I/O)   **Data byte A**. These contain 9 data bits (8 data bits and parity bit) for reading and writing between the controller and the direct RDRAM. RSL levels. This is one of the 8 bits that make up the 16-bit data bus.

DQB[8:0] (I/O)   **Data byte B**. These contain 9 data bits (8 data bits and parity bit) for reading and writing between the controller and the direct RDRAM. RSL levels. This is one of the 8 bits that make up the 16-bit data bus.

RQ[7:5] or ROW[2:0] (O)

   Row access control. These pins contain control and address information for row accesses. RSL levels.

CQ[4:0] or COL[4:0] (O)

   Column access control. These pins contain control and address information for column accesses. RSL levels.

CTM (I)	**Clock to master**. Differential transmit clock for direct RDRAM operation. It is an input to the controller and is generated from an external clock synthesizer. RSL levels.
CTM# (I)	**Clock to master Complement**. Complement to CTM. RSL levels.
CFM (O)	**Clock from master**. Differential receive clock for direct RDRAM operations. It is an output from the controller. RSL levels.
CFM# (O)	**Clock from master Complement**. Complement to CFM. RSL levels.
CMD (O)	**Command**. A command output used for power mode control, configuring the SIO daisy chain, and framing SIO operations. CMOS levels.
SCK (O)	**Serial clock**. Used to provide clocking for register accesses, and selecting direct RDRAM devices for power management. CMOS levels.
SIO (I/O)	**Serial input/output**. Used for device initialization, register operations, power mode control and device reset. CMOS levels.

Packets

The protocol used to pass data and control information is based on packet-oriented approach, which has the following advantages:

- Reduction in the number of pins required for the RDRAM, thus making the channel physically small, with an overall cost saving and improved electrical response (800 MB/s for each pin).
- Reserved bits have been placed in the command packets so that direct Rambus can support memory devices from 32 MB to 1 GB using the same control signals. There is thus little need to add extra addressing lines in the future as new sizes or types of memory become available.

Each packet contains a burst of 8 bits over the corresponding signal lines of the channel. For example, a row packet is a burst of 8 bits over the three-signal row bus, giving the row command a total of 24 bits. Correspondingly, a column packet consists of 40 bits and a data packet is 128 bits.

RIMMs

The direct Rambus RIMM is the expansion memory module that contains one or more direct RDRAMs and the channel wiring. RIMMSs are similar to SDRAM DIMMs, and have a connector with 168 contacts (84 contacts on either side of the RIMM), as illustrated in Figure 12.9, which illustrates an eight-chip RIMM. They have the same form factor and can replace the existing SDRAM slots without any changes in the size of the memory slots. The channel enters the RIMM on one end, crosses all of the direct RDRAMs, and exits out the other end of the RIMM (as shown in Figure 12.8). Each RIMM thus connects the channel from one end of the connector to the other. As the channel must be terminated, there must be no empty RIMM slots. To overcome this, RIMMs with only the channel and no RDRAMs. These are named *continuity modules*, and must be inserted into unpopulated RIMM sockets.

Other factors include:

- SPD. RIMMs support SPD, which allows the BIOS to read the characteristics of the memory and configure it properly.
- Single or doubly populated RIMMs. Direct RDRAMs can be mounted on either side of the RIMM. A single-sided board can have between one and eight direct DRAMs, while a double-sided RIMM can hold up to 16 direct RDRAMs.

A single direct Rambus channel supports up to 32 direct RDRAMS on up to three direct Rambus RIMMs. The maximum capacity per channel is 256MB, 512MB and 1GB, using 64Mbit, 128Mbit, and 256Mbit RDRAM devices, respectively. Up to two repeaters can be used to expand the channel beyond 32 devices. With one repeater chip, up to 64 devices can be supported on six RIMMs; with two repeater chips, 128 devices can be supported on 12 RIMMs.

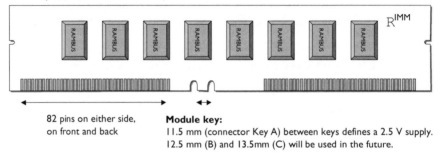

RIMMs are similar to SDRAM, and fit into the same area. They have SPD, and
can any number of direct RDRAM chips (up to the maximum number allowed).
Single-sided RIMMs can contain up to eight direct RDRAMS, while double-sided
RIMMs can contain up to 16 direct RDRAMs. Each controller can contain
up to three RIMMs.

82 pins on either side,
on front and back

Module key:
11.5 mm (connector Key A) between keys defines a 2.5 V supply.
12.5 mm (B) and 13.5mm (C) will be used in the future.

Figure 12.9   RIMM containing eight direct DRAMs

12.3   Memory Subsystem

Figure 12.10 illustrates the main components of the P6 memory subsystem. The main elements are:

- **MC-DC (memory controller DRAM control).** The control interface between the DRAMs and the processor bus is provided by the MC-DC. It provides the multiplexed memory address (MA), RAS# and CAS# signals to the DIMMs. It controls the movement of data through the memory controller data path (MC-DP) and memory interface component (MIC), and provides processor bus address and data parity checking.
- **MC-DP.** The MC-DP provides a data path to move data between the processor data bus and the memory data bus. It also performs ECC checking on data provided from the processor bus and data provided from the memory interface components.
- **MIC.** The MIC provides a data path between the MC-DP and the DIMMs.
- **DIMM.** These are the DRAM modules; they support 64 data bits and 8 ECC bits.

12.3.1 Memory address/control interface signals

These signals provide access DIMMs, and include:

- **MA[12:0] memory address bits**. The MA signals provide the system memory row and column addresses. They are derived from the processor address signals, A[35:3]#.
- **RAS# (row address strobe).** The RAS# signal strobes the row address, on the MA bus into DRAM.
- **CAS# (column address strobe).** The CAS# signal strobes the column address on the MA bus into DRAM.

- **WE# (write enable).** The WE# signal indicates that the current transaction is a write transaction when low, and a read transaction when high.

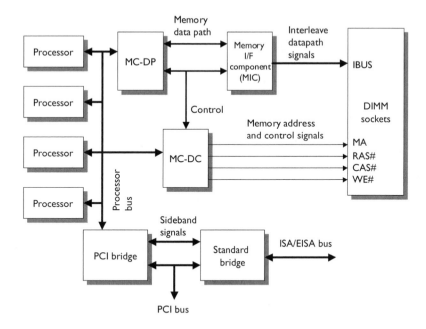

Figure 12.10 Memory subsystem

12.3.2 Interchip control signals

This group of signals consists of command and error reporting signals. Figure 12.11 shows the command signals. These are:

- **SYSCMD[4:0]# (system side command signals).** The SYSCMD# signals are generated by the MC-DC to the MC-DP; they control the transfer of data between the processor bus and the MC-DP internal buffers. They carry information about the type of operation, for example, read, write and the byte enables. They control the movement of data on the processor side of the MC-DP.
- **SYSDEN (system side data enable).** The movement of data between the processor bus and the MC-DP is controlled by the SYSDEN# signal.
- **MEMCMD[7:0]# (memory side command signals).** The MEMCMD# signals are generated by the MC-DC to the MC-DP; they control the transfer of data between the MIC and the MC-DP internal buffers. They carry information about the type of operation, for example, read and write. They control the movement of data on the memory side of the MC-DP.
- **MICCMD[6:0]# (memory interface component command).** The MICCMD# signals are generated by the MC-DC to the MIC; they control the transfer of data between the MIC and DIMMs. They carry information about the type of operation, for example, read and write.
- **MICMWC# (memory interface component memory write command signal).** The MICMWC# signal is used during a write cycle to command the MIC to drive data onto the interleave bus to the DIMMs.

- **MEMERR[1:0]# (memory error signals).** The MEMERR[1:0]# signals are used to report when a memory data error is detected on the memory data bus, that is, an error on the memory side of the MC-DP. The error information is sent from the MC-DP to the MC-DC; the encoding of the MEMERR[1:0]# signals is:

MEMERR[1:0]#	*Type of error*
00	No error on MDE[71:0]
01	Correctable error on MDE[71:0]
10	Uncorrectable error on MDE[71:0]
11	Reserved

If a single-bit ECC error (a correctable error) is detected the MC-DC generates SBCERR#. If a multiple-bit ECC error (an uncorrectable error) is detected, the MC-DC generates BERR#. The central agent will then cause an NMI to be generated.

- **SBCERR# (single-bit correctable memory error).** SBCERR# indicates when a single bit memory error was detected and corrected.
- **SYSERR# (system error).** The SYSERR# signal is used to report when a processor data bus error is detected during a write transaction, that is, an error on the processor side of the MC-DP. The encoding of the SYSERR# signal is:

SYSERR#	*Type of error*
1	No error
0	Error detected

If SYSERR# is active for one clock, the error is correctable and the MC-DC generates SBCERR#. If SYSERR# is active for two clocks, the error is uncorrectable, and the MC-DC generates BERR#. The central agent will then cause an NMI to be generated.

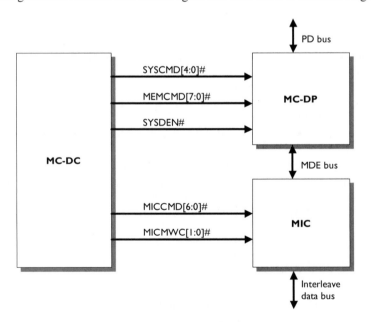

Figure 12.11   Memory subsystem

12.3.3 Memory data path signals

- **MDE[71:0] (memory data and ECC bus).** The MDE bus provides a bidirectional path for transferring D[63:0]# and the 8 ECC bits. The MDE[71:0] bits are all supported directly by the MC-DP. Four MICs are required to support the entire MDE bus; each one supports 18 MDE bits. Figure 12.14 shows the translation between the MDE bus and the processor data and DEP bits.
- **MD-RDY# (memory data ready).** MD-RDY# is generated by the MC-DP to the MIC during a memory write. It indicates to the MIC to accept the data on MDE[71:0].

12.3.4 Interleave data path signals

This group of signals is for moving data between the MICs and the DIMMs; the group consists of data/ECC signals. These are:

- **I0-D[17:0] (input 0 data bus) (bidirectional).** A bidirectional data path for 18 bits comprising of data and ECC information is provided between the MIC and DRAMs by I0-D[17:0].
- **I1-D[17:0] (input 1 data bus) (bidirectional).** A bi-directional data path for 18 bits comprising of data and ECC information is provided between the MIC and DRAMs by I1-D[17:0].
- **I2-D[17:0] (input 2 data bus) (bidirectional).** A bidirectional data path for 18 bits comprising of data and ECC information is provided between the MIC and DRAMs by I2-D[17:0].
- **I3-D[17:0] (input 3 data bus) (bidirectional).** A bidirectional data path for 18 bits comprised of data and ECC information is provided between the MIC and DRAMs by I3-D[17:0].

Figure 12.13 illustrates a memory set-up, banks and data paths that support four DIMM sockets. DIMM 1 and 2 make up the first bank, and DIMM 3 and 4 make up the second bank; DIMM 1 and 3 store data for interleave 0, and DIMM 2 and 4 store data for interleave 1.

P6 bits	MDE bus	P6 bits	MDE bus
D[25:0]	MDE[25:0]	D[57:32]	MDE[61:36]
DEP 2	MDE 26	DEP 6	MDE 62
DEP 5	MDE 27	DEP 1	MDE 63
D[31:26]	MDE[33:28]	D[63:58]	MDE[69:64]
DEP 3	MDE 34	DEP 7	MDE 70
DEP 4	MDE 35	DEP 0	MDE 71

Figure 12.12 Translation between the MDE bus and the processor data and DEP bits

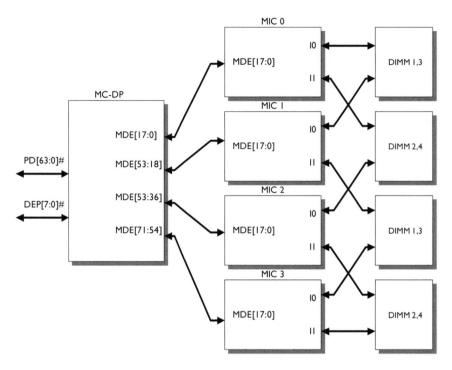

Figure 12.13   Memory set-up, banks and data paths

12.4 Memory Errors

If the board does not boot, and the last write to the milestone checkpoint indicates that a memory error has occurred, the error format is as follows:

XXXXXXXX YY DIMM Z

XXXXXXXX is the address that has failed. The address points to a byte and the interleave.

YY is the failing data; a high identifies a failing bit(s).

Z indicates the DIMM that may have provided the bad data.

Use the following steps to isolate a memory error:

1. The processor byte lane/bits is identified using the failing address; the byte lane is identified by A[2:0]#.
2. Example: A[2:0]# = 010b = 2h. The error is associated with byte 2 of the PD bus, which is PD[23:16]#.
3. Using the byte/data bits identified in step 1, determine the failing data bit(s) on the processor data bus from the failed byte in the error message, that is, convert the failed error byte to binary, and beginning with the least significant bit, start counting from the least significant processor data bit identified in step 1.
4. Example: byte 2 is made up of PD[23:16]#, and the failed byte is 20h = 0010 0000b.

The failing data bit is PD21# on the processor side of the MC_DP.

5. Use the failing processor data bit identified in step 3 to determine the failing MDE bit; use the table in Figure 12.12, that is, MDE21 is the failing bit on the memory side of the MC_DP.

6. Identify the MIC associated with the failing MDE bit in step 3. Trace the failing MDE bit from the MC_DP to the connected MIC. MDE21 is connected to MIC1.

7. Determine which interleave the error is associated with. In a 2:1 interleave environment A[3]# identifies the interleave; A[3]# high → interleave 1, A[3]# low → interleave 0. If A[3]# is high, then the error is associated with interleave 1, MIC1.

8. Determine the interleave data bit. The relationship between the MDE[17:0] and Ix_D[17:0] signals on the MIC is one to one. MDE21 is attached to MIC1, MDE03. It is associated with I1_D03, which is MD25.

12.4.1 Transaction examples

Memory read

Figure 12.14 shows memory read in a 2:1 interleave environment. The operation is as follows:

T_1 A row address is driven on the MA bus by the MC-DC; MA is valid at the DIMMs.

T_2 RAS# is generated by the MC-DC; the row address is latched by the DIMMs.

T_3 A column address is driven on the MA bus by the MC-DC; MA is valid at the DIMMs. The MC-DC keeps WE# inactive, indicating that this is a read operation; the DIMMs know a read is in progress.

T_4 CAS# is generated by the MC-DC; the column address is latched by the DIMMs.

T_5 Two quadwords of data and the ECC bits are provided by the DIMMs; data is on the interleave buses. The MEMCMD[7:0]# signals are generated by the MC-DC to the MC-DP to tell it the cycle type (read and length, i.e. four quadwords); the MC-DP keeps MICMWC# inactive. The MICCMD[6:0]# signals are generated by the MC-DC to the MICs, to tell it the cycle type (read and length i.e. quadword) and the starting interleave location defined by A3#; the MIC knows which quadword is the critical chunk, that is, the one the processor wants first.

T_6 The two quadwords on the interleave buses are latched by the MICs on the rising edge of T_6, and the critical chunk is provided to the MC-DP on MDE[71:0]; the first quadword is available to the MC-DP.

T_7 The MC-DP latches the data on the rising edge of T7; the MC-DP then provides the first quadword to the processor data bus. The CAS# signal is deasserted by the MC-DC, and a new column address is generated; a new column address is available at the DIMMs.

T_8 CAS# is generated by the MC-DC again; the new column address is latched by the DIMMs. The next chunk (quadword) is provided by the MICs to the MC-DP on MDE[71:0]; the second quadword is available to the MC-DP.

T_9 The MC-DP latches the data on the rising edge of T_9; the MC-DP provides the second quadword to the processor data bus. Two quadwords and ECC bits are provided by the same two DIMMs; data is on the interleave buses. The MICCMD[6:0]# signals are generated by the MC-DC to the MICs to tell it the cycle type (read and length, i.e. quadword) and the starting interleave location defined by A3#; the MIC knows which quadword is the critical chunk, that is, the one the processor wants first.

T_{10} The second two quadwords on the interleave busses are latched by the MICs on the rising edge of T_{10}, and the next chunk is provided to the MC-DP on MDE[71:0]; the third quadword is available to the MC-DP.

T_{11} The MC-DP latches the data on the rising edge of T_{11}; the MC-DP then provides the third quadword to the processor data bus.

T_{12} The next chunk (quadword) is provided by the MICs to the MC-DP on MDE[71:0]; the fourth quadword is available to the MC-DP.

T_{13} The MC-DP latches the data on the rising edge of T_{13}; the fourth quadword is provided by the MC-DP to the processor data bus.

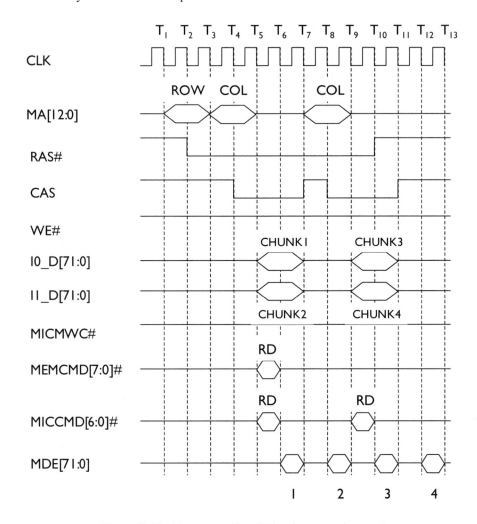

Figure 12.14   Memory read in a 2:1 interleave environment

Memory write

Figure 12.15 shows memory write in a 2:1 interleave environment. The operation is as follows:

T_1 The MEMCMD[7:0]# signals are generated by the MC-DC to the MC-DP, to tell it the cycle type (write and length, i.e. four quadwords); the MC-DP keeps MICMWC# inactive.

T_3 The MICCMD[6:0]# signals are generated by the MC-DC to the MICs to tell it the cycle type (write and length, i.e. quadword) and the starting interleave location defined by A3#; the MIC knows which quadword is the critical chunk, that is, the one the processor wants first.

T_4 The first quadword to be written to the MICs is provided by the MC-DP on MDE[71:0]. MD_RDY# is generated to the MICs by the MC-DP.

T_5 The MICs latch MDE[71:0] on the rising edge of T_5, with MD_RDY# active; the first quadword is accepted. The second quadword to be written is provided to the MICs on MDE[71:0] by the MC-DP.

> **Pipeline burst cache**
>
> Pipeline burst cache is a synchronous cache which minimizes processor wait states using:
>
> **Burst mode.** This prefetches memory contents before they are requested.
> **Pipelining.** One memory value can be accessed in the cache at the same time that another memory value is accessed in DRAM.

T_6 The MICs latch MDE[71:0] on the rising edge of T_6, with MD_RDY# active; the second quadword is accepted. The third quadword to be written is provided to the MICs on MDE[71:0] by the MC-DP. A row address is generated by the MC-DC on the MA bus; the MA bus at the DIMMs is valid.

T_7 The MICs latch MDE[71:0] on the rising edge of T_7, with MD_RDY# active; the third quadword is accepted. The fourth quadword to be written is provided to the MICs on MDE[71:0] by the MC-DP. The MC-DC generates a RAS# signal; the DIMMs latch the row address and MICMWC# to the MICs, that is, data will be provided to the interleave bus by the MICs.

T_8 The MICs latch MDE[71:0] on the rising edge of T_8, with MD_RDY# active; the fourth quadword is accepted. The MC-DC generates the WE# signals; the DIMMs know to accept data. A column address is generated by the MC-DC on the MA bus; the MA bus at the DIMMs is valid. The MICs drive the first two quadwords onto the interleave buses; data is available to the DIMMs.

T_9 The CAS# signals are generated by the MC-DC; the column address and data are latched by the DIMMs.

$T_{10/11}$ The row and column address, a write enable and data has been provided to the DIMMs; the DRAM on the DIMMs accepts the data. MICMWC# is generated to the MICs by the MC-DC; the MICs will provide data to the interleave bus.

T_{12} The CAS# signals are deasserted by the MC-DC, and a column address is generated on the MA bus; a column address is available at the DIMMs. The MICs drive the second two quadwords over the interleave buses; data is available at the DIMMs.

> **Burst mode**
>
> Bursting allows for a rapid data-transfer, which automatically generates a block of data (a series of consecutive addresses) each time, the processor requests a single address. In burst mode, it is assumed that the processor will sequentially access the next data address from the previous one, and can be applied to reading and writing operations.

T_{13} CAS# is generated by the MC-DC; the column address and data are latched by the DIMMs.

$T_{14/15}$ The row and column address, a write enable and data have been provided to the DIMMs; the DRAM on the DIMMs accepts the data.

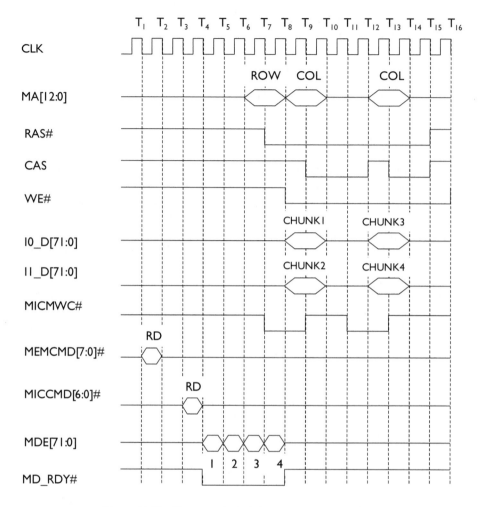

Figure 12.15   Memory write in a 2:1 interleave environment

12.4.2 Miscellaneous signals

- **RCLK (reference clock).** The RCLK frequency is the same as the processor frequency; it is a phase lock loop clock used to synchronize the MC-DC, MC-DP and MIC operations.
- **GTL-REFV (gunning transceiver logic reference voltage).** This is the reference voltage input, that is, 1V, used by the MC-DC, and MC-DP for the gunning transceivers.
- **PWR-GD (power good).** This signal, when low, resets the MC_DC, and causes it to generate a reset to the other components in the memory subsystem, that is, MC_DP and the MICs.

> **Burst EDO DRAM**
>
> Burst EDO DRAM is a type of EDO DRAM that can process four memory addresses in one burst. Unlike SDRAM, however, BEDO DRAM can only stay synchronized with the CPU clock for short periods (bursts) and cannot operate at clock speeds above 66 MHz.

12.4.3 Test signals

This group of signals are used for boundary scan testing.

- **TCK (test clock).** This clock is used for boundary scan testing; it clocks state information in and out of the device.
- **TDI (test data).** This signal is the boundary scan serial test data input signal.
- **TDO (test data).** This signal is the boundary scan serial test data output signal.
- **TMS (test mode).** This signal is used for boundary scan test purposes.
- **TRST# (test reset).** This signal is used for boundary scan test purposes.

Debug hints

Fault: Last write to the milestone checkpoint indicates that a memory error has occurred. Use the memory error code to identify the problem if possible.

Causes/check:
- Bad data path between the MICs and the DIMM connector; check the interleave data path.
- Bad data through MIC; stress the MIC with the heat gun/freezer spray.
- Bad data path between the MC-DP and the MICs; check the MDE data path.
- Bad data through MC-DP; stress the MC-DP with the heat gun/freezer spray.
- Bad data path between the processor and the MC-DP; check the PD data path.

12.5 Exercises

12.5.1 Which is a typical access time for DRAM memory?
    (a)   1 ns   (b)   7 ns
    (c)   70 ns   (d)   120 ns

12.5.2 For a memory that has a burst timing of 5-3-3-3, how long will it take to access four memory elements with a 66 MHz clock?
    (a)   2.12 ns   (b)   181.8 ns
    (c)   15 ns   (d)   212.1 ns

12.5.3 Which of the following burst rate timings will give the fastest overall memory access?
    (a)   5-3-3-3   (b)   6-1-1-1
    (c)   5-2-2-2   (d)   7-3-3-3

12.5.4 What is the size of a single channel RDRAM data bus?
    (a)   8 bits   (b)   16 bits
    (c)   32 bits   (d)   64 bits

Debug hints

Fault: Last write to the milestone checkpoint indicates that the processor cannot communicate with the MC-DC registers properly.

Causes/check:
- The MC-DC registers cannot be accessed by the processor; check the processor transaction signals at the MC-DC.
- DIMM access problem; check the signals between the MC-DC and the DIMMs, that is, MA bus, RAS#, CAS# and WE#.
- Data path control problem; check the control signals between the MC-DC and the MC-DP. MIC control problem; check the control signals between the MC-DC and the MICs.
- Data path problem between the processor and the interleave data bus; check 1) the PD data path between the processor and the MC-DP; 2) the MDE data path between the MC-DP and the MICs; 3) the interleave data path between the MIC and the DIMM.

12.5.5 What is special about the way that RDRAM signals are routed from the RIMM module?
    (a)   They carry signals in a single direction.
    (b)   The signal lines travel from one end of the module to the other.
    (c)   They vary in size for each data line.
    (d)   The cross-over each other.

12.5.6 Outline the main differences between EDO, SDRAM and RDRAM memory.

12.6 Additional diagrams

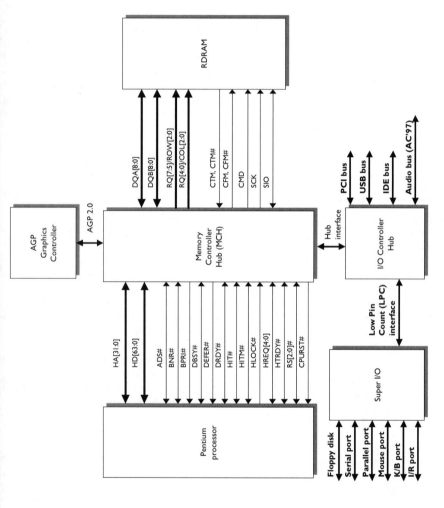

Figure 12.16 820-based chip interface to DRAM

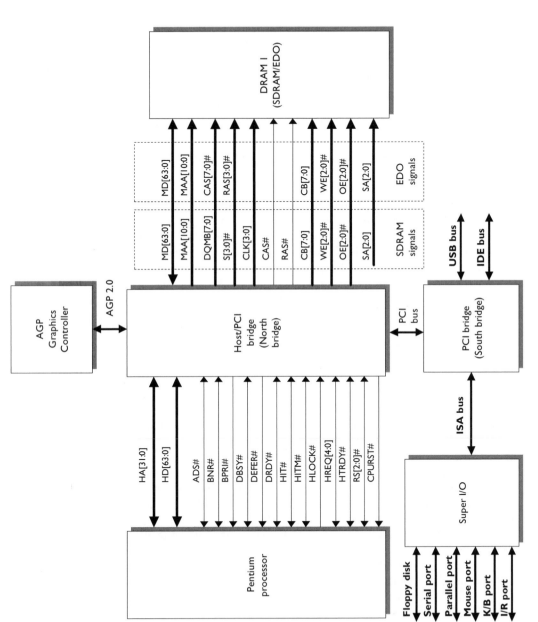

Figure 12.17 SDRAM/EDO interface

13 MMX Technology

13.1 Introduction

This and subsequent chapters introduce some of the advanced features provided by the Pentium II/III processors, including enhanced features, MMX technology, enhanced bus architecture and operation methods. The PII processor combined the power of the Pentium Pro processor with the capabilities of MMX technology. Its features include:

- Compatibility with applications running on previous members of the Intel microprocessor line.
- Dynamic execution micro-architecture.
- Dual independent bus architecture: separate dedicated external system bus and dedicated internal high-speed cache bus.
- Combines the power of the P6 processor with the capabilities of MMX technology.
- Power management capabilities (system management mode and multiple low-power states).
- Single edge contact (SEC) cartridge packaging technology, which delivers high-performance processing and bus technology, with improved handling protection and socketability. The SEC cartridge allows the L2 cache to remain coupled tightly to the processor.
- Integrated high-performance 16 kB instruction and 16 kB data, non-blocking level-one cache.
- Available with integrated 512 kB unified, non-blocking level-two cache.
- Enables systems that are scaleable up to two processors and 64GB of physical memory.
- Error-correcting code for system bus data.
- Optimized for 32-bit applications running on advanced operating systems. 32 kB (16 kB/16 kB) L1 cache. 512 kB L2 cache.
- GTL+ signal technology. This is similar to the GTL specification, but has been enhanced to provide larger noise margins and reduced ringing. The improvements are accomplished by increasing the termination voltage level and controlling the edge rates. This specification is different from the standard GTL specification, and is referred to as GTL+. The GTL+ inputs require a reference signal, (VREF). VREF is used to determine whether a signal is a logical 0 or a logical 1, and is generated on the SEC cartridge for the processor core.
- Data integrity and reliability features include system bus ECC, fault analysis, recovery, and functional redundancy checking.

13.2 PII Technology Profile

The PII processor contains the following architecture functions:

- Superpipelined.
- Superscalar.

- Speculative execution.
- Multiple branch prediction.
- Out-of-order.
- GTL+ system bus.
- JTAG boundary scan and tap connection.
- 16 kB/16 kB L1 cache.
- 512 kB L2 cache.

> **Monster or the great unifier?**
> With the growth in the Internet and global communications, we have created a global village, but have we also created an unregulated monster that is out of control? Albert Einstein sums it up well:
>
> *"Concern for man himself and his fate must always be the chief interest of all technical endeavors ... in order that the creations of our minds shall be a blessing and not a curse to mankind. Never forget that in the midst of your diagrams and equations."*

The L1 cache is a 16 kB/16 kB split similar to the Pentium processor L1 8 kB/8 kB split, with the crucial difference that the cache is non-blocking. The non-blocking cache feature is an important one because in an out-of-order engine a speculative access that missed in the cache would stall all the accesses behind it. This, in turn, would result in the potential for performance boost being lost, so the PII L1 cache is non-blocking. The L2 cache is also non-blocking. If a miss occurs, then the access is parked, and other cache accesses can be made. The L2 cache can support four concurrent cache misses before store buffers are used.

13.2.1 PII technology profile descriptions

The PII implements a dynamic execution micro-architecture, a combination of multiple branch prediction, speculative execution and data flow analysis. The PII executes MMX technology instructions for enhanced media and communication performance. The PII utilizes multiple low-power states such as AutoHALT, Stop-Grant, Sleep and Deep Sleep to conserve power during idle times.

Multiple branch prediction predicts the flow of the program through several branches: using a branch prediction algorithm, the processor can anticipate jumps in the instruction flow. It predicts where the next instruction can be found in memory with an amazing 90 per cent or greater accuracy. This is made possible because, while the processor is fetching instructions, it is also looking at instructions further ahead in the program.

Data flow analysis analyzes and schedules instructions to be executed in an optimal sequence, independent of the original program order; the processor looks at decoded software instructions and determines if they are available for processing or if they are dependent on other instructions.

Speculative execution increases the rate of execution by looking ahead of the program counter and executing instructions that are likely to be needed later. When the processor executes instructions (up to five at a time), it does so using speculative execution. The instructions being processed are based on predicted branches and the results are stored as speculative results. Once their final state can be determined, the instructions are returned to their proper order and committed to permanent machine state. Up to 512 MB of addressable memory space is cacheable.

13.3 MMX Technology

Intel's MMX technology is designed to accelerate multimedia and communications applications. The MMX technology retains its full compatibility with the original Pentium processors. It contains five architectural design enhancements:

- New instructions.

- SIMD.
- More cache. Intel has doubled on-chip cache size to 32k. That way, more instructions and data can be stored on the chip, reducing the number of times the processor has to access slower, off-chip memory area for information.
- Improved branch prediction. The MMX processor contains four prefetch buffers that can hold up to four successive code streams.
- Enhanced pipeline and deeper write buffers. An additional pipeline stage has been added and four write buffers are shared between the dual pipelines to improve memory write performance.

The following discussion is intended to provide only a brief introduction to MMX technology. MMX is an internal processor function that is worthy of a mention, although it is transparent from an external hardware point of view.

The PII processor incorporates MMX technology, which:

- **Improves video compression/decompression, image manipulation, and IO processing**. Today's multimedia and communication applications often use repetitive loops that, while occupying 10 per cent or less of the overall application code, can account for up to 90 per cent of the execution time. A technique called single instruction multiple data (SIMD), enables one instruction to perform the same function on multiple pieces of data, similar to a drill sergeant telling an entire platoon, "about face", rather than addressing each soldier one at a time. SIMD allows the chip to reduce compute-intensive loops common to video, audio, and graphics.
- **New instructions**. Fifty-seven new instructions designed specifically to manipulate and process video, audio and graphical data more efficiently have been added. These instructions are oriented to the highly parallel, repetitive sequences often found in multimedia operations.
- **Efficient processing techniques of dynamic execution**. Dynamic execution is an innovative combination of three processing techniques designed to help the processor manipulate data more efficiently. The three techniques are speculative execution, data flow analysis, and multiple branch prediction. Dynamic execution enables the processor to be more efficient by manipulating data rather than simply processing a list of instructions. It enables the processor to streamline and predict the order of instructions.
- **Multimedia**. The volume and complexity of data processed by today's PCs is increasing exponentially, placing incredible demands on the microprocessor. New communications, games and educational applications feature video, 3D graphics, animation, audio and virtual reality, all of which demand ever-increasing levels of performance. MMX technology is designed to accelerate multimedia and communications applications. The technology includes new instructions and data types that allow applications to achieve a new level of performance. It exploits the parallelism inherent in many multimedia and communications algorithms, yet maintains full compatibility with existing operating systems and applications.
- **Improved architecture**. MMX technology is the most significant enhancement to the architecture since the 386 processor, which extended the architecture to 32 bits. Processors enabled with MMX technology will deliver enough performance to execute compute-intensive communications and multimedia tasks with headroom left to run other tasks or applications. They allow software developers to design richer, more exciting applications for the PC.

MMX technology is designed as a set of basic, general-purpose integer instructions that can be applied easily to the needs of the wide diversity of multimedia and communications applications. The highlights of the technology are:

- SIMD technique.
- 57 new instructions.
- Eight 64-bit wide MMX registers.
- Four new data types.

13.3.1 Data types

The principal data type of the MMX instruction set is the packed, fixed-point integer, where multiple integer words are grouped into single 64-bit quantities. These 64-bit quantities are moved into the 64-bit MMX registers. The decimal point of the fixed-point values is implicit and is left for the programmer to control for maximum flexibility. The supported data types are signed and unsigned fixed-point integers, bytes, words, doublewords and quadwords.
The four MMX technology data types are:

- Packed byte: eight bytes packed into one 64-bit quantity.
- Packed word: four 16-bit words packed into one 64-bit quantity.
- Packed doubleword: two 32-bit double words packed into one 64-bit quantity.
- Quadword: one 64-bit quantity.

As an example, graphics pixel data are generally represented in 8-bit integers, or bytes. With MMX technology, eight of these pixels are packed together in a 64-bit quantity and moved into an MMX register. When an MMX instruction executes, it takes all eight of the pixel values from the MMX register, performs the arithmetic or logical operation on all eight elements in parallel, and writes the result into an MMX register.

13.3.2 Detecting the presence Of MMX technology

Detecting the existence of MMX technology on an Intel microprocessor is done by executing the CPUID instruction and checking a set bit. This gives software developers the flexibility to determine the specific code in their software to execute. During install or run time the software can query the microprocessor to determine whether MMX technology is supported and install or execute the code that includes, or does not include, MMX instructions based on the result.

13.3.3 Instructions

The MMX instructions cover several functional areas including:

- Basic arithmetic operations such as add, subtract, multiply, arithmetic shift and multiply-add.
- Comparison operations.
- Conversion instructions to convert between the new data types–pack data together, and unpack from small to larger data types.
- Logical operations such as AND, NOT, OR and XOR.
- Shift operations.
- Data Transfer (MOV) instructions for MMX register-to-register transfers, or 64-bit and 32-bit load/store to memory.

Arithmetic and logical instructions are designed to support the different packed integer data types. These instructions have a different op code for each data type supported. As a result, the new MMX technology instructions are implemented with 57 op codes.

MMX technology uses general-purpose basic instructions that are fast and are easily assigned to the parallel pipelines in Intel processors. By using this general-purpose approach, MMX technology provides performance that will scale well across current and future generations of Intel processors.

13.3.4 MMX instruction set summary

Table 13.1 lists MMX instructions and corresponding mnemonics that are grouped by function categories. If an instruction supports multiple data types – byte (B), word (W), doubleword (DW), or quadword (QW) – the datatypes are listed in brackets. Only one data type may be chosen for a given instruction. For example, the base mnemonic PADD (packed add) has the following variations: PADDB, PADDW and PADDD. The number of op codes associated with each base mnemonic is listed.

The first major extension to the x86 instruction will greatly improve the handling of multimedia applications. The 57 new instructions, known as MMX, accelerate calculations in audio, 2D and 3D graphics, video, speech synthesis and recognition, and data communications algorithms by as much as 8×. Users will see at least 50–100 per cent performance improvement on these types of programs when using MMX instructions. MMX is designed to have no impact on the operating system, making it compatible with existing x86-based OSs. The new instructions will provide PC users with a highly visible performance boost on many of today's performance-critical applications.

13.3.5 Simple software model

From the programmer's view, there are eight new MMX registers (MM0–MM7) along with new instructions that operate on these registers. But to avoid adding new state, these registers are mapped onto the existing floating-point registers (FP0–FP7). When a multitasking operating system (or application) executes an FSAVE instruction, as it does today to save state, the contents of MM0–MM7 are saved in place of FP0–FP7 if MMX instructions are in use.

The obvious drawback is that programs cannot use both FP and MMX instructions within the same routines, as both share the same register set. This is rarely an issue, since most programs do not use FP at all, and those that do typically use these calculations to generate data, while MMX is typically used in separate routines that display data.

13.3.6 Single instruction, multiple data

The new instructions use a SIMD model, operating on several values at a time. Using the 64-bit MMX registers, these instructions can operate on eight bytes, four words, or two doublewords at once, greatly increasing throughput.

MMX adds three new data types: packed byte, packed word, and packed doubleword. For example, audio data is usually stored in 8-, 12-, or 16-bit samples; the average person cannot appreciate further precision. Video is represented in pixels, commonly encoded as RGB (red, green, blue) triplets. Each of the three color values can be stored in 4, 6, or 8 bits; the last provides 16.7 million possible colors (24-bit), more than most people can discern.

Most of the new mnemonics begin with P for packed; for example, PADD means packed add. The op codes all begin with the byte 0Fh, as do existing long jump and set byte instructions. MMX uses previously reserved values for the second byte (none of which is used by other x86 vendors). The next two (or more) bytes provide the two operands, using the same encodings as other x86 instructions, except the target registers are the MMX registers, not the integer registers (EAX, and so on). For example, the MOVD and MOVQ instructions can move data to and from memory using the same multitude of addressing modes as the standard MOV instruction; they also move data from one MMX register to another. The MOVD instruction can even exchange data with the integer registers. Likewise, PADD performs register-to-register or memory-to-register operations, just like the integer ADD instruction. One exception is that register-to-memory mode is not supported in MMX.

Table 13.1 MMX instructions

Mnemonic	Opcodes	Description
Arithmetic		
PADD[B,W,D]	3	Add with wrap-around on [byte, word, doubleword]
PADDS[B,W]	2	Add signed with saturation on [byte, word]
PADDUS[B,W]	2	Add unsigned with saturation on [byte, word]
PSUB[B,W,D]	3	Subtract with wrap-around on [byte, word, doubleword]
PSUBS[B,W]	2	Subtract signed with saturation on [byte, word]
PSUBUS[B,W]	2	Subtract unsigned with saturation on [byte, word]
PMULHW	1	Packed multiply high on words
PMULLW	1	Packed multiply low on words
PMADDWD	1	Packed multiply on words and add resulting pairs
Comparison		
PCMPEQ[B,W,D]	3	Packed compare for equality [byte, word, doubleword]
PCMPGT[B,W,D]	3	Packed compare greater than [byte, word, doubleword]
Conversion		
PACKUSWB	1	Pack words into bytes (unsigned with saturation)
PACKSS[WB,DW]	2	Pack [words into bytes, doublewords into words] (signed with saturation)
PUNPCKH [BW,WD,DQ]	3	Unpack (interleave) high-order [bytes, words, doublewords] from MMXTM register
PUNPCKL [BW,WD,DQ]	3	Unpack (interleave) low-order [bytes, words, doublewords] from MMX register
Logical		
PAND	1	Bitwise AND
PANDN	1	Bitwise AND NOT
POR	1	Bitwise OR
PXOR	1	Bitwise XOR
Shift		
PSLL[W,D,Q]	6	Packed shift left logical [word, doubleword, quadword] by amount specified in MMX register or by immediate value
PSRL[W,D,Q]	6	Packed shift right logical [word, doubleword, quadword] by amount specified in MMX register or by immediate value
PSRA[W,D]	4	Packed shift right arithmetic [word, doubleword] by amount specified in MMX register or by immediate value
Data transfer		
MOV[D,Q]	4	Move [doubleword, quadword] to MMX register or from MMX register
FP and MMX state management		
EMMS	1	Empty MMX state

13.3.7 Saturating and unsaturating arithmetic

The add and subtract instructions have three variations. The default (no suffix) option is simple, non-saturating arithmetic. The other two options apply saturating arithmetic; as with the saturating PACK instructions, any overflow causes the result to be clamped to its maximum value, and underflows set the result to the minimum value. The suffix S indicates signed saturating arithmetic; the most significant bit in each field is treated as a sign bit.

The third case is unsigned saturating (US) arithmetic, typically used for pixel operations. When two intensities, for example, are added, the result can never be whiter than white or blacker than black; saturating arithmetic handles this automatically, avoiding the long series of overflow and underflow checks needed with traditional instruction sets. In fact, a single PADDUSB instruction could replace 40 non-MMX x86 instructions.

These options are not completely orthogonal, a fact that should not surprise any x86 programmer. Although the non-saturating form supports bytes, words and doubles, the saturating forms cannot handle 32-bit data. The combination of the extra logic required to perform saturation with the longer carry chain of the 32-bit adder failed to meet the cycle-time requirement.

For most situations, the saturating and non-saturating forms are equivalent. In fact, it is dangerous to use the non-saturating form for values that might cause an overflow, as it has no overflow trap. Of the non-saturating adds and subtracts, only the 32-bit versions are typically used to compensate for the lack of 32-bit saturating instructions.

13.3.8 Two instructions perform 16-bit multiplication

Simple multiplication is handled by PMULHW and PMULLW instructions. These instructions operate only on 16-bit values. Because the result of a multiplication can be twice the width of its operands, PMULHW stores only the high-order word of the result in the destination register (of course, it generates and stores four results in parallel). In some situations, this 16-bit result will provide adequate precision.

For full 32-bit precision, the second half of the result is generated by PMULLW. The results of the two instructions must then be combined using PUNPCKWD, which interleaves the two destination registers. The following code multiplies the four words in MM1 by the four words in MM2, storing the four products as two doublewords in MM1 and two doublewords in MM2:

```
MOVQ        MM0, MM1 ; Make copy of MM1
PMULHW      MM0, MM2 ; Calculate high bits in MM0
PMULLW      MM1, MM2 ; Calculate low bits in MM1
MOVQ        MM2, MM1 ; Make copy of low bits
PUNPCKHWD   MM1, MM0 ; Merge first two dwords
PUNPCKLWD   MM2, MM0 ; Merge second dwords
```

This code calculates four products in six cycles, whereas a non-MMX processor requires 10 cycles to complete a single 16×16 32-bit integer multiplication.

13.3.9 Parallel comparisons eliminate branches

The MMX extensions include parallel compare operations that seem awkward at first but will produce big performance savings. The PCMPEQW instruction, for example, compares two packed words; the fields in the result are set to zero if the comparison is false (not equal, in this case) or all ones if the comparison is true (equal).

This function is useful when combining or overlaying two images. For example, a common video technique known as chroma keying allows an object (such as the weather presenter) in front of a blue screen to be superimposed on another image (such as the weather map). In a digital implementation, this technique combines two images such that any blue pixels in the first image are replaced by the corresponding pixels in the second image.

Assume that X[i] is the first image, Y[i] is the background image, and the result is put back into X[i]. Using traditional x86 code, a single iteration might look like this:

```
CMP        X[i], BLUE ; Check if blue
JNE        next_pixel ; If not, skip ahead
MOV        X[i], Y[i] ; If blue, use second image
```

In this case, three instructions are needed per pixel. Using MMX instructions, this sequence can be recoded as follows, assuming 16-bit pixels:

```
MOV        MM1, X[i] ; Make a copy of X[i]
PCMPEQW    MM1, BLUE ; Check four pixels in X[i]
PAND       Y[i], MM1 ; Zero out non-blue pixels in Y
PANDN      MM1, X[i] ; Zero out blue pixels in X
POR        MM1, Y[i] ; Combine two images
```

Note that this sequence assumes all pixels are in MMX registers. The compare instruction generates four results in register MM1, setting each to zero if the corresponding pixel is not blue. The PAND combines this result with Y[i], zeroing any pixels corresponding to non-blue values in X[i]. Conversely, the PANDN zeroes the blue pixels in X[i].

At first glance, this routine appears to be about 2.5 times faster than the non-MMX routine, processing four pixels in five instructions. The actual performance will be even better, however, because the second routine eliminates a branch. Although modern processors predict branches, they mispredict perhaps 10–20 per cent of the time. PII takes an average of 15 cycles to recover from a misprediction. Thus, eliminating branches in this way significantly improves performance.

13.3.10   *Instruction examples*

The following section will describe briefly five examples of MMX instructions. For illustration, the data type shown in this section will be the 16-bit word data type; most of these operations also exist for 8-bit or 32-bit packed data types.

The following example shows a packed add word with wrap around. It performs four additions of the eight, 16-bit elements, with each addition independent of the others and in parallel. In this case, the right-most result exceeds the maximum value that can be represented in 16 bits, thus it wraps around. This is how regular arithmetic behaves. FFFFh + 8000h would be a 17-bit result. The seventeenth bit is lost because of wrap-around, so the result is 7FFFh.

The following example is for a packed add word with unsigned saturation. This example uses the same data values from before. The

> **Converting from RGB**
>
> Video cameras have sensors for red, green and blue (the primary colors for video information). Before color television these colors where converted into luminance (Y). When color television arrived, the extra color information had to be hidden and sent it as U and V (redness and blueness). Thus, RGB is converted into YUV.
>
> With images, the human eye is very sensitive to changes in brightness in any object, and not so sensitive to color changes. Thus color changes can be compressed more than the luminance. This is why RGB is converted in YC_bC_r. For example, 4:2:2 uses twice as many samples for luminance than redness and blueness, and 4:1:1 uses four times as many samples.

right-most add generates a result that does not fit into 16 bits; consequently, in this case saturation occurs. Saturation means that if addition results in overflow or subtraction results in underflow, the result is clamped to the largest or the smallest value that can be represented.

For an unsigned, 16-bit word, the largest and the smallest values that can be represented are FFFFh and 0000h; for a signed word the largest and the smallest values that can be represented are 7FFFh and 8000h. This is important for pixel calculations where this would prevent a wrap-around add from causing a black pixel to suddenly turn white while, for example, doing a 3D graphics Gouraud shading loop.

The specific instruction here is packed add unsigned saturation word (PADDUSW). A complete set of ADD operations exists for signed and unsigned cases. The number FFFFh, treated as unsigned (65 535 decimal), is added to 8000h unsigned (32 768), and the result saturates to FFFFh–the largest unsigned 16-bit value that can be represented.

There is no saturation mode bit as a new mode bit would require a change to the operating system. Separate instructions are used to generate wrap-around and saturating results.

The next example shows the key instruction used for multiply-accumulate operations, which are fundamental to many signal processing algorithms like vector-dot-products, matrix multiplies, FIR and IIR filters, FFTs, DCTs, and so on. This instruction is the packed multiply add (PMADD).

The PMADD instruction starts from a 16-bit packed data type and generates a 32-bit packed data type result. It multiplies all the corresponding elements generating four 32-bit results, and adds together the two products on the left together for one result and the two products on the right for the other result. To complete a multiply-accumulate operation, the results would then be added to another register, which is used as the accumulator.

The following example is a packed parallel compare. This example compares four pairs of 16-bit words. It creates a result of true (FFFFh) or false (0000h). This result is a packed mask of ones for each true condition, or zeroes for each false condition. The following example shows an example of a compare greater than on packed word data. There are no new condition code flags, nor are any existing condition code flags affected by this instruction.

The packed compare result can be used as a mask to select elements from different inputs using a logical operation, eliminating the need for a branch or a set of branch instructions. The ability to do a conditional move instead of using branch instructions is an important performance enhancement in advanced processors that have deep pipelines and employ branch prediction. A branch based on the result of a compare operation on the incoming data is usually difficult to predict, as incoming data in many cases can change randomly. Eliminating branches that are used to perform data selection by using the conditional select capability, together with the parallelism of the MMX instruction set, is an important performance enhancement feature of the MMX technology.

Displayable colors

The number of displayable colors depends on the number of bits used to store the intensity of the red, green and blue colors (RGB). For example:

Bits	Packed pixel	Number of colors
4-bit	12-bit color	4096
	16-bit color	65 636
8-bit	24-bit color	16.7 million
	32-bit color	4.3 billion

The amount of video data that must be stored for each screen depends on the number of pixels. For example:

640×480 at 16.7 million colors gives 900 kB.
1024×800 at 65 636 colors gives 1.56 MB.

If animation is used, then the screen must be updated at a certain refresh rate. For USATV systems, the refresh rate is 60 Hz (60 times per second). For 640×480 at 16.7 million, gives a data throughput of 52.7 MB/s.

This can be reduced using an interlaced monitor where the screen is written to for every second line. This reduces the actual screen update rate to 30 Hz, giving half the data rate (26 MB/s).

The following is an example of a pack instruction. It takes four 32-bit values and packs them into four 16-bit values, performing saturation if one of the 32-bit source values does not fit into a 16-bit result. There are also instructions that perform the opposite – unpack, for example, a packed byte data type into a packed word data type.

The pack and unpack instructions exist to facilitate conversion between the new packed data types. These are especially important when an algorithm needs higher precision in its intermediate calculations, as in image filtering. A filter on an image usually involves a set of multiply operations between filter coefficients and a set of adjacent image pixels, accumulating all the values together. These multiplies and accumulations need more precision than 8 bits, the original data type of the pixels. The solution is to unpack the image's 8-bit pixels into 16-bit words, perform the calculations in 16-bit words without concern for overflow, then pack back to 8-bit pixels before storing the filtered pixels to memory.

13.3.11 *Application examples*

The following section describes example MMX instruction set uses to implement basic coding structures:

> **MP-3**
>
> MP-3 audio is set to revolutionize the way that music is distributed and licensed. A typical audio track is sampled at 44,100 times per second, for two channels at 16 bits per sample. Thus the data rate is 1.411 Mbps (176,400 B/s), giving a total of 52,920,000 B (50.47 MB) for a five minute song. As the storage of a CD is around 650 MB, it is possible to get 64 minutes from the CD.
>
> Obviously it would take too long with present bandwidths to download a five-minute audio file from the Internet in its raw form (over three hours with a 56 kbps modem). If the audio file is compressed with MP-3, it can be reduced to one-tenth of its original size, without losing much of its original content.
>
> So, it is now possible, with MP-3, to get over 10 hours of hi-fi quality music on a CD. But the big change is likely to occur with songs being sampled and downloaded over the Internet. Users would then pay for the license to play the music, and not for purchasing the CD.

Conditional select

Multimedia applications must process large sets of data. In some cases there is a need to select the data based on a condition query performed on the incoming data. Intel has been able to improve performance in its family of processors by implementing micro-architectural features for increased performance and deeper pipelines. Branch prediction is an important part of making the pipelines run efficiently, as a misprediction can cause the pipelines to flush and degrade performance.

Vector dot product

The vector dot product is one of the most basic algorithms used in signal processing of natural data such as images, audio, video and sound. The following example shows how the PMADD instruction helps speed up algorithms using vector dot products. The PMADD instruction will handle four multiplies and two additions at a time. Coupled with a PADD instruction, as described before, eight multiply-accumulate operations are performed. These eight element vectors fit nicely into two PMADD instructions and two PADD instructions.

Assuming that the precision supported by the PMADD instruction is sufficient, this dot-product example on eight-element vectors can be completed using eight MMX instructions: two PMADDs, two more PADDs, two shifts (if needed to fix the precision after the multiply operation), and two memory moves to load one of the vectors (the other vector is loaded by the PMADD instruction, which can have one of its operands come from memory).

Comparing instruction counts with and without MMX technology for this operation yields the following:

	Number of instructions without MMX technology	Number of instructions
Load	16	4
Multiply	8	2
Shift	8	2
Add	7	1
Miscellaneous	–	3
Store	1	1
Total	*40*	*13*

With MMX technology, one third of the number of instructions is needed. Most MMX instructions can be executed in one clock cycle, so the performance improvement will be more dramatic than the simple ratio of instruction counts.

Matrix multiply

Exciting new 3D games are coming to market every day. Typically, computations that manipulate 3D objects are based on 4×4 matrices that are multiplied with four element vectors many times. The vector has the X, Y, Z and perspective corrective information for each pixel. The 4×4 matrix is used to rotate, scale, translate and update the perspective corrective information for each pixel. This 4×4 matrix is applied to many vectors.

Applications that already use 16-bit integer or fixed-point data are able to make extensive use of the PMADD instruction. There would be one PMADD instruction per row in the matrix, for a total of four. Comparing instruction counts with and without MMX technology for this operation yields the following:

	Number of instructions without MMX technology	Number of instructions
Load	32	6
Multiply	16	4
Add	12	2
Miscellaneous	8	12
Store	4	4
Total	*72*	*28*

With MMX technology, less than one-half of the number of instructions without MMX technology is needed.

13.3.12   MMX summary

MMX technology brings more power to multimedia and communication applications. It adds new data types and instructions that can process data in parallel. MMX technology is fully compatible with existing operating systems and application software.

The technology brings a step improvement to the PC platform and enables new applications and usage of PCs. It has helped to overcome the PC's big weakness – graphics performance.

Instruction Execution

14.1 Introduction

The chapter mainly discusses the Pentium II and Pentium Pro processors, whose operation and architecture have been used in the Pentium III and Pentium 4 processors. The Pentium II and Pentium Pro introduced many new enhancements to microprocessor technology, including:

- **Superscalar model**. The processor can process up to three instructions at a time, as long as the instructions do not depend on each other.
- **Superpipelined model**. The processor can pipeline up to four transactions. These transactions are split into sequential phases; more than one transaction can be executed at the same time; each transaction is in a different phase.
- **Register renaming**. Multiple instructions not dependent on each other, using the same registers, allow the source and destination registers to be temporarily renamed. The original register names are used when instructions are retired; program flow is maintained.
- **Out-of-order execution**. Instructions that are not dependent on each other can be executed out of order. The original program flow is maintained.
- **Speculative execution**. Instructions are executed ahead of their normal sequence. The results are temporarily stored because they may be discarded, for example, due to a jump instruction.
- **Integrated L2 cache**. The PII has an 8 kB L1 instruction cache, and an 8 kB L1 data cache. The PII module also has an integrated L2 cache. Depending on the processor version, the L2 cache will be either 256 kB or 512 kB.

It also brought many new terms, such as:

AMD Processors

1969	AMD incorporates with $100,000.
1975	AMD manufactures 8080A processor.
1976	AMD and Intel sign patent cross-license agreement.
1981	AMD and Intel expand their original cross-licensing agreement.
1982	AMD and Intel sign technology exchange agreement for iAPX86 processor family.
1987	AMD initiates arbitration action against Intel.
1991	AM386 microprocessor range introduced.
1992	Five-year arbitration with Intel ends. AMD awarded full rights to make and sell the entire Am386 family of microprocessors.
1993	Am486 microprocessor range introduced, and AMD announce plans for the AMD-K5 project.
1994	Federal court jury confirms AMD's right to Intel microcode in 287 math coprocessor trial.
1997	AMD introduces AMD-K6 processor
1998	AMD Athlon processor range introduced (which had been named K7).
2000	AMD announce x86-64 architecture which expands data and address buses to 64 bits, and will be an open standard. Product range expanded to include the AMD-K6 range (AMD-K6-2, the mobile AMD-K6-2, and the AMD-K6-III), the AMD Athlon (to compete against the Intel Pentium II/III) and the AMD Duron (to complete against the Intel Celeron).
2001	64-bit processors (codenamed 'Hammer') for x86-64 architecture, which will automatically detect the requirement for 32-bit or 64-bit transfers.

- **Transaction**. This is what was previously called a bus cycle. A transaction consists of a set of phases, which are related to a single bus request.
- **Bus agents**. Devices that reside on the processor bus, that is, processor, host-to-PCI bridge, and memory controller.
- **Priority agent**. The device handling reset, configuration, initialization, error detection and handling; generally the host-to-PCI bridge.
- **Requesting agent**. The device driving the transaction, that is, busmaster.
- **Addressed agent**. The slave device addressed by the transaction, that is, target agent.
- **Responding agent**. The device that provides the transaction response on RS[2:0]# signals.
- **Snooping agent**. A caching device that snoops on the transactions to maintain cache coherency.
- **Implicit write-back**. When a hit to a modified line is detected during the snoop phase, an implicit write back occurs. This is the mechanism used to write back the cache line.

> **AMD Athlon**
>
> - First 7th generation x86 processor.
> - PC industry's first fully pipelined,
> - superscalar floating point unit.
> - High-performance cache technology, with 128 KB of on-chip L1 cache.
> - 3DNow! technology for enhanced multimedia performance.
> - First 200 MHz system bus for x86 systems.
> - First 1 GHz x86 processor clock speed.

14.2 Typical Processor Approach to Instruction Execution

Figure 14.1 illustrates the instruction flow in a typical processor. The prefetcher causes instructions to be read from memory. Instructions read into the processor are provided to the instruction decoder, which feeds instructions to the execution unit. The execution unit performs the instruction execution. The retire unit commits the result of an instruction to its appropriate location, for example, an internal register, a memory location, etc. Using this method, instructions are executed by the execution unit in the original program flow order.

For example, the following instructions have been prefetched and decoded:

Instruction 1: MOV AX, [100]
Instruction 2: ADD CX, BX
Instruction 3: ADD DX, BX

Assume the data needed for Instruction 1 is not in the cache that is offset location 100 of the current data segment. A cache miss occurs. The execution unit stalls while waiting for the data to be returned from memory. Once the data is returned, the execution Unit will execute Instruction 1 then proceed to Instruction 2, then Instruction 3.

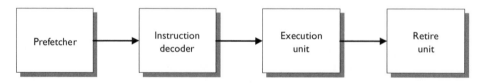

Figure 14.1   Instruction execution

14.3 PII Approach to Instruction Execution

Figure 14.2 illustrates the flow of instructions in the PII processor. The prefetcher causes instructions to be read from memory. Once instructions are inside the processor, the instruction decoder feeds an instruction pool. To ensure that the execution unit is not stalled, the instruction pool reorders the flow of instructions to the execution unit, that is, instructions are provided to the execution unit in an order that is different to the original program flow. The execution unit performs the instruction execution. The execution unit then provides the executed instructions back to the instruction pool where they are stored. The instruction pool sends the executed instructions to the retire unit in the original program flow order. The retire unit commits the result of an instruction to its appropriate location, for example, an internal register, a memory location etc. Using this method, instructions are not executed by the execution unit in the original program flow order; however, the instructions are retired in the original program flow order.

For example, assume the following instructions are prefetched and decoded.

Instruction 1: `MOV AX, [100]`
Instruction 2: `ADD CX, BX`
Instruction 3: `ADD DX, BX`

Assume the data needed in Instruction 1 is not in cache, that is, offset location 100 of the current data segment. A cache miss occurs. The instruction pool provides Instruction 2 to the execution unit while the cache linefill occurs. Once Instruction 2 is completed, the execution unit provides the result back to the instruction pool; it is not retired yet. It is likely that the requested data from Instruction 1 is still not available. The instruction pool provides Instruction 3 to the execution unit. Once Instruction 3 is completed, the execution unit provides the result back to the instruction pool; it is not retired yet. Assume the requested data for Instruction 1 is now available. The instruction pool provides Instruction 1 to the execution unit. Once Instruction 1 is completed, the execution unit provides the result back to the instruction pool. The instruction pool sends Instructions 1, 2 and 3 to the retire unit, in that order, for retirement.

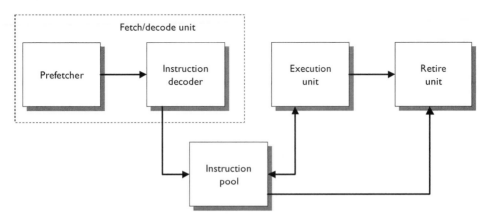

Figure 14.2   Instruction execution

14.4　PII Processor Block Diagram

Figure 14.3 illustrates the major blocks within the PII processor. The elements are:

- **Bus interface unit**. The interface between the processor and external logic. This provides an interface for controlling processor operations, like resets, cache control and interrupts. It also handles all processor transactions that involve accessing external memory and I/O.
- **APIC unit**. Provides logic for handling interrupts in a multiprocessor environment.
- **L1 instruction cache**. An 8k look-through cache, which stores frequently used instructions. The L1 instruction cache supports the shared and invalid states of the MESI protocol.
- **L1 data cache**. An 8k look-through cache, which stores frequently used data. The L1 data cache fully supports the MESI protocol, that is, all four states.
- **L2 cache** (not shown). A unified cache, that is, stores both data and instructions, which fully supports the MESI protocol. Any instructions or data stored in the L1 caches is also stored in the L2 cache
- **Fetch/decode unit**. Provides instructions to the instruction pool. The fetch/decode unit is comprised of:

Intel Processors

1971	4004 processor. First 4-bit processor.
1972	8008 processor. First 8-bit processor.
1974	8080 processor.
1978	8086/8088 processors. Intel's first 16-bit processor.
1982	80286 processor.
1985	80386 processor. Intel's first 16-bit processor.
1989	80486 processor.
1993	Pentium processor.
1995	Pentium Pro processor. Used in high-processing applications.
1997	Pentium II. Used SEC (single-edged connector).
1998	Pentium II Xeon. Used in high-processing applications, such as in server, and supports systems which can be configured to scale to four or eight processors and beyond.
1999	Celeron. Stripped-down version of the Pentium II.
1999	Pentium III, which speed of over 1Gz, 70 New Instructions, P6 Architecture, 133- or 100-MHz System Bus, 512K L2 Cache or 256K Advanced Transfer Cache.
1999	Pentium III Xeon. Used in high-processing application, such as in servers.
2000	Pentium 4 (formerly code named Willamette)
2000	Itanium. The first processor using the new IA-64 architecture.

Prefetcher. Retrieves instructions from memory before they are requested. The prefetcher works in conjunction with the branch prediction logic.

Branch prediction. Logic that predicts future program flow. If a branch instruction is fetched, the branch prediction logic predicts whether or not the branch will be taken. If the branch is predicted to be taken, prefetching begins filling the prefetch queue. The branch prediction logic operates with 90 per cent accuracy.

- **Instruction decoder**. Decodes instructions fed to it by the prefetch unit. The processor instruction decoder is comprised of three parallel decoders.
- **Instruction pool**. Stores decoded instructions fed to it by the instruction decoder. The instruction pool renames sources and destinations to eliminate register reuse, reorders instructions to keep the execution unit from stalling when possible, and stores the results of executed instructions until they can be retired.
- **Execution unit**. Executes the instructions provided to it. The execution unit consists of two integer execution units and one floating-point execution unit.
- **Retire unit**. Commits the results of instructions to their respective locations. This may be an internal register, a memory or an I/O location.

- **In-order queue**. Keeps track of pipelined transactions. The processor can pipeline up to four transactions, and can track up to eight transactions. The transaction waiting for a response is the one at the top of the in-order queue. All bus agents contain an in-order queue.

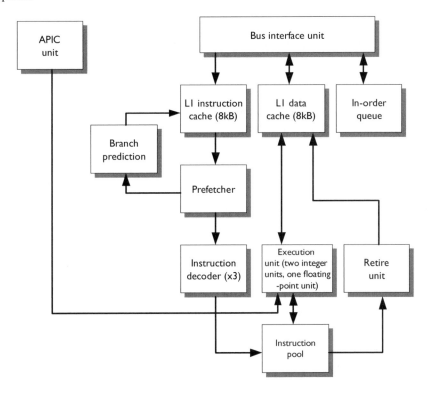

Figure 14.3 PII blocks

14.5 PII Dynamic Execution Implementation

Fig 14.4 shows the basic blocks, which include the cache and memory interfaces. The main units are:

- **Fetch/decode unit**. This is an in-order unit that takes as input the user program instruction stream from the instruction cache, and decodes them into a series of micro-operations that represent the data flow of that instruction stream. The program prefetch is speculative.
- **Dispatch/execute unit**. This is an out-of-order unit that accepts the data flow stream, schedules execution of the micro-ops subject to data dependencies and resource availability and temporarily stores the results of these speculative executions.
- **Retire unit**. This is an in-order unit that knows how and when to commit, retire, the temporary, speculative results to permanent architectural state.
- **Bus interface unit**. This is responsible for connecting the internal units to the real world. It communicates directly with the L2 cache, and also controls a transaction bus, with MESI snooping protocol, to system memory.

Fig 14.4 shows how the core engines interface with the memory subsystem using 8k/8k unified caches.

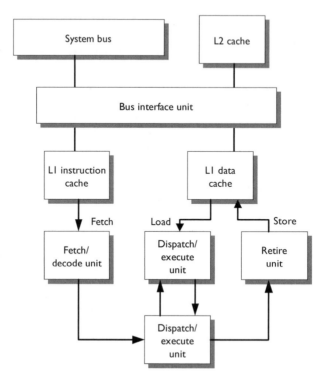

Figure 14.4   PII internal blocks

14.6 PII Bus Features

The PII bus supports up to two processors on the same bus without support logic. Integrated into the bus structure are cache coherency signals, advanced programmable interrupt control signals, and bus arbitration. The PII supports only uni- and dual-processor configurations, as illustrated in Figure 14.5.

The dual-independent bus architecture is available with the PII processor to aid processor bus bandwidth. Two dual-independent buses enable the PII processor to access data from either bus simultaneously, rather than in a singular sequential manner, as in a single-bus system.

- Two buses make up the dual-independent bus architecture; the processor to main memory system bus, and the L2 cache bus.
- The PII processor can use both buses simultaneously.

The pipelined system bus enables multiple simultaneous transactions, instead of singular sequential transactions, increasing the flow of information within the system, boosting overall performance.

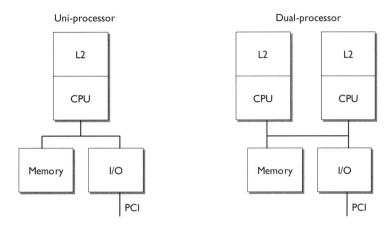

Figure 14.5 PII dual-independent bus architecture

The system bus has a 36-bit physical address bus and a 64-bit data bus, and uses a transaction-based bus protocol. An access that is looking for data gets on the bus with the request, and gets off the bus until the data is being returned. In the meantime, other agents on the bus can use it. There is also snooping support built in for multiprocessing.

The PII bus is highly pipelined, that is, it can have many overlapping transactions; the Pentium processor does not have a pipelined bus apart from the NA# signal. To understand the format of the PII bus communication proper understanding of the PII bus transaction phases.

Other features of the PII bus include:

- **MESI protocol**.
- **Gunning transceiver logic**. To reduce both power consumption and electromagnetic interference, the PII bus uses a low voltage swing. Signals that use the GTL logic are terminated to 1.5 V. GTL requires a 1 V reference signal. If a signal is 0.2 V above the reference voltage, that is, 1.2 V, then it is considered high. If a signal is 0.2 V below the reference voltage, that is, 0.8 V, then it is considered low.
- **Data error detection and correction**. The PII bus detects and corrects single bit data bus errors. It also detects multiple-bit errors on the data bus.
- **Address and control bus signals parity protection**. The PII bus supports address and control bus parity protection.
- **Modified line write-back performed without backing off the current bus owner**. The processor must perform a write-back to memory when it detects a hit to a modified line. The following mechanism eliminates the need to back-off the current bus master. If a memory write is being performed by the current bus owner, two writes will be seen on the bus, that is, the original one followed by the write-back. The memory controller latches, and merges the data from the two cycles, and performs one write to DRAM. If a memory read is being performed by the current bus owner, it accepts the data when it is being written to memory.
- **Deferred reply transactions**. This stops the processor from having to wait for slow devices; transactions that require a long time can be completed later, that is, deferred.
- **Deeply pipelined bus transactions**. The processor bus supports up to eight outstanding pipelined transactions.

Figure 14.6 outlines the main blocks of the PII system, which includes:

- **Processor**. A PII system may contain up to two processors.
- **PCI bridge/memory controller**. The PCI bridge provides the interface between the processor bus and the PCI bus. The memory control logic provides the memory control signals, that is, memory address, RAS# and CAS# signals.
- **Memory data buffer**. The data buffer moves the data between the processor bus and the memory data bus.
- **Memory DRAMS**. The memory consists of single or dual in line memory modules, that is, SIMMs or DIMMs. A module supports 64 bits of data, and 8 parity or ECC bits.
- **Standard Bridge**. The standard bridge provides an interface between the PCI bus and the EISA/ISA bus.
- **EISA/ISA support component**. This component provides the EISA/ISA bus support functions, for example, timers, interrupt control, flash ROM, keyboard/mouse interface, system address translation, and XD bus control.

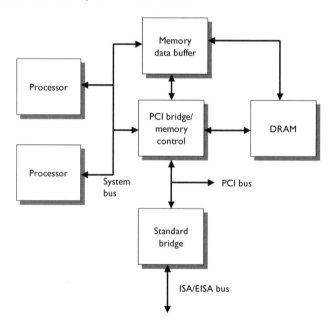

Figure 14.6   PII dual independent bus architecture

14.7 PII/III Bus Transactions

A processor bus transaction contains up to six phases; each phase uses a particular set of signals to communicate information. The six phases are:

- **Arbitration**. A transaction begins with the arbitration phase when the requesting agent does not already own the buses. The bus agent generates the appropriate bus request signals to get ownership of the buses. This phase is skipped if the bus agent already owns the buses.
- **Request**. The bus agent enters the request phase once it owns the buses. This phase con-

sists of two clocks. During the first CLK, the bus agent drives ADS# and an address on the bus; this allows other agents to snoop. During the second CLK, other transaction information is driven, for example, byte enables. All bus agents latch the information provided during the request phase, and store it in their in-order queues.

- **Error**. If a bus agent detects an address or control bus parity error, it must generate the appropriate error signals during the error phase timeframe. If an error is indicated during the error phase, then the rest of the transactions phases are cancelled.
- **Snoop**. If a transaction is not cancelled during the error phase, then it will have a snoop phase. During this phase, all snooping agents must indicate whether a hit was detected to a line in the shared or modified state.
- **Response**. If the transaction is not cancelled during the error phase, then it will have a response phase. The response phase indicates the status of the transaction. A hard failure response is provided if a transaction is retired due to an error, and then fails again on a retry. A no data response will be provided if the transaction is complete, for example, a write transaction. A normal data response will be provided if the transaction has to contain a data phase, for example, a read transaction. A deferred response is provided if the transaction is to be completed later, for example, an I/O read from a slow device. An implicit write-back response will be provided if modified data has to be written back, for example, a snooping agent detects a hit to a modified line during a read-from or a write-to memory. A retry response is provided if a bus agent decides that a transaction must be retired.
- **Data**. If a transaction is not cancelled during the error phase, and did not get a hard failure, deferred or retry response during the response phase, then it will contain a data phase. Data is transferred during the data phase, for example, read data, write data, or implicit write-back data.

14.7.1 Arbitration phase

The processor supports only two agents, BR0# – bus request 0, and BR1# – bus request 1. The chipset uses BPRI#, which is a priority arbitration request and BPRI#, a priority bus request. For example, after reset, the agent with an ID of 0 asserts the first cycle by asserting its BR0# signal, as illustrated in Figure 14.7.

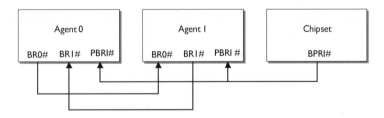

Figure 14.7   Arbitration phase

14.7.2 Request phase

The request phase consists of two packets, that is, packet 'a' and packet 'b'. The first packet, 'a', goes with ADS#; packet 'b' goes with the clock after ADS#.

Signals used during the request phase are:

ADS#   Address strobe
A[31:3]#   Address bus
AP[1:0]#   Address parity
REQ[4:0]#   Request type

RP#   Request parity

Request phase signals, REQ[4:0]#, definitions during packet 'a':

REQa 4 3 2 1 0

      0 1 0 0 0   Int Ack
      0 1 0 0 1   Branch Msg
      1 0 0 0 0   IO Read
      1 0 0 0 1   IO Write
      0 0 0 1 0   Mem Read & Inv
      0 0 1 0 0   Fetch
      0 0 1 1 0   Mem Data Read
      0 0 1 0 1   Mem Write (Cannot Defer)
      0 0 1 1 1   Mem Write (Cannot Defer)

> **Debug hint:**
>
> If ADS# does not go active,
> check the BR0# signal goes active
> from that processor.

Request phase signals, REQ[4:0]#, definitions during packet 'b':

REQb 4 3 2 1 0

      1 0 x 0 0   Use byte enables
      1 0 x 0 1   16 bytes
      1 0 x 1 0   32 bytes

During packet 'b' the address bus is defined as:

    A[31:24]#   Cache attribute
    A[23:16]#   Deferred ID
    A[15:8]#   Byte enables
    A[7:3]#   Extended functions

14.7.3 Error phase

If a parity error is detected by any bus agent, the AERR# signal will be asserted two clocks after ADS#, that is, during the error phase.

    AERR#   Parity error detected

14.7.4 Snoop phase

The following three signals are used during the snoop phase. If any of them go active during the snoop phase they indicate as follows,

    HIT#   Snoop agent has cache data.
    HITM#   Snoop agent has modified cache data.
    DEFER#   Try again later.

> **Debug hint:**
>
> The snoop phase is extended by
> another two clocks if both HIT#
> and HITM# are active. together.
> This can also be an indication of a
> PCI bus hang.

14.7.5 Response phase

During the response phase the following signals are:

    RS[2:0]# Response bus
    RSP#   Response parity
    TRDY#   Target ready

The response phase signals, RS[2:0]#, are defined during the response phase as:

RS 2 1 0
0 0 0	Idle
0 0 1	Retry
0 1 0	Defer
1 0 0	Hard fail
1 0 1	No data (write)
1 1 0	Writeback
1 1 1	Normal data

14.7.6 Data phase

During the data phase the following signals are used,

D[63:0]#	Data bus	DEP[7:0]#	Data parity
DBSY#	Data busy	DRDY#	Data bus valid

The DEP[7:0]# signals provide parity protection over the data bus D[63:0]#. They can be configured to provide one bit per byte parity protection or encoded using an algorithm to provide, error corrective coding (ECC) protection for the data bus D[63:0]#.

14.8 Transaction Types

The PII can perform the following types of transactions:

* I/O write.   I/O read.
* Memory write.   Memory read.
* Interrupt acknowledge. Special.
* Deferred.

14.8.1 Special transactions

The type of special transaction being requested is determined by the active byte enable in conjunction with the transaction type signals indicating a special transaction. Note: A[15:8]# become the BE#'s during the second CLK of the request phase. Special transaction types are:

* Shutdown.   Flush.
* Halt.   SMI acknowledge.
* Flush acknowledge.   Sync.
* Stop CLK acknowledge.

14.8.2 Deferred transactions

This allows the processor to move onto the next transaction instead of waiting for a response from a slow device. The processor is notified during the response phase of the current transaction, by a bus agent, that the transaction will be deferred, that is, will be completed at a later time.

The bus agent that deferred the transaction will perform a deferred reply transaction, when the original transaction can be completed, for example, the deferred reply transaction will return data to complete an earlier I/O read.

During the request phase of a deferred reply transaction, the bus agent identifies who the original requesting agent was, and which transaction the reply is for.

If the original transaction was a read, then a normal data response would be provided during the deferred reply transaction, that is, a data phase would follow the response phase. If the original transaction was a write, then a no-data response would be provided during the deferred reply transaction, that is, the deferred reply transaction will not contain a data phase because the write took place during the data phase of the original transaction.

Pentium bus transaction:
```
Cycle 1
        Request ------ Data    Cycle 2
                                Request ------ Data    Cycle 3
                                                        Request ------ Data
```
PII bus transaction:
```
Cycle 1
        Request - Error - Snoop - Response - Data
          Cycle 2
                   Request - Error - Snoop - Response - Data
                     Cycle 3
                              Request - Error - Snoop - Response - Data
```

14.9 Transaction Phases

Each transaction on the PII bus consists of up to six phases:

1. **Arbitration phase**. During the arbitration Phase, the request agent arbitrates for bus ownership, to allow it to begin the transaction.
2. **Request phase**. During the request Phase, the request agent issues a request, which is latched by the other agents.
3. **Error phase.** During the error phase, any agent that detected an error reports it.
4. **Snoop phase.** During the snoop phase, any agent that has a cache, that is, a snoop agent, looks up the request address in its cache.
5. **Response phase.** During the response phase, the target agent responds with how it intends to handle the request.
6. **Data phase.** During the data phase, data is transferred if required.

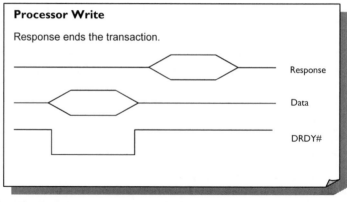

Processor Write

Response ends the transaction.

Response
Data
DRDY#

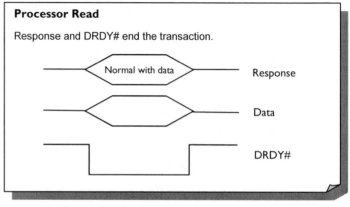

Processor Read

Response and DRDY# end the transaction.

Normal with data

Response
Data
DRDY#

14.9.1 Transaction completion

There is no equivalent to RDY# or BRDY#. (DRDY# = "data ready").

14.9.2 Request phase – two CLKs

First CLK: ADS# and snooping information.
Second CLK: Byte enables and transaction information on the address bus at this point.

14.9.3 Error phase

1 CLK; error = abort transaction.

14.9.4 Snoop phase

1 CLK; agents indicate whether it is a hit/modified hit using the HIT#/HITM# signals.

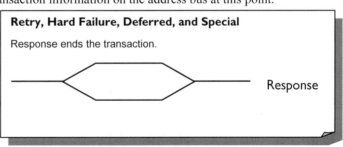

Retry, Hard Failure, Deferred, and Special

Response ends the transaction.

Response

14.9.5 Response phase

RS[2:0]# indicate response type

- Hard failure response; no data.
- Normal without data.
- Normal with data.
- Deferred.
- Implicit write-back.
- Retry.

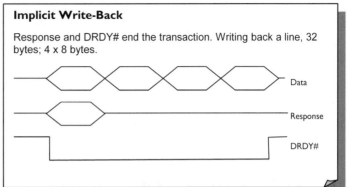

Implicit Write-Back

Response and DRDY# end the transaction. Writing back a line, 32 bytes; 4 x 8 bytes.

Data

Response

DRDY#

14.9.6 Deferred transaction

This transaction will not take place on the PII bus in-order.

Deferred read
This occurs if:

- DEN# = 0; deferred enable.
- I/O cycle, non-local memory cycle.
- PCI bridge is enabled to defer.

A suffix a and b indicate during the first and second CLKs, respectively. During the second CLK of the request phase, DEN# is the same as A4#; Ab[31:3]# provide transaction information. If the PCI bridge sends back a deferred response to free up the PII bus, the cycle continues on the PCI bus until it is completed, and then a deferred reply is returned.

Deferred reply
This is the responsibility of the original responding agent; the request line status REQa[4:0]# indicate a deferred reply.

14.10 Processor Bus Transaction Signals Diagram

Figure 14.8 shows the PII transaction phase signals.

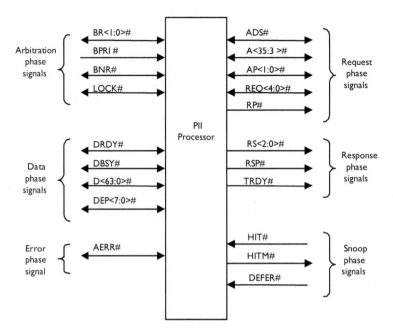

Figure 14.8   Transaction phase signals

14.10.1   *Arbitration phase*

The arbitration phase signals are used to get control of the bus. The following defines the signals used in the arbitration phase.

BR[1:0]# – bus request signals
BR[1:0]# are the physical bus request pins that drive the BREQ[1:0]# signals in the system. The BREQ[1:0]# signals are interconnected in a rotating manner to individual processors. Table 14.1 shows the rotating interconnect between the bus signals and the processor.

Table 14.1   Bust request pins

Bus signal	Agent ID0 pins	Agent ID1 pins
BREQ0#	BR0#	BR1#
BREQ1#	BR1#	BR0#

Symmetric agents have equal arbitration with more than one other device. The central agent has a higher arbitration priority than any other device.

During reset the central agent asserts BREQ0#, that is, BREQ0# is driven low. The processors, symmetric agents, sample their BR[1:0]# pins on a low-to-high transition of RESET#; the value on the BR[1:0]# pins at this time identify the agent's ID number. All agents then configure their pins to match the appropriate bus signal protocol, as given below:

Pin sampled active on RESET#	*Agent ID*
BR0#	0
BR1#	1

At reset, a rotating ID value of 1 is set in all the processors; the rotating ID identifies the processor with the lowest priority, that is, after reset processor 0 has the highest priority. A round-robin rotating priority scheme is used. The BR[1:0]# signals are used by the processors to keep track of the rotating ID number, and to determine which processor should get the buses next. The processor requests bus ownership by generating its BR0# signal. All processors in the system sample the BR[1:0]# signals on the rising edge of the next CLK; the new bus owner is determined by the rotating priority. The rotating ID changes as long as BPRI# remains inactive. The requesting processor owns the buses when its agent number equals the rotating ID.

For example, assume the rotating ID is 1. This means that agent 0 has the highest priority, followed by agent 1. If agent 1 wants control of the buses it drives its BR0# pin active, that is, board signal BREQ1#. All processors sample their BR# pins and decide that the next bus owner will be agent 1. All processors change the rotating ID to 1; agent 1 can begin its transaction. The priority order is now agent 0, and 1, starting from the agent with the highest priority. If agents 0 and 1 want control of the buses they will generate their BR0# signals. The processors sample their BR# signals and decide that the next bus owner is agent 0, because the rotating ID is currently 1. On the next CLK the rotating ID is set to 0, the priority order becomes, starting with the highest, 1, 0, and agent 0 begins its transaction.

Each processor in the system is identified by its agent ID number. The processor provides its agent ID during the transaction phase of a transaction; this allows all bus agents to track each transaction.

If one processor owns the buses, when another one requests them by generating its BR0# signal, the current bus owner must deassert its BR0# signal when the current transaction is finished.

Note that if functional redundancy checking is being used on the system then the processors are combined in pairs; agent 0 and 1 form an FRC master and slave respectively. Also, in the single processor environment the agent is configured to have an agent ID number of 0. When the processor wants control of the buses it monitors the BPRI# signal, and if it is inactive, automatically takes control of the buses.

If AERR#, BINIT# or RESET# go active, BR[1:0]# must be de-asserted in the next CLK. The BPRI# signal has priority over the BR[1:0]# signals.

BSEL# – bus select

The BSEL# signal is used for future Slot 1 processors and motherboards. This signal must be tied to GND for proper processor operation.

SLOTOCC#

The SLOTOCC# signal is defined to allow a system design to detect the presence of a terminator card or processor in a PII connector. Combined with the VID combination of VID[4:0 = 11111, a system can determine whether a PII connector is occupied, and whether a processor core is present.

SLP# – sleep

The SLP# signal, when asserted in stop grant state, causes processors to enter the sleep state. During sleep state, the processor stops providing internal clock signals to all units, leaving only the phase-locked loop (PLL) still operating. Processors in this state will not recognize snoops or interrupts. The processor will recognize only assertions of the SLP#, STPCLK# and RESET# signals while in sleep state. If SLP# is deasserted, the processor exits sleep state and returns to stop grant state, restarting its internal clock signals to the bus and APIC processor core units.

BPRI# – bus request priority

The BPRI# signal going active indicates that a device with higher priority than the ones connected to the BR[1:0]# signals, that is, processor(s), wants control of the buses. The device could be a PCI master, DMA, EISA master etc. If the processor is performing an un-locked transaction, and the BPRI# signal is sampled active, it must release the buses when the transaction is complete. The central agent is always the next bus owner.

The processor-to-PCI bus bridge chip is generally the central agent, that is, drives BPRI# to get control of the buses from the processor. Also, if a processor is busmaster, and a PCI master, EISA master, ISA master or DMA wants control of the buses then REQ#, MREQ# or DRQ is generated respectively. For EISA, ISA or DMA masters, the standard bridge, that is, PCI-to-EISA bridge, would generate a request for the buses to the processor-to-PCI bridge chip. It will back the processor off, and respond with a grant signal, GNT#, allowing the requesting master to get control of the buses.

If AERR#, BINIT# or RESET# go active, BPRI# must be de-asserted in the next CLK. The BPRI# signal has priority over the BR[1:0]# signals.

BNR# – block next request

The BNR# signal is driven by a bus agent to assert a bus stall. The current bus owner cannot start a new transaction because the agent that is driving the BNR# signal is indicating that it is unable to accept new transactions, to avoid an internal queue overflow.

The relation is:

- After RESET#. Bus agents that wish to stall the buses to perform hardware initialization must assert BNR# in the CLK after reset is sampled inactive.
- After BINIT#. Bus agents that wish to stall the buses to perform hardware initialization must assert BNR# four CLKs after BINIT# is sampled inactive.

LOCK# – lock

LOCK# indicates that new bus requests should not be generated because the current bus owner is performing a locked transaction. LOCK# takes priority over an active BPRI# or BR[1:0]# signal(s).

14.10.2   Request phase

The current busmaster starts a transaction in the request phase, which is two clocks long. During these two clocks, signals are driven which provide address, agent ID, control, parity and cacheability information about the transfer.

ADS# – address strobe

The current bus owner generates ADS# for one CLK, which identifies the beginning of a new transaction. The transaction address and control signals, A[35:3]#, RP#, AP[1:0]# and REQ[4:0]#, are generated at the same time and validated by the active ADS#. Other transaction phases, that is, error, snoop, response, and data, are defined with respect to the active ADS#.

The signals A[35:3]#, RP#, AP[1:0]# and REQ[4:0]# are all sampled with respect to ADS#.

A[35:3]# – address bus

A[35:3]# form the quadword address that identifies the location being accessed. This allows the processor to address 64 GB of address space. The current bus owner drives the quadword address of the location being accessed on A[35:3]#, during the first CLK of the request phase.

A[35:3]# contain byte enables, transaction length information, cache attributes connected with the location being accessed, deferred ID information, and other information related to the transaction, during the second clock of the request phase. During the second CLK of the request phase, A[35:3] are defined next.

A[31:24]# are outputs that contain cache attribute information, ATTR[7:0]#. The lower 3 bits are defined below; the rest are reserved for future expansion.

> ATTR[2:0]#
> 000   Write-back
> 001   Write-protected
> 010   Write-through
> 011   Write-combining, (reads are non-cacheable, writes can be delayed and combined)
> 111   Non-cacheable

A[23:16]# contain deferred ID information, DID[7:0]#; they are valid only if DEN# is active. If the transaction is deferred, DID[7:0]# keep track of the transaction. DID[7:0]# are provided in the first clock of the request phase during a deferred reply transaction. The deferred ID provides:

DID[7:0]#
> 7#   Requesting agent type, low for symmetric, high for priority
> [6:4]#   Requesting agent ID, defined at reset
> [3:0]#   Transaction ID; used to track the transaction

A[15:8]# contain byte enable information, BE[7:0]#. They identify the location in the quad-word address being accessed. During special cycles, they identify the type of special cycle being run:

Active BE#s
> none   No operation
> 0   Shutdown
> 1   Flush
> 1,0   Halt
> 2   Sync
> 2,0   Flush acknowledge
> 2,1   Stop clock acknowledge
> 2,1,0   SMI acknowledge

A[7:3]# contain current transaction information, EXF[4:0]#.

Table 14.2   Extended function pin functions

Extended function pin	Signal	Function
EXF4#	SMMEM#	SMRAM space is being accessed; in system management mode.
EXF3#	SPLCK#	Indicates that a locked transaction is split.
EXF2#	reserved	
EXF1#	DEN#	Defer enable indicates that the transaction can be deferred by the responding agent.
EXF0#		Reserved.

During the snoop phase, HIT# is generated if a hit is detected by snooping A[35:3]#. During the snoop phase, HITM# is generated if a hit to a modified line is detected by snooping A[35:3]#. A[23:16]# carry the deferred ID for deferred reply transactions, defined by REQ[4:0]# = 0h. A[11:5]# contain processor configuration information during RESET#.

AP[1:0]# – address parity bits

AP[1:0]# provide address bit, A[35:3]#, parity protection during both clocks of the transaction request phase. AP0# is the parity bit for A[23:3]#, and AP1# is the parity bit for A[35:24]. The parity bit is high if the number of zeros in the covered range is even. The parity bit is low if the number of zeros in the covered range is odd.

For example:

Address 13C1C6928h; A[35:24]# contains seven lows, AP1# is low, and A[23:3]# contains 12 lows, AP0# is high.

AERR# is generated in the error phase of a transaction if a bus agent detects an address parity error. AP[1:0]# are driven in the same CLK as address strobe.

REQ[4:0]# – request command signals

The REQ[4:0]# signals are generated, during the request phase by the current bus owner. During the first CLK, REQa[4:0]# identify the type of transaction taking place, and during the second CLK, REQb[4:0]# identify the data transfer length.

Type of transaction	REQa[4:0]#					REQb[4:0]#				
	1	2	3	4	5	1	2	3	4	5
Deferred reply	1	1	1	1	1	x	x	x	x	x
Interrupt acknowledge	1	0	1	1	1	x	x	x	1	1
Special transaction	1	0	1	1	1	1	1	x	1	0
Branch trace message	1	0	1	1	0	1	1	x	1	1
I/O read	0	1	1	1	1	1	1	x	LEN#	
I/O write	0	1	1	1	0	1	1	x	LEN#	
Memory read and invalidate	ASZ#	1	0		1	1	1	x	LEN#	
Memory read	ASZ#	0	D/C#		1	1	1	x	LEN#	
Memory write	ASZ#	0	W/WB#		0	1	1	x	LEN#	

ASZ# indicates the memory address space being accessed, that is, 11 [4 GBytes, 10] 4 GBytes. LEN# identifies the length of the transaction, that is, 11 0-8 bytes, 01 32 bytes. D/C#, data or code read. W/WB#, write or write-back.

REQa[4:0]# are generated in the same CLK as ADS#. RP# provides parity protection for REQ[4:0]#, and ADS#. AERR# is generated by any bus agent that detects a parity error during either of the two request phase CLKs.

RP# – request parity

Parity protection on ADS# and REQ[4:0]# is provided by RP# during both CLKs of the request phase. RP# is high if the number of zeroes in the covered signals is even, and low if the number of zeroes in the covered signals is odd.

For example:

- During the first CLK of the request phase, ADS# is active, and assume REQ[4:0]# is 2h; the number of zeroes is odd, RP# will be low.

- During the second CLK of the request phase, ADS# goes inactive; the number of zeroes is even, RP# will be high.

AERR# is generated in the error phase of a transaction if a bus agent detects a parity error in either of the two request phase CLKs.

14.10.3   Error phase

Once a transaction has been started by a bus agent, the other bus agents check parity on the supported signals. If an error is detected, the AERR# signal must be generated during the error phase.

AERR# – address parity error
If an address parity error or request parity error occurs, AERR# is generated during the error phase. All bus agents abort the transaction and remove it from their in-order queues when AERR# is sampled active. The current bus owner will retry the transaction once. If AERR# is sampled active on the retry, the processor treats it as a hard error, goes into shutdown, and generates BERR#.

AERR# is generated if an address parity error is detected; A[35:3]# and AP[1:0]#. AERR# is generated if a request parity error is detected; ADS#, REQ[4:0]#, and RP#.

14.10.4   Snoop phase

All snooping agents must provide the result of their snoop during the snoop phase.

HIT# and HITM# – hit and hit modified
A snooping agent performs a cache directory search when it observes the beginning of a memory transaction, that is, the generation of ADS#, REQ[4:0]# and A[35:3]#. The snoop result is provided using HIT# and HITM# during the snoop phase.

HIT# will be active when the directory search results in a hit to a line in the exclusive or shared state. HITM# will be active when the directory search results in a hit to a line in the modified state. The implicit write-back data is provided by the agent that detected the hit. If a write transaction is in progress, the bus owner provides the write data, the snooping agent provides the implicit write-back data, and the memory agent merges the data before writing it to memory. If a read transaction is in progress, the bus owner accepts the data, and the memory agent writes the modified data to memory.

DEFER# – defer
DEFER# can be used to suspend the current transaction, with the corresponding transaction reply being completed later. It indicates to the processor that the current transaction will not be completed in order on the processor's bus.

DEN# and DID[7:0]# are sent out during the second clock of the request (refer to the A[35:3]# signals in the request phase section) and are latched by the responding agent. The deferred ID, DID[7:0]# identifies the transaction ID and the agent ID. The agent ID identifies the requester, and the transaction ID is different for each transaction, allowing the transaction to be tracked if it is deferred. DEN# indicates whether the processor will allow the transaction to be deferred.

Once the addressed agent is able to complete the transaction, the PCI bridge will become the bus owner and perform a deferred reply transaction. The bus agent that originated the original transaction will use the information in the current transaction to locate the original one, and the transaction is retired.

The transaction will not be deferred if HITM# and DEFER# are both active during the snoop phase; HITM# has priority, ensuring that the implicit write-back will occur.

14.10.5   Response phase

During the response phase, the responding agent provides information about the current transaction back to the requesting agent. The information indicates whether the current transaction should be deferred or retired, a hard failure has been detected, an implicit write-back will occur, and whether there will be a data phase.

RS[2:0]# – response status signals

RS[2:0]# are driven by the agent responsible for the completion of the transaction, that is, the response agent, at the top of the in-order queue. Table 14.3 shows possible response codes and their meanings. Note that it shows the actual logic levels for the RS[2:0]# signals for each of the conditions described; it does not use the true/false notation, where all the levels indicated would be reversed.

- Retry response – provided when an error, not parity, is detected.
- Deferred response – provided for an I/O read/write, a memory read/write, or an interrupt acknowledge, if the function is enabled and DEN# was active during the request phase of the transaction.
- Hard failure response – provided when a non-parity error is detected during a transaction that is being retired due to an earlier error.
- No data response – provided for a write transaction.
- Implicit write-back response – provided when a caching agent detects a hit to a modified line.
- Normal data response – provided for a read transaction.

RSP# – response phase

RSP# provides parity protection for RS[2:0]#. For example, if RS[2:0]# is 3h, RSP# will be low; if an odd number of covered signals are low, then RSP# is low, and if an even number of covered signals are low, then RSP# is high.

Table 14.3   Response codes table

RS[2:0]#	Description	HITM#	DEFER#
7h	Idle state; the current transaction has been cancelled and must be re-issued by the initiator.	NA	NA
6h	Retry response; RS[2:0]# indicate the end of the transaction; it has been cancelled, and must be re-issued by the initiator.	1	0
5h	Defer response; RS[2:0]# indicate the end of the transaction; it has been suspended; the defer agent will complete it with a defer reply.	1	0
4h	Reserved.		
3h	Hard failure; RS[2:0]# indicate the end of the transaction; a hard error was received, and exception handling is required by the initiator.	1	1
2h	No data; RS[2:0]# indicate the end of the transaction; it is complete at this time.	1	1
1h	Implicit writeback response; snooping agent will transfer the modified cache data.	0	x
0h	Normal with data; transaction completed.	1	1

If a parity error is detected by a bus agent BINIT# will be generated if the function has been enabled during configuration.

TRDY# – target ready

The target agent generates TRDY# during the response phase when it is ready to accept write or write-back data; the requesting or snooping agent can begin the data transfer.

During a write or write-back transaction, TRDY# active enables the requesting agent to provide D[63:0]# and DRDY#.

14.10.6   Data phase

A transaction that is going to transfer data will contain a data phase. During the data phase, data and parity or ECC information are provided.

DRDY# – data ready

DRDY# indicates that valid data have been placed on the bus by the agent driving the data. When TRDY# is sampled active during a write transaction, the processor generates DRDY#. During a processor read transaction, DRDY# is driven by the memory controller or the processor-to-PCI bridge when valid data have been placed on the processor's data bus.

During multiple data transfers, DBSY# is generated before the first DRDY# and between DRDY# assertions.

DBSY# – data bus busy

DBSY# is asserted by the agent responsible for driving the processor's data bus, when the data phase requires more than one clock, for example, cache linefill. It is driven at the start of the data phase. DBSY# is generated during a processor write transaction, when TRDY# is sampled active, if the transaction requires multiple data transfers. During a processor read transaction, DBSY# is driven by the memory controller or the host to PCI bridge if the transaction requires multiple data transfers.

A hold is placed on the data bus, D[63:0]#, that is, no other agent will try to use it when DBSY# is active.

D[63:0]# – data bus

D[63:0]# provide a bidirectional data path for the transfer of information between the processor and other devices on the processor bus. During the second clock of the request phase, A[15:8]# represent the byte enables. The byte enables indicate which data bits are transferring valid information.

A15#, BE7#	Byte lane 7, D[63:56]#	A14#, BE6#	Byte lane 6, D[55:48]#
A13#, BE5#	Byte lane 5, D[47:40]#	A12#, BE4#	Byte lane 4, D[39:32]#
A11#, BE3#	Byte lane 3, D[31:24]#	A10#, BE2#	Byte lane 2, D[23:15]#
A9#, BE1#	Byte lane 1, D[15:8]#	A8#, BE0#	Byte lane 0, D[7:0]#

DEP[7:0]# provide parity or ECC protection, determined by configuration, for the data bus. DBSY# indicates that the data bus is in use. DRDY# indicates that information on the data bus should be latched.

DEP[7:0]# – data bus error correction/parity bits

DEP[7:0]# signals provide data bus parity or ECC protection. The post software sets up the type of protection required. If parity protection is required, then each DEP# signal is associated with one byte of the data bus. The following are some of the error conditions:

- If an odd number of covered signals are low, then the DEP# bit should be low, and if an even number of covered signals are low, then the DEP# bit should be high.
- If ECC protection is required then an algorithm is used to generate, check and correct errors. The DEP# signals are not associated with specific data bus bytes.
- If a single bit ECC error is detected by the processor, it can correct the error; a record of the error is kept in an error log.
- If a double bit ECC error is detected by the processor, a record of the error is kept in an error log. The processor cannot correct double bit errors, and BERR# is generated.

The processor, host-to-PCI bridge and the memory controller can all generate and check ECC data errors; they can correct single-bit errors.

The DEP[7:0]# signals provide parity or ECC protection for the data bus, D[63:0]#. BERR# is generated if multiple bit ECC data errors are detected.

14.11 Exercises

14.11.1　Which of the following is not a feature of the Pentium II/III?
　　(a)　　Register renaming
　　(b)　　Out-of-order execution
　　(c)　　Support for up to eight processors connected on the same bus
　　(d)　　Speculative execution

14.11.2　Outline the architecture of the Pentium II/III processor, giving the function of each of its units.

SC242 Signals

15.1 Introduction

The basic Pentium II/III/4 processor has 242 main pins and its interface is typically known as SC242. This section discusses additional SC242 signals that were not covered in Chapter 14. The additional signals cannot be associated directly with a particular transaction phase. Figure 15.1 shows that they can be divided into four groups.

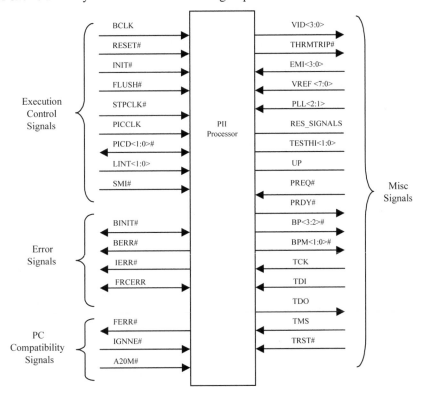

Figure 15.1   Write-back transaction block diagram

The connections of the processor to the rest of the components on a motherboard will be discussed in Chapter 27. This section gives an outline of the interface between the processor and the bridge devices. The architecture of a Pentium-based processor differs from a Pentium II/III processor, as the Pentium II/III has an on-package level-2 controller and cache memory. Figure 15.2 shows that the processor connects to the North bridge, which then connects to the level-2 cache, the DRAM memory and the PCI bus. The South bridge connects the PCI bus to the other major buses, such as the ISA bus, the IDE bus, and so on. A problem with this type of architecture is that the AGP graphics port requires a very high data throughput, especially with the DRAM memory. The architecture shown in Figure 15.2 does not really allow for high-speed transfers between DRAM and the AGP interface as it must go through the PCI bus as an intermediate interface, and an improved architecture is given in Figure 15.3, where the Level-2 cache has been closely coupled to the processor, and the AGP port now connects to the North bridge. As we will see the AGP interface is based on the PCI bus, but has much higher data throughputs. Note that the level-2 cache will still operate at the system speed as the host clock, whereas the level-1 cache will operate at the speed of the processor.

The ISA bus is seen as a legacy bus, and its use will eventually be phased-out. Figure 15.4 shows a more modern SC242 architecture, which uses a hub architecture. The interface between the North hub and the South hub is achieved with a special hub interface (as there is no need for the full functionality of the PCI bus). This allows for faster and more dynamic interchanges.

Figure 15.4 shows that the connection to the SC242 has no external connections to the level-2 cache, as the Pentium II/III has an integrated on-package level-2 cache. The processor interfaces mainly to the North bridge (host/PCI bridge, such as the PAC), which interfaces the processor to the AGP interface (for graphics), the DRAM interface and the PCI interface. The South bridge (such as the PIIX4) then connects to the PCI bus, and then provides an interface to other buses, such as the ISA bus, the IDE bus, and so on. The South bridge handles the main interrupts, such as the ISA bus interrupts (IRQ0 to IRQ15) and the PCI steerable interrupts (INTA to INTE). Thus the South bridge integrates the PIC, and generates the main interrupt lines for the processor (such as INIT, NMI, FERR, and so on). Figure 15.5 shows an example of the connections to a Pentium processor. Notice that the level-2 cache connects to the North bridge (TXC).

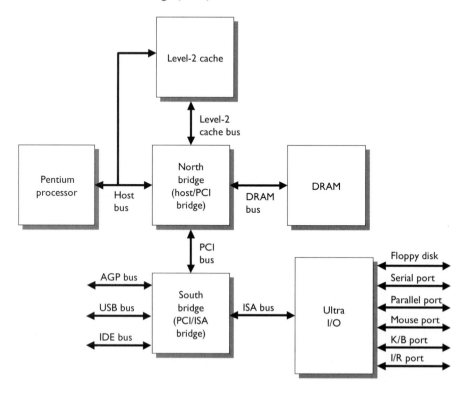

Figure 15.2   Pentium system architecture (such as the 440 HX chipset)

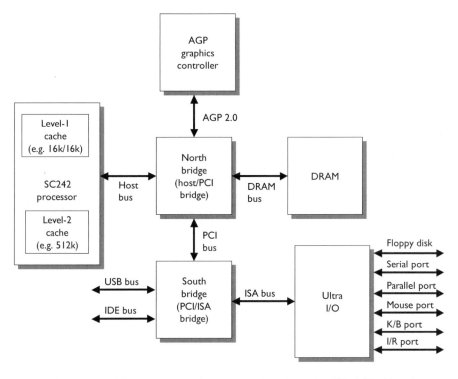

Figure 15.3 SC242 system architecture (such as the 440 LX/BX AGP chipset)

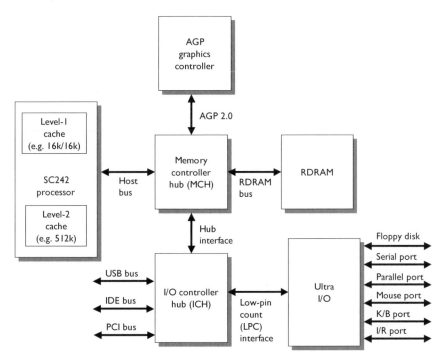

Figure 15.4 SC242 system architecture (such as the 820/840 chipset)

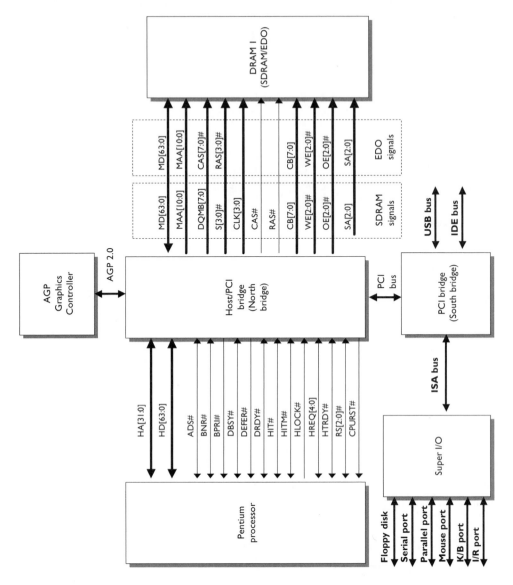

Figure 15.5   SC242 connections

15.2 Additional SC242 signals

15.2.1 Execution control group

The execution control signals control how the SC242 handles the flow of transactions.

STPCLK# – stop clock (input)
The SC242 is placed in a low power state by STPCLK#; most of the processor's internal CLKs are stopped by this operation. The processor still snoops on bus transactions in the stop clock state. The processor restarts its internal clock to all units, and continues executing, when STPCLK# is de-asserted.

15.2.2 Clock control and low power states

The processor allows the use of AutoHALT, stop-grant, sleep and deep sleep states to reduce power consumption by stopping the clock to internal sections of the processor. These are:

- **Normal state** – state 1. This is the normal operating state for the processor.
- AutoHALT power down state – state 2. AutoHALT is a low power state entered when the processor executes the HALT instruction. The processor will transition to the normal state upon the occurrence of SMI#, BINIT#, INIT# or LINT[1:0] (NMI, INTR). RESET# will cause the processor to immediately initialize itself.
- **Stop-grant state** – state 3. The stop-grant state on the processor is entered when the STPCLK# signal is asserted.
- **HALT/grant snoop state** – state 4. The processor will respond to snoop transactions on the Slot 1 processor system bus while in stop-grant state or in autoHALT power down state. During a snoop transaction, the processor enters the HALT/grant snoop state.
- **Sleep state** – State 5. The sleep state is a very low power state in which the processor maintains its context, maintains the phase-locked loop (PLL), and has stopped all internal clocks. The sleep state can be entered only from stop-grant state. Once in the stop-grant state, the SLP# pin can be asserted, causing the processor to enter the sleep state. The SLP# pin is not recognized in the normal or autoHALT states.
- **Deep sleep state** – State 6. The deep sleep state is the lowest power state the processor can enter while maintaining context. The deep sleep state is entered by stopping the BCLK input (after the sleep state was entered from the assertion of the SLP# pin). The processor is in deep sleep state immediately after the BCLK is stopped. It is recommended that the BCLK input be held low during the deep sleep state. Stopping of the BCLK input lowers the overall current consumption to leakage levels. To re-enter the sleep state, the BCLK input must be restarted. While in deep sleep state, the processor is incapable of responding to snoop transactions or latching interrupt signals. No transitions or assertions of signals are allowed on the system bus while the processor is in deep sleep state.

The processor provides the clock signal to the L2 cache. During autoHALT power down and stop-grant states, the processor will process the snoop phase of a system bus cycle. The processor will not stop the clock data to the L2 cache during autoHALT power down or stop-grant states. Entrance into the HALT/grant snoop state will allow the L2 cache to be snooped. When the processor is in sleep and deep sleep states, it will not respond to interrupts or snoop transactions. During sleep state, the clock to the L2 cache is not stopped. During the deep sleep state, the clock to the L2 cache is stopped.

15.2.3 SC242 processor system bus clock and processor clocking

The BCLK input controls directly the operating speed of the SC242 processor system bus interface. All SC242 processor system bus timing parameters are specified with respect to the rising edge of the BCLK input.

- **BCLK** – bus CLK (input). Bus CLK determines the SC242 bus frequency, and determines indirectly the processor's internal CLK frequency, that is, the processor's core frequency is a multiple of BCLK. The SC242 samples LINT1/NMI, LINT0/INTR, IGNNE# and A20M# on a high-to-low transition of RESET# to determine the ratio of the bus frequency to the processor core frequency; these values are latched on a low-to-high RESET# transition, so that the signals can then be used for their normal function.

Table 15.1 shows the bus to core frequency ratio determined by the power-on configuration conditions. External timing parameters are measured from the rising edge of BCLK.

Table 15.1   Bus to core frequency ratio

Bus/core frequency ratio	LINT1/NMI	LINT0/INTR	IGNNE#	A20M#
2/4	0	0	0	0
2/5	0	1	0	0
2/6	0	0	1	0
2/7	0	0	1	0
2/8	0	0	0	1
2/9	0	1	0	1
2/10	0	0	1	1
2/11	0	1	1	1

- **RESET#** – reset (input). The SC242 registers are set to their default values, the internal caches are invalidated, and certain signals are sampled for configuration purposes when RESET# is active. Signals that are sampled and latched on a low-to-high reset transition for configuration are discussed in their own section.
- **INIT#** – initialize (input). The SC242 registers are set to their default values when INIT# goes active; the internal caches are not invalidated. The SC242 executes its built in self test, if INIT# is active, on a low-to-high reset transition.
- **FLUSH#** – flush (input). The SC242 writes back all cache lines in the modified state to memory, and then invalidates all lines in both caches, when FLUSH# is sampled active. A flush acknowledge transaction is performed to indicate to external logic that the cache flush operation is complete. The SC242 enters tristate test mode, if FLUSH# is active, on a low-to-high reset transition. In a multiprocessor system, FLUSH# is generated in an attempt to allow another processor to take over as the boot processor if the boot processor fails to boot.
- **LINT[1:0]** – local interrupt signals (inputs). The processor contains a local advanced programmable interrupt controller (APIC) with two interrupt inputs, LINT[1:0]. The LINT[1:0] are local interrupt inputs, which default to INTR, LINT0 and NMI, LINT1, when the APIC is disabled. LINT[1:0] are programmed as local interrupt inputs when the APIC is enabled; the system requires an I/O APIC, which handles EISA and PCI interrupts, to make full use of the local APIC (EISA and PCI interrupts are then handled via PICD[1:0]#).The bus to core frequency ratio is determined by sampling LINT[1:0], IGNNE# and A20M# on a low-to-high reset transition.
- **PICD[1:0]#** – programmable interrupt controller data bus (bidirectional). The SC242 APIC bus operations are synchronized by the PICCLK input. The PICCLK is used as a reference for sampling the APIC data signals, PICD[1:0]#, which provide a bidirectional serial data path for the SC242 to read messages from and send messages to another APIC. APIC logic allows any interrupt to be serviced by any processor in a multiprocessor environment. The advantages of using an APIC are that the processor does not have to perform an interrupt acknowledge cycle to get the interrupt vector ID, because it is part of the message sent, and that interrupt servicing is shared by all the processors. Its logic consists of a local APIC and an I/O APIC. The I/O APIC resides in the I/O subsystem, and has interrupt input pins that allow I/O devices to request servicing. The local APIC resides in the SC242, and decides who should service the interrupt when a message is received from the I/O APIC. The processor handles the interrupt in the normal manner.

- **PICCLK** – programmable interrupt controller clock (input).
- **SMI#** – system management interrupt (input). SMI# is generated by an I/O agent that wants to be placed in power conservation mode, or wants to come out of power conservation mode. The processor saves its registers and enters system management mode when SMI# is active. An SMI acknowledge transaction is issued by the processor. It then executes the SMM handler. The error signals group indicate when a catastrophic error has occurred.
- **BINIT#** – bus initialization (bidirectional). BINIT# resets the bus state machines when an error occurs that prevents reliable operation. Note that BINIT# can be enabled or disabled through the processor power-on configuration register. As an output, BINIT# is output by a bus agent, if enabled, when an error is detected, for which BINIT# is a valid response, for example:

  - ADS# active when the in-order queue is full.
  - HIT# or HITM# active out-with the snoop phase.
  - Response parity error is detected.

As an input, BINIT# is an input to all bus agents. If a bus agent sees BINIT# active, it must:

- De-assert all signals on the bus.
- Reset the transaction queues.
- Reset the arbitration IDs to the power-on reset value, and begin a new arbitration sequence to request the busses.

Note that if the processor samples BINIT# active, it fetches its first instruction from the power-on restart vector address. If A10# is active at reset, BINIT# sampling is enabled.

- **BERR#** – bus error (output). BERR# is generated by the processor when a bus protocol violation occurs; the processor will shut down, and the priority agent will generally generate an NMI. Examples of when BERR# would be generated are:

  - On a transaction retry, AERR# is active.
  - A hard error response during a transaction.
  - An internal parity error.
  - An FRCERR error.
  - Multiple-bit ECC errors on the data bus.

Fault finding

Bad first fetch address:

- No processor RESET#: check RESET#.
- No processor CLK: check BCLK.
- Processor is in stop CLK mode, tristate mode, or shutdown mode: check STPCLK#, FLUSH# and BERR#/IERR# for each fault, respectively.
- Overheating: THRMTRIP#.

Video post lock-up:

- Interrupts not functioning correctly: check LINT[1:0]

Lock-up:

- Internal error detected: check IERR#.

Processor speed fails:

- Switch settings: check the processor frequency switches.

BERR# is generated if multiple bit ECC errors are detected on the data bus, D[63:0]# and DEP[7:0]#.

- **IERR#** – internal error (output). IERR# is generated by the SC242 when it detects an internal error. Note that IERR# can be mapped to BERR#. Examples of when IERR# would be generated are:

  - Multiple bit ECC errors on the data bus.
  - On a transaction retry, AERR# is active.
  - A hard error response during a transaction.
  - An internal parity error.
  - An FRCERR error.

- **FRCERR** – functional redundancy check error (bidirectional). If there are two SC242 processors in a system, they can be configured as an FRC pair. The master processor executes all the instructions, while the second processor (checker) mirrors the operations but does not drive the buses. The checker compares the masters outputs with its own internally sampled ones when a transaction is being performed. If the checker detects an error, it generates FRCERR to the master FRCERR input. The master enters into a machine check. After reset, FRCERR is generated, indicating the status and result of the BIST.

15.2.4 PC compatibility group

- **FERR#** – floating point error (output). FERR# is generated by the SC242 processor when an unmasked floating-point error is detected.
- **IGNNE#** – ignore numeric error (input). The SC242 processor ignores numeric errors, and continues to executing floating-point instructions, when IGNNE# is active. The bus to core frequency ratio is determined by sampling IGNNE# at RESET#, along with A20M# and LINT[1:0].
- **A20M#** – address 20 mask (input). A20M# goes active only in real mode. It ensures that the SC242 masks out A20#, that is, it is low, before it performs a transaction. A20M# is used to emulate the 8086 address wrap around at 1 MB. The bus to core frequency ratio is determined by sampling A20M# at RESET#, along with IGNNE# and LINT[1:0].

15.2.5 Miscellaneous group

The miscellaneous group of signals provide a boundary scan interface and other miscellaneous functions. These are:

- **VID[3:0]** – voltage ID signals (outputs). The SC242 generates the VID[3:0] signals to an adjustable DC to DC converter, to set its voltage reference requirements. The following VID[3:0] patterns identify the voltage settings. 0000h : 3.5 V, incrementing in steps of one to 1110h : 2.1 V; as the hex patterns increment, the voltage settings decrement in steps of 0.1V, for example, 0100 : 3.1 V.
- **THRMTRIP#** – thermal trip (output). If the processor's internal temperature reaches approximately. 130°C, it shuts down to prevent any damage.
- **EMI[3:0]** – emissions signals (inputs). These pins are tied to the package heat spreader, and should be connected to ground.
- **VREF[7:0]** – voltage reference signals (input). These are voltage reference signals used by the internal gunning transceiver logic.
- **PLL[2:1]** – phase lock loop signals (input). These pins provide decoupling for an internal phase lock loop; they should be attached to a 0.1 µF capacitor.
- **TESTHI[2:1]** – test high. These should be pulled high.
- **UP** – upgrade present. UP is linked to the voltage regulators to prevent harmful voltages

from damaging the overdrive processor (if fitted).

- **PREQ#** –probe request (input). This signal places the processor in probe mode for emulation purposes.
- **PRDY#** –probe ready (output). This signal indicates that the processor is in probe mode, and its test access port is ready to accept a boundary scan command.
- **BP[3:2]#** – break point bits (output). These bits indicate when a condition identified by the debug registers has occurred.
- **BPM[1:0]#** – breakpoint performance bits (output). When programmed as breakpoint bits, they indicate when a condition identified by the debug registers has occurred. These bits can also be configured as performance monitoring bits.
- **TCK** – test clock (input). This clock is used to CLK data into, and out of, the SC242 during boundary scan mode operation.
- **TDI** – test data in (input). This is the boundary scan serial data input. On the rising edge of TCK, data is shifted into the SC242.
- **TO** – test data out (output). This is the boundary scan serial data output. On the rising edge of TCK, data is shifted out of the SC242.
- **TMS** – test mode select (input). This is a boundary scan test logic control input.
- **TRST#** – tap reset (input). This is a boundary scan test logic asynchronous reset or initialization pin.

15.3 Exercises

15.3.1 Which of the following is one of the main differences between the Pentium and the Pentium II/III (SC242)?
    (a)   Integrated on-package Level-2 cache
    (b)   Increased number of interrupts lines
    (c)   Improved compatibility with previous processors
    (d)   Increased size of data bus

15.3.2 How many pins does the Pentium III package have?
    (a)   100   (b)   242
    (c)   350   (d)   500

15.3.3 Which device provides an interface between the processor and DRAM?
    (a)   North bridge   (b)   South bridge
    (c)   Ultra I/O   (d)   Level-2 cache

15.3.4 Which device handles the interrupts on the motherboard?
    (a)   North bridge   (b)   South bridge
    (c)   Ultra I/O   (d)   Level-2 cache

15.3.5 Which state is used when the processor maintains its context, but stops all clocks?
    (a)   Normal state   (b)   Stop-grant state
    (c)   Steep state   (d)   Halt state

15.3.6 Which clock signal determines the speed of the bus?
    (a)   BLCK   (b)   PICCLK
    (c)   BERR#   (d)   SMI#

15.3.7 Which signal lines define the PC compatibility grouping?
    (a)   FERR#, IGNNE#, A20M#   (b)   FERR#, RESET#, A20M#
    (c)   FERR#, FRCERR#, IERR#   (d)   FERR#, IGNNE#, IERR#

Processor Developments

16

16.1 Introduction

The processor within the PC has evolved continually, with each processor being compatible with all the previous ones. The mistakes that Zilog made with the update from the Z80 to the Z8000 have been learned. Compatibility with previous systems and software means more than outstanding processor architecture or speed.

The major milestones for the PC have been the 8086 processor, the 80386 processor (the first 32-bit device), the 80486 (the first PC processor to properly run a graphical user interface), the Pentium (the processor that allowed Windows 95 and NT to bloom), the PCI bus (which changed the architecture of the PC with the introduction of bridges that moved slow devices away from the main system bus), and the Pentium II/III (which allowed the PC to become a supercomputer). Processor speeds have moved from under 4.77 MHz to over 1 GHz, and memory has increased from 640 KB to many hundreds of MB. The motherboard speed has also increased from 4.77/8 MHz (with the 8086), to 33 MHz (with the 80386), on to 66 MHz (with Pentium) and 133 MHz, and more. It has been Intel's processors that have defined how the processor interfaces with the rest of the devices on the PC, and this has left other companies to follow their designs with pin-compatible version. Few modern companies have the strength to force major changes in technology.

16.1.1 0th generation

The 0th generation spans the time between the very first integrated microprocessor, and the adoption of the Intel 8086 by IBM for their PC. In 1969, as man first walked on the moon, Intel were busy producing their first memory chips. By 1970, Intel had produced the first DRAM memory. In the same year, they were

---

Processor generations

First generation
16-bit processors
8086 and 8088 (1978–81): 29,000 transistors, 1 MB addressable memory.

Second generation
16-bit processors with enhanced memory organization
80286 (1984): 134,000 transistors.

Third generation
32-bit processors
80386DX and 80386SX (1987–88) 275,000 transistors, 16 MB addressable memory (SX) or 4 GB address memory (DX).

Fourth generation
32-bit processors with cache
80486SX, 80486DX, 80486DX2 and 80486DX4 (1990–92): 1,200,000 transistors.

Fifth generation
32-bit processors with integrated controllers/superscaler (more than one instruction at a time)
Pentium (1993–95), Cyrix 6x86 (1996), AMD K5 (1996), IDT WinChip C6 (1997): 3,500,000, enhanced Pentium MMX (1997), 4,500,000 transistors.

Sixth generation
Enhanced system transactions and multiprocessor systems
Pentium Pro (1995), AMD K6 (1997), Pentium II (1997), AMD K6-2 (1998).

Seventh generation
Ultra-high speed architecture
AMD K7 Athlon, Pentium III.

Eight generation
64-bit architecture.

developing another product that would change the world: the 4004 microprocessor. Intel, at the time, had viewed the microprocessor as a small diversification from their main memory line. It has since turned out that it was one of the best business moves ever, projecting Intel into the leading electronics manufacturer in the world. The 4004 was a 4-bit device that had only 2300 transistors and a clock speed of 108 kHz. It was released as part of the 4000 series, which included a 4k PROM, a 4kbit RAM, and a register device. Within one year, Intel released the world's first 8-bit device: the 8008 (0.2 MHz, 0.06 MIPS, 3,500 transistors, 10-micron technology, 16 kB memory) and the 8080 (2 MHz, 0.64 MIPS, 6,000 transistors, could address up to 64 kB memory). Most people, even Intel, still viewed the microprocessor as a useful tool in selling memory devices and support chips. It took another two years before Intel released the

> ### It's hot!
>
> The Pentium processor initially ran with a voltage supply of 5 V at 60 MHz and 66 MHz. Unfortunately, the larger the clock frequency, the larger the power dissipation, and the larger processor supply voltage, the larger the power dissipation. It ran so hot that it required a fan to sit on top of the processor. Initially, the processor did not have thermal shutdown, and a failing fan would cause the processor to melt. New processor and memory designs use 3.3 V rather than 5 V. The power dissipation is reduced by over 56 per cent (as power dissipation varies with the square of the voltage).

enhanced 8080 (2 MHz, 0.64 MIPS, 6,000 transistors, could address up to 64 kB memory). Other manufacturers had started to produce their own microprocessors. The main competitor was the Motorola 6800. These two devices held most of the market for microprocessors, and the duopoly allowed for large mark-up to be made on the microprocessors. This changed with the introduction in 1976 of two new designs that emulated the 8080 and the 6800, and were software-compatible and pin-compatible with their equivalents. These were the 2.5 MHz Z80 from Zilog (which was compatible with the 8080), and the 1 MHz 6502 from MOS Technologies (which was compatible with the 6800). These inexpensive devices allowed microcomputer designers to produce relatively cheap computers based around the Z80 and 6502 processors. The new microcomputers, such as the Apple II, the Commodore PET and the Sinclair/Timex ZX80/81 computers were all based on the 6502 or the Z80.

Zilog threw away their advantage with the development of the technologically superior, but totally incompatible, Z8000. To ensure a good supply of the 6502, Commodore International bought MOS Technology. With the advent of the 16-bit processors, the 6502 struggled. These new devices were the Intel 8086 and the Motorola 68000. It would take almost two years from the release of the Intel 8086/8088 (in 1979) for IBM to release their first PC.

16.1.2 First generation (8086/8088)

IBM adopted the 8088 for their PC system. It had an 8-bit data bus and a 20-bit address bus. This gave a maximum addressing limit of 1 MB. The 8086 had the same internal architecture as the 8088, but an external data bus of 16 bits. They used a 4.77 MHz or 8 MHz clock speed.

16.1.3 Second generation (80286)

Intel enhanced the 8086 further with the 80286. It was still a 16-bit device, but allowed an increased access to physical memory, and reduced the number of clock cycles of processor operations. It was released in 1984 (the year of the release of the Apple Mac). IBM initially adopted it for their AT and some of their PS/2 range, which used the new MCA bus. The 80286 increased the clock speed to 8 MHz, 10 MHz and 12 MHz. It kept compatibility with the 8086, but could now run in protected mode, which allowed a 24-bit virtual address mode (giving a virtual memory of up to 16 MB). Unfortunately, at the time, DOS or Microsoft Windows could not use this enhancement, while OS/2 could.

16.1.4 Third generation (80386)

Intel released the 80386 in 1985. It was adopted immediately by Compaq, who developed their Compaq Deskpro range around it, and immediately headed off IBM's PS/2 range (which initially used the 80286 processor for most of the range). The 80386 helped Compaq to establish a new standard for PC-compatible systems. The SX and DX processor were both 32-bit devices, but the SX device had only a 24-bit address bus (giving it an address range of 16 MB). The clock speed evolved from 16 MHz, to 20 MHz and then to 33 MHz. It worked in either a real-mode, protected-mode or a virtual-8086 mode, which allowed the multitasking of several virtual 8086 programs running in their own memory space. For the first time, serious cloners started to produce pin-compatible and software-compatible devices that were not direct copies of the Intel processor. These included designs from Cyrix and AMD.

16.1.5 Fourth generation (80486)

In 1989, Intel released the 80486, which had many enhancements over the 80386. It ran approximately twice as fast as the 80386, as many of the instructions were completed in fewer clock cycles (RISC technology). It also had an integrated math coprocessor (although the SX version did not allow access to it) and an integrated L1 cache (8 KB). The cache was a considerable enhancement as it allowed data and code to be loaded from the relatively slow DRAM into the SRAM cache. The clock speed of the processor was moving to 50 MHz (20 ns), while the DRAM memory had a delay of 70 ns before it presented its contents to the processor. Thus, the processor had to insert at least four wait states when it accessed memory. The cache overcame this, if the cache controller guessed the next piece of code or data to be accessed next.

The 80486 was released around the same time as Microsoft released Windows Version 3.0. Luckily for Microsoft, the 80486 was the first PC-processor that could properly run a graphical user interface, and Windows shone brightly. Windows, though, did not use the full capabilities of the processor as it could not properly run more than one user program at a time.

As the processor increased, it was starting to be held back by the limiting speed of the motherboard (typically, at the time this was either 33 MHz or 50 MHz). The processor broke the link by multiplying the clock by a given factor, for example the DX2 multiplied the 33 MHz clock to give 66 MHz, and the DX4 multiplied the clock to 100 MHz.

16.1.6 Fifth generation (Pentium)

In 1983, Intel introduced the amazing Pentium processor. It allowed superscaler design, which allowed the execution of more than one instruction at a time (typically two instructions at a time). It also increased the data bus to 64 bits and initially ran at a speed of 60 MHz and 66 MHz. The Pentium was an excellent processor that competed well against other com-

---

The 586

After the 80486, most people expected to see the 80586, but it never happened. The reason for this was that Intel had tried to make the 386 one of their trademarks. Unfortunately, the US courts believed that the 386 number was so prevalent that it was almost a generic name (which led to the introduction of the term Intel386 for an Intel 386 processor). Instead of 586, they used the Pentium, so that they could trademark the name. This allowed Intel to invest their own money into developing the Pentium brand. Few users actually understand the technical specifications of the processors, and will typically buy a computer using the following judgements:

1. Brand name of the computer, such as IBM, Dell or Compaq.
2. Computer type is chosen depending on the brand name of the processor, such as Intel or AMD, and its clock speed.
3. Memory and hard disk capacities.
4. Software packages pre-installed.
5. Support and delivery times.

peting processors, but lacked in one area: its graphics and multimedia capabilities. Intel addressed this, in 1997, with MMX extensions, which introduced 57 new integer instructions, four new data types and eight 64-bit registers.

The number of compatible devices increased with AMD, IDT and Cyrix all producing Pentium-like devices. Intel, though, had an excellent marketing strategy, Intel Inside, where OEMs (original equipment manufacturers) such as IBM, Dell and Compaq carried the Intel logo on their cases if they were based on the Intel processor.

16.1.7 Sixth generation (Pentium Pro)

The Pentium Pro raised the performance of the PC and was a pure RISC device, where many instructions were completed in a single clock cycle; it was fully optimized for 32-bit processor

> **Intel Inside**
>
> With the Pentium processor, Intel promoted the Intel Inside logo, which allowed OEMs to display the Intel Inside logo if they contained the Intel Pentium processor. Consumers soon started to look for the logo, so that they knew that the computer was 100 per cent Intel compatible. Few products have ever carried the logo of another company (apart, from advertising brands). Other brands that have achieved this include Dolby (for noise reduction), Teflon (for non-stick frying-pans), and Nutrasweet, (low-calorie drinks).

(especially with Windows NT and OS/2). The best new feature was a level-2 cache, which allowed an SRAM cache to be inserted onto the motherboard, allowing easy upgrades of the cache with plug-in chips (256 kB/512 kB). This connected to the processor using a 64-bit data bus, and ran synchronously. It also had:

- **Multiple branch prediction**. The processor anticipates the next instruction.
- **Data flow analysis**. Reduces data dependence.
- **Speculative execution**. The processor attempts to anticipate instruction results.
- **Four pipelines**. Allows for simultaneous instruction execution.
- **RISC instructions,** with concurrent x86 CISCO code to MicroOps RISC instruction decoding.

The Pentium II could address up to 64 GB of main memory, but had cache limitations preventing memory use above 512 MB. With the introduction of the sub-$1,000 PC, Intel had to introducte a cheaper processor version that did not compete directly with the top-of-the-range Pentium II/III. For this, they produced the Celeron processor, which was basically a stripped down version of the Pentium II (the Celeron is sometimes affectionately known as 'the Castrated one'. The Celeron is offered without any second-level cache, giving it a slower performance than the Pentium II. Other processors competing with the Pentium II and Pentium Pro were the AMD K6 and the AMD K6-2 (typically used in mobile computing applications).

16.1.8 Seventh generation (Pentium III/Athlon K7)

New features added with the AMD K7 Athlon include:

- Ultra-high clock speeds of over 1 GHz.
- Up to 8 MB for level-2 cache.
- 128 KB level-1 cache.
- New system bus, which operates at 200 MHz (using enhanced AMD 756 chipset).
- Can use and rearrange up to 72 instructions simultaneously.
- Three instruction decoders, which translate x86 instructions into RISC instructions.
- Up to nine instructions can be executed simultaneously.

The Pentium III (Xeon) processor contains many enhancements over the Pentium II, including a new feature for streaming SIMD (single instruction multiple data) extensions for enhanced application performance extensions. It also included a robust, new instruction set and architecture enhancements, including:

- Clock frequencies of over 1 GHz.
- Integrated PBSRAM L2 cache (512 k).
- 100 MHz/133 MHz system bus.
- 70 new instructions, including streaming SIMD.
- Memory streaming architecture.
- Concurrent SIMD-FP architecture.
- New media instructions.

16.2 Other Processors

Processors come and go, but most manufacturers now know, especially with the advent of the Pentium, the importance of developing a strong brand name, with differing models to differentiate up-market products from mass-market products. Important differences are often processor clock speeds and cache sizes. Level-1 cache is obviously important for system speed, but it is expensive to integrate the cache into the same package as the processor.

16.2.1 Merced and IA-64 bus

IA-32 processors, such as the Pentium II/III, provide excellent performance, but are still limited in their scope. In the future, processors based on the IA-64 architecture will extend the Intel architecture for servers and workstations to even higher levels of performance and functionality to serve the needs of the most demanding applications.

The Merced processor will be the first IA-64 processor. As with all IA-64 processors, the Merced processor will have full IA-32 binary compatibility in hardware for end user investment protection.

The IA-64 architecture, on which the Merced processor is based, is a unique combination of innovative features, including explicit parallelism, predication and speculation. The architecture has been designed to be highly scalable to fulfill the requirements of various server and workstation market segments. A key design criterion of the IA-64 architecture is full IA-32 binary compatibility in hardware to allow end users a seamless software environment for their IA-32 software. The result is an architecture that is inherently scalable, enables industry-leading performance, and is fully compatible with existing IA-32 software.

The future is likely to involve an increase in real-time audio and video over the Internet. While the performance of today's processors continue to improve, existing architectures based on an out-of-order execution model require increasingly complex hardware mechanisms and are impeded increasingly by performance limiters such as branches and memory latency. The IA-64 processor architecture has been designed to overcome these limitations. The IA-64 architecture also provides additional performance headroom and scalability needed for future compute-intensive applications. It features a revolutionary 64-bit instruction set architecture (ISA), which applies a new processor architecture technology called explicitly parallel instruction computing (EPIC). EPIC embodies a set of advanced computer architecture techniques, such as explicit parallelism, predication and speculation. These techniques, as applied to Intel's IA-64 architecture, enable a much higher degree of instruction-level parallelism (ILP), and enable IA-64 processors to execute more instructions per clock cycle to deliver superior performance relative to today's out-of-order based RISC processors.

Explicit parallelism

In today's processor architectures, the compiler creates sequential machine code that attempts to imply parallelism to the hardware. The processor's hardware must then reinterpret this machine code and try to identify opportunities for parallel execution – the key to higher performance. This process is inefficient not only because the hardware doesn't always interpret the compiler's intentions correctly, but also because it uses valuable die area that could be better used to do real work – like executing instructions. Even today's fastest and most efficient processors devote a significant percentage of hardware resources to this task of extracting more parallelism from software code.

The IA-64 architecture's use of explicit parallelism enables far more effective parallel execution of software instructions. In the new IA-64 architecture model, the compiler analyzes and explicitly identifies parallelism in the software at compile time. This allows the most optimal structuring of the machine code to deliver maximum ILP before the processor executes it, rather than potentially wasting valuable processor cycles at run time. The result is significantly improved processor utilization. Also, there is no wasting of precious die area for the hardware reorder engine used in out-of-order RISC processors.

Predication enhances parallelism

Simple decision structures, or *code branches,* are a severe performance challenge to out-of-order RISC architectures. In the simple if-then-else decision code sequence, traditional architectures view the code in four basic blocks. In order to continuously feed instructions into the processor's instruction pipeline, a technique called *branch prediction* is commonly used, to predict the correct path. With this technique, mispredicts commonly occur five to ten per cent of the time, causing the entire pipeline to be purged and the correct path to be re-loaded. A misprediction rate of just five to ten per cent can slow processing speed as much as 30 to 40 per cent.

To address this problem and to improve performance, the IA-64 architecture uses a technique known as predication. Predication begins by assigning special flags called predicate registers to both branch paths – p1 to the 'then' path and p2 to the 'else' path. At run time, the compare statement stores either a true or false value in the 1-bit predicate registers. Both paths are then executed by the processor but only the results from the path with a true predicate flag are used. Branches, and the possibility of associated mispredicts, are removed, the pipeline remains full, and performance is increased.

Predication is widely applicable. According to a study based on popular software benchmarks, predication can, on average, reduce the number of branches by more than 50 per cent and reduce mispredicts by as much as 40 per cent. In contrast to some existing architectures, the IA-64 architecture allows all instructions to be predicated.

Speculation minimizes the effect of memory latency

Overcoming memory latency is another major performance challenge for today's processor architectures. Because memory speed is significantly slower than processor speed, the processor must attempt to load data from memory as early as possible to insure the data is available when needed. Traditional architectures allow compilers and the processor to schedule loads before data is needed, but branches act as barriers to this *load hoisting*.

IA-64 architecture employs a technique known as *speculation* to initiate loads from memory earlier in the instruction stream – even before a branch. Because loads can generate exceptions, a mechanism to ensure that exceptions are properly handled is needed to support speculation that hoists loads before branches.

The memory load is scheduled speculatively above the branch in the instruction stream so as to start the memory access as early as possible. If an exception occurs, this event is stored and the *checks* instruction causes the exception to be processed. The elevation of the load allows more time to account for memory latency, without stalling the processor pipeline.

Branches occur with great frequency in common software code sequences. The unique ability of the IA-64 architecture to schedule loads before branches increases significantly the number of loads that can be speculated relative to traditional architectures. On average, over half of all loads can be executed speculatively resulting in significant performance improvement for today's software.

IA-64 architecture innovations enable greater parallelism than traditional architectures. In order to realize the performance improvements of this greater parallelism, the processor must provide massive hardware resources. IA-64 processors include:

- 128 general-purpose integer registers.
- 128 floating-point registers.
- 64 predicate registers.

The IA-64 architecture is also inherently scalable to allow for the expansion of the number of hardware execution units and increased parallel execution in new IA-64 processor implementations.

Sample crash

A crash within Windows shows the location of a fault, and the current state of the registers. The following shows an example Windows message. It can be seen that Windows uses a paged memory, where each page has a 32-bit address (in this case the fault occurred at BFF87EDEh), within a 16-bit page address (in this case 0167h). It can also be see that the system uses 32-bit registers (for example, EAX contains C00309C4h).

```
IEXPLORE caused an invalid
page fault in module
KERNEL32.DLL at 0167:bff87ede.

Registers:
EAX=c00309c4  CS=0167
EIP=bff87ede  EFLGS=00010206
EBX=0058fb1c  SS=016f
ESP=0054fff0  EBP=0055005c
ECX=00000000  DS=016f
ESI=81792b24  FS=4c0f
EDX=81792b2c  ES=016f
```

16.3 x84-64 Architecture

The x84-64 architecture is AMD's attempt to introduce a 64-bit open architecture for the PC. It uses a 64-bit data and address bus for 64-bit processors, which will be able to detect whether the transfer is 32-bit or 64-bit. An important factor is that it keeps compatibility with existing 16-bit and 32-bit technology, and allows a gradual migration in software from 32-bit to 64-bit.

x84-64 uses the x86 instruction set as a foundation, and is designed to support applications that address large amounts of physical and virtual memory, such as high performance servers, database management systems, and CAD tools. The current x86 instruction set has been enhanced with:

- **64-bit flat virtual addressing**.
- **64-bit extension called long mode**. Long mode consists of two sub-modes: 64-bit mode, and compatibility mode. 64-bit mode supports new 64-bit code through the addition of eight general-purpose registers and increases their size, along with the instruction pointer
- **Register extensions**. This has added eight 128-bit floating point registers streaming SIMD extensions (SSE).
- **Compatibility mode**. This supports existing 16-bit and 32-bit applications under a 64-bit operating system. In addition to long mode, the architecture also supports a pure x86 legacy mode, which preserves binary compatibility with existing 16-bit and 32-bit applications and operating systems.

17 Interface Buses

17.1 Introduction

The type of interface card used greatly affects the performance of a PC system. Early PC models relied on expansion options to improve their specification. These expansion options were cards that plugged into an expansion bus. Eight slots were usually available and these added memory, video, fixed and floppy disk controllers, printer output, modem ports, serial communications, and so on.

There are eight main types of interface buses available for the PC. The number of data bits they handle at a time determines their classification. They are:

- PC (8-bit)   ISA (16-bit)
- EISA (32-bit)   MCA (32-bit)
- VL-local bus (32-bit)   PCI bus (32/64-bit)
- SCSI (16/32-bit)   PCMCIA (16-bit)

> **Golden rules**
>
> Three golden rules at Dell:
>
> 1. Disdain inventory. Dell now measures its inventory in terms of hours rather than days or weeks.
> 2. Always listen to the customer.
> 3. Never sell indirect.

17.2 PC Bus

The PC bus uses the architecture of the Intel 8088 processor, which has an external 8-bit data bus and 20-bit address bus. A PC bus connector has a 62-pin printed circuit card edge connector and a long narrow or half-length plug-in card. As it uses a 20-bit address bus, it can address a maximum of 1 MB of memory. The transfer rate is fixed at 4.772 727 MHz, thus, a maximum of 4,772,727 bytes can be transferred every second. Dividing a crystal oscillator frequency of 14.318 18 MHz by three derives this clock speed. Figure 17.1 shows a PC card. Figure 17.2 defines the signal connections. The direction of the signal is taken as input if a signal comes from the ISA bus controller. An output comes from the slave device and input/output identifies that the signal can originate from either the ISA controller or the slave device.

The following gives the 8-bit PC bus connections:

SA0–SA19   Address bus (input/output). The lower 20 bits of the system address bus.

D0–D7   Data bus (input/output). The eight data bits that allow a transfer between the busmaster and the slave.

AEN   Address enable (output). The address enable allows for an expansion bus board to disable its local I/O address decode logic. It is active high. When active, address enable indicates that either DMA or refresh are in control of the buses.

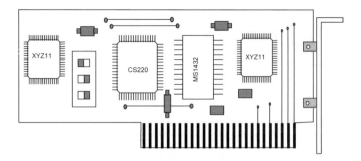

Figure 17.1   PC card

CLK

Clock (output). The bus CLK is set to 4.772 727 MHz (for PC bus and 8.33 MHz for ISA bus) and provides synchronization of the data transmission (it is derived from the OSC clock).

ALE

Address latch (output). The bus address latch indicates to the expansion bus that the address bus and bus cycle control signals are valid. It thus indicates the beginning of a bus cycle on the expansion bus.

$\overline{\text{IOR}}$

I/O read (input/output). I/O read command signal indicates that an I/O read cycle is in progress.

$\overline{\text{IOW}}$

I/O write (input/output). I/O write command signal indicates that an I/O write bus cycle is in progress.

$\overline{\text{SMEMR}}$

System memory read (output). System memory read signal indicates a memory read bus cycle for the 20-bit address bus range (0h to FFFFFh).

$\overline{\text{SMEMW}}$

System memory write (output). System memory write signal indicates a memory read bus cycle from the 20-bit address bus range (0h to FFFFFh).

IO CH RDY

Bus ready (input). The bus ready signal allows a slave to lengthen the amount of time required for a bus cycle.

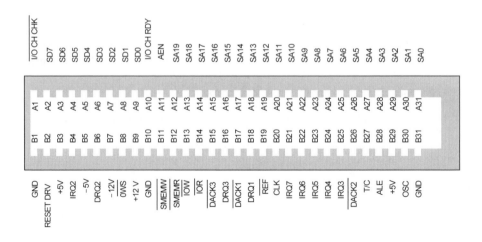

Figure 17.2   PC card connections

$\overline{\text{OWS}}$	Zero wait states (input). The zero wait states (or no wait state) allows a slave to shorten the amount of time required for a bus cycle.
DRQ1–DRQ3	DMA request (input). The DMA request indicates that a slave device is requesting a DMA transfer.
$\overline{\text{DACK1}}$ – $\overline{\text{DACK3}}$	DMA acknowledge (output). The DMA acknowledge indicates to the requesting slave that the DMA is handling its request.
T/C	Terminal count (input). The terminal count indicates that the DMA transfer has been successful and all the bytes have been transferred.
$\overline{\text{REF}}$	Refresh (output). The refresh signal is used to inform a memory board that it should perform a refresh cycle.
IRQ2–IRQ7	Interrupt request. The interrupt request signals indicate that the slave device is requesting service by the processor.
RESET DRV	Reset drive (output). The reset drive resets plug-in boards connected to the ISA bus.
OSC	Crystal oscillator (output). The crystal oscillator signal is 14.318 18 MHz signal provided for use by expansion boards. This clock speed is three times the CLK speed.
$\overline{\text{IO CH CHK}}$	I/O check (input). The I/O check signal indicates that a memory slave has detected a parity error.
±5V, ±12V and GND	Power (output).

17.3 ISA Bus

IBM developed the ISA (industry standard architecture) for their 80286-based AT (advanced technology) computer. It had the advantage of being able to deal with 16 bits of data at a time. An extra edge connector gives compatibility with the PC bus. This gives an extra 8 data bits and four address lines. Thus, the ISA bus has a 16-bit data and a 24-bit address bus. This gives a maximum of 16 MB of addressable memory and, like the PC bus, it uses a fixed clock rate of 8 MHz. The maximum data rate is thus 2 bytes (16 bits) per clock cycle, giving a maximum throughput of 16 MB/sec. In machines that run faster than 8 MHz, the ISA bus runs slower than the rest of the computer.

A great advantage of PC bus cards is that they can be plugged into an ISA bus connector. ISA cards are very popular as they give good performance for most interface applications. The components used are extremely cheap and it is a well-proven reliable technology. Typical applications include serial and parallel communications, networking cards and sound cards. Figure 17.3 illustrates an ISA card and Figure 17.4 gives the pin connections for the bus. It can be seen that there are four main sets of connections (the A, B, C and D sections). The standard PC bus connection contains the A and B sections. The A section includes the address lines A0–A19 and eight data lines, D0–D7. The B section contains interrupt lines, IRQ0–IRQ7, power supplies and various other control signals. The extra ISA lines are added with the C and D section; these include the address lines, A17–A23, data lines D8–D15 and interrupt lines IRQ10–IRQ14.

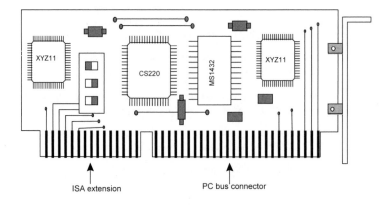

Figure 17.3   ISA card

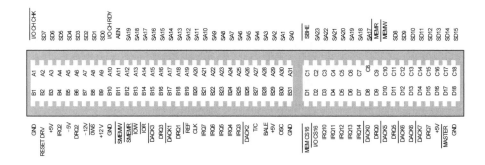

Figure 17.4   ISA bus connections

The ISA bus uses a 16-bit data bus (D0-D15) and a 24-bit address bus (A0–A24), and the CLK signal is set to 8.33 MHz. The $\overline{\text{SMEMR}}$ and $\overline{\text{SMEMW}}$ lines are used to transfer data for the lowest 1 MB (0h to FFFFFh) of memory (where the S prefix can be interpreted as small memory model) and the signals $\overline{\text{MEMR}}$ and $\overline{\text{MEMW}}$ are used to transfer data between 1 MB (FFFFFh) and 16 MB (FFFFFFh). For example, if reading from the address is 001000h, then the $\overline{\text{SMEMR}}$ the line is made active low; if the address is 1F0000h, then the $\overline{\text{MEMR}}$ line is made active. For a 16-bit transfer the $\overline{\text{M16}}$ and $\overline{\text{IO16}}$ lines are made active.

The extra 16-bit ISA bus connections are:

A17–A23	Address bus (input/output). The upper 7 bits of the address of the system address bus.
$\overline{\text{SBHE}}$	System byte high enable (output). The system byte high enable indicates that data is expected on the upper 8 bits of the data bus (D8–D15).
D8–D15	Data bus (input/output). The upper 8 bits of the data bus provides for the second half of the 16-bit data bus.
$\overline{\text{MEMR}}$	Memory read (input/output). The memory read command indicates a memory read when the memory address is in the range 100000h–FFFFFFh (16 MB of memory).
$\overline{\text{MEMW}}$	Memory write (input/output). The memory write command indi-

cates a memory write when the memory address is in the range 100000h–FFFFFFh (16 MB of memory).

$\overline{\text{M16}}$ — 16-bit memory slave. Indicates that the addressed slave is a 16-bit memory slave.

$\overline{\text{IO16}}$ — 16-bit I/O slave (input/output). Indicates that the addressed slave is a 16-bit I/O slave.

DRQ0, DRQ5–DRQ7 — DMA request lines (input). Extra DMA request lines that indicate that a slave device is requesting a DMA transfer.

$\overline{\text{DACK0}}$, $\overline{\text{DACK5}}$ – $\overline{\text{DACK7}}$ — DMA acknowledge lines (output). Extra DMA acknowledge lines that indicate to the requesting slave that the DMA is handling its request.

$\overline{\text{MASTER}}$ — Bus ready (input). This allows another processor to take control of the system address, data and control lines.

IRQ9–IRQ12, IRQ14, IRQ15 — Interrupt requests (input). Additional interrupt request signals that indicate that the slave device is requesting service by the processor. Note that the IRQ13 line is normally used by the hard disk and included in the IDE bus.

17.3.1 Handshaking lines

Figure 17.5 shows a typical connection to the ISA bus. The ALE (sometimes known as BALE) controls the address latch; when active low, it latches the address lines A2–A19 to the ISA bus. The address is latched when ALE goes from a high to a low.

The Pentium's data bus is 64 bits wide, whereas the ISA expansion bus is 16 bits wide. It is the bus controller's function to steer data between the processor and the slave device for either 8-bit or 16-bit communications. For this purpose, the bus controller monitors $\overline{\text{BE0}}$ – $\overline{\text{BE3}}$, $\text{W}/\overline{\text{R}}$, $\overline{\text{M16}}$ and $\overline{\text{IO16}}$ to determine the movement of data.

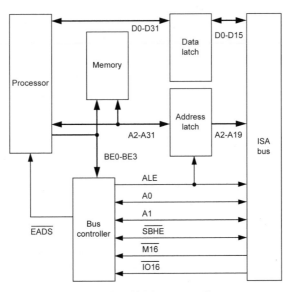

Figure 17.5 ISA bus connections

When the processor outputs a valid address, it sets address lines (AD2–AD31), the byte enables ($\overline{BE0}$ – $\overline{BE3}$) and sets ADS active. The bus controller then picks up this address and uses it to generate the system address lines, SA0–SA19 (which are just a copy of the lines A2–A19. The bus controller then uses the byte enable lines to generate the address bits SA0 and SA1.

The EADS signal returns an active low signal to the processor if the external bus controller has sent a valid address on address pins A2–A21.

It can be seen from Figure 17.6 that the BE0 line accesses the addresses ending with 0h, 4h, 8h and Ch, the BE1 line accesses addresses ending with 1h, 5h, 9h and Dh, the BE2 line accesses addresses ending with 02, 5h, Ah and Eh, and so on.

Thus, if the BE0 line is asserted and the SBHE line is high, then a single byte is accessed through the D0–D7. If a word is to be accessed then SBHE is low and D0–D15 contains the data.

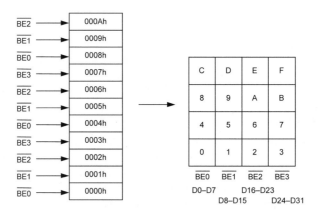

Figure 17.6   Address decoding

Table 17.1 shows three examples of handshaking lines. The first is an example of a byte transfer with an 8-bit slave at an even address. The second example gives a byte transfer for an 8-bit slave at an odd address. Finally, the table shows a 2-byte transfer with a 16-bit slave at an even address.

Table 17.1   Example handshaking lines

BE0	BE1	BE2	BE3	IO16	M16	SBHE	SA0	SA1	Data
0	1	1	1	1	1	1	0	0	SD0–SD7
1	0	1	1	1	1	0	1	0	SD8–SD15
0	0	1	1	0	1	0	0	0	SD0–SD15

If 32-bit data is to be accessed, then BE0–BE3 will each be 0000, which makes 4 bytes active. The bus controller will then cycle through SA0, SA1 = 00 to SA0, SA1 = 11. Each time, the 8-bit data is placed into a copy buffer, which is then passed to the processor as 32 bits.

17.3.2 82344 IC

Much of the electronics in a PC has been integrated onto single ICs. The 82344 IC is one that interfaces directly to the ISA bus. Figure 17.7 shows its pin connections.

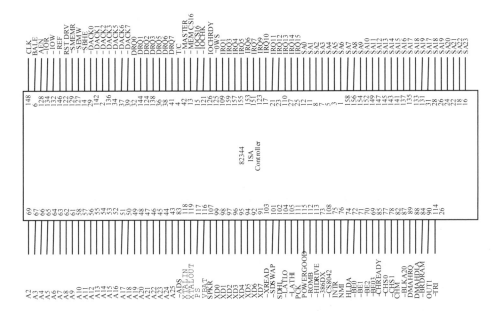

Figure 17.7   82344 IC connections

17.4 Other Legacy Buses

Two other buses that were used in the past are:

- **MCA**. IBM developed the Microchannel Interface Architecture (MCA) bus for their PS/2 computers. This bus is completely incompatible with ISA bus. It can operate as a 16-bit or 32-bit data bus. The main technical difference between the MCA and PC/ISA (and EISA) is that the MCA is an asynchronous bus whereas PC/ISA/EISA use a synchronous bus. A synchronous bus works at a fixed clock rate whereas an asynchronous bus data transfer is not dependent on a fixed clock. Asynchronous buses take their timings from the devices involved in the data transfer (that is, the processor or system clock). The original MCA specification resulted in a maximum transfer rate of 160 MB/sec. Very few manufacturers have adopted MCA technology and it is mainly found in IBM PS/2 computers.

- **EISA**. Several manufacturers developed the EISA (extended industry standard architecture) bus in direct competition to

Typical I/O Addresses

Address	Device
0000–000F	Slave DMA controller
0020–0021	Master PIC
0040–0043	System timer
0060	Keyboard
0061	Speaker
0064	Keyboard
0070–0071	Real-time clock
0080–008F	DMA
00A0–00A1	Slave PIC
00F0–00FF	Numeric processor
0170–0177	Secondary H/D
0200–020F	Game port
0220–022F	Soundcard
0294–0297	PCI bus
02F8–02FF	COM2
0330–0331,	Soundcard
0370–0371	Soundcard
0376	Secondary IDE
0378–037A	LPT1
0388–03B8	Soundcard
03B0–03BB	VGA
03C0–03DF	VGA
03F6	Primary IDE
03F8–03FF	COM1
0480–048F	PCI bus
04D0–04D1	PCI bus
0530–0537	Soundcard
0778–077A	ECP Port (LPT1)
0CF8–0CFF	PCI bus
4000–403F	PCI bus
5000–5018	PCI bus
D000–DFFF	AGP controller
E000–E01F	USB controller
E400–E4FF	VGA

the MCA bus. It provides compatibility with PC/ISA but not MCA. The EISA connector looks like an ISA connector. It is possible to plug an ISA card into an EISA connector, but a special key allows the EISA card to be inserted deeper into the EISA bus connector. It then makes connections with a 32-bit data and address bus. An EISA card has twice the number of connections over an ISA card and there are extra slots that allow it to be inserted deeper into the connector. The ISA card connects only with the upper connectors because it has only a single key slot. EISA uses a synchronous transfer at a clock speed of 8 MHz. It has a full 32-bit data and address bus and can address up to 4 GB of memory. In theory, the maximum transfer rate is 4 bytes for every clock cycle. As the clock runs at 8 MHz, the maximum data rate is 32 MB/s.

17.5 Summary of Interface Bus Types

Devices connect to the microprocessor using a computer bus. The specification of this bus defines the transfer speed between the microprocessor and the connected device. Peripherals can connect to the computer using either an internal or an external interface. Some buses, especially internal buses have a separate address bus, such as AGP, EISA and ISA, whereas others such as Ethernet, IDE and ISDN do not have an address line. Table 17.2 outlines typical computer buses and their maximum throughputs. Tables 17.3 and 17.4 give some examples of typical PC interfaces.

Table 17.2   Examples of computer buses

Bus	Maximum throughput	Data bus (bits)	Address bus (bits)	Notes
AGP	500 MB/s	64	32	
EISA	32 MB/s	32	32	4 GB maximum address, 8 MHz clock
Ethernet	1.25 MB/s	1	N/A	10 Mbps (10BASE)
Fibre Channel	132.5 MB/s	1	N/A	1.06 Gbps
Firewire	50 MB/s	1	N/A	400 Mbps (S400)
IDE	16.6 MB/s	16	N/A	Mode 4, EIDE, maximum four devices
IEEE-488	1 MB/s	8	N/A	
ISA	16 MB/s	16	24	16 MB maximum address, 8 MHz clock
ISDN	16 kB/s	1	N/A	2×64 kbps
MCA	100 MB/s	32	32	
Modem	7 kB/s	1	N/A	56 kbps
Parallel port	150 kB/s	8	N/A	150 kB/s is equivalent to 1.2 Mbps, which is the required transfer rate for stereo, 44.1kHz, 16-bit sampled audio
Parallel port (ECP/EPP)	1.2 MB/s	8	N/A	×8
PC	8 MB/s	8	20	1 MB maximum address, 8 MHz clock
PCI (32-bit)	132 MB/s	32	32	33 MHz clock
PCI (64-bit)	264 MB/s	64	32	33 MHz clock
PCMCIA	16 MB/s	16	26	64 MB maximum address
RS-232	14.4 kB/s	1	N/A	115.2 kbps
RS-485	1.25 MB/s	1	N/A	10 Mbps

SCSI (Fast/wide)	40 MB/s	16	N/A	20 MHz clock
SCSI-I	5 MB/s	8	N/A	
SCSI-II (Wide)	20 MB/s	16	N/A	10 MHz clock
SCSI-II (Fast)	10 MB/s	8	N/A	10 MHz clock
USB 1.0	1.5 MB/s	1	N/A	12 Mbps
USB 2.0	60 MB/s	1	N/A	480 Mbps
VL	132 MB/s	32	32	33 MHz clock

Table 17.3 Internal PC buses

Bus	Description	Typical devices connected
ISA	The ISA bus uses an interface card, which has two edge connectors (as one of the connectors was used on the original PC bus). Typical ISA connections are network interface adaptors, video camera interfaces and sound cards. It can transfer up to 16 bits at a time, and uses a fixed transfer rate of 8 MHz (8,000,000 transfers every second). Maximum: 16 MB/s.	Network adaptor Video camera adaptor Sound card
PCI	The PCI bus is used to connect internal devices in the PC. Typically, modern PCs have at least four PCI adaptors, which are used to connect to network interface cards, graphics adaptors and sound cards. It can transfer up to 32 bits at a time. Maximum: 132 MB/s (more typically, 66 MB/s).	Network adaptor Video camera adaptor Sound card
AGP	The AGP bus is used solely to connect to video cards. It uses a special connector, but builds on the standard PCI bus. It is optimized so that it uses the main memory of the computer, and does not depend on memory on the graphics card. Maximum: 500 MB/s.	Graphics adaptor
IDE	The integrated drive electronics (IDE) bus is used solely to connect to either hard disk drives or CD-ROM drives. There are two IDE connections: IDE0 and IDE1. Up to two devices can connect to each IDE connector, thus up to four disk drives can connect to the IDE bus. Maximum: 16.6 MB/s (IDE, Mode 4).	Hard disk drive CD-ROM drive
PCMCIA	The Personal Computer Memory Card International Association (PCMCIA) interface allows small thin cards to be plugged into laptop, notebook or palmtop computers. It was originally designed for memory cards (Version 1.0) but has since been adopted for many other types of adapters (Version 2.0), such as fax/modems, sound cards, local area network cards, CD-ROM controllers, digital I/O cards, and so on. Most PCMCIA cards comply with either PCMCIA Type II or Type III. Type I cards are 3.3 mm thick; Type II take cards are up to 5 mm thick; Type III allows cards up to 10.5 mm thick. A new standard, Type IV, takes cards that are thicker than 10.5 mm. Type II interfaces can accept Type I cards, Type III accept Types I and II, and Type IV interfaces accept Types I, II and III. It uses a 16-bit data transfer.	Network adaptor Modem adaptor Sound card CD-ROM drive Memory upgrade Hard disk drive

Table 17.4   External PC buses

Bus	Description	Typical devices connected
SCSI	The SCSI (small computer system interface) bus is used to connect to a wide range of device, and is typically used in workstations and Apple computers. It allows devices to connect using cables, which connect from one to the next (a daisy chain). In its standard form, it allows for up to seven devices to be connected (SCSI-I), but new standards (SCSI-II/III) allow up to 15 devices to connect. It can also be used as an internal or external bus system. In Apple Macs and workstations, SCSI is used to connect hard disk drives. Maximum: 5 MB/s (SCSI-I), 20 MB/s (SCSI-II), 40 MB/s (SCSI-III).	Hard disk drive CD-ROM drive Scanner Back-up device
RS-232	RS-232 is a standard interface on most computer systems. It uses serial communications to send data one bit at a time. The speed of the transfer is set by the bit rate. Typical bit rates are 9,600 bps (bits per second), 14,400 bps, 28,800 bps and 56,000 bps. It is typically used to transfer files from one computer to another, and to connect to a modem. In the past, it was also used to connect to a serial mouse, but mice typically connect using the PS/2 mouse connector. Typically, PCs have one or two serial ports, which are given the names COM1: and COM2. Maximum 7 kB/s (56,000 bps)	Modem Mouse File Transfer (with null modem cable)
Parallel port	The parallel port transfers 8 bits of data at a time. In its standard form, it supports a maximum rate of 150 kbps, with only one connected device. It also slows down the processor, as it must involve itself with the transfer of the data. In its standard form, it uses a 25-pin D-type connector to connect to the PC. As technology has improved, a new standard named ECP (extended capabilities port protocol)/EPP (enhanced parallel port) has been developed to increase the data rate, and also to connect multiple devices (as the SCSI bus). These allow the transfer of data to be controlled automatically by the system, not the processor. Typically with ECP/EPP, several devices can connect to the port, such as a printer, external CD-ROM drive, scanner, and so on. Its main advantage is that it is standard on most PCs, but it does have many disadvantages. Typically, PCs have a single parallel port, which is given the name LPT1. In many cases, it is being replaced by USB. Maximum 150 kbps (standard), 1.5 Mbps (ECP/EPP)	Printer CD-ROM drive Scanner File transfer (with parallel port cable)
USB	USB 1.0 allows for the connection of medium bandwidth peripherals such as keyboards, mice, tablets, modems, telephones, CD-ROM drives, printers and other low-to-moderate speed external peripherals in a tiered-star topology. It is typically used to connect to printers, scanners, external CD-ROM drives, digital speakers, and so on. It is likely to replace the printer port and the serial port for connecting external devices. USB 2.0 is aimed at medium-to-high bandwidth devices. Maximum 12 Mbps (USB 1.0), 480 Mbps (USB 2.0)	Digital speakers Scanner Printer Video camera Modem Joystick Monitor
PS/2 Port/ Keyboard	Initially on PCs, the serial port was used to connect a mouse, which reduced the number of connections to the serial port. These days, a mouse typically connects to the PS/2 mouse port, which has a small 5-pin DIN-like connector. This is the same connector that is used to connect to the keyboard.	Keyboard Mouse

17.6 Comparison of Different Interface Bus Types

Data throughput depends on the number of bytes being communicated for each transfer and the speed of the transfer. With the PC, ISA and EISA buses, this transfer rate is fixed at 8 MHz, whereas the PCI and VL local buses use the system clock. For many applications, the ISA bus offers the best technology as it has been around for a long time, it gives a good data throughput and it is relatively cheap and reliable. It has a 16-bit data bus and can thus transfer data at a maximum rate of 16 MB/s. The EISA bus can transfer four bytes for each clock cycle, thus if four bytes are transferred for each clock cycle, it will be twice as fast as ISA. The maximum data rates for the different interface cards are:

PC	8 MB/s	
ISA	16 MB/s	
EISA	32 MB/s	
VL-local bus	132 MB/s	(33 MHz system clock using 32-bit transfers)
PCI	264 MB/s	(33 MHz system clock using 64-bit transfers)
MCA	20 MB/s	(160 MB/s burst)

The type of interface technology used depends on the data throughput. Table 17.5 shows some typical transfer data rates. The heaviest use the system are microprocessor-to-memory and graphics adaptor transfers. These data rates depend on the application and the operating system used. GUI programs have much greater data throughput than programs running in text mode. Notice that a high-specification sound card with recording standard quality (16-bit samples at 44.1 kHz sampling rate) requires a transfer rate of only 172 kB/s. The transfer rate for audio is:

$$\text{Transfer rate} = \text{Number of samples per second} \times \text{Number of bytes per sample}\ (\text{B/s})$$
$$= (44,100 \times 2) \times 2\ \text{B/s}$$
$$= 176,400\ \text{B/s}$$
$$= \frac{166,400}{1,024} = 172.26\ \text{kB/s}$$

A standard Ethernet local area network card transfers at data rates of up 10 Mbps (about 1 MB/s), although new, fast Ethernet cards can transfer at data rates of up to 100 Mbps (about 10 MB/s). These transfers thus require local bus type interfaces.

Table 17.5 Example transfer rates

Device	Transfer rate	Application
Hard disk	4 MB/s	Typical transfer
Sound card	88 kB/s	16-bit, 44.1 kHz sampling
LAN	1 MB/s	10 Mbps Ethernet
RAM	66 MB/s	Microprocessor to RAM
Serial communications	1 kB/s	9,600 bps
Super VGA	15 MB/s	1,024×768 pixels with 256 colors

For a graphics adaptor with a screen resolution of 1024×640, 64k colors (16-bit color), which is updated 20 times per second (20 Hz), the maximum transfer rate will be:

Transfer rate (maximum) = Number of pixels per screen × Number of bits per pixel

$$× \text{Number of screen updates (b/s)}$$

$$= (1{,}024 × 640) × 16 × 20 \text{ b/s}$$

$$= 209{,}715{,}200 \text{ b/s}$$

$$= \frac{209{,}715{,}200}{8} = 26{,}214{,}400 \text{ B/s}$$

$$= \frac{26{,}214{,}400}{1{,}024 × 1{,}024} = 246.2 \text{ MB/s}$$

The PCI local bus has become a standard on most new PC systems and has replaced the VL-local bus for graphics adaptors. It has the advantage over the VL-local bus in that it can transfer at much higher rates. Unfortunately, most available software packages cannot use the full power of the PCI bus because they do not use the full 64-bit data bus. PCI and VL-local buses are discussed in the next chapter.

17.7 Exercises

17.7.1   How many bits are transferred in a single clock operation with the PC bus?
(a)   1   (b)   8
(c)   16   (d)   32

17.7.2   What is the standard clock frequency used in ISA transfers?
(a)   4.77 MHz   (b)   8 MHz
(c)   10 MHz   (d)   16 MHz

17.7.3   What is the maximum transfer rate for the ISA bus?
(a)   8 MB/s   (b)   16 MB/s
(c)   32 MB/s   (d)   64 MB/s

17.7.4   What is the maximum transfer rate for the EISA bus?
(a)   8 MB/s   (b)   16 MB/s
(c)   32 MB/s   (d)   64 MB/s

17.7.5   What is the main disadvantage of PC, ISA and EISA buses?
(a)   They are incompatible with each other
(b)   They use a fixed clock frequency
(c)   They are not supported in PC systems
(d)   They are expensive to implement

17.7.6   What is the maximum transfer rate for a 10 Mbps Ethernet adaptor?
(a)   1 MB/s   (b)   1.221 MB/s
(c)   10 MB/s   (d)   100 MB/s

17.7.7   Prove, apart from the MCA bus, the transfer rates given in section 3.6.

17.7.8   If an audio card is using 16-bit sampling at a rate of 44.1 kHz, prove that the transfer rate for stereo sound will be 176.4 k B/sec. Show also that this is equivalent to 1.411 Mbps (note that this is approximately the standard rate for CD-ROMs). Can this rate be transferred using the ISA bus? Using this transfer rate, determine the maximum transfer speed of a ×32 CD-ROM drive.

17.7.9   Determine the amount of data for a single screen that must be transferred for the following screen resolutions:

(a)   800×600, 65,5536 colors (960,000 B/s).
(b)   800×600, 16,777,216 colors (1,440,000 B/s).
(c)   1,024×768, 65,536 colors (1,572,864 B/s).

Determine the maximum number of screen updates that is required for a 32-bit PCI bus for each of the above.

17.7.10   Identify the main ISA signal lines and explain how they are used to transfer data.
(a)   What are the main differences between a PC card and an ISA card?
(b)   How the byte enable lines are used?
(c)   How is a read or write transfer identified?
(d)   How is a memory read/write or isolated memory read/write transfer identified?
(e)   Identify the interrupt lines that are available on a PC card and an ISA card.

Typically, what devices could be supported by a PC card (that is, what devices use the interrupts that a PC card can support)? How does this related to the original specification of the PC?

Typical DMA channels	
0	Any
1	Any
2	Floppy disk
3	Parallel port
4	Cascaded DMA
5	Any
6	Any
7	Any

17.8 The Fall of the MCA Bus

The leading computer companies of 1987 were Intel, IBM, Compaq and Microsoft, but a special mention must go to Apple, Commodore and Sun Microsystems, who fought bravely against the growing IBM PC market. With the release of the IBM AT and now the PS/2, IBM had presented Intel with a large market for their 80286 design, but it was Compaq who increased it even more with the release of the DeskPro 386. The new Intel processors were now so successful that Intel had little to do, but try to keep up with demand, and try to stop cloners from copying their designs. They could now consolidate on their success with other support devices, such as the 80387math coprocessor. By the end of the year, their only real mass-market competitor was Motorola, who released their excellent Motorola 68030 microprocessor, which would become the foundation of many Apple Mac computers. Within a few years, Motorola would become extremely reliant on the Apple Mac, while Intel held onto the PC market.

At IBM, things were hectic. They were phasing out their IBM PC range, and introducing their new computer range, the PS/2. IBM realized that the open architecture of the IBM PC held few long-term advantages for them, as clone manufacturers could always sell computers at much less cost than themselves. IBM had large development teams, sales staff, distribution centers, training centers, back-up support, and so on. They thus needed to make enough profit on each computer to support all these functions. The PS/2 was their attempt to close the open system and make one that had to be licensed through themselves. It was also an attempt to reduce some of the problems that were caused with the limited technology of the IBM PC. One of the main problems was the PC bus, which allowed users to easily add peripherals to the computer by plugging them into the system with a standard card that had a standard edge connector. Initially, this used an 8-bit data bus, and operated at 8 MHz, which gave a data throughput of 8 MB/s. This was upgraded on the AT computer with the AT bus, which used a 16-bit data bus, giving a data throughput of 16 MB/s. The great advantage of the AT bus was that it was still compatible with the PC bus, so PC bus cards could still be slotted into AT bus connectors (soon to be renamed the ISA).

The AT bus was fine for slow devices, such as printers, modems, and so on. However, for color graphics, it was far to slow. For example, a color monitor with a resolution of 640×480 with 256 colors (8 bits per color) and a screen refresh of 25 Hz requires a data throughput of 7,680,000 B/s (640×480×1×25 B/s).

IBM's concept was to use a bus that intentionally had a different connector to the PC and the AT buses and did not use a fixed clock rate, and could thus operate at the speed of the processor, which was now moving above 20 MHz. The MCA (micro channel architecture) bus also used a 32-bit data bus, which allowed data throughputs of 100 MB/s.

The PS/2 was an excellent concept, and was boosted by an extensive advertising campaign. It was the right move, and the system looked good, with 3.5-inch disk drives, and a rugged gray plastic case. Computers had never look so professional. For many businesses, they were heaven-sent. However, the fly in the ointment for IBM was Compaq, who had previously released their DeskPro 386. The big problem with the PS/2 range was that the lower-end PCs were based on the 8086 and the 80286, and against the 80386-based Compaq they seemed slow. The initial range was:

- Model 30, which used the relatively slow 8 MHz 8086. IBM also introduced the Model 25, also with an 8 MHz Intel 8086, which had no hard drive, and a reduced keyboard, for $1,350.
- Models 50 and 60, which used a 10 MHz 80286 with MCA.
- Model 80, which used a 20 MHz 80386 with MCA.

The battle lines had been drawn in 1987. IBM was trying to pull the market towards their architecture. The strength of this was highlighted by John Akers, the then IBM Chairman: 'We're trying to change the habits of an awful lot of people. That won't happen overnight, but it will bloody well happen'.

IBM thought they would win the battle, and the older IBM PC architecture would die off. Several companies went with IBM, including Tandy (Tandy 5000MC), Dell and Olivetti. But the first signs of problems for IBM came when 61 companies developed the 32-bit version of the ISA bus, the EISA. This allowed 32 bits to be transferred at a time. Unfortunately, it was still based on an 8 MHz clocking rate, which gave it a data throughput of 32 MB/s. It was supported by the leading computer companies, such as Compaq Computer, AST, Epson, Hewlett-Packard, NEC Technologies, Olivetti, Tandy, Wyse, Zenith and Microsoft. Along with this, Compaq Computer and eight other companies started developing the ISA standard to improve the AT-bus. Rod Canion, the Compaq Computer CEO, showed his company's resistance to the MCA bus: 'If people are going to buy Micro Channel, they're going to buy it from IBM'.

The market would eventually reject the MCA bus, mainly because of the weight of the new 80386 computers on the market. It would take a company such as Intel to develop a totally new bus system: the PCI bus.

17.9 Notes from the Author

There are three main reasons for the number of buses available: legacy, compatibility and efficiency. Buses exist because they have existed in the past, and are required to be supported for the time being. Buses allow the segmentation of a system and provide, most of the time, a standard interface that allows an orderly flow of data and allows manufactures to interconnect their equipment. If allowed, many manufacturers would force users to use their own versions of buses, but the trend these days is to use internationally defined buses. Efficient buses have been designed to take into account the type of data that is being transmitted.

Manufacturers who try to develop systems on their own can often fail miserably. This has been shown with the MCA bus, which was an excellent step in bus technology, and made up for the mistakes made in the original PC design. But IBM tried to force the market, and failed. These days, it is international standards that are important. Products to be accepted in the market or the industry require an international standards body to standardize them, such as the IEEE, the ISO, ANSI, and so on. Without them, very few companies will accept the product. A classic case of an open standard winning against a closed system was VHS video, which was an open standard, against Betamax, which was a closed standard, produced by Sony. VHS was the inferior technology, but won because there were more companies willing to adopt it.

The days of having a single computer bus for internal and external connections are a long way off as there will always be some peripherals that need to transmit data in a certain way that differs from other peripherals. Also, standard technology always tends to win over newer, faster technology. Few companies can now define new standards on their own.

Before we start to look at

Best buses of all time

1. **PCI bus**. An excellent internal bus that provides the backbone to most modern PCs. It has been a complete success, and provides for many modern enhancements, such as plug-and-play technology, steerable interrupts, and so on. The VL-local bus held the fort for a short time, and gave a short-term fix for high-speed graphics transfers, but Intel busily developed a proper bus that could support other high-speed devices. With local bus technology, low-speed devices were pushed away from the processor, and could communicate with it only over a bridge. The PCI bus that is the bedrock of modern computing , and it still has a few trump cards left to play (increasing its transfer rate, integration with the AGP port, and increasing its data bus size).

2. **SCSI bus**. The most general-purpose of the external buses and in many respects as g as the PCI bus, but it loses out to the PCI bus in that it is not used in as many computers. It provides an easy method of connecting external devices in a daisy-chain connection. New standards for the SCSI bus support fast transfer rates (over 40 MB/s), and allow up to 15 internal or external devices to be connected.

3. **USB**. An external bus that shows great potential in the way that it integrates many of the low-and medium-bit rate devices onto a single bus system. New standards for USB are trying to also integrate high-bit rate devices. It supports hot plug-and-play, which allows users to connect and disconnect peripherals from the bus while the computer is still on.

4. **AGP port**. Overcomes the last great problem area of the PC: the graphics adaptor. AGP provides for fast transfer rates using the PCI bus as a foundation, and allows the PC to use local memory for graphics transfers.

5. **PCMCIA**. An external bus that provides for easy upgrades on notebook technology. It highlights how small and compact interface devices can be. Typical additions are modem and network adaptors. Its future will depend on how the USB bus is going to be used.

---

the technology behind computer buses, the list above gives what I believe to be the best buses (in order of their current and future usefulness).

And let's not forget the buses that have helped us get to this point. We may call them legacy buses, but they still provide useful functions. Thus, the awards for the Most Helpful Busses of the Past (in order of their previous usefulness) are given on the right-hand side.

Let's not forget about the great-grandfather of all the PC buses: the PC bus, the bus that has launched a million computers.

Finally, on the insert on the next page, the relegation zone for computer buses (in order of the problems that they have caused or for their lack of adoption).

Before covering the main buses Table 17.6 grades some of the main buses for their usefulness, availability, data throughput, cost and configuration.

From the table, it can be seen that the 'winners' are the PCI bus and Ethernet (100BASE). Over the years, the PCI has moved up the table rapidly and takes away the top position from the ISA bus; it does everything well, and beats the ISA bus for its ease of configuration. Its only problem is that it costs a bit more than the ISA bus, but it's worth it. The one to watch for is the USB bus. This is sure to rise further as more applications use it, and its bit rate increases. Buses such as the keyboard, joypad and PS/2 mouse port are not included as they are too specific to single applications. One of the oldest of the buses given here is the Ethernet bus. It has withstood a lot of pressure from other buses that would like to take control of the networking applications, and beaten of all of them. Its main strengths are its

Most Helpful Buses of the Past

1. **ISA bus**. The ISA bus competed head to head with the MCA, and, although it was much slower, it triumphed as it was compatible with the older PC bus. For many years, its performance was acceptable (16 MB/s), but the advent of the GUI was the beginning of the end for it. Sadly, it has seen the number of PCI slots increasing, while its own connections have been reduced from over five to less than two.

2. **RS-232 port**. A classic bus that is compatible (almost) with all the other RS-232 ports on every computer in the world. It provides a standard way to talk to devices, such as instruments, other computers and modems.

3. **IDE bus**. A rather quiet and unassuming internal bus, which does its job of interfacing to disk drives well, without much trouble. It has reasonable performance (over 14MB/s) and has no intention of ever becoming anything other than a disk-interfacing bus. Like Ethernet, it has overcome early retirement by increasing its transfer rate, but still keeping compatibility with previous systems. Its main competitor is SCSI, which is unlikely ever to beat it for compatibility and cost, thus it is likely to stay around for much longer than some of its earlier PC partners. For systems with fewer than four disk drives (in a combination of CD-ROM or hard disks), it is still the best choice, and is often integrated in the PC motherboard.

4. **VL-local bus**. The bus that showed the way for local bus technology, especially the PCI bus. It was always going to be a short-term fix, but it did its job effectively and quietly. Apart from the 80486, it was one of the leading factors that increased the adoption of Microsoft Windows (as it allowed the fast transfer to graphical data).

5. **Parallel port**. Another classic bus that was created purely to interface to an external printer, but has now been developed to support multi-attachment buses with reasonable transfer rates (over 150 kB/s).

cheapness and its general usage. In networking in particular, standardness counts more than virtually anything else. If a company were to adopt a new network bus for their network, and within five years that technology was either too expensive to maintain, or was not even available, it would take a major investment to redesign the network. So, Ethernet wins because it has a virtual monopoly on the connection of computers to corporate networks. Its shortcomings have been overcome with gradual migration. Its slowness has been overcome with new standard such as 100BASE (100MBps) and 1000BASE (1Gbps). Its connection and grounding problems have been solved with hubs, twisted-pair cables and fibre-optic cables.

Relegation zone for buses

1. ***ISA bus****. Like the 8088 processor and DOS, this has a Dr Jekyll and Mr Hyde appearance. It is probably both the best and worst computer bus. It is the bus which, in the past, has provided the foundation for upgrading the PC, and has gently handed over its mantel to the PCI bus. But it has caused lots of problems as it quickly fossilized the connection between the processor and the peripherals. Its major problems were its fixed rate transfer rate, the way that it handled interrupts, its lack of address lines (a maximum of 24), its lack of data lines (a maximum of 16), and the way that fast, medium and slow devices all connected to the same bus (thus allowing slow devices to 'hog' the bus). It started to show its age when 32-bit processors appeared and the motherboard speeds increased. The beginning of its end was the introduction of Microsoft Windows 3, which started to properly use a GUI. The VL-local bus quickly came in as a stand-in. From there on, local bus technology became the standard way to transfer large amounts of data.*

2. ***MCA bus****. IBM tried to pull the standard for bus technology back to a closed system with the MCA bus. It failed as it came up against the ISA, which, although technologically inferior, was an open standard.*

3. ***VME bus****. Powerful, complex and very misunderstood. The designers decided to create a bus that had everything.*

4. ***RS-232 port.*** *An extremely useful bus that suffers because of a lack of speed and its incompatibility (even although everyone is working to the same standard, the level of implementation of the standard varies).*

5. ***Keyboard connection/serial port mouse connection****. Two extremely limited connectors. The keyboard connector has virtually no intelligence built into it, and provides for limited sensing of the keyboard type, or extra functionality. Its only real advantages are that it looks different from other connectors, and that is has allowed the integration of the new PS/2-type mouse connector. Serial port mouse connections have always caused problems, mainly because they use up one of the serial port connections.*

Table 17.6   Comparison of the main buses: (mark out of 10)

		Usefulness	Availability	Data throughput	Cost	Configuration	Total
=1	PCI	9	9	8	6	9	41
=1	Ethernet (100BASE)	10	9	5	10	7	41
=3	ISA	10	9	5	10	5	39
=3	Ethernet (10BASE)	10	9	3	10	7	39
=5	IDE	5	9	6	9	8	37
=5	USB	10	7	4	8	8	37
7	RS-232	10	10	2	10	3	35
8	Parallel port (ECP/EPP)	8	8	5	8	4	33
=9	Parallel port	7	8	3	8	5	31
=9	SCSI-I	8	6	5	5	7	31
=9	AGP	5	6	9	3	8	31
12	SCSI-II	8	4	7	4	7	30
13	PC	5	9	3	7	3	27
14	IEEE-488	7	5	3	6	5	26
15	ISDN	3	6	5	2	5	21
=16	Modem	3	9	1	3	4	20
=16	RS-485	4	5	4	3	4	20
=18	Firewire	3	3	7	2	4	19
=18	PCMCIA	4	5	5	1	4	19
=20	Fibre channel	2	2	8	2	4	18
=20	MCA	4	1	6	2	5	18
=20	VL	5	1	6	1	5	18
23	EISA	1	1	3	2	5	12

PCI Bus

18.1 Introduction

The PC was conceived at a time when processor clock speeds were measured in several MHz. Initially this was set at 4.77 MHz, and then increased to 8 MHz. The PC and ISA buses fossilized with these clock frequencies. In the first few years of its design, the motherboard ran at the same speed as the processor. Soon, with improvements in silicon design, the speed of the processor was increased to tens of megahertz. Shortly afterwards, the maximum limit of the motherboard was reached and the only way to break this limit was to double or treble the motherboard clock speed. This limit was set at 33 MHz or 50 MHz. Processor speed has since been risen to over 500 MHz. Local bus technology uses the speed of the motherboard, rather than a fixed rate. Most new PCs have a motherboard speed of 100 MHz, which is at least twice as fast as 50 MHz motherboards.

The greatest need for greater data throughput is in video adaptors. A high-resolution video screen with high screen update rate can require burst rates of over 100 MB/s. For example a screen of 1024×640 with 16.7 million colors (24-bit color) will require the following amount of memory for a single screen:

$$
\begin{aligned}
\text{Memory} &= 1,024 \times 640 \times 3 \ \text{B} \\
&= 1,966,080 \, \text{B} \\
&= \frac{= 1,966,080}{1,024 \times 1,024} = 1.875 \, \text{MB}
\end{aligned}
$$

If this screen is updated 10 times every second (10 Hz) then the data throughput is :

$$
\begin{aligned}
\text{Data transfer} &= 1.875 \times 20 \ \text{MB/s} \\
&= 37.5 \, \text{MB/s}
\end{aligned}
$$

This transfer rate is far too fast for buses such as ISA and EISA, and the only solution is a fast 32-bit bus, transferring at a rate of at least 33 MHz. The maximum transfer rates for various local bus transfers are as follows:

Data bus size	Transfer clock (MHz)	Data transfer rate (MB/s)
16	33	66
16	50	100
32	33	132
32	50	200
32	100	320
64	50	400

Intel have developed a standard interface, named the PCI (Peripheral Component Interconnection) local bus, for the Pentium processor. This technology allows fast memory, disk and video access. A standard set of interface ICs known as the 82430 PCI chipset is available to interface the bus. Figure 18.1 shows how the PCI bus integrates into the PC. The processor runs at a multiple of the motherboard clock speed, and is closely coupled to a local SRAM cache (first-level, or primary, cache). If the processor requires data it will first look in the primary cache for its contents. If it is in this cache, it will read its contents, and there is thus no need to either read from the second level cache or from DRAM memory. If the data is not in the primary cache then the processor slows downs to the motherboard clock speed, and contacts the system controller (which contains a cache controller). The controller then examines the second-level cache and if the contents are there, it passes the data onto the processor. If it does not have the contents then DRAM memory is accessed (which is a relatively slow transfer).

The system controller also interfaces to PCI bus, which is running at the motherboard clock frequency. This then bridges onto other buses, such as ISA, IDE and USB, each of which is running at different clock rates. The PCI bus thus provides a foundation bus for most of the internal and external buses.

Local bus design involves direct access to fast address and data buses. The ISA bus was a great bottleneck because it could only run at 8 MHz. This chapter discusses the VL-local bus and the PCI bus. The PCI bus is now the main interface bus used in most PCs, and is rapidly replacing the ISA bus for internal interface devices. It is a very adaptable bus and most of the external buses, such as SCSI and USB connect to the processor via the PCI bus.

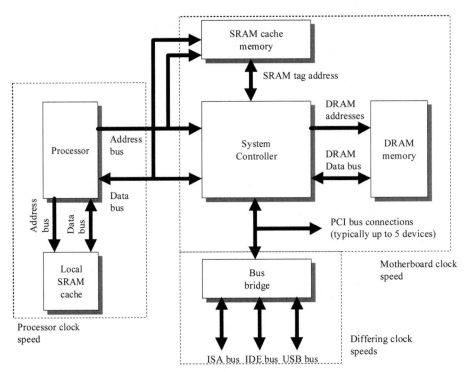

Figure 18.1   Local bus architecture

The PCI bus transfers data using the system clock, and can operate over a 32- or 64-bit data path. The high transfer rates used in PCI architecture machines limit the number of PCI bus interfaces to two or three (normally the graphics adapter and hard disk controller). If data is transferred at 64 bits (8 bytes) at a rate of 33 MHz then the maximum transfer rate is 264 MB/s. Figure 18.1 shows the PCI architecture. Notice that a bus bridge gives access to

ISA, IDE and USB. Unfortunately, to accommodate for the high data rates and for a reduction in the size of the interface card, the PCI connector is not compatible with PC, ISA or EISA.

The maximum data rate of the PCI bus is 264 MB/s, which can only be achieved using 64-bit software on a Pentium-based system. On a system based on the 80486 processor this maximum data rate will only be 132 MB/s (that is, using a 32-bit data bus).

The PCI local bus is a radical redesign of the PC bus technology. Table 18.1 lists the pin connections for the 32-bit PCI local bus and it shows that there are two lines of connections, the A and the B side. Each side has 64 connections giving a total of 128 connections. A 64-bit, 2×94-pin connector version is also available. The PCI bus runs at the speed of the motherboard which for the Pentium processor is typically 33 MHz.

Table 18.1 32-bit PCI local bus connections

Pin	Side A	Side B	Pin	Side A	Side B
1	−12V	$\overline{\text{TRST}}$	32	AD17	AD16
2	TCK	+12V	33	$\overline{\text{C/BE2}}$	+3.3V
3	GND	TMS	34	GND	$\overline{\text{FRAME}}$
4	TDO	TDI	35	$\overline{\text{IRDY}}$	GND
5	+5V	+5V	36	+3.3V	$\overline{\text{TRDY}}$
6	+5V	$\overline{\text{INTA}}$	37	$\overline{\text{DEVSEL}}$	GND
7	$\overline{\text{INTB}}$	$\overline{\text{INTC}}$	38	GND	$\overline{\text{STOP}}$
8	$\overline{\text{INTD}}$	+5V	39	$\overline{\text{LOCK}}$	+3.3V
9	$\overline{\text{PRSNT1}}$	Reserved	40	$\overline{\text{PERR}}$	SDONE
10	Reserved	+5V(I/O)	41	+3.3V	$\overline{\text{SBO}}$
11	$\overline{\text{PRSNT2}}$	Reserved	42	$\overline{\text{SERR}}$	GND
12	GND	GND	43	+3.3V	PAR
13	GND	GND	44	$\overline{\text{C/BE1}}$	AD15
14	Reserved	Reserved	45	AD14	+3.3V
15	GND	$\overline{\text{RST}}$	46	GND	AD13
16	CLOCK	+5V(I/O)	47	AD12	AD11
17	GND	$\overline{\text{GNT}}$	48	AD10	GND
18	$\overline{\text{REQ}}$	GND	49	GND	AD09
19	+5V(I/O)	Reserved	50	KEY	KEY
20	AD31	AD30	51	KEY	KEY
21	AD29	+3.3V	52	AD08	$\overline{\text{C/BE0}}$
22	GND	AD28	53	AD07	+3.3V
23	AD27	AD26	54	+3.3V	AD06
24	AD25	GND	55	AD05	AD04
25	+3.3V	AD24	56	AD03	GND
26	$\overline{\text{C/BE3}}$	IDSEL	57	GND	AD02
27	AD23	+3.3V	58	AD01	AD00
28	GND	$\overline{\text{FRAME}}$	59	+5V(I/O)	+5V(I/O)
29	AD21	AD20	60	$\overline{\text{ACK64}}$	$\overline{\text{REQ64}}$
30	AD19	GND	61	+5V	+5V
31	+3.3V	$\overline{\text{TRDY}}$	62	+5V	+5V

18.2 PCI Operation

The PCI bus cleverly saves lines by multiplexing the address and data lines. It has two modes (Figure 18.2):

- **Multiplexed mode** – the address and data lines are used alternately. First, the address is sent, followed by a data read or write. Unfortunately, this requires two or three clock cycles for a single transfer (either an address followed by a read *or* write cycle, or an address followed by read *and* write cycle). This causes a maximum data write transfer rate of 66 MB/s (address, then write) and a read transfer rate of 44 MB/s (address, write then read), for a 32-bit data bus width.

- **Burst mode** – the multiplexed mode obviously slows down the maximum transfer rate. Additionally, it can be operated in burst mode, where a single address can be initially sent, followed by implicitly addressed data. Thus, if a large amount of sequentially addressed memory is transferred then the data rate approaches the maximum transfer of 133 MB/s for a 32-bit data bus and 266 MB/s for a 64-bit data bus.

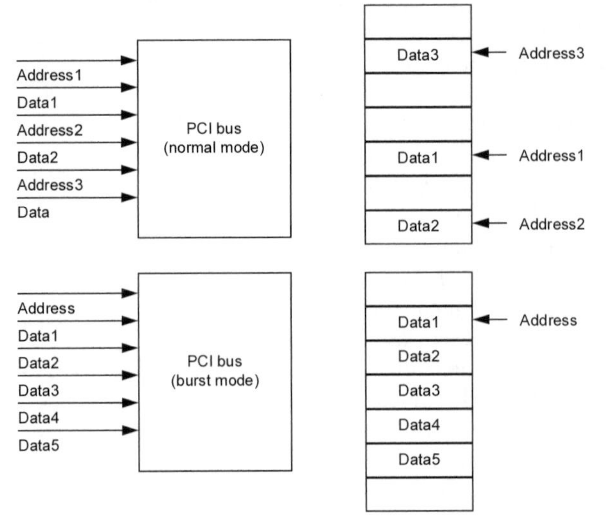

Figure 18.2 PCI bus transfer modes

If the data from the processor is sequentially addressed information then PCI bridge buffers the incoming data and then releases it to the PCI bus in burst mode. The PCI bridge may also use burst mode when there are gaps in the addressed data and use a handshaking line to identify that no data is transferred for the implied address. For example in Figure 18.2 the burst mode could involve Address+1, Address+2 and Address+3 and Address+5, then the byte enable signal can be made inactive for the fourth data transfer cycle.

To accommodate the burst mode, the PCI bridge has a prefetch and posting buffer on both the host bus and the PCI bus sides. This allows the bridge to build the data access up into burst accesses. For example, the processor typically transfers data to the graphics card with sequential accessing. The bridge can detect this and buffer the transfer. It will then transfer the data in burst mode when it has enough data. Figure 18.3 shows an example where the PCI bridge buffers the incoming data and transfers it using burst mode. The transfers between the processor and the PCI bridge,

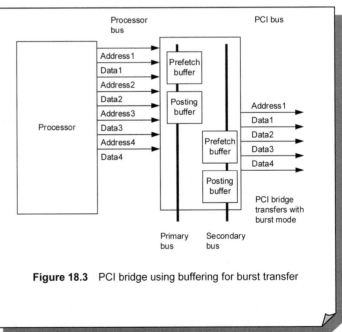

Figure 18.3 PCI bridge using buffering for burst transfer

and between the PCI bridge and the PCI bus can be independent where the processor can be transferring to its local memory while the PCI bus is transferring data. This helps to decouple the PCI bus from the processor.

The primary bus in the PCI bridge connects to the processor bus and the secondary bus connects to the PCI bus. The prefetch buffer stores incoming data from the connected bus and the posting buffer holds the data ready to be sent to the connected bus.

The PCI bus also provides for a configuration memory address (along with direct memory access and isolated I/O memory access). This memory is used to access the configuration register and 256-byte configuration memory of each PCI unit.

18.2.1 PCI bus cycles

The PCI has built-in intelligence where the command/byte enable signals ($\overline{C/BE3} - \overline{C/BE0}$) are used to identify the command. They are given by:

$\overline{C/BE3}$	$\overline{C/BE2}$	$\overline{C/BE1}$	$\overline{C/BE0}$	*Description*
0	0	0	0	INTA sequence
0	0	0	1	Special cycle
0	0	1	0	I/O read access
0	0	1	1	I/O write access
0	1	1	0	Memory read access
0	1	1	1	Memory write access
1	0	1	0	Configuration read access
1	0	1	1	Configuration write access
1	1	0	0	Memory multiple read access
1	1	0	1	Dual addressing cycle
1	1	1	0	Line memory read access
1	1	1	1	Memory write access with invalidations

The PCI bus allows any device to talk to any other device, thus one device can talk to another without the processor being involved. The device that starts the conversion is known as the initiator and the addressed PCI device is known as the target. The sequence of operation for write cycles, in burst mode, is:

- Address phase – the transfer data is started by the initiator activating the $\overline{\text{FRAME}}$ signal. The command is set on the command lines ($\overline{C/BE3} - \overline{C/BE0}$) and the address/data pins (AD31–AD0) are used to transfer the address. The bus then uses the byte enable lines ($\overline{C/BE3} - \overline{C/BE0}$) to transfer a number of bytes.
- The target sets the $\overline{\text{TRDY}}$ signal (target ready) active to indicate that the data on the AD31–AD0 (or AD62–AD0 for a 64-bit transfer) lines is valid. In addition, the initiator indicates its readiness to the PCI bridge by setting the $\overline{\text{IRDY}}$ signal (indicator ready) active. Figure 18.4 illustrates this.
- The transfer continues using the byte enable lines. The initiator can block transfers if it sets $\overline{\text{IRDY}}$ and the target with $\overline{\text{TRDY}}$.
- Transfer is ended by deactivating the $\overline{\text{FRAME}}$ signal.

The read cycle is similar but the $\overline{\text{TRDY}}$ line is used by the target to indicate that the data on the bus is valid.

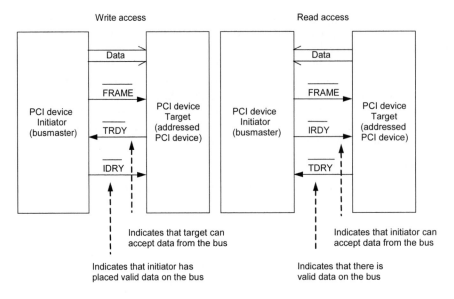

Figure 18.4   PCI handshaking

18.2.2 PCI commands

The first phase of the bus access is the command/addressing phase. Its main commands are:

- INTA sequence – addresses an interrupt controller where interrupt vectors are transferred after the command phase.
- Special cycle – used to transfer information to the PCI device about the processor's status. The lower 16 bits contain the information codes, such as 0000h for a processor shutdown, 0001h for a processor halt, 0002h for x86specific code and 0003h to FFFFh for reserved codes. The upper 16 bits (AD31–AD16) indicate x86specific codes when the information code is set to 0002h.
- I/O read access – indicates a read operation for I/O address memory, where the AD lines indicate the I/O address. The address lines AD0 and AD1 are decoded to define whether an 8-bit or 16-bit access is being conducted.
- I/O write access – indicates a write operation to an I/O address memory, where the AD lines indicate the I/O address.
- Memory read access – indicates a direct memory read operation. The byte-enable lines ($\overline{C/BE3} - \overline{C/BE0}$) identify the size of the data access.
- Memory write access – indicates a direct memory write operation. The byte-enable lines ($\overline{C/BE3} - \overline{C/BE0}$) identify the size of the data access.
- Configuration read access – used when accessing the configuration address area of a PCI unit. The initiator sets the IDSEL line activated to select it. It then uses address bits AD7–AD2 to indicate the addresses of the double words to be read (AD1 and AD0 are set to 0). The address lines AD10–AD18 can be used for selecting the addressed unit in a multi-function unit.
- Configuration write access – similar to the configuration read access, but data is written from the initiator to the target.
- Memory multiple read access – used to perform multiple data read transfers (after the initial addressing phase). Data is transferred until the initiator sets the $\overline{FRAME}$ signal inactive.

- Dual addressing cycle – used to transfer a 64-bit address to the PCI device (normally only 32-bit addresses are used) in either a single or a double clock cycle. In a single clock cycle the address lines AD63–AD0 contain the 64-bit address (note that the Pentium processor only has a 32-bit address bus, but this mode has been included to support other systems). With a 32-bit address transfer the lower 32 bits are placed on the AD31–AD0 lines, followed by the upper 32 bits on the AD31–AD0 lines.
- Line memory read access – used to perform multiple data read transfers (after the initial addressing phase). Data is transferred until the initiator sets the $\overline{\text{FRAME}}$ signal inactive.
- Memory write access with invalidations – used to perform multiple data write transfers (after the initial addressing phase).

18.2.3 PCI interrupts

The PCI bus support four interrupts ($\overline{\text{INTA}} - \overline{\text{INTD}}$). The $\overline{\text{INTA}}$ signal can be used by any of the PCI units, but only a multifunction unit can use the other three interrupt lines ($\overline{\text{INTB}} - \overline{\text{INTD}}$). These interrupts can be steered, using system BIOS, to one of the IRQx interrupts by the PCI bridge. For example, a 100 Mbps Ethernet PCI card can be set to interrupt with $\overline{\text{INTA}}$ and this could be steered to IRQ10.

18.3 Bus Arbitration

Busmasters are devices on a bus which are allowed to take control of the bus. For this purpose, PCI uses the $\overline{\text{REQ}}$ (request) and $\overline{\text{GNT}}$ (grant) signals. There is no real standard for this arbitration, but normally the PCI busmaster activates the $\overline{\text{REQ}}$ signal to indicate a request to the PCI bus, and the arbitration logic must then activate the $\overline{\text{GNT}}$ signal so that the requesting master gains control of the bus. To prevent a bus lock-up, the busmaster is given 16 clock cycles before a time-overrun error occurs.

18.3.1 Arbitration timing diagram

Figure 18.5 shows that two devices are requesting the buses at the same time. They are referred to as device-a, and device-b. The sequence is:

1. PCI clock – All signals are sampled on the rising edge of the PCI clock.
2. In this example REQ#-a was asserted prior to the 1st clock.
3. Device-a is granted access to the PCI bus when GNT#-a is asserted.
4. Device-a's transaction begins when FRAME# is sampled active, (low), on the rising edge of clock. Device-a leaves REQ#-a asserted since it wants to perform another transaction.
5. The arbiter decides that device-b should get the buses next, it deasserts GNT#-a, and asserts GNT#-b.
6. Device-a completes its transaction, FRAME# and IRDY#, (not shown), are inactive, and device-b now owns the buses.
7. Device-b completes its transaction. The arbiter has granted the buses to device-a again since its REQ# signal is still active.

18.3.2 Exclusive access

An exclusive access or a resource lock, allows a master to 'lock' a specific target until the master has completed its accesses. By locking a target no other master will be able to access the target until the master that locked it is finished with its series of accesses.

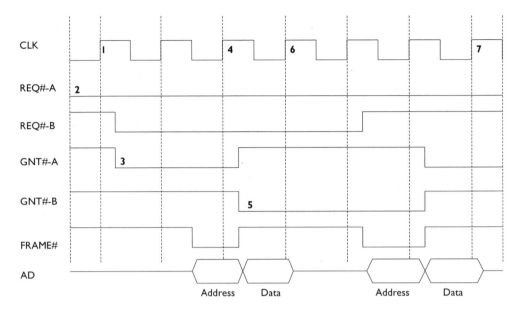

Figure 18.5   Arbitration

18.3.3 Locked targets

PCI allows exclusive access while allowing other masters to access targets other than the locked targets. The sequence is:

1. PCI targets that support exclusive accesses sample LOCK# when sampling the address.
2. If LOCK# is asserted during the address phase, the target of the transaction will not mark itself as locked (since there is already another exclusive access taking place).
3. If LOCK# is deasserted during the address phase, then the target of the transaction marks itself as locked.
4. The target stays locked until FRAME# and LOCK# are deasserted.

A true lock, (a target is locked for several transactions), occurs when LOCK# is de-asserted during the address phase and asserted on the following clock.

18.3.4 Establishing a lock on a target

An agent that intends to lock a target must wait until any other locked transactions have ended before requesting and gaining control of the buses.

1. If an agent requires an exclusive operation, then the agent checks the state of the LOCK#.
2. If lock is already asserted, then the agent waits until FRAME#, and LOCK# are de-asserted, (previous lock is released).
3. If LOCK# is not asserted, and FRAME# is not asserted, then the agent asserts its unique REQ# in order to gain control of the buses.
4. When the agent is given control of the buses, (its GNT# is asserted by the arbiter), and LOCK# is not asserted, then the agent, (which is now a master), can assert LOCK#, the clock following the address phase.
5. The lock is established after the first data phase is complete.

18.3.5 Maintaining a lock on a target

Once a lock is established, LOCK# is kept asserted by the controlling agent, (master), until the locked operation is completed or an error or early termination occurs. Other masters may perform transactions to targets other than the one that is locked.

18.3.6 Ending a lock on a target

Once the exclusive operation has been accomplished, the agent controlling LOCK# deasserts it at the same time as it deasserts IRDY#. The target unlocks itself when LOCK#, and FRAME# are deasserted.

18.3.7 LOCK# timing diagram

Figure 18.5 shows a LOCK# established and maintained. The sequence is:

1. All signals are sampled on the rising edge of the PCI clock.
2. The agent, (master), that requires an exclusive transfer has been granted the buses and begins the transaction by asserting FRAME# and leaving LOCK# deasserted.
3. The target samples LOCK# deasserted when address is sampled and marks itself as locked.
4. The master asserts LOCK#, the clock following the address phase.
5. The LOCK# is established after the first data phase is complete.
6. If the master wishes to continue the exclusive access it will continue to drive LOCK# until the LOCK# operation is complete; otherwise, the master will deassert LOCK#.

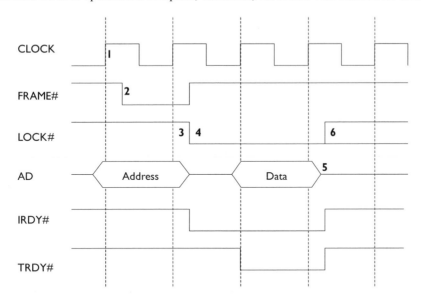

Figure 18.6 LOCK# timing diagram

18.4 PCI I/O Write Data Cycle Timing Diagram Section

Figure 18.6 shows the timing of some of the control signals on each of the three buses, that is, Processor, PCI, and ISA/X, with respect to each other, when a PCI write cycle is in progress. Note that the time difference between ADS# and FRAME# is approximately 136 ns, the time difference between FRAME# and KEYCS#, going active, is approximately 136 ns, and the time difference between FRAME# and BRDY# is approximately 1.872 μs.

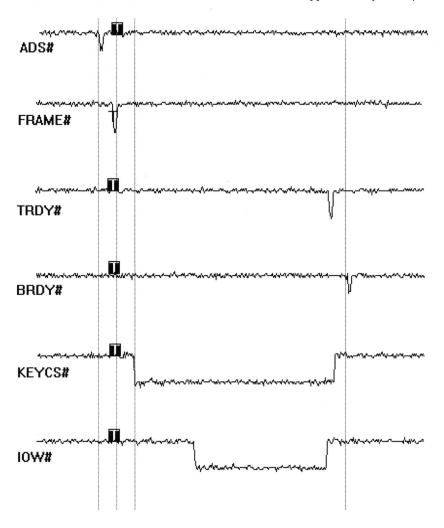

Figure 18.7   System signals

18.4.1 Example : ISA X-bus section

The following discussion shows the timing and signals involved on the ISA / X- bus when an I/O write data 55h to address 64h cycle is performed, on a board with a PCI bus. Note that the scope timebase was set at 400 ns/division for the following signals. The top signal is FRAME#, and the bottom one is the keyboard chipselect, KEYCS#.

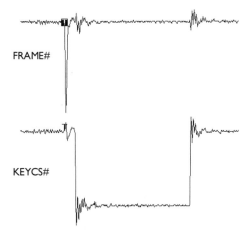

FRAME#

KEYCS#

IOW#, indicates when the data is being written into the keyboard controller, in conjunction with an active KEYCS#.

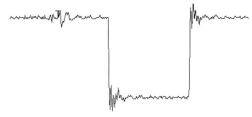

XAD2 at the keyboard controller:

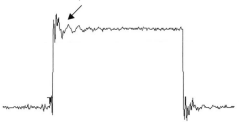

XAD2 is high, to select port 64h in the keyboard controller instead of port 60h.

XD0 at the keyboard controller:

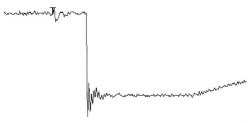

XD1 at the keyboard controller:

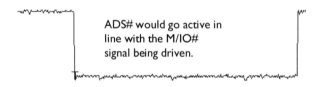

Note that XD0 is low, and XD1 is high; 1010 → Ah.

18.4.2 Example: processor bus section

The following discussion shows the timing and signals involved on the processor bus when an I/O write data 55h to address 64h cycle is performed, on a board with a PCI bus. Note that the scope timebase was set at 400 ns/division for the following signal. The top signal is FRAME#, and the bottom one is address strobe, ADS#. Note that the scope timebase has been changed to 10 µs/division for the following signals in this section.

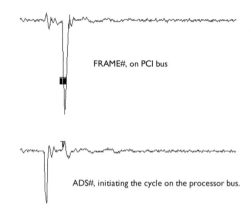

FRAME#, on PCI bus

ADS#, initiating the cycle on the processor bus.

M/IO#

ADS# would go active in line with the M/IO# signal being driven.

D/C#

W/R#

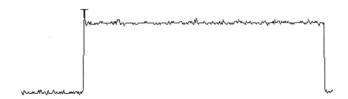

Note that the bus cycle definition signals above, define an I/O data write cycle.

BRDY#

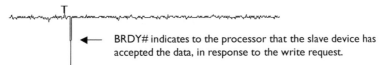

BRDY# indicates to the processor that the slave device has accepted the data, in response to the write request.

BE4#

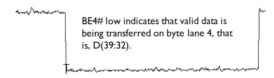

BE4# low indicates that valid data is being transferred on byte lane 4, that is, D(39:32).

PA4

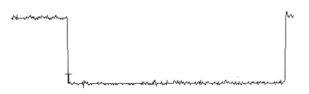

PA5

PA4 is low, and PA5 is high, that is, 0110 → 6h

PD0

PD1

PD0 is low, and PD1 is high, that is, 1010 → Ah

18.4.3 Example: PCI bus section

The following discussion shows the timing and signals involved on the PCI bus when an I/O write data 55h to address 64h cycle is performed. FRAME#, driven by the current master to indicate the beginning of an access.

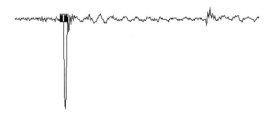

IRDY#, initiator ready indicates the busmaster's ability to complete the data phase of the transaction.

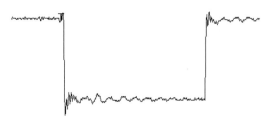

TRDY#, target ready indicates the target agent's ability to complete the data phase of the transaction.

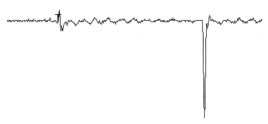

DEVSEL#, device select indicates that a target device has decoded the current address as an access to it.

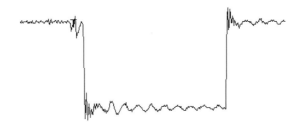

C/BE(3:0)#, bus command and byte enable are multiplexed; they define the bus command during the address phase of a transaction, and which byte lanes carry valid data during the data phase of a transaction.

C/BE2#

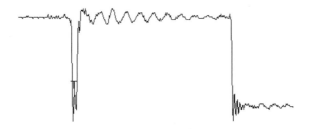

Note that C/BE2# is low during the address phase, that is, indicating the C/BE2# bus command state for an I/O write cycle. Refer to the bus command definition table. It is high during data time indicating that valid data is not being transferred on byte lane two.

C/BE0#

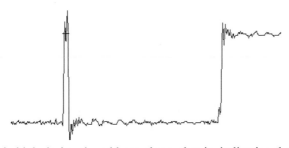

Note that C/BE0# is high during the address phase, that is, indicating the C/BE0# bus command state for an I/O write cycle. Refer to the bus command definition table. It is low during data time indicating that valid data is being transferred on byte lane zero.

The address and data are multiplexed; they contain the address during the first clock of a transaction, that is, address phase; and then data during subsequent clocks. The AD(7:0) lines during address time form the address 64h, and the data AAh during data time. Note that AD1, and 0 indicate the burst type.

AD0

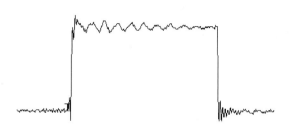

AD1

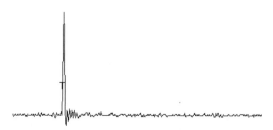

AD2

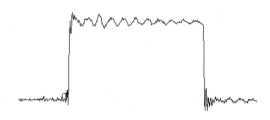

Note that AD2 is high during address time, that is, 0100 → 4h, and low during data time, that is, 1010 → Ah.

AD3

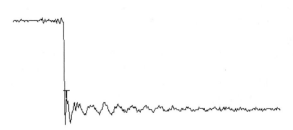

AD4

AD5

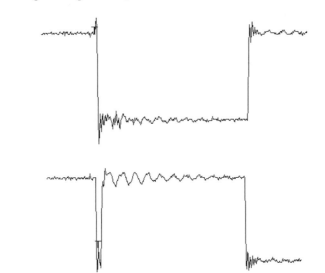

Note that AD5 is high during address, and data time.

AD6

AD7

Note that AD7 is low during address time, that is, $0110 \rightarrow$ 6h, and high during data time, that is, $1010 \rightarrow$ Ah.

18.5 Other PCI Pins

The other PCI pins are:

- $\overline{\text{RST}}$ (Pin A15) – resets all PCI devices.
- $\overline{\text{PRSNT1}}$ and $\overline{\text{PRSNT2}}$ (Pins B9 and B11) – these, individually, or jointly, show that there is an installed device and what the power consumption is. A setting of 11 (that is, $\overline{\text{PRSNT1}}$ is a 1 and $\overline{\text{PRSNT2}}$ is a 1) indicates no adapter installed, 01 indicates maximum power dissipation of 25 W, 10 indicates a maximum dissipation of 15 W and 00 indicate a maximum power dissipation of 7.5 W.
- $\overline{\text{DEVSEL}}$ (Pin B37) – indicates that an addressed device is the target for a bus operation.
- TMS (test mode select), TDI (test data input), TDO (test data output), $\overline{\text{TRST}}$ (test reset), and TCK (test clock) – used to interface to the JTAG boundary scan test.
- IDSEL (Pin A26) – used for a device initialization select signal during the accessing of the configuration area.
- $\overline{\text{LOCK}}$ (Pin A15) – indicates that an addressed device is to be locked-out of bus transfers. All other unlocked devices can still communicate.

- PAR, $\overline{PERR}$ (Pins A43 and B40) – The parity pin (PAR) is used for even parity for AD31–AD0 and C/BE3–C/BE0, and $\overline{PERR}$ indicates that a parity error has occurred.
- SDONE, $\overline{SBO}$ (Pins A40 and A41) – used in snoop cycles. SDONE (snoop done) and $\overline{SBO}$ (snoop back off signal).
- $\overline{SERR}$ (Pin B42) – used to indicate a system error.
- $\overline{STOP}$ (Pin A38) – used by a device to stop the current operation.
- $\overline{ACK64}$, $\overline{REQ64}$ (Pins B60 and A60) – the $\overline{REQ64}$ signal is an active request for a 64-bit transfer and $\overline{ACK64}$ is the acknowledgement for a 64-bit transfer.

18.6 Configuration Address Space

Each PCI device has 256 bytes of configuration data, which is arranged as 64 registers of 32 bits. It contains a 64-byte predefined header followed by an extra 192 bytes which contain extra configuration data. Figure 18.8 shows the arrangement of the header. The definitions of the fields are:

- Unit ID and Man. ID – a Unit ID of FFFFh defines that there is no unit installed, while any other address defines its ID. The PCI SIG, which is the governing body for the PCI specification, allocates a Man. ID. This ID is normally shown at BIOS start-up. Section 4.8 gives some example Man. IDs (and plug-and-play IDs).
- Status and command.
- Class code and Revision – the class code defines PCI device type. It splits into two 8-bit values with a further 8-bit value that defines the programming interface for the unit. The first defines the unit classification (00h for no class code, 01h for mass storage, 02h for network controllers, 03h for video controllers, 04h for multimedia units, 05h for memory controllers and 06h for bridges), followed by a subcode which defines the actual type. Typical codes are:

  - 0100h – SCSI controller
  - 0102h – Floppy controller
  - 0201h – Token ring network adapter
  - 0280h – Other network adapter
  - 0301h – XGA video adapter
  - 0400h – Video multimedia device
  - 0480h – Other multimedia device
  - 0501h – Flash memory controller
  - 0600h – Host
  - 0602h – EISA bridge
  - 0604h – PCI–PCI bridge

  - 0101h – IDE controller
  - 0200h – Ethernet network adapter
  - 0202h – FDDI network adapter
  - 0300h – VGA video adapter
  - 0380h – Other video adapter
  - 0401h – Audio multimedia device
  - 0500h – RAM memory controller
  - 0580h – Other memory controller
  - 0601h – ISA bridge
  - 0603h – MAC bridge
  - 0680h – Other bridge

- BIST, header, latency, CLS – the BIST (built-in self test) is an 8-bit field, where the most significant bit defines if the device can carry out a BIST, the next bit defines if a BIST is to be performed (a 1 in this position indicates that it should be performed) and bits 3–0 define the status code after the BIST has been performed (a value of zero indicates no error). The header field defines the layout of the 48 bytes after the standard 16-byte header. The most significant bit of the header field defines whether the device is a multi-function device or not. A 1 defines a multifunction unit. The CLS (cache line size) field defines the size of the cache in units of 32 bytes. Latency indicates the length of time for a PCI bus operation, where the amount of time is the latency+8 PCI clock cycles.

- Base address register – this area of memory allows the device to be programmed with an I/O or memory address area. It can contain a number of 32- or 64-bit addresses. The format of a memory address is

Bit 64–4	Base address.
Bit 3	PRF. Prefetching, 0 identifies not possible, 1 identifies possible.
Bit 2, 1	Type. 00 – any 32-bit address, 01 – less than 1MB, 10 – any 64-bit address and 11 – reserved.
Bit 0	0. Always set to a 0 for a memory address.

For an I/O address space it is defined as:

Bit 31–2	Base address.
Bit 1, 0	01. Always set to a 01 for an I/O address.

- Expansion ROM base address – allows a ROM expansion to be placed at any position in the 32-bit memory address area.
- MaxLat, MinGNT, INT-pin, INT-line – the MinGNT and MaxLat registers are read-only registers that define the minimum and maximum latency values. The INT-Line field is a 4-bit field that defines the interrupt line used (IRQ0–IRQ15). A value of 0 corresponds to IRQ0 and a value of 15 corresponds to IRQ15. The PCI bridge can then redirect this interrupt to the correct IRQ line. The 4-bit INT-pin defines the interrupt line that the device is using. A value of 0 defines no interrupt line, 1 defines $\overline{\text{INTA}}$, 2 defines $\overline{\text{INTB}}$, and so on.

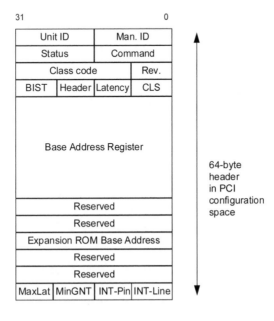

Figure 18.8   PCI configuration space

18.7 I/O Addressing

The standard PC I/O addressing ranges from 0000h to FFFFh, which gives an addressable space of 64 KB, whereas the PCI bus can support a 32- or 64-bit addressable memory. The PCI device can be configured using one of two mechanisms.

Configuration mechanism 1

Passing two 32-bit values to two standard addresses configures the PCI bus:

Address	Name	Description
0CF8h	Configuration address	Used to access the configuration address area.
0CFCh	Configuration data	Used to read or write a 32-bit (double word) value to the configuration memory of the PCI device.

The format of the configuration address register is

Bit 31	ECD (Enable CONFIG_DATA) bit. A 1 activates the CONFIG_DATA register, while a 0 disables it.
Bit 30–24	Reserved.
Bit 23–16	PCI bus number. Defines the number of the PCI bus (to a maximum of 256).
Bit 15–11	PCI unit. Selects a PCI device (to a maximum of 32). PCI thus supports a maximum of 256 attached buses with a maximum of 32 devices on each bus.
Bit 10–8	PCI function. Selects a function within a PCI multifunction device (one of eight functions).
Bit 7–2	Register. Selects a Dword entry in a specified configuration address area (one of 64 Dwords).
Bit 1, 0	Type. 00 – decode unit, 01 – CONFIG_ADDRESS value copy to AD*x*.

Configuration mechanism 2

In this mode, each PCI device is mapped to a 4 kB I/O address range between C000h and CFFFh. This is achieved by used in the activation register CSE (configuration space enable) for the configuration area at the port address 0CF8h. The format of the CSE register is located at 0CF8h and is defined as

Bit 7–4	Key. 0000 – normal mode, 0001...1111 – configuration area activated. A value other than zero for the key activates the configuration area mapping, that is, all I/O addresses to the 4 KB range between C000h and CFFFh would be performed as normal I/O cycles.
Bit 3–1	Function. Defines the function number within the PCI device (if it represents a multifunction device).
Bit 0	SCE. 0 defines a configuration cycle, 1 defines a special cycle.

The forward register is stored at address 0CFAh and contains

Bit 7–0	PCI bus.

The I/O address is defined by:

Bit 31–12 Contains the bit value of 0000Ch.
Bit 11–8 PCI unit.
Bit 7–2 Register index.
Bit 1, 0 Contains the bit value of 00 (binary).

18.7.2 Sample test program

An example BASIC program to test the PCI bridge device is given in Program 18.1. The code:

```
170   IOWRITE
      &CF8,2,&80000000
180   IOREAD &CFC,2
190   IF B1<>&10008086
      THEN GOTO 410
```

writes the value 80000000h (1000 0000 … 0000b) to the CF8h register (configuration address), where the most signification bit activates the configuration data register. Next the program reads from the CFCh register (configuration data), after this the B1 value contains the 32-bit value read from the configuration data register. In this case the value

```
      Program 18.1
130   Print "Host PCI bridge test"
160   Print "PCI Configuration Address &80000000"
170   IOWRITE &CF8,2,&80000000
180   IOREAD &CFC,2
190   IF B1<>&10008086 THEN GOTO 410
200   Print "Test1 Passed….Component ID Test"

210   Dim TEST(4)
220   TEST(1)=&FFFFFFFF
230   TEST(2)=&AAAAAAAA
240   TEST(3)=&O55555555
250   TEST(4)=&OO

260   D9=&80000000
270   REG = &O60

280   REPEAT
290     TST = &O1
300     IOWRITE &CF8,2,D9 + REG
310     REPEAT
320        IOWRITE &CFC,2,TEST(TST)
330        IOREAD &CFC,2
340        If B1 <> TEST(TST) Then GoTo 450
350        TST = TST + &O1
360     UNTIL TST=&5
370     REG = REG + &O4
380   UNTIL REG=&68

390   Print "Test2 Passed…Internal Register Test"
400   GoTo 480
410   Print "Test1 Failed…."
420   Print "Component ID Test…."
430   PRINT "Expected ID &10008086  Actual ID "~B1
440   GoTo 480
450   Print "Test2 Failed…."
460   Print "Internal register test…."
470   PRINT "Register "~REG", Expected "
                      ~TEST(TST)"  Actual "~B1
```

will be the first 32 bits from the configuration memory of the PCI device. The value tested in this case is 10000E11h, where 1000h identifies the unit ID and 8086h identifies the manufacturer ID (Intel).

The values written to the registers are FFFFFFFFh (1111 1111 … 1111), AAAAAAAAh (1010 1010 … 1010), 55555555h (0101 0101 … 0101) and 00000000h. These values are then read back and tested to determine if they match the values that were written.

Program 18.2 is a sample BASIC program to test the video adaptor on the PCI bus. The code:

```
122   IOWRITE &CF8,2,&80005000
124   IOR.EAD &CFC,2
126   IF B1<>&00A81013 THEN PRINT : GOTO 172
```

The above code writes the value 80005000h (1000 0000 … 0000b) to the CF8h register (configuration address), where the most signification bit activates the configuration data register. Next the program reads from the CFCh register (configuration data), after this the B1 value contains the 32-bit value read from the configuration data register. In this case the value will be the first 32 bits from the configuration memory of the PCI device. The value tested in this case is 00A81013h, where 00A8h identifies the Unit ID and 1013h identifies the manufacturer ID (Cirrus Logic).

The following code tests four 32-bit words from the configuration memory. The values written are:

FF000000h,   AA000000h, 55000000h, 00h

These values are then read back and tested against the values actual written. It should be noted that the least significant 24 bits are read-only registers, thus they cannot be written to.

```
144   REPEAT
146     TST = 1
148     IOWRITE
        &CF8,2,ADDR + REG
150     REPEAT
152       IOWRITE &CFC,2,TEST(TST)
154       IOREAD &CFC,2
156       If B1 <> TEST(TST) Then Print: GoTo 180
158       TST = TST + 1
160     UNTIL TST=5

162     REG = REG + &O20
164   UNTIL REG=&50
```

Note, C/C++ can only access 8 or 16 bits at a time, thus the code:

```
122   IOWRITE &CF8,2,&80005000
124   IOREAD &CFC,2
126   IF B1<>&00A81013 THEN PRINT : GOTO 172
```

would be replaced with:

```
#include <conio.h>

int main(void)
{
unsigned int        val1, val2, val3, val4;
unsigned long int   val;

    _outp(0xcf8,0x00);    /* least significant byte */
    _outp(0xcf9,0x00);
    _outp(0xcfa,0x00);
```

📄 **Program 18.2**

```
112   Print "PCI test: Component ID and PCI Register"
122   IOWRITE &CF8,2,&80005000
124   IOREAD &CFC,2
126   IF B1<>&00A81013 THEN PRINT : GOTO 172
128   Print "Passed....Component ID Test"
130   Dim TEST(4)
132   TEST(1)=&FF000000
134   TEST(2)=&AA000000
136   TEST(3)=&O55000000
138   TEST(4)=&OO
140   ADDR=&80005000
142   REG =&O10
144   REPEAT
146     TST = &O1
148     IOWRITE &CF8,2,ADDR + REG
150     REPEAT
152       IOWRITE &CFC,2,TEST(TST)
154       IOREAD &CFC,2
156       If B1 <> TEST(TST) Then Print: GoTo 180
158       TST = TST + &O1
160     UNTIL TST=&5
162     REG = REG + &O20
164   UNTIL REG=&50
166   Print "Test02 Passed....PCI Register Test"
168   GoTo 188
172   Print "FAIL: Component ID Test"
174   PRINT "Expected ID &00A81013  Actual ID "~B1
176   Print:      GoTo 130
180   Print "FAIL: PCI Register Test...."
182   PRINT "Register "~REG", Expected "
                 ~TEST(TST)"  Actual "~B1

188     etc
```

```
    _outp(0xcfb,0x80);        /* most significant byte */

    val1=_inp(0xcfc) & 0xff;     val2=_inp(0xcfd) & 0xff;
    val3=_inp(0xcfe) & 0xff;     val4=_inp(0xcff) & 0xff;

    val= val1 + (val2<<8) + (val3<<16)+ (val4<<24);

    if (val==0x00a81013)
    {
        printf("Success");
    }

    etc
    return(0);
}
```

18.7.3 Basic configuration read cycle

A basic configuration read cycle is given in Figure 18.9:

1. PCI clock – All signals are sampled on the rising edge of the PCI clock.
2. Host performs an I/O write to the configuration address port.
3. Host/PCI bridge decodes the access as a configuration access and decodes the address in order to determine the IDSEL signal to assert.
4. Host/PCI bridge (master) asserts FRAME#, and the address and command signals are driven.
5. Address, AD (31...00), command, C/BE (3...0)#, (contain the command codes), and IDSEL are stable and valid on the 1st clock that samples FRAME# active; this is the address phase.
6. The master asserts IRDY# to indicate that it is prepared to accept data, and asserts the byte enables, C/BE (3...0)#. The updated value is valid on the next clock.
7. When the master intends to complete one more data phase, FRAME# is deasserted. FRAME# cannot be deasserted unless IRDY# is asserted. IRDY# must always remain asserted on the first clock edge that FRAME# is deasserted.
8. Byte enables, C/BE (3...0)# are stable and valid, on the clock following the address phase, (this is the first data phase), and every clock during the entire data phase regardless of the number of wait states inserted. Due to the fact that this is a read transaction the first data phase requires a turnaround cycle. The turnaround cycle is enforced by the target not asserting TRDY# until after the 1st data phase.
9. An agent claiming to be the target of the access by asserting DEVSEL#. DEVSEL# must be asserted with, or prior, to the edge when the target enables its outputs; TRDY# cannot be driven until DEVSEL# is asserted. Once DEVSEL# has been asserted, it cannot be deasserted until the last data phase has been completed; except to signal target abort. The amount of time that it takes to decode the address will depend on the device. The target asserts TRDY# to indicate that the data the target is driving is valid.
10. Data, AD (31...00) is stable and valid on reads when TRDY# is active and on writes when IRDY# is active. The AD lines cannot change until the current data phase completes, that is, When IRDY# is asserted on a write transaction, or when TRDY# is asserted on a read transaction. Data is transferred between master and target on each clock edge when both IRDY# and TRDY# are asserted. The last data phase completes when FRAME# is deasserted and TRDY# is asserted; when FRAME# and IRDY# are both deasserted, the transaction has ended.

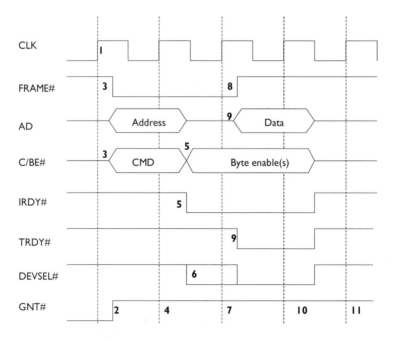

Figure 18.9   Configuration read cycle

18.8 Bus Cycles

C/BE (3...0)# determine the bus cycle types.

- 0000 – Interrupt Acknowledgment. A read addressed to the system interrupt controller. Address bits are don't care during the address phase, byte enables indicate the size of the vector to be returned.
- 0001 – Special Cycle. PCI message broadcast mechanism. Used as an alternative to physical signals when sideband communication is necessary.
- 0010 – I/O Read. Used to read data from an agent mapped in the I/O address space. Byte enables indicate transfer size. AD (31...0) provide the byte address, (all 32-bits must be decoded).
- 0011 – I/O Write. As above, except used to write data to an agent in I/O space.
- 0100, 0101, 1000,1001 – Reserved. Reserved for future use. Targets must not respond to a reserved encoding. If one is used on the i/f, the access will be terminated with master abort.
- 0110 – Memory Read. Used to read data from an agent mapped in the memory address space.
- 0111 – Memory Write. Used to write data to an agent mapped in the memory address space.
- 1010 – Configuration Read. Used to read an agent's configuration space. An agent is selected, when AD (1...0) are 00, and IDSEL is asserted. During the address phase of a configuration cycle, AD (7...2) address one of 64 dword registers, (where the byte enables address the bytes within each dword), in the configuration space of each device, and AD (31...11), are don't care. AD (10...8), indicate which device of a multifunction agent is being addressed.

- 1011 – Configuration Write. Used to transfer data to the configuration space of each agent. IDSEL signal is used to select an agent, and AD (1…0) are 00. During address phase of configuration cycle, AD (7…2) address one of 64 dword registers, (where byte enables address the bytes within each dword), in the config space of each device and AD (31…11), are don't care. AD (10…8), indicate which device of a multifunction agent is being addressed.
- 1100 – Memory Read Multiple. Used to read data from an agent mapped in the memory address space, except that it additionally indicates that the master may intend to fetch more than one cache line before disconnecting.
- 1101 – Dual Address Cycle. Used to transfer 64-bit address to devices that support 64-bit addressing. Targets that only support 32-bit addresses, treat as reserved and do not respond.
- 1110 – Memory Read Line. Used to read data from an agent mapped in the memory address space, except that it indicates that the master intends to complete more than two 32-bit PCI data phases.
- 1111 - Memory Write And Invalidate. Used to write data to an agent mapped in memory address space, except that it guarantees transfer of one cache line, that is, the master intends to write all bytes within the addresses cache line in a single PCI transaction.

18.8.1 PCI bus cycles - basic read/write cycle

The basic transfer mechanism on the PCI bus is a burst cycle. A burst cycle consists of an address phase and one or more data phases. The host/PCI bridge, under certain circumstances, may merge memory write accesses into a single transaction. I/O accesses by the CPU will normally have a single data phase.

PCI data transfers are controlled by three signals:

- FRAME# . Driven by the master, to indicate the beginning and end of a transaction.
- IRDY#. Driven by the master, allowing it to force wait cycles.
- TRDY#. Driven by the target, allowing it to force wait cycles.

18.8.2 Basic read cycle

Simple read operation, not incorporating wait states, from either the initiator or the target (Figure 18.10). The sequence is:

1. PCI clock – Signals are sampled on the rising edge.
2. Once the requesting agents, (master's), GNT# signal has been asserted by the arbiter, (occurs in previous bus cycle), the agent, (master), may start an access when FRAME# and IRDY# are deasserted, (bus is in the idle state).
3. A transaction starts when FRAME#, (driven by the master), is sampled active for the 1st time. Address and command signals are driven by the master.
4. Address, AD (31…0) and command, C/BE (3…0)#, contains the command codes, are stable and valid on the first clock that samples FRAME# active. This is the address phase.
5. Master asserts IRDY#, indicating that it is prepared to accept data, and asserts the byte enables, C/BE (3…0)#. During a burst, the master updates the byte enables from clock, for each data phase. IRDY# and TRDY# are active.
6. An agent claims to be the target by asserting DEVSEL#. DEVSEL# must be asserted with, or before, target enables its outputs. TRDY# is not driven until DEVSEL# is asserted. Once DEVSEL#, is asserted it cannot be deasserted until the last data phase has completed, except to signal terminal abort.

7. The byte enables, C/BE (3...0)# are stable and valid on the clock following the address phase, (1st data phase), and every clock during the entire data phase regardless of the number of wait states. Due to the fact that this is a read cycle, the 1st data phase requires a turnaround cycle. The turnaround cycle is enforced by the target not asserting TRDY# until after the first data phase.

8. When the master intends to complete one more data phase, FRAME# is deasserted. FRAME# cannot be deasserted unless IRDY# is asserted. IRDY# must be asserted on 1st clock edge that FRAME# is deasserted.

9. The source of the data is required to assert its xRDY# signal unconditionally when data is valid. (IRDY# – write, TRDY# – read). The receiving agent may assert its xRDY# as it chooses. In the above example, target drives data on the AD lines and asserts TRDY# to indicate that the data the target is driving is valid.

10. Data, AD (31...0) is stable and valid on reads when TRDY# is asserted, and on writes when IRDY# is asserted. The AD lines cannot change, (to carry new address or data), until the current data phase completes; IRDY# – write, TRDY# – reads. Data is transferred between master and target on each clock edge that both IRDY# and TRDY# are active. The last data phase completes when FRAME# is deasserted and TRDY# is asserted.

11. When FRAME# and IRDY# are deasserted the transaction has ended.

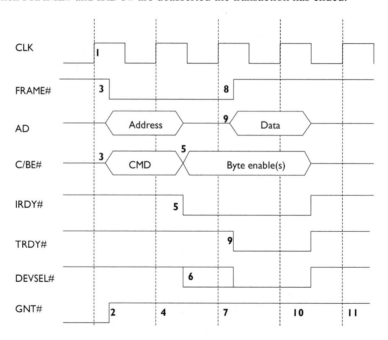

Figure 18.10   Basic read cycle

18.8.3 Basic write cycle

Simple write cycle, no wait states (Figure 18.11). The sequence is:

1. PCI clock – Signals are sampled on the rising edge.

2. Once the requesting agent's, (master's) GNT# signal has been asserted by the arbiter, (occurs in previous bus cycle), the agent, (master), may start an access when

FRAME# and IRDY# are deasserted, (bus is in the idle state).

3.   A transaction starts when FRAME#, (driven by the master), is sampled active for the 1st time. Address and command signals are driven by the master.

4.   Address, AD (31...0) and command, C/BE (3...0)#, contains the command codes, are stable and valid on the first clock that samples FRAME# active. This is the address phase.

5.   The data source asserts xRDY# signal, data valid, (IRDY# - writes, TRDY# - read), the receiving agent asserts xRDY#, as it chooses. In this case the master drives data on AD (31...0), asserts byte enables C/BE (3...0)# and asserts IRDY#, indicating that it is driving data. During a burst, the master updates the byte enables, (on clock), for each data phase, (IRDY#, TRDY# asserted); the updated value is valid on the next clock.

6.   An agent claims to be the target by asserting DEVSEL#. DEVSEL# must be asserted with, or before, target enables its outputs. TRDY# is not driven until DEVSEL# is asserted. Once DEVSEL#, is asserted it cannot be deasserted until the last data phase has completed; except to signal terminal abort.

7.   Target asserts TRDY# when it is prepared to accept data.

8.   Byte enables, C/BE (3...0)# are valid on the clock following the address phase, (1st data phase), and every clock during the data phase, regardless of the number of wait states. Data, AD (31...00) is valid on reads when TRDY# is asserted, and on writes when IRDY# is asserted. AD cannot change until current data phase completes. Data is transferred on a rising clock edge, when both TRDY# and IRDY# are asserted.

9.   When the master intends to complete one more data phase, FRAME# is deasserted. FRAME# cannot be deasserted unless IRDY# is asserted. IRDY# must be asserted on 1st clock edge that FRAME# is deasserted.

10. Last data phase completes when FRAME# is deasserted and TRDY# is asserted.

11. When FRAME# and IRDY# are deasserted the transaction has ended.

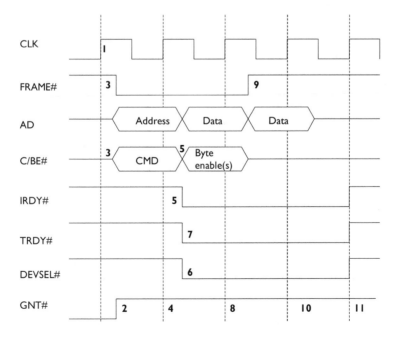

Figure 18.11   Basic write cycle

18.9 PCI Faults

There is a set protocol for a bus cycle, which must be followed. This is made up of control, address and data signals. The complete cycle cannot be performed if there are communication problems in any of these areas:

- **PCI control faults**. The processor bus to PCI bus bridge chip must decode the processor control signals, for example, Bus cycle definition signals, and from them generate the PCI bus control signals, for example, FRAME#. The cycle will not run, if any of the control signals are not being generated properly.
- **PCI address faults**. The PCI address should be on the AD lines during address time, that is, when FRAME# is active. Trigger the scope of the FRAME# signal and check the AD lines during this time to locate the bad address bit(s).
- **PCI data faults**. The PCI data should be on the AD lines during data time, that is, when both IRDY# and TRDY# are active. Trigger the scope of the FRAME# signal and check the AD lines during data time, that is, when both signals are active, to locate the bad data bit(s).

18.9.1 PCI error and interrupt handling

PCI devices generate parity for every transaction, including configuration cycles, special cycles, and interrupt acknowledge cycles. For example:

Number of '1s' on AD (31...00), C/BE (3...0)#, and PAR equals an even number.

In order for parity to be calculated consistently, during each transaction all addresses, data, command, and byte enable lines must be driven to a stable value, even though all lines may not carry meaningful data. PAR must be driven by the initiator one clock after the addresses and data phase. If a parity error is detected, agents that support parity checking must set the detected parity error bit in the configuration space status register. The signals are:

- **PERR# and SERR#**. PERR# and SERR# are used to report errors in the system.
- **PERR#**. Used for reporting data parity errors on all transactions except data parity errors involving special cycle commands.
- **SERR#**. Used for 1) address parity errors on all transactions, 2) reporting data parity errors on special cycle commands, 3) may be used on other non-parity or system errors, system dependent.

18.9.2 Error responses and reporting on PERR#

When a data parity error is detected:

1. If a read data parity error occurs, the master must report it. If a write data parity error occurs, the target must report it.
2. If a parity error occurs, agents that support parity checking must set the detected parity error bit in the configuration space status register.
3. Parity error signaling and response is controlled by the parity error response bit. If the bit is cleared, the agent ignores all parity errors and completes the transaction as if parity was correct. PERR# is not generated. If the bit is set, the agent is required to assert PERR# when a parity error is detected.
4. When a master detects a parity error and asserts PERR#, (on a read transaction), or samples PERR# asserted, (on a write transaction), it must set the data parity reported bit. Tar-

gets never set the data parity reported bit.

5. PERR# will be driven by only one bus agent at a time. If an error occurs the agent must assert PERR# two PCI clock cycles after the data transfer, in which the error occurred.
6. Only the master of the corrupted data transfer is allowed to report the parity errors to the system, (by using an interrupt or setting a bit in a device specific register or asserting SERR#).

18.9.3 PAR And PERR# timing diagram

Figure 18.12 shows when PAR and PERR# will be generated, if appropriate. The sequence is:

1. PAR generated as a result of the address phase.
2. PAR generated as a result of the data phase.
3. If a parity error is detected as a result of the data phase, PERR# must be asserted two clock cycles after the transfer that caused the parity error.

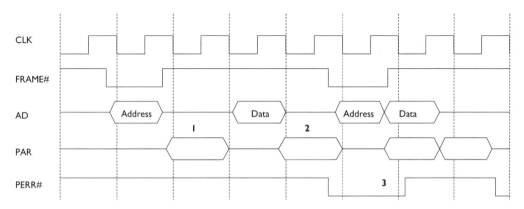

Figure 18.12   Basic write cycle

18.9.4 Error response and reporting on SERR#

Occurs when a data parity error is detected. The sequence is:

1. Any agent can check and signal address parity errors on SERR#.
2. If an address parity error is detected, the address parity error detected bit must be set.
3. The generation of SERR# is controlled by the serr enable bit.

   If this bit is cleared, SERR# cannot be generated regardless of the type of error. If this bit is set, SERR# may be generated under the following conditions:

   • The master, (which does not have a driver), was involved in a transaction that was abnormally terminated.
   • A catastrophic error that left the agent questioning its ability to operate correctly.

4. If an address parity error is detected, reporting the error on SERR# is controlled by the parity error response bit in the command register.

   If this bit is cleared, SERR# cannot be generated as a result of an address parity error.

PERR# is not generated. If this bit is set, and the serr enable bit is set, SERR# may be generated under the following conditions: address parity error or data parity error on special cycles detected.

The detection of a parity error that is not reported by some other mechanism, (current busmaster only).

5. If an agent asserts SERR# it must set the signaled system error bit in the configuration space status register, regardless of the error type.
6. SERR# may be driven by multiple agents at the same time.
7. The only agent monitoring SERR# is the agent whose function is to convert it to a signal to the processor.

18.10 Interrupt Handling

The host / PCI bus bridge, (if the 8259s are on its secondary bus side), will transfer the interrupt acknowledgment cycle from the processor to the PCI bus. The family of x86 processors can run two interrupt acknowledgment cycles as a result of an interrupt. The PCI bus performs only one interrupt acknowledgment cycle per interrupt. Only one device may respond to the interrupt acknowledgment; that device must assert DEVSEL# indicating that it is claiming the interrupt acknowledgment.

Figure 18.13 shows an example of an interrupt acknowledgment cycle on the PCI bus, where a single byte enable is asserted. The sequence is:

1. During the address phase, the AD signals do not contain a valid address; they must be driven with stable data so that PAR will be valid, and parity can be checked. The C/BE# signals contain the interrupt acknowledge command code.
2. IRDY# and the BE#s are driven by the host/PCI bus bridge to indicate that the bridge, (master), is ready for a response.
3. The target will drive DEVSEL#, (not shown), and TRDY# along with the vector, (on the data bus).

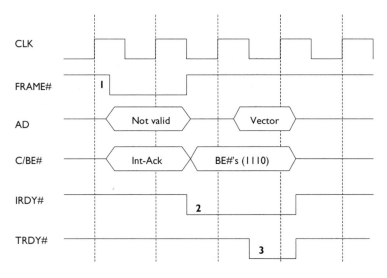

Figure 18.13   Interrupt acknowledgement timing diagram

18.11 Exercises

18.11.1   What is the maximum data throughput for a 33 MHz, 32-bit data PCI bus?
    (a)   33 MB/s   (b)   66 MB/s
    (c)   132 MB/s   (d)   264 MB/s

18.11.2   Which I/O register address is used to access PCI configuration address space?
    (a)   1F8h   (b)   CF8h
    (c)   3F8h   (d)   2F8h

18.11.3   Which I/O register address is used read and write to registers in the PCI configuration address space?
    (a)   1FCh   (b)   CFCh
    (c)   3FCh   (d)   1FCh

18.11.4   How many bits can be accessed, at a time, with the configuration address register?
    (a)   8   (b)   16
    (c)   32   (d)   64

18.11.5   Which company has the manufacture ID of 8086?
    (a)   Compaq   (b)   Motorola
    (c)   NCR   (d)   Intel

18.11.6   Explain how PCI architecture uses bridges.

18.11.7   Outline the operation of Program 18.1 and Program 18.2. Highlight the range of addresses used. Why does Program 18.2 write the bit pattern FF000000h and not FFFFFFFFh?

18.11.8   Explain how the 32-bit PCI bus transfers data. Prove that the maximum data rate for a 32-bit PCI in its normal mode is only 66 MB/s. Explain the mechanism that the PCI bus uses to increase the maximum data rate to 132 MB/s.

18.11.9   How does buffering in the PCI bridge aid the transfer of data to and from the processor?

18.11.10   Explain how the PCI bus uses the command phase to set up a peripheral.

18.11.11   How are interrupt lines used in the PCI bus? Explain how these interrupts can be steered to the ISA bus interrupt lines.

18.11.12   Outline the concept of bus mastering and how it occurs on the PCI bus. What signal lines are used?

18.11.13   Explain how the PCI bus uses configuration addresses.

18.11.14   Which of the following is true about PCI arbitration?

    (i)   The arbitration process occurs during the previous access so that no separate bus cycles are necessary.
    (ii)   Each device capable of being a PCI bus master has a unique GNT# and REQ# signal.
    (iii)   A master may assert LOCK# at anytime.
    (iv)   LOCK# should be de-asserted.

18.12 PCI Functional Signal Groups

All devices on the PCI bus must have the ability to be targets. Any device on the PCI bus may be a master. A target device must have 47 pins, and a master device must have 49 pins. Figure 18.14 illustrates the pin connections.

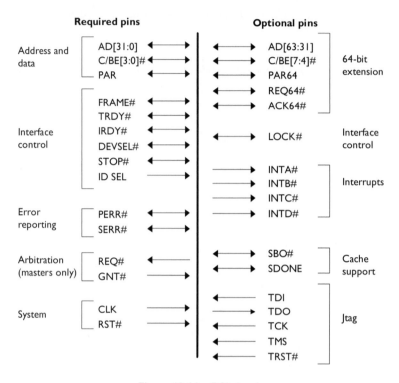

Figure 18.14 PCI signals

Address And Data

AD (31...00) The address and data bus are multiplexed. During the first clock of a transaction, (address phase), they are a 32-bit physical address. During subsequent clocks, they are data. Address bits AD0 and AD1 have no meaning; they are encoded to indicate the burst type.

C/BE (3...0)# The bus command and byte enables are multiplexed. During the address phase, they define the bus command. During the data phase they determine which byte lanes carry valid data.

PAR Parity indicates even parity across AD (31...00) and C/BE (3...0)#.

Error Reporting

PERR# Parity error reports a data parity error on all commands except special cycles.

SERR# System error reports address parity errors, data parity errors on special cycle commands, or any other system error where the result would be catastrophic.

Interface Control

FRAME# Cycle frame is driven by the current master to indicate the beginning and duration of an access.

TRDY# Target ready indicates the target agent's, (selected device's), ability to complete the current data phase of the transaction. During a read TRDY# indicates that valid data is present. During a write it indicates the target is prepared to accept data.

IRDY#   Initiator ready indicates the initiating agent's, (busmaster's), ability to complete the current data phase of the transaction. During a write IRDY# indicates that valid data is present. During a read, it indicates that the master is prepared to accept data.

DEVSEL#   Device select, when actively driven, indicates the driving device has decoded its address as the target of the current access. As an input it indicates that a device on the bus has been selected.

STOP#   The current target, (output of the target), asserts STOP# in order to request that the master, (input to the master), terminates the current transaction.

IDSEL   Initialization device select is used as a chip select instead of the upper 24 address lines during configuration read and write transactions.

Arbitration (Masters Only)

REQ#   Request indicates to the arbiter that this agent requires use of the bus. This is a point to point signal. Every master has its own REQ#.

GNT#   Grant indicates to an agent that the arbiter has granted it access to the bus. This is a point to point signal. Every master has its own GNT#.

System

CLOCK   PCI clock – The signals on the PCI bus only have significance on the rising edge of the PCI clock.

RST#   Reset forces the PCI sequencer of each device to a known state.

64-bit Extension

AD (63…32) 64-bit address and data provide additional support for full 64-bit transfers.

C/BE (7…4)#The upper byte-enable lines determine which of the upper byte lanes carry meaningful data during 64-bit data transfers. The 64-bit bus command lines only contain a valid bus command if a dual address cycle command is present on C/BE (3…0)#.

PAR64   Parity upper dword indicates even parity across AD (63…32) and C/BE (7…4)#.

REQ64#   Requests 64-bit transfer, when actively driven by the current bus master, indicates its desire to transfer data using 64-bits.

ACK64#   Acknowledge 64-bit transfer indicates that the PCI target is willing to transfer data using 64-bits.

Interface Control

LOCK#   Lock indicates an atomic transaction that may require multiple transactions to complete.

Interrupts

INTA#   Interrupt A is used to request an interrupt.

INTB#   INTB# is used to request an interrupt and only has meaning on a multi-function device.

INTC#   As above.

INTD#   As above.

Cache Support

SBO#   Snoop backoff indicates whether the current memory access may proceed or is required to be retired.

SDONE Snoop done indicates the status of the snoop for the current cache access.

Jtag

TDI   Test input shifts data and instructions into the tap in a serial manner.

TDO   Test output shifts data out of the device. If an add-in card does not implement tap; TDI and TDO should be tied together.

TCK   Test clock clocks state information into and out of the device during boundary scan. All of the test related pins conform to the test access port, (tap), and boundary scan architecture specs.

TMS   Test mode select controls the state of the tap controller.

TRST# Test reset is used to force the tap controller into a test logic reset state.

18.13 Example Manufacturer and Plug-and-play IDs

Manufacturer	man. ID	PNP ID	Manufacturer	Man. ID	PNP ID
NCR	1000	4096	ULSI	1003	4099
VLSI	1004	4100	ALR	1005	4101
Reply Group	1006	4102	Netframe	1007	4103
EPSON	1008	4104	Phoenix	100a	4106
National Semi	100b	4107	Tseng Labs	100c	4108
AST	100d	4109	Weitek	100e	4110
Video Logic Ltd	1010	4112	Digital	1011	4113
Micronics	1012	4114	Cirrus Logic	1013	4115
IBM	1014	4116	ICL	1016	4118
Spea Software	1017	4119	UNISYS	1018	4120
Elite	1019	4121	NCR	101a	4122
Vitesse	101b	4123	Western Digital	101c	4124
American Mega	101e	4126	PictureTel	101f	4127
Hitachi	1020	4128	Oki	1021	4129
AMD	1022	4130	Trident	1023	4131
Acer	1025	4133	Dell	1028	4136
Siemens	1029	4137	LSI	102a	4138
Matrox	102b	4139	Chips and Tech.	102c	4140
Wyse	102d	4141	Olivetti	102e	4142
Toshiba	102f	4143	Miro Computer	1031	4145
Compaq	1032	4146	NEC	1033	4147
Future Domain	1036	4150	HITACHI	1037	4151
AMP	1038	4152	Seiko Epson	103a	4154
Tatung	103b	4155	HP	103c	4156
Genoa	1047	4167	Fountain	1049	4169
SGS Thomson	104a	4170	Buslogic	104b	4171
TI	104c	4172	SONY	104d	4173
OAK	104e	4174	Hitachi	1054	4180
ICL	1056	4182	Motorola	1057	4183
Vtech	105e	4190	United Micro	1060	4192
Mitsubishi	1067	4199	Apple	106b	4203
Hyundai	106c	4204	Sequent	106d	4205
Daewood	1070	4208	Mitac	1071	4209
Yamaha	1073	4211	Nexgen	1074	4212
Cyrix	1078	4216	I-BUS	1079	4217
Networth	107a	4218	Gateway 2000	107b	4219
Goldstar	107c	4220	Leadtek	107d	4221
Interphase	107e	4222	Tulip	1085	4229
Data General	1089	4233	Elonex	108c	4236
Intergraph	1091	4241	Diamond	1092	4242
National Instruments	1093	4243	Quantum Designs	1098	4248
Samsung	1099	4249	Packard Bell	109a	4250
Gemlight	109b	4251	Megachips	109c	4252
3COM	10b7	4279	SMC	10b8	4280
Acer	10b9	4281	Mitsubishi	10ba	4282

Tsenglabs	10be	4286	Samsung	10c3	4291
Award	10c4	4292	Xerox	10c5	4293
Neomagic	10c8	4296	Fujitsu	10ca	4298
Fujitsu	10d0	4304	Newbridge	10e3	4323
Tandem	10e4	4324	Micro Industries	10e5	4325
Xilinx	10ee	4334	Creative	10f6	4342
Matsushita	10f7	4343	Altos	10f8	4344
PC Direct	10f9	4345	Truevision	10fa	4346
Creative Labs	1102	4354	Santa Cruz	1111	4369
Rockwell	1112	4370	Zilog	1121	4385
S3	5333	21299	Intel	8086	32902
Adaptec	9004	36868			

18.14 Note from the author

There is an amusing statement that was made in 1981, in the book 30 Hour BASIC Standard, 1981:

Microcomputers are the tool of the 80s. BASIC is the language that all of them use. So the sooner you learn BASIC, the sooner you will understand the microcomputer revolution

Now it is clear that a good knowledge of BASIC will not really help your understanding of microcomputers, but if there is one bus that you need to understand in the PC, it is the PCI bus. This is because it is the main interface bus within the PC. Most external devices eventually connect to the PCI through bridge devices. There were several short-term fixes for local bus technology, but the PCI was the first attempt at a properly designed system bus. It allows the PC to be segmented into differing data transfer rates. PCI provides a buffer between the main system core, such as the processor and its memory, and the slower peripherals, such as the hard-disk, serial ports, and so on.

With interrupts, the PCI has the great advantage over ISA in that it allows interrupts to be properly assigned at system start-up. The BIOS or the operating system can communicate with the PCI-connected bus with the configuration address area. From this, the system can determine which type of device it is, whether it be a graphics card or a network card. The system can then properly configure the device and grant it the required resources. The days of users having to assign interrupts (using card jumpers, in some cases) and I/O addresses are reducing.

The great leap forward in PC systems happened with local bus technology. The demand came from graphics cards as Windows 3.0 was being adopted. The ISA bus was far too slow, as it only supported 8MHz transfers. Graphic card manufacturers got together and developed the VESA-backed VL-local bus standard. It showed how fast transfer devices could be connected to a local bus, while other slower devices had to access the processor through a bridge, which allowed a different clock speed, and a different data and address bus. Most PCs are now based around this local bus idea, and they can be split into there main areas:

- *Local processor bus. Direct connection of the processor to its local cache memory (either Level-1 or Level-2 cache.*
- *Local bus. Connection onto the PCI bus. This connects to the local processor bus via a bridge.*
- *External bus. ISA, IDE, RS-232, and so on. This connects to the local bus via a bridge.*

There is great potential in the PCI bus. At present, most systems use 32-bit data transfers, but there is scope for 64-bit data transfers. Also, the 33 MHz clock can be increased to 66MHz with double edge clocking. A new enhanced PCI-based system called the AGP (Advanced Graphics Port) has been developed which allows for data transfers of over 500 MB/s.

19 IDE

19.1 Introduction

Chapters 19 and 20 discuss IDE and SCSI interfaces, which are used to interface to disk drives and mass storage devices. Disks are used to store data reliably in the long term. Typical disk drives store binary information as magnetic fields on a fixed disk (as in a hard disk drive), a plastic disk (as in a floppy disk or tape drive), or as optical representation (on optical disks).

The main sources of permanent read/writeable storage are:

- **Magnetic tape**. The digital bits are stored with varying magnetic fields. Typical devices are tape cartridges, DAT and 8 mm video tape.
- **Magnetic disk**. As with the magnetic tape, the bits are stored as varying magnetic fields on a magnetic disk. This disk can be permanent (such as a hard disk) or flexible (such as a floppy disk). Large-capacity hard disks allow storage of several gigabytes of data. Normally, fixed disks are designed to a much higher specification than floppy disks and can thus store much more information.
- **Optical disk**. The digital bits are stored as pits on an optical disk. A laser then reads these bits. This information can be read-only (CD-ROM) or write once, read many (WORM), or it can be reprogrammable. A standard CD-ROM stores up to 650 MB of data (whereas DVD can store many gigabytes of data). The main disadvantage was the relative slowness, as compared with Winchester hard disks; this is now much less of a problem as speeds have increased steadily over the years.

19.2 Tracks and Sectors

A disk must be formatted before it is used, to allow data to be stored in a logical manner. The format of the disk is defined by a series of tracks and sectors on one or two sides. A track is a concentric circle around the disk where the outermost track is track 40 and the innermost track is 0. The next track is track 1, and so on, as shown in Figure 19.1. Each of these tracks is divided into a number of sectors. The first sector is named sector 1, the second is sector 2, and so on. Most disks have two sides: the first side

is called side 0 and the other is side 1. Figure 19.1 also shows how each track is split into a number of sectors; in this case, there are eight sectors per track. Typically each sector stores

512 bytes. The total disk space, in bytes, will thus be given by

Disk space = Number of sides × Tracks × Sectors per track × Bytes per sector

For example, a typical floppy disk has two sides, with 80 tracks per side, 18 sectors per track and 512 bytes per sector:

$$
\begin{aligned}
\text{Disk capacity} \quad &= 2{\times}80{\times}18{\times}512 &&= 1{,}474{,}560 \text{ B} \\
&= 1{,}474{,}560/1{,}024 \text{ kB} &&= 1{,}440 \text{ kB} \\
&= 1{,}440/1{,}024 \text{ MB} &&= 1.4 \text{ MB}
\end{aligned}
$$

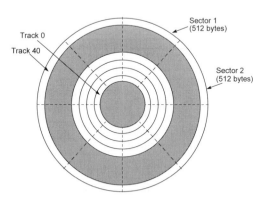

Figure 19.1   Tracks and sectors on a disk

19.3 Fixed Disks

Fixed disks store large amounts of data and vary in their capacity, from several megabytes to several gigabytes. A fixed disk (or hard disk) consists of one or more platters that spin at about 3000 rpm (10 times faster than a floppy disk); these platters are mounted on a central axle or spindle, which rotates all the platters at the same speed. Data is read from the disk by a flying head, which sits just above the surface of the platter. This head does not actually touch the surface as the disk is spinning so fast. The distance between the platter and the head is about $10\,\mu\text{in}$ (no larger than the thickness of a human hair or a smoke particle). It must thus be protected from any outer particles by sealing it in an airtight container. A floppy disk is prone to wear as the head touches the disk as it reads, but a fixed disk has no wear as its heads never touch the disk.

> **Floppy disks**
>
> A 3.5-inch double density disk (DD) can be formatted with two sides, nine sectors per track and 40 tracks per side. This gives a total capacity of 720 kB. A 3.5 inch high density (HD) disk has a maximum capacity, when formatted, with 80 tracks per side.
>
> A 5.25-inch DD disk can be formatted with two sides, nine sectors per disk, and either 40 or 80 tracks per side. The maximum capacity of these formats is 360 kB (40 tracks) or 720 kB (80 tracks). A 5.25-inch HD disk can be formatted with 15 sectors per track, which gives a total capacity of 1.2 MB. When reading data, the disks rotate at 300 rpm.

One problem with a fixed disk is head crashes, typically caused when the power is interrupted abruptly or the disk drive is jolted. This can cause the head to crash into the disk surface. In most modern disk drives, the head is automatically parked when the power is taken away. Older disk drives that do not have automatic head parking require a program to park the heads before the drive is powered down.

There are two sides to each platter and, like floppy disks, each side divides into a number of tracks, which are subdivided into sectors. A number of tracks on fixed disks are usually named cylinders. For example a 40-megabyte hard disk has two platters with 306 cylinders, four tracks per cylinder, 17 sectors per track and 512 bytes per sector, thus each side of a platter stores

$$
\begin{aligned}
306 \times 4 \times 17 \times 512 \text{ B} \quad &= \quad 10{,}653{,}696 \text{ B} \\
&= \quad 10{,}653{,}696/1{,}048{,}576 \text{ MB} \\
&= \quad 10.2 \text{ MB}
\end{aligned}
$$

19.4 Drive Specifications

Access time is the time taken for a disk to locate data. Typical access times for modern disk drives range from 10 to 30 ms. The average access time is the time for the head to travel half way across the platters. Once the head has located the correct sector, then there may be another wait until it locates the start of the data within the sector. If it is positioned at a point after the start of the data, it requires another rotation of the disk to locate the data. This average wait, or latency time, is usually taken as half of a revolution of the disk. If the disk spins at 3600 rpm, then the latency is 8.33 ms. Newer disk drives spin at 7200 rpm, which allows for faster data transfers.

The main parameters that affect the drive specification are the data transfer rate and the average access time. The transfer rate is dependent upon the interface for the controller/disk drive and system/controller and the access time is dependent upon the disk design.

Extended partition

An extended partition allows a physical drive to be physically divided so that it creates other logical partitions. The partition itself does not directly contain data, and must have a logical partition for data to be stored to it.

Logical partition

These existing within extended partition and are meant to contain only data files and OSs that can be booted from a logical partition, such as OS/2, Linux, Windows NT, and so on. Once created, logical partitions must be logically formatted, but each can use a different file system.

19.5 Hard Disk and CD-ROM Interfaces

There are two main interfaces involved with hard disks and CD-ROMs. One connects the disk controller to the system (system–controller interface) and the other connects the disk controller to the disk drive (disk–controller interface).

The controller can be interfaced by standards such as ISA, EISA, MCA, VL-local bus or PCI bus. For the interface between the disk drive and the controller, standards such as ST-506, ESDI, SCSI or IDE can be used. ST-506 was developed by Seagate Technologies and is used in many older machines with hard disks with a capacity of less than 40 MB. The enhanced small disk interface (ESDI) is capable of transferring data between itself and the processor at rates approaching 10 MB/s.

The small computer system interface (SCSI) allows up to seven different disk drives or other interfaces to be connected to the system through the same interface controller. SCSI is a common interface for large-capacity disk drives; it is illustrated in Figure 19.2.

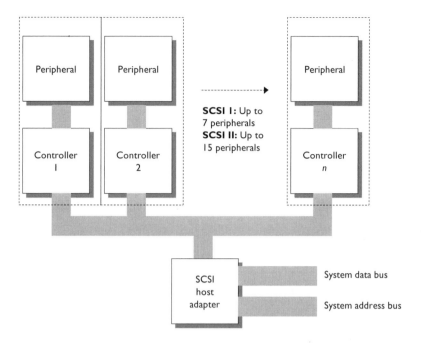

Figure 19.2 SCSI interface

The most popular type of PC disk interface is the integrated drive electronics (IDE) standard. It has the advantage of incorporating the disk controller in the disk drive, and attaches directly to the motherboard through an interface cable. This cable allows many disk drives to be connected to a system without worrying about bus or controller conflicts. The IDE interface is also capable of driving other I/O devices besides a hard disk. It also normally contains at least 32k of

Table 19.1 Capacity of different disk types

Interface	Maximum data rate (MB/s)
ST-506	0.6
ESDI	1.25
IDE	8.3
E-IDE	16.6
SCSI	4.0
SCSI-II	10.0

disk cache memory. Common access times for an IDE are often less than 16 ms, whereas access times for a floppy disk are about 200 ms. With a good disk cache system, the access time can reduce to less than 1 ms. A comparison of the maximum data rates is given in Table 19.1.

A typical modern PC contains two IDE connections on the motherboard, IDE0 and IDE1. The IDE0 connection connects to the master drive (C:) and IDE1 connects to the slave drive (D:). These could connect either to two hard disks or to one hard disk and a CD-ROM drive (or even a tape back-up system). Unfortunately, the IDE standard allows disk access up to only 528 MB. A new standard called enhanced-IDE (E-IDE) allows for disk capacities above this limit. The connector used is the same as IDE but the computer's BIOS must be able to recognize the new standard. Most computers manufactured since 1993 are able to access E-IDE disk drives fully.

The specifications for the IDE are:

- Maximum of two devices (hard disks).

- Maximum capacity for each disk of 528 MB.
- Maximum cable length of 18 inches.
- Data transfer rates of 3.3, 5.2 and 8.3 MB/s.

The specifications for the EIDE are:

- Maximum of four devices (hard disks, CD-ROM and tape).
- Uses two ports (for master and slave).
- Maximum capacity for each disk is 8.4 GB.
- Maximum cable length of 18 inches.
- Data transfer rates of 3.3, 5.2, 8.3, 11.1 and 16.6 MB/s.

19.6 IDE Interface

The most popular interface for hard disk drives is the integrated drive electronics (IDE) interface. Its main advantage is that the hard disk controller is built into the disk drive and the interface to the motherboard consists simply of a stripped-down version of the ISA bus. The most common standard is the ANSI-defined ATA-IDE standard. It uses a 40-way ribbon cable to connect to 40-pin header connectors. Table 19.2 lists the pin connections. It has a 16-bit data bus (D0–D15) and the only available interrupt line used is IRQ14 (the hard disk uses IRQ14).

Table 19.2   IDE connections

Pin	IDE signal	AT signal	Pin	IDE signal	AT signal
1	RESET	RESET DRV	2	GND	–
3	D7	SD7	4	D8	SD8
5	D6	SD6	6	D9	SD9
7	D5	SD5	8	D10	SD10
9	D4	SD4	10	D11	SD11
11	D3	SD3	12	D12	SD12
13	D2	SD2	14	D13	SD13
15	D1	SD1	16	D14	SD14
17	D0	SD0	18	D15	SD15
19	GND	–	20	KEY	–
21	DRQ3	DRQ3	22	GND	–
23	$\overline{\text{IOW}}$	$\overline{\text{IOW}}$	24	GND	–
25	$\overline{\text{IOR}}$	$\overline{\text{IOR}}$	26	GND	–
27	IOCHRDY	IOCHRDY	28	CSEL	–
29	$\overline{\text{DACK3}}$	$\overline{\text{DACK3}}$	30	GND	–
31	IRQ14	IRQ14	32	$\overline{\text{IOCS16}}$	$\overline{\text{IOCS16}}$
33	Address bit 1	SA1	34	$\overline{\text{PDIAG}}$	–
35	Address bit 0	SA0	36	Address bit 2	SA2
37	$\overline{\text{CS1FX}}$	–	38	$\overline{\text{CS3FX}}$	–
39	$\text{SP}/\overline{\text{DA}}$	–	40	GND	–

The standard allows for the connection of two disk drives in a daisy-chain configuration. This can cause problems because both drives have controllers within their drives. The primary drive (Drive 0) is assigned as the master, and the secondary driver (Drive 1) is the slave. A drive is set as a master or a slave by setting jumpers on the disk drive. They can also be set by software using the cable select (CSEL) pin on the interface.

EIDE has various modes (ANSI modes) of operation:

- Mode 0 – 600 ns read/write cycle time, 3.3 MB/s burst data transfer rate.
- Mode 1 – 383 ns read/write cycle time, 5.2 MB/s burst data transfer rate.
- Mode 2 – 240 ns read/write cycle time, 8.3 MB/s burst data transfer rate.
- Mode 3 – 180 ns read/write cycle time, 11.1 MB/s burst data transfer rate.
- Mode 4 – 120 ns read/write cycle time, 16.6 MB/s burst data transfer rate.

The PC is now a highly integrated system. The main elements of modern systems are the processor, the system controller and the PCI IDE/ISA accelerator, as illustrated in Figure 19.3 The system controller provides the main interface between the processor and the level-2 cache, the DRAM and the PCI bus. It is one of the most important devices in the system and allows data to flow to and from the processor in the correct way. The PCI bus links to interface devices and also the PCI IDE/ISA accelerator (such as the PIIX4 device). The PCI IDE/ISA device then interfaces to other buses, such as IDE and ISA. The IDE interface has separate signals for both the primary and second IDE drives, these are electrically isolated, which allows drives to be swapped easily without affecting the other port. Figure 19.4 illustrates the connections to the on-board connector for IDE0 (the primary IDE port) and IDE1 (the secondary IDE port). Up to four devices can be connected to the port, where each port has a master and a slave.

HPFS

HPFS (high performance file system) is used by OS/2 and older versions of Windows NT. Its main features are:

- **Sorts directory based on filename**. HPFS uses B-tree format to store the file system directory structure. The B-tree format stores directory entries in an alphabetic tree, and binary searches are used to search for the target file in the directory list. This makes file access faster, and space is used more efficiently than with the FAT file system

- **Sectors**. HPFS uses sectors rather than clusters. HPFS organizes a disk or partition into 8 MB bands, with 2 kB allocation bitmaps between the bands (this improves performance as the disk heads do not have to return to track zero every time information is required about the available space or a files location).

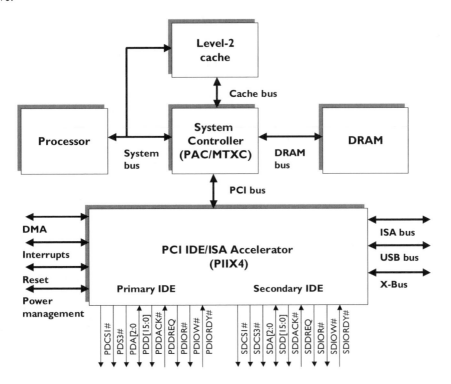

Figure 19.3   IDE system connections

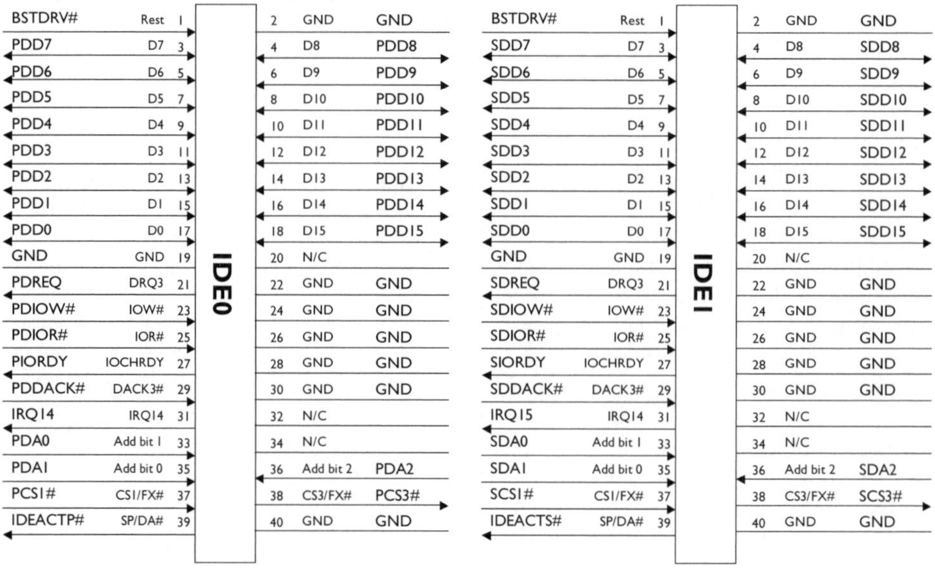

IDE0

Signal	Pin name	Pin	Pin	Pin name	Signal
BSTDRV#	Rest	1	2	GND	GND
PDD7	D7	3	4	D8	PDD8
PDD6	D6	5	6	D9	PDD9
PDD5	D5	7	8	D10	PDD10
PDD4	D4	9	10	D11	PDD11
PDD3	D3	11	12	D12	PDD12
PDD2	D2	13	14	D13	PDD13
PDD1	D1	15	16	D14	PDD14
PDD0	D0	17	18	D15	PDD15
GND	GND	19	20	N/C	
PDREQ	DRQ3	21	22	GND	GND
PDIOW#	IOW#	23	24	GND	GND
PDIOR#	IOR#	25	26	GND	GND
PIORDY	IOCHRDY	27	28	GND	GND
PDDACK#	DACK3#	29	30	GND	GND
IRQ14	IRQ14	31	32	N/C	
PDA0	Add bit 1	33	34	N/C	
PDA1	Add bit 0	35	36	Add bit 2	PDA2
PCS1#	CS1/FX#	37	38	CS3/FX#	PCS3#
IDEACTP#	SP/DA#	39	40	GND	GND

IDE1

Signal	Pin name	Pin	Pin	Pin name	Signal
BSTDRV#	Rest	1	2	GND	GND
SDD7	D7	3	4	D8	SDD8
SDD6	D6	5	6	D9	SDD9
SDD5	D5	7	8	D10	SDD10
SDD4	D4	9	10	D11	SDD11
SDD3	D3	11	12	D12	SDD12
SDD2	D2	13	14	D13	SDD13
SDD1	D1	15	16	D14	SDD14
SDD0	D0	17	18	D15	SDD15
GND	GND	19	20	N/C	
SDREQ	DRQ3	21	22	GND	GND
SDIOW#	IOW#	23	24	GND	GND
SDIOR#	IOR#	25	26	GND	GND
SIORDY	IOCHRDY	27	28	GND	GND
SDDACK#	DACK3#	29	30	GND	GND
IRQ15	IRQ14	31	32	N/C	
SDA0	Add bit 1	33	34	N/C	
SDA1	Add bit 0	35	36	Add bit 2	SDA2
SCSI#	CS1/FX#	37	38	CS3/FX#	SCS3#
IDEACTS#	SP/DA#	39	40	GND	GND

Figure 19.4   IDE0 and IDE1 interface

The PCI IDE/ISA accelerator is a massively integrated device (the PIIX4 has 324 pins) and provides for an interface to other buses, such as the USB and X-Bus. It also handles the interrupts from the PCI bus and ISA bus. It thus has two integrated 82C59 interrupt controllers, which support up to 15 interrupts (IRQ1 to IRQ15). IRQ14 and IRQ15 are directed to IDE0 and IDE1, respectively. The PCI IDE/ISA accelerator also handles DMA transfers (on up to eight channels), and thus has two integrated 82C37 DMA controllers. Along with this, it has an integrated 82C54, which provides for the system timer, DRAM refresh signal and the speaker tone output. The DMA channels supports ultra DMA33 (ATA-33), which is a synchronous DMA mode where transfers up to 33 MB/s can be supported, whereas PIO Mode 4 only allows up to 14 MB/s. Some newer systems allows for Ultra DMA66 (ATA-66), which transfers at 66 MB/s (possibly using high-speed disks which spin at 7200 rpm).

19.7 IDE Communication

The IDE (or AT bus) is the de facto standard for most hard disks in PCs. It has the advantage over older type interfaces that the controller is integrated into the disk drive. Thus, the computer only has to pass

---

NTFS

Windows NT/2000 uses the NTFS (new technology file system). It uses a master file table (MFT) to record the file system (and also multiple copies of the critical portion of the MFT to protect against corruption and data loss). It can support files systems up to 16 EB.

Its main features are:

- **Clusters**. As with FAT and FAT32, NTFS uses clusters to store data files. With FAT and FAT32, the cluster size is dependent on the size of the disk or partition. In NTFS, the cluster size is as small as 512 B, regardless of the disk size. Smaller cluster sizes reduces the amount of wasted disk space, and also reduces file fragmentation, which results from files being broken up into many non-contiguous clusters (resulting in slower file access).

- **Hot fixing**. NTFS allows hot fixing, where bad sectors are automatically detected and marked so that they will not be used.

- **Enhanced security**. Each file has uniquely defined attributes.

high-level commands to the unit and the actual control can be achieved with the integrated controller. Several companies developed a standard command set for an AT attachment (ATA). Commands include:

- Read sector buffer – reads contents of the controller's sector buffer.
- Write sector buffer – writes data to the controller's sector buffer.
- Check for active.
- Read multiple sectors.
- Write multiple sectors.
- Lock drive door.

The control of the disk is achieved by passing a number of high-level commands through a number of I/O port registers. Table 19.2 outlines the pin connections for the IDE connector. Typically, pin 20 is missing on the connector cable so that it cannot be inserted the wrong way, although most systems buffer the signals so that the bus will not be damaged if the cable is inserted the wrong way. The five control signals that are unique to the IDE interface (and not the AT bus) are:

- $\overline{\text{CS3FX}}$, $\overline{\text{CS1FX}}$ – used to identify either the master or the slave.
- $\overline{\text{PDIAG}}$ (passed diagnostic) – used by the slave drive to indicate that it has passed its diagnostic test.
- $\text{SP}/\overline{\text{DA}}$ (slave present/drive active) – used by the slave drive to indicate that it is present and active.

The other signals are:

- IOCHRDY – this signal is optional and is used by the drive to tell the processor that it requires extra clock cycles for the current I/O transfer. A high level informs the processor that it is ready, while a low informs it that it needs more time.
- DRQ3, $\overline{\text{DACK3}}$ – these are used for DMA transfers.

19.7.1 AT task file

The processor communicates with the IDE controller through data and control registers (typically known as the AT task file). The base registers used are between 1F0h and 1F7h for the primary disk (170h and 177h for secondary), and 3F6h (376h for secondary), as shown in Figure 19.5. Their functions are shown in Table 19.3.

Table 19.3   IDE registers

Port	Function	Bits	Direction
1F0h	Data register	16	R/W
1F1h	Error register	8	R
	Precompensation	8	W
1F2h	Sector count	8	R/W
1F3h	Sector number	8	R/W
1F4h	Cylinder LSB	8	R/W
1F5h	Cylinder MSB	8	R/W
1F5h	Drive/head	8	R/W
1F6h	Status register	8	R
	Command register	8	W
3F6h	Alternative status register	8	R
	Digital output register	8	W
3F7h	Drive address	8	R

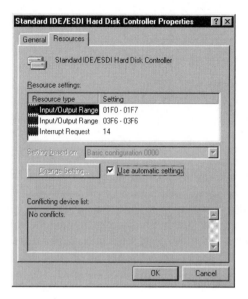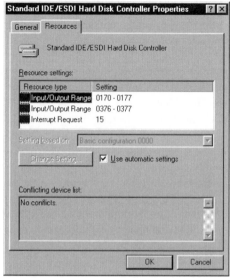

Figure 19.5   Typical hard-disk controller settings for the primary and secondary drive

Data register (1F0h)
The data register is a 16-bit register used to read/write data from/to the disk.

Error register (1F1h)
The error register is read-only and contains error information relating to the last command. Its definitions are:

b_7	b_6	b_5	b_4	b_3	b_2	b_1	b_0
BBK	UNC	MC	NID	MCR	ABT	NT0	NDM

where:

- BBK is set to 1 if the sector is bad.
- UNC is set to 1 if there is an unrecoverable error.
- NID is set to 1 if mark not found.
- ABT is set to 1 if command aborted.
- NT0 is set to 1 if track 0 not found.
- MC is set to 1 to show that the medium has changed (EIDE only). The EIDE standard support disks that can be changed while the system is running (such as CD-ROMs, tape drives, and so on).
- MCR is set to 1 to show that the medium requires to be changed (EIDE only).

Sector count register (1F2h)
This is a read/write 8-bit register that defines the number of sectors to be read, written or verified. After each transfer to/from the disk, causes the register value is decremented by one.

Sector number register (1F3h)
This is a read/write 8-bit register that defines the start sector to be read, written or verified. After each transfer to/from the disk, the register contains the last processed sector.

Cylinder register (1F4h/1F5h)

These are read/write 8-bit registers that define the LSB (1F4h) and MSB (1F5h) of the cylinder number. The two registers are capable of containing a 16-bit value. In standard IDE, the cylinder number is 10-bit and can vary from 0 to 1,023 (0 to $2^{10}-1$). For E-IDE, the value can be a 16-bit value and can thus vary from 0 to 65,535 (0 to $2^{16}-1$). This is one of the main reasons that E-IDE can address much more data than IDE.

Drive/head register (1F6h)

This is a read/write 8-bit register that defines the currently used head. Its definitions are:

b_7	b_6	b_5	b_4	b_3	b_2	b_1	b_0
1	L	1	DRV	HD_3	HD_2	HD_1	HD_0

where:

- L is set to 1 if LBA (logical block addressing) mode, else set to 0 if CHS (EIDE only).
- DRV is set to 1 for the slave, else it is master.
- HD_3–HD_0 identifies the head number, where 0000 identifies head 0, 0001 identifies head 1, and so on.

Status register (1F7h)

The 1F7h register has two modes. If it is written to, then it is a command register (see next section); if it is read from, then it is a status register. The status register is a read-only 8-bit register that contains status information from the previously issued command. Its definitions are:

b_7	b_6	b_5	b_4	b_3	b_2	b_1	b_0
BUSY	RDY	WFT	SKT	DRQ	COR	IDX	ERR

where:

- BUSY is set to 1 if the drive is busy.
- RDY is set to 1 if the drive is ready.
- WFT is set to 1 if there is a write fault.
- SKT is set to 1 if head seek positioning is complete.
- DRQ is set to 1 if data can be transferred.
- COR is set to 1 if there is a correctable data error.
- IDX is set to 1 to show that the disk index has just passed.
- ERR is set to 1 to show that the error register contains error information.

Command register (1F7h)

If the 1F7h register is written to, then it is a command register. The command register is an 8-bit register that can contain commands such as given in Table 19.4, where R is set to 0 if the command is automatically retried and L identifies the long bit.

Digital output register (3F6h)

This is a write-only 8-bit register that allows drives to be reset and also IRQ14 to be masked. Its definitions are

b_7	b_6	b_5	b_4	b_3	b_2	b_1	b_0
–	–	–	–	–	SRST	$\overline{\text{IEN}}$	–

Table 19.4   Command registers

Command registers	b_7	b_6	b_5	b_4	b_3	b_2	b_1	b_0	Related
Calibrate drive	0	0	0	1	–	–	–	–	1F6h
Read sector	0	0	1	0	–	–	L	R	1F2h–1F6h
Write sector	0	0	1	1	–	–	L	R	1F2h–1F6h
Verify sector	0	1	0	0	–	–	–	R	1F2h–1F6h
Format track	0	1	0	1	–	–	–	–	1F3h–1F6h
Seek	0	1	1	1	–	–	–	–	1F4h–1F6h
Diagnostics	1	0	0	1	–	–	–	–	1F2h, 1F6h
Read sector buffer	1	1	1	0	0	1	0	0	1F6h
Write sector buffer	1	1	1	0	1	0	0	0	1F6h
Identify drive	1	1	1	0	1	1	–	–	1F6h

where

- SRST is set to a 1 to reset all connected drives, else accept the command.
- $\overline{\text{IEN}}$ controls the interrupt enable. If set to 1, then IRQ14 is always masked, else interrupted after each command.

Drive address register (3F7h)

The drive address register is a read-only register that contains information on which drive and head are currently active. Its definitions are:

b_7	b_6	b_5	b_4	b_3	b_2	b_1	b_0
–	$\overline{\text{WTGT}}$	$\overline{\text{HS3}}$	$\overline{\text{HS2}}$	$\overline{\text{HS1}}$	$\overline{\text{HS0}}$	$\overline{\text{DS1}}$	$\overline{\text{DS0}}$

where

- $\overline{\text{WTGT}}$ is set to 1 if the write gate is closed, else the write gate is open.
- $\overline{\text{HS3}} - \overline{\text{HS0}}$ – 1s complement value of currently active head.
- $\overline{\text{DS1}} - \overline{\text{DS0}}$ identifies the selected drive.

19.7.2 Command phase

The IRQ14 line is used by the disk when it wants to interrupt the processor, to read or write data to/from memory. For example, Program 19.1 uses Microsoft C++ (for Borland replace _outp() and _inp() with outport() and inport()) to write to a disk at cylinder 150, head 0 and sector 7.

Note that if the L bit is set, then an extra four ECC (error correcting code) bytes must be written to the sector (thus a total of 516 bytes are written to each sector). The code used is cyclic redundancy check, which, while it cannot correct them, is very powerful at detecting errors.

19.7.3 E-IDE

The original IDE BIOS only allowed up to 1,024 cylinders to be defined on a partition, thus any cylinders over this could not be seen by IDE. There was also a limit on the number of heads and sectors that could be defined. This gives a limit of 504 MB. In 1994, a new specification named enhanced-IDE (E-IDE) was developed, which increased the number of supported heads, cylinders and sectors.

📄 **Program 19.1**

```
#include <conio.h>
int main(void)
{
int        sectors=4, sector_no=7, cylinder=150, drive=0, command=0x33, i,
unsigned   int buff[1024], *buff_pointer;
      do
      {
         /* wait until BSY signal is set to a 1 */

      } while (( _inp(0x1f7) & 0x80) != 0x80);

      _outp(0x1f2,sectors);              /* set number of sectors    */
      _outp(0x1f3,sector_no);            /* set sector number        */
      _outp(0x1f4,cylinder & 0x0ff);     /* set cylinder number LSB  */
      _outp(0x1f5,cylinder & 0xf00);     /* set cylinder number MSB  */
      _outp(0x1f6,drive);                /* set DRV=0 and head=0      */
      _outp(0x1f7,command);              /* 0011 0011 (write sector) */

      do
      {
         /* wait until BSY signal is set to a 1 and DRQ is set to a 1 */

      } while ( (( _inp(0x1f7) & 0x80) != 0x80) &&
                                    (( _inp(0x1f7) & 0x08) !=0x08) );
      buff_pointer= buff;
      for (i=0;i<512;i++,buff_pointer++)
      {
         _outp(0x1f0,*buff_pointer); /* output 16-bits at a time */
      }
      return(0);
}
```

The main differences between IDE and E-IDE are:

- E-IDE support removable media.
- E-IDE supports a 16-bit cylinder value, which gives a maximum of 65,636 cylinders.
- Higher transfer rates. In mode 4, E-IDE has a 120 ns read/write cycle time, which gives a 16.6 MB/s burst data transfer rate.
- E-IDE supports LBA (logical block addressing), which differs from CHS (cylinder head sector) in that the disk drive appears to be a continuous stream of sequential blocks. The addressing of these blocks is achieved from within the controller and the system does not have to bother about which cylinder, header and sector is being used.

IDE is limited to 1,024 cylinders, 16 heads (drive/head register has only four bits for the number of heads) and 63 sectors, which gives:

$$\text{Disk capacity} = 1,024 \times 16 \times 63 \times 512 \quad = 504 \text{ MB}$$

With enhanced BIOS, this is increased to 1,024 cylinders, 256 heads (8-bit definition for the number of heads) and 63 sectors, to give:

Disk capacity $= 1{,}024 \times 256 \times 63 \times 512 = 7.88\,\text{GB}$

With E-IDE, the maximum possible is 65,536 cylinders, 256 heads and 63 sectors, to give:

Disk capacity $= 65{,}536 \times 256 \times 63 \times 512 = 128\,\text{GB}$

A 3.5-inch hard disk with two platters and four heads would give a capacity of around 8.1GB.

ATA (advanced technology attachment)

ATA is a standard used by hard disk drives to communicate with the controller ports, allowing the drive to interface with the computer. ATA is now the official ANSI name for integrated drive electronics (IDE). Before ATA, there were numerous incompatible methods for interfacing hard disk drives to computers.

ATA-2 (or fast-ATA), which is the common name for a new E-IDE, extends the ATA interface but keeps compatibility with previous IDE BIOS.

19.8 Optical Storage

Optical storage devices can store extremely large amounts of digital data. They use a laser beam, which reflects from an optical disk. If a pit exists in the disk, then the laser beam does not reflect back. Figure 19.6 shows the basic mechanism for reading from optical disks. A focusing lens directs the laser light to an objective lens, which focuses the light onto a small area on the disk. If a pit exists, then the light does not reflect back from the disk. If the pit does not exist, then it is reflected and directed through the objective lens and a quarter-wave plate to the polarized prism. The quarter-wave polarizes the light by 45 degrees thus the reflected light will have a polarization of 90 degrees, with respect to the original incident light in the prism. The polarized prism then directs this polarized light to the sensor.

19.8.1 CD-ROM

In a permanent disk (compact disk or CD), the pits are set up by pressing them onto the disk at production. The data on this type of disk is permanent and cannot be reprogrammed to store different data, and is known as CD-ROM (compact disk read-only memory). This type of disk is normally cost-effective only in large quantities.

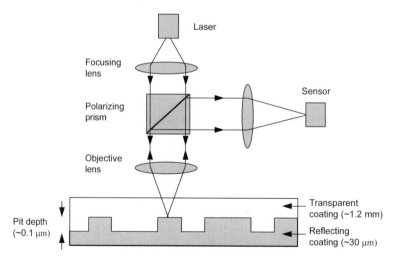

Figure 19.6   Reading from an optical disk

Standard CD-ROMs have a diameter of 120 mm (4.7 inch) and a thickness of 1.2 mm. They can store up to 650 MB of data, which gives around 74 minutes of compressed video (MPEG format with near VCR quality) or uncompressed hi-fi audio. The reflective coating (normally aluminum) on the disk is approximately 30 µm and the pits are approximately 0.1 µm long and deep. A protective transparent coating is applied on top of the reflective coating in a depth of 1.2 mm (the approximate thickness of the disk). The protective coating also helps to focus the light beam from about

> **Master boot record (MBR)**
>
> The MBR is located at the first sector of the first physical hard disk. It consists of a master boot program and a partition table (which describes the disk partitions). When booted, the master boot program looks at the partition table to determine which primary partition is active. After it finds it, it starts the boot program from the boot sector of the active partition. A useful command to restore the MBR is `fdisk /mbr`.

0.7 mm on the surface of the coating to the 0.1 µm pit. Data is stored on the disk as a spiral, starting from the inside and ending at the outside (opposite to hard disk. The thickness of the track is 1.6 µm, which gives a total spiral length of 5.7 km.

19.8.2 WORM drives

WORM (write once read many) disks allow data to be written to the optical disk once. The data is then permanent and cannot be altered. They are typically used in data logging applications and in making small volumes of CD-ROMs. A 350 mm (14 inch) WORM disk can store up to 10 GB of data (5 GB per side). This gives around 15 hours of compressed video (MPEG format with near VCR quality).

WORM disks consist of two pieces of transparent material (normally glass) with a layer of metal (typically tellurium) sandwiched in between. Initially, the metal recording surface is clear. A high-intensity laser beam then writes information to the disk by burning small pits into the surface.

19.8.3 CD-R and CD-RW disks

CD-R (CD-recordable) disks are write-once disks that can store up to 650 MB of data or 74 minutes of audio. For a disk to be read by any CD-ROM drive, they must comply with ISO 9660 format. A CD-R disk can also be made multisession where a new file system is written each time the disk is written to. Unfortunately, this takes up around 14 MB of header data for each session. Typical parameters for sessions are given in Table 19.4. Typically, CD recorders write at two (or even four) times the standard writing/playback speed of 150 kB (75 sectors) per second.

A CD-RW (CD-rewriteable) disk allows a disk to be written to many times, but the file format is incompatible with standard CD-ROM systems (ISO 9660). The formatting of the CD-RW disk (which can take a few hours) takes up about 157 MB of disk space, which leaves only about 493 MB for data.

Table 19.5 CD-R sessions

Number of sessions	Header information	Data for each session
1	About 14 MB	636 MB one session
5	About 70 MB	116 MB each session
10	About 140 MB	51 MB each session
30	About 420 MB	7.7 MB each session

New CD-R and CD-RW writing systems incorporate a smart laser system that eradicates the problem of dirt on the disk. It does this by adjusting the write power of the laser using automatic power control. This allows the unit to continue to write when it encounters minor media errors such as dirt, smudges, small scratches, and so on.

19.8.4 CD-ROM disk format

The two main standards for writing a CD-ROM are ISO 9660 and UDF (universal disk format). The ISO 9660 disk unfortunately uses 14 MB for each write to the disk. In 1980, Philips NV and Sony Corporation first announced the CD-DA (digital audio) and, in 1983, released the standard for CD-ROM. Then in 1988, they released the Red Book standard for recordable CD audio disks. This served as a blueprint for the Yellow Book specification for CD-ROMs (CD-ROM and CD-ROM-XA data format) and the Orange Book Parts 1 and 2 specifications for CD-recordable (CD-R/CD-E (CD-recordable/CD-erasable)). In the Red Book standard, a disk is organized into a number of segments:

- Lead in contains the table of contents for the disk that specifies the physical location of each track.
- Program area contains the actual disk data or audio data and is divided up into 99 tracks, with a two-second gap between each track.
- Lead out contains a string of zeros, which is a legacy of the old Red Book standard. These zeros enabled old CD players to identify the end of a CD.

The CD is laid out in a number of sectors. Each of these sectors contains 2,352 bytes, made up of 2,048 bytes of data and other information such as headers, subheaders, error detection codes and so on. The data is organised into logical blocks. After each session, a logical block has a logical address, which is used by the drive to find a particular logical block number (LBN).

Within the tracks, the CD can contain either audio or computer data. The most common formats for computer data are ISO 9660, hierarchical file system (HFS) and the Joliet file system.

The ISO 9660 was developed at a time when disks required to be mass replicated. It thus wrote the complete file system at the time of creation, as there was no need for incremental creation. Now, with CD-R technology, it is possible to incrementally write to a disk. This is described as multisession. Unfortunately, after each session a new lead in and lead out must be written (requiring a minimum of 13 MB of disk space). This consists of:

- 13.2 MB for the lead out for the first session and 4.4 MB for each subsequent session.
- 8.8 MB for lead in for each session comprising 8.8 MB.

Boot process

After switch-on, the processor executes the following:

- **Reads instructions from the BIOS.** The BIOS contains the start up procedures. Typically BIOS is now Flash BIOS, which allows for software updates.

- **Executes master boot program.** The last part of BIOS contains the boot routine, which then reads the master boot record (MBR) from the first sector of the first physical hard disk, which contains the master boot program and a partition table. The BIOS boot routine executes the master boot program, which then continues the boot process.

- **Reads partition table.** The master boot program looks at the partition table to see which primary partition is active. On systems with only one primary partition, the system is booted from it, otherwise the boot record holds a boot program designed specifically to start that partition's installed OS.

- **Start boot program.** This program is read from the primary partition.

Note that DOS, Windows 3.x and Windows 95/98 must boot from an active primary partition on the first hard disk drive (C:), where Windows NT/2000 can boot from a logical partition, but the Windows NT/2000 boot program must be in the active primary partition on the first hard disk (C:).

Thus multisession is useful for writing large amounts of data for each session, but is not efficient when writing many small updates. Most new CD-R systems now use a track-at-once technique, which stores the data one track at a time and only writes the lead in and lead out data when the session is actually finished. In this technique, the CD can be built up with

> **Ext2 and Swap**
>
> These are file systems developed for the Linux operating systems. They support a maximum disk or partition size of 4TB (a thousand, thousand million bytes). Linux Swap provides for a Linux swap file.

data over a long period of time. Unfortunately, the disk cannot be read by standard CD-ROM drives until the session is closed (and written with the ISO 9660 format). Another disadvantage is that the Red Book only specifies up to 99 tracks for each CD. Unfortunately, the ISO 9660 is not well suited for packet writing and is likely to be phased out over the coming years.

19.8.5 Magneto-optical disks

As with CD-R disks, magneto-optical (MO) disks allow the data to be rewritten many times. These disks use magnetic and optical fields to store the data. Unfortunately, the disk must first be totally erased before data is written (although new developments are overcoming this limitation).

19.8.6 Transfer rates

Optical disks spin at variable speeds. They spin at a lower rate on the outside of the disk than on the inside. Thus the disk increases its speed progressively as the data is read from the disk. The actual rate at which the drive reads the data is constant for the disk. The basic transfer rate for a typical CD-ROM is 150 kB/s (approximately 1.2 Mbps). This has recently been increased to 300 kB/s ($\times$2 CD drives), 600 kB/s ($\times$4), 900 kB/s ($\times$6), 1.5 MB/s ($\times$10) and even 6 MB/s ($\times$40).

19.8.7 Silver, green, blue or gold

CD-ROMs are available in a number of colors:

> **Standards**
>
> Data disks are described in the following standards books, each of them specific to an area or type of data application. These books can be obtained by becoming a licensed CD developer with Philips. These standards apply to media, hardware, operating systems, file systems and software.
>
> - **Red Book**. World standard for all compact disks (CD-DA) (audio).
> - **Yellow Book**. Covers CD-ROM and CD-ROM-XA data formats.
> - **Green Book**. Covers CD-I data formats and operating systems (photo).
> - **White Book**. CD-I (video).
> - **Orange Book**. Covers CD-R/CD-E.
> - **Blue Book**. CD-enhanced (CD extra, CD plus).

- **Silver**. These are read-only disks, which are a stamped as an original disk.
- **Gold**. These are recordable disks, which use a basic phthalocyanine formulation patented by Mitsui Toatsu Chemicals (MTC) of Japan, and is licensed to other phthalocyanine media manufacturers. They generally work better with 2 m writing speeds as some models of disk can not be written to at 1 m writing speed.
- **Green**. These are recordable disks, which are based on cyanine-based formulations. They are not covered by a governing patent, and are more or less unique to the individual manufacturers. An early problem was encountered with cyanine-based disk as the dye became chemically unstable in the presence of sunlight. Other problems included a wide variation in electrical performance depending on write speed and location (inner or outer portion of the disk). Eventually, in 1995 some stabilizing compounds were added. The best attempt produced a metal-stabilized cyanine dye formulation that gave excellent

overall performance. Gradually, the performance of these disks is approaching gold disk performance.

- **Blue**. These are recordable disks based on an azo media. This was designed and manufactured by Mitsubishi Chemical Corporation (MCC) and marketed through its US subsidiary, Verbatim Corporation.

19.9 Magnetic Tape

Magnetic tapes use a thin plastic tape with a magnetic coating (normally of ferric oxide). Most modern tapes are either reel-to-reel or cartridge type. A reel-to-reel tape normally has two interconnected reels of tape with tension arms (similar to standard compact audio cassettes). The cartridge type has a drive belt to spin the reels; this mechanism reduces the strain on the tape and allows faster access speeds.

FAT cluster size

Files are stored in cluster segments. The larger the cluster size, the more space that will be wasted. For example 10 files with 1 kB in them will take-up 640 kB on the disk if a 64 kB cluster size is used. Typical cluster sizes for partition sizes are.

Partition size (MB)	Cluster size	Sectors per cluster
16– 27	2 kB	2
128– 255	4 kB	4
256– 511	8 kB	8
512– 1,023	16 kB	16
1,024– 2,047	32 kB	32
2,048– 4,096	64 kB	64

Thus one way of reducing the amount of wastage is to partition the disk so that it uses smaller cluster sizes. FAT32 uses:

Partition size (GB)	Cluster size	Sectors per cluster
0.256– 8.01	4 kB	8
8.02– 16.02	8 kB	16
16.03– 32.04	16 kB	32
32.04	32 kB	64

Magnetic tapes have an extremely high capacity and are relatively cheap. Data is saved in a serial manner with one bit (or one record) at a time. This has the disadvantage that they are relatively slow when moving back and forward within the tape to find the required data. Typically, it may take many seconds (or even minutes) to search from the start to the end of a tape. In most applications, magnetic tapes are used to back up a system. This type of application requires large amounts of data to be stored reliably over time but the recall speed is not important.

The most common types of tape are:

- **Reel-to-reel tapes.** The tapes have two interconnected reels with an interconnecting tape that is tensioned by tension arms. They were used extensively in the past to store computer-type data but have been replaced by 8 mm, QIC and DAT tapes.
- **8 mm video cartridge tapes.** This type of tape was developed for use in video cameras; it is extremely compact. As with videotapes, the tape wraps round the read/write head in a helix.
- **Quarter-inch cartridge (QIC) tapes.** QIC is available in two main sizes: 5.25 inch and 3.5 inch. They give capacities of 40 MB to tens of gigabytes.
- **Digital audio tape (DAT).** This type of tape was developed to be used in hi-fi applications, and is extremely compact. As with the 8 mm tape, the tape wraps round the read/write head in a helix. The tape itself is 4 mm wide and can store several gigabytes of data with a transfer rate of several hundred kbps.

19.9.1 QIC tapes

QIC tapes are available in two sizes: 5.25-inch and 3.5-inch. The tape length ranges from 200 to 1000 feet, with a tape width of 0.25-inch. Typical capacities range from 40 MB to tens of GB. A single capstan drive is driven by the tape drive.

19.9.2 8 mm video tape

The 8 mm video tape is a high-specification tape and was originally used in video cameras. These types are also known as Exabyte after the company that originally developed a back - up system using 8 mm videotapes. They can be used to store several gigabytes of data with a transfer rate of 500 kbps. In order to achieve this high transfer rate, the read/write head spins at 2000 rpm and the tape passes it at a relatively slow speed.

19.10 File Systems

Microsoft Windows (NT/2000) supports three different types of file system:

- FAT (file allocation table) – as used by MS-DOS, OS/2 and Windows NT. A single volume can be up to 2 GB (now increased to over 4 GB). It has no built-in security but can be accessed through Windows 95/98, MS-DOS and Windows NT/2000.
- HPFS (high-performance file system) – a UNIX-style file system used by OS/2 and Windows NT. A single volume can be up to 8 GB. MS-DOS applications cannot access files.
- NTFS (NT file system) – as used by Windows NT. A single volume can be up to 64 TB (based on current hardware, but theoretically 16 exabytes). It has built-in security and also supports file compression/decompression. MS-DOS applications cannot access the file system except when run with Windows NT/2000; Windows 95/98 cannot access the file system.

The FAT file system is used widely and is supported by a variety of operating systems, such as MS-DOS, Windows NT and OS/2. If a system is to use MS-DOS, it must be installed with a FAT file system.

FAT

The FAT (file allocation table) file system uses a root directory (\), with a maximum allowable number of entries. It uses:

- **The FAT**. This defines the files on the drive. The FAT records which clusters are used, which are unused, and where files are located within the clusters. The FAT must be located at a specific place on the disk or partition. For back up there is a copy of the FAT.
- **Clusters**. These define the smallest unit of data storage on the FAT file system. One cluster consists of a fixed number of disk sectors.

FAT supports disk or partition sizes up to 2 GB, and allows a maximum of 65,525 clusters. In general, the larger the size of the clusters, the more space will be wasted.

With FAT, the root directory stores information about each subdirectory and file in the form of individual directory entries. The file's directory entry holds information on its name, size, a data and time stamp, the starting cluster number (which cluster holds the first portion of the file), and the file's attributes (such as read-only, hidden or system).

FAT

The standard MS-DOS FAT file and directory-naming structure allows an 8-character file name and a 3-character file extension with a dot separator (.) between them (the 8.3 file name). It is not case sensitive and the file name and extension cannot contain spaces and other reserved characters, such as:

```
" / \ : ; | = , ^ * ? .
```

With Windows NT/2000 and Windows 95/98, the FAT file system supports long file names of up to 255 characters. The name can also contain multiple spaces and dot separators. File names are not case sensitive, but the case of file names is preserved (a file named `FredDocument.XYz` will be displayed as `FredDocument.XYz` but can be accessed with any of the characters in upper or lower case.

Each file in the FAT table has four attributes or properties: read-only, archive, system and hidden. The FAT uses a linked list, where the file's directory entry contains its beginning FAT entry number. This FAT entry in turn contains the location of the next cluster if the file is larger than one cluster, or a marker that designates this is included in the last cluster. A file that occupies 12 clusters will have 11 FAT entries and 10 FAT links.

HPFS (high-performance file system)

HPFS is supported by OS/2 and is typically used to migrate from OS/2 to Microsoft Windows. It allows long file names of up to 254 characters with multiple extensions. As with Microsoft Windows FAT system, the file names are not case sensitive but do preserve the case. HPFS uses B-tree format to store the file system directory structure. The B-tree format stores directory entries in an alphabetic tree, and binary searches are used to search for the target file in the directory list.

> **FAT32**
>
> FAT32 is an enhanced version of FAT and was used to overcome the 2 GB limit in FAT. It was first used with Windows 95 OSR 2 and has since been used with Windows 98/2000. It enhancements are:
>
> - **32-bit allocation table**. FAT 32 based on a 32-bit file allocation table entries, rather than the 16-bit entries used by the FAT system. As a result, FAT32 supports much larger disk or partition sizes (up to 2 TB).
> - **Smaller clusters**. The FAT32 file system uses smaller clusters than the FAT file system.
> - **Duplicate boot records**.
> - **Any number of entries in the root.**

NTFS (NT file system)

NTFS is the preferred file system for Windows NT/2000 as it makes more efficient usage of the disk and offers increased security. It allows for file systems up to 16 EB (16 exabytes, or 1 billion gigabytes, or 2^{64} bytes). As with HPFS, it uses B-tree format for storing the file system's directory structure. Its main objectives are:

- To increase *reliability*. NTFS automatically logs all directory and file updates, which can be used to redo or undo failed operations resulting from system failures such as power losses, hardware faults, and so on.
- To provide sector sparing (or *hot fixing*). When NTFS finds errors in a bad sector, it causes the data in that sector to be moved to a different section and the bad sector to be marked as bad. No other data is then written to that sector. Thus, the disk fixes itself as it is working and there is no need for disk repair programs (FAT only marks bad areas when formatting the disk).
- Increases file system size (up to 16 EB).
- To enhance security permissions.
- To support POSIX requirements, such as case-sensitive naming, addition of a time stamp to show when the file was last accessed, and hard links from one file (or directory) to another.

19.10.2   Security model

Microsoft Windows (NT/2000) treats all its resources as objects that can only be accessed by authorized users and services. Examples of objects are directories, printers, processes, ports, devices and files. On an NTFS partition, the access to an object is controlled by the security descriptor (SD) structure, which contains an access control list (ACL) and security identifier (SI). The SD contains the user (and group) accounts that have access and permissions to the object. The system always checks the ACL of an object to determine whether the user is allowed to access it.

The main parts of the SI are:

OWNER	Indicates the user account for the object.
GROUP	Indicates the group the object belongs to.
User ACL	The user-controller ACL.
System ACL	System manager controlled ACL.

The ACL file access rights are:

```
Full control      (All)    Change                (RWXD)
Read              (RX)     Add                   (WX)
List              (RX)     Change Permissions    (P)
```

where R identifies read access, W identifies write access, X identifies execute, D identifies delete, and P identifies change permissions. There is also another attribute, named O, which identifies take ownership.

Full control gives all access to all file permissions, and takes ownership of the NTFS volume. The Change rights allows creation of folders and adding files to them, changing data in files, appending data to files, changing file attributes, deleting folders and files, and performing all tasks permitted by the Read permission. The Read permission allows the display of folder and file names, display of the data and attributes of a file, run program files, and access to other subfolders. For example a directory could have the following permissions:

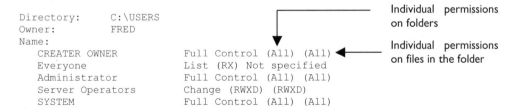

```
Directory:     C:\USERS
Owner:         FRED
Name:
   CREATER OWNER        Full Control (All) (All)
   Everyone             List (RX) Not specified
   Administrator        Full Control (All) (All)
   Server Operators     Change (RWXD) (RWXD)
   SYSTEM               Full Control (All) (All)
```

Individual permissions on folders

Individual permissions on files in the folder

It can be seen in this example that the owner has full control over the directory, but everyone else (apart from the Administrator, Server Operators and SYSTEM) have only list rights (that is, they can only view or run programs or get access to subfolders).

19.11 Exercises

19.11.1 Which of the following is a typical data capacity for a CD-ROM disk?
   (a)   100 MB   (b)   650 MB
   (c)   800 MB   (d)   1 GB

19.11.2 Which interface is most often used in PCs to connect to hard disk drives?
   (a)   ST-506   (b)   ISA
   (c)   EISA   (d)   IDE

19.11.3 Which bus does the IDE share many of its signals with?
   (a)   ST-506   (b)   ISA
   (c)   EISA   (d)   PCI

19.11.4   How many devices can a single IDE bus support?
(a)   1   (b)   2
(c)   4   (d)   7

19.11.5   What is the base address for the primary IDE controller?
(a)   1F0h   (b)   170h
(c)   2F0h   (d)   270h

19.11.6   What is the base address for the secondary IDE controller?
(a)   1F0h   (b)   170h
(c)   2F0h   (d)   270h

19.11.7   What is the main advantage of E-IDE over IDE?
(a)   It is compatible with more hard disk drives
(b)   It allows for larger hard disk capacities
(c)   It is easier to interface to
(d)   It has a large data bus size

19.11.8   What is the main advantage, apart from increased transfer rate, that IDE has over older interface standards, such as ST-506 and ESDI?

19.11.9   Explain how IDE differs from E-IDE and how E-IDE supports larger disk capacities. How does E-IDE use modes to define the maximum transfer rate. Which mode is the fastest?

19.11.10   Show that the maximum capacity of IDE is 528 MB and that the maximum capacity (per disk) is 8.4 GB for E-IDE.

19.11.11   Which IRQ does an IDE connected disk drive normally use and what is the size of its data bus?

19.11.12   A floppy disk ribbon cable has a cable twist to differentiate between the A: drive and the B: drive. How does the ribbon cable that connects two IDE connected drives differ? In addition, how many wires does the ribbon cable have?

19.11.13   Outline how three hard disks and a CD-ROM can be connected to the IDE bus. What settings are required for the disks to connect properly? Which signal line differentiates between a master and a slave?

19.11.14   How are I/O addresses used to communicate with hard disks? How is data transferred to and from the disk? What are the standard address ranges for the primary and the secondary? If possible, check these on an available PC.

19.11.15   Which register is used to identify a hard disk error? Explain its operation.

19.11.16   Which is the IDE signal line that identifies whether a slave device exists?

19.11.17   Prove that 16-bit, 44.1 kHz sampled stereo audio gives over 65 minutes for a 650 MB optical disk.

19.12 Note from the author

There is not much to say about the IDE bus. It works, it's reliable, it's standard, it's cheap, and it's relatively easy to set up. IDE is not very fast, but it doesn't really have to be, as disk drives do not require high data rates. E-IDE improved IDE a great deal and required only a simple change in the BIOS. In conclusion, SCSI is the natural choice for disk drives and allows for much greater flexibility in configuration and also high data rates. But, it tends to be more expensive.

In Chapter 17, we listed the IDE bus as one of the most helpful buses of all time. Over the years, it has interfaced to disk drives, and has even supported the addition of CD-ROM drives. By the flick of a BIOS chip, it supported large capacity disk drives (EIDE). It also requires very little to set it up, as the BIOS is able to determine the capacity of the disk drive and set it up properly. At present, there are no real plans to phase out the IDE bus, thus it is likely to stay a standard part of the motherboard. New synchronous DMA transfers now allow data rates of 33 MB/s and even 66 MB/s.

DVD

Digital versatile disks (DVDs) use the MPEG-2 video format, which allows movies to fit onto a CD-ROM. There are two ways of playing a DVD movie:

- **Hardware-based decoding**. This uses special hardware to decode the MPEG-2 video stream.
- **Software-based decoding**. This uses software to decode the MPEG-2 video stream. Unfortunately, this method requires the processor to process the video stream. It is less expensive than hardware decoding, but ties up the processor.

UNIX workstations and Apple computers, ever since the Mac, have always used the SCSI bus, as it gives easy external disk upgrades but, as few users of PC require to add external disk drives to their computer, there has never really been a great demand for SCSI-based disk drives for the PC. IDE drives have two interrupts lines set aside for themselves, so why not use them to interface to disk drives. The SCSI bus, though, now offers high data rates, improved connectivity, improved command and message structure, and easy upgrades. So why isn't it the standard bus for PC system? Well, it costs more, and it's an Apple thing.

20 SCSI

20.1 Introduction

SCSI (small computer systems interface) has many advantages over IDE, including:

- A single bus system for up to seven connected devices (with SCSI-I).
- It supports many different peripherals, such as hard disks, tape drives, CD-ROMs, and so on.
- It supports device priority where a higher SCSI-ID has priority over a lower SCSI-ID.
- It supports both high-quality connectors and cables, and low-quality connection and ribbon cable.
- It supports differential signals, which gives longer cable lengths.
- Extended support for commands and messaging.
- Devices do not need individual IRQ lines (as they do in IDE) as the controller communicates with the devices.
- It has great potential for faster transfer and enhanced peripheral support.

20.2 SCSI Types

SCSI has an intelligent bus subsystem and can support multiple devices cooperating currently. Each device is assigned a priority. The main types of SCSI are:

- **SCSI-I.** Transfer rate of 5 MB/s with an 8-bit data bus and seven devices per controller.
- **SCSI-II.** Support for SCSI-1 and with one or more of the following:
  - Fast SCSI, which uses a synchronous transfer to give 10 MB/s transfer rate. The initiator and target initially negotiate to see if they can both support synchronous transfer. If they can they, then go into a synchronous transfer mode.
  - Fast/wide SCSI-2, which doubles the data bus width to 16 bits to give 20 MB/s transfer rate.
  - 15 devices per master device.
  - Tagged command queuing (TCQ), which greatly improves performance and is supported by Windows, NetWare and OS/2.
  - Multiple commands sent to each device.
  - Commands executed in whatever sequence will maximize device performance.
- **Ultra SCSI** (SCSI-III). Operates either as 8-bit or 16-bit with either 20 MB/s or 40 MB/s transfer rate.

20.2.1 SCSI-II

SCSI-II supports fast SCSI, which is basically SCSI-I operating at a rate of 10 MB/s (using synchronous versus asynchronous) and wide SCSI, which uses a 64-pin connector and a 16-bit data bus. The SCSI-II controller is also more efficient and processes commands up to seven times faster than SCSI-I.

The SCSI-II drive latency is also much less than SCSI-I due mainly to tag command queuing (TCQ), which allows multiple commands to be sent to each device. Each device then holds its own commands and executes them in whatever sequence will maximize performance (such as by minimizing the latency associated with disk rotation). Table 20.1 contrasts fast SCSI-II and fast/wide SCSI-II. It can be seen that both disks have predictive failure analysis (PFA) and automatic defect reallocation (ADR).

The normal 50-core cable is typically known as A-cable, while the 68-core cable is known as B-cable.

Table 20.1   Comparison of SCSI-II disks

	Seek time (ms)	Latency (ms)	Rotational speed (rpm)	Sustained data read (MB/s)	PFA	ADR
1 GB SCSI-II fast	10.5	5.56	5400	4	✓	✓
4.5 GB SCSI-II fast/ wide	8.2	4.17	7200	12	✓	✓

20.2.2 Ultra SCSI

Ultra SCSI (SCSI-III) allows for 20 MB/s burst transfers on an 8-bit data path and 40 MB/s burst transfer on a 16-bit data path. It uses the same cables as SCSI-II and the maximum cable length is 1.5 m. Ultra SCSI disks are compatible with SCSI-2 controllers; however, the transfer will be at the slower speed of the SCSI controller. SCSI disks are compatible with ultra SCSI controllers; however, the transfer will be at the slower speed of the SCSI disk.

SCSI-I and fast SCSI-II use a 50-pin 8-bit connector, whereas fast/wide SCSI-II and ultra SCSI use a 68-pin 16-bit connector. The 16-bit connector is physically smaller than the 8-bit connector and the 16-bit connector cannot connect directly to the 8-bit connector. The cable used is called P-cable and replaces the A/B-cable.

Note that SCSI-II and Ultra SCSI require an active terminator on the last external device. Table 20.2 compares the main types of SCSI.

Table 20.2   SCSI types

	Data bus (bits)	Transfer rate (MB/s)	Tagged command queuing	Parity checking	Maximum devices	Pins on cable and connector
SCSI-I	8	5	×	×/✓ (optional)	7	50
SCSI-II fast	8	10 (10MHz)	✓	✓	7	50
SCSI-II fast/ wide	16	20 (10MHz)	✓	✓	15	68
Ultra SCSI	16	40 (20MHz)	✓	✓	15	68

20.3 SCSI Interface

In its standard form, SCSI standard uses a 50-pin header connector and a ribbon cable to connect to up to eight devices. It overcomes the problems of the IDE, where devices have to be assigned as a master and a slave. SCSI and fast SCSI transfer one byte at a time with a parity check on each byte. SCSI-II, wide SCSI and ultra SCSI use a 16-bit data transfer and a 68-pin connector. Table 20.3 lists the pin connections for SCSI-I (single-ended cable) and fast SCSI (differential cable), and Table 20.4 lists the pin connections for SCSI-II, wide SCSI and ultra SCSI.

Table 20.3 SCSI-I and Fast SCSI connections

	Single-ended cable				Differential cable		
Pin	Signal	Pin	Signal	Pin	Signal	Pin	Signal
1	GND	2	$\overline{D0}$	1	GND	2	GND
3	GND	4	$\overline{D1}$	3	$+\overline{D0}$	4	$-\overline{D0}$
5	GND	6	$\overline{D2}$	5	$+\overline{D1}$	6	$-\overline{D1}$
7	GND	8	$\overline{D3}$	6	$+\overline{D2}$	8	$-\overline{D2}$
9	GND	10	$\overline{D4}$	8	$+\overline{D3}$	10	$-\overline{D3}$
11	GND	12	$\overline{D5}$	11	$+\overline{D4}$	12	$-\overline{D4}$
13	GND	14	$\overline{D6}$	13	$+\overline{D5}$	14	$-\overline{D5}$
15	GND	16	$\overline{D7}$	15	$+\overline{D6}$	16	$-\overline{D6}$
17	GND	18	$\overline{\text{D(PARITY)}}$	17	$+\overline{D7}$	18	$-\overline{D7}$
19	GND	20	GND	19	D(PARITY)	20	$-\overline{\text{D(PARITY)}}$
21	GND	22	GND	21	DIFFSEN	22	GND
23	RESERVED	24	RESERVED	23	RESERVED	24	RESERVED
25	Open	26	TERMPWR	25	TERMPWR	26	TEMPWR
27	RESERVED	28	RESERVED	27	RESERVED	28	RESERVED
29	GND	30	GND	29	$+\overline{\text{ATN}}$	30	$-\overline{\text{ATN}}$
31	GND	32	$\overline{\text{ATN}}$	31	GND	32	GND
33	GND	34	GND	33	$+\overline{\text{RST}}$	34	$-\overline{\text{RST}}$
35	GND	36	$\overline{\text{BSY}}$	35	$+\overline{\text{ACK}}$	36	$-\overline{\text{ACK}}$
37	GND	38	$\overline{\text{ACK}}$	37	$+\overline{\text{RST}}$	38	$-\overline{\text{RST}}$
39	GND	40	$\overline{\text{RST}}$	39	$+\overline{\text{MSG}}$	40	$-\overline{\text{MSG}}$
41	GND	42	$\overline{\text{MSG}}$	41	$+\overline{\text{SEL}}$	42	$-\overline{\text{SEL}}$
43	GND	44	$\overline{\text{SEL}}$	43	$+\overline{\text{C}}/\text{D}$	44	$-\overline{\text{C}}/\text{D}$
45	GND	46	$\overline{\text{C}}/\text{D}$	45	$+\overline{\text{REQ}}$	46	$-\overline{\text{REQ}}$
47	GND	48	$\overline{\text{REQ}}$	47	$+\overline{\text{I}}/\text{O}$	48	$-\overline{\text{I}}/\text{O}$
49	GND	50	$\overline{\text{I}}/\text{O}$	49	GND	50	GND

20.3.1 Signals

A SCSI bus is made up of a SCSI host adapter connected to a number of SCSI units via a SCSI bus. As all units connect to a common bus, only two units can transfer data at a time, either from one SCSI unit to another or from one SCSI unit to the SCSI host. The great advantage of this transfer is that is does not involve the processor.

Each unit on a SCSI is assigned a SCSI ID address. In the case of SCSI-I, this ranges from 0 to 7 (where 7 is normally reserved for a tape drive). The host adapter takes one of the addresses, thus a maximum of seven units can connect to the bus. Most systems allow the units to take on any SCSI ID address, but older systems required boot drives to be connected to a specific SCSI address. When the system is initially booted, the host adapter sends out a Start Unit command to each SCSI unit. This allows each of the units to start in an orderly manner (and not overloading the local power supply). The host will start with the highest priority address (ID=7) and finishes with the lowest address (ID=0). Typically, the ID is set with a rotating switch selector or by three jumpers.

SCSI defines an initiator control and a target control. The initiator requests a function from a target, which then executes the function, as illustrated in Figure 20.1. The initiator effectively takes over the bus for the time to send a command and the target executes the command and then contacts the initiator and transfers any data. The bus will then be free for other transfers.

The main signals are:

- $\overline{\text{BSY}}$ – indicates that the bus is busy, or not (an OR-tied signal).
- $\overline{\text{ACK}}$ – activated by the initiator to indicate an acknowledgement for a $\overline{\text{REQ}}$ information transfer handshake.
- $\overline{\text{RST}}$ – when active (low) resets all the SCSI devices (an OR-tied signal).
- $\overline{\text{ATN}}$ – activated by the initiator to indicate the attention state.
- $\overline{\text{MSG}}$ – activated by the target to indicate the message phase.
- $\overline{\text{SEL}}$ – activated by the initiator, and used to select a particular target device (an OR-tied signal).
- $\overline{\text{C}}$ / D (control/data) – activated by the target to identify whether there is data or control on the SCSI bus.
- $\overline{\text{REQ}}$ – activated by the target to acknowledge to indicate a request for an $\overline{\text{ACK}}$ information transfer handshake.
- $\overline{\text{I}}$ / O (input/output) – activated by the target to show the direction of the data on the data bus. Input defines that data is an input to the initiator, else it is an output.

Each of the control signals can be true or false. They can be:

- **OR-tied driven**, where the driver does not drive the signal to the false state. In this case, the bias circuitry of the bus terminators pulls the signal false whenever it is released by the drivers at every SCSI device. If any driver is asserted, then the signal is true. The $\overline{\text{BSY}}$, $\overline{\text{SEL}}$ and $\overline{\text{RST}}$ signals are OR-tied. In the ordinary operation of the bus, the $\overline{\text{BSY}}$ and $\overline{\text{RST}}$ signals may be simultaneously driven true by several drivers.
- **Non-OR-tied driven**, where the signal may be actively driven false. No signals other than $\overline{\text{BSY}}$, $\overline{\text{RST}}$ and $\overline{\text{D(PARITY)}}$ are driven simultaneously by two or more drivers.

Table 20.4 SCSI-II, wide SCSI and ultra SCSI

Pin	Signal	Pin	Signal
1	GND	35	GND
2	GND	36	$\overline{\text{D8}}$
3	GND	37	$\overline{\text{D9}}$
4	GND	38	$\overline{\text{D10}}$
5	GND	39	$\overline{\text{D11}}$
6	GND	40	$\overline{\text{D12}}$
7	GND	41	$\overline{\text{D13}}$
8	GND	42	$\overline{\text{D14}}$
9	GND	43	$\overline{\text{D15}}$
10	GND	44	$\overline{\text{D(PARITY1)}}$
11	GND	45	$\overline{\text{ACKB}}$
12	GND	46	GND
13	GND	47	$\overline{\text{REQB}}$
14	GND	48	$\overline{\text{D16}}$
15	GND	49	$\overline{\text{D17}}$
16	GND	50	$\overline{\text{D18}}$
17	TERMPWR	51	TERMPWR
18	TERMPWR	52	TERMPWR
19	GND	53	$\overline{\text{D19}}$
20	GND	54	$\overline{\text{D20}}$
21	GND	55	$\overline{\text{D21}}$
22	GND	56	$\overline{\text{D22}}$
23	GND	57	$\overline{\text{D23}}$
24	GND	58	$\overline{\text{D(PARITY2)}}$
25	GND	59	$\overline{\text{D24}}$
26	GND	60	$\overline{\text{D25}}$
27	GND	61	$\overline{\text{D26}}$
28	GND	62	$\overline{\text{D27}}$
29	GND	63	$\overline{\text{D28}}$
30	GND	64	$\overline{\text{D29}}$
31	GND	65	$\overline{\text{D30}}$
32	GND	66	$\overline{\text{D31}}$
33	GND	67	$\overline{\text{D(PARITY3)}}$
34	GND	68	GND

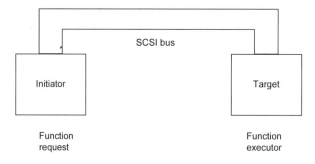

Figure 20.1   Initiator and target in SCSI

20.4 SCSI Operation

The SCSI bus allows any unit to talk to any other unit, or the host to talk to any unit. Thus there must be some way of arbitration where units capture the bus. The main phases that the bus goes through are:

- **Free-bus**. In this state, there are no units that either transfer data or have control of the bus. It is identified by deactivate $\overline{SEL}$ and $\overline{BSY}$ (both will be high). Thus, any unit can capture the bus.
- **Arbitration**. In this state, a unit can take control of the bus and become an initiator. To do this, it activates the $\overline{BSY}$ signal and puts its own ID address on the data bus. After a delay, it tests the data bus to determine whether a high-priority unit has put its own address on the bus. If it has, then it will allow the other unit access to the bus. If its address is still on the bus, then it asserts the $\overline{SEL}$ line. After a delay, it then has control of the bus.
- **Selection**. In this state, the initiator selects a target unit and gets the target to carry out a given function, such as reading or writing data. The initiator outputs the OR value of its SCSI-ID and the SCSI-ID of the target onto the data bus (for example, if the initiator is 2 and the target is 5 then the OR-ed ID on the bus will be 00100100). The target then determines that its ID is on the data bus and set the $\overline{BSY}$ line active. If this does not happen within a given time, then the initiator deactivates the $\overline{SEL}$ signal, and the bus will be free. The target determines that it is selected when the $\overline{SEL}$ signal and its SCSI ID bit are active and the $\overline{BSY}$ and $\overline{I/O}$ signals are false. It then asserts the $\overline{BSY}$ signal within a selection abort time.
- **Reselection**. When the arbitration phase is complete, the winning SCSI device asserts the $\overline{BSY}$ and $\overline{SEL}$ signals and has delayed at least a bus clear delay plus a bus settle delay. The winning SCSI device sets the DATA BUS to a value that is the logical OR of its SCSI ID bit and the initiator's SCSI ID bit. Sometimes, the target takes some time to reply to the initiator's request. The initiator determines that it is reselected when the $\overline{SEL}$ and $\overline{I/O}$ signals and its SCSI ID bit are true and the $\overline{BSY}$ signal is false. The reselected initiator then asserts the $\overline{BSY}$ signal within a selection abort time of its most recent detection of being reselected. An initiator does not respond to a reselection phase if other than two SCSI ID bits are on the data bus. After the target detects that the $\overline{BSY}$ signal is true, it also asserts the $\overline{BSY}$ signal and waits a given time delay and then releases the $\overline{SEL}$ signal. The target may then change the $\overline{I/O}$ signal and the data bus. After the reselected initiator detects the $\overline{SEL}$ signal is false, it releases the $\overline{BSY}$ signal. The target continues to assert

the $\overline{BSY}$ signal until it gives up the SCSI bus.

- **Command**. The command phase is used by the target to request command information from the initiator. The target asserts the $\overline{C}/D$ signal and negates the $\overline{I}/O$ and $\overline{MSG}$ signals during the $\overline{REQ}/\overline{ACK}$ handshake(s) of this phase.

- **Data**. The data phase covers both the data-in and data-out phases. In the data-in phase, the target requests that data be sent to the initiator from the target. For this purpose, the target asserts the $\overline{I}/O$ signal and negates the $\overline{C}/D$ and $\overline{MSG}$ signals during the $\overline{REQ}/\overline{ACK}$ handshake(s) of this phase. In the data-out phase, the target requests that data be sent from the initiator to the target. The target negates the $\overline{C}/D$, $\overline{I}/O$ and $\overline{MSG}$ signals during the $\overline{REQ}/\overline{ACK}$ handshake(s) of this phase.

- **Message**. The message phase covers both the message-out and message-in phases. The first byte transferred in either of these phases can be either a single-byte message or the first byte of a multiple-byte message. Multiple-byte messages are contained completely within a single message phase.

- **Status**. The status phase allows the target to request that status information be sent from the target to the initiator. The target shall assert the $\overline{C}/D$ and $\overline{I}/O$ signals and negate the $\overline{MSG}$ signal during the $\overline{REQ}/\overline{ACK}$ handshake of this phase.

Typical times are:

- **Arbitration delay**, 2–4 μs. This is the minimum time that a SCSI device waits from asserting $\overline{BSY}$ for arbitration until the data bus can be examined to see whether arbitration has been won.

- **Power-on to selection time**, 10 s. This is the maximum time from power start-up until a SCSI target is able to respond with appropriate status and sense data.

- **Selection abort time**, 200 μs. This is the maximum time that a target (or initiator) takes from its most recent detection of being selected (or reselected) until asserting a $\overline{BSY}$ response. This is required to ensure that a target (or initiator) does not assert $\overline{BSY}$ after a select (or reselection) phase has been aborted.

- **Selection time-out delay**, 250ms. The minimum time that a SCSI device should wait for a $\overline{BSY}$ response during the selection or reselection phase before starting the time-out procedure.

- **Disconnection delay**, 200 μs. The minimum time that a target shall wait after releasing $\overline{BSY}$ before participating in an arbitration phase when honouring a disconnect message from the initiator.

- **Reset hold time**, 25 μs. The minimum time for which $\overline{RST}$ is asserted.

The signals $\overline{C}/D$, $\overline{I}/O$ and $\overline{MSG}$ distinguish between the different information transfer phases, as summarized in Table 20.5 (where a 1 identifies an active signal and a 0 identifies a false signal). The target drives these

Table 20.5 Information transfer phases

$\overline{MSG}$	$\overline{C}/D$	$\overline{I}/O$	*Phase*	*Direction*
0	0	0	Data out	Initiator→target
0	0	1	Data in	Initiator←target
0	1	0	Command	Initiator→target
0	1	1	Status	Initiator←target
1	0	0	–	–
1	0	1	–	–
1	1	0	Message out	Initiator→target
1	1	1	Message in	Initiator←target

three signals and therefore controls all changes from one phase to another. The initiator can request a message out phase by asserting the $\overline{\text{ATN}}$ signal, while the target can cause the bus free phase by releasing the $\overline{\text{MSG}}$, $\overline{\text{C}}/\text{D}$, $\overline{\text{I}}/\text{O}$ and $\overline{\text{BSY}}$ signals.

The information transfer phases use one or more $\overline{\text{REQ}}/\overline{\text{ACK}}$ handshakes to control the information transfer. Each $\overline{\text{REQ}}/\overline{\text{ACK}}$ handshake allows the transfer of one byte of information. During the information transfer phases, the $\overline{\text{BSY}}$ signal shall remain true and the $\overline{\text{SEL}}$ signal shall remain false. Additionally, during the information transfer phases, the target shall continuously envelope the $\overline{\text{REQ}}/\overline{\text{ACK}}$ handshake(s) with the $\overline{\text{C}}/\text{D}$, $\overline{\text{I}}/\text{O}$ and $\overline{\text{MSG}}$ signals in such a manner that these control signals are valid for a bus settle delay before the assertion of the $\overline{\text{REQ}}$ signal of the first handshake and remain valid until after the negation of the $\overline{\text{ACK}}$ signal at the end of the handshake of the last transfer of the phase.

The $\overline{\text{I}}/\text{O}$ signal allows the target to control the direction of information; when its $\overline{\text{I}}/\text{O}$ signal is true, then the information is transferred from the target to the initiator; when false, the transfer is from the initiator to the target.

The handshaking operation for a transfer to the initiator is as follows:

- The $\overline{\text{I}}/\text{O}$ signal is asserted as a true.
- The target sets the data bus lines.
- The target asserts the $\overline{\text{REQ}}$ signal.
- The initiator reads the data bus.
- The initiator then indicates its acceptance of the data by asserting the $\overline{\text{ACK}}$ signal.
- The target may change or release the data bus.
- The target negates the $\overline{\text{REQ}}$ signal.
- The initiator shall then negate the $\overline{\text{ACK}}$ signal.
- The target may continue the transfer by driving the data bus and asserting the $\overline{\text{REQ}}$ signal, and so on.

The handshaking operation for a transfer from the initiator is as follows:

- The $\overline{\text{I}}/\text{O}$ signal is asserted as a false.
- The target asserts the $\overline{\text{REQ}}$ signal (requesting information).
- The initiator sets the data bus lines.
- The initiator asserts the $\overline{\text{ACK}}$ signal.
- The target then reads the data bus.
- The target negates the $\overline{\text{REQ}}$ signal (acknowledging transfer).
- The initiator may then set the data bus, and so on.

> **SCSI pointers**
>
> SCSI provides for three pointers for each I/O process (called saved pointers), for command, data and status. When an I/O process becomes active, its three saved pointers are copied into the initiator's set of three current pointers. These current pointers point to the next command, data or status byte to be transferred between the initiator's memory and the target.

20.5 Message System Description

The message system allows the initiator and the target to communicate over the interface connection. Each message can be one, two or multiple bytes in length. In a single message phase, one or more messages can be transmitted (but a message cannot be split between multiple message phases). Table 20.6 lists the message format, where the first byte of the message determines the format. The initiator ends the message out phase (by negating $\overline{\text{ATN}}$)

when it sends certain messages, identified in Table 20.7. Single-byte messages consist of a single byte transferred during a message phase.

Table 20.6 Message format

Value	Message format
00h	One-byte message (command complete)
01h	Extended messages
02h–1Fh	One-byte messages
20h–2Fh	Two-byte messages
30h–7Fh	Reserved
80h–FFh	One-byte message (identify)

Table 20.7 Message codes

Code	Message	Direction	Description
00h	Command complete	In	Sent from a target to an initiator to indicate that the execution of an I/O process has completed and that valid status has been sent to the initiator. After successfully sending this message, the target shall go to the bus-free phase by releasing the $\overline{\text{BSY}}$ signal. The target considers the message transmission to be successful when it detects the negation of $\overline{\text{ACK}}$ for the command complete message with the $\overline{\text{ATN}}$ signal false.
03h	Restore pointers	In	
04h	Disconnect	In/out	Sent from a target to inform an initiator that the present connection is going to be broken (the target plans to disconnect by releasing the $\overline{\text{BSY}}$ signal), but that a later reconnect will be required in order to complete the current I/O process. This message shall not cause the initiator to save the data pointer. After successfully sending this message, the target shall go to the bus-free phase by releasing the $\overline{\text{BSY}}$ signal. The target shall consider the message transmission to be successful when it detects the negation of the $\overline{\text{ACK}}$ signal for the disconnect message with the $\overline{\text{ATN}}$ signal false.
05h	Initiator-detected error	Out	
06h	Abort	Out	Sent from the initiator to the target to clear any I/O process. The target goes to the bus-free phase following successful receipt of this message.
07h	Message reject	Out	Sent from either the initiator or target to indicate that the last message or message byte it received was inappropriate or has not been implemented.

08h	No operation	Out	Sent from an initiator in response to a target's request for a message when the initiator does not currently have any other valid message to send.
09h	Message parity error	Out	
0Ah	Linked command complete	In	
0Bh	Linked command complete (with flag)	In	
0Ch	Bus device reset	Out	Sent from an initiator to direct a target to clear all I/O processes on that SCSI device. This message forces a hard reset condition to the selected SCSI device.
0Dh	Abort tag	Out	
0Eh	Clear queue	Out	
0Fh	Initiate recovery	In/out	
10h	Release recovery	Out	
11h	Terminate I/O process	Out	
12h–1Fh	Reserved		
23h	Ignore wide residue (2 bytes)		
24h–2Fh	Reserved for two-byte messages		
30h–7Fh	Reserved		
80h–FFh	Identify	In/out	

20.6 SCSI Commands

A command is sent from the initiator to the target. The first byte of all SCSI commands contains an operation code, followed by a command descriptor block and finally the control byte.

The format of the command descriptor block for 6-byte commands is:

- Byte 0 – operation code.
- Byte 1 – logical unit number (MSB, if required).
- Byte 2 – logical bock address.
- Byte 3 – logical bock address (LSB, if required).
- Byte 4 – transfer length (if required) / parameter list length (if required) / allocation length (if required).
- Byte 5 – control.

20.6.1 Operation code

Figure 20.2 shows the operation code of the command descriptor block. It has a group code field and a command code field. The 3-bit group code field provides for eight groups of command codes and the 5-bit command code field provides for 32 command codes in each group.

The group code specifies one of the following groups:

- Group 0   – 6-byte commands.
- Group 1/2 – 10-byte commands.
- Group 3/4 – reserved.
- Group 5   – 12-byte commands.
- Group 6/7 – vendor-specific.

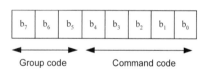

Figure 20.2   Operation code

20.6.2 Logical unit number

The logical unit number (LUN) is defined in the identify message. The target ignores the LUN specified within the command descriptor block if an identify message was received (normally the logical unit number in the command descriptor block is set to zero).

20.6.3 Logical block address

The logical block address (LBA) on logical units or within a partition on device volumes begins with block zero and is contiguous up to the last logical block on that logical unit or within that partition.

10-byte and 12-byte command descriptor blocks contain 32-bit logical block addresses, whereas a 6-byte command descriptor block contains a 21-bit logical block address.

20.6.4 Transfer length

The transfer length field specifies the amount of data to be transferred (normally the number of blocks). For several commands, the transfer length indicates the requested number of bytes to be sent as defined in the command description. A command that uses 1 byte for the transfer length will thus allow up to 256 blocks of data for one command (a value of 0 identifies a transfer bock of 256 blocks).

20.6.5 Parameter list length

The parameter list length specifies the number of bytes to be sent during the data-out phase. It is typically used in command descriptor blocks for parameters that are sent to a target, such as mode parameters, diagnostic parameters, log parameters, and so on.

20.6.6 Control field

The control field is the last byte of every command descriptor block. Its format is shown in Figure 20.3. The flag bit specifies which message the target returns to the initiator if the link bit is a 1 and the command completes without error. If the link bit is 0, then the flag bit should be a 0, else the target returns check condition status.

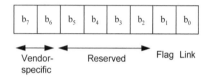

Figure 20.3   Control field

20.6.7 Allocation length

The allocation length field specifies the maximum number of bytes that an initiator has allocated for returned data. The target terminates the data-in phase when allocation length bytes have been transferred or when all available data have been transferred to the initiator, whichever is less. The allocation length is used to limit the maximum amount of data (for example, sense data, mode data, log data, diagnostic data, and so on) returned to an initiator.

20.6.8 Command code

Commands for all device types are (bold type identifies the mandatory commands and the operation code is given in brackets):

- Change definition (40h). This command modifies the operating definition of the selected logical unit or target with respect to commands from the selecting initiator or for all initiators.
- Compare (39h). This command allows for a compare operation of data on one logical unit with another or the same logical unit in a manner similar to the copy command.
- Copy (18h). This command allows the copying of data from one logical unit to another or the same logical unit. The logical unit that receives and performs the copy command is the copy manager. It is responsible for copying data from the source device to the destination device.
- Copy and compare (3Ah). This command performs the same function as the COPY command, except that a verification of the data written to the destination logical unit is performed after the data is written.
- **Inquiry** (12h). This command requests that information regarding parameters of the target and its attached peripheral device(s) be sent to the initiator.
- Log select (4Ch). This command provides a means for the initiator to manage statistical information maintained by the device about the device or its logical units. Targets that implement the log select command shall also implement the log sense command. Structures in the form of log parameters within log pages are defined as a way to manage the log data. The log select command provides for sending zero or more log pages during a data out phase.
- Log sense (4Dh). This command allows the initiator to retrieve statistical information maintained by the device about the device or its logical units. It is a complementary command to the log select command.
- Mode select (15h). This command provides a means for the initiator to specify medium, logical unit, or peripheral device parameters to the target. Targets that implement the mode select command shall also implement the mode sense command.
- Mode sense (1Ah). This command allows a target to report parameters to the initiator and is a complementary command to the mode select command.
- Read buffer (3Ch). This command is used in conjunction with the write buffer command as a diagnostic function for testing target memory and the SCSI bus integrity.
- Receive diagnostic results (1Ch). This command requests analysis data be sent to the initiator after completion of a send diagnostic.
- **Send diagnostic** (1Dh). This command requests the target to perform diagnostic operations on itself, on the logical unit, or on both.
- **Test unit ready** (00h). This command provides a means to check if the logical unit is ready. This is not a request for a self-test. If the logical unit would accept an appropriate medium-access command without returning check condition status, this command shall return a good status.

- Write buffer (3Bh). This command is used in conjunction with the read buffer command as a diagnostic for testing target memory and the SCSI bus integrity.

20.7 Status

The status phase normally occurs at the end of a command (although in some cases may occur before transferring the command descriptor block). Figure 20.4 shows the format of the status byte and Table 20.8 defines the status byte codes. This status byte is sent from the target to the initiator during the status phase at the completion of each command unless the command is terminated by one of the following events:

- Abort message.
- Abort tag message.
- Bus device reset message.
- Clear queue message.
- Hard reset condition.
- Unexpected disconnect.

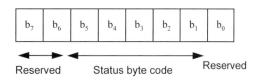

Figure 20.4 Status field

Table 20.8 Status byte codes

Bit values of status byte								Status	Description
7	6	5	4	3	2	1	0		
R	R	0	0	0	0	0	R	Good	Indicates that the target has successfully completed the command.
R	R	0	0	0	0	1	R	Check condition	Indicates that a contingent allegiance condition has occurred.
R	R	0	0	0	1	0	R	Condition met	This status or INTERMEDIATE-CONDITION MET is returned whenever the requested operation is satisfied.
R	R	0	0	1	0	0	R	Busy	Indicates that the target is busy. This status shall be returned whenever a target is unable to accept a command from an otherwise acceptable initiator (that is, no reservation conflicts).
R	R	0	1	0	0	0	R	Immediate	This status or INTERMEDIATE-CONDITION MET shall be returned for every successfully completed command in a series of linked commands (except the last command).
R	R	0	1	0	1	0	R	Immediate-condition met	This status is the combination of the CONDITION MET and INTERMEDIATE statuses.
R	R	0	1	1	0	0	R	Reservation conflict	This status occurs whenever an initiator attempts to access a logical unit that is reserved with a conflicting reservation type for another SCSI device.
R	R	1	0	0	0	1	R	Command conflict	This status occurs whenever the target terminates the current I/O process after receiving a TERMINATE I/O PROCESS message.
R	R	1	0	1	0	0	R	Queue full	This status shall be implemented if tagged queuing is implemented.
R	R	R	R	R	R	R	R	Reserved	

20.8 Exercises

20.8.1   What is the maximum number of devices that can connect to a standard SCSI bus?
    (a)   1   (b)   4
    (c)   7   (d)   8

20.8.2   How many data bits does the SCSI-I bus use?
    (a)   8   (b)   16
    (c)   32   (d)   64

20.8.3   How many data bits does the SCSI-II fast/wide bus use?
    (a)   8   (b)   16
    (c)   32   (d)   64

20.8.4   How is device priority implemented on the SCSI bus?
    (a)   By active polling   (b)   By interrupt priority
    (c)   By brute force   (d)   By unit IDs

20.8.5   What method does the SCSI bus use to prevent devices from hogging the bus?
    (a)   Time-outs   (b)   Interrupts
    (c)   Active polling   (d)   Memory mapping

20.8.6   The transfer clock for a SCSI bus is 20 MHz. Which is the transfer rate for a 16-bit data bus?
    (a)   10 MB/s   (b)   20 MB/s
    (c)   40 MB/s   (d)   80 MB/s

20.8.7   Explain the main differences between SCSI-I, SCSI-II and ultra SCSI. Outline their maximum data throughput, the connectors used and the size of their data buses. Outline some of the advantages of SCSI over buses such as the ISA bus.

20.8.8   State the SCSI lines that are used for simple error detection. Why is it not possible to detect which bits are in error?

20.8.9   Discuss the main system lines that are used in the SCSI bus and the operation of OR-tied driven signals.

20.8.10   Outline the main phases that the initiator and target go through in setting up a connection. Outline the importance of device time-outs for the different SCSI phases.

20.8.11   Discuss how the $\overline{\text{MSG}}$, $\overline{C}/D$ and $\overline{I}/O$ signals are used to set up different transfer phases.

20.8.12   Explain how SCSI uses the SCSI-ID address to set up a device priority system.

20.8.13   Discuss the use of the message phase in SCSI and cite typical examples of its usage.

20.8.14   Discuss the use of the command phase in SCSI and cite typical examples of its usage.

20.8.15   Discuss the use of the status phase in SCSI and cite typical examples.

20.9 Note from the Author

SCSI is a massive area, and one which could fill this book three or four times over. Here, we have, tried to give a flavor of the bus. SCSI stands for 'small computer systems interface'. It is difficult to define exactly what a small computer system is, but SCSI has outgrown its original application of interfacing to 'small' systems and to external disk drives. It now has the potential of being able to interface to virtually any external peripheral to a system. It can also be used to connect devices internally within a system. Typically, it takes a bit longer to initially boot the system, but once it has, it should be as reliable as any non-SCSI device.

An important concept in SCSI is the prioritization of devices using SCSI IDs. Few buses allow the system to prioritize peripherals. Thus, in a properly configured system, fast devices that require to be quickly serviced will always get access onto the bus before slow devices that do not require fast servicing. Unfortunately, the method SCSI uses limits the number of devices to one less than the number of bits on the data bus (seven for an 8-bit data bus and 15 for a 16-bit data bus). In most cases, this is not a major problem. For example, two hard disks, two CD-ROM drives, a tape back-up system, a zip drive and a midi keyboard could all be attached to a standard SCSI-I bus.

In most PCs the IDE drive is still used as it is relatively easy to set up and it is cheap. It is also dedicated to interfacing to the disk drives; thus, no other peripheral can 'hog' the disk drive bus. However, for most general-purpose applications, SCSI is best. New standards for SCSI give a 16-bit data bus, at a transfer rate of 20 MHz, giving a maximum data throughput of 40 MB/s, which is much faster than IDE. It is also much easier to configure a SCSI system than it is to connect peripherals internally in a PC. A SCSI system requires only a single interrupt line for all the devices that are connected.

Ask anyone who has set up a UNIX network, or who has configured an Apple computer, and they will tell you that little to beat a well set-up SCSI bus. It is reliable, and it is easy to upgrade.

PCMCIA (PC Card)

21.1 Introduction

The Personal Computer Memory Card International Association (PCMCIA) interface allows small thin cards to be plugged into laptop, notebook or palm-top computers. The interface was originally designed for memory cards (Version 1.0), but it has since been adopted for many other types of adapters (Version 2.0), such as fax/modems, sound cards, local area network cards, CD-ROM controllers, digital I/O cards, and so on. Most PCMCIA cards comply with either PCMCIA Type II or Type III. Type I cards are 3.3 mm thick, Type II take cards up to 5 mm thick, Type III allows cards up to 10.5 mm thick. A new standard, Type IV, takes cards that are thicker than 10.5 mm. Type II interfaces can accept Type I cards, Type III accept Types I and II, and Type IV interfaces accept Types I, II and III.

The PCMCIA standard uses a 16-bit data bus (D0–D15) and a 26-bit address bus (A0–A25), which gives an addressable memory of 2^{26} bytes (64 MB). The memory is arranged as:

- Common memory and attribute memory, which gives a total addressable memory of 128 MB.
- I/O addressable space of 65,536 (64 k) 8-bit ports.

The PCMCIA interface allows the PCMCIA device to map into the main memory or into the I/O address space. For example, a modem PCMCIA device would map its registers into the standard COM port addresses (such as 3F8h–3FFh for COM1 or 2F8h–2FF for COM2). Any accesses to the mapped memory area will be redirected to the PCMCIA rather than the main memory or I/O address space. These mapped areas are called windows. A window is defined with a START address and a LAST address. The PCMCIA control register contains these addresses.

Table 21.1 shows the pin connections. The main PCMCIA signals are:

Maximum throughput
CardBus (32 bit burst mode)   • Byte mode: 33 MB/sec   • Word mode: 66 MB/sec   • DWord mode: 132 MB/sec   **16-bit Memory Transfers (100 ns minimum cycle)**   • Byte mode: 10 MB/sec   • Word mode: 20 MB/sec   **16-bit I/O Transfers (255 ns minimum cycle)**   • Byte mode: 3.92 MB/sec   • Word mode: 7.84 MB/sec

- A25–A0, D15–D0 – data bus (D15–D0) and a 26-bit memory address (A25–A0) or 16-bit I/O memory address (A15–A0).
- $\overline{\text{CARD DETECT 1}}$, $\overline{\text{CARD DETECT 2}}$ – used to detect whether a card is present in a socket. When a card is inserted one of these lines is pulled to a low level.
- $\overline{\text{CARD ENABLE 1}}$, $\overline{\text{CARD ENABLE 2}}$ – used to enable the upper 8 bits of the data bus ($\overline{\text{CARD ENABLE 1}}$) and/or the lower 8 bits of the data bus ($\overline{\text{CARD ENABLE 2}}$).
- $\overline{\text{OUTPUT ENABLE}}$ – set low by the computer when reading data from the PCMCIA unit.
- $\overline{\text{REGISTER SELECT}}$ – set high when accessing common memory, or set low when accessing attribute memory.
- RESET – used to reset the PCMCIA card.
- REFRESH – used to refresh PCMCIA memory.

- $\overline{WAIT}$ – used by the PCMCIA device when it cannot transfer data fast enough and requests a wait cycle.
- $\overline{WRITE\ ENABLE\ /\ PROGRAM}$ – used to program the PCMCIA device.
- Vpp1, Vpp2 – programming voltages for flash memories.
- READY / $\overline{BUSY}$ – used by the PCMCIA card when it is ready to process more data (when a high) or is still occupied by a previous access (when it is a low).
- $\overline{IOIS16}$ – used to indicate the state of the write-protect switch on the PCMCIA card. A high level indicates that the write-protect switch has been set.
- $\overline{INPACK}$ – used by the PCMCIA card to acknowledge the transfer of a signal.
- $\overline{IOR}$ – used to issue an I/O read access from the PCMCIA card (must be used with an active $\overline{REGISTER\ SELECT}$ signal).
- $\overline{IOW}$ – used to issue an I/O write access to the PCMCIA card (must be used with an active $\overline{REGISTER\ SELECT}$ signal).
- $\overline{SPKR}$ – used by PCMCIA card to send audio data to the system speaker.
- $\overline{STSCHG}$ – used to identify that the card has changed its status.

Table 21.1   PCMCIA connections

Pin	Signal	Pin	Signal	Pin	Signal	Pin	Signal
1	GND	18	Vpp1	35	GND	52	Vpp2
2	D3	19	A16	36	*See below*	53	A22
3	D4	20	A15	37	D11	54	A23
4	D5	21	A12	38	D12	55	A24
5	D6	22	A7	39	D13	56	A25
6	D7	23	A6	40	D14	57	RFU
7	$\overline{CARD\ ENABLE\ 1}$	24	A5	41	D15	58	RESET
8	A10	25	A4	42	*See below*	59	$\overline{WAIT}$
9	$\overline{OUTPUT\ ENABLE}$	26	A3	43	REFRESH	60	$\overline{INPACK}$
10	A11	27	A2	44	$\overline{IOR}$	61	$\overline{REGISTER\ SELECT}$
11	A9	28	A1	45	$\overline{IOW}$	62	$\overline{SPKR}$
12	A8	29	A0	46	A17	63	$\overline{STSCHG}$
13	A13	30	D0	47	A18	64	D8
14	A14	31	D1	48	A19	65	D9
15	*See below*	32	D2	49	A20	66	D10
16	READY / $\overline{BUSY}$	33	$\overline{IOIS16}$	50	A21	67	$\overline{CARD\ DETECT\ 2}$
17	+5V	34	GND	51	+5V	68	GND

Pin 15 $\overline{WRITE\ ENABLE\ /\ PROGRAM}$ Pin 33 $\overline{IOIS16}$ (write protect)
Pin 36 $\overline{CARD\ DETECT\ 1}$ Pin 42 $\overline{CARD\ ENABLE\ 2}$

21.2 PCMCIA Registers

A typical PCMCIA interface controller (PCIC) is the 82365SL. Figure 21.1 shows the main registers for the first socket. The second socket index values are simply offset by 40h. Figure 21.2 shows that the base address of the PCIC is, in Windows, set to 3E0h, by default. Figure 21.2 also shows an example of a FIRST and LAST memory address. The PCIC is accessed using two addresses: 3E0h and 3E1h. The I/O windows 0/1 are accessed through:

- 08h/0Ch for the low byte of the FIRST I/O address.
- 09h/0Dh for the high byte of the FIRST I/O address.

- 0Ah/0Eh for the high byte of the LAST I/O address.
- 0Bh/0Fh for the high byte of the LAST I/O address.

The registers are accessed by loading the register index into 3E0h and then the indexed register is accessed through the 3E1h. The memory windows 0/1/2/3/4 are accessed through:

- 10h/18h/20h/28h/30h for the low byte of the FIRST memory address.
- 11h/19h/21h/29h/31h for the high byte of the FIRST memory address.
- 12h/1Ah/22h/2Ah/32h for the low byte of the LAST memory address.
- 13h/1Bh/23h/2Bh/33h for the high byte of the LAST memory address.
- 14h/1Ch/24h/2Ch/34h for the low byte of the card offset.
- 15h/1Dh/25h/2Dh/35h for the high byte of the card offset.

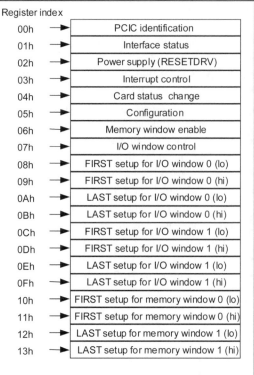

Figure 21.1   PCMCIA controller registers

For example, to load a value of 22h into the Card status change register, the following would be used:

```
_outp(0x3E0,5h);  /* point to Card status change register  */
_outp(0x3E1,22h);  /* load 22h into Card status change register */
```

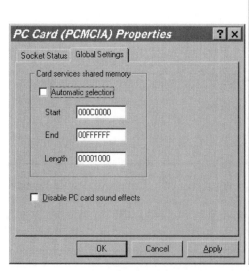
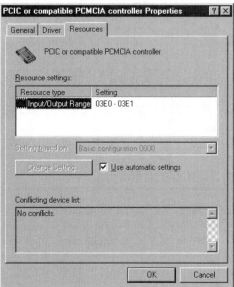

Figure 21.2   Start and end of shared memory and base address of the PCIC

21.2.1 Window enable register

The window enable register has a register index of 06h (and 46h for the second socket). The definition of the register is:

Bit 7   IOW1   I/O window 1 enable (1)/ disable (0).
Bit 6   IOW0   I/O window 0 enable (1)/ disable (0).
Bit 5   DEC   If active (1) $\overline{\text{MEMCS16}}$ generated from A23–A12, else from A23–A17.
Bit 4   MW4   Memory window 4 enable (1)/disable (0).
Bit 3   MW3   Memory window 3 enable (1)/disable (0).
Bit 2   MW2   Memory window 2 enable (1)/disable (0).
Bit 1   MW1   Memory window 1 enable (1)/disable (0).
Bit 0   MW0   Memory window 0 enable (1)/disable (0).

21.2.2 FIRST set up for memory window

The FIRST window memory address is made up of a low byte and a high byte. The format of the high-byte register is:

Bit 7   DS   Data bus size: 16-bit (1)/ 8-bit (0).
Bit 6   0WS   Zero wait states: no wait states (1)/ additional wait states (0).
Bit 5   SCR1   Scratch bit (not used).
Bit 4   SCR0   Scratch bit (not used).
Bit 3–0   Window start address A23–A20.

The format of the low-byte register is:

Bit 7–0   A19–A12. Window start address A19–A12.

21.2.3 LAST set up for memory window

The LAST window memory address is made up of a low byte and a high byte. The format of the high-byte register is:

Bit 7, 6   WS1, WS0   Wait state.
Bit 5, 4   Reserved.
Bit 3–0   A23–A20   Window start address A23–A20.

The format of the low-byte register is:

Bit 7–0   Window start address A19–A12.

21.2.4 Card offset set up for memory window

The card offset memory address is made up of a low byte and a high byte. The format of the high-byte register is:

Bit 7   WP   Write protection: protected (1)/unprotected (0).
Bit 6   REG $\overline{\text{REGISTER SELECT}}$ enabled. If set to a 1, then access to attribute memory, else common memory.
Bit 5–0   Window start address A25–A20.

The format of the low-byte register is:

Bit 7–0   Window start address A19–A12

21.2.5 FIRST set up for I/O window

The FIRST window I/O address is made up of a low byte and a high byte. The format of the high-byte register is:

Bit 7–0   A15–A8

The format of the low-byte register is:

Bit 7–0   A7–A8

21.2.6 LAST setup for I/O window

The LAST window I/O address is made up of a low byte and a high byte. The format of the high-byte register is:

Bit 7–0   A15–A8.

The format of the low-byte register is:

Bit 7–0   A7–A8

21.2.7 Control register for I/O address window

The control register for the I/O address window is made up from a single byte. Its format is:

Bit 7, 3   WS1, WS0   Wait states for window 1 and 0.
Bit 6, 2   0WS1, 0WS0   Zero wait states for window 1 and 0.
Bit 5, 1   CS1, CS0 $\overline{IOIS16}$ source. Select $\overline{IOIS16}$ from PC (1) or select data size from DS1 and DS0 (0).
Bit 4, 0   DS1, DS0.   Data size: 16-bit (1)/ 8-bit (0).

21.2.8 Examples

A typical application of the PCMCIA socket is to use it for a modem. This is an example of a program to set up a modem on the COM2 port. For this purpose, the socket must be set up to map into the I/O registers from 02F8h to 02FFh. Program 21.1 gives some code to achieve this.

```
   Program 21.1
/* load 02f8 into FIRST and 02FFh into LAST registers   */
_outp(0x3E0,08h); /* point to FIRST low byte             */
_outp(0x3E1,f8h); /* load f8h into FIRST low byte        */
_outp(0x3E0,09h); /* point to FIRST high byte            */
_outp(0x3E1,02h); /* load 02h into FIRST high byte       */

_outp(0x3E0,0Ah); /* point to LAST low byte              */
_outp(0x3E1,ffh); /* load ffh into LAST low byte         */

_outp(0x3E0,0Bh); /* point to LAST high byte             */
_outp(0x3E1,02h); /* load 02h into LAST high byte        */
/*setup control register:
      no wait states, 8-bit data access   */
_outp(0x3E0,07h); /* point to I/O Control register       */
_outp(0x3E1,00h); /* load 00h into register              */
/* enable window 0 */
_outp(0x3E0,06h); /* point to memory enable window       */
_outp(0x3E1,04h);
    /* load 0100 0000b to enable I/O window 0*/
```

21.3 Exercises

21.3.1 How many data bits does the PCMCIA bus have?
- (a) 8
- (b) 16
- (c) 24
- (d) 32

21.3.2 How are devices typically added to the system?
- (a) They are mapped into the I/O memory address
- (b) They connect directly into the physical address of the system
- (c) They use polled interrupts
- (d) They interface to a main controller

21.3.3 What is the base address of the registers that are used to program the PCMCIA device?
- (a) 1E0h
- (b) 2E0h
- (c) 3E0h
- (d) 4E0h

21.3.4 Prove that the maximum address memory with PCMCIA is 64 MB.

21.3.5 Explain how I/O registers are used to program the PCMCIA device.

21.3.6 Show the lines of C code that would be required to mount a primary serial port (3F8h–3FFh) and an ECP printer port (378h–37Ah).

21.3.7 Show the lines of C code that would be required to mount a primary (1F0h–1F7h) and a secondary hard disk (170h–177h).

21.3.8 How would the programming for extra memory differ from an isolated I/O device?

> **Minature card**
>
> Miniature Card provides for a Linear Flash interface, which requires no ASICs, microcontrollers, or hardware overhead. The low-cost connector reduces costs by requiring no connector on the card and no ejection mechanism on the host. It is 73 per cent smaller than a PC card (38mm x 33mm x 3.5mm). Typical applications are memory expansions (Flash/DRAM) for PDA/Palmtops, and image data storage for digital cameras.

> **SmartMedia card**
>
> PCMCIA has, in the past, added the Small PC Card form factor specifications to the PC Card Standard, along with the Miniature Card Standard. Soon, PCMCIA will be publishing the SmartMedia Card Standard which should provides memory modules with one of the smallest modular peripheral form factors.

21.4 Additional: PCMCIA Types and Pin Connections

Table 21.2   PCMCIA connections

	PC Card	Small PC card	Miniature card	SmartMedia card	MulitMedia card	CompactFlash
Length (mm)	85.6	45.0	33.0	45.0	32.0	36.0
Width (mm)	54.0	42.8	38.0	37.0	24.0	43.0
Height (mm)	3.3/5.0/10.5	3.3/5.0/10.5	3.5	0.76	1.4	3.3/5.0
Connector	Pin/socket	Pin/socket	Elastomeric	Surface	Surface	Pin/socket
Contacts	68	68	60	22	7	50
Interfaces	Memory, I/O, CardBus	Memory, I/O	Memory (DRAM, Flash, ROM)	Memory (Flash, ROM)	Memory (Flash, ROM)	Memory

Pin	16-Bit Memory	16-Bit I/O and Mem	32-Bit CardBus	Pin	16-Bit Memory	16-Bit I/O and Mem	32-Bit CardBus
1	GND	GND	GND	35	GND	GND	GND
2	D3	D3	CAD0	36	CD1#	CD1#	CCD1#
3	D4	D4	CAD1	37	D11	D11	CAD2
4	D5	D5	CAD3	38	D12	D12	CAD4
5	D6	D6	CAD5	39	D13	D13	CAD6
6	D7	D7	CAD7	40	D14	D14	RSRVD
7	CE1#	CE1#	CCBE0#	41	D15	D15	CAD8
8	A10	A10	CAD9	42	CE2#	CE2#	CAD10
9	OE#	OE#	CAD11	43	VS1#	VS1#	CVS1
10	A11	A11	CAD12	44	RSRVD	IORD#	CAD13
11	A9	A9	CAD14	45	RSRVD	IOWR#	CAD15
12	A8	A8	CCDE1#	46	A17	A17	CAD16
13	A13	A13	CPAR	47	A18	A18	RSRVD
14	A14	A14	CPERR#	48	A19	A19	CBLOCK#
15	WE#	WE#	CGNT#	49	A20	A20	CSTOP#
16	READY	IREQ#	CINT#	50	A21	A21	CDEVSEL#
17	Vcc	Vcc	Vcc	51	Vcc	Vcc	Vcc
18	Vpp1	Vpp1	Vpp1	52	Vpp2	Vpp2	Vpp2
19	A16	A16	CClk	53	A22	A22	CTRDY
20	A15	A15	CIRDY#	54	A23	A23	CFRAME#
21	A12	A12	CCBE2#	55	A24	A24	CAD17
22	A7	A7	CAD18	56	A25	A25	CAD19
23	A6	A6	CAD20	57	VS2#	VS2#	CVS2
24	A5	A5	CAD21	58	RESET	RESET	CRST#
25	A4	A4	CAD22	59	WAIT#	WAIT#	CSERR#
26	A3	A3	CAD23	60	RSRVD	INPACK#	CREQ#
27	A2	A2	CAD24	61	REG#	REG#	CCBE3#
28	A1	A1	CAD25	62	BVD2	SPKR#	CAUDIO
29	A0	A0	CAD26	63	BVD1	STSCHG#	CSTSCHG
30	D0	D0	CAD27	64	D8	D8	CAD28
31	D1	D1	CAD29	65	D9	D9	CAD30
32	D2	D2	RSVD	66	D10	D10	CAD31
33	WP	IOIS16#	CCLKRUN#	67	CD2#	CD2#	CCD2#
34	GND	GND	GND	68	GND	GND	GND

21.5   Note from the Author

PCMCIA devices are good, but they tend to be relatively expensive. Their principal use is to add a network adapter or a modem to a notebook computer. They are typically not used to add to the memory of the notebook or to increase its hard disk space (an internal upgrade is much better for these). Their growth in the future are likely to be in PDAs and Palmtop computers. Personally, I find them a little too thin, and I do not believe they can hold all the required electronics, but I remember when transistors were the size of your thumb, whereas now you can get 100 million transistors on your thumb.

22 USB and Firewire

22.1 Introduction

USB (universal serial bus) allows for the connection of medium bandwidth peripherals such as keyboards, mice, tablets, modems, telephones, CD-ROM drives, printers and other low-to-moderate speed external peripherals in a tiered-star topology. Its basic specification is:

- Isochronous ('continuous') transfers, which supports audio and video. With isochronous data transfers, devices transmit and receive data in a guaranteed and predictable fashion. USB also supports non-isochronous devices (the highest priority); both isochronous and non-isochronous can exist at the same time.

- Standardized industry-wide plug-and-play specification, cables and connections.

- Multiple-tiered hubs with almost unlimited expansion (with up to 127 physical devices), and concurrent operations.

- 12 Mbps transfer rate and different packet sizes. It supports many device bandwidth requirements from a few kbps to 12 Mbps.

- Wide range of device data rates by accommodating packet buffer size and latencies.

- A hot-plug capability, which allows peripherals to be connected without powering down the computer. Dynamically attachable and reconfigurable peripherals.

- Enhanced power management with system hibernation and sleep modes.

- Self-identifying peripherals, automatic mapping of function to driver and configuration.

- Support for compound devices that have multiple functions.

- Flow control for buffer handling built into protocol.

- Error handling/fault recovery mechanism.

- Support for identification of faulty devices.

- Simple protocol to implement and integrate.

> **PC evolution**
>
> The PC is now evolving into a powerful system through:
>
> - Microprocessor developments.
> - Improved graphics systems, such as AGP.
> - Faster processor and system clocks.
> - The PCI bus architecture, especially the PCI bridge.
> - Improved plug-and-play technology and automated set-up. The USB port aids in its ease of connection.

> **USB connected devices**
>
> Typical examples of USB connected devices are:
>
> - Digital speakers/microphones.
> - Joysticks.
> - Scanners/modems/printers/ monitors.
> - Game controllers/graphics tablets.
> - Video conferencing cameras.
> - Musical interfaces, such as MIDI.

USB is a balanced bus architecture that hides the complexity of the operation from the devices connected to the bus. The USB host controller controls system bandwidth. Each device is assigned a default address when the USB device is first powered or reset. Hubs and functions are assigned a unique device address by USB software.

22.2 USB

USB uses a four-wire cable to connect to devices. One pair of the twisted-pair lines gives the differential data lines (D+ and D–), while the other two gives a 5 V and a GND supply rail, as given in Table 22.1.

Table 22.1	USB connections	
Pin	Name	Description
1	V_{CC}	$+5\,V_{DC}$
2	D–	Data–
3	D+	Data+
4	GND	Ground

With USB 1.0, data transfer rate is up to 12 Mbps, with a 1.5 Mbps subchannel for low data rate devices (such as a mouse). A single unit can connect directly to the PC, but a hub is required when more than one device is connected. Each peripheral can extend up to 5 m from each hub connection, with a maximum of 127 different devices to a single PC.

22.2.1 Bus protocol

Each bus transaction involves the transmission of up to three packets. These are

USB features

- Easy to use.
- Self-identifying peripherals with automatic mapping of function to driver and configuration.
- Dynamically attachable and reconfigurable peripherals.
- Low/medium-speed transfer rate of 1.5 Mbps or 12 Mbps.

- **Token packet transmission.** On a scheduled basis, the host controller sends a USB packet that describes the type and direction of a transaction, the USB device address and endpoint number. The addressed USB device selects itself by decoding the appropriate address fields.
- **Data packet transmission.** The source of the transaction then sends a data packet, or indicates it has no data to transfer.
- **Handshake packet transmission.** Destination device responds with a handshake packet to indicate whether the transfer was successful.

USB supports two types of transfers: stream and message. A stream has no defined structure, whereas a message does. At start-up, one message pipe, control pipe 0, always exists as it provides access to the device's configuration, status and control information.

The USB protocol supports hardware or software error handling. In hardware error handling, the host controller retries three times before informing the client software of the error. Each packet includes a CRC field, which detects all single-and double-bit errors, as well as many multi-bit errors. Typically, error conditions are short-term.

A major advantage of USB is the hot attachment and detachment of devices. USB does this by sensing when a device is attached or detached. When this happens, the host system is notified, and system software interrogates the device. It then determines its capabilities, and automatically configures the device. All the required drivers are then loaded and applications can immediately make use of the connected device.

22.2.2 Data transfers types

USB optimizes large data transfers and real-time data transfers. When a pipe is established for an endpoint, most of the pipe's transfer characteristics are determined and remain fixed for the lifetime of the pipe. Transfer characteristics that can be modified are described for each transfer type.

USB defines four transfer types:

- **Control transfers.** Bursty, non-periodic, host-software-initiated request/response communication typically used for command/status operations.

- **Isochronous transfers.** Periodic, continuous communication between host and device typically used for time-relevant information. This transfer type also preserves the concept of time encapsulated in the data. This does not imply, however, that the delivery needs of such data are always time-critical.

- **Interrupt transfers.** Small data, non-periodic, low frequency, bounded latency, device- initiated communication typically used to notify the host of device service needs.

- **Bulk transfers.** Non-periodic, large bursty communication typically used for data that can use any available bandwidth and also is delayed until bandwidth is available.

22.2.3 USB implementation

There are two main ways to implement USB. These are:

> **Attachment of USB devices**
>
> All USB devices attach to the USB via a port on specialized USB devices known as hubs. Hubs indicate the attachment or removal of a USB device in its per port status. The host queries the hub to determine the reason for the notification. The hub responds by identifying the port used to attach the USB device. The host enables the port and addresses the USB device with a control pipe using the USB default address. All USB devices are addressed using the USB default address when initially connected or after they have been reset. The host determines whether the newly attached USB device is a hub or a function and assigns a unique USB address to the USB device. The host establishes a control pipe for the USB device using the assigned USB address and endpoint number zero. If the attached USB device is a hub and USB devices are attached to its ports, then the above procedure is followed for each of the attached USB devices. If the attached USB device is a function, then attachment notifications will be dispatched by USB software to interested host software.

- **OHCI (open host controller interface).** This method defines the register level interface that enables the USB controller to communicate with the host computer and the operating system. OHCI is an industry standard hardware interface for operating systems, device drivers, and the BIOS to manage the USB. It optimizes performance of the USB bus while minimizing CPU overhead to control the USB. Its main features are:

  - Scatter/gather busmaster hardware support reduces CPU overhead to handle multiple data transfers across the USB.
  - Efficient isochronous data transfers allow for high USB bandwidth without slowing down the host CPU.
  - Assurance of full compatibility with all USB devices.

- **UHCI (universal host controller interface).** This method defines how the USB controller talks to the host computer and its operating system. It is optimized to minimize host computer design complexity and uses the host CPU to control the USB bus. Its main features are:

  - Simple design reduces the transistor count required to implement the USB interface on the host computer, thus reducing system cost.
  - Assurance of full compatibility with all USB devices.

The PCI bridge device (PIIX3/PIIX4) contains a USB host controller (HC) with a root hub with two USB ports. This allows two USB peripheral devices to communicate directly with the PCI bridge without an external hub. When more than two USB devices need to be connected, then an external hub can be added. The USB's PCI configuration registers are located in the PCI configuration space.

The host controller uses the UHCI standard and thus uses UHCI standard software drivers. It basically consists of two parts:

- **Host controller driver (HCD)**. This is the software that manages the host controller operation and is responsible for scheduling the traffic on USB by posting and maintaining transactions in system memory. It interprets requests from the USBD and builds frame list, transfer descriptor, queue head and data buffer data structures for the host controller. These data structures are built in system memory and contain all necessary information to provide end-to-end communication between client software in the host and devices on the USB. The host controller moves data between system memory and devices on the USB by processing these data structures and generating the transaction on USB. The host controller executes the schedule lists generated by HCD and reports the status of transactions on the USB to HCD. Command execution includes generating serial bus token and data packets based on the command and initiating transmission on USB. For commands that require the host controller to receive data from the USB device, the host controller receives the data and then transfers it to the system memory pointed to by the command. The UHCI's HCD provides sufficient commands and data to keep ahead of the host controller execution and analyzes the results as the commands are completed.

- **Host controller (HC)**. The host controller interfaces to the USB system software in the host via the HCD.

USB host: hardware and software

The USB host interacts with USB devices through the host controller. The host is responsible for the following:

- Detecting the attachment and removal of USB devices.
- Managing control flow between the host and USB devices.
- Managing data flow between the host and USB devices.
- Collecting status and activity statistics.
- Providing a limited amount of power to attached USB devices.

USB system software on the host manages interactions between USB devices and host-based device software. There are five areas of interactions between USB system software and device software:

- Device enumeration and configuration.
- Isochronous data transfers.

> **Removal of USB devices**
>
> When a USB device has been removed from one of its ports, the hub automatically disables the port and provides an indication of device removal to the host. Then the host removes knowledge of the USB device. If the removed USB device is a hub, then the removal process must be performed for all of the USB devices that were previously attached to the hub. If the removed USB device is a function, removal notifications are sent to interested host software.

> **USB host controller registers**
>
> VID (vendor identification register):
>
> | | |
> |---|---|
> | Address offset | 00–01h |
> | Default value | 8086h |
> | Attribute | Read only |
>
> The VID register contains the vendor identification number. This register, along with the device identification register, uniquely identifies any PCI device. Writes to this register have no effect. Bit description 15:0 vendor identification number. This is a 16-bit value assigned by Intel.

- Asynchronous data transfers.
- Power management.
- Device and bus management information.

Whenever possible, USB software uses existing host system interfaces to manage the above interactions. For example, if a host system uses advanced power management (APM) for power management, USB system software connects to the APM message broadcast facility to intercept suspend and resume notifications.

> **USB host controller registers**
>
> DID (device identification register):
>
> | | |
> |---|---|
> | Address offset | 02–03h |
> | Default value | 7112h |
> | Attribute | Read only |
>
> The DID register contains the device identification number. This register, along with the VID register, defines the USB host controller.

22.2.4 USB system connection

Figure 22.1 shows an example connection of the USB port into the system. The CLK48 input is fed by a 48 MHz crystal clock (2500 ppm tolerance) and is used to create a data rate of 12 MHz (±0.25%) and an initial frame interval of 1.0 ms (500 ppm). The PCI IDE/ISA accelerator device (PCI bridge) has an integrated UHCI design with either 1.5 Mbps or 12 Mbps transfer rate. The power for the device is fed from the supply on the +5 V motherboard supply (V_{cc}), thus there must be some protection for a short circuit; this is provided for with a 2.0 A fuse. The system also monitors the status of the USB power supply lines with the OC#1 and OC#0 lines. When the PCI bridge device detects a fault on the supply line it disables the corresponding USB port.

On the data lines there are 27 Ω serial resistors, which will also limit the current when there is a short circuit to ground (GND). The current will thus be limited to less than 185 mA (5 V/27 Ω). Series inductors are also included on the power supply line, so that electrical noise on external devices does not affect the power supply on the motherboard.

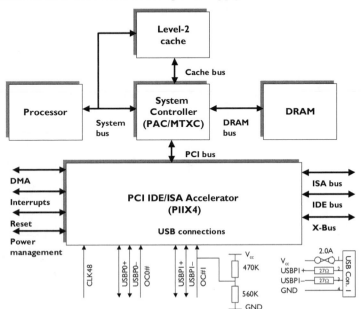

Figure 22.1 USB system connections

22.2.5 USB 2.0

The USB Version 1 port has been a great success and is now a standard port on most PCs. Its main problem is that it is still relatively slow to truly integrate many of the peripherals onto a single interconnection. This has been overcome with USB 2.0, which allows a data transfer rate of up to 480 Mbps, while keeping compatibility with USB 1.0. The main classifications for USB 2.0 are:

- **Low-speed** (1.5 Mbps): interactive devices. Typically 10–100 kbps.
- **Full-speed** (12 Mbps): phone and audio applications. Typically 500 kbps to 10 Mbps.
- **High-speed** (480 Mbps): video and storage applications. 25–400 Mbps.

The USB 2.0 port will accelerate the move toward a totally legacy-free PC. Figure 22.2 shows a possible PC of the future, where a memory hub is used to provide a fast data transfer (GB/s), while the Firewire connection gives an ultra-high-speed connection for video transfers. The USB connection provides low-high and full-speed connections to most of the peripherals that connect to the system. The USB connections can be internal or can connect to an external hub. The great advantage of USB is that it allows for peripherals to be added and deleted from the system without causing any system upsets. The system will also automatically sense the connected device and load the required driver.

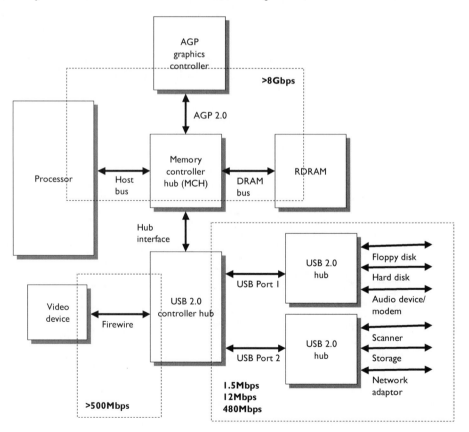

Figure 22.2   Legacy-free system

22.3 Firewire

The main competitor to USB is the Firewire standard (IEEE 1394–1995), which is a high-speed serial bus for desktop peripheral devices, typically for video transfers. It supports rates of approximately 100, 200 and 400 Mbps, known as S100, S200 and S400 respectively. Future standards promise higher data rates, and ultimately it is envisaged that rates of 3.2 Gbps will be achieved when optical fiber is introduced into the system. It is generally more expensive than USB to implement for both the host computer and peripherals.

Firewire also complements USB in that it

> **Firewire features**
>
> - 100/200/400 Mbps transfer rate.
> - Point-to-point interconnect with a tree topology; 1,000 buses with 64 nodes gives 64,000 nodes.
> - Automatic configuration and hot-plugging.
> - Isochronous data transfer, where a fixed bandwidth is dedicated to a particular peripheral.
> - Maximum cable length of 4.5 m.

supports high-speed peripherals, whereas USB supports low-to-medium-speed peripherals. It is an attractive alternative to technologies such as SCSI, and it may provide a universal connection to replace many of the older connectors normally found at the back of a standard PC. This should subsequently reduce the costs of production of computer interfaces and peripheral connectors, as well as simplifying the requirements placed on users when setting up their devices. This is made possible by the following features of the IEEE-1394 bus:

- Hot-pluggable – devices can be added or removed while the bus is still active.
- Easy to use – there are no terminators, device addressing or elaborate configuration often associated with technologies like SCSI.
- Flexible topology – devices can be connected together in many configurations, thus the user need not consider logical locations on the network.
- Fast – suitable for high-bandwidth applications.
- Rate mixing – a single cable medium can carry a mix of different speed capabilities at the same time.
- Inexpensive – targeted at consumer devices.

22.3.1 Topology

There are two bus categories:

- **Cable**. This is a bus that connects external devices via a cable. The cable environment is a non-cyclic network with finite branches consisting of bus bridges and nodes (cable devices). Non-cyclic networks contain no loops and results in a tree topology, with devices daisy-chained and branched (where more than one device branch is connected to a device). Figure 22.3 shows an example of an IEEE-1394 splitter, which has three branches and the telephone is daisy-chained from the digital camera.

   The finite branches restriction imposes a limit of 16 cable hops between nodes. Therefore branching should be used to take advantage of the maximum number of nodes on a bus. 6-bit node addressing allows up to 63 nodes on each bus, while 10-bit bus addressing allows up to 1,023 buses, interconnected using IEEE-1394 bridges. Devices on the bus are identified by node IDs. Configuration of the node IDs is performed by the self ID and tree ID processes after every bus reset. This happens every time a device is added to or removed from the bus, and is invisible to the user.

   A final restriction is that, using standard cables, the length between nodes is limited to 4.5 m. This can be increased by adding repeaters between nodes, but lengths are expected to improve as work on the standard ensues. Although a PC is shown in Figure 22.3, a principal advantage of IEEE-1394 is that, unlike USB, no PC is actually required to form a bus, and devices can talk to each other without intervention from a computer.

- **Backplane**. This type is an internal bus. An internal IEEE-1394 device can be used alone, or incorporated into another backplane bus. For example, two pins are reserved for a serial bus by various ANSI and IEEE bus standards. Implementation of the back-plane specification lags the development of the cable environment, but one could image internal IEEE-1394 hard disks in one computer being directly accessed by another IEEE-1394 connected computer.

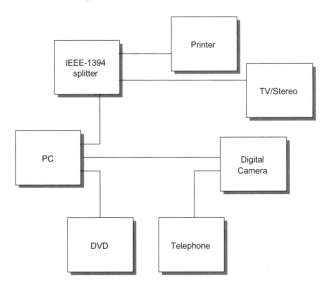

Figure 22.3   IEEE-1394 topology example

22.3.2 Asynchronous and isochronous transfer

One of the key capabilities of IEEE-1394 is isochronous data transfer. Both asynchronous and isochronous are supported, and are useful for different applications. Isochronous transmission transmits data like real-time speech and video, both of which must be delivered uninterrupted, and at the rate expected, whereas asynchronous transmission is used to transfer data that is not tied to a specific transfer time. With IEEE-1394, asynchronous transmission is the conventional transfer method of sending data to an explicit address, and receiving confirmation when it is received. Isochronous, however, is an unacknowledged guaranteed bandwidth transmission method, useful for just-in-time delivery of multimedia-type data.

An isochronous 'talker' requests an amount of bandwidth and a channel number. Once the bandwidth has been allocated, it can transmit data preceded by a channel ID. The isochronous *listeners* can then listen for the specified channel ID and accept the data following. If the data is not intended for a node, it will not be set to listen on the specific channel ID. Up to 64 isochronous channels are available, and these must be allocated, along with their respective bandwidths, by an isochronous resource manager on the bus.

Figure 22.4 shows an example situation where two isochronous channels are allocated. These have a guaranteed bandwidth, and any remaining bandwidth is used by pending asynchronous transfers. Thus, isochronous traffic takes some priority over asynchronous traffic.

By comparison, asynchronous transfers are sent to explicit addresses on the 1394 bus (Figure 22.5). When data is to be sent, it is preceded by a destination address, which each node checks to identify packets for itself. If a node finds a packet addressed to itself, it copies it into its receive buffer. Each node is identified by a 16-bit ID, containing the 10-bit bus ID and 6-bit node or physical ID. The actual packet addressing, however, is 64 bits wide, providing a further 48 bits for addressing a specific offset within a node's memory. This addressing conforms to the control and status register (CSR) bus architecture standard. The ISO/IEC 13213:1994 minimizes the amount of circuitry required by 1394 ICs to interconnect with standard parallel buses. The 48-bit offset allows for the addressing of 256 terabytes of memory and registers on each node.

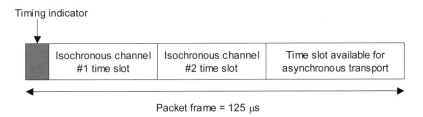

Figure 22.4   Bandwidth allocation on the IEEE-1394 bus

22.3.3 IEEE-1394 packet formats

There are a number of different packet formats specified in 1394–1995. However, only the asynchronous block write will be presented here, as it is the main transaction type used within this project.

The asynchronous block write is described in the 1394–1995 specification as a packet type that requests that a data block be written to the specified destination address. It is the packet type used on asynchronous transmits for a variable length of data (Figure 22.5).

The destination_ID field should contain the 16-bit destination node ID, while the destination_offset field contains the remaining 48 bits required for CSR addressing. The data is sent in the data field, which can be any quadlet-aligned length up to a maximum given by the transmission speed. At 200 Mbps, for example, the data field may hold anything from 0 to 1,024 bytes, in stages of 4 bytes. The header information is followed by a CRC (cyclic redundancy check) for error checking, as is the block of data.

22.3.4 Bus management

Two bus management entities are available in the cable environment: the isochronous resource manager and the bus manager. They provide services such as maintaining topology maps, or acting as a central resource from which bandwidth and channel allocations can be made. Further information on bus management can be found in the 1394–1995 specification.

22.3.5 Cable

Figure 22.6 shows that the 1394 cable consists of three individually shielded cable pairs. There are two power lines and two (screened) twisted pairs for data and strobe transmission.

22.3.6 Transmission rates

As discussed already, the cable rate definitions for 1394–1995 are termed S100, S200 and S400; they give data rates of 98.304 Mbps, 196.608 Mbps and 393.216 Mbps, respectively. The high data rates are achieved by using differential non-return to zero (nrz), signalling on each shielded twisted pair.

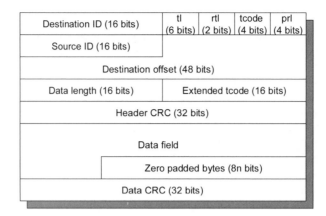

Destination ID (16 bits)	tl (6 bits)	rtl (2 bits)	tcode (4 bits)	prl (4 bits)
Source ID (16 bits)				
Destination offset (48 bits)				
Data length (16 bits)	Extended tcode (16 bits)			
Header CRC (32 bits)				
Data field				
Zero padded bytes (8n bits)				
Data CRC (32 bits)				

Figure 22.5 Asynchronous write data block payload

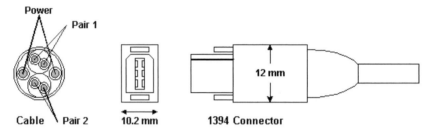

Figure 22.6 IEEE-1394 cable and connectors

22.4 Exercises

22.4.1 How many USB ports are available from the host controller on a PC (PIIX3/4)?
(a) 1   (b) 2
(c) 4   (d) 8

22.4.2 What is the maximum data rate for USB 1.0?
(a) 1 Mbps   (b) 10 Mbps
(c) 12 Mbps   (d) 100 Mbps

22.4.3 What is the maximum data rate for USB 2.0?
(a) 400 Mbps   (b) 480 Mbps
(c) 800 Mbps   (d) 1 Gbps

22.4.4 What is likely to be the main application for Firewire?
(a) Memory transfers   (b) Real-time video
(c) Text   (d) Networking

22.4.5 Which of the following are isochronous?
(a) File transfer   (b) Network transfer
(c) Mouse data   (d) Digital audio

22.4.6 Which of the following is the most likely to burst data:
(a) Text chat   (b) Network transfer
(c) Teletex   (d) Digital audio

22.4.7   Discuss the advantages of USB connected devices over:

(i)   ISA devices
(ii)   PCI devices
(iii)   Serial/parallel port connected devices

22.4.8   Outline the main difference between isochronous and asynchronous data traffic. In which applications is it isochronous?

22.4.9   Outline the main types of data transfer on the USB port.

22.4.10   By searching the Internet or a computer catalogue, locate some USB connected devices.

22.5 Note from the Author

Congratulations go to the USB port. It was the first truly generic, easy-to-use, connection bus for the PC that had mechanisms for non-real-time data (such as printer data) and real-time data (such as video, audio and speech). It allows for the easy addition and removal of devices from the system, and it also supports hot-plugging (adding or removing a device while the computer is on). Microsoft first supported USB in Windows 95 OSR2, and it has since become one of the most used ports for devices such as video cameras, CD-ROM drives, printers, digital speakers, monitors, and so on. The only problem with USB is that it only gives a data throughput of 12 Mbps, and thus cannot be used for high-speed devices. Over time, this rate may be increased, or other faster buses, such as Firewire, could be used for high-speed applications, such as Fast Ethernet, multimedia communications, hard disk inter-faces, and so on.

23 Games Port, Keyboard and Mouse

23.1 Introduction

The games port, the keyboard and the mouse are also relatively slow devices, which, in their standard forms, all have different connectors. In the future, PCs may standardize these low- and medium-speed devices on the USB port. The keyboard port and mouse port are now standard items on a PC, and most PCs now have a games port, which supports up to two joysticks.

Most PCs support either a PS/2-style mouse or a mouse connected to the serial port (COM1: or COM2:). The operating system automatically scans all the mouse and keyboard ports to determine where the mouse is connected to, and whether there is a keyboard connected.

Typically, these days, a mouse connects to the PS/2 port, which is basically an extension of the keyboard port. The keyboard connects to either a 5-pin DIN plug or, more typically on modern PCs, to a smaller 5-pin plug. With the smaller connector, the PS/2 mouse and the keyboard can share the same port (this is typical in new PCs and also for notebooks).

23.2 Games Port

The PC was never really designed to provide extensive games support, but as it is so general-purpose, it is now used to run arcade-style games. A mouse is well designed for precise movements and to select objects, but it is not a good device to play

PC setup

PCs have traditionally been difficult to connect to and set up, for reasons such as:

- **Different connectors.** There are many different types of connectors for many different types of devices that connect to the PC. For example, the keyboard uses a 5-pin DIN plug, the parallel port uses a 25-pin D-type connector, the primary serial port uses a 9-pin D-type connector, the video adaptor uses a 15-pin D-type connector, and so on. The future is likely to bring a standardization of these connectors, possibly with the USB port.

- **Different configurations.** Typically, different peripherals required assigned interrupts and I/O addresses. For example, the keyboard uses IRQ1 and I/O ports at 60h and 64h. This is now being overcome by buses such as SCSI and USB, which require only a single interrupt and a limited range of addresses. They also cope better with hot plug-and-play devices and operating system configurable devices.

- **Different data traffic rates.** Relatively low-speed interfaces, such as the ISA bus, have often reduced the rate of other faster buses, such as the PCI bus. This is now being overcome by the use of bridges and the USB bus.

Table 23.1 Game adapter connections

Pin	Description
1	+5V
2	First button for joystick A (BA1)
3	X-potentiometer of joystick A (AX)
4	GND
5	GND
6	Y-potentiometer of joystick A (AY)
7	Second button for joystick A (BA1)
8	+5V
9	+5V
10	First button for joystick B (BB1)
11	X-potentiometer of joystick B (BX)
12	GND
13	Y-potentiometer of joystick B (BY)
14	Second button for joystick B (BB1)
15	+5V

games with; thus, a joystick is typically used. The games port adapter supports up to two joysticks connected to the same port. It has 15 pins, which are outlined in Table 23.1 and connects to the system via:

- Lower 8 bits of the data bus.
- Lower 10 bits of the address bus.
- $\overline{\text{IOR}}$ and $\overline{\text{IOW}}$.

Each joystick has two buttons, which are normally open circuit, and two potentiometers, which give a variable resistance from 0 to $100\,\text{k}\Omega$, to indicate the x- and y-positions of the joystick handle. Figure 23.1 shows its connections. An unpressed button corresponds to a high level, while a button press corresponds to a low level.

The status of the button can be determined by reading the 201h address (see Figure 23.2); its format is given in Figure 23.3. Thus, to test for a button press, the upper four bits of the register are tested to determine whether they are a zero. Figure 23.4 shows a simple C program to test the status of the buttons.

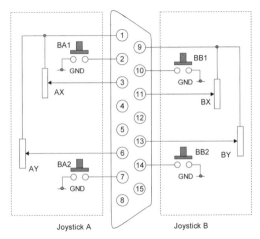

Figure 23.1 Joystick interface

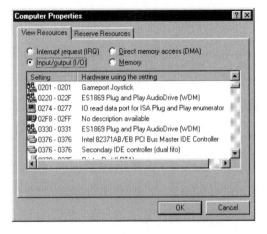

Figure 23.2 Memory map showing Gameport I/O address

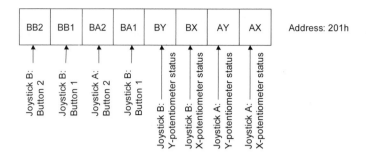

Figure 23.3 Joystick status register format

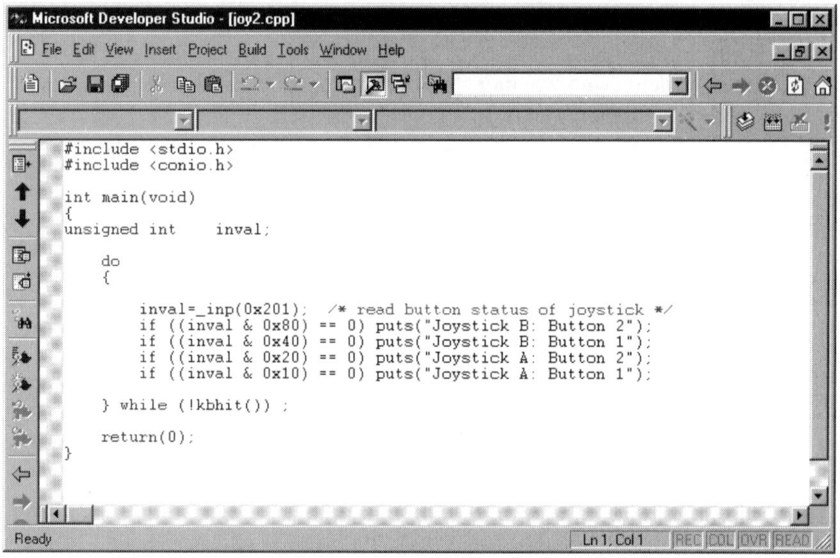

```
#include <stdio.h>
#include <conio.h>

int main(void)
{
unsigned int    inval;

    do
    {
        inval=_inp(0x201);   /* read button status of joystick */
        if ((inval & 0x80) == 0) puts("Joystick B: Button 2");
        if ((inval & 0x40) == 0) puts("Joystick B: Button 1");
        if ((inval & 0x20) == 0) puts("Joystick A: Button 2");
        if ((inval & 0x10) == 0) puts("Joystick A: Button 1");

    } while (!kbhit()) ;

    return(0);
}
```

Figure 23.4 Simple C program to test joystick button status

The reading of the position of the joystick is a little more difficult. For this, an event is triggered by writing to the status register. This triggers a one-shot multivibrator, the status of which is given on the lower 4 bits of the status register, which change from a zero to a one when it has completed the single shot. The resistance is given by:

$$\text{Resistance} = \frac{\text{Time interval}\left(\mu s\right) - 24.2}{0.011}\,\Omega$$

Thus, the timing values will change from 24.2 µs (for 0 kΩ) to 1.124 ms (for 100 kΩ). A simple program that determines the time it takes for AX to be set is given next:

📄 **Program 23.1**
```
#include <stdio.h>
#include <conio.h>

int main(void)
{
unsigned int    inval, start1, start2, start, end1, end2, end;
    do
```

```
{
    _outp(0x43,0);          /* Specify Counter 0      */
    start1=_inp(0x40);      /* get LSB of Counter 0   */
    start2=_inp(0x40);      /* get MSB of Counter 0   */
    _outp(0x201,0);         /* start one-shot         */
    do
    {
        inval=_inp(0x201);    /* read button status of joystick */
    } while ((inval & 1)==1); /* wait till set to a 0 */
    _outp(0x43,0); /* Specify Counter 0 */
    end1=_inp(0x40);  /* get LSB of Counter 0 */
    end2=_inp(0x40);  /* get MSB of Counter 0 */

    start=(start1 &0xff)+((start2 &0xff)<<8);
    end=(end1 & 0xff)+((end2 & 0xff)<<8);

    if (start>end) printf("Value = %u\n",start-end);
    else  /* roll-over has occurred */
        printf("Value = %u\n",start+(0xffff-end));
} while (!kbhit()) ;
return(0);
}
```

Program 23.1 uses Counter 0, which is loaded from address 40h. It has a 16-bit counter register and has a 1.2 MHz clock as its input. It thus rolls over every 55 ms.

In a sample test run of the above program, the output value varied from 62 to 2,740, with a static value of 1,400. The joystick could be easily calibrated with these values, which are the extremes for either x or y. Note that AY is tested with:

```
do
{
    inval=_inp(0x201);      /* read button status of joystick */
} while ((inval & 2)==1); /* wait till set to a 0 */
```

and BX is tested with:

```
do
{
    inval=_inp(0x201);      /* read button status of joystick */
} while ((inval & 4)==1); /* wait till set to a 0 */
```

23.3 Mouse

Typically, on modern PCs the PS/2-style mouse is preferred over serial port mice. PS/2-style mice free up the serial port for other uses, such as data transfers, modem connections, and so on. Table 23.3 outlines the commands that can be used to program the mouse.

The PS/2 mouse is programmed by:

> **Quick keyboard test**
>
> A quick test for the keyboard controller is to perform the following:
>
> - I/O write data AAh to port 64h.
> - I/O read from port 60h; expected data 55h.

- Sending the write auxiliary device (d4h) command to 64h (control register).
- The next byte is a command code that is sent to port 60h, and then transferred to the mouse port (valid codes are given in Table 23.3). This command transfer only occurs for a single transfer.

Table 23.2 Control register commands

Code	Command	Description
e6h	Reset scaling	
e7h	Set scaling	
e8h	Set resolution	Sets the resolution: 00h = 1 count/mm, 01h = 2 counts/mm, 02h = 4 counts/mm and 03 = 8 counts/mm.
e9h	Determine status	3 status bytes
		Byte 1:
		Bit 0: right mouse button pressed (if 1).
		Bit 2: left mouse button pressed (if 1).
		Bit 4: scaling (0=1:1, 1=1:2).
		Bit 5: mouse (0=enabled, 1= disabled).
		Bit 6: mode (0=stream, 1=remote).
		Byte 2: resolution.
		Byte 3: sample rate.
eah	Set stream mode	
ebh	Read data	Reads an 8-byte data packet from the mouse.
ech	Resets mouse to normal mode	
eeh	Sets mouse to wrap mode	In wrap mode, all the commands or data sent to the mouse.
f0h	Set remote mode	
f2h	Identify unit	00h = mouse
f3h	Set sampling rate	Sampling rate is then set by the value put into output buffer: 0ah = 10 samples/s, 14h = 20 samples/s, 28h = 40 samples/s, 3c = 60 samples/s, 50h = 80 samples/s, 64h = 100 samples/s and c8h = 200 samples/s.
f4h	Enable mouse	
f5h	Disable mouse	
f6h	Set standard mouse to standard values	
feh	Resend	
ffh	Reset	

The mouse can be set into either a stream mode or a remote mode, and writes movement data into the keyboard buffer. In stream mode, the mouse transmits movement data when it is moved by a given amount (set by the sample rate). In remote mode, the mouse transfers movement data only when there is a specific read data command.

When the read data command is sent, the 8-byte data packet is read from the addresses as specified in Table 23.3. An example of programming the mouse is given next:

```
_outp(0x64,0xd4);                      /* Write aux. device          */
do
{
    inval=_inp(0x64);
} while ((inval & 0x02)==0x02); /* wait until input buffer empty  */
_outp(0x60,0xe7);                      /* set scaling                */
```

Table 23.3 Control register commands

Offset	Description
00h	Bit 7: YOV (Y-data overflow), Bit 6: XOV (X-data overflow), Bit 5: YNG (Y-value negative), Bit 4: XNG (X-value negative), Bit 1: RIG (right button pressed), Bit 0: LEF (left button pressed).
02h	X-data movement since last access
04h	Y-data movement since last access

23.4 Keyboard

Figure 23.5 shows the main connections in the keyboard interface. It uses a 5-pin DIN socket for the connection. The data is sent from the keyboard to the PC in an 11-bit SDU (serial data unit) format over the KBD data line. When a key has been pressed, the IRQ1 interrupt line is activated. The keyboard interface IC scans the keys on the keyboard by activating the X-decoder lines and then sensing the Y-decoder lines to see if there has been a keypress. It then decodes this to sense whether a key has changed its state. It then converts the keypress or release to a code, which it sends to the keyboard controller on the PC. The format of the code is in the form of an RS-232 interface with 8 data bits, 1 parity bit, 1 start bit and 1 stop bit. Unlike RS-232, it uses a synchronous transfer where the clock speed is defined by the KDB clock line.

It is very unlikely that a programmer would ever need to interface directly with the keyboard, as there are a whole host of standard functions that are well tested and interface well with the operating system. It is always advisable to use the standard input keyboard functions, over direct interfacing. Typically, the operating system takes over control of all input key presses and sends these to the required process, thus it is not a good idea to interrupt the flow.

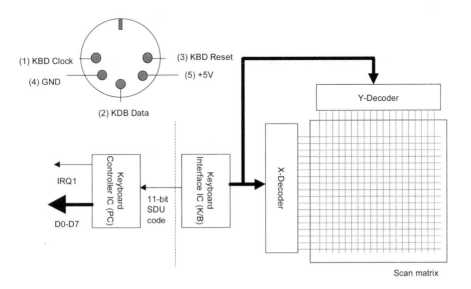

Figure 23.5 Keyboard interface

The keyboard uses two I/O addresses (shown in Figure 23.6):

- Input/output buffer (address: 60h) – used to read the code from the keyboard.
- Control/status register (address: 64h) – used either to determine the status of the keyboard (when a value is read from the register) or to set up the keyboard (when a value is written to the register). The commands used are listed in Table 23.2. On a read operation, it acts as a status register. Figure 23.7 shows the bit definitions, which are:

PARE   **Parity bit.** 1 = last byte has a parity error, 0 = no error.
TIM   **General time-out.** 1 = error, 0 = no error.
AUXB   **Output buffer for auxiliary device.** 1 = holds data for auxiliary device, 0 = holds keyboard data.
KEYL   **Keyboard lock status.** 1 = keyboard unlocked, 0 = keyboard locked.
C/D   **Command/data.** 1 command byte written via port 64h, data byte written via port 60h.
SYSF. **System flag.** 1 = self-test successful, 0 = power-on reset.
INPB. **Input buffer status.** 0 = data in input buffer, 0 = no data.
OUTB. **Output buffer status.** 0 = controller data in output buffer, 0 = buffer empty.

The auxiliary device is typically a PS/2 style mouse. Program 23.2 shows an example program that reads from the keyboard buffer. It disables the IRQ1 interrupt. (Note that this may cause some systems to not respond to the keyboard if the program does not terminate properly.)

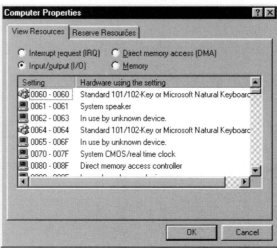

Figure 23.6   Keyboard I/O addresses (60h and 64h)

PARE	TIM	AUXB	KEYL	C/D	SYSF	INPB	OUTB

Address: 64h
Status register

Figure 23.7   Status register bits

📄 Program 23.2

```c
/* This program may not work in Windows 95/98/NT/2000   */
/* as it tries to take direct control of the keyboard   */

#include <stdio.h>
#include <conio.h>
int main(void)
{
unsigned int   inval, hit=0;
char           ch;

        _outp(0x21,0x02); /* disable IRQ1 */
        do
        {
           do
           {
              inval=_inp(0x64); /* read status register */
              if ((inval & 0x01)==0x01) /* set for output buffer */
              {
                 puts("Key pressed");
                 ch=_inp(0x60); /* read key from buffer */
                 printf("%c",ch);
                 hit=1;
              }
           } while (hit==0);
           hit=0;
           if (ch==0x1) break;  /* wait for ESC key */
        } while (1);
        _outp(0x21,0); /* enable IRQ1 */
        return(0);
}
```

Table 23.4 Control register commands

Code	Command	Return value (in output buffer)
a7h	Disable auxiliary device	
a8h	Enable auxiliary device	
a9h	Check interface to auxiliary device	00h = no error, 01h = clock line low, 02h = clock line high, 03h = data line low, 04h = data line high and ffh = no auxiliary device.
aah	Self-test	55h, on success.
abh	Check keyboard interface	00h = no error, 01h = clock line low, 02h = clock line high, 03h = data line low, 04h = data line high and ffh = no auxiliary device.
adh	Disable keyboard	
aeh	Enable keyboard	
c0h	Read input port	
c1h	Read input port (low)	
c2h	Read input port (high)	
d0h	Read output port	
d1h	Write output port	
d2h	Write keyboard output buffer	
d3h	Write output buffer of auxiliary device	
d4h	Write auxiliary device	
e0h	Read test input port	

23.5 Mouse and Keyboard Interface

Modern PCs typically use the 8242 device to provide for a PS/2 mouse and keyboard function, as illustrated in Figure 23.8. It can be seen that the two interrupts that are available are IRQ1 (the keyboard interrupt) and IRQ12 (PS/2 style mouse). If the mouse connects to the serial port, then the IRQ12 line does not cause an interrupt. All clock frequencies are derived from the keyboard clock frequency. Notice that the interface for the PS/2-style mouse is identical to the keyboard connection. They are interfaced through the same registers (60h and 64h).

The keyboard controller contains a microcontroller, which is used to scan for pressed keys. The keyboard controller uses the two I/O address locations:

Keyboard fault

Last write to the milestone checkpoints is the keyboard controller test.

Possible cause:
- Keyboard controller not getting the correct address, data or control lines.
- Keyboard not getting or sending correct clock or data signals.

Check:
- Address, data, and control inputs to the keyboard controller.
- Clock and data signals to and from the keyboard.
- Keyboard connector pins.

- Port 60h. Data I/O register; used to send data to, and get data from, the keyboard controller.
- Port 64h. Command/status register; when writing, this register contains a command for the keyboard controller. When reading, this register contains status information.

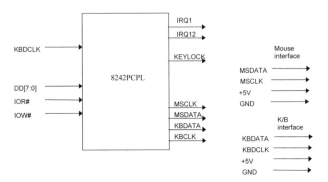

Figure 23.8 Mouse and keyboard interface

Figure 23.9 shows the connection of the PS/2-style mouse and keyboard to the main system board. The ultra I/O device bridges between the ISA bus and other devices, such as the floppy disk, serial ports, parallel ports and the infrared port. The interrupt lines for the PS/2-stype mouse and keyboard are IRQ12 and IRQ1, respectively.

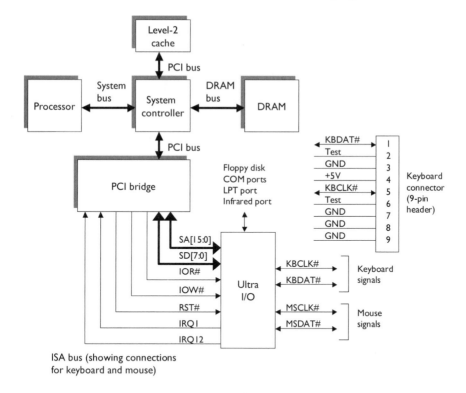

Figure 23.9 Mouse and keyboard interface

When a key is pressed the following occur:

1. Key pressed.
2. The keyboard sends a scan code to the keyboard controller using the KBDDATA input; the KBDCLK synchronizes the keyboard and the keyboard controller, and provides the sample points for the serial data.
3. The scan code is captured (an 11-bit code consisting of a start bit, a byte of data, a parity bit, and a stop bit), and the keyboard controller checks for odd parity. Note that if the parity is bad, the keyboard will be asked to send the data again.
4. IRQ1 is generated by the keyboard controller.
5. The interrupt service routine is run; it reads the scan code from port 60h, translates it to ASCII, and writes the ASCII to video memory in order for it to be displayed on the screen.

> **Keyboard fault**
>
> No keyboard response.
>
> **Possible Cause**
> - Bad KBDCLK or KBDDATA signals
> - Keyboard controller not generating IRQ1
>
> **Check**
> - KBDCLK and KBDDATA paths between the connector and the controller
> - IRQ1 path between the interrupt controller and the keyboard controller

23.6 Exercises

23.6.1   What is the base address of the joystick port?
   (a)   101h   (b)   201h
   (c)   301h   (d)   401h

23.6.2   Which I/O port addresses are used for the keyboard?
   (a)   60h, 64h   (b)   160h, 164h
   (c)   260h, 264h   (d)   360h, 364h

23.6.3   How are the x and y positions determined?
   (a)   The time for a single shot   (b)   A voltage level
   (c)   An electrical current   (d)   A value in a register

23.6.4   What interrupt does the keyboard use?
   (a)   IRQ1   (b)   IRQ3
   (c)   IRQ4   (d)   IRQ12

23.6.5   What interrupt does the PS/2 style mouse use?
   (a)   IRQ1   (b)   IRQ3
   (c)   IRQ4   (d)   IRQ12

23.6.6   Run the program shown in Figure 23.4, and show that the joystick buttons are working. Modify the program so that it only displays a change of status in a button press (rather that scrolling down the screen). For example:

```
if ((inval & 0x80) == 1) && (button==0)) { button=1; puts("B:Button 2 Press");}
if ((inval & 0x80) == 0) && (button==1)) { button=0; puts("B:Button 2 Reset");}
```

23.6.7   Run Program 23.1 and test the movement detection. Modify it so that it detects the y movement.

23.6.8   Run Program 23.1 so that the user can calibrate the joystick. The user should be asked to move the joystick to its maximum x and y directions. From this, write a program that displays the joystick movement as a value from -1 to $+1$.

23.7 Note from the Author

The three interfaces covered in this chapter are all based on a legacy-type system. Over time, the USB port should replace each interface type, but as they work well at the present they may be around for a while longer.

The method that the games port uses to determine position is rather cumbersome, as it uses a single-shot monostable timer to determine the x and y positions. An improved method is to pass the data using a serial interface, just as the mouse does. The keyboard and PS/2-style mouse connections have proved popular, as they are both small 5-pin DIN-style connectors; as the software scans the port automatically for devices, they can be plugged into either socket. This allows for an extra keyboard or mouse to be used with a notebook.

24.1 Introduction

The AGP (accelerated graphics port) is a major advancement in the connection of 3D graphics applications, and is based on an enhancement of the PCI bus. One of the major motivating factors is to improve the speed of transfer between the main system memory and the local graphics card. This reduces the need for large areas of memory on the graphics card, as illustrated in Figure 24.1.

The main gain in moving graphics memory from the display buffer (on the graphics card) to the main memory is the display of text information because:

- It is generally read-only, and does not have to be displayed in any special order.
- Shifting text does not require a great deal of data transfer and can be easily cached in memory, thus reducing data transfer. A shift in text can be loaded from the cached memory.
- It is dependent on the graphics quality of the application, rather than the resolution of the display. There is thus great scope in the future for improvement in the quality of graphics images, rather than their resolution.
- It is not persistent, as it resides in memory only for the duration that it is required. When it has completed the main memory, it can be assigned to another application. A display buffer, on the other hand, is permanent.

The 440LX was the first AGP set product designed to support the AGP interface. The HOST BRIDGE AGP implementation is compatible with the accelerated graphics port specification 1.0. HOST BRIDGE supports only a synchronous AGP interface, coupling to the host bus frequency. The AGP 1.0 interface can reach a theoretical 528 MB/s transfer rate (for two transfers for every 66 MHz clock cycle) and AGP 2.0 can achieve a theoretical 1.056 GB/s transfer rate (for four transfers for every 66 MHz clock cycle). The actual bandwidth will be limited by the capability of the HOST BRIDGE memory subsystem.

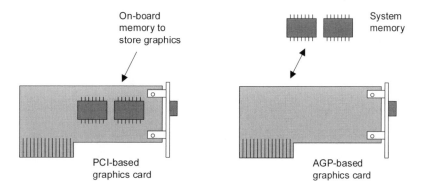

Figure 24.1   AGP card using main system memory

24.1.1 PCI interface

The HOST BRIDGE PCI interface is 33-MHz revision 2.1 compliant and supports up to five external PCI bus masters in addition to the I/O bridge (PIIX4). HOST BRIDGE supports only synchronous PCI coupling to the host bus frequency.

HOST BRIDGE defines a sophisticated data buffering scheme to support the required level of concurrent operations and provide adequate sustained bandwidth between the DRAM subsystem and all other system interfaces (CPU, AGP and PCI).

24.2 PCI and AGP

AGP defines the master as the graphics controller and the corelogic as the graphics card. The AGP interface is based on the 66 MHz PCI standard, but has four additional extensions/enhancements. These extensions are:

- Deeply pipelined memory read and write operations, which fully hide memory access latency.
- Address bus and data bus demultiplexing, allowing for nearly 100 per cent bus efficiency.
- Extension to the PCI timing cycle, which allows for one or two data transfers per 66 MHz clock cycle. This provides a maximum data rate of 500 MB/s.
- Extension to the PCI timing cycle, which allows for four data transfers per 66 MHz clock cycle. This provides for a maximum data rate of 1 GB/s.

All these enhancements are implemented using extra signal lines (sideband signals), and it is not intended as a replacement to the PCI bus. The AGP is physically, logically and electrically independent of the PCI bus, and has its own connector that is reserved solely for graphics devices (and is not interchangeable with the AGP connector). Figure 24.2 shows the main AGP signal lines.

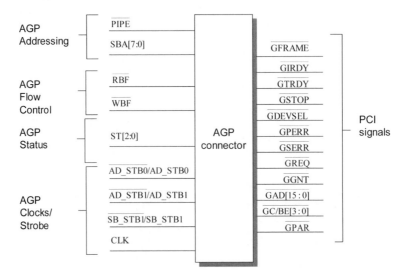

Figure 24.2   The main AGP signal lines

24.3 Bus Transactions

AGP uses two types of bus operations:

- **Queuing requests**. This can be done over the SBA port or the AD bus, and is set up using Bit 9 for the status register (only one type at a time can be used). With the SBA port, the AD bus cannot be used, and vice versa. The sideband signals (SBA[7:0]) are used exclusively to transmit AGP access requests (all PCI transactions use the AD pins for both data and address), and are sent from the master to the core logic (the AGP requests are the same when sent over the AD bus or the SBA bus). A master that uses the SBA port does not require the $\overline{\text{PIPE}}$ signal, which is used only to frame requests on the AD pins.
- **Address demultiplexing option**. This allows the complete AGP access request to be transmitted over the 8-bit SBA port. For this, the request is broken into three parts: low-order address bits and length (type 1), mid-order address bits and command (type 2), and high-order address bits (type 3).

24.4 Pin Description

AGP adds an extra 21 signal lines to the PCI specification. The basic implementation of AGP should support ×1 and ×2 transfer rates, and may optionally support ×4 data transfer rates. All devices should support low-priority (LP) data writes, but optionally support fast-write (FW) data transfers.

The signal lines split into four main groups:

- AGP requests.
- AGP flow control.
- AGP status.
- AGP clocking.

Also, the PCI lines are identified with a preceding G, such as GAD[31:0] for the PCI AD bus, $\overline{\text{GSTOP}}$ for $\overline{\text{STOP}}$, and so on.

24.4.1 Requests

AGP supports two methods of queuing requests by an AGP master. A master selects the required method during start-up and is not allowed to change when set up. The methods use either the $\overline{\text{PIPE}}$ signal line or the SBA port. These signals cannot be used at the same time. These lines are defined as:

$\overline{\text{PIPE}}$	On the master (the graphics controller), $\overline{\text{PIPE}}$ is a sustained tristate signal and is an input to the target (the core logic). When assessed by the current master, it indicates a pipelined request, so that the full width request is to be queued by the target. The master queues one request each rising edge of CLK while $\overline{\text{PIPE}}$ is asserted.
SBA[7:0]	These signals are outputs from the master and are inputs to the target, and they indicate the sideband address (SBA) port, which gives an additional bus to pass requests (address and command) to the target from the master.

24.4.2 Flow control

Apart from the normal PCI flow control lines, the following have been added to AGP:

$\overline{\text{RBF}}$ The read buffer full (RBF) signal indicates whether the master is ready to accept previously requested LP read data or not. When it is active (LOW), the arbiter is not allowed to initiate the return of LP read data to the master. It is made inactive by either the AGP target or motherboard.

$\overline{\text{WBF}}$ The write buffer full (WBF) signal indicates that the master is ready to accept FW data. When it is active (LOW), the core logic arbiter is not allowed to initiate a transaction to provide FW data. It is made inactive by either the AGP target or motherboard.

24.4.3 Status signals

The AGP status signals indicate how the AD bus is used in future transactions, such as using it to queue new requests, return previously requested read data, or send previously queued write data. These lines are always an output from the corelogic and an input to the master, and are:

ST[2:0]   These provide information from the arbiter to the master on the mode of operation, and they only have a meaning when $\overline{\text{GNT}}$ is asserted (else they are ignored). Their settings are:

000   Previously requested low-priority read or flush data is being returned to the master.
001   Previously requested high-priority read data is being returned to the master.
010   Master is to provide low-priority write data for a previous queued write command.
011   Master is to provide high-priority write data for a previous queued write command.
100   Reserved.
101   Reserved.
110   Reserved.
111   Master has been given permission to start a bus transaction.

24.4.4 Clocks

The CLK signal provides the basic clock signal for all control signals and is based on the ×1 transfer mode. Two other strobes are used to transfer data on the AD bus or the SBA port. As the AD bus has 32 bits, then two copies of the AD_STB are required. If ×4 mode is used, the complements of the strobes are also required.

CLK   Basic clock information for both AGP and PCI control signals.
AD_STB0   This strobe provides for timing in a ×2 data transfer mode on GAD[15:0] and is provided by the agent that is providing data.
$\overline{\text{AD\_STB0}}$ This strobe provides for timing in a ×4 data transfer mode on GAD[15:0] and is provided by the agent that is providing data.
AD_STB1   This strobe provides for timing in a ×2 data transfer mode on GAD[31:16] and is provided by the agent that is providing data.

$\overline{\text{AD\_STB1}}$ This strobe provides for timing in a ×4 data transfer mode on GAD[31:16] and is provided by the agent that is providing data.

SB_STB   This strobe provides the strobe for the SBA[7:0] (when required). It is driven by the AGP master.

$\overline{\text{SB\_STB}}$ This strobe provides the strobe for the SBA[7:0] (when required) at ×4 data transfer mode. It is driven by the AGP master.

24.4.5 USB signals

USB+   Used to send USB data and control packets to an externally connected USB capable video monitor.

USB−   Inverse of USB+.

$\overline{\text{OVRCNT}}$ The USB overcurrent indicator is set low when there is too much current being taken from the 5 V supply.

24.4.6 Other signals

$\overline{\text{PME}}$ Power management event. Not used by the AGP bus; used by the PCI bus.

TYPEDET   The type detect signal identifies whether the interface is 1.5 V or 3.3 V.

24.4.7 PCI signals and AGP

AGP supports most of the PCI signals. IDSEL, $\overline{\text{LOCK}}$, $\overline{\text{INTC}}$ and $\overline{\text{INTD}}$ are not supported on the AGP connector, whereas $\overline{\text{FRAME}}$, IDSEL, $\overline{\text{STOP}}$ and $\overline{\text{DEVSEL}}$ are used in FW transactions, but not in AGP pipelined operations.

$\overline{\text{FRAME}}$ Used for FW transactions, but not for AGP pipelined transaction.

$\overline{\text{IRDY}}$ Used by the AGP master to indicate that it is ready to provide all write data for the current transaction. When the master asserts it, then it cannot insert any wait states either when reading or writing blocks of data (but it can in between blocks). In FW transactions, the core logic sets the line to indicate that there is write data on the bus. The core logic cannot insert wait states with data blocks.

$\overline{\text{TRDY}}$ Used by an AGP target to indicate that it is ready to provide read data for the entire transaction or is ready to transfer a block of data when the transfer/transaction requires more than four clocks to complete the operation. In FW transactions, the AGP master uses it to indicate when it is willing to transfer a subsequent block.

$\overline{\text{STOP}}$ Used in FW transactions to signal a device disconnection.

$\overline{\text{DEVSEL}}$ Used in FW transactions to signal that a transaction cannot complete during the block.

IDSEL   Not used in the AGP connector, and generated internally in the graphics device.

$\overline{\text{PERR}}$ Not used in the AGP transaction.

$\overline{\text{SERR}}$ As PCI bus.

$\overline{\text{REQ}}$ Used to request access to the bus to initiate an AGP request.

$\overline{\text{GNT}}$ Same meaning as PCI (but extra information is added by ST[2:0]).

$\overline{\text{RST}}$ As PCI bus.

AD[31:00]   As PCI bus.

$\overline{\text{C/BE}[3:0]}$ AGP command information (see section 24.5).

PAR   Not valid during an AGP transaction.

$\overline{\text{LOCK}}$ Not supported on the AGP interface.

$\overline{\text{INTA}}$, $\overline{\text{INTB}}$ As PCI bus.

$\overline{\text{INTC}}$, $\overline{\text{INTD}}$ Not supported on the AGP connector.

24.5   AGP Connections

Figure 24.3 shows the main connections for a PC motherboard to the AGP and PCI buses. The AGP bus and PCI bus have separate, electrically isolated signals on the system controller. Figure 24.4 shows the connector used with the AGP port. The AGP port has different pin names for the AGP port, such as GAD[31:0] instead of AD[31:0] and GC/BE#[3:0] instead of C/BE#[3:0]. Note that the SC242 connection has an on-package level-2 cache, thus there are no external connections from the processor to the cache.

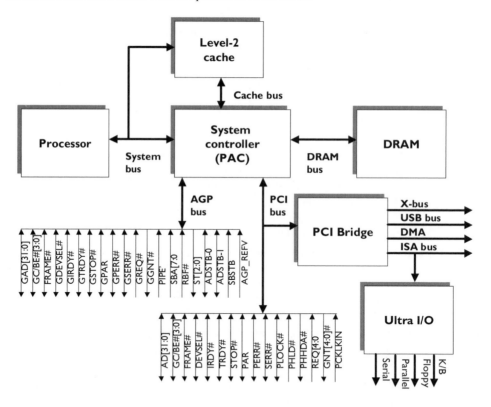

Figure 24.3   AGP/PCI system connections

24.6   AGP Master Configuration

The AGP master is configured in the same way as a device on the PCI bus, which requires that it responds to a PCI configuration transaction. This occurs when:

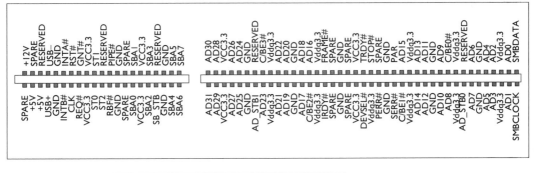

Figure 24.4 AGP signal lines

- A configuration command is decoded.

- AD01 and AD00 are '00'.

- The IDSEL signal is asserted. As the AGP connector does not support IDSEL, then it is connected to AD16. This is done by connecting it internally for AGP operation, but externally for PCI operation.

Initially, the AGP device asserts $\overline{\text{DEVSEL}}$ when the bus command is configuration (read or write). AD16 is set to a '1' and AD1 and AD0 are '00'. These cause the device's configuration space to be accessed. The system software then scans all configuration spaces by asserting different AD signals between AD16 and AD31, and using PCI configuration read or write commands.

24.7 Bus Commands

The AGP bus uses the command lines ($\overline{\text{C/BE}[3:0]}$) to indicate the type of pipelined transaction on the AD bus or SBA port. These are:

0000	**Read.** Starting at the specified address, read n sequential Qwords, where $n =$ (length_field + 1). The length_field is provided by the lower 3 bits on the AD bus (A2–A0).
0001	**Read (high priority).** As Read, but the request is queued in the high-priority queue. The reply data may be returned out of order with respect to other requests.
0010	Reserved.
0011	Reserved.
0100	**Write.** Starting at the specified address, write n sequential Qwords, as enabled by the $\overline{\text{C/BE}[3:0]}$, where $n =$ (length_field + 1).
0101	**Write (high priority).** As Write, but indicates that the write data must be transferred from the master within the maximum latency window established for high priority accesses.
0110/0111	Reserved.

1000	**Long read.** As Read, except for access size, in this case, $n = 4\times$ (length_field + 1) allowing up to 256 byte transfers.
1001	**Long read (high priority).** As Read (high priority) except for access size, which is the same as for Long Read.
1010	**Flush.** Similar to Read. Forces all low-priority write accesses ahead of it to the point that all the results are fully visible to all other system agents.
1011	Reserved.
1100	**Fence.** Creates a boundary in a single master's low-priority access stream around which writes may not pass reads.
1101	**Dual address cycle (DAC).** Used by the master to transfer a 64-bit address to the core logic when using the AD bus.
1110/1111	Reserved.

The master uses two clock periods to transfer the entire address using AD[31:0] and $\overline{C/BE[3:0]}$. Within the first clock period, the master provides the lower address bits (A31–A03) and the length encoding on (A2–A0), as with a 32-bit request, but uses the 1101 command (DAC) encoding on $\overline{C/BE[3:0]}$ instead of the actual command. The second clock of the request contains the upper address bits (A63–A32) on AD[31:0] and the actual command on $\overline{C/BE[3:0]}$.

24.8 Addressing Modes and Bus Operations

AGP transactions differ from PCI transactions in several ways:

- In AGP, pipelined read/write transactions are disconnected from their associated access request, where the request and associated data may be separated by other AGP operations. Conversely, a PCI data phase is connected to its associated address phase, with no interventions allowed. This helps to maintain the pipe depth and allows the core logic to ensure a sufficiently large buffer for receiving the write data, before locking up the bus on a data transfer that could be blocked awaiting buffer space. The rules for the order of accesses on the AGP bus are not based on the order of the data transfer, but on the arrival order of access requests.

- AGP has different bus commands that allow access only to the main system memory. PCI allows access to multiple address spaces: memory, I/O and configuration.

- In AGP, memory addresses are always aligned in 8-byte references, whereas PCI uses 4-byte, or lower, references (the number of bytes addressed is defined with the $\overline{C/BE[3:0]}$). The reason for the increased AGP addressing granularity (from four in the PCI bus to eight in AGP) is because modern processors use a 64-bit data bus and can manipulate 64 bits at a time. The memory systems are also 64 bits wide.

- In AGP, pipelined access requests have an explicitly defined access length or size. In PCI transfer, lengths are defined by the duration of $\overline{FRAME}$.

24.9 Register Description

The PCI bridge supports AGP through two sets of registers, which are accessed via I/O addresses. These are:

- **Configuration address (CONFADD).** Enables/disables the configuration space and determines what portion of configuration space is visible through the configuration data window.
- **Configuration data (CONFDATA).** 32-bit/16-bit/8-bit read/write window into configuration space.

Configuration address register

I/O address	0CF8h accessed as a DWord (32-bit)
Default value	00000000h
Access	Read/write

CONFADD is accessed with an 8-bit or a 16-bit value, then it will 'pass through' this register and go onto the PCI bus as an I/O cycle. The register contains the bus number, device number, function number, and register number for which a subsequent configuration access is intended. Its format is:

Bit	Description
31	Configuration enable (CFGE) 1=enable, 0=disable.
30:24	Reserved.
23:16	**Bus number (BUSNUM).** – If it has a value of 00h then the target of the configuration cycle is either the HOST BRIDGE or the PCI bus that is directly connected to the HOST BRIDGE.
15:11	**Device number (DEVNUM).** Selects one agent on the PCI bus selected by the bus number. In the configuration cycles, this field is mapped to AD[15:11].
10:8	**Function number (FUNCNUM).** This field is mapped to AD[10:8] during PCI configuration cycles. It allows for the configuration of a multifunction device.
7:2	**Register number (REGNUM).** This field selects one register within a particular bus, device, and function as specified by the other fields in the configuration address register. This field is mapped to AD[7:2] during PCI configuration cycles.
1:0	Reserved.

Configuration data register

I/O address	0CFCh
Default value	00000000h
Access	Read/Write

CONFDATA is a 32-bit/16-bit/8-bit read/write window into configuration space. The portion of configuration space that is referenced by CONFDATA is determined by the settings in the CONFADD register.

24.9.2 *Configuration access*

The routing of configuration accesses to PCI or AGP is controlled by PCI-to-PCI bridge standard mechanism using the following:

- Primary bus number register.
- Secondary bus number register.
- Subordinate bus number register.

The PCI bus 0 is frequently known as the primary PCI.

Maximum transfer rates

32-bit PCI, 33 MHz   → 132 MB/s (burst)
32-bit PCI, 33 MHz   → 66 MB/s (multiplexed)
32-bit AGP, 66 MHz, 2 transfers/clock
→ 528 MB/s
32-bit AGP, 66 MHz, 4 transfers/clock
→ 1.056 GB/s

PCI bus configuration mechanism

The PCI bus has a slot based configuration space that allows each device to contain up to eight functions, with each function containing up to 256 8-bit configuration registers.

PCI configuration is achieved with two bus cycles: configuration read and configuration write. A device can be configured using the CONFADD and CONFDATA registers. First, a Dword value is placed into the CONFADD register that enables the configuration (CONFADD[31]=1), specifies the PCI bus (CONFADD[23:16]), the device on that bus (CONFADD[15:11]), the function within the device (CONFADD[10:8]). CONFDATA then becomes a window for which four bytes of configuration space are specified by the contents of CONFADD. Any read or write to CONFDATA results in the host bridge translating CONFADD into a PCI configuration cycle.

If the bus number is 0, then a Type 0 configuration cycle is performed on primary PCI bus, where:

- CONFADD[10:2] (FUNCNUM and REGNUM) are mapped directly to AD[10:2].
- CONFADD[15:11] (DEVNUM) is decoded onto AD[31:16].

The host bridge entity within HOST BRIDGE is accessed as a Device 0 on the primary PCI bus segment and a virtual PCI-to-PCI bridge entity is accessed as a Device 1 on the primary PCI bus.

24.9.3 PCI configuration space

HOST BRIDGE is implemented as a dual PCI device residing within a single physical component, where:

- Device 0 is the host-to-PCI bridge, and includes PCI bus number 0 interface, main memory controller, graphics aperture control and HOST BRIDGE's specific AGP control registers.

AGPCMD register

The AGPCMD register reports AGP device capability/status. Its main parameters are:

Address offset	A8–ABh
Default value	00000000h
Access	Read/write

Bit	Description
31:10	Reserved.
9	AGP side band enable. – 1=enable; 0=disable (default).
8	AGP enable. – 1=enable; 0=disable (default). When this bit is set to a 0, the HOST BRIDGE ignores all AGP operations. Any AGP operations received (queued) while this bit is 1 will be serviced, even if this bit is subsequently reset to 0. If it is 1, then the HOST BRIDGE responds to AGP operations delivered via $\overline{\text{PIPE}}$ (or responds to the SBA, if the AGP side band enable bit is set to 1).
7:2	Reserved.
1:0	AGP data transfer rate. One bit in this field must be set to indicate the desired data transfer rate. Bit 0 identifies ×1, and bit 1 identifies ×2.

- Device 1 is the virtual PCI-to-PCI bridge, and includes mapping of AGP space and standard PCI interface control functions of the PCI-to-PCI bridge.

Table 24.1 shows the configuration space for Device 0. Corresponding configuration registers for both devices are mapped as devices residing at the primary PCI bus (bus #0). The configuration registers layout and functionality for Device 0 and is implemented with a high level of compatibility with a previous generation of PCIsets (i.e. 440FX). Configuration registers of HOST BRIDGE Device 1 are based on the standard configuration space template of a PCI-to-PCI bridge.

Table 24.1 PCI configuration space (Device 0)

Address	Reference	Register name
00–01h	VID	Vendor identification
02–03h	DID	Device identification
04–05h	PCICMD	PCI command register
06–07h	PCISTS	PCI status register
08h	RID	Revision identification
0Ah	SUBC	Subclass code
0Bh	BCC	Base class code
0Dh	MLT	Master latency timer
0Eh	HDR	Header type
10–13h	APBASE	Aperture base address
34h	CAPPTR	Capabilities pointer
50–51h	HOST BRIDGECFG	Host bridge configuration
53h	DBC	Data buffering control
55–56h	DRT	DRAM row type
57h	DRAMC	DRAM control
58h	DRAMT	DRAM timing
59–5Fh	PAM[6:0]	Programmable attribute map (seven registers)
60–67h	DRB[7:0]	DRAM row boundary (eight registers)
68h	FDHC	Fixed DRAM hole control
6A-6Bh	DRAMXC	DRAM extended mode select
6C-6Fh	MBSC	Memory buffer strength control register
70h	MTT	Multitransaction timer
71h	CLT	CPU latency timer register
72h	SMRAM	System management RAM control
90h	ERRCMD	Error command register
91h	ERRSTS0	Error status register 0
92h	ERRSTS1	Error status register 1
93h	RSTCTRL	Reset control register
A0–A3h	ACAPID	AGP capability identifier
A4–A7h	AGPSTAT	AGP status register
A8–ABh	AGP	Command register
B0–B3h	AGPCTRL	AGP control register
B4h	APSIZE	Aperture size control register
B8–BBh	ATTBASE	Aperture translation table base register
BCh	AMTT	AGP MTT control register
BDh	LPTT	AGP low-priority transaction timer register

24.9.4 AGP memory address ranges

The HOST BRIDGE can be programmed for direct memory accesses of the AGP bus interface when addresses are within the appropriate range. This uses two subranges:

- AMBASE/AMLIMIT. This method is controlled with the memory base register (AMBASE) and the memory limit register (AMLIMIT).
- APMBASE/APMLIMIT. This method is controlled with the prefetchable memory base register (APMBASE) and AGP prefetchable memory limit register (APMLIMIT).

The decoding of these addresses is based on the top 12 bits of the memory base and memory limit registers, which correspond to address bits A[31:20] of a memory address. When address decoding, the HOST BRIDGE assumes that address bits A[19:0] of the memory address are zero and that address bits A[19:0] of the memory limit address are FFFFFh. This forces the memory address range to be aligned to 1 MB boundaries and to have a size granularity of 1 MB. The base and limit addresses define the minimum and maximum ranges of the addresses.

> **Graphics aperture**
>
> AGP supports a graphic aperture that uses memory-mapped graphics data structures. Its starting address is defined by APBASE configuration register of HOST BRIDGE and its range is defined by the APSIZE register, such as 4 MB (default), 8 MB, 16 MB, 32 MB, 64 MB, 128 MB and 256 MB.

24.9.5 AGP address mapping

HOST BRIDGE directs I/O accesses to the AGP port in the address range defined by AGP I/O address range. This range is defined by the AGP I/O base register (AIOBASE) and AGP I/O limit register (AIOLIMIT). These are decoded where the top 4 bits of the I/O base and I/O limit registers correspond to address bits A[15:12] of an I/O address. For address decoding, the HOST BRIDGE assumes that the lower 12 address bits A[11:0] of the I/O base are zero and that address bits A[11:0] of the I/O limit address are FFFh. This forces the I/O address range to be aligned to 4 kB boundary and to have a size granularity of 4 kB.

24.10 Exercises

24.10.1   Which bus is the AGP bus based on?
   (a)   PCI   (b)   IDE
   (c)   ISA   (d)   USB

24.10.2   What is likely to be a *typical* maximum data throughput for PCI operating at 33 MHz:
   (a)   66 MB/s   (b)   132 MB/s
   (c)   528 MB/s   (d)   1.056 MB/s

24.10.3   What is the maximum throughput for 66 MHz AGP which uses 2 transfers per clock cycle:
   (a)   66 MB/s   (b)   132 MB/s
   (c)   528 MB/s   (d)   1.056 MB/s

24.10.4   What is the maximum throughput for 66 MHz AGP which uses 4 transfers per clock cycle:
(a)   66 MB/s   (b)   132 MB/s
(c)   528 MB/s   (d)   1.056 MB/s

24.10.5   How does AGP increase the data rate by x2 (and even x4)?
(a)   Extra clock signals   (b)   Increased data bus size
(c)   Direct memory accesses   (d)   Increased address bus size

24.10.6   Which of the following is *not* an advantage of using the AGP bus?
(a)   Faster transfers between memory and the graphics devices
(b)   Increased use of main memory (with reduced need for localized memory)
(c)   Reduced requirement for interrupts
(d)   Increase throughput compared with the standard PCI bus

24.10.7   Which of the following identifies the address/data lines on the AGP bus?
(a)   HAD[31:0]   (b)   GAD[31:0]
(c)   AAD[31:0]   (d)   AD[31:0]

24.10.8   Explain the main objectives of the AGP bus and outline the advantages of moving textural information into main memory.

24.10.9   Contrast the PCI and AGP buses and explain how AGP increases the data throughput. Discuss the extra signal lines used with AGP, and how they are used.

24.11 Note from the Author

In the past, the biggest weakness of the PC has probably been the graphics facilities. This is mainly because the bus systems within the PC did not support large data throughput (ISA/EISA is too slow). The design of the graphics system also required that the video card had to store all the data that was to be displayed on the screen. Thus, regardless of the amount of memory on the system, it was still limited by the amount of memory on the graphics card. AGP overcomes this by allowing graphical images to be stored in the main memory and then transferred to the video displayed over a fast bus.

The data demand for graphical displays is almost unlimited, as the faster they can be driven, the greater their applications. The AGP bus is an excellent extension to the PCI bus, and gives data throughput of over 500 MB/s, whereas standard PCI devices can typically only be run at less than 100 MB/s. AGP is now a standard part of most PC motherboards, but it is still to be seen whether many systems will start to use this port.

25 RS-232

25.1 Introduction

RS-232 is one of the most popular techniques used to interface external equipment to computers. It uses serial communications where one bit is sent along a line, at a time. This differs from parallel communications which send one or more bytes, at a time. The main advantage that serial communications has over parallel communications is that a single wire is needed to transmit and another to receive. RS-232 is a de facto standard that most computer and instrumentation companies comply with. It was standardized in 1962 by the Electronics Industries Association (EIA). Unfortunately this standard only allows short cable runs with low bit rates. The standard RS-232 only allows a bit rate of 19,600 bps for a maximum distance of 20 m. New serial communications standards, such as RS-422 and RS-449, allow very long cable runs and high bit rates. For example, RS-422 allows a bit rate of up to 10 Mbps over distances up to 1 mile, using twisted-pair, coaxial cable or optical fiber. The new standards can also be used to create computer networks. This chapter introduces the RS-232 standard and gives simple programs which can be used to transmit and receive using RS-232.

> **PC serial port connectors**
>
> All PCs have at least one serial communications port. The primary port is named COM1: and the secondary is COM2:. There are two types of connectors used in RS-232 communications, 25- and 9-way D-type. Most modern PCs use either a 9-pin connector for the primary (COM1:) serial port. The serial port can be differentiated from the parallel port in that the 25-pin parallel port (LPT1:) is a 25-pin female connector on the PC and a male connector on the cable. The 25-pin serial connector is a male on the PC and a female on the cable. The different connector types can cause problems in connecting devices.

25.2 Electrical Characteristics and Connectors

The electrical characteristics of RS-232 defines the minimum and maximum voltages of a logic '1' and '0'. A logic '1' ranges from –3 V to –25 V, but will typically be around –12 V. A logical '0' ranges from 3 V to 25 V, but will typically be around +12 V. Any voltage between –3 V and +3 V has an indeterminate logical state. If no pulses are present on the line the voltage level is equivalent to a high level, that is –12 V. A voltage level of 0 V at the receiver is interpreted as a line break or a short circuit. Figure 25.1 shows an example transmission.

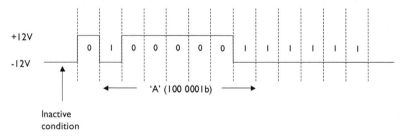

Figure 25.1 RS-232 voltage levels

The DB25S connector is a 25-pin D-type connector and gives full RS-232 functionality. Figure 25.2 shows the pin number assignment. A DCE (the terminating cable) connector has a male outer casing with female connection pins. The DTE (the computer) has a female outer casing with male connecting pins. There are three main signal types: control, data and ground. Table 25.1 lists the main connections. Control lines are active HIGH, that is they are HIGH when the signal is active and LOW when inactive.

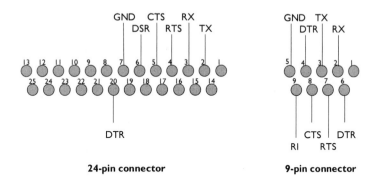

Figure 25.2   RS-232 9-pin and 25-pin connection

The 25-pin connector is the standard for RS-232 connections but as electronic equipment becomes smaller, there is a need for smaller connectors. For this purpose most PCs now use a reduced function 9-pin D-type connector rather than the fully functional 25-way D-type. As with the 25-pin connector the DCE (the terminating cable) connector has a male outer casing with female connection pins. The DTE (the computer) has a female outer casing with male connecting pins. Figure 25.2 shows the main connections.

Table 25.1   Main pin connections used in 25-pin connector

25-pin	9-pin	Name	Abbreviation	Functionality
1		Frame ground		This ground normally connects the outer sheath of the cable and to earth ground.
2	3	Transmit data	TD	Data is sent from the DTE (computer or terminal) to a DCE via TD.
3	2	Receive data	RD	Data is sent from the DCE to a DTE (computer or terminal) via RD.
4	7	Request to send	RTS	DTE sets this active when it is ready to transmit data.
5	8	Clear to send	CTS	DCE sets this active to inform the DTE that it is ready to receive data.
6	6	Data set ready	DSR	Similar functionality to CTS but activated by the DTE when it is ready to receive data.
7	5	Signal ground	SG	All signals are referenced to the signal ground (GND).
20	4	Data terminal ready	DTR	Similar functionality to RTS but activated by the DCE when it wishes to transmit data.

25.3 Communications Between Two Nodes

RS-232 is intended to be a standard but not all manufacturers abide by it. Some implement the full specification while others implement just a partial specification. This is mainly because not every device requires the full functionality of RS-232, for example a modem requires many more control lines than a serial mouse.

The rate at which data is transmitted and the speed at which the transmitter and receiver can transmit/receive the data dictates whether data handshaking is required.

25.3.1 Handshaking

In the transmission of data, there can either be no handshaking, hardware handshaking or software handshaking. If no handshaking is used then the receiver must be able to read the received characters before the transmitter sends another. The receiver may buffer the received character and store it in a special memory location before it is read. This memory location is named the receiver buffer. Typically, it may only hold a single character. If it is not emptied before another character is received then any character previously in the buffer will be overwritten. An example of this is illustrated in Figure 25.3 In this case, the receiver has read the first two characters successfully from the receiver buffer, but it did not read the third character as the fourth transmitted character has overwritten it in the receiver buffer. If this condition occurs then some form of handshaking must be used to stop the transmitter sending characters before the receiver has had time to service the received characters.

Hardware handshaking involves the transmitter asking the receiver if it is ready to receive data. If the receiver buffer is empty it will inform the transmitter that it is ready to receive data. Once the data is transmitted and loaded into the receiver buffer the transmitter is informed not to transmit any more characters until the character in the receiver buffer has been read. The main hardware handshaking lines used for this purpose are:

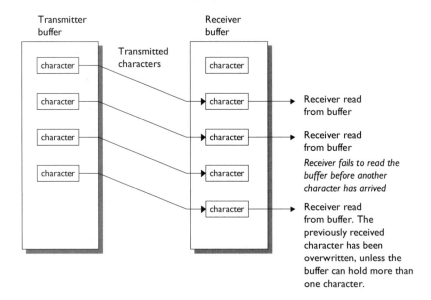

Figure 25.3   Transmission and reception of characters

- CTS – Clear to send.
- DTR – Data terminal ready.
- RTS – Ready to send.
- DSR – Data set ready.

Software handshaking involves sending special control characters. These include the DC1 (Xon)-DC4 (Xoff) control characters.

25.3.2 RS-232 set-up

Microsoft Windows allows the serial port setting to be set by selecting control panel → system → device manager → ports (COM and LPT) → port settings. The settings of the communications port (the IRQ and the port address) can be changed by selecting control panel → system → device manager → ports (COM and LPT) → resources for IRQ and addresses. Figure 25.4 shows example parameters and settings. The selectable baud rates are typically 110, 300, 600, 1,200, 2,400, 4,800, 9,600 and 19,200 baud for an 8250-based device. A 16650 UART also gives enhanced speeds of 38,400, 57,600, 115,200, 230,400, 460,800 and 921,600 baud. Notice that the flow control can either be set to software handshaking (Xon/Xoff), hardware handshaking or none. The parity bit can either be set to none, odd, even, mark or space. A mark in the parity option sets the parity bit to a '1' and a space sets it to a '0'. In this case COM1: is set at 9600 baud, 8 data bits, no parity, 1 stop bit and no parity checking.

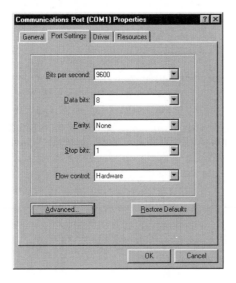
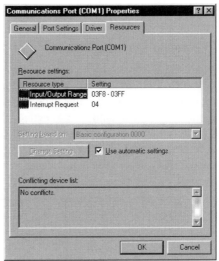

Figure 25.4   Changing port setting and parameters

25.3.3 Simple no-handshaking communications

In this form of communication it is assumed that the receiver can read the received data from the receive buffer before another character is received. Data is sent from a TD pin connection of the transmitter and is received in the RD pin connection at the receiver. When a DTE (such as a computer) connects to another DTE, then the transmit line (TD) on one is connected to the receive (RD) of the other and vice versa. Figure 25.5 shows the connections between the nodes.

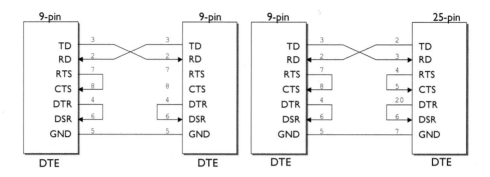

Figure 25.5 RS-232 connections with no hardware handshaking

25.3.4 Software handshaking

There are two ASCII characters that start and stop communications. These are X-ON (^S , Cntrl-S or ASCII 11) and X-OFF (^Q, Cntrl-Q or ASCII 13). When the transmitter receives an X-OFF character it ceases communications until an X-ON character is sent. This type of handshaking is normally used when the transmitter and receiver can process data relatively quickly. Normally, the receiver will also have a large buffer for the incoming characters. When this buffer is full, it transmits an X-OFF. After it has read from the buffer the X-ON is transmitted, see Figure 25.6.

25.3.5 Hardware handshaking

Hardware handshaking stops characters in the receiver buffer from being overwritten. The control lines used are all active HIGH. Figure 25.7 shows how the nodes communicate. When a node wishes to transmit data it asserts the RTS line active (that is, HIGH). It then monitors the CTS line until it goes active (that is, HIGH). If the CTS line at the transmitter stays inactive then the receiver is busy and cannot receive data, at the present. When the receiver reads from its buffer the RTS line will automatically go active indicating to the transmitter that it is now ready to receive a character.

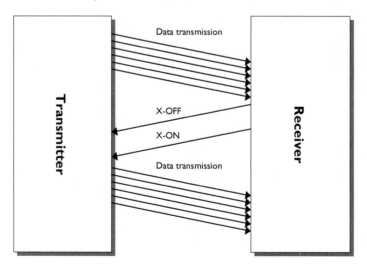

Figure 25.6 Software handshaking using X-ON and X-OFF

Receiving data is similar to the transmission of data, but the lines DSR and DTR are used instead of RTS and CTS. When the DCE wishes to transmit to the DTE the DSR input to the receiver will become active. If the receiver cannot receive the character, it will set the DTR line inactive. When it is clear to receive it sets the DTR line active and the remote node then transmits the character. The DTR line will be set inactive until the character has been processed.

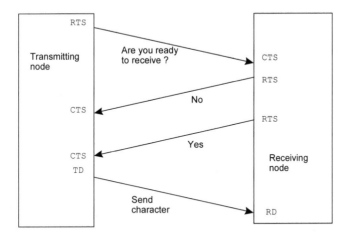

Figure 25.7 Handshaking lines used in transmitting data

25.3.6 Two-way communications with handshaking

For full handshaking of the data between two nodes the RTS and CTS lines are crossed over (as are the DTR and DSR lines). This allows for full remote node feedback (see Figure 25.8).

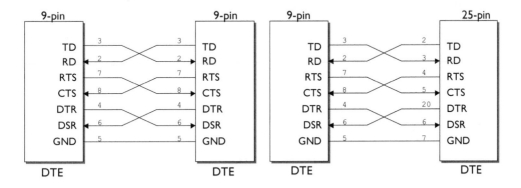

Figure 25.8 RS-232 communications with handshaking (null modem connection)

25.3.7 DTE-DCE connections (PC to modem)

A further problem occurs in connecting two nodes. A DTE/DTE connection requires cross-overs on their signal lines, whereas DTE/DCE connections require straight-through lines. An example computer to modem connection is shown in Figure 25.9.

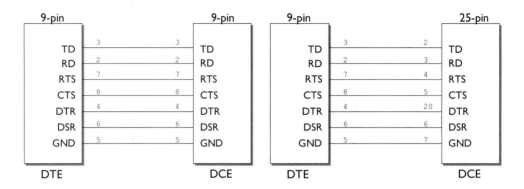

Figure 25.9   DTE to DCE connections

25.4 Programming RS-232

See Section 8.2.2.

25.5 RS-232 Programs

Figure 25.10 shows the main RS-232 connections for 9-and 25-pin connections without hardware handshaking. The loopback connections are used to test the RS-232 hardware and the software, while the null modem connections are used to transmit characters between two computers. Program 25.1 uses a loop back on the TD/RD lines so that a character sent by the computer will automatically be received into the receiver buffer. This set-up is useful in testing the transmit and receive routines. The character to be sent is entered via the keyboard. A CNTRL-D (^D) keystroke exits the program.

Program 25.2 can be used as a sender program (send.c) and Program 25.3 can be used as a receiver program (receive.c). With these programs, the null modem connections shown in Figure 25.10 are used.

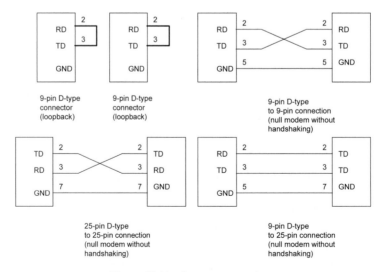

Figure 25.10   System connections

Note that programs 25.1 to 25.3 are written for Microsoft Visual C++. For early versions of Borland C/C++ program change _inp for inportb and _outp for outportb.

📄 Program 25.1

```
/*    This program transmits a character from COM1: and receives   */
/*    it via this port. The TD is connected to RD.                 */

#define   COM1BASE    0x3F8
#define   COM2BASE    0x2F8
#define   TXDATA      COM1BASE
#define   LCR         (COM1BASE+3) /*   0x3FB line control          */
#define   LSR         (COM1BASE+5) /*   0x3FD line status           */

#include <conio.h>   /* required for getch()                        */
#include <dos.h>     /*     */
#include <stdio.h>

/* Some ANSI C prototype definitions   */
void   setup_serial(void);
void   send_character(int ch);
int    get_character(void);

int       main(void)
{
int       inchar,outchar;

      setup_serial();
      do
      {
         puts("Enter char to be transmitted (Cntrl-D to end)");
         outchar=getch();
         send_character(outchar);
         inchar=get_character();
         printf("Character received was %c\n",inchar);
      } while (outchar!=4);
      return(0);
}

void      setup_serial(void)
{
      _outp( LCR, 0x80);
      /* set up bit 7 to a 1 to set Register address bit   */

      _outp(TXDATA,0x0C);
      _outp(TXDATA+1,0x00);
      /* load TxRegister with 12, crystal frequency is 1.8432MHz    */

      _outp(LCR, 0x0A);
      /* Bit pattern loaded is 00001010b, from msb to lsb these are:*/
      /* 0 - access TD/RD buffer ,  0 - normal output               */
      /* 0 - no stick bit  , 0 - even parity                        */
      /* 1 - parity on,  0 - 1 stop bit                             */
      /* 10 - 7 data bits                                           */
}

void send_character(int ch)
{
char  status;
      do
      {
         status = _inp(LSR) & 0x40;
      } while (status!=0x40);
      /*repeat until Tx buffer empty ie bit 6 set*/
```

```
        _outp(TXDATA,(char) ch);
}

int   get_character(void)
{
int   status;
      do
      {
         status = _inp(LSR) & 0x01;
      } while (status!=0x01);
      /* Repeat until bit 1 in LSR is set */
      return( (int)_inp(TXDATA));
}
```

📄 Program 25.2

```
/*        send.c                                        */
#define   TXDATA    0x3F8
#define   LSR       0x3FD
#define   LCR       0x3FB

#include    <stdio.h>
#include    <conio.h>   /* included for getch          */
#include    <dos.h>

void      setup_serial(void);
void      send_character(int ch);

int       main(void)
{
int       ch;
      puts("Transmitter program. Please enter text (Cntl-D to end)");
      setup_serial();
      do
      {
         ch=getche();
         send_character(ch);
      } while (ch!=4);
      return(0);
}

void   setup_serial(void)
{
      _outp( LCR, 0x80);
      /* set up bit 7 to a 1 to set Register address bit       */
      _outp(TXDATA,0x0C);
      _outp(TXDATA+1,0x00);
      /* load TxRegister with 12, crystal frequency is 1.8432MHz   */
      _outp(LCR, 0x0A);
      /* Bit pattern loaded is 00001010b, from msb to lsb these are:*/
      /* Access TD/RD buffer, normal output, no stick bit          */
      /* even parity, parity on, 1 stop bit, 7 data bits           */
}
void   send_character(int ch)
{
char   status;
      do
      {
         status = _inp(LSR) & 0x40;
      } while (status!=0x40);
      /*repeat until Tx buffer empty ie bit 6 set*/
      _outp(TXDATA,(char) ch);
}
```

📄 Program 25.3

```
/*         receive.c                                              */
#define  TXDATA    0x3F8
#define  LSR       0x3FD
#define  LCR       0x3FB
#include   <stdio.h>
#include   <conio.h>   /* included for getch                      */
#include   <dos.h>
void     setup_serial(void);
int      get_character(void);
int      main(void)
{
int      inchar;
       setup_serial();
       do
       {
          inchar=get_character();
          putchar(inchar);
       } while (inchar!=4);
       return(0);
}
void setup_serial(void)
{
       _outp( LCR, 0x80);
       /* set up bit 7 to a 1 to set Register address bit         */
       _outp(TXDATA,0x0C);
       _outp(TXDATA+1,0x00);
       /* load TxRegister with 12, crystal frequency is 1.8432MHz  */
       _outp(LCR, 0x0A);
       /* Bit pattern loaded is 00001010b, from msb to lsb these are:*/
       /* Access TD/RD buffer, normal output, no stick bit         */
       /* even parity, parity on, 1 stop bit, 7 data bits          */
}
int   get_character(void)
{
int   status;
       do
       {
          status = _inp(LSR) & 0x01;
       } while (status!=0x01);    /* Repeat until bit 1 in LSR is set */
       return( (int)_inp(TXDATA));
}
```

25.6   Interface to the Motherboard

The serial ports typically connect to the system through an Ultra I/O device, as illustrated in Figure 25.11. The signal lines for the serial ports connect to a 10-pin header on the motherboard, which then connects to the serial port connector through a ribbon cable.

25.7   Exercises

25.7.1   Which is the maximum cable length for a standard RS-232 connection?

(a)   2 m   (b)   20 m
(c)   200 m   (d)   2 km

25.7.2   Which enhancement to RS-232 allows for 1 Mbps bit rates and increased cable lengths?

(a)   RS-232x   (b)   RS-422
(c)   RS-444   (d)   RS-233

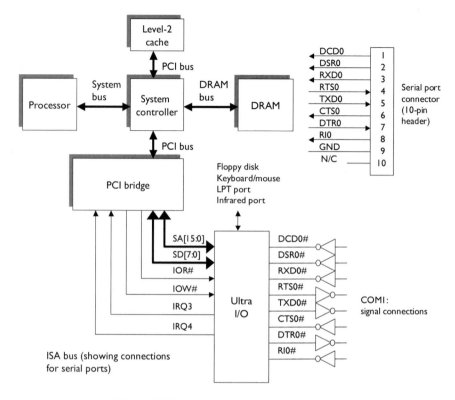

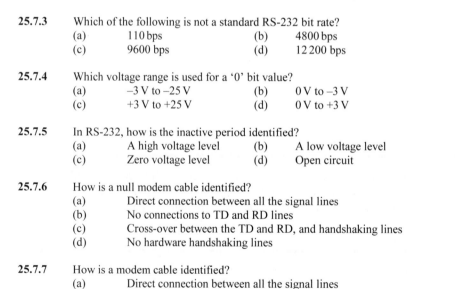

Figure 25.11 System connections for serial ports

25.7.3 Which of the following is not a standard RS-232 bit rate?
(a) 110 bps   (b) 4800 bps
(c) 9600 bps   (d) 12 200 bps

25.7.4 Which voltage range is used for a '0' bit value?
(a) −3 V to −25 V   (b) 0 V to −3 V
(c) +3 V to +25 V   (d) 0 V to +3 V

25.7.5 In RS-232, how is the inactive period identified?
(a) A high voltage level   (b) A low voltage level
(c) Zero voltage level   (d) Open circuit

25.7.6 How is a null modem cable identified?
(a) Direct connection between all the signal lines
(b) No connections to TD and RD lines
(c) Cross-over between the TD and RD, and handshaking lines
(d) No hardware handshaking lines

25.7.7 How is a modem cable identified?
(a) Direct connection between all the signal lines
(b) No connections to TD and RD lines
(c) Cross-over between the TD and RD, and handshaking lines
(d) No hardware handshaking lines

25.7.8 The main connections used to transmit data over a null modem cable with no hardware handshaking are?

(a)	TD, RD, GND	(b)	RTS, CTS, GND
(c)	DSR, DTR, GND	(d)	TD, RD, RTS, CTS

25.7.9 If a device transmits at 9600 bps, approximately how many characters are transmitted every minute?

(a)	5 760	(b)	57 600
(c)	576 000	(d)	5 760 000

25.7.10 If a device transmits at 4800 bps, approximately what is the period of a single bit?

(a)	2.08 µs	(b)	20.8 µs
(c)	208 µs	(d)	2.08 ms

25.7.11 Which handshaking line is used by a transmitter to identify that it is read to send data?

(a)	RTS	(b)	CTS
(c)	DTR	(d)	DTE

25.7.12 Which handshaking line is used by a receiver to identify that it is ready to receive data?

(a)	RTS	(b)	CTS
(c)	DTR	(d)	DTE

25.7.13 Which characters are used to start and stop data transfer in software handshaking?

(a)	X-ON, X-OFF	(b)	OFF, ON
(c)	IN, OUT	(d)	LF, CR

25.7.14 Which is the standard I/O port address for COM1?

(a)	1F8h	(b)	2F8h
(c)	3F8h	(d)	4F8h

25.7.15 Which is the standard I/O port address for COM2?

(a)	1F8h	(b)	2F8h
(c)	3F8h	(d)	4F8h

25.7.16 The standard IC used in RS-232 communications is?

(a)	8232	(b)	8086
(c)	8088	(d)	8250

25.7.17 Which register is used to determine the status of the RS-232 connection?

(a)	LSR	(b)	LCR
(c)	STATUS	(d)	TD/RD buffer

25.7.18 Which register is used to configure the RS-232 connection?

(a)	LSR	(b)	LCR
(c)	STATUS	(d)	TD/RD buffer

25.7.19 Write a program that continuously sends the character 'A' to the serial line. Observe the output on an oscilloscope and identify the bit pattern and the baud rate.

25.7.20 Write a program that continuously sends the characters from 'A' to 'Z' to the serial line. Observe the output on an oscilloscope.

25.7.21 Modify Program 25.2 so that the program prompts the user for the baud rate when the program is started. A sample run is shown in Sample run 25.1.

25.7.22 Complete Table 25.2 to give the actual time to send 1000 characters for the given baud rates. Compare these values with estimated values. Note that approximately 10 bits are used for each character thus 960 characters per second will be transmitted at 9600 baud.

🖳 Sample run 25.1

```
Enter baud rate required:
1    110      2  150     3   300      4   600
5    1200     6  2400    7   4800     8   9600
>> 8
RS232 transmission set to 9600 baud
```

25.7.23   Modify the `setup_serial()` routine so that the RS232 parameters can be passed to it. These parameters should include the comport (either `COM1:` or `COM2:`), the baud rate, the number of data bits and the type of parity. An outline of the modified function is given in Program 25.4.

25.7.24   One problem with Programs 25.2 and 25.3 is that when the return key is pressed only one character is sent. The received character will be a carriage return which returns the cursor back to the start of a line and not to the next line. Modify the receiver program so that a line feed will be generated automatically when a carriage return is received. Note a carriage return is an ASCII 13 and line feed is a 10.

Table 25.2   Baud rate divisors

Baud rate	Time to send 1000 characters (s)
110	
300	
600	
1200	
2400	
4800	
9600	
19200	

📄 Program 25.4

```c
#define     COM1BASE 0x3F8
#define     COM2BASE 0x2F8
#define     COM1        0
#define     COM2        1
enum     baud_rates  {BAUD110,BAUD300,BAUD600,BAUD1200,
                       BAUD2400,BAUD4800,BAUD9600};
enum     parity      {NO_PARITY,EVEN_PARITY,ODD_PARITY};
enum     databits    {DATABITS7,DATABITS8};
#include <conio.h>
#include <dos.h>
#include <stdio.h>
void  setup_serial(int comport, int baudrate, int parity,
                    int databits);
void  send_character(int ch);
int   get_character(void);
int   main(void)
{
int   inchar,outchar;

    setup_serial(COM1,BAUD2400,EVEN_PARITY,DATABITS7);
    :::::::::::::etc.
}
void  setup_serial(int comport, int baudrate, int parity, int databits)
{
int   tdreg,lcr;
    if (comport==COM1)
```

```
    {
        tdreg=COM1BASE;    lcr=COM1BASE+3;
    }
    else
    {
        tdreg=COM2BASE;    lcr=COM2BASE+3;
    }
    _outp( lcr, 0x80);
    /* set up bit 7 to a 1  to set Register address bit      */
    switch(baudrate)
    {
    case BAUD110: _outp(tdreg,0x17);_outp(tdreg+1,0x04); break;
    case BAUD300: _outp(tdreg,0x80);_outp(tdreg+1,0x01); break;
    case BAUD600: _outp(tdreg,0x00);_outp(tdreg+1,0xC0); break;
    case BAUD1200: _outp(tdreg,0x00);_outp(tdreg+1,0x40);break;
    case BAUD2400: _outp(tdreg,0x00);_outp(tdreg+1,0x30);break;
    case BAUD4800: _outp(tdreg,0x00);_outp(tdreg+1,0x18);break;
    case BAUD9600: _outp(tdreg,0x00);_outp(tdreg+1,0x0C);break;
    }
        :::::::::: etc.
}
```

25.7.25   Modify the `get_character()` routine so that it returns an error flag if it detects an error or if there is a time-out. Table 25.3 lists the error flags and the returned error value. An outline of the C code is given in Program 25.5. If a character is not received within 10 s an error message should be displayed.

Table 25.3   Error returns from get_character().

Error condition	Error flag return	Notes
Parity error	−1	
Overrun error	−2	
Framing error	−3	
Break detected	−4	
Time out	−5	`get_character()` should time out if no characters are received with 10 seconds.

Test the routine by connecting two PCs together and set the transmitter with differing RS-232 parameters.

📄 Program 25.5

```
#include <stdio.h>
#include <dos.h>
#define   TXDATA    0x3F8
#define   LSR       0x3FD
#define   LCR       0x3FB
void      show_error(int ch);
int       get_character(void);
enum      RS232_errors   {PARITY_ERROR=-1, OVERRUN_ERROR=-2,
          FRAMING_ERROR=-3, BREAK_DETECTED=-4, TIME_OUT=-5};
int       main(void)
{
int       inchar;
    do
    {
        inchar=get_character();
        if (inchar<0) show_error(inchar);
        else printf("%c",inchar);
    } while (inchar!=4);
```

```
            return(0);
      }
      void      show_error(int ch)
      {
         switch(ch)
         {
         case PARITY_ERROR: printf("Error: Parity error/n"); break;
         case OVERRUN_ERROR: printf("Error: Overrun error/n"); break;
         case FRAMING_ERROR: printf("Error: Framing error/n"); break;
         case BREAK_DETECTED: printf("Error: Break detected/n");break;
         case TIME_OUT: printf("Error: Time out/n"); break;
         }
      }
      int   get_character(void)
      {
      int   instatus;
         do
         {
            instatus = _inp(LSR) & 0x01;
            if (instatus & 0x02) return(BREAK_DETECTED);
                           :::: etc
         } while (instatus!=0x01 );
         return( (int) _inp(TXDATA) );
      }
```

25.8 Note from the Author

Good old RS-232. I have made more consultancy income with it than any other piece of computer equipment. I have also run more RS-232 training courses than all the more topical subjects areas (such as Java and C++) put together The reason for this is because it is one of the least understood connections on computer equipment. I've interfaced PCs to gas chromatographs (using an 8-port RS-232 card), a PC to a VAX, a Sun workstation to a PC, a PC to another PC, a Honeywell TDC to a PC, a PC to a PLC, and so on. For most applications, a serial port to serial port connection is still the easiest method to transfer data from one computer to another.

RS-232 is one of the most widely used 'standards' in the world. It is virtually standard on every computer and, while it is relatively slow, it is a reliable device. This over-rules its slowness, its non-standardness, its lack of powerful error checking, its lack of address facilities, and, so on. It shares its gold stars with solid performers, such as Ethernet and the parallel port. Neither of these are star performers and are far from perfect, but they are robust performers who will outlast many of their more modern contenders. When their position is challenged by a young contender, the standards agency simply invest a lot of experience and brainpower to increase their performance. Who would believe that the data rate over copper wires could be increased to 1 Gbps for Ethernet and to 1 MBps for RS-422. One trusted piece of equipment I could have never done without is an RS-232 transmitter/receiver. For this, I used an old 80386-based laptop computer (which weighs as much as a modern desktop computers) which ran either a simple DOS-based transmitter/receiver program (see previous chapter), or the Windows 3.1 Terminal program. These I could use just as an electronic engineer would use a multimeter to test the voltages and currents in a circuit. A sign that I was transmitting at the wrong bit rate or using an incorrect number of data bits was incorrectly received characters (but at least it was receiving characters, which was an important test).

Parallel Port

26.1 Introduction

This chapter discusses parallel communications. The Centronics printer interface transmits 8 bits of data at a time to an external device, normally a printer. A 25-pin D-type connector is used to connect to the PC and a 36-pin Centronics interface connector normally connects to the printer. This interface is not normally used for other types of interfacing as the standard interface transmits data over the data lines in only one direction, that is, from the PC to the external device. Some interface devices overcome this problem by using four of the input handshaking lines to input data and then multiplexing using an output handshaking line to multiplex them to produce 8 output bits.

As technology has improved, there has arisen a great need for a bidirectional parallel port to connect to devices such as tape back-up drives, CD-ROMs, and so on. The Centronics interface unfortunately lacks speed (150 kbps) and has limited length of lines (2 m), and very few computer manufacturers comply with an electrical standard.

Thus, in 1991, several manufacturers (including IBM and Texas Instruments) formed a group called NPA (National Printing Alliance). Their original objective was to develop a standard for controlling printers over a network. To achieve this, a bidirectional standard was developed, which was compatible with existing software. This standard was submitted to the IEEE so that they could standardize it. The committee that the IEEE set up was known as the IEEE 1284 committee and the standard they produced is known as the IEEE 1284–1994 Standard (as it was released in 1994).

With this standard, all parallel ports use a bidirectional link in either a compatible, nibble or byte mode. These modes are relatively slow as the software must monitor the handshaking lines (up to 100 kbps). To allow high speeds, the EPP (enhanced parallel port) and ECP (extended capabilities port protocol) modes which allows high-speed data transfer using automatic hardware handshaking. In addition to the previous three modes, EPP and ECP are being implemented on the latest I/O controllers by most of the super I/O chip manufacturers. These modes use hardware to assist in the data transfer. For example, in EPP mode, a byte of data can be transferred to the peripheral by a simple OUT instruction. The I/O controller handles all the handshaking and data transfer to the peripheral.

Figure 26.1 shows the pin connections on the PC connector. The data lines (D0–D7) output data from the PC and each of the data lines has an associated ground line (GND).

26.2 Data Handshaking

The main handshaking lines are $\overline{\text{ACK}}$, BUSY and $\overline{\text{STROBE}}$. Initially, the computer places the data on the data bus; it then sets the $\overline{\text{STROBE}}$ line low to inform the external device that the data on the data bus is valid. When the external device has read the data, it sets the $\overline{\text{ACK}}$ lines low to acknowledge that it has read the data. The PC then waits for the printer to set the BUSY line inactive, that is, low. Figure 26.2 shows a typical handshaking operation and Table 26.1 outlines the definitions of the pins.

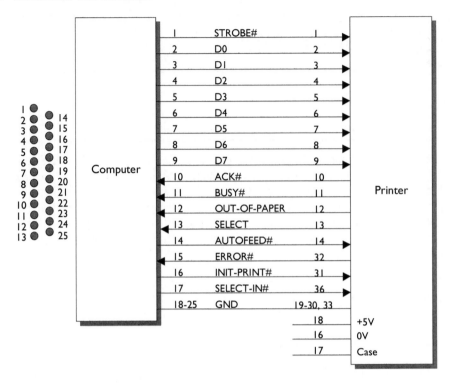

Figure 26.1   Centronics parallel interface showing pin numbers on PC connector

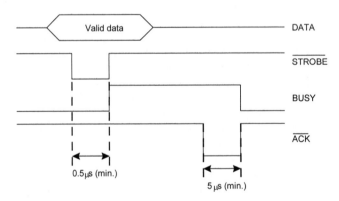

Figure 26.2   Data handshaking with the Centronics parallel printer interface

The parallel interface can be accessed by either direct reads to, and writes from, the I/O memory addresses or with a program that uses the BIOS printer interrupt. This interrupt allows a program either to get the status of the printer or to write a character to it. Table 26.2 outlines the interrupt calls.

26.2.1 BIOS printer

Program 26.1 uses the BIOS printer interrupt to test the status of the printer and output characters to the printer.

Table 26.1 Signal definitions

Signal	In/out	Description
$\overline{\text{STROBE}}$	Out	Indicates that valid data is on the data lines (active low).
$\overline{\text{AUTO FEED}}$	Out	Instructs the printer to insert a linefeed for every carriage return (active low).
$\overline{\text{SELECT INPUT}}$	Out	Indicates to the printer that it is selected (active low).
INIT	Out	Resets the printer.
$\overline{\text{ACK}}$	In	Indicates that the last character was received (active low).
BUSY	In	Indicates that the printer is busy and thus cannot accept data.
OUT OF PAPER	In	Out of paper.
SELECT	In	Indicates that the printer is online and connected.
$\overline{\text{ERROR}}$	In	Indicates that an error exists (active low).

Table 26.2 BIOS printer interrupt

Description	Input registers	Output registers
Initialize printer port	AH = 01h DX = printer number (00h–02h)	AH = printer status bit 7: not busy bit 6: acknowledge bit 5: out of paper bit 4: selected bit 3: I/O error bit 2: unused bit 1: unused bit 0: timeout
Write character to printer	AH = 00h AL = character to write DX = printer number (00h–02h)	AH = printer status
Get printer status	AH = 02h DX = printer number (00h–02h)	AH = printer status

📄 **Program 26.1**

```c
#include <dos.h>
#include <stdio.h>
#include <conio.h>

#define  PRINTERR -1

void  print_character(int ch);
int   init_printer(void);

int   main(void)
```

```
{
int    status,ch;

        status=init_printer();
        if (status==PRINTERR) return(1);
        do
        {
           printf("Enter character to output to printer");
           ch=getch();
           print_character(ch);
        } while (ch!=4);
        return(0);
}


int    init_printer(void)
{
union REGS inregs,outregs;

        inregs.h.ah=0x01; /* initialize printer */
        inregs.x.dx=0; /* LPT1: */
        int86(0x17,&inregs,&outregs);
        if (inregs.h.ah & 0x20)
        { puts("Out of paper"); return(PRINTERR); }
        else if (inregs.h.ah & 0x08)
        { puts("I/O error"); return(PRINTERR); }
        else if (inregs.h.ah & 0x01)
        { puts("Printer timeout"); return(PRINTERR); }
        return(0);
}

void  print_character(int ch)
{
union REGS inregs,outregs;

        inregs.h.ah=0x00; /* print character */
        inregs.x.dx=0; /* LPT1: */
        inregs.h.al=ch;
        int86(0x17,&inregs,&outregs);
}
```

26.3 I/O Addressing

The printer port has three I/O addresses assigned for the data, status and control ports. These addresses are normally assigned to:

Printer	Data register	Status register	Control register
LPT1	378h	379h	37ah
LPT2	278h	279h	27ah

The DOS debug program can be used to display the base addresses for the serial and parallel ports by displaying the 32 memory location starting at 0040:0008. For example:

```
-d 40:00
0040:0000  F8 03 F8 02 00 00 00 00-78 03 00 00 00 00 29 02
```

  The first four 16-bit addresses give the serial communications ports. In this case, there are two COM ports at address 03F8h (COM1) and 02F8h (for COM2). The next four 16-bit addresses gives the parallel port addressees. In this case, there are two parallel ports: one at 0378h (LPT1) and one at 0229h (LPT4).

26.3.1 *Output lines*

Figure 26.3 shows the bit definitions of the registers. The data port register links to the output lines. Writing a 1 to the bit position in the port sets the output high, while a 0 sets the corresponding output line to a low. Thus, to output the binary value 1010 1010b (AAh) to the parallel port data using Visual C++:

```
_outp(0x378,0xAA);   /* in Visual C this is _outp(0x378,0xAA); */
```

The output data lines are each capable of sourcing 2.6 mA and sinking 24 mA; it is thus essential that the external device does not try to pull these lines to ground.

The control port also contains five output lines, of which the lower 4 bits are $\overline{\text{STROBE}}$, $\overline{\text{AUTO FEED}}$, INIT and $\overline{\text{SELECT INPUT}}$, as illustrated in Figure 26.3. These lines can be used as either control lines or as data outputs. With the data line, a 1 in the register gives an output high, while the lines in the control port have inverted logic. Thus a 1 to a bit in the register causes an output low.

Program 26.2 outputs the binary pattern 0101 0101b (55h) to the data lines and sets $\overline{\text{SELECT INPUT}}$=0, INIT=1, $\overline{\text{AUTO FEED}}$=1 and $\overline{\text{STROBE}}$=0; the value of the data port will be 55h and the value written to the control port will be XXXX 1101 (where X represents 'don't care'). The value for the control output lines must be inverted, so that the $\overline{\text{STROBE}}$ line will be set to a 1 so that it will be output as a LOW.

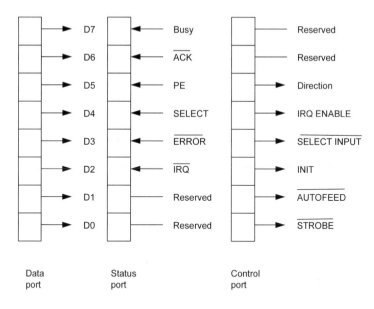

Figure 26.3 Port assignments

📄 Program 26.2

```
#define DATA       0x378
#define STATUS     DATA+1
#define CONTROL    DATA+2

int   main(void)
```

```
{
int out1,out2;

        out1 = 0x55;                   /* 0101 0101 */
        _outp(DATA, out1);
        out2 = 0x0D;                   /* 0000 1101 */
        _outp(CONTROL, out2);          /* STROBE=LOW, AUTOFEED=HIGH, etc */
        return(0);
}
```

The setting of the output value (in this case, out2) looks slightly confusing as the output is the inverse of the logical setting (that is, a 1 sets the output low). An alternative method is to exclusive-OR (EX-OR) the output value with $B which will invert the first, second and fourth least significant bits ($\overline{\text{SELECT INPUT}}$ =0, $\overline{\text{AUTO FEED}}$ =1, and $\overline{\text{STROBE}}$ =0), while leaving the third least significant bit (INIT) untouched. Thus the following will achieve the same as the previous program:

```
        out2 = 0x06;                   /* 0000 0110 */
        _outp(CONTROL, out2 ^ 0xb);    /* STROBE=LOW, AUTOFEED=HIGH, etc */
```

If the fifth bit on the control register (IRQ enable) is written as 1, then the output on this line will go from a high to a low, which will cause the processor to be interrupted.

The control lines are driven by open collector drivers pulled to +5 Vdc through 4.7 kΩ resistors. Each can sink approximately 7 mA and maintain 0.8 V down-level.

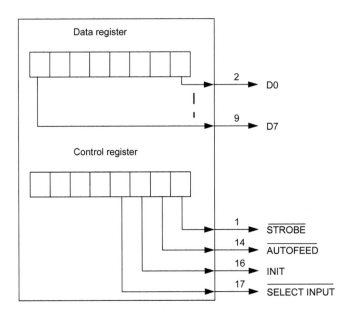

Figure 26.4   Output lines

26.3.2 Inputs

There are five inputs from the parallel port (BUSY, $\overline{\text{ACK}}$, PE, SELECT and $\overline{\text{ERROR}}$). The status of these lines can be found by simply reading the upper 5 bits of the status register, as illustrated in Figure 26.5.

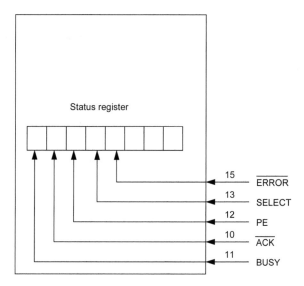

Figure 26.5 Input lines

Unfortunately, the BUSY line has an inverted status. Thus, when a LOW is present on BUSY, the bit will actually be read as a 1. For example, Program 26.3 reads the bits from the status register, inverts the BUSY bit and then shifts the bits three places to the right so that the 5 input bits are in the 5 least significant bits.

📄 **Program 26.3**

```
#include         <stdio.h>
#define DATA      0x378
#define STATUS    DATA+1
int    main(void)
{
unsigned int in1;

        in1 = _inp(STATUS); /* read from status register */
        in1 = in1 ^ 0x80        /* invert  BUSY bit  */
        in1 = in1 >> 3;            /* move bits so that the inputs are the least
                                    significant bits */
        printf("Status bits are %d\n",in1);
        return(0);
}
```

26.3.3 Electrical interfacing

The output lines can be used to drive LEDs. Figure 26.6 shows an example circuit where a LOW output will cause the LED to be ON while a HIGH causes the output to be OFF. For an input, an open push button causes a HIGH on the input.

26.3.4 Simple example

Program 26.4 uses a push button connected to pin 11 (BUSY). When the button is open, then the input to BUSY will be a HIGH and the most significant bit in the status register will thus be a 0 (as the BUSY signal is inverted). When the button is closed, then this bit will be a 1. This is tested with

```
    if (in1&0x80)==1)
```

When this condition is TRUE (that is, when the button is closed), then the output data lines (D0–D7) will flash on and off with a delay of 1 second between flashes. An output of all 1s to the data lines causes the LEDs to be off; all 0s causes the LEDs to be on.

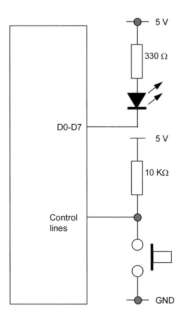

Figure 26.6 Interfacing to inputs and outputs

Program 26.4

```
/*    Flash LEDs on and off when the push button connected to BUSY   */
/*    is closed                                                       */
#include <stdio.h>
#include <dos.h>

#define DATA        0x378
#define STATUS      DATA+1
#define CONTROL     DATA+2

int main(void)
{
int in1;
    do
    {
        in1 = _inp(STATUS);

        if (in1&0x80)==1)  /* if switch closed this is TRUE  */
        {
            _outp(DATA,0x00);   /* LEDs on */
            delay(1000);
            _outp(DATA, 0xff);    /* LEDs off    */
            delay(1000);
        }
        else
            _outp(DATA,0x01); /* switch open */
    } while (!kbhit());
    return(0);
}
```

26.4 Interrupt-driven Parallel Port

We have discussed previously how the parallel port is used to output data. This section discusses how an external device can interrupt the processor. It does this by hooking onto the interrupt server routine for the interrupt that the port is attached to. Normally, this interrupt routine serves as a printer interrupt (such as lack of paper, paper jam and so on). Thus, an external device can use the interrupt service routine to transmit data to or from the PC.

26.4.1 Interrupts

Each parallel port is hooked to an interrupt. Normally, the primary parallel port is connected to IRQ7. It is assumed in this section that this is the case. As with the serial port, this interrupt line must be enabled by setting the appropriate bit in the interrupt mask register (IMR), which is based at address 21h. The bit for IRQ7 is the most significant bit, and it must be set to a 0 to enable the interrupt. As with the serial port, the end of interrupt signal must be acknowledged by setting the EOI signal bit of the interrupt control register (ICR) to a 1.

The interrupt on the parallel port is caused by the $\overline{\text{ACK}}$ line (pin 10) going from a high to a low (just as a printer would acknowledge the reception of a character). For this interrupt to be passed to the PIC, then bit 4 of the control port (IRQ Enable) must be set to a 1.

26.4.2 Example program

Program 26.5 is a simple interrupt-driven parallel port Borland C program. The program interrupts the program each time the $\overline{\text{ACK}}$ line is pulled LOW. When this happens, the output value should change corresponding to a binary count (0000 0000 to 1111 1111, and then back again). The user can stop the program by pressing any key on the keyboard. Figure 26.7 shows a sample set-up with a push button connected to the $\overline{\text{ACK}}$ line and LEDs connected to the output data lines.

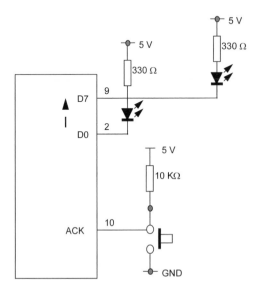

Figure 26.7 Example set-up for interrupt-driven parallel port

🖹 Program 26.5

```
/* Program to sample data from the parallel port   */
/* when the ACK line goes low                       */
#include <stdio.h>
#include <bios.h>
#include <conio.h>
#include <dos.h>
#define   TRUE     1
#define   FALSE    0
#define   DATA     0x378
#define   STATUS   DATA+1
#define   CONTROL  DATA+2
#define   IRQ7     0x7F  /* LPT1 interrupt */
#define   EOI      0x20  /* End of Interrupt */
#define   ICR      0x20  /* Interrupt Control Register */
#define   IMR      0x21  /* Interrupt Mask Register */

void  interrupt far pl_interrupt(void);
void  setup_parallel (void);
void  set_vectors(void);
void  enable_interrupts(void);
void  disable_interrupts(void);
void  reset_vectors(void);
void  interrupt far (*oldvect)();
int   int_flag = TRUE;
int   outval=0;

int main(void)
{
      set_vectors();
      setup_parallel();
      do
      {
         if (int_flag)
         {
            printf("New value sent\n");
            int_flag=FALSE;
         }
      } while (!kbhit());
      reset_vectors();
      return(0);
}

void  setup_parallel(void)
{

   outportb(CONTROL, inportb(CONTROL) | 0x10);
                  /* Set Bit 4 on control port to a 1 */
}

void interrupt far pl_interrupt(void)
{
      disable();
      outportb(DATA,outval);
      if (outval!=255) outval++; else outval=0;
      int_flag=TRUE;
      outportb(ICR,EOI);
      enable();
}

void set_vectors(void)
{
int int_mask;
```

```
         disable();                    /* disable all ints           */
         oldvect=getvect(0x0f);        /* save any old vector         */
         setvect (0x0f,pl_interrupt);  /* set up for new int serv     */
}

void  enable_interrupts(void)
{
int ch;
         disable();
         ch=inportb(IMR);
         outportb(IMR, ch & IRQ7);
         enable();
}


void  disable_interrupts(void)
{
int ch;
         disable();
         outportb(IMR, ch & ~IRQ7);
         enable();
}

void  reset_vectors(void)
{
         setvect(0x0f,oldvect);
}
```

26.4.3 Program explanation

The initial part of the program enables the interrupt on the parallel port by setting bit 4 of the control register to 1:

```
void  setup_parallel(void)
{

   outportb(CONTROL, inportb(CONTROL) | 0x10); /* Set Bit 4 on control port*/
}
```

After the serial port has been initialized, the interrupt service routine for the IRQ7 line is set to point to a new 'user-defined' service routine. The primary parallel port LPT1: normally sets the IRQ7 line active when the $\overline{\text{ACK}}$ line goes from a high to a low. The interrupt associated with IRQ7 is 0Fh (15). The getvect() function gets the ISR address for this interrupt, which is then stored in the variable oldvect so that at the end of the program it can be restored. Finally, in the set_vectors() function, the interrupt assigns a new 'user-defined' ISR (in this case it is the function pl_interrupt()):

```
void set_vectors(void)
{
int int_mask;
         disable();  /* disable all ints */
         oldvect=getvect(0x0f);  /* save any old vector */
         setvect (0x0f,pl_interrupt);  /* set up for new int serv */
}
```

At the end of the program the ISR is restored with the following code:

```
void  reset_vectors(void)
{
         setvect(0x0f,oldvect);
}
```

To enable the IRQ7 line on the PIC, bit 5 of the IMR (interrupt mask register) is to be set to a 0. The statement

```
ch = inportb(IMR) & 0x7F;
```

achieves this as it bitwise ANDs all the bits, except for bit 7, with a 1. This is because any bit that is ANDed with a 0 results in a 0. The bit mask 0x7F has been defined with the macro IRQ7:

```
void  enable_interrupts(void)
{
int ch;
      disable();
      ch=inportb(IMR);
      outportb(IMR, ch & IRQ7);
      enable();
}
```

At the end of the program, the interrupt on the parallel port is disabled by setting bit 7 of the IMR to a 1; this disables IRQ7 interrupts:

```
void  disable_interrupts(void)
{
int ch;
      disable();
      outportb(IMR, ch & ~IRQ7);
      enable();
}
```

The ISR for the IRQ7 function is set to pl_interrupt(). It outputs the value of outval, which is incremented each time the interrupt is called (note that there is a roll-over statement that resets the value of outval back to zero when its value is 255). At the end of the ISR, the end of interrupt flag is set in the interrupt control register with the statement outportb(ICR, EOI);, as follows:

```
void interrupt far pl_interrupt(void)
{
      disable();
      outportb(DATA,outval);
      if (outval!=255) outval++; else outval=0;
      int_flag=TRUE;
      outportb(ICR,EOI);
      enable();
}
```

The main() function calls the initialization and the de-initialization functions. It also contains a loop that continues until any key is pressed. Within this loop, the keyboard is tested to determine whether a key has been pressed. The interrupt service routine sets int_flag. If the main routine detects that it is set, it displays the message 'New value sent' and resets the flag:

```
int main(void)
{
   set_vectors();
   outportb(CONTROL, inportb(CONTROL) | 0x10);
                /* set bit 4 on control port to logic one */
```

```
     do
     {
        if (int_flag)
        {
           printf("New value sent\n");
           int_flag=FALSE;
        }
  } while (!kbhit());
  reset_vectors();

  return(0);
}
```

26.5 ECP/EPP Mode

The Centronics parallel port only allows data to be sent from the host to a peripheral. To overcome this, the IEEE published the 1284 standard, entitled 'Standard Signaling Method for a Bidirectional Parallel Peripheral Interface for Personal Computers'. It allows for bidirectional communication and high communication speeds, while being backwardly compatible with existing parallel ports.

The IEEE-1284 standard defines the following modes:

* Compatibility mode (forward direction only). This mode defines the transfer of data between the PC and the printer (Centronics mode, as covered in the previous chapter).
* Nibble mode (reverse direction). This mode defines how 4 bits are transferred at a time, using status lines for the input data (sometimes known as Hewlett-Packard Bi-tronics). The Nibble mode can thus be used for bidirectional communication, with the data lines being used as outputs. To input a byte requires two nibble cycles.
* Byte mode (reverse direction). This mode defines how 8 bits are transferred at a time.
* Enhanced parallel port (EPP). This mode defines a standard bidirectional communication and is used by many peripherals, such as CD-ROMs, tape drives, external hard disks, and so on.

In the IEEE 1284 standard, the control and status signal for nibble, byte and EPP modes have been renamed. It also classifies the modes as forward (data goes from the PC), reverse (data is input into the PC) and bidirectional. Both the compatibility and nibble modes can be implemented with all parallel ports (as the nibble mode uses the status lines and the compatibility mode only outputs data). Some parallel ports support input and output on the data lines and thus support the byte mode. This is usually implemented by the addition of a direction bit on the control register.

26.5.1 Compatibility mode

The compatibility mode was discussed in the previous section. In this mode, the program sends data to the data lines and then sets the $\overline{\text{STROBE}}$ LOW and then HIGH. These then latch the data to the printer. The operations that the program does are:

1. Data is written to the data register.
2. The program reads from the status register to test whether the BUSY signal is LOW (that is, the printer is not busy)
3. If the printer is not busy, then the program sets the $\overline{\text{STROBE}}$ line active LOW.
4. Program then makes the $\overline{\text{STROBE}}$ line HIGH by deasserting it.

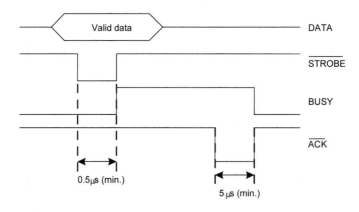

Figure 26.8   Compatibility mode transfer

26.5.2 Nibble mode

This mode defines how 4 bits are transferred at a time, using status lines for the input data (sometimes known as Hewlett-Packard Bitronics). The Nibble mode can thus be used for bi-directional communication, with the data lines being used as outputs. To input a byte requires two nibble cycles. As seen in the previous section, there are five inputs from the parallel port (BUSY, $\overline{\text{ACK}}$, PE, SELECT and $\overline{\text{ERROR}}$). The status of these lines can be found simply by reading the upper 5 bits of the status register. The BUSY, PE, SELECT and $\overline{\text{ERROR}}$ are normally used as $\overline{\text{ACK}}$ used to interrupt the processor.

Table 26.3 defines the names of the signal in the nibble mode and Figure 26.9 shows the handshaking for this mode.

Table 26.3   Nibble mode signals

Compatibility signal name	Nibble mode name	In/out	Description
STROBE	STROBE	Out	Not used.
$\overline{\text{AUTO FEED}}$	HostBusy	Out	Host nibble mode handshake signal. It is set LOW to indicate that the host is ready for nibble and set HIGH when the nibble has been received.
$\overline{\text{SELECT INPUT}}$	1284Active	Out	Set HIGH when the host is transferring data.
$\overline{\text{INIT}}$	$\overline{\text{INIT}}$	Out	Not used.
$\overline{\text{ACK}}$	PtrClk	In	Indicates valid data on the status lines. It is set low to indicate that there is valid data on the control lines and then set HIGH when the HostBusy going high.
BUSY	PtrBusy	In	Data bit 3 for one cycle, then data bit 7.
PE	AckDataReq	In	Data bit 2 for one cycle, then data bit 6.
SELECT	Xflag	In	Data bit 1 for one cycle, then data bit 5.
$\overline{\text{ERROR}}$	DataAvail	In	Data bit 0 for one cycle, then data bit 4.
D0–D7	D0–D7		Not Used.

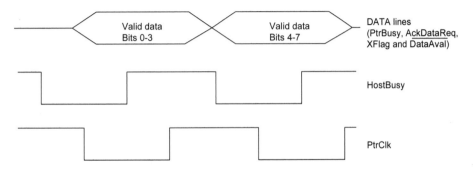

Figure 26.9 Nibble mode data transfer cycle

The nibble mode has the following sequence:

1. Host (PC) indicates that it is ready to receive data by setting HostBusy LOW.
2. The peripheral places the first nibble on the status lines.
3. The peripheral indicates that the data is valid on the status line by setting PtrClk low.
4. The host reads from the status lines and sets HostBusy high to indicate that it has received the nibble, but it is not yet ready for another nibble.
5. The peripheral sets PtrClk HIGH as an acknowledgement to the host.
6. Repeat steps 1–5 for the second nibble.

These operations are software-intensive as the driver has to set and read the handshaking lines. This limits transfer to about 50 kBps. Its main advantage is that it will work with all printer ports because it uses the standard Centronics set-up and is normally used in low-speed bidirectional operations, such as ADC adapters, reading data from switches, and so on.

Figure 26.10 illustrates the operation of the nibble mode, where 4 data bits are read into the parallel port using the 4 input handshaking lines. The status of these lines is then read by interrogating the upper four bits of the status register. This method is fine when there is no handshaking and when there are 4, or less, data bits to be read in. If there are more, or if there is handshaking, then extra circuitry is required.

Figure 26.11 shows how the nibble mode can be used to read-in 8 bits at a time. For this, 1 bit of the data output lines (D0) is used to select either the upper 4 bits or the lower 4 bits of the 8-bit data byte. If D0 is a low (0) then the lower 4 bits are selected. If it is a high (1), then the upper 4 bits are selected. The D0 output line connects to a multiplexor, which will select the lower or upper 4 bits. If A is the multiplexor selector line, X[1:4] are the input data bits and Z[1:4] the output from the multiplexor, then the equation for the multiplexor is:

$$Z[1] = AX[5] + \overline{A}X[1]$$

$$Z[2] = AX[6] + \overline{A}X[2]$$

$$Z[3] = AX[7] + \overline{A}X[3]$$

$$Z[4] = AX[8] + \overline{A}X[4]$$

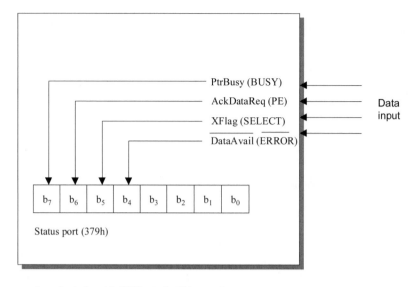

```
inval=(_inp(0x379) & 0xf0) >> 4
```

Figure 26.10   Nibble mode interfacing

26.5.3 Byte mode

The byte mode is often known as a bidirectional port and it uses bidirectional data lines. It has the advantage over nibble mode in that it only takes a single cycle to transfer a byte. Unfortunately, it is only compatible with newer ports. Table 26.4 defines the names of the signal in the nibble mode and Figure 26.12 shows the handshaking for this mode.

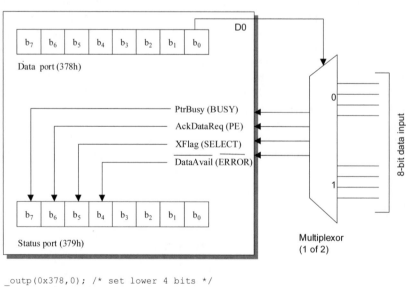

```
_outp(0x378,0); /* set lower 4 bits */
inval1=(_inp(0x379) & 0xf0) >> 4;
_outp(0x378,1); /* set upper 4 bits */
inval=(_inp(0x379) & 0xf0) +inval1;
```

Figure 26.11   Nibble mode for 8-bit input

The byte mode has the following sequence:

1. Host (PC) indicates that it is ready to receive data by setting HostBusy LOW.
2. The peripheral places the byte on the status lines.
3. The peripheral indicates that the data is valid on the status line by setting PtrClk LOW.
4. The host reads from the data lines and sets HostBusy HIGH to indicate that it has received the nibble, but it is not yet ready for another nibble.
5. The peripheral sets PtrClk HIGH as an acknowledgement to the host.
6. The host acknowledges the transfer by pulsing HostClk.

Table 26.4 Byte mode signals

Compatibility signal name	Byte mode name	In/Out	Description
$\overline{\text{STROBE}}$	HostClk	Out	Used as an acknowledgment signal. It is pulsed low after each transferred byte.
$\overline{\text{AUTO FEED}}$	HostBusy	Out	It is set LOW to indicate that the host is ready for nibble and set HIGH when the nibble has been received.
$\overline{\text{SELECT INPUT}}$	1284Active	Out	Set HIGH when the host is transferring data.
$\overline{\text{INIT}}$	$\overline{\text{INIT}}$	Out	Not used.
$\overline{\text{ACK}}$	PtrClk	In	Indicates valid data byte. It is set LOW to indicate that there is valid data on the data lines and then set HIGH when the HostBusy going high.
BUSY	PtrBusy	In	Busy status (for forward direction).
PE	AckDataReq	In	Same as $\overline{\text{DataAvail}}$.
SELECT	Xflag	In	Not used.
$\overline{\text{ERROR}}$	$\overline{\text{DataAvail}}$	In	Indicates that there is reverse data available.
D0–D7	D0–D7	In/Out	Input/output data lines.

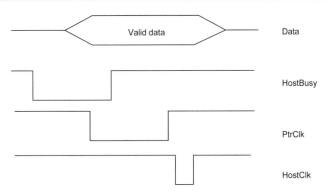

Figure 26.12 Byte mode data transfer cycle

26.5.4 EPP

The EPP mode defines a standard bidirectional communications mode and is used by many peripherals, such as CD-ROMs, tape drives, external hard disks and so on.

The EPP protocol provides four types of data transfer cycles:

1. Data read and write cycles. These involve transfers between the host and the peripheral.
2. Address read and write cycles. These pass address, channel, or command and control information.

Table 26.5 defines the names of the signal in the nibble mode. The $\overline{\text{WRITE}}$ occurs automatically when the host writes data to the output lines.

The data write cycle has the following sequence:

1. Program executes an I/O write cycle to the base address port + 4 (EPP data port) (see Table 26.4). Then the following occur with hardware:
2. The $\overline{\text{WRITE}}$ line is set LOW, which puts the data on the data bus.
3. The $\overline{\text{DATASTB}}$ is then set LOW.
4. The host waits for peripheral to set the $\overline{\text{WAIT}}$ line HIGH.
5. The $\overline{\text{DATASTB}}$ and $\overline{\text{WRITE}}$ are then HIGH and the cycle ends.

The important parameter is that it takes just one memory-mapped I/O operation to transfer data. This gives transfer rates of up to 2 million bytes per second. Although it is not as fast as a peripheral transferring over the ISA, it has the advantage that the peripheral can transfer data at a rate that is determined by the peripheral.

Table 26.5   EPP mode signals

Compatibility signal name	EPP mode name	In/out	Description
STROBE	WRITE	Out	A LOW for a write operation while a HIGH indicates a read operation.
$\overline{\text{AUTO FEED}}$	$\overline{\text{DATASTB}}$	Out	Indicates a data read or write operation.
$\overline{\text{SELECT INPUT}}$	$\overline{\text{ADDRSTROBE}}$	Out	Indicates an address read or write operation.
$\overline{\text{INIT}}$	$\overline{\text{RESET}}$	Out	Peripheral reset when LOW.
$\overline{\text{ACK}}$	$\overline{\text{INTR}}$	In	Peripheral sets this line LOW when it wishes to interrupt to the host.
BUSY	$\overline{\text{WAIT}}$	In	When it is set LOW it indicates that it is valid to start a cycle, else if it is HIGH then it is valid to end the cycle.
PE	User defined	In	Can be set by each peripheral.
SELECT	User defined	In	Can be set by each peripheral.
$\overline{\text{ERROR}}$	User defined	In	Can be set by each peripheral.
D0–D7	AD0–AD7	In/out	Bidirectional address and data lines.

EPP registers

Several extra ports are defined: these include the EPP address register and EPP data register. The EPP address register has an offset of 3 bytes from the base address and the EPP data register is offset by 4 bytes. Table 26.6 defines the registers.

Table 26.6 EPP register definitions

Port Name	I/O address	Read/ write	Description
Data register	BASE_AD	W	
Status register	BASE_AD +1	R	
Control register	BASE_AD +2	W	
EPP address port	BASE_AD+3	R/W	Generates EPP address read or write cycle
EPP data port	BASE_AD+4	R/W	Generates EPP data read or write cycle

26.5.5 ECP

The ECP protocol was proposed by Hewlett-Packard and Microsoft as an advanced mode for communication with printer and scanner type peripherals. It provides a high-performance bidirectional data transfer between a host and a peripheral.

The standard provides for two cycle types in both forward and reverse directions:

1. Data cycles.
2. Command cycles, which can either be a run length count or a channel address.

It has many advantages over the EPP standard, including:

- Standard addresses. ECP has standard register addresses; Figure 26.13 shows that the addresses from 0778h to 077Ah have been defined for the extra functionality of ECP.
- Run length encoding (RLE). RLE allows for compression. It allows high compression rates when there is a great deal of repetitive information in a file (typically with graphics files). A repetitive sequence is identified by a count followed by the repeated byte.
- FIFOs for both the forward and reverse channels.
- DMA as well as programmed I/O for the host register interface.
- Channel addressing. This allows multiple logical devices to be located within a single physical device. This channel address is passed in the command phase and can support up to 128 devices (addresses 0 to 127). For example, a single unit could have an integrated printer, fax and modem. ECP channel address allows them all to be accessed over a single connection. Within one physical package, having a single parallel port attached, there is a printer, fax and modem. This has the advantage that the printer can be busy printing while the modem can be accessed at the same time.

ECP redefines the SPP signals to be consistent with the ECP handshake. Table 26.7 describes these signals.

Figure 26.14 shows two forward data transfer cycles. It has data followed by a command phase. A high on the HostAck line indicates a data cycle, whereas a low indicates a command cycle. In the low state (command cycle), the data represents either an RLE count or a channel address. The most significant bit of the data byte indicates whether it is an RLE count or a channel address. If it is a 0, then the other 7 bits represent a RLE count (from 0 to 127), else a 1 represents a channel address (from 0 to 127).

In the forward mode, the transfer of the data is from the host to the peripheral. Initially the host places its data on the data bus. It sets the HostAck line high to indicate a data cycle and sets HostClk low to indicate valid data. Next, the peripheral acknowledges the host by setting PeriphAck high. The host sets HostClk high which clocks the data into the peripheral. After this, the peripheral sets PeriphAck low to indicate that it is ready for the next byte.

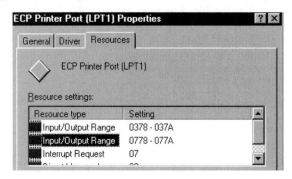

Figure 26.13   ECP input/output address ranges

Table 26.7   ECP mode signals

Compatibility signal name	ECP mode name	In/out	Description
STROBE	HostClk	I	Transfers data or address information in the forward direction (along with PeriphAck).
AUTO FEED	HostAck	O	Command/Data status in the forward direction. Data transfer in reverse direction (along with PeriphClk).
SELECT INPUT	1284Active	O	Set high when host is in a 1284 transfer mode.
INIT	ReverseRequest	O	A low puts channnel in reverse direction.
ACK	PeriphClk	I	Transfer data in the reverse direction (along with HostAck).
BUSY	PeriphAck	I	Transfer data or command information (along with HostClk).
PE	nAckReverse	I	Acknowledgement to nReverseRequest.
SELECT	Xflag	I	Extensibility flag.
ERROR	nPeriphRequest	I	Set low by peripheral to indicate that reverse data is available.
D0–D7	Data[8:1]	I/O	Data lines.

Figure 26.15 illustrates an example of the reverse channel transfer where the peripheral transfers information to the host. As before, it shows a command cycle followed by a data cycle. It is similar to the forward phase except that the host requests a reverse channel by setting the nReverseRequest low. The peripheral then sets the nAckReverse line low to indicate that it is ready to transfer data, then it puts the data on the data bus. It then sets the PeriphAck high to indicate that it is a data cycle and sets PeriphClk low to indicate valid data. After this the host sets HostAck high to acknowledge these events and the peripheral sets PeriphClk high. This clock edge then clocks the data into the host. Finally, the host sets HostAck low to indicate that it is ready for the next byte.

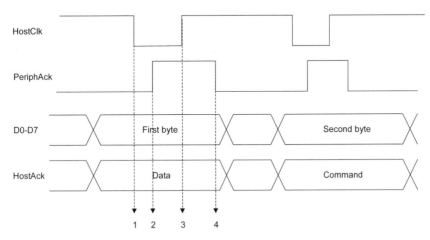

Figure 26.14 ECP forward data and command cycle

ECP software and register interface

The ECP specification ('The IEEE 1284 Extended Capabilities Port Protocol and ISA Interface Standard') defines a number of operational modes. These are defined in Table 26.8 The registers used to program ECP are based on the standard parallel port setting, and use an address that is offset by 1024 (400h) from the standard port address. Thus:

Standard port base address = 378h
ECP extended registers   = 378h + 400h = 778h

There are six extra registers defined for ECP; these are given in Table 26.9. These six registers are mapped into three memory addresses and are shown in Figure 26.15 (778h, 779h and 77Ah). The ECR register is used to set the current operational mode, and can also be used to determine whether an ECP-capable port is installed in the PC. Detection software can try to access any ECR registers by adding 402h to the base address of the LPT ports identified in the BIOS LPT port table.

The operation of the ECP port is similar to the EPP port. The ECR register is used to set an operational mode, after which an I/O port is used to transfer data (the actual port depends on the mode). Handshaking is done automatically by the hardware and there is no need for the software to control it.

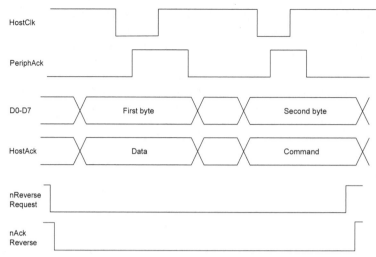

Figure 26.15   ECP Reverse data and command cycle

Table 26.8   ECR register modes

Mode	Description	Mode	Description
000	SPP mode	100	EPP parallel port mode (note 1)
001	Bidirectional mode (byte mode)	101	Reserved
010	Fast Centronics	110	Test mode
011	ECP parallel port mode	111	Configuration mode

Table 26.9   ECP register descriptions

Offset	Name	Read/Write	ECP Mode	Function
000	Data	R/W	000-001	Data register
000	ecpAfifo	R/W	011	ECP address FIFO
001	dsr	R/W	all	Status register
002	dcr	R/W	all	Control register
400	cFifo	R/W	010	Parallel port data FIFO
400	ecpDfifo	R/W	011	ECP data FIFO
400	tfifo	R/W	110	Test FIFO
400	cnfgA	R	111	Configuration register A
401	cnfgB	R/W	111	Configuration register B
402	ecr	R/W	all	Extended control register

26.6 Interface to the Motherboard

Figure 26.16 shows the connection of the parallel port to the system motherboard. Normally, this is achieved through an ultra I/O device, which provides the main signal connections. The connection on the motherboard is a 26-pin header connection, which then typically connects to the parallel port connect using a ribbon cable. The interrupt line from the parallel port is IRQ7.

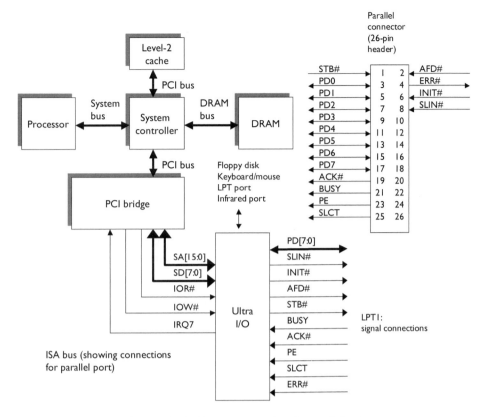

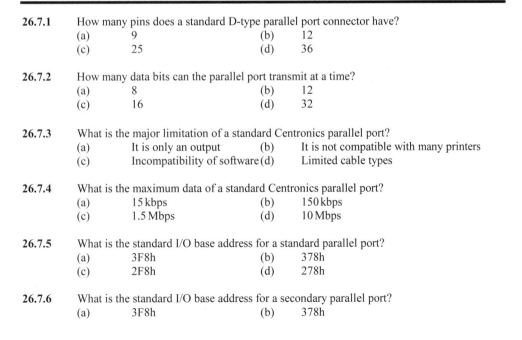

Figure 26.16 System connections for parallel port

26.7 Exercises

26.7.1 How many pins does a standard D-type parallel port connector have?
(a)　　9　　　　　　　　　　(b)　　12
(c)　　25　　　　　　　　　(d)　　36

26.7.2 How many data bits can the parallel port transmit at a time?
(a)　　8　　　　　　　　　　(b)　　12
(c)　　16　　　　　　　　　(d)　　32

26.7.3 What is the major limitation of a standard Centronics parallel port?
(a)　　It is only an output　　(b)　　It is not compatible with many printers
(c)　　Incompatibility of software (d)　　Limited cable types

26.7.4 What is the maximum data of a standard Centronics parallel port?
(a)　　15 kbps　　　　　　　(b)　　150 kbps
(c)　　1.5 Mbps　　　　　　(d)　　10 Mbps

26.7.5 What is the standard I/O base address for a standard parallel port?
(a)　　3F8h　　　　　　　　(b)　　378h
(c)　　2F8h　　　　　　　　(d)　　278h

26.7.6 What is the standard I/O base address for a secondary parallel port?
(a)　　3F8h　　　　　　　　(b)　　378h

(c)   2F8h   (d)   278h

26.7.7   What is the standard interrupt line for a standard parallel port?
(a)   IRQ3   (b)   IRQ4
(c)   IRQ5   (d)   IRQ7

26.7.8   How many pins does a standard D-type parallel port connector have?
(a)   9   (b)   12
(c)   25   (d)   36

26.7.9   What is the maximum transfer rate for ECP/EPP mode?
(a)   100 kB/s   (b)   150 kB/s
(c)   1 MB/s   (d)   1.2 MB/s

26.7.10   Outline the operation of the nibble mode. How does the parallel port allow data to be input?

26.7.11   Design a circuit for nibble mode operation, which will sample data bits. The design should include ground connections (GND), connector types and pin numbers. If possible, implement the design by adding switches to simulate input levels (power can be supplied by the parallel port connection).

26.7.12   Explain how several devices can be connected to the parallel port, and explain how the operating system identifies each of the devices.

26.7.13   Write a program that sends a 'walking-ones' code to the parallel port. The delay between changes should be 1 second. A 'walking-ones' code is as follows:

```
00000001
00000010
00000100
00001000
  :  :
10000000
00000001
00000010
```
and so on.

Hint: Use a `do...while` loop with either the shift left operators ($<<$) or output the values 0x01, 0x02, 0x04, 0x08, 0x10, 0x20, 0x40, 0x80, 0x01, 0x02, and so on.

26.7.14   Write separate programs that output the patterns in the following sequence:

```
(a)   00000001    (b)    10000001
      00000010           01000010
      00000100           00100100
      00001000           00011000
      00010000           00100100
      00100000           01000010
      01000000           10000001
      10000000           01000010
      01000000           00100100
      00100000           00011000
      00010000           00100100
        : :        and so on.
      00000001
      00000010
      and so on.
```

26.7.15   Write separate programs that output the following sequences:

(a)	1010 1010	(b)	1111 1111
	0101 0101		0000 0000
	1010 1010		1111 1111
	0101 0101		0000 0000
	and so on.		and so on.

(c)	0000 0001	(d)	0000 0001
	0000 0011		0000 0011
	0000 1111		0000 0111
	0001 1111		0000 1111
	0011 1111		0001 1111
	0111 1111		0011 1111
	1111 1111		0111 1111
	0000 0001		1111 1111
	0000 0011		0111 1111
	0000 0111		0011 1111
	0000 1111		0001 1111
	0001 1111		0000 1111
	and so on.		and so on.

(e)   The inverse of (d) above.

26.7.16 Binary coded decimal (BCD) is used mainly in decimal displays and is equivalent to the decimal system where a 4-bit code represents each decimal number. The first 4 bits represent the units, the next 4 the tens, and so on. Write a program that outputs to the parallel port a BCD sequence with a 1-second delay between changes. A sample BCD table is given in Table 26.3. The output should count from 0 to 99.

Hint: One possible implementation is to use two variables to represent the units and tens. These would then be used in a nested loop. The resultant output value will then be (tens << 4)+units. An outline of the loop code is given next.

```
for (tens=0;tens<10;tens++)
   for (units=0;units<10;units++)
      {
      }
```

Table 26.10 BCD conversion

Digit	BCD
00	00000000
01	00000001
02	00000010
03	00000011
04	00000100
05	00000101
06	00000110
07	00000111
08	00001000
09	00001001
10	00010000
11	00010001
.	.
.	.
.	.
97	10010111
98	10011000
99	10011001

26.7.17   Write a program that interfaces to a seven-segment display and displays an incremented value every second. Each of the segments should be driven from one of the data lines on the parallel port. For example:

Value	Segment						Hex
	A	B	C	D	E	F	G	value
0	1	1	1	0	1	1	1	77h
1	0	0	1	0	0	1	0	12h
2	1	1	0	1	0	1	1	6Bh
:				:	:		
9	0	0	1	1	1	1	1	1Fh

Two ways of implementing this are to determine the logic for each segment, and to have a basic look-up table, such as:

```
int seg_val[8]={0x77, 0x12, 0x6B, ... 0x1F};
        val=seq_val(count % 10);
                                /* mask-off the least-significant digit
*/
                outportb(0x378,seg_val[val]);
```

26.7.18   Write a program that counts the number of pushes of a button. The display should show the value.

26.7.19   Modify the program developed in Exercise 26.7.16 so that it outputs the count value to the parallel port.

26.7.20   Modify the program developed in Exercise 26.7.16 so that the display is incremented when the user presses a button.

26.7.21   Write a program in which the user presses a button, which causes the program to read from the parallel port.

26.7.22   Write a printer driver in which a string buffer is passed to it and this is then output to the printer. The driver should include all the correct error checking (such as out-of-paper, and so on).

26.8 Note from the Author

The parallel port is hardly the greatest piece of technology. In its standard form, it allows only for simplex communications from the PC outwards. However, like the RS-232 port, it is a standard part of the PC, and it is cheap. So, interface designers have worked under difficult circumstances to improve its specifications, such as increasing its bit rate and allowing multiple devices to connect to it at the same time, but it still suffers from a lack of controllability. Anyone who has changed the interface of a device from the parallel port to the USB will know how much better the USB port is over the parallel port.

So why has the serial port become more popular than the parallel port? For one reason: since PCs first became available, the serial port has always been a standard port and most manufacturers abide with it, whereas the parallel port was a quick fix so that the original PC could communicate with a printer. In its standard form, it can only send information in a single direction, and, even worse, only 8 bits can be sent at a time. Nevertheless, it has survived, and now has several uses, especially with printers, scanners and external CD-ROMs. So it will hold the fort for a few years yet before the USB port takes over in creating a truly integrated bus system. But, the USB port is serial, so why transmit 1 bit at a time when you can transmit 8 or 16 or even 32 bits at a time? This is to do with the number of wires that must be connected. A serial bus always has the advantage over a parallel bus in that you need only one signal line in a serial bus to transmit all the data. This saves space in both the connector and the cable. It is also cheaper to install.

Personally, I think that there is no better bus for a student learning how to interface to external devices. It is relatively easy to build the interface electronics and to connect a few LEDs. In the past, especially in the 1970s and 1980s electronic engineers used breadboards and wires to prototype circuits. Sometimes, the circuits blew up, sometimes they would stop working, but at least you knew where you were with the electronics. These days, with massively integrated circuits, it is difficult to know one end of a microchip from another. They normally work first time, they're easy to connect to, and when they don't work you just throw them in the bin. Image the size of the bin that would have been required if someone had built a Pentium processor from the discrete transistors (over 20 million of them). Imagine the heat that would have been generated. Assuming 15 mW for each transistor, the total power would be 300 kW, which is equivalent to the heat given off by 3,000 100 W light builds, or 300 1 kW heaters. Now, we can touch the processor, and it just feels a little hot.

So, as the technology has moved on, the parallel port seems like an old friend. It has watched the PC develop as the inners have become more integrated and faster, but it has never really been a high flier, preferring instead to perform its duties quietly without much bother. From CGA and EGA to VGA, from the serial port to the USB port, from 5.25 inch floppy disks to 6,550 MB CD-ROMs, and so on. But, there's no way that the parallel port could be allowed to stay as it was in the original parallel specification. It has potential, but that potential is severely limited because it must always maintain compatibility with previous ports. So, how is it possible to connect a printer on the parallel port, and other devices, without the printer reading communications that are destined for another device? In the next chapter, we will see how the parallel port has been dragged into the modern age. The prize for the best upgrade goes to Ethernet, which has increased its transmission rate by a factor of 100 (10 Mbps to 1 Gbps).

The parallel port was never destined for glory. It is basically a legacy port, which, in the past, was only really useful in connecting printers. The future for printer connections is either with network connections, such as Ethernet, or with a USB connection. In its standard form, it has a large, bulky connector that in many systems, is never even used.

It has always struggled against the serial port because it lacks the flexibility of RS-232 and, until recently, had no standards agency to support it. However, it's there and it has great potential for fast data transfers. RS-232 has always been a great success and has many of the large manufacturers supporting it; importantly, it is now defined by several standards agencies. The key to its current success was due to the intervention of the NPA, which brought together many of the leading computer and printer manufacturers. Now, there are only a few major companies, such as Intel and Microsoft, who can lead the market and define new standards (such as the PCI bus, with Intel).

The main difficulties are how to keep compatibility with previous implementations and software, and how to connect multiple devices on a bus system, and allow them to pass data back and forward without interfering with other devices. This has finally been achieved with ECP/EPP mode. It is a bit complex, but it works, and it even supports data compression. At present, my notebook connects to a CD-R drive, a scanner and a printer, all on the same parallel port (just like SCSI). This arrangement works well most of the time and is a relatively cheap way of connecting devices, but it is in no way as flexible and as fast a SCSI.

PC Motherboards

27.1 Introduction

Chapters 27 and 28 analyze several Pentium-based motherboards. Most PC system motherboards are similar in their architecture, and are based around three main devices:

- **Processor**. This provides the main processing element for the system.
- **System controller**. This provides the interface between the processor and its DRAM memory, SRAM level-2 cache (if not integrated with the processor) and the PCI bus.
- **PCI bridge device**. This bridges between the PCI bus and other buses, such as ISA, IDE, and USB.

Figure 27.1 shows a typical PC architecture, which uses an on-motherboard, level-2. With the SC242, the level-2 cache and its controller are integrated into the processor package. It can be seen that the system controller has one of the most important functions as it interfaces the processor to its memory and its buses. Each bus runs at different speeds, and possibly uses different supply voltages. For example, the system bus typically uses a 3.3 V or a 2.5 V supply (to reduce power dissipation) and the PCI, IDE and ISA buses use 5 V supplies.

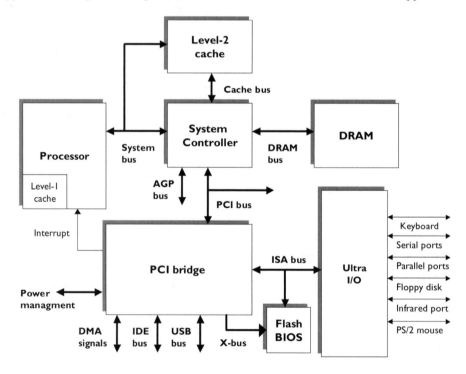

Figure 27.1 System architecture (using a level-2 cache on the motherboard)

Two important speeds are the processor speed and the system motherboard speed. These are two important because a fast processor will be slowed down by a slow system clock speed. It will also be slowed down by lack of level-1 cache. Different clock speeds are:

- **System speed**. This is the clock speed of the main system devices, such as the system controller, the DRAM and the level-2 cache. Typical motherboard board speeds are 50 MHz, 66 MHz, 100 MHz, 133 MHz and 200 MHz.
- **Processor speed**. This is typically a multiple of the system clock (such as 1 GHz).
- **PCI bus**. This typically operates at 33 MHz, and can transfer 32 bits at a time, giving a transfer rate of 132 MB/s.
- **ISA bus**. This runs at 8 MHz and can transfer over 16-bits, giving a transfer rate of 16 MB/s.
- **USB**. This transfers at a rate of 12 Mbps (for USB Version 1) or 480 Mbps (for USB Version 2).
- **AGP bus**. This runs at 66 MHz, and can run at a rate of 266 Msamples/sec (using four samples per clock period), which gives a maximum data rate of 1,066 MB/s ($\times 4$ AGP).

The future is likely to involve a migration from legacy buses, such as ISA, the serial port, the parallel port and the IDE bus, towards plug-and-play buses such as USB. With USB Version 2, there is the capacity for up to 480 Mbps. This should allow for most low-and medium-speed devices to communicate with the main system; Firewire could be used for high-speed audio and video applications.

27.1.1 Pentium-II/III processor

Appendix A outlines the connections for a Slot 1/SC242 processor, and Figure 27.2 illustrates its main connections. It can be seen that it has:

- 64-bit data bus (D0–D63), which connects to the TXC (HD0–HD63).
- 32-bit address bus (A0–A31), which connects to the TXC (HA0–HA31).
- 8-byte address lines (BE0#–BE7#) to allow the processor to access from 1 to 8 bytes (64 bits) at a time, which connects to TXC (HBE0#–HBE7#).
- Read/write line (W/R#), which connects to TXC (HW/R#).
- Memory/IO (M/IO#), which connects to TXC (HM/IO#).
- Data/control (D/C#), which connects to TXC (HD/C#).

The following sections outline some Pentium-based motherboards. A common factor is the reduction of the support for ISA slots, and the increase in the support for PCI and AGP. Faster system clocks are also a feature with the traditional clock speed of 66 MHz increasing to 100 MHz, and even 200 MHz.

27.2 Intel HX

An example board is the Intel 430HX motherboard, which supports most Pentium processors and has the following component parts:

- PCIset components – 82438 System Controller (TXC) and 82371SB PCI ISA Xcelerator (PIIX3).
- 82091AA (AIP) for serial and parallel ports, and floppy disk controller.
- DRAM main memory and L2 cache SRAM.
- Universal serial bus (USB).

- Interface slots (typically 4 PCI and 3 ISA).
- 1 Mbit flash RAM.

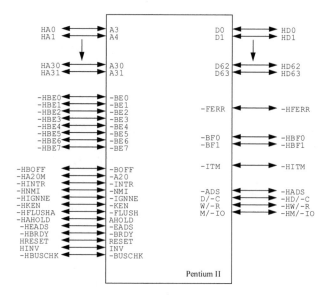

Figure 27.2 Pentium II/III connections

Figure 27.3 illustrates the main connections of the PCIset (the TXC and PIIX3 devices). The TCX allows for a host-to-PCI bridge, whereas the PIIX3 device supports:

- PCI-to-ISA bridge.
- Fast IDE.
- APIC interface.
- USB host/hub controller and power management.

The 430HX board has 3 V and 5 V buses. PCI bus connections are 5 V and the Pentium bus is 3 V.

27.2.1 *82371SB PCI ISA Xcelerator (PIIX3)*

The PIIX3 is a 208-pin QFP (quad flat pack) IC that integrates much of the functionality of the ISA bus interface onto a single device. Table 27.1 outlines the main connections to the PIIX3 IC. Its functionality includes:

- Enhanced seven-channel DMA with two 8237 controllers. This is supported with the handshaking lines DRQ0–DRQ7 and DRQ0#–DRQ7#.
- ISA-to-PCI bridge.
- Fast IDE support for up to four disk drives (two masters and two slaves). It supports mode four timings, which gives transfer rates of up to 22 MB/s.
- I/O APIC (advanced programmable interrupt controller) support.
- Implementation of PCI 2.1.
- Incorporates 82C54 timer for system timer, refresh request and speaker output tone.
- Non-maskable interrupts (NMI).
- PCI clock speed of 25/33 MHz. Motherboard configurable clock speed (normally

33 MHz).

- Plug-and-play support with one steerable interrupt line and one programmable chip select. The motherboard interrupt MIRQ0 can be steered to any one of 11 interrupts (IRQ3–IRQ7, IRQ9–IRQ12, IRQ14 and IRQ15).

- Steerable PCI interrupts for PCI device plug-and-play. The PCI interrupt lines (PIRQA–PIRQD) can be steered to one of 11 interrupt (IRQ3–IRQ7, IRQ9–IRQ12, IRQ14 and IRQ15).

- Support for PS/2-type mouse and serial port mouse. IRQ12/M can be enabled for the PS/2-type mouse or disable for a serial port mouse.

- Support for five ISA slots. Typical applications for ISA include 10 Mbps Ethernet adaptor cards, serial/parallel port cards, sound cards, and so on.

- System power management. Allows the system to operate in a low power state without being powered down. This can be triggered by a software, hardware or external event.

- Math coprocessor error function. The FERR# line goes active (LOW) when a math coprocessor error occurs. The PIIX3 device automatically generates an IRQ13 interrupt and sets the INTR line to the processor. The PXII3 device then sets the IGNNE# active and INTR inactive when there is a write to address F0h.

- Two 82C59 controllers with 14 interrupts. The interrupts lines IRQ1, IRQ3–IRQ15 are available (IRQ0 is used by the system time and IRQ2 by the cascaded interrupt line).

- Universal serial bus with root hub and two USB ports. With the USB the host controller transfers data between the system memory and USB devices. This is achieved by processing data structures set up to by the host software and generated the transaction on USB.

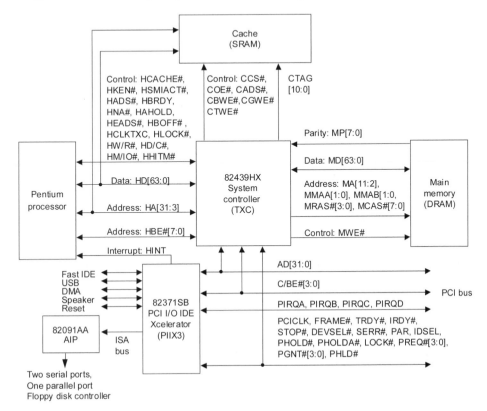

Figure 27.3 PCIset system architecture

Table 27.1 PIIX3 connections

Address lines		IRQ lines		ISA lines		ISA lines	
Signal	*Pin*	*Signal*	*Pin*	*Signal*	*Pin*	*Signal*	*Pin*
AD0	206	IRQ1	4	BALE	64	SA8/DD0 55	
AD1	205	IRQ3	58	AEN	20	SA9/DD1 50	
AD2	204	IRQ4	56	LA17	86	SA10/DD2	49
AD3	203	IRQ5	34	LA18	84	SA11/DD3	48
AD4	202	IRQ6	33	LA19	82	SA12/DD4	47
AD5	201	IRQ7	32	LA20	80	SA13/DD5	46
AD6	200	-IRQ8	5	LA21	76	SA14/DD6	45
AD7	199	IRQ9	10	LA22	74	SA15/DD7	44
AD8	197	IRQ10	73	LA23	72	SA16/DD8	43
AD9	194	IRQ11	75	SA0	69	SA17/DD9	41
AD10	193	IRQ12/M	77	SA1	68	SA18/DD10	40
AD11	192	IRQ14	83	SA2	67	SA19/DD11	39
AD12	191	IRQ15	81	SA3	66	SA20/DD12	38
AD13	190			SA4	63	SA21/DD13	37
AD14	189			SA5	61	SA22/DD14	36
AD15	188			SA6	59	SA23/DD15	35
AD16	177			SA7	57	-OWS	15
AD17	176			DRQ0	87	-SMEMW	22
AD18	175			DRQ1	30	-SMEMR	19
AD19	174			DRQ2	12	-IOW	24
AD20	173			DRQ3	25	-IOR	23
AD21	172			DRQ5	91	-REFRESH	31
AD22	171			DRQ6	95	T/C	62
AD23	168			DRQ7	99	OSC	
AD24	166			-DACK0	85	-MEMCS16	70
AD25	165			-DACK1	29	-IOCS16	71
AD26	164			-DACK2	60	-MASTER	
AD27	163			-DACK3	21	IOCHK	6
AD28	162			-DACK5	89	IOCHRDY	18
AD29	161			-DACK6	93	-SBHE (DD12)	
AD30	160			-DACK7	97	-MEMR	88
AD31	159			RSTISA		MEMW	90

USB	
Signal	Pin
USBP1-	143
USBP1+	142
USBP0-	145
USBP0+	144

The address lines (AD0–AD22) connect to the TXC IC and the available interrupt lines at IRQ1, IRQ2–IRQ12, IRQ14 and IRQ15 (IRQ0 is generated by the system timer and IRQ2 is the cascaded interrupt line). The PS/2-type mouse uses the IRQ12/M line.

27.2.2 82438 System Controller (TXC)

The 324-pin TXC BGA (ball grid array) provides an interface between the processor, DRAM and the external buses (such as the PCI, ISA, and so on). Table 27.2 outlines its main pin connections. The TXC's functionality includes:

- Supports 50 MHz, 60 MHz and 66 MHz host buses.
- Integrated DRAM controller. Supports four CAS lines and eight RAS lines. The memory supports symmetrical and asymmetrical addressing for 1 MB, 2 MB and 4 MB-deep SIMMs and symmetrical addressing for 16 MB-deep SIMMs.
- Integrated second level cache controller. Supports up to 512 MB of second-level cache with synchronous pipelined burst SRAM.
- Dual processor support.

- Optional parity.
- Optional error checking and correction on DRAM. The ECC mode is software configurable and allows for single-bit error correction and multi-bit error detection on single nibbles in DRAM. Also, supports swapable memory bank support, which allows memory banks to be swapped out.
- PCI 2.1-compliant bus and supports USB.

The TXC controls the processor cycles for:

- Second-level cache transfer – the processor sends data to the second-level cache directly and the TXC controls its operation.
- All other processor cycles – the TXC directs all other processor cycles to their destinations (DRAM, PCI or internal TXC configuration space).

Table 27.2   TXC connections

PCI memory addresses		Cache memory addresses		cache memory data			
Signal	*Pin*	*Signal*	*Pin*	*Signal*	*Pin*	*Signal*	*Pin*
AD0	15			HD0	305	HD32	179
AD1	14			HD1	307	HD33	178
AD2	33			HD2	306	HD34	149
AD3	13	HA3	275	HD3	308	HD35	180
AD4	52	HA4	315	HD4	285	HD36	136
AD5	32	HA5	252	HD5	286	HD37	135
AD6	12	HA6	316	HD6	265	HD38	138
AD7	51	HA7	312	HD7	212	HD39	125
AD8	11	HA8	272	HD8	245	HD40	126
AD9	50	HA9	271	HD9	287	HD41	115
AD10	30	HA10	311	HD10	267	HD42	137
AD11	10	HA11	291	HD11	288	HD43	117
AD12	49	HA12	251	HD12	225	HD44	128
AD13	29	HA13	310	HD13	268	HD45	114
AD14	9	HA14	270	HD14	247	HD46	127
AD15	48	HA15	290	HD15	266	HD47	102
AD16	47	HA16	250	HD16	248	HD48	101
AD17	27	HA17	309	HD17	247	HD49	116
AD18	7	HA18	289	HD18	246	HD50	104
AD19	46	HA19	269	HD19	214	HD51	103
AD20	26	HA20	249	HD20	228	HD52	81
AD21	6	HA21	273	HD21	213	HD53	84
AD22	45	HA22	254	HD22	226	HD54	82
AD23	25	HA23	253	HD23	201	HD55	61
AD24	66	HA24	294	HD24	215	HD56	83
AD25	44	HA25	293	HD25	203	HD57	63
AD26	24	HA26	274	HD26	202	HD58	62
AD27	4	HA27	313	HD27	191	HD59	41
AD28	23	HA28	314	HD28	204	HD60	42
AD29	3	HA29	255	HD29	193	HD61	43
AD30	22	HA30	295	HD30	192	HD62	21
AD31	2	HA31	292	HD31	194	HD63	1
PCI control lines							
C/BE0#	21	FRAME#	86	PREQ0#	67	PGNT0#	68
C/BE1#	31	DEVSEL#	89	PREQ1#	69	PGNT1#	70
C/BE2#	8	IRDY#	88	PREQ2#	71	PGNT2#	72
C/BE3#	5	STOP#	91	PREQ3#	73	PGNT3#	74
		LOCK#	85				
		PHOLD#	64				
		PHLDA#	65				
		PAR	92				
		SERR#	93				

Cache memory tag		Parity		Address lines			
Signal	*Pin*	*Signal*	*Pin*	*Signal*	*Pin*	*Signal*	*Pin*
CTAG0	207	MP0	133	MD32	74		
CTAG1	260	MP1	123	MD33	75		
CTAG2	261	MP2	146	MA2	317	MD34	76
CTAG3	281	MP3	113	MA3	297	MD35	76
CTAG4	238	MP4	132	MA4	277	MD36	76
CTAG5	282	MP5	124	MA5	257	MD37	76
CTAG6	302	MP6	134	MA6	237	MD38	76
CTAG7	322	MP7	122	MA7	298	MD39	76
CTAG8	303			MA8	258		
CTAG9	323			MA9	319		
CTAG10	324			MA10	318		
				MA11	278		

Cache address lines

MRASR0#	121	MCASR0#	145	MAA0	300
MRASR1#	110	MCASR1#	159	MAA1	300
MRASR2#	109	MCASR2#	131	MAB0	300
MRASR3#	96	MCASR3#	173	MAB1	300
		MCASR4#	130		
		MCASR5#	144		
		MCASR6#	120		
		MCASR7#	172		

Cache control lines

CBWE#	321	COE#	259	CCS#	300	CADS#	299
CGWE#	320	CADV#	279				

27.2.3 82091AA (AIP)

The AIP device integrates the serial ports, parallel ports and floppy disk interfaces. Figure 27.4 shows its connections and Figure 27.5 shows the interconnection between the AIP and the PIIX3 device. The OSC frequency is set to 14.218 18 MHz. It can be seen that the range of interrupts for the serial, parallel and floppy disk drives is IRQ3, IRQ4, IRQ5, IRQ6 and IRQ7. Normally the settings are IRQ3 – secondary serial port

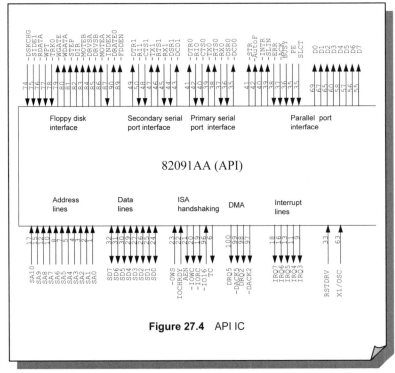

Figure 27.4   API IC

(COM2/COM4); IRQ4 – primary serial port (COM1/COM3); IRQ6 – floppy disk controller; and IRQ7 – parallel port (LPT1).

Figure 27.5 shows the main connections between the TXC, PIIX3 and the AIP. It can be seen that the AIP uses many of the ISA connections (such as 0WS#, IOCHRDY, and so on). The interface between the TCX and the PIIX3 defines the PCI bus and the interface between the PIIX3 and AIP defines some of the ISA signals.

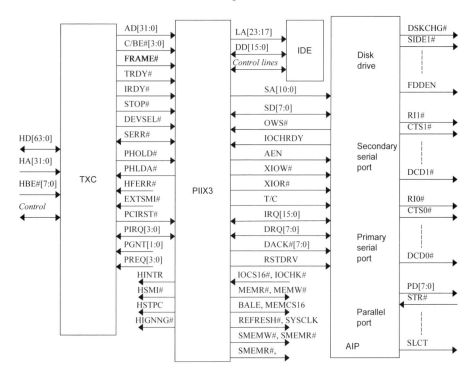

Figure 27.5 Connections between TXC, PIIX3 and AIP

27.2.4 DRAM interface

The DRAM interface supports from 4–512 MB with eight RAS lines (RAS0–RAS7) and a 64-bit data path with 8 parity bits. It can use either a 3.3 V or a 5 V power supply and both standard page mode and extended data out (EDO) memory are supported with a mixture of memory sizes for 1 MB, 2 MB and 4 MB-deep SIMMs and symmetrical addressing for 16 MB-deep SIMMs.

Each SIMM has 12 input address lines and a 32-bit data output. They are normally available with 72 pins (named tabs) on each side. These pins can read the same signal because they are shorted together on the board. For example, tab 1 (pin 1) on side A is shorted to tab 1 on side B. Thus, the 144 tabs give only 72 usable signal connections.

Figure 27.6 shows how the DRAM memory is organized. It shows banks 1 and 2 (but does not show banks 3 and 4). Each bank has two modules, such as modules 0 and 1 are in bank 0. The bank is selected with the MRAS lines, for example bank 1 is selected with MRAS0 and MRAS1, bank 1 by MRAS2 and MRAS3, and so on. An even-numbered module gives the lower 32 bits (MD0–MD31) and the odd number modules give the upper 32 bits (MD32–MD63). Each module also provides 4 parity bits (MP0–MP3 and MP4–MP7).

DIMMs have independent signal lines on each side of the module and are available with

72 (36 tabs on each side), 88 (44 tabs on each side), 144 (72 tabs on each side), 168 (84 tabs on each side) or 200 tabs (100 tabs on each side). They give greater reliability and density and are used in modern high-performance PC servers.

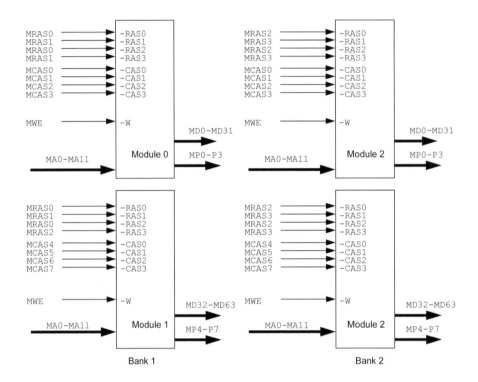

Figure 27.6   DRAM memory interface

27.2.5 Clock rates

The system board runs at several clock frequencies. These are:

- Processor speed – the processor, TXC and SRAM run at the system frequency (such as 66 MHz).
- PCI bus speed – TCX, PIIX3 and PCI slots. Typically the PCI bus runs at 33 MHz.
- 24 or 48 MHz – USB.
- 12 MHz – keyboard.
- 24 MHz – floppy clock.
- 14 MHz – ISA bus OSC.
- 8 MHz – ISA bus clock.

27.2.6 ISA/IDE interface

The IDE and ISA buses share several data, address and control lines. Figure 27.7 shows the connections to the buses. The IDE interface uses the DD[12:0] and LA[23:17] lines, and the ISA uses these lines as SBHE#, SA[19:8], CS1S, CS3S, CS1P, CS3P and DA[2:0]. A multi-plexor (MUX) is used to select either the ISA or IDE interface lines.

27.2.7 DMA interface

The PIIX3 device incorporates the functionality of two 8237 DMA controllers to give seven independently programmable channel (channels 0–3 and Channels 5–7). DMA channel 4 is used to cascade the two controllers and defaults to cascade mode in the DMA channel mode (DCM) register. Figure 27.8 shows the interface connections.

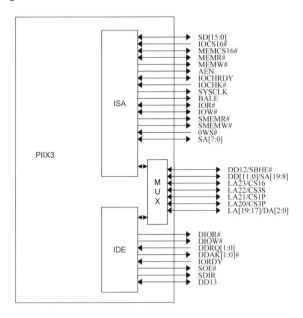

Figure 27.7   IDE/ISA interface with PIIX3

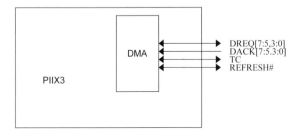

Figure 27.8   DMA interface

27.2.8 Interval timer

The PIIX3 contains three 8251-compatible counters. The three counters are contained in one PIIX3 timer unit, referred to as Timer 1. Each counter provides an essential system function. The functions of the counters are:

- Counter 0 – connects to the IRQ0 line and provides a system timer interrupt for a time-of-day, diskette time-out, and so on. The input to the counter is a 14.218 18 MHz clock (OSC). This is then used to increment a 16-bit register, which rolls over every 55 ms.
- Counter 1 – generates a refresh request signal.
- Counter 2 – generates the speaker tone.

27.2.9 Interrupt controller

The PXII3 incorporates two 8259-compatible interrupt controllers, which provide an ISA-compatible interrupt controller. These are cascaded to give 13 external and three internal interrupts. The primary interrupt controller connects to IRQ0–IRQ7 and the secondary connects to IRQ8–IRQ15. The three internal interrupts are:

- IRQ0 – used by the system timer; connected to Timer 1, Counter 0.
- IRQ2 – used by the primary and secondary controllers (see Figure 2.2).
- IRQ13 – used by the math coprocessor, which is connected to the FERR pin on the processor.

The PC uses IRQ0 as the system timer and IRQ2 by the programmable interrupt controller.

The interrupt unit also supports interrupt steering. The four PCI active low interrupts (PIRQ#[D:A]) can be routed internally in the PIIX3 to one of 11 interrupts (IRQ15, IRQ14, IRQ12–IRQ9, IRQ7–IRQ3).

27.2.10   Mouse function

The mouse normally connects either to one of the serial ports (COM1: or COM2:) or a PS/2-type connector. If it connects to the PS/2-type connector then IRQ12 is used, else a serial port connected mouse uses the serial interrupts (such as IRQ4 for COM1 and IRQ3 for COM2). Thus, a system with a serial connected mouse must have the IRQ12/M interrupt disabled. This is normally done with a motherboard jumper (to enable or disable the mouse interrupt). Power management

PIIX3 has extensive power management capability permitting a system to operate in a low power state without being powered down. In a typical desktop PC, there are two states – power on and power off. Leaving a system powered on when not in use wastes power. PIIX3 provides a fast on/off feature that creates a third state called fast off. When in the fast off state, the system consumes less power when in the power-on state.

The PIIX3's power management function is based on two modes:

- System management mode (SMM).
- Advanced power management (APM).

Software (called SMM code) controls the transitions between the power-on state and the fast-off state. PIIX3 invokes this software by generating an SMI (system management interrupt) to the CPU (asserting the $\overline{\text{SMI}}$ signal). The SMM code places the system in either the power on state or the fast off state.

27.2.11   Graphics subsystem

The 430HX incorporates the S3 ViRGE graphics device with 2 MB of graphics memory, which has:

- High performance 64-bit 2D/3D graphics engine.
- RAMDAC/clock synthesizer capable of pixel rates of 135 MHz.
- S3 streams processor, enabling the device to convert YUV formatted video data to RGB format.
- 3D features, including flat shading and texture mapping support.
- Fast linear addressing scheme.
- VESA (Video Electronics Standards Association) capability.

27.3 TX Motherboard

The Intel 430HX motherboard only supports up to 128 MB of memory and has a relatively small second-level cache (256 kB). The Intel 430TX board has many enhanced devices, such as standardized USB connections and enhanced super I/O device. Figure 27.9 shows the main layout. The 430TX board uses 168-pin DIMM sockets for memory addition. It supports both EDO DRAM and SDRAM (synchronous DRAM). SDRAM synchronous data transfers using the system clock. This simplifies memory timing, leading to an increase in memory transfer. The 430TX motherboard supports a 64-bit data path to memory.

The 430TX board uses the 82430TX PCI chipset, which has:

- 82439TX Xcelerated Controller (MTXC), which replaces the TXC (82439HX) in the HX board.

- 82371AB PCI/ISA IDE Xcelerator (PIIX4), which replaces the PIIX3 (82371SB) in the HX board. This is a 324-pin BGA that integrates PCI-to-ISA bridge (two 82C37 DMA controllers, two 82C59 interrupt controllers, an 82C54 timer/counter and a real-time clock), PCI/IDE interface, USB host/hub function and power management functions.

27.3.1 PIIX4

The PIIX4 supports two types of PCI DMA protocol: PC/PCI DMA, which uses dedicated request and grant signals to permit PCI devices to request transfers associated with specific DMA channels; and distribute DMA, which is based on monitoring CPU accesses to the 8237 controller (this was not implemented on the PIIX3). The architecture of the TX chipset is given in Figure 27.10.

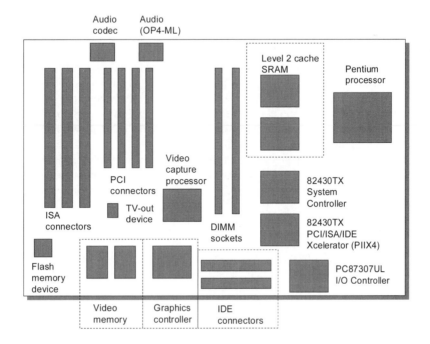

Figure 27.9 AN430TX board

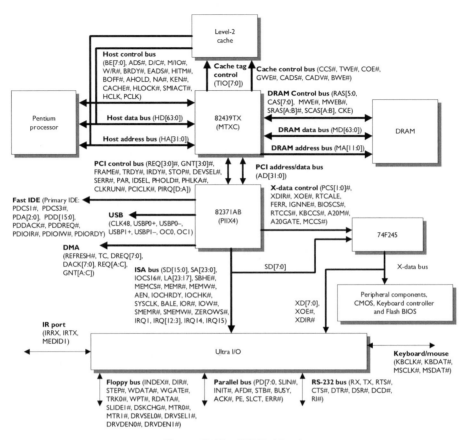

Figure 27.10 430TX chipset

The PIIX4 also supports ultra DMA/33 synchronous DMA mode transfers up to 33MB/s. Ultra DMA is a newer protocol for the IDE hard drive interface, which doubles the burst data rate from 16.6MB/s (as supported by the PIIX3). Ultra DMA widens the path to the hard drive by transferring twice as much data per clock cycle, so doubling the performance. The ultra DMA protocol lets host computers send and receive data faster, removing bottlenecks associated with data transfers.

In addition to speed improvements, the protocol brings new data integrity capabilities to the IDE interface, such as improved timing margins and data protection verification. Ultra DMA protocol also allows drives and system to retain backward compatibility with the previous ATA standard.

Real-time clock

The real-time clock (RTC) provides a data-and-time keeping device with alarm features and battery- backed operation. The RTC counts seconds, minutes, hours, days, day of the week, date, month and year. It counts 256 bytes of battery-backed SRAM in two banks. The RTC module requires an external oscillator source of 32.768kHz connected between TXCX1 and RTCX2.

27.3.2 I/O controller

The PC87306B I/O controller is similar to the 82091AA (AIP) used in the 430HX board. It has:

- Floppy disk interface – provides support for several different floppy disk capacities and sizes.

- Multimode parallel port – supports for output-only compatibility mode, bidirectional mode, EPP mode and ECP mode.

- Two FIFO serial ports giving transfers rates up to 921 kbps.

- Real-time clock – provides time-of-day, 100-year calendar and alarm features.

- Keyboard and mouse controller – keyboard and mouse interfaces (as well as power-on/reset password protection).

- Infrared support – connection to infrared transmitter/receiver.

Graphics subsystem

The 430HX motherboard incorporates the ATI-241 Rage II+ graphics controller, which has:

- Drawing coprocessor that operates concurrently with the host processor.

- Video coprocessor.

- Video scalar, color space converter, true color palette.

- ATI multimedia.

- Enhanced power features.

- VGA/VESA capability.

The 430HX has an optional video capture processor for digitizing analogue inputs from VCRs, cameras, TVs, and so on. It also has an optional ATI-ImpactTC NSTC/PAL encoder, which provides a TV output for the graphics accelerators.

27.3.3 DRAM interface

The DRAM interface is a 64-bit data path that supports fast page mode (FPM) and extended data out (EDO) memory. The integrated DRAM controller supports from 4 MB to 256 MB of main memory. The 12 multiplexed address lines (MA[11:0]) allow the chips to support 4-bit, 16-bit and 64-bit memory, both symmetrical and asymmetrical addressing. The MTXC has six RAS lines, which enables support of up to six rows of DRAM (the TXC has eight RAS lines).

The MTXC supports SRAM. The 14 multiplexed address lines (MA[13:0]) allow the MTXC to support 16-bit and 64-bit SDRAM devices. The MTXC has six chip select (CS) lines (mixed into RAS[5:0]), which allows six rows of the faster SDRAM modules to be installed. These memory types (FPM, EDO and SDRAM) can all be mixed on the 430TX, but only the FPM and EDO are supported in the 430HX board. The extra lines that have been added in the MTXC are:

- SRAS [A,B] – SRAM row address strobe.
- SCAS [A,B] – DRAM column address.

27.3.4 Second- level cache

The MTXC supports cache memory area of 64 MB using either 8 k×8 or 16 k×8 SRAM blocks to store the cache tags for either 256 kB or 512 kB SRAM cache. (8 k×8 is used for 256 kB and 16 k×8 is used for 512 kB). Each cache entry is 32 bits (4 bytes) thus the total cache memory size is 512 kB (16 k×8×4). The signals are:

CCS   Cache chip select – set active upon power-up and allows access to the cache.

TWE	Tag write enable – allows new state and tag addresses to be written into the cache.
COE	Cache output enable – puts the cache data onto the data bus.
GWE	Global write enable – causes all bytes to be written to.
CADS	Cache address strobe – cache loads the address register from the address pins.
CADV	Cache advance – the address is automatically increment to the next word.
TIO[7:0]	Tag address – input lines for tag addresses.
KRQAK/CS4_64 .	Cache chip select – KRQAK specifies DRAM cache, else implements a 64 MB main memory cache.
BWE	Byte write enable – enables up to 8 bytes from the data bus.

Figure 27.11 shows the interface between the MTXC and the second-level cache. Note that four 32k×32 devices make up the 512 kB (4×32×4) SRAM cache. Only two are shown in Figure 27.11, as the other two are connected in parallel with the two shown.

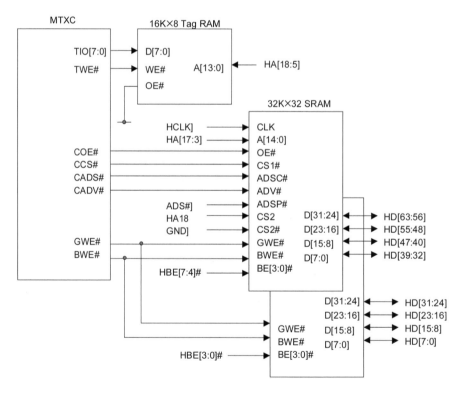

Figure 27.11   Second-level cache interface

Cache control register (CC)

This is an 8-bit register located at 52h in the I/O memory. It defines secondary cache operations. Its format is:

Bit	Description
7:6	Secondary cache size – 00 (disabled), 01 (256 k), 10 (512 k), 11 (reserved).
5:4	SRAM cache type – 00 (pipelined burst SRAM), 01 (reserved), 10 (reserved), 11 (two banks of pipelined burst).
3	NA disable – 1 (disable), 0 (enabled); normally enabled.
2	Reserved.
1	Secondary cache force miss or invalidated (SCFMI). When set to a 1, the level 2 hit/miss facility is disabled, else it is enabled.
0	First-level cache enable (FLCE) – 1 (enable), 0 (disable). When it is set to a 1, the control responds to processor cycles with KEN# active. Normal mode for FLCE, SCFMI is 1, 0.

Extended cache control register (CEC)

This is an 8-bit register located at 53h in the I/O memory. It defines the refresh rate for DRAM Level 2. Its format is:

Bit	Description
7:6	Reserved.
5	Defines whether DRAM cache is present – 1 (present), 0 (not present).
4:0	DRAM cache refresh timer value.

27.3.5 Power management

The PIIX4 has enhanced power management over the PIIX3 and can detect when a specific device is idle. The system management software is then informed, which then can place the idle device into a power-managed condition (such as local standby or powered off). Accesses targeted to that device are then monitored. When detected, an $\overline{\text{SMI}}$ is generated to allow the software to restore the device to operation.

The PIIX4 supports the advanced configuration and power interface (ACPI) specification. The software consists of system management mode (SMM) BIOS for legacy control and operating system for ACPI. The basic operation consists of software setting up the desired configurations and power management mode and corresponding power-saving levels. The hardware then performs the necessary actions to maintain the power mode. The I/O chip also monitors the system for events that may require changing the system power mode.

27.4 450NX PCIset

The 440NX PCIset chipset is aimed at the enterprise server market. It was introduced to be used with the Pentium Xeon (36-bit address, 64-bit data), and can support up to four processors. Its main features include:

- Support for up to four processors.
- Allows for the support of up to 8 GB of main memory.
- Optimizes memory bandwidth using address bit permuting (ABP), card to card (C2C) interleaving, and four-way interleaved memory, which gives up to 1 GB/s memory transfers.
- Either four 32-bit PCI slots or two 64-bit PCI slots.
- Optimized for multiprocessor systems and standard high-volume (SHV) servers.
- Based on P6 microarchitecture family.

The 450NX PCIset consists of four main components:

- Memory and I/O bridge controller (MIOC – 82451NX, 540-pin PLGA). This connects the processor to the memory and PCI bus, using a 100 MHz bus.
- PCI expander bridge (PXB – 82454NX, 540-pin PLGA). This interfaces the MIOC and the PCI buses. Each PXB provides the interface to two independent 32-bit, 33 MHz PCI buses, or a single 64-bit, 33 MHz PCI bus. See the section on the 840 chipset on how different PCI buses are used. Two PXBs are required for a system.

Other chipsets

Chipset	Features
440 LX AGPset	• First chipset to introduce AGP. • Quad port acceleration (to support up to four processors). • Distributed arbitration.
440 BX AGPset	• First chipset to be optimized for Pentium III for 3D graphics and video performance. • 100 MHz system bus. • 100 MHz SDRAM. • AGP interface, with speeds from 66 MHz to 100 MHz. • ATA/66 ID interface. • Dual independent bus (supports two processors).

- RAS/CAS generate (RCG – 82452NX, 324-pin PLGA). This is responsible for getting memory requests from the MIOC and converting them into the signals required for DRAM, and supports up to four banks of memory. Two RCGs are required for a system.
- Data path multiplexor (MUX – 82453NX, 324-pin PLGA). This provides the multiplexing and timing for memory interleaving between the DRAMs and the MIOC. Each MUX provides the data path for one-half of a quadword for each of four interleaves. Four MUXs are required for a system.

The 450NX PCIset can use either the PIIX3 or PIIX4E as its South bridge to provide IDE, USB, ISA, DMA, and so on.

Other chipsets

Chipset	Features
440 GX AGPset	• Evolved from BX, and optimized for Pentium III Xeon. • 100 MHz system bus, and 100MHz AGP/SDRAM. • 2 GB for SDRAM.
440EX AGPset	• Aimed at the value PC market, especially for the Celeron processor. • Based on 440LX AGPset. • 66 MHz system/SDRAM speed.
440MX	• Used typically in mobile applications. • Supports AC-97.
440ZX AGPset	• Enhancement to 440BX AGPset, with pin-compatibility. • 100 MHz system bus/SDRAM. • ATA/66 IDE. • ×2 AGP.

27.5 450KX and 450GX PCISET

The 450KX PCIset and 450GX PICset are aimed at the server market, and are based on a reliable and robust chipset. They use a PCI bus as a basis of connecting devices to, and consists of:

- PCI bridge (PB – 82454). This is a single-device host bus-to-PCI bridge. It has a synchronous interface with the Pentium Pro processor bus and supports a derived clock for the synchronous PCI interface. The PB derives either a 30 or 33 MHz PCI clock output from the Pentium Pro processor bus clock.
- Memory controller (MC). The MAC consists of an 82453 DRAM controller (DC), an 82452 data path (DP), and four 82451 memory interface components (MIC), as illustrated in Figure 27.12. The DC provides control for the DRAM memory subsystem, the DP provides the data path, and the four MICs are used to interface the MC datapath with the DRAM memory subsystem. The memory configuration can be either two-way interleaved or non-interleaved. The memory can consist of four-way interleaved, two-way interleaved, or non-interleaved. Asymmetric DRAM is supported by up to 2 bits of asymmetry (such as 12 row address lines and 10 column address lines). The maximum memory size is 4 GB for the four-way interleaved configuration, 2 GB for the two-way interleaved configuration, and 1 GB for the non-interleaved configuration, with a 64-bit data path to main memory.

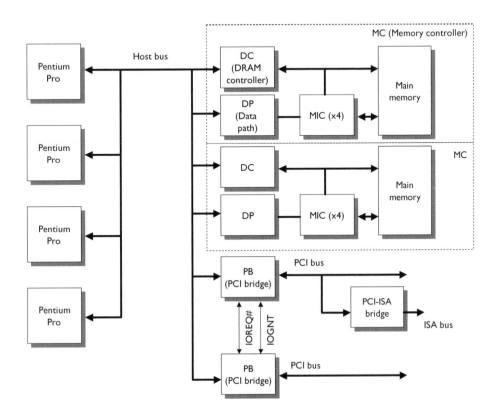

Figure 27.12   GX architecture

The main differences are:

	450KX	450GX	*Notes*
Pentium Pro Processors	2	4	
PCI bridges	1	2	Figure 27.12 shows that two arbitration lines are required between the PCI bridges in order for them to ask for control of the bus (IOREQ# and IOGNT).
Memory Controllers	1	2	

27.6 Exercises

27.6.1 The data bus signals that connect to the processor are:

(a) HD0–HD63 (b) D0–D63
(c) HA0–HA63 (d) AD0–AD63

27.6.2 Which device provides the bridge between the processor, second-level cache, DRAM and the PCI bus?

(a) PIIX3/4 (b) HXC
(c) RFC/MRFC (d) TXC/MTXC

27.6.3 Which device provides the bridge between the PCI bus and other buses, such as the IDE, ISA and USB?

(a) PIIX3/4 (b) HXC
(c) RFC (d) TXC

27.6.4 Which chipset best supports a standard high-volume (SHV) server?

(a) 440BX (b) 440AX
(c) 400EX (d) 450NX

27.6.5 The maximum achievable data throughput for a 33 MHz, 32-bit PCI is 132 MB/s. Why is this not achievable in the normal multiplexed mode?

(a) Half of the bus is used for addresses, the other half for data
(b) The bus must slow down because of synchronization problems
(c) The address and data line are shared (multiplexed address then data)
(d) The clock rate is halved for all transfers

27.6.6 How does a cache identify the address of the data it has in its memory?

(a) The full address is stored along with the data
(b) It is tagged (CTAG)
(c) It guesses the address
(d) It checks the address with the contents of the DRAM

27.6.7 How many data bits are transferred between the processor and the second-level cache?

(a) 16 (b) 32
(c) 64 (c) 128

27.6.8 Outline the importance of the TXC (system controller) device in the PC. Outline the main ICs that are used in a PC.

27.6.9 Describe, in detail, the architecture of the HX PCI chip set, and how the Pentium processor communicates with: DRAM memory, level-2 SRAM cache, the PCI bus, the ISA bus and the IDE bus.

27.6.10   Explain, with reference to the PIIX3 and Pentium processor, how interrupts on the PCI and ISA buses are dealt with.

27.6.11   Explain, with reference to the level-1 cache, the level-2 cache and DRAM, how the processor accesses memory. What advantage does level-1 have over level-2 cache, and what advantage do these have over DRAM.

27.6.12   Discuss the power management modes supported by the PXII3 and the PXII4.

27.6.13   Which interrupts are supported with the AIP, and where are they typically used?

27.6.14   Explain how the ISA and IDE buses share the same control and data lines.

27.6.15   Contrast the HX motherboard with the LX motherboard.

27.7 Interface to Flash

Figure 27.13 shows the interface between the PIIX4 and Flash memory, which stores the boot program for the system. Jump B allows the Flash memory to be reprogrammed. Jump A defines whether a 1 Mb memory or a 2 Mb memory is used.

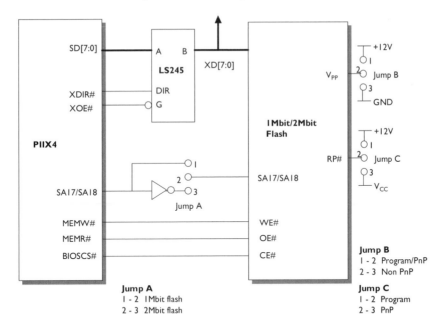

Figure 27.13   Interface to Flash

27.8 Note from the Author

It is important to realize that it is not just the speed of the processor that defines the performance of a system – it is the cache controllers, the bridge devices, the PCI bus, and so on. I have tried to give you an understanding of the segmentation that is used in typical PCs. The devices used will change, but the basic concept is likely to stay the same. The days of a PC on a chip will happen, some day.

The great thing about modern PC systems is that they are almost completely compatible with the original PC; the big change has happened in the integration of many of the component parts. The great strength of the PC is its availability, durability and upgradeability of its components. I find it amazing that you can disconnect the cable to the disk drives, turn it round and connect it and the system will not be damaged in any way (although it won't start). I can even put the processor in the wrong way, and it will not damage it.

The other amazing thing about PCs is the way that new peripherals are quickly adopted, and become standard parts of the PC. This has included CD-ROM drives, USB connectors, PS/2-type mouse connectors, PCMCIA connectors (in notebooks), VGA graphics adaptors, TV output, DVD drives, network cards, sound cards, and so on. Who would have believed that such a basic system as the original PC would support all this expansion, without ever the need to redesign it?

28 Hub-based Architecture

28.1 Introduction

The overall performance of a PC depends on the architecture and the chipset that are used. As we have seen, the architecture of the PC has changed drastically. The main evolution has been:

1. ISA architecture.
2. Addition of the PCI bus, for improved automated configuration.
3. Addition of an on-chip level-1 cache.
4. Addition of a level-2 cache onto the motherboards.
5. Usage of the North/South bridge approach, for faster interfaces to memory.
6. Enhancements of DRAM from EDO to SDRAM.
7. Addition of the AGP interface, for faster interfaces to graphics.
8. Movement of level-2 cache from motherboard to an on-package memory.
9. Faster DRAM memory transfers with 100MHz and 133MHz SDRAM.
10. Hub-based architecture, for faster transfers between the processor, graphics and memory.
11. Fast RDRAM, for ultra-high data transfers between the processor and memory, and the AGP interface and memory.

All of these architectures have been supported by a range of chipsets. Tables 28.1 and 28.2 outlines some of the most recent ones. It can be seen that the 840, 820, 810E and 810 chipsets are based on hub architecture and use RDRAM memory modules, whereas the 450/440 series is based on the PIIX4E south bridge. The 450NX is well matched to server applications as it supports up to four processors, whereas most of the other chipsets support two processors.

Some of the devices used with the chipset include:

810: 82801 I/O controller hub (ICH), 82802 firmware hub (FWH) and 82810 graphics memory controller hub (GMCH). This GMCH has an integrated graphics controller that uses direct AGP (integrated AGP) for ultrafast 2D and 3D effects and images. The 82810 also has an integrated hardware motion compensation to improve soft DVD video quality and a digital TV out port.

820: 82820 memory controller hub (MCH), 82801 ICH, 82802 FWH.

840: 82840 MCH 82801 I/O ICH 82802 FWH 82806 64-bit PCI controller hub and 82803 RDRAM-based memory repeater hub (MRH-R) or 82804 SDRAM-based memory repeater hub.

Table 28.1 Example chipsets

	Servers/workstation			Performance desktop			
	450NX	840	440GX	820	810E	440BX AGP	440ZX AGP
Processors	Pentium II/III Xeon	Pentium II/III Xeon	Pentium II/III Xeon	Pentium II/III	Pentium II/III	Pentium II/III	Pentium II/III
Bus signals	AGTL+	AGTL+	GTL+	AGTL+	AGTL+	GTL+	GTL+
Maximum number of processors	4	2	2	2	I	2	2
DRAM refresh	CAS-before-RAS	RDRAM Active Refresh	CAS-before-RAS	N/A	CAS-before-RAS	CAS-before-RAS	CAS-before-RAS
Memory support	8 rows	32 RDRAM devices per channel	8 rows	32 RDRAM	4 rows	8 rows	4 rows
DRAM chips supported	Yes	64/128/256 Mbit	64/128 Mbit	64/128/256 Mbit	Yes	Yes	Yes
Maximum memory	8 GB	8 GB	2 GB	I GB	512 MB	I GB	256 MB
Memory types	SDRAM / EDO	PC800/PC600 RDRAM PC100 SDRAM	SDRAM	RDRAM	PC100 SDRAM	SDRAM	SDRAM
PCI type	PCI 2.1	PCI 2.2	PCI 2.1	PCI 2.2	PCI 2.2	PCI 2.1	PCI 2.1
Integrated graphics	No	No	No	No	Yes	No	No
AGP type	No	AGP 1×/2×/4×	AGP 1×/2×	AGP	AGP	AGP	AGP
AGP pipe	No	PIPE	PIPE	PIPE	Integrated	PIPE	PIPE
AGP SBA	No	SBA	SBA	SBA	Integrated	SBA	SBA
South bridge	PIIX4E	ICH	PIIX4E	ICH	ICH	PIIX4E	PIIX4E
IDE type	ATA/33	ATA/66	ATA/33	ATA/66	ATA/66	ATA/33	ATA/33

Table 28.2   Example chipsets (Value PCs)

	810	440LX	440EX AGP	440ZX AGP
Processors	Pentium II/III	Pentium Celeron	Pentium Celeron	Pentium Celeron
Bus signals	AGTL+	GTL+	GTL+	AGTL+
Maximum number of processors	I	2	I	I
DRAM refresh	CAS-before-RAS	CAS-before-RAS	CAS-before-RAS	CAS-before-RAS
Memory support	4 rows	8 rows	4 rows	4 rows
DRAM chips supported	16/ 64/128 Mbit	Yes	Yes	Yes
Maximum memory	512MB	I GB	256 MB	256 MB
Memory types	PC100 SDRAM	EDO SDRAM	SDRAM	EDO SDRAM
PCI type	PCI 2.2	PCI 2.1	PCI 2.1	PCI 2.1
Integrated graphics	Yes	No	No	No
AGP type	Integrated	AGP I×/ 2×	AGP I×/ 2×	AGP I×/ 2×
AGP pipe	Integrated	PIPE	PIPE	PIPE
AGP SBA	Integrated	SBA	SBA	SBA
South bridge	ICH	PIIX4E	PIIX4E	PIIX4E
IDE type	ATA/66	ATA/33	ATA/33	ATA/33

28.2 820 Chipset

The Intel 820 chip supports the third-generation desktop architecture (Intel SC242). Its main features are:

- Enhanced graphics performance. A ×4 AGP 2.0 interface gives up to 1GB/s for graphics transfers (four transfers for each of the 66 MHz clock cycles).
- Increased data throughput for direct RDRAM. A 400MHz direct RDRAM (Rambus) uses a 16-bit, double-clock, 400 MHz, direct RDRAM interface, which gives up to 1.6GB/s transfer rates.
- New architecture based on hubs.
- Improved security and manageability using the firmware hub component.

> **RDRAM**
>
> RDRAM uses fast DRAM accesses for clock speeds at 266 MHz, 300 MHz, 356 MHz, and 400 MHz. This allows for transfers of up to 1.6 GB/s (twice the transfer rate of 100 MHz SDRAM).

- Enhanced power management functions. The ACPI compliant Intel 820 chipset platform supports the full-on, stop grant, suspend to RAM, suspend to disk, and soft-off power management states.
- Possible deletion of the ISA expansion bus. The deletetion of the ISA bus increases the plug-and-play technology for devices. An ISA bus can be added with the use of the optional 82380AB PCI-ISA bridge.

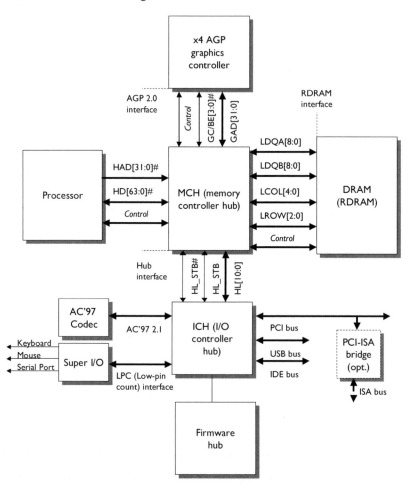

Figure 28.1   820-based motherboard

The main elements of the systems are illustrated in Figure 28.1; they are:

- **Memory controller hub** (MCH). This integrates a 133 MHz processor system bus controller, AGP 2.0 controller, 400 MHz direct RDRAM controller and a high-speed hub interface for communication with the ICH. An example device is the 82820.
- **I/O controller hub** (ICH). This integrates an ultraATA/66 IDE controller, a USB host controller, an LPC (low pin count) interface controller (which replaces the ISA interface to the ultra I/O device with a seven-line connection), on FWH (firmware hub) interface controller, PCI interface controller, AC'97 digital controller and a hub interface for the MCH. An example device is the 82801AA.

- **Firmware Hub** (FWH). This supports enhanced security and manageability, and operates under the FWH interface and protocol. It uses a random number generator (RNG), register-based locking, and hardware-based locking. An example device is the 82802.

and additionally the 82380AB PCI-ISA bridge, if ISA is required.

It can be seen that the ISA interface has been phased-out in favor of the LPC interface to the Super I/O device.

Transfer rates				
	Clock Speed (MHz)	Clocking	Data Rate (million samples/s)	Transfer rate (MB/s)
AGP 2.0 (32 bits)	66	Quad (4 samples/ clock)	266	1066
CPU bus (64 bits)	133	Single	133	1066
Hub interface (8 bits)	66	Quad	266	266
PCI 2.2 (32 bits)	33	Single	33	133
RDRAM (16 bits)	266/300/ 356/400	Double	533/600/ 711/800	1066/1200 /1422/1600

28.2.1 System connections

The processor connections are given in section 28.5 (SCS242 – 242-pin connector); Figure 28.2 outlines the main connections to and from the MCD. In the HX-board, the system controller interfaced to the PCI bus, which had a complex interface. This has been replaced with the hub interface, which uses 12 data/address lines (HL[10:0]) and two strobe signals (HL_STB and HL_STB#). The other interfaces are to the main high-bandwidth devices: the memory (using RDRAM) and the graphics port (using AGP 2.0). These are both high-transfer ports and are closed coupled so that the graphics controller can load data from the RDRAM quickly, without the processor becoming involved in the transfer. In the RDRAM the main connections are (refer to section 12.2.5):

- LDQA[8:0]. Data byte A with 1 bit for parity.
- LDQB[8:0]. Data byte B with 1 bit for parity.
- LROW[2:0]. Row access control to access a given row.
- LCOL[4:0]. Column access control to access a given column.
- Clocks, (refer to section 12.2.5).

> **Single instruction multiple data (SIMD)**
>
> The Pentium III processor brought 70 new streaming SIMD (single instruction, multiple data) floating-point extensions, which expand the MMX extensions (which are integer based).

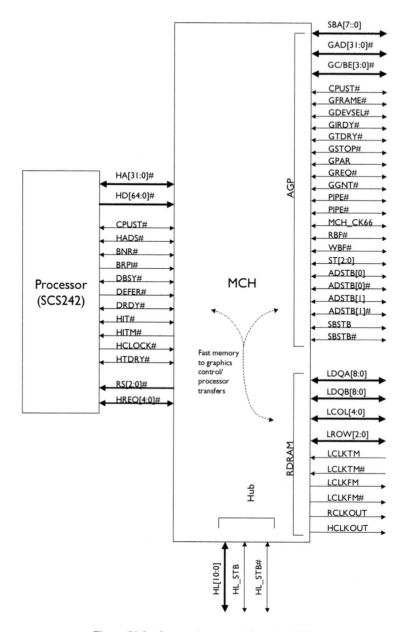

Figure 28.2   Connections to and from the MCD

28.2.2 RIMM sockets

The RDRAM memory devices are mounted on the 168-pin RIMM. Data passes in either direction using two 8-bit data buses (LDQA[8:0] and LDQB[8:0]) with an extra bit added for parity (LDQA[8] and LDQV[8]). The memory is addressed with five column (LCOL[4:0]) and three row address lines (LROW[2:0]). As the clocking rates are high (up to 400MHz), care must be taken when routing lines to and from RIMM sockets (see section 12.2.5). Figure 28.3 illustrates the connections between two RIMM sockets. The signal lines run through the RIMM modules and are then terminated at either end (either with the TERMINATOR or the MCH). One of the clocks runs from the MCH to the TERMINATOR (clock from master – CFM), or to the master (clock to master – CTM). The CTM provides for data traveling from the memory to the MCH (data output from memory), and the CFM provides for data traveling from the MCH to the memory (data input to memory).

> **Termination for RIMMs**
>
> RDRAM uses RSL signals that must be terminated to 1.8 V (V_{term}) using 27 Ω resistors at the end of the channel opposite the MCH. V_{term} must be decoupled using 0.1 μF high-speed bypass capacitors near the terminating resistors.

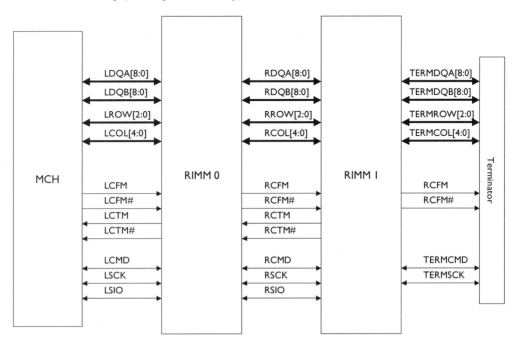

Figure 28.3 RIMM connections

28.2.3 I/O controller hub

Figure 28.4 illustrates the connection to the I/O controller hub. It can be seen that many of the connections, such as the PCI bus connections, have been moved from the system controller to the controller hub. The main connections are to the PCI bus, the processor (mainly interrupt lines), IDE bus, AC'97, LPC and the USB.

Notice, that there is little support for IRQ lines, apart from IRQ14 and IRQ15, which are used in the IDE bus. The only other interrupts that are

> **AC'97**
>
> The Audio Code 97 (AC'97) specification defines the digital link that is used to connect a mixture of audio codecs (ACs) and modem codecs (MCs). This allows for cost-effective audio and modem connects, which do not involve the ISA bus, and are configurable by software.

supported are the steerable interrupts (PIRQA, PIRQB, PIRQC and PIRQD). It can be seen that the 820 architecture supports more plug-and-plug technology and that ISA will eventually be phased-out. Busmastering on the PCI bus is performed with the PREQ[5:0] and PGNT[5:0] lines. Up to four PCI add-in slots can be supported (using PREQ[3:0] and PGNT[3:0] lines). As with previous designs, the system board supports two USB connectors.

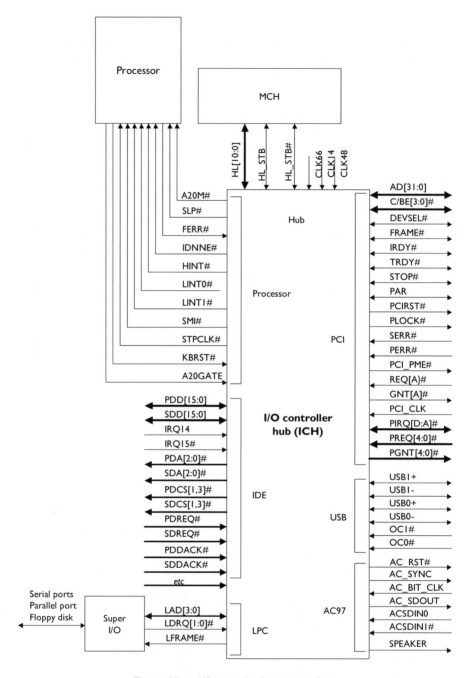

Figure 28.4   I/O controller hub connections

28.2.4 Super I/O

Figure 28.5 shows the connections to the super I/O device (LPC47B27X). It can be seen that it supports two serial ports, a parallel port, two joypad connections (although only one is shown in the diagram), a floppy disk connection and an infrared connection.

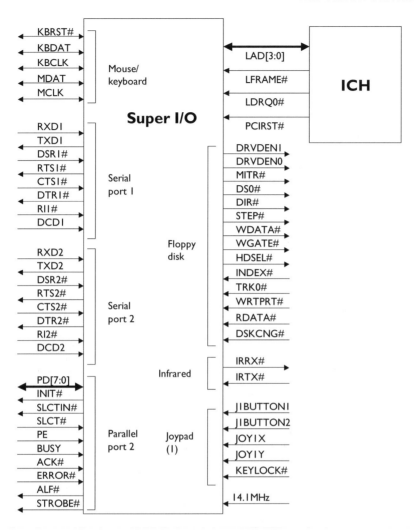

Figure 28.5 Super I/O connections

28.2.5 Network connection

Network connections have been important in computer systems, and the 820 chipset supports a special network device: the 82559 (LAN controller). This device provides a 32-bit connection onto the PCI bus.

28.2.6 Audio connection

The AC'97 interface allows for a standard connection between the audio device and the ICH. Figure 28.6 shows example connections. The interface from the ICH consists of four signals for handshaking, clocking and transferring audio data. The audio device (such as the AD1881) interfaces to these signal lines and provides line in/out, CD left/right and microphone input. With the AC'97 interface, it is also possible to interface to a modem codec, or even a combined modem/audio codec that combines the functionality of a modem with an audio device. Thus, the audio and the modem codec do not require any interrupts as they would on the ISA bus.

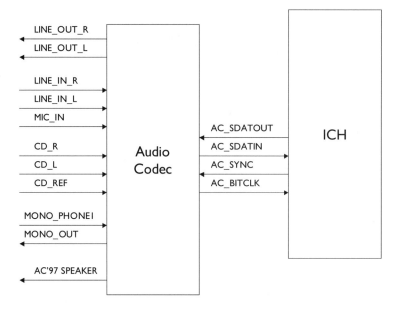

Figure 28.6   Audio connections

28.3   840 Chipset

The 810, 820 and 840 are based on a hub architecture that allows for optimized interfaces between each of the main components. The 840 is another enhancement on a hub-based design. Figure 28.7 shows an example system. It is based on:

Hi-tech's most influential

1. Chris Gent, CEO, Vodafone.
2. Steve Case, Chairman, Time Warner.
3. Rupert Murdoch, Chairman, News Corp.
4. Steve Balmer, CEO, Microsoft.
5. Michael Dell, CEO, Dell Computers.
6. Jeff Bezos, CEO, Amazon.com.
7. John Chambers, CEO, Cisco Systems.
8. Jiang Zemin, President, China.
9. Jack Welch, CEO, General Electric.
10. Stelios Haji-Ioannou, Owner, EasyGroup.

Silicon.com survey, 2000

- **Memory controller hub** (82820, 324-pin BGA). This connects the processor to the AGP port (x4 AGP), RDRAM and the I/O controller hub (ICH). As with the 820-based system, the interface between the MCH and the ICH is an optimized, low-pin-count interface. The host clock speed is either 100 MHz or 133 MHz, with up to two processors. The addressing bus can operate as either a 32-bit or a 36-bit address bus.
- **I/O controller hub** (82801AA or 82801AB, 241-pin BGA). This connects the MCH to the IDE, PCI, USB, AC'97, and the super I/O device. The IDE interface is either ATA/66 (for the 82801AA) or ATA/33 (for the 82801AB). The 82801AB is known as ICH0 and supports ATA/66 for the IDE bus, and wake on LAN. The 82801AA is known as ICH and supports ATA/33.
- **PC64H** (82806A, 241pin BGA). This allows for the connection of either two 66 MHz PCI slots or four 33 MHz PCI slots, which can either transfer at 32 or 64 data bits. At a rate of 66 MHz, with a burst mode, the maximum transfer rate will be increased from 132 MB/s (with 32 bits at 33 MHz) to 396 MB/s (with 64 bits at 66 MHz). It has integrated I/O APIC, which provides for up to 24 interrupts. The PC64H also allows hot-plugging.

- **Super I/O**. This connects the ICH to buses such as the serial port, parallel port and the keyboard. This devices are typically slow and their interfaces, have been pushed away from the main high-speed interfaces, such as the PCI and AGP buses.
- **Firmware hub** (82802AB/AC, 32-pin PLCC). Provides security with a random number generate (RNG).

The MCH can also interface to SDRAM (to allow migration from SDRAM to RDRAM) using a SDRAM memory repeater hub (MRH-S) running at either 100 MHz or 133 MHz. The MCH supports up to 64 RDRAM devices without an RDRAM memory repeater hub (MRH-D), and up to eight RDRAM channels with four external MRH-Ds.

Each repeater connects onto a branch of the Channel A and Channel B of the RDRAM bus connection. The interfaces from the MCH and the ICH and the P64H are via Hub interface A and hub interface B. The A interface operates at 266 MB/s and the B interface operates at 533 MB/s.

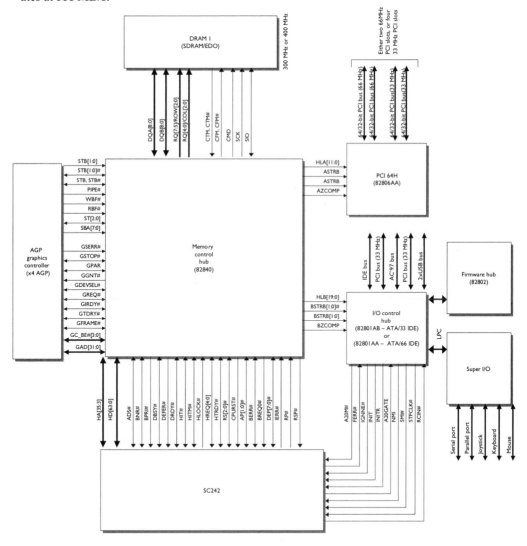

Figure 28.7   840-based system

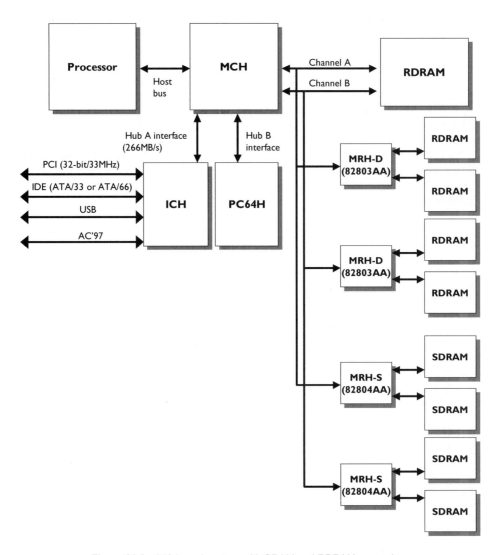

Figure 28.8 840-based system with SRAM and RDRAM expansions

Figure 28.9 shows the interface to the 64-bit/66 MHz PCI bus. The extra signals over the 32-bit PCI bus are:

- AD[63:32]. PCI address/data. These provide the additional 32 bits for the 64-bit data/address bus. In the address phase, when REQ64# is asserted, the upper 32 bits are transferred. During the data phase, an additional 32 bits of data are transferred when REQ64# and ACK64# are both asserted.

ANSI ASCII code

In 1963, ANSI defined the 7-bit ASCII standard code for characters. At the time, IBM had developed the 8-bit EBCDIC code, which allowed for up to 256 characters, (ASCII allows 128 characters). It is thought that the 7-bit code was used for the standard as it was reckoned that eight holes in punched paper tape would weaken the tape. Thus, the world has had to use the 7-bit ASCII standard, which is still popular in the days of global communications and large-scale disk storage.

- C/BE[7:4]#. Bus command and byte enables. These provide the additional bus enable and command lines. In an address phase, they identify the command; in a data phase, they identify the byte enables.
- PAR64. Carries even parity for AD[63:32] and C/BE[7:4]#.
- REQ64#. PCI 64-bit transfer. Identifies a 64-bit data transfer.
- ACK64#. Acknowledge 64-bit transfer. Indicates the target's ability to receive a 64-bit data transfer.
- REQ[5:0]#. Support for up to six busmasters; used to request a busmaster.
- M66E. 66 MHz enable. If low, the bus speed is 66 MHz, else it is 33 MHz.
- GNT[5:0]#. Support for up to six busmasters; used to grant busmaster requests.
- IRQ[23:0]. APIC interrupts. These are not supported by an 8259 (PIC).
- APICD[1:0]. APIC data. These are used to send and receive data over the APIC bus. The IOAPIC resides on the secondary PCI bus (which is within the ICH).

The interrupt lines (PIRQ[A:D]) can be routed to interrupts IRQ3-IRQ7, IRQ9-IRQ12, IRQ14 or IRQ15 (with interrupt steering). In APIC mode, these signals are connected to the internal I/O APIC, PIRQA# is connected to IRQ16, PIRQB# to IRQ17, PIRQC# to IRQ18, and PIRQD# to IRQ19, which frees up ISA interrupts (IRQ0-IRQ15).

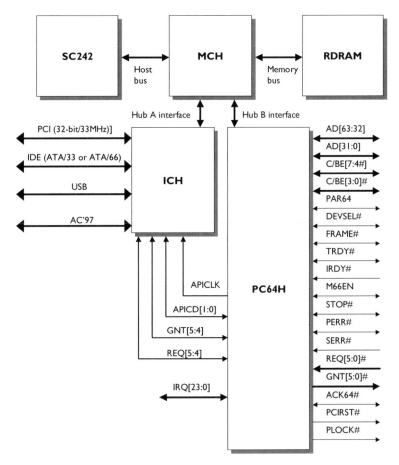

Figure 28.9 64-bit/66 MHz PCI interface

28.4 810E Chipset

The 810E chipset uses a memory controller hub with a built-in graphics facility. Its main components are:

- **Graphics memory controller hub** (GMCH – 82810, 421-pin BGA). As with the MCH in the 820/840, this connects the processor to the memory and the I/O controller hub. It also contains a graphics controller, which uses direct AGP (integrated AGP) for ultrafast 2D and 3D effects and images. The 82810 also has an integrated hardware motion compensation to improve soft DVD video quality and a digital TV out port.
- **I/O controller hub** (ICH – 82801, 241-pin BGA). This connects to the main buses, such as the IDE controllers, USB ports, and PCI bus. It also contains an integrated AC'97 controller.
- **Firmware Hub** (FWH – 82802, 32-pin PLCC). This provides security with a hardware random number generate (RNG), for stronger encryption, digital signing, and security protocols. It also stores system BIOS and video BIOS, eliminating a redundant nonvolatile memory component.

The 810E chipset supports either a 100 MHz or a 133 MHz system bus, and uses systems manageability bus (SMB) to networked equipment to monitor the 810 chipset. Figure 28.10 shows a typical architecture. The GMCH supports only a single processor; it has the following specifications:

- Integrated 2D and 3D graphics engines.
- Integrated hardware motion compensation engine.
- Integrated 230 MHz DAC. The DAC converts digital color information into an analogue voltage for the red, green and blue signals.
- Integrated digital video out port.
- Display Cache DRAM controller with a 32-bit 100/133 MHz DRAM array. It uses SDRAM to give a 4 MB display cache.

> **Full circle**
>
> The IBM System/360 was one of the classic computers. It was used by many large organizations in the 1960s and the 1970s. It gained its name because it was aimed at the full circle (360°) of customers, from business to science.

The SRAM cache interface include the following signal lines:

LCS#	**Chip Select**. Used to select a particular SDRAM block.
LDQM[3:0]	**Input/Output data mask**. These control the memory array and synchronize output enables during read cycles and as byte enables during write cycles.
LSRAS#	**SDRAM row address strobe**. Used to identify a row address.
LSCAS#	**SDRAM column address strobe**. Used to identify a column address.
LMA[11:0]	**Memory Address**. Used to provide the multiplexed row and column address.
LWE#	**Write enable signal**. Used to identify a memory write.
LMD[31:0]	**Memory Data**. DRAM data bus.

The digital TV signals are:

TVCLKIN	**Low voltage TV Clock In**

CLKOUT[1:0]	**LCD/TV port clock out**
BLANK#	**Flicker blank or border**
	Period indication
LTVDATA[11:0]	**LCD/TV data**
TVVSYNC	**Vertical sync**
TVHSYNC	**Horizontal Sync**
LTVCL	**LCD/TV clock**
LTVDA	**LCD/TV data**

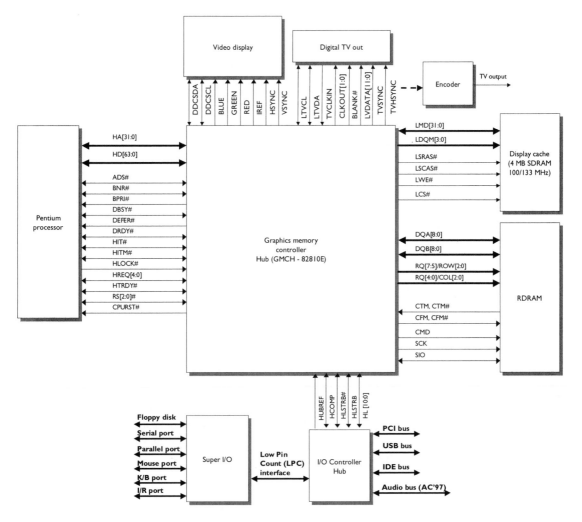

Figure 28.10 810E architecture

28.5 Exercises

28.5.1 Which of the following is the most advanced chipset?

(a)	810E	(b)	820
(c)	840	(d)	440

28.5.2   Which of the following chipsets has an integrated graphics
controller?
  (a)   810E
  (b)   820
  (c)   840
  (d)   440

28.5.3   Which of the following is the
main function of the firmware
hub:
  (a)   To generate a random
         number, by hardware
  (b)   To allow networking
  (c)   To handle hardware
         interrupts
  (c)   To allow parallel
         processing

28.5.4   Which of the following is one
of the main advances with the
840 chipset over the 820 chipset?
  (a)   66MHz/32-bit PCI bus
  (b)   Faster interface to
         AGP
  (c)   Less power dissipation
  (d)   Support for RDRAM

28.5.5   How are SDRAM modules
added to the 840 chipset?
  (a)   They interface
         directly to the
         memory hub
  (b)   They are not supported
  (c)   They connect to the
         PCI interface
  (d)   With repeater hubs

28.5.6   How are RDRAM modules
normally added to the 840
chipset?
  (a)   They interface
         directly to the
         memory hub
  (b)   They are not supported
  (c)   They connect to the
         PCI interface
  (d)   With repeater hubs

Snow White and the Seven Dwarfs

In the 1960s and the 1970s, IBM was so pow-
erful that it held a larger market share than all
of its competitors combined (at least 70%).
There were seven main rivals, thus the term
Snow White and the Seven 'dwarfs' was often
used. The Dwarfs were General Electric,
RCA, Burroughs, UNIVAC, NCR, Control
Data and Honeywell. In the face of the IBM
System/370, RCA left the computer market.
UNIVAC became a division of Sperry, GE sold
its computer business to Honeywell, and
AT&T bought over NCR (which changed the
meaning of its name from National Cash Register to National Computing Resources), In
1986, Burroughs bought UNIVAC from
Sperry and, at the time, became the second
largest computer company. In the same year,
AT&T spun off NCR into an independent
company. Control Data was taken over by a
finance company called Commercial Credit,
who never really exploited the dynamic na-
ture of Control Data.

It is to IBM's credit that they are still one
of the largest computing companies, while the
other 'dwarfs' have mainly left the mainstream
computer business. In the era of the PC, the
RCAs, UNIVACs, and Burroughs were replaced by the Commodores, the Radio
Shacks, the Osbornes, who have since been
replaced by the Dells, the Compaqs and the
Packard Bells. The great survivors of the PC
revolution have been:

1.   **IBM** (for holding their own in a difficult
      market).
2.   **Compaq** (for doing the same as IBM).
3.   **Sun** (who have refused to be drawn
      down the PC market/Microsoft/Intel
      road).
4.   **Apple** (for doing the same as Sun).

Appendices

A.1 SIMM/DIMM Pin Connections

Table A.1 30-pin SIMM connections

Pin	Signal name	Pin	Signal name
1	+5V	16	D4
2	CAS	17	A8
3	D0	18	A9
4	A0	19	
5	A1	20	D5
6	D1	21	R/W
7	A2	22	GND
8	A3	23	D6
9	GND	24	
10	D2	25	D7
11	A4	26	
12	A5	27	RAS
13	D3	28	
14	A6	29	
15	A7	30	+5V

Table A.2 72-pin SIMM connections

Pin	Signal name	Pin	Signal name	Pin	Signal name
1	GND	25	BLOCK SEL 0	49	D8
2	D0	26	+5V	50	D24
3	D16	27	A8	51	D9
4	D1	28	A9	52	D25
5	D17	29	RAS3	53	D10
6	D2	30	RAS2	54	D26
7	A10	31		55	D11
8	+5V	32	D6	56	D27
9		33		57	D12
10	A0	34		58	D28
11	A1	35		59	+5V
12	A2	36		60	D29
13	A3	37		61	D13
14	A4	38		62	D30
15	A5	39	GND	63	D14
16	A6	40	CAS0	64	D31
17		41	CAS2	65	D15
18	D4	42	CAS3	66	BLOCK SEL 2
19	D20	43	CAS1	67	PRES DET 0
20	D5	44	RAS0	68	PRES DET 1
21	D21	45	RAS1	69	PRES DET 2
22	D6	46	BLOCK SEL 1	70	PRES DET 3
23	D22	47	R/W	71	BLOCK SEL 3
24	D7	48		72	GND

A 168-pin DIMM connector is arranged as front side (left side 1–42, right side 43–84) and a back side (left side 85–126, right side 127–168).

Table A.3   168-pin DIMM connections

(Front, left)

Pin	Non-Parity	Parity	72 ECC	80 ECC	Description
1	VSS	VSS	VSS	VSS	Ground
2	DQ0	DQ0	DQ0	DQ0	Data 0
3	DQ1	DQ1	DQ1	DQ1	Data 1
4	DQ2	DQ2	DQ2	DQ2	Data 2
5	DQ3	DQ3	DQ3	DQ3	Data 3
6	VCC	VCC	VCC	VCC	+5 VDC or +3.3 VDC
7	DQ4	DQ4	DQ4	DQ4	Data 4
8	DQ5	DQ5	DQ5	DQ5	Data 5
9	DQ6	DQ6	DQ6	DQ6	Data 6
10	DQ7	DQ7	DQ7	DQ7	Data 7
11	DQ8	DQ8	DQ8	DQ8	Data 8
12	VSS	VSS	VSS	VSS	Ground
13	DQ9	DQ9	DQ9	DQ9	Data 9
14	DQ10	DQ10	DQ10	DQ10	Data 10
15	DQ11	DQ11	DQ11	DQ11	Data 11
16	DQ12	DQ12	DQ12	DQ12	Data 12
17	DQ13	DQ13	DQ13	DQ13	Data 13
18	VCC	VCC	VCC	VCC	+5 VDC or +3.3 VDC
19	DQ14	DQ14	DQ14	DQ14	Data 14
20	DQ15	DQ15	DQ15	DQ15	Data 15
21	n/c	CB0	CB0	CB0	Parity/check bit input/output 0
22	n/c	CB1	CB1	CB1	Parity/check bit input/output 1
23	VSS	VSS	VSS	VSS	Ground
24	n/c	n/c	n/c	CB8	Parity/check bit input/output 8
25	n/c	n/c	n/c	CB9	Parity/check bit input/output 9
26	VCC	VCC	VCC	VCC	+5 VDC or +3.3 VDC
27	/WE0	/WE0	/WE0	/WE0	Read/write input
28	/CAS0	/CAS0	/CAS0	/CAS0	Column address strobe 0
29	/CAS1	/CAS1	/CAS1	/CAS1	Column address strobe 1
30	/RAS0	/RAS0	/RAS0	/RAS0	Row address strobe 0
31	/OE0	/OE0	/OE0	/OE0	Output enable
32	VSS	VSS	VSS	VSS	Ground
33	A0	A0	A0	A0	Address 0
34	A2	A2	A2	A2	Address 2
35	A4	A4	A4	A4	Address 4
36	A6	A6	A6	A6	Address 6
37	A8	A8	A8	A8	Address 8
38	A10	A10	A10	A10	Address 10
39	A12	A12	A12	A12	Address 12
40	VCC	VCC	VCC	VCC	+5 VDC or +3.3 VDC
41	VCC	VCC	VCC	VCC	+5 VDC or +3.3 VDC
42	DU	DU	DU	DU	Don't use

(Front, right)

Pin	Non-Parity	Parity	72 ECC	80 ECC	Description
43	VSS	VSS	VSS	VSS	Ground
44	/OE2	/OE2	/OE2	/OE2	
45	/RAS2	/RAS2	/RAS2	/RAS2	Row address strobe 2
46	/CAS2	/CAS2	/CAS2	/CAS2	Column address strobe 2
47	/CAS3	/CAS3	/CAS3	/CAS3	Column address strobe 3
48	/WE2	/WE2	/WE2	/WE2	Read/write input
49	VCC	VCC	VCC	VCC	+5 VDC or +3.3 VDC
50	n/c	n/c	n/c	CB10	Parity/check bit input/output 10
51	n/c	n/c	n/c	CB11	Parity/check bit input/output 11
52	n/c	CB2	CB2	CB2	Parity/check bit input/output 2
53	n/c	CB3	CB3	CB3	Parity/check bit input/output 3
54	VSS	VSS	VSS	VSS	Ground

55	DQ16	DQ16	DQ16	DQ16	Data 16
56	DQ17	DQ17	DQ17	DQ17	Data 17
57	DQ18	DQ18	DQ18	DQ18	Data 18
58	DQ19	DQ19	DQ19	DQ19	Data 19
59	VCC	VCC	VCC	VCC	+5 VDC or +3.3 VDC
60	DQ20	DQ20	DQ20	DQ20	Data 20
61	n/c	n/c	n/c	n/c	Not connected
62	DU	DU	DU	DU	Don't Use
63	n/c	n/c	n/c	n/c	Not connected
64	VSS	VSS	VSS	VSS	Ground
65	DQ21	DQ21	DQ21	DQ21	Data 21
66	DQ22	DQ22	DQ22	DQ22	Data 22
67	DQ23	DQ23	DQ23	DQ23	Data 23
68	VSS	VSS	VSS	VSS	Ground
69	DQ24	DQ24	DQ24	DQ24	Data 24
70	DQ25	DQ25	DQ25	DQ25	Data 25
71	DQ26	DQ26	DQ26	DQ26	Data 26
72	DQ27	DQ27	DQ27	DQ27	Data 27
73	VCC	VCC	VCC	VCC	+5 VDC or +3.3 VDC
74	DQ28	DQ28	DQ28	DQ28	Data 28
75	DQ29	DQ29	DQ29	DQ29	Data 29
76	DQ30	DQ30	DQ30	DQ30	Data 30
77	DQ31	DQ31	DQ31	DQ31	Data 31
78	VSS	VSS	VSS	VSS	Ground
79	n/c	n/c	n/c	n/c	Not connected
80	n/c	n/c	n/c	n/c	Not connected
81	n/c	n/c	n/c	n/c	Not connected
82	SDA	SDA	SDA	SDA	Serial Data
83	SCL	SCL	SCL	SCL	Serial Clock
84	VCC	VCC	VCC	VCC	+5 VDC or +3.3 VDC

(Back, left)

Pin	Non-Parity	Parity	72 ECC	80 ECC	Description
85	VSS	VSS	VSS	VSS	Ground
86	DQ32	DQ32	DQ32	DQ32	Data 32
87	DQ33	DQ33	DQ33	DQ33	Data 33
88	DQ34	DQ34	DQ34	DQ34	Data 34
89	DQ35	DQ35	DQ35	DQ35	Data 35
90	VCC	VCC	VCC	VCC	+5 VDC or +3.3 VDC
91	DQ36	DQ36	DQ36	DQ36	Data 36
92	DQ37	DQ37	DQ37	DQ37	Data 37
93	DQ38	DQ38	DQ38	DQ38	Data 38
94	DQ39	DQ39	DQ39	DQ39	Data 39
95	DQ40	DQ40	DQ40	DQ40	Data 40
96	VSS	VSS	VSS	VSS	Ground
97	DQ41	DQ41	DQ41	DQ41	Data 41
98	DQ42	DQ42	DQ42	DQ42	Data 42
99	DQ43	DQ43	DQ43	DQ43	Data 43
100	DQ44	DQ44	DQ44	DQ44	Data 44
101	DQ45	DQ45	DQ45	DQ45	Data 45
102	VCC	VCC	VCC	VCC	+5 VDC or +3.3 VDC
103	DQ46	DQ46	DQ46	DQ46	Data 46
104	DQ47	DQ47	DQ47	DQ47	Data 47
105	n/c	CB4	CB4	CB4	Parity/check bit input/output 4
106	n/c	CB5	CB5	CB5	Parity/check bit input/output 5
107	VSS	VSS	VSS	VSS	Ground
108	n/c	n/c	n/c	CB12	Parity/check bit input/output 12
109	n/c	n/c	n/c	CB13	Parity/check bit input/output 13
110	VCC	VCC	VCC	VCC	+5 VDC or +3.3 VDC
111	DU	DU	DU	DU	Don't use
112	/CAS4	/CAS4	/CAS4	/CAS4	Column address strobe 4
113	/CAS5	/CAS5	/CAS5	/CAS5	Column address strobe 5

Pin	Non-Parity	Parity	72 ECC	80 ECC	Description
114	/RAS1	/RAS1	/RAS1	/RAS1	Row address strobe 1
115	DU	DU	DU	DU	Don't use
116	VSS	VSS	VSS	VSS	Ground
117	A1	A1	A1	A1	Address 1
118	A3	A3	A3	A3	Address 3
119	A5	A5	A5	A5	Address 5
120	A7	A7	A7	A7	Address 7
121	A9	A9	A9	A9	Address 9
122	A11	A11	A11	A11	Address 11
123	A13	A13	A13	A13	Address 13
124	VCC	VCC	VCC	VCC	+5 VDC or +3.3 VDC
125	DU	DU	DU	DU	Don't use
126	DU	DU	DU	DU	Don't use

(Back, right)

Pin	Non-Parity	Parity	72 ECC	80 ECC	Description
127	VSS	VSS	VSS	VSS	Ground
128	DU	DU	DU	DU	Don't use
129	/RAS3	/RAS3	/RAS3	/RAS3	Column address strobe 3
130	/CAS6	/CAS6	/CAS6	/CAS6	Column address strobe 6
131	/CAS7	/CAS7	/CAS7	/CAS7	Column address strobe 7
132	DU	DU	DU	DU	Don't use
133	VCC	VCC	VCC	VCC	+5 VDC or +3.3 VDC
134	n/c	n/c	n/c	CB14	Parity/check bit input/output 14
135	n/c	n/c	n/c	CB15	Parity/check bit input/output 15
136	n/c	CB6	CB6	CB6	Parity/check bit input/output 6
137	n/c	CB7	CB7	CB7	Parity/check bit input/output 7
138	VSS	VSS	VSS	VSS	Ground
139	DQ48	DQ48	DQ48	DQ48	Data 48
140	DQ49	DQ49	DQ49	DQ49	Data 49
141	DQ50	DQ50	DQ50	DQ50	Data 50
142	DQ51	DQ51	DQ51	DQ51	Data 51
143	VCC	VCC	VCC	VCC	+5 VDC or +3.3 VDC
144	DQ52	DQ52	DQ52	DQ52	Data 52
145	n/c	n/c	n/c	n/c	Not connected
146	DU	DU	DU	DU	Don't use
147	n/c	n/c	n/c	n/c	Not connected
148	VSS	VSS	VSS	VSS	Ground
149	DQ53	DQ53	DQ53	DQ53	Data 53
150	DQ54	DQ54	DQ54	DQ54	Data 54
151	DQ55	DQ55	DQ55	DQ55	Data 55
152	VSS	VSS	VSS	VSS	Ground
153	DQ56	DQ56	DQ56	DQ56	Data 56
154	DQ57	DQ57	DQ57	DQ57	Data 57
155	DQ58	DQ58	DQ58	DQ58	Data 58
156	DQ59	DQ59	DQ59	DQ59	Data 59
157	VCC	VCC	VCC	VCC	+5 VDC or +3.3 VDC
158	DQ60	DQ60	DQ60	DQ60	Data 60
159	DQ61	DQ61	DQ61	DQ61	Data 61
160	DQ62	DQ62	DQ62	DQ62	Data 62
161	DQ63	DQ63	DQ63	DQ63	Data 63
162	VSS	VSS	VSS	VSS	Ground
163	CK3	CK3	CK3	CK3	
164	n/c	n/c	n/c	n/c	Not connected
165	SA0	SA0	SA0	SA0	Serial address 0
166	SA1	SA1	SA1	SA1	Serial address 1
167	SA2	SA2	SA2	SA2	Serial address 2
168	VCC	VCC	VCC	VCC	+5 VDC or +3.3 VDC

Table A.4   168-pin RIMM connections

Pin	Name	Pin	Name	Pin	Name	Pin	Name
A1	Gnd	B1	Gnd	A47	RSRV17-(NC)	B47	RSR18V-(NC)
A2	LDQA8	B2	LDQA7	A48	RSRV19-(NC)	B48	RSRV20-(NC)
A3	Gnd	B3	Gnd	A49	RSRV21-(NC)	B49	RSRV22-(NC)
A4	LDQA6	B4	LDQA5	A50	RSRV23-(NC)	B50	RSRV24-(NC)
A5	Gnd	B5	Gnd	A51	Vref	B51	Vref
A6	LDQA4	B6	LDQA3	A52	Gnd	B52	Gnd
A7	Gnd	B7	Gnd	A53	SCL	B53	SA0
A8	LDQA2	B8	LDQA1	A54	Vdd	B54	Vdd
A9	Gnd	B9	Gnd	A55	SDA	B55	SA1
A10	LDQA0	B10	LCFM	A56	SVdd	B56	SVdd
A11	Gnd	B11	Gnd	A57	SWP	B57	SA2
A12	LCTMN	B12	LCFMN	A58	Vdd	B58	Vdd
A13	Gnd	B13	Gnd	A59	RSCK	B59	RCMD
A14	LCTM	B14	RSRV1	A60	Gnd	B60	Gnd
A15	Gnd	B15	Gnd	A61	RDQB7	B61	RDQB8
A16	RSRV2	B16	LROW2	A62	Gnd	B62	Gnd
A17	Gnd	B17	Gnd	A63	RDQB5	B63	RDQB6
A18	LROW1	B18	LROW0	A64	Gnd	B64	Gnd
A19	Gnd	B19	Gnd	A65	RDQB3	B65	RDQB4
A20	LCOL4	B20	LCOL3	A66	Gnd	B66	Gnd
A21	Gnd	B21	Gnd	A67	RDQB1	B67	RDQB2
A22	LCOL2	B22	LCOL1	A68	Gnd	B68	Gnd
A23	Gnd	B23	Gnd	A69	RCOL0	B69	RDQB0
A24	LCOL0	B24	LDQB0	A70	Gnd	B70	Gnd
A25	Gnd	B25	Gnd	A71	RCOL2	B71	RCOL1
A26	LDQB1	B26	LDQB2	A72	Gnd	B72	Gnd
A27	Gnd	B27	Gnd	A73	RCOL4	B73	RCOL3
A28	LDQB3	B28	LDQB4	A74	Gnd	B74	Gnd
A29	Gnd	B29	Gnd	A75	RROW1	B75	RROW0
A30	LDQB5	B30	LDQB6	A76	Gnd	B76	Gnd
A31	Gnd	B31	Gnd	A77	RSRV7	B77	RROW2
A32	LDQB7	B32	LDQB8	A78	Gnd	B78	Gnd
A33	Gnd	B33	Gnd	A79	RCTM	B79	RSRV8 (NC)
A34	LSCK	B34	LCMD	A80	Gnd	B80	Gnd
A35	Vcmos	B35	Vcmos	A81	RCTMN	B81	RCFMN
A36	SOUT	B36	SIN	A82	Gnd	B82	Gnd
A37	Vcmos	B37	Vcmos	A83	RDQA0	B83	RCFM
A38	RSRV3 (NC)	B38	RSRV4	A84	Gnd	B84	Gnd
A39	Gnd	B39	Gnd	A85	RDQA2	B85	RDQA1
A40	RSRV5 (NC)	B40	RSRV6	A86	Gnd	B86	Gnd
A41	Vdd	B41	Vdd	A87	RDQA4	B87	RDQA3
A42	Vdd	B42	Vdd	A88	Gnd	B88	Gnd
A43	RSRV9	B43	RSRV10	A89	RDQA6	B89	RDQA5
A44	RSRV11	B44	RSRV12	A90	Gnd	B90	Gnd
A45	RSRV13	B45	RSRV14	A91	RDQA8	B91	RDQA7
A46	RSRV15	B46	RSRV16	A92	Gnd	B92	Gnd

Table A.5   SPD byte locations

Byte No.	Function described	Example	Notes
0	Number of serial PD bytes written during module production	128 bytes (80h)	
1	Total number of bytes in serial PD device	256 bytes (08h)	01h – 2 bytes, 02h – 4 bytes, 03h – 8 bytes, and so on.
2	Fundamental memory type (FPM, EDO, SDRAM, and so on)	04 (SDRAM)	01h – FPM DRAM 02h – EDO 04h – SDRAM
3	Number of row addresses	0D (13 address lines – RA[0:12])	
4	Number of column addresses	0B (11 address lines – CA[0:10])	
5	Number of DIMM banks	2	
6–7	Data width	4800h (72-bit)	Used to designate the module's data width. The data width is presented as a 16-bit word: Bit 0 of byte 6 is the LSB of the 16-bit width identifier, and bit 7 of byte 7 becomes the MSB. For example, 4800h would become: 0000 0000 0100 1000 Others include: 64-bit (4000h), 128-bit (8000h), 144-bit (9000h), 256-bit (FF00h) and 512-bit (0002h).
8	Voltage interface level of this assembly	1 (LVTTL)	0 TTL/5V tolerant 1 LVTTL (not 5V tolerant) 2 HSTL 1.5V 3 SSTL 3.3V 4 SSTL 2.5V
9	SDRAM cycle time at maximum supported CAS latency (CL)	7.5ns (75h)	Defines the minimum cycle time for the SDRAM module at the highest CAS latency, CAS latency =X, defined in byte 18. The higher order nibble (bits 4–7) define the number of ns while the lower order nibble (bits 0–3) defines the number of 0.1ns. For example: 10.5ns (10+0.5ns) → A5h 15.2ns (12+0.2ns) → F2h
10	SDRAM access from clock	5.4ns (54h)	As above
11	DIMM configuration type (non-parity, parity or ECC)	ECC (02h)	00h – None, 01 – Parity, 02h – ECC.
12	Refresh rate/type	SR/1X(7.813µs)	Defines refresh rate/type. Bit 7 defines whether the DRAM is self-refresh. An example is: 82h – reduced (0.5x)...7.8µs

13	Primary SDRAM width	04h (x4)	Bits 0 – 6 of this byte indicate the width of the primary data SDRAM. Bit 7 defines whether the second physical bank on the module is a different size from the first physical bank.
14	Error checking SDRAM width	04h (x4)	As above.
15	SDRAM device attributes: minimum clock delay, back-to-back random column access	01h (one clock)	
16	SDRAM device attributes: burst lengths supported	0F (1,2,4 and 8)	
17	SDRAM device attributes: number of banks on SDRAM	04 (4)	
18	SDRAM device attributes: CAS latency	06 (2, 3)	
19	SDRAM device attributes: CS latency	04 (4)	
20	SDRAM device attributes: write latency 4	01 (0)	
21	SDRAM module attributes	1Fh (Registered/Buffered with PLL)	
22	SDRAM device attributes: general	0Eh (Write-1/Read Burst, Precharge All, Auto-Precharge)	
23	Minimum clock cycle at CLX-1	F0 (15.0ns)	
24	Maximum data access time (t_{AC}) from clock at CLX-1		
25	Minimum clock cycle at CLX-2 (ns)		
26	Maximum data access time (t_{AC}) from clock at CLX-2		
27	Minimum row precharge time (t_{RP})		
28	Minimum row active to row active delay (t_{RRD})		
29	Minimum RAS to CAS delay (t_{RCD})		
30	Minimum RAS pulse width (t_{RAS})		
31	Module bank density		
32	Address and command setup time before clock		
33	Address and command hold time after clock		
34	Data input setup time before clock		
35	Data input hold time after clock		
36–61	Superset information (may be used in future)		
62	SPD revision		
63	Checksum for Bytes 0-62		
64–71	Manufacturer's JEDEC ID Code		
72	Module manufacturing location		
73–90	Module part number		
91–92	Module revision code		
93–94	Module manufacturing date		
95–98	Module serial number		
99–125	Manufacturer's specific data		

A.2   Slot 1/SC242 Connections

The Pentium II/III processor is sometimes known as SC242 as it uses 242 pins, either using a Slot 1 connection, or a zero-insertion force connector. The connections for a connection are given below:

B01	EMI	A01	VCC_VTT
B02	**FLUSH#**	A02	GND
B03	SMI#	A03	VCC_VTT
B04	**INIT#**	A04	ERR#
B05	VCC_VTT	A05	**A20M#**
B06	**STPCLK#**	A06	GND
B07	TCK	A07	**FERR#**
B08	**SLP#**	A08	**IGNNE#**
B09	VCC_VTT	A09	TDI
B10	TMS	A10	GND
B11	TRST#	A11	TDO
B12	N/C	A12	PWRGOOD
B13	VCC_VD	A13	TESTHI
B14	N/C	A14	GND
B15	N/C THERMTRIP#	A15	
B16	LINT1	A16	N/C
B17	VCC_VD	A17	LINT0
B18	PICCLK	A18	GND
B19	N/C	A19	PICD0
B20	N/C	A20	**PREQ[0]#**
B21	N/C	A21	N/C
B22	PICD1	A22	GND
B23	**PRDY[0]#**	A23	N/C
B24	N/C	A24	N/C
B25	N/C	A25	N/C
B26	N/C	A26	GND
B27	N/C	A27	N/C
B28	N/C	A28	N/C
B29	VCC_VD	A29	N/C
B30	HD62#	A30	GND
B31	HD58#	A31	N/C
B32	HD63#	A32	HD61#
B33	VCC_VD	A33	HD55#
B34	HD56#	A34	GND
B35	HD50#	A35	HD60#
B36	HD54#	A36	HD53#
B37	VCC_VD	A37	HD57#
B38	HD59#	A38	GND
B39	HD54#	A39	HD46#
B40	HD52#	A40	HD49#
B41	EMI	A41	HD51#
B42	HD41#	A42	GND
B43	HD47#	A43	HD42#
B44	HD44#	A44	HD45#
B45	VCC_VD	A45	HD39#
B46	HD36#	A46	GND
B47	HD40#	A47	N/C
B48	HD34#	A48	HD43#

INIT# [I] initialization: used to generate a soft reset to the processor.

INTR [O] interrupt: used to identify an interrupt request.

A20M# [I] mask A20. Goes active based on either setting the appropriate bit in the Port 92h register.

SLP [I] processor sleep.

STPCLK# [I] stop clock request: used to ask the processor to stop its internal clock.

FERR# [O] numeric coprocessor error: if FERR# is asserted, an internal IRQ13 is generated on the interrupt controller unit.

IGNNE# [I] ignore numeric error.

NMI [I] non-maskable interrupt.

FLUSH# [I]: when asserted, it causes the processor to stop caching new lines, write back all cache lines in the modified state, and disable further caching until FLUSH# is negated.

PREQ[0]# [I] PCI request: used by a PCI device to request the PCI bus.

PRDY[0]# [I] PrePCI Target Ready: asserted by the target to indicate that it is able to complete the current data transfer.

HD[63:0]# [I/0] host data: used for the data lines on the system bus.

B49	VCC_VD	A49	HD37#
B50	HD38#	A50	GND
B51	HD32#	A51	HD33#
B52	HD28#	A52	HD35#
B53	VCC_VD	A53	HD31#
B54	HD29#	A54	GND
B55	HD26#	A55	HD30#
B56	HD25#	A56	HD27#
B57	VCC_VD	A57	HD24#
B58	HD22#	A58	GND
B59	HD19#	A59	HD23#
B60	HD18#	A60	HD21#
B61	FM1	A61	HD16#
B62	HD20#	A62	GND
B63	HD17#	A63	HD13#
B64	HD15#	A64	HD11#
B65	VCC_VD	A65	HD10#
B66	HD12#	A66	GND
B67	HD7#	A67	HD14#
B68	HD6#	A68	HD9#
B69	VCC_VD	A69	HD8#
B70	HD4#	A70	GND
B71	HD2#	A71	HD5#
B72	HD0#	A72	HD3#
B73	VCC_VD	A73	HD1#
B74	HRESET#	A74	GND
B75	N/C	A75	CPUHCLK
B76	N/C	A76	BREQ[0]#
B77	VCC_VD	A77	N/C
B78	N/C	A78	GND
B79	N/C	A79	N/C
B80	HA29#	A80	N/C
B81	EMI	A81	HA30#
B82	HA26#	A82	GND
B83	HA24#	A83	HA30#
B84	HA28	A84	HA27#
B85	VCC_VD	A85	HA22#
B86	HA20#	A86	GND
B87	HA21#	A87	HA23#
B88	HA25#	A88	N/C
B89	VCC_VD	A89	HA19#
B90	HA15#	A90	GND
B91	HA17#	A91	HA18#
B92	HA11#	A92	HA16#
B93	VCC_VD	A93	HA13#
B94	HA12#	A94	GND
B95	HA8#	A95	HA14#
B96	HA7#	A96	HA10#
B97	VCC_VD	A97	HA5#
B98	HA3#	A98	GND
B99	HA6#	A99	HA9#
B100	EMI	A100	HA4#
B101	S_0#	A101	**BNR#**
B102	**HREQ[0]#**	A102	GND
B103	**HREQ[1]#**	A103	**BPRI#**
B104	**HREQ[4]#**	A104	HTRDY#

Intel changed the address and data lines to an inverted state so that it saved power dissipation. For example, HA31 changed to HA31#.

HA[31:3]# [I/O] host address bus: connects to host address bus. During host cycles, HA[31:3]# are inputs.

BNR# [I/O] block next request: used to block the current request bus owner from issuing new requests. This signal is used to dynamically control the host bus pipeline depth.
BPRI# [O] priority agent bus request: indicates to the processor when there is only one priority agent on the host bus, and is asserted when the agent requires ownership of the address bus. This signal has priority over symmetric bus requests and will cause the current symmetric owner to stop issuing new transactions unless the HLOCK# signal was asserted.
DRDY# data ready: asserted for each cycle that data is transferred.
DEFER# defer: used to indicate to the processor that there is a deferred response, or can be used to indicate a host retry response.
DBSY# data bus busy: used by the data bus owner to hold the data bus for transfers requiring more than one cycle.

HREQ[4:0]# [I/O] host request command: set active during both clocks of request phase. On the first clock, the signals define the transaction type for a snoop request. On the next clock, the signals carry additional information to define the complete transaction type.

HLOCK# host lock: all processor bus cycles sampled with the assertion of HLOCK# and ADS#.

B105	VCC_VD	A105	**DEFER#**
B106	**HLOCK#**	A106	GND
B107	**DRDY#**	A107	**HREQ[2]#**
B108	**RS[0]#**	A108	**HREQ[3]#**
B109	VCC_5	A109	**HITM#**
B110	**HIT#**	A110	GND
B111	**RS[2]#**	A111	**DBSY#**
B112	N/C	A112	**RS[1]#**
B113	VCC_3	A113	N/C
B114	N/C	A114	GND
B115	N/C	A115	**ADS#**
B116	N/C	A116	N/C
B117	VCC_3	A117	N/C
B118	N/C	A118	GND
B119	VID[3]	A119	VID[2]
B120	VID[0]	A120	VID[1]
B121	VCC_3	A121	VID[4]

HIT# hit: Indicates that a caching agent holds an un-modified version of the requested line.
HITM# hit modified: Indicates that a caching agent holds a modified version of the requested line and that this agent assumes responsibility for providing the line.

RS[2:0] response type:
000	Idle state	001	Retry response
010	Deferred response		
011	Reserved	100	Hard failure
101	No data response		
110	Implicit writeback		
111	Normal data response		

ADS# [I/O] address strobe: The host bus owner asserts ADS# to indicate the first of two cycles of a request phase.

A.3   Quick Reference

Parallel port

Pin	Name	Pin	Name
1	Strobe	14	GND
2	Auto Feed	15	D6
3	D0	16	GND
4	Error	17	D7
5	D1	18	GND
6	INIT	19	ACK
7	D2	20	GND
8	SLCT IN	21	BUSY
9	D3	22	GND
10	GND	23	PE
11	D4	24	GND
12	GND	25	SLCT
13	D5		

Serial port

Pin	Name	Pin	Name
1	DCD	6	CTS
2	DSR	7	DTR
3	RX	8	RI
4	RTS	9	GND
5	TX		

IDE

Pin	Name	Pin	Name
1	Reset	2	GND
3	D7	4	D8
5	D6	6	D9
7	D5	8	D10
9	D4	10	D11
11	D3	12	D12
13	D2	14	D13
15	D1	16	D14
17	D0	18	D15
19	GND	20	Key
21	DRQ3	22	GND
23	-I/O W	24	GND
25	-I/O R	26	GND
27	IOCHRDY	28	BALE
29	-DACK3	30	GND
31	IRQ14	32	IOCS16
33	ADD 1	34	GND
35	ADD 0	36	ADD 2
37	-CS 0	38	CS 1
39	ACTIVITY	40	GND

Floppy disk

Pin	Name	Pin	Name
1	GND	2	FDHDIN
3	GND	4	Reserved
5	Key	6	FDEDIN
7	RTS	8	-Index
9	GND	10	Motor En A
11	GND	12	Drive Sel B
13	GND	14	Drive Sel A
15	GND	16	Motor En B
17	GND	18	DIR
19	GND	20	STEP
21	GND	22	Write Data
23	GND	24	Write Gate
25	GND	26	Track 00
27	GND	28	Write Protect
29	GND	30	Read Data
31	GND	32	Side 1 Sel
33	GND	34	Diskette

Typical IRQs

0	Internal timer	1	Keyboard
2	Cascaded interrupt	3	COM2
4	COM1	5	(Soundcard)
6	Floppy disk	7	LPT1
8	Real-time clock	9	User available
10	User available	11	(PCI steering)
12	Serial bus mouse (if any)	13	Math coprocessor
14	Primary IDE	15	Secondary IDE

Typical DMA channels

0	Any
1	Any
2	Floppy disk
3	Parallel port
4	Cascaded DMA
5	Any
6	Any
7	Any

Example I/O map

0000–000F	Slave DMA controller	0020–0021	Master PIC
0040–0043	System timer	0060	Keyboard
0061	Speaker	0064	Keyboard
0070–0071	Real-time clock	0080–008F	DMA
00A0–00A1	Slave PIC	00F0–00FF	Numeric processor
0170–0177	Secondary H/D	0200–020F	Game port
0220–022F	Soundcard	0294–0297	PCI bus
02F8–02FF	COM2	0330–0331	Soundcard
0370–0371	Soundcard	0376	Secondary IDE
0378–037A	LPT1	0388–03B8	Soundcard
03B0–03BB	VGA	03C0–03DF	VGA
03F6	Primary IDE	03F8–03FF	COM1
0480–048F	PCI bus	04D0–04D1	PCI bus
0530–0537	Soundcard	0778–077A	ECP Port (LPT1)
0CF8–0CFF	PCI bus	4000–403F	PCI bus
5000–5018	PCI bus	D000–DFFF	AGP controller
E000–E01F	USB controller	E400–E4FF	VGA

Bus specification

Bus	Maximum throughput	Data bus (bits)	Address bus (bits)	Notes
AGP	500 MB/s	64	32	
EISA	32 MB/s	32	32	4 GB maximum address, 8 MHz clock
Ethernet	1.25 MB/s	1	N/A	10 Mbps (10BASE)
Fibre Channel	132.5 MB/s	1	N/A	1.06 Gbps
Firewire	50 MB/s	1	N/A	400 Mbps (S400)
IDE	16.6 MB/s	16	N/A	Mode 4, EIDE, maximum four devices
IEEE-488	1 MB/s	8	N/A	
ISA	16 MB/s	16	24	16 MB maximum address, 8 MHz clock
ISDN	16 kB/s	1	N/A	2×64 kbps
MCA	100 MB/s	32	32	
Modem	7 kB/s	1	N/A	56 kbps
Parallel port	150 kB/s	8	N/A	150 kB/s is equivalent to 1.2 Mbps which is the required transfer rate for stereo, 44.1kHz, 16-bit sampled audio
Parallel port (ECP/EPP)	1.2 MB/s	8	N/A	×8
PC	8 MB/s	8	20	1 MB maximum address, 8 MHz clock
PCI	132 MB/s	32	32	33 MHz clock
PCI (32-bit)	132 MB/s	32	32	33 MHz clock
PCI (64-bit)	264 MB/s	64	32	33 MHz clock
PCMCIA	16 MB/s	16	26	64 MB maximum address
RS-232	14.4 kB/s	1	N/A	115.2 kbps
RS-485	1.25 MB/s	1	N/A	10 Mbps
SCSI (Fast/wide)	40 MB/s	16	N/A	20 MHz clock
SCSI-I	5 MB/s	8	N/A	
SCSI-II (Wide)	20 MB/s	16	N/A	10 MHz clock
SCSI-II (Fast)	10 MB/s	8	N/A	10 MHz clock
USB	1.5 MB/s	1	N/A	12 Mbps
VL	132 MB/s	32	32	33 MHz clock

A.4 ASCII

ANSI defined a standard alphabet known as ASCII. This has since been adopted by the CCITT as a standard, known as IA5 (International Alphabet No. 5). The following tables define this alphabet in binary, as a decimal value, as a hexadecimal value and as a character. Unfortunately, standard ASCII character has 7 bits and the basic set ranges from 0 to 127. This code is rather limited as it does not contain symbols such as Greek letters, lines, and so on. For this purpose the extended ASCII code has been defined, which uses character numbers 128 to 255.

Binary	Decimal	Hex	Character	Binary	Decimal	Hex	Character
00000000	0	00	NUL	00010000	16	10	DLE
00000001	1	01	SOH	00010001	17	11	DC1
00000010	2	02	STX	00010010	18	12	DC2
00000011	3	03	ETX	00010011	19	13	DC3
00000100	4	04	EOT	00010100	20	14	DC4
00000101	5	05	ENQ	00010101	21	15	NAK
00000110	6	06	ACK	00010110	22	16	SYN
00000111	7	07	BEL	00010111	23	17	ETB
00001000	8	08	BS	00011000	24	18	CAN
00001001	9	09	HT	00011001	25	19	EM
00001010	10	0A	LF	00011010	26	1A	SUB
00001011	11	0B	VT	00011011	27	1B	ESC
00001100	12	0C	FF	00011100	28	1C	FS
00001101	13	0D	CR	00011101	29	1D	GS
00001110	14	0E	SO	00011110	30	1E	RS
00001111	15	0F	SI	00011111	31	1F	US
00100000	32	20	SPACE	00110000	48	30	0
00100001	33	21	!	00110001	49	31	1
00100010	34	22	"	00110010	50	32	2
00100011	35	23	#	00110011	51	33	3
00100100	36	24	$	00110100	52	34	4
00100101	37	25	%	00110101	53	35	5
00100110	38	26	&	00110110	54	36	6
00100111	39	27	/	00110111	55	37	7
00101000	40	28	(	00111000	56	38	8
00101001	41	29	)	00111001	57	39	9
00101010	42	2A	*	00111010	58	3A	:
00101011	43	2B	+	00111011	59	3B	;
00101100	44	2C	,	00111100	60	3C	<
00101101	45	2D	–	00111101	61	3D	=
00101110	46	2E	.	00111110	62	3E	>
00101111	47	2F	/	00111111	63	3F	?
01000000	64	40	@	01010000	80	50	P
01000001	65	41	A	01010001	81	51	Q
01000010	66	42	B	01010010	82	52	R
01000011	67	43	C	01010011	83	53	S
01000100	68	44	D	01010100	84	54	T
01000101	69	45	E	01010101	85	55	U
01000110	70	46	F	01010110	86	56	V
01000111	71	47	G	01010111	87	57	W
01001000	72	48	H	01011000	88	58	X
01001001	73	49	I	01011001	89	59	Y
01001010	74	4A	J	01011010	90	5A	Z
01001011	75	4B	K	01011011	91	5B	[

Binary	Dec	Hex	Char	Binary	Dec	Hex	Char
01001100	76	4C	L	01011100	92	5C	\
01001101	77	4D	M	01011101	93	5D	]
01001110	78	4E	N	01011110	94	5E	`
01001111	79	4F	O	01011111	95	5F	_
01100000	96	60		01110000	112	70	p
01100001	97	61	a	01110001	113	71	q
01100010	98	62	b	01110010	114	72	r
01100011	99	63	c	01110011	115	73	s
01100100	100	64	d	01110100	116	74	t
01100101	101	65	e	01110101	117	75	u
01100110	102	66	f	01110110	118	76	v
01100111	103	67	g	01110111	119	77	w
01101000	104	68	h	01111000	120	78	x
01101001	105	69	i	01111001	121	79	y
01101010	106	6A	j	01111010	122	7A	z
01101011	107	6B	k	01111011	123	7B	{
01101100	108	6C	l	01111100	124	7C	:
01101101	109	6D	m	01111101	125	7D	}
01101110	110	6E	n	01111110	126	7E	~
01101111	111	6F	o	01111111	127	7F	DEL
10000000	128	80	Ç	10010000	144	90	É
10000001	129	81	ü	10010001	145	91	æ
10000010	130	82	é	10010010	146	92	Æ
10000011	131	83	â	10010011	147	93	ô
10000100	132	84	ä	10010100	148	94	ö
10000101	133	85	à	10010101	149	95	ò
10000110	134	86	å	10010110	150	96	û
10000111	135	87	ç	10010111	151	97	ù
10001000	136	88	ê	10011000	152	98	ÿ
10001001	137	89	ë	10011001	153	99	Ö
10001010	138	8A	è	10011010	154	9A	Ü
10001011	139	8B	ï	10011011	155	9B	¢
10001100	140	8C	î	10011100	156	9C	£
10001101	141	8D	ì	10011101	157	9D	¥
10001110	142	8E	Ä	10011110	158	9E	₧
10001111	143	8F	Å	10011111	159	9F	ƒ
10100000	160	A0	á	10110000	176	B0	░
10100001	161	A1	í	10110001	177	B1	▒
10100010	162	A2	ó	10110010	178	B2	▓
10100011	163	A3	ú	10110011	179	B3	│
10100100	164	A4	ñ	10110100	180	B4	┤
10100101	165	A5	Ñ	10110101	181	B5	╡
10100110	166	A6	ª	10110110	182	B6	╢
10100111	167	A7	º	10110111	183	B7	╖
10101000	168	A8	¿	10111000	184	B8	╕
10101001	169	A9	⌐	10111001	185	B9	╣
10101010	170	AA	¬	10111010	186	BA	║
10101011	171	AB	½	10111011	187	BB	╗
10101100	172	AC	¼	10111100	188	BC	╝
10101101	173	AD	¡	10111101	189	BD	╜
10101110	174	AE	«	10111110	190	BE	╛

10101111	175	AF	»	10111111	191	BF	⌐
11000000	192	C0	└	11010000	208	D0	╨
11000001	193	C1	┴	11010001	209	D1	╤
11000010	194	C2	┬	11010010	210	D2	╥
11000011	195	C3	├	11010011	211	D3	╙
11000100	196	C4	─	11010100	212	D4	╘
11000101	197	C5	┼	11010101	213	D5	╒
11000110	198	C6	╞	11010110	214	D6	╓
11000111	199	C7	╟	11010111	215	D7	╫
11001000	200	C8	╚	11011000	216	D8	╪
11001001	201	C9	╔	11011001	217	D9	┘
11001010	202	CA	╩	11011010	218	DA	┌
11001011	203	CB	╦	11011011	219	DB	█
11001100	204	CC	╠	11011100	220	DC	▄
11001101	205	CD	=	11011101	221	DD	▌
11001110	206	CE	╬	11011110	222	DE	▐
11001111	207	CF	╧	11011111	223	DF	▀
11100000	224	E0	α	11110000	240	F0	Ξ
11100001	225	E1	ß	11110001	241	F1	$\pm$
11100010	226	E2	Γ	11110010	242	F2	$\geq$
11100011	227	E3	π	11110011	243	F3	$\leq$
11100100	228	E4	Σ	11110100	244	F4	$\int$
11100101	229	E5	σ	11110101	245	F5	$\int$
11100110	230	E6	μ	11110110	246	F6	$\div$
11100111	231	E7	τ	11110111	247	F7	$\approx$
11101000	232	E8	Φ	11111000	248	F8	$\circ$
11101001	233	E9	Θ	11111001	249	F9	·
11101010	234	EA	Ω	11111010	250	FA	·
11101011	235	EB	δ	11111011	251	FB	$\sqrt{}$
11101100	236	EC	φ	11111100	252	FC	^{n}
11101101	237	ED	ϕ	11111101	253	FD	^{2}
11101110	238	EE	ϵ	11111110	254	FE	■
11101111	239	EF	Λ	11111111	255	FF	

A.5 Additional WWW material

Additional WWW material is available at:

    http://www.dcs.napier.ac.uk/~bill/ad_arc.html

Index